D1104647
U.S. FRIGATE
"CONSTITUTION"
DRAWN FROM THE OFFICIAL PLANS FOR
THE 1927 RESTORATION LENT THROUGH THE
COURTESY OF THE COMMANDANT, NAVY YARD, BOSTON
F. Alexander Magoun
MASSACHUSETTS INSTITUTE OF TECHNOLOGY
CAMBRIDGE MASS.
FORE ROYAL
FORE TOPGALLANT
TOPSAIL
FORESAIL
FORE ROYAL STAY
FLYING JIB STAY
FORE TOPGALLANT STAY
STANDING JIB STAY
FORE TOPMAST STAY
FORE TOPMAST PREVENTER STAY
FORE STAY
PREVENTER
FORE-TOPSAIL BRACE
FORE LIFT
FORE BRACE
FLYING JIB BOOM
JIB BOOM
BOWSPRIT
DOLPHIN STRIKER
SPRITSAIL YARD
ORLOP DECK
FEET
COPYRIGHT 1927 BY F.A.M.

SHIPS OF OAK
GUNS OF IRON

SHIPS OF OAK

GUNS OF IRON

THE WAR OF 1812 AND THE FORGING OF THE AMERICAN NAVY

RONALD D. UTT

Cataloging-in-Publication data on file with the Library of Congress
ISBN 978-1-62157-002-8

Published in the United States by
Regnery History
An imprint of Regnery Publishing, Inc.
One Massachusetts Avenue NW
Washington, DC 20001
www.RegneryHistory.com

Manufactured in the United States of America

10 9 8 7 6 5 4 3 2 1

Books are available in quantity for promotional or premium use. Write to Director of Special Sales, Regnery Publishing, Inc., One Massachusetts Avenue NW, Washington, DC 20001, for information on discounts and terms, or call (202) 216-0600.

Images of the *Constitution* on endpapers reprinted from *The Frigate Constitution and Other Historic Ships*, courtesy of Dover Publications, Inc.

Distributed to the trade by
Perseus Distribution
250 West 57th Street
New York, NY 10107

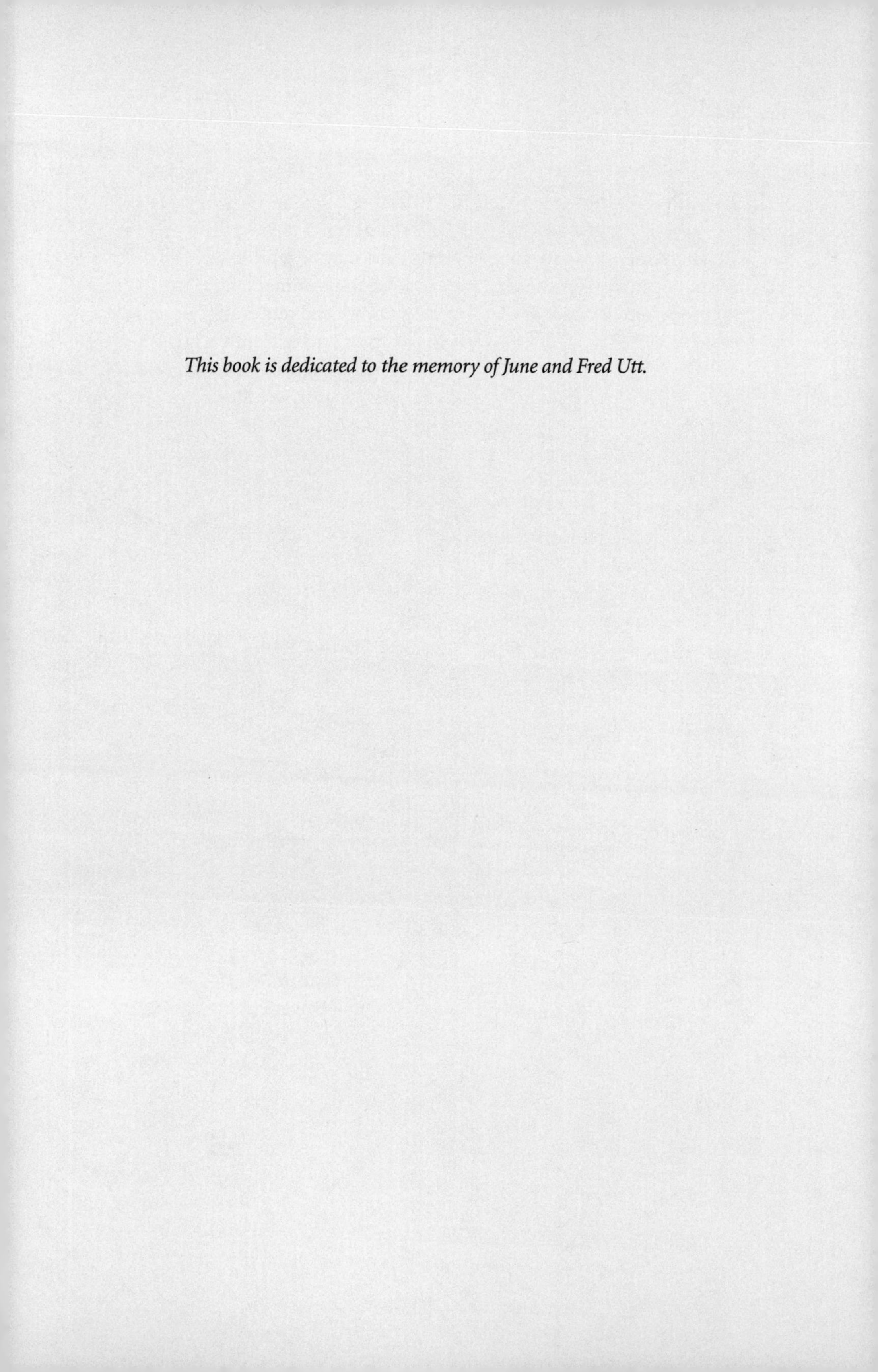

This book is dedicated to the memory of June and Fred Utt.

CONTENTS

PARTICIPANTS IN THE WAR OF 1812

William Henry Allen. Lieutenant, USN. Served on the *Chesapeake* in her confrontation with *Leopard* in June 1806 and with Decatur on the *United States* when she captured *Macedonian* on 25 October 1812. Allen commanded *Argus* during its predatory voyage in the seas around the British Isles in the summer of 1813. He was mortally wounded in *Argus*'s defeat to HMS *Pelican* on 14 August 1813.

George Armistead. Major, USA. Commander of Fort McHenry, Baltimore, during the British bombardment of 13–14 September 1814.

John Armstrong. Veteran of the Revolutionary War, senator from New York, and Jefferson's minister to France. Madison appointed Armstrong as secretary of war on 5 February 1813 to replace William Eustice. Armstrong resigned from the position in late August 1814 after the burning of Washington.

Joseph Bainbridge. Master commandant, USN. Younger brother of William Bainbridge. Given command of the brig *Frolic* in 1814.

William Bainbridge. Captain, USN. Served in the Quasi-War against France, lost the frigate *Philadelphia* to the Tripolitans during the Barbary Wars, and was in command of *Constitution* in its fight with *Java* off the coast of Brazil, 29 December 1812.

Robert H. Barclay. Captain, RN. Commander of the British squadron on Lake Erie in the battle of Put-in-Bay against Oliver Hazard Perry's squadron on 10 September 1813.

Joshua Barney. On-and-off officer in the USN. Veteran of the Revolutionary War and privateer early in the War of 1812. He was reinstated in the navy in August 1813 to organize the naval defense of Baltimore and Washington.

James Barron. Commodore, USN. In command of the *Chesapeake* when it was attacked by *Leopard* off the Virginia Capes, 22 June 1807. An 1808 court-martial found him guilty of negligence and suspended him from service for five years without pay. Barron killed Stephen Decatur in a duel in 1820.

Henry Bathurst, third Earl Bathurst. Secretary of state for war and the colonies during the War of 1812.

James Biddle. Captain, USN. As a lieutenant under Captain Jacob Jones on the *Wasp*, participated in the fight with *Frolic* on 17 October 1812 and later commanded *Hornet* in the fight with *Penguin* on 23 March 1815.

Johnston Blakely. Captain, USN. Commanded *Wasp* in fight with HMS *Reindeer* on 28 June 1814, and with HMS *Avon* on 1 September 1814.

Sir Isaac Brock. Major general, British Army. Led British forces in attack on Fort Detroit, 16 August 1812, and in their counter-attack at Queenston, in which he was killed, 13 October 1812.

Sir Philip Bowes Vere Broke. RN. Captain of the frigate *Shannon.* Led the pursuit of *Constitution* off the coast of New Jersey in July 1812 and commanded the frigate in her fight with *Chesapeake* on 1 June 1813.

Jacob Brown. Brigadier general, USA. Defended the naval base at Sackets Harbor, New York, from British attack on 29 May 1813. He later participated in several battles along the New York–Canadian frontier, notably the advance on Montreal, Chippawa, Lundy's Lane, and the defense of Fort Erie.

James Buchanan. Lieutenant, Pennsylvania militia. Served in the defense of Baltimore, fifteenth president of the United States.

William Bush. Lieutenant, USMC. Led the marine contingent aboard the *Constitution* in the fight with *Guerriere* on 19 August 1812.

John Surman Carden. Captain, RN. Captain of the *Macedonian* in her fight with Decatur's *United States* on 25 October 1812. Eventually achieved rank of admiral.

John Cassin. Captain, USN. Commanded the naval artillery forces on Craney Island, Virginia, against a British attack on 22 June 1813.

Isaac Chauncey. Commodore, USN. In command of all U.S. naval forces on the Great Lakes from his base at Sackets Harbor and in direct command of the squadron on Lake Ontario.

Henry Clay. Member of U.S. House of Representatives from Kentucky, elected speaker of the House in 1808. Leader of the "War Hawk" faction agitating for war with Britain in response to impressments and the encouragement of Indian uprisings along the western frontier.

Sir Alexander Cochrane. Vice admiral, RN. Commander in chief of North American Station. Planned and commanded the August–September 1814 attacks on Washington and Baltimore and the January 1815 attack on New Orleans.

Sir George Cockburn. Rear admiral, RN. Led British forces that invaded the Chesapeake Bay in the summers of 1813 and 1814. With Major General Robert Ross, he led the capture and burning of Washington, 24 August 1814.

Sir Edward Codrington. Rear admiral, RN. Commanded and directed the British fleet in the attacks on Washington, Baltimore, and New Orleans.

John Coffee. Colonel, Tennessee militia. General Andrew Jackson's second in command during the Creek campaigns in Alabama, 1813–1814 and at New Orleans, December–January 1815.

George Croghan. Major, USA. Defended Fort Stephenson, Ohio, against combined British and Indian forces, 1–2 August 1813, and on 4 August 1814, led the land attack to retake Fort Michilimackinac, Michigan.

Benjamin W. Crowninshield. Replaced William Jones as secretary of the navy in December 1814.

James Richard Dacres. Captain, RN. Commanded the frigate *Guerriere* on patrol off the coast of the United States in the months leading up to the war; fought *Constitution* on 19 August 1812.

Henry Dearborn. General, USA. Veteran of the Revolutionary War, secretary of war and customs collector during the Jefferson administration. After war was declared, Madison offered Dearborn the rank of senior major general and command over the northern theater. He held overall command of several of the early campaigns from Queenston to York but suffered from poor health. Relieved of command on 6 July 1813.

Stephen Decatur. Commodore, USN. As a lieutenant during the Barbary Wars he defeated a squadron of Tripolitan gunboats and recaptured and destroyed the frigate *Philadelphia* in Tripoli Harbor. Promoted to commodore in 1807, he commanded the frigate *United States* in her fight with *Macedonian* on 29 October 1812 and the frigate *President* in her fight with a British squadron led by the frigate *Endymion* on 15 January 1815. Slain in a duel with Commodore James Barron, 1820.

George Downie. Captain, RN. Commanded the British squadron on Lake Champlain against Thomas Macdonough on 11 September 1814.

Sir Gordon Drummond. Lieutenant general, British Army. Appointed to command of the forces in Upper Canada in 1813, the Canadian-born Drummond moved aggressively to attack the American forces arrayed against him. During his tenure he was in overall command during the battles along the Niagara frontier (Lundy's Lane and Fort Erie), and the 6 May 1814 raid on Oswego, New York.

Jesse Elliott. Lieutenant, USN. Initial commander of the brig *Niagara* at the battle of Put-in-Bay, Lake Erie, 10 September 1813, and Perry's second in command on the lake.

Matthew Elliott. British Indian agent active in encouraging Indians to resist U.S. encroachment in Northwest Territories. Elliott led the Indians at the attack on Frenchtown, 22 January 1813.

William Eustis. Secretary of the army, March 1809–December 1812.

David Glasgow Farragut. Midshipman, USN. Nominally adopted by Captain David Porter and later commissioned as a midshipman, he served aboard the frigate *Essex* during its Pacific voyage in 1813.

Archibald Hamilton. Midshipman, USN. Son of Secretary of the Navy Paul Hamilton, he served under Decatur on the *United States* and the *President* and presented *Macedonian*'s flag to Dolley Madison at a naval ball in Washington, December 1812.

Paul Hamilton. South Carolina planter, governor, and veteran of the Revolutionary War. Secretary of the navy from 7 March 1809 to 31 December 1812.

Wade Hampton. Major general, USA. Veteran of the Revolutionary War and South Carolina planter. Hampton was assigned command of an army stationed in Plattsburgh, New York., but became subordinate to General James Wilkinson, a bitter rival. Involved in the attempt to capture Montreal in late 1813, Hampton subsequently resigned.

Thomas Masterman Hardy. Admiral, RN. Captain of Nelson's flagship *Victory* at Trafalgar, 21 October 1805, and commanded a squadron blockading the U.S. coast during the War of 1812.

William Henry Harrison. One-time aid to General Anthony Wayne in the Northwest Territories, appointed governor of the Indiana territory. Harrison expanded white settlement in the region, escalating tensions with Indian tribes led by Tecumseh. Destroyed Prophet's Town after narrow victory in battle of Tippecanoe, 7 November 1811. After William Hull's surrender at Detroit, Harrison secured the military command in the Northwest, ahead of Brigadier General James Winchester, by obtaining the higher rank of major general in the Kentucky militia. Harrison was instrumental in defending the Northwest against further British incursion, and in late September 1813 he went on the offensive against Procter's force in the Detroit region.

James Hillyar. Captain, RN. Commanded the frigate *Phoebe* against the frigate *Essex* under Captain David Porter's command on 28 March 1814.

Samuel Houston. Lieutenant/ensign in the Tennessee militia under General Andrew Jackson during the campaign against the Creeks in Alabama. He was badly wounded at the battle of Horseshoe Bend.

Isaac Hull. Captain, USN. As a new lieutenant aboard *Constitution*, Hull fought in the Quasi-War with France. He commanded *Enterprise* and *Argus* in the Barbary Wars. Promoted to captain in 1806, Hull commanded the frigates *Chesapeake* and *President* until June 1810, when the more senior Commodore Rogers, then in command of *Constitution*, expressed an interest in commanding the *President* and exchanged ships with Hull. On 19 August 1812, Hull led the *Constitution* to victory over *Guerriere* in the North Atlantic.

William Hull. Brigadier general, USA. Uncle of Captain Isaac Hull, veteran of the Revolutionary War, appointed governor of the Michigan Territory in 1805. In 1812 Hull assumed command of the "North Western Army," and Fort Detroit served as his headquarters in the early days of the war.

Joshua Humphrey. Philadelphia-based naval architect and shipbuilder whose innovative designs and strategic thinking were incorporated into America's big frigates.

Salusbury Pryce Humphreys. Captain, RN. Commanded the *Leopard* in its confrontation with *Chesapeake* on 22 June 1806.

George Izard. Major general, USA. Appointed to command of land forces on the Canadian border in January 1814.

Andrew Jackson. Veteran of the Revolutionary War, Nashville lawyer, and general in the Tennessee militia. Jackson led the attacks on the Creek Indians in Alabama following the massacre at Fort Mims on 30 August 1813. Appointed a major general in the regular army on 18 June 1814, Jackson attacked and seized Pensacola from the Spanish and defended New Orleans against the British.

Thomas Jefferson. President of the United States, 1801–1809, a period of rising tensions with England over impressment and free trade. Responded with a program to expand the fleet of gunboats, which were largely ineffective during the subsequent war. His 1806 embargo of British imports inflicted more harm on the United States than on Britain.

Richard Mentor Johnson. A member of Congress from Kentucky and a colonel in the militia. He created a highly trained mounted force of Kentucky volunteers that patrolled the Northwest Territories and played a major role in the battle of the Thames, 5 October, 1813, at which he was credited with slaying Tecumseh.

Jacob Jones. Captain, USN. Lieutenant aboard *Philadelphia* when she ran aground in Tripoli Harbor. Promoted to master commandant and given command of the sloop *Wasp*, which fought the sloop *Frolic* on 18 October 1812.

Thomas ap Catesby Jones. Lieutenant, USN. Jones commanded five gunboats at the entrance to Lake Borgne, Louisiana, and on 14 December 1814 fought against a larger British assault force attempting to cross the lake and attack New Orleans.

William Jones. Veteran of the Revolutionary War, merchant, member of Congress from Pennsylvania, secretary of the navy from 12 January 1813 to 1 December 1814.

Francis Scott Key. Lawyer and officer in the militia of the District of Columbia. While attempting to secure the release of a civilian imprisoned by the British, Key witnessed the British bombardment of Fort McHenry in Baltimore. His poem commemorating the event—the future national anthem—became popular throughout the country.

Jean Lafitte. A French pirate-privateer-smuggler operating out of Barataria Bay, Louisiana. Aided Andrew Jackson during the British attack on New Orleans.

Henry Lambert. Captain, RN. Commanded the frigate *Java* in its fight with *Constitution* on 29 December 1812.

James Lawrence. Captain, USN. Decatur's second in command in the recapture and destruction of the frigate *Philadelphia* in Tripoli Harbor. Lawrence commanded the sloop *Hornet* in its fight with the brig *Peacock*, 24 February 1813, and the frigate *Chesapeake* in its fight with *Shannon*, 1 June 1813. Remembered for his dying command on the *Chesapeake*, "Don't give up the ship!"

Samuel Leech. Served aboard the *Macedonian* as a boy. Captured by the Americans, the fourteen-year-old Leech stayed in the U.S. and became a citizen. His book, *A Voice from the Main Deck*, is one of the few detailed accounts of the gruesome nature of ship-to-ship combat during the war.

Uriah Levy. Sailing master on *Argus*. A merchant captain in his family's business, Levy asked to join the *Argus* under Henry Allen's command. He was provided nominal officer status and given command of one of the prizes during the ship's cruise in the English Channel and Irish Sea.

Thomas Macdonough. Master commandant, USN. One of "Preble's Boys" in the Barbary Wars, he was a midshipman under Decatur in the recapture of the frigate *Philadelphia* in Tripoli Harbor. As a lieutenant, he built and commanded the U.S. squadron on Lake Champlain. He defeated the British squadron on 11 September 1814.

Alexander Macomb. Brigadier general, USA. When his superior, Major General George Izard, took half of the force at Plattsburg, New York, to the Niagara front, Macomb was left in command. He defended the town against a larger British force under General Sir George Prevost on 11 September 1814.

James Madison. President of the United States, 1809–1817. As commander in chief, he appointed incompetent but politically connected generals to important commands.

John Fordyce Maples. Captain, RN. Commanded *Pelican* against the *Argus*, August 1813.

James Monroe. Secretary of state (and for several months, 1814–1815, simultaneously secretary of war) under President Madison.

Charles Morris. Lieutenant commander, USN. Served with Decatur in the recapture of the frigate *Philadelphia* and as a lieutenant under Isaac Hull on the *Constitution* in her fight with *Guerriere*, in which he was severely wounded. He later assumed command of the small frigate *John Adams*.

Charles James Napier. Colonel, British Army. Participated in Chesapeake campaign of 1813.

Sir Edward Pakenham. Major general, British Army. Brother-in-law of the duke of Wellington, Pakenham served with distinction in Spain during the Napoleonic Wars. He was given command of the army in North America and led the British force at New Orleans on 8 January 1814.

Sir Peter Parker. Captain, RN. A nephew of Lord Byron, Parker commanded the frigate *Menelaus* during the British incursion into the Chesapeake under Cockburn during the summer of 1814.

Oliver Hazard Perry. Master commandant, USN. Assembled and commanded the seven ship squadron on Lake Erie, which defeated the British squadron under Captain Robert Barclay at Put-in-Bay on 10 September 1813.

Zebulon Montgomery Pike. Brigadier general, USA. A career army officer, Pike achieved early fame in his 1806–1807 exploration of the newly acquired Louisiana Territory. Pike led the ground forces in the attack on York, Ontario, on 27 April 1813.

David Porter. Captain, USN. Imprisoned at Tripoli when the *Philadelphia* was captured in the Barbary Wars. Commander of the frigate *Essex* during the War of 1812, Porter was the first American to capture a British ship (*Alert* on 13 August 1812). Cruising the Pacific during 1813 and early 1814, Porter captured fourteen British whalers. On 28 March 1814 he fought *Phoebe* and *Cherub* near Valparaiso, Chile.

William Preble. Commodore, USN. Preble commanded the U.S. naval forces during part of the Barbary Wars. He was a mentor to many of the young naval officers who later assumed major roles during the War of 1812, known as "Preble's Boys."

Sir George Prevost. Lieutenant general, British Army. Given command of British forces in North America on 4 July 1811, he later led a force from Canada to attack the American land and naval forces at Plattsburgh, New York, in September 1814.

Henry Procter (or Proctor). Major general, British Army. Leading the British forces on Canada's western frontier, Procter had overall command of the attack on Fort Detroit, 16 August 1812, and thwarted American efforts to retake lost territory in the Northwest. Procter was in command of British forces when Harrison attacked on 5 October 1813 in the battle of the Thames (Ontario).

Samuel Chester Reid. Captain of the American privateer *General Armstrong* during its fight against a British squadron at Fayal in the Portuguese Azores on 26 September 1814.

Stephen Van Rensselaer. Major general, USA. In overall command of U.S. forces at the battle of Queenston, 13 October 1812.

Phineas Riall. Major general, British Army. Commander on the Niagara front in early 1814, Riall led the British forces in the battles of Chippawa and Lundy's Lane, July 1814.

John Rodgers. Commodore, USN. After service in the Quasi-War and the Barbary Wars, Rodgers commanded the frigate *President* in its confrontation with the sloop *Little Belt* on 16 May 1811. Rodgers captured numerous merchant ships during the war but never saw action against another warship of comparable strength.

Robert Ross. Major general, British Army. After serving in Egypt and Spain during the Napoleonic Wars, Ross took command in June 1814 of a new army being assembled for North America. Ross led this force in its attack on Washington and Baltimore, August–September 1814.

Hercules Scott. Colonel, British Army. Fought at Lundy's Lane and Fort Erie during the summer of 1814.

Winfield Scott. Brigadier general, USA. Led forces in numerous battles along the Niagara front, beginning with Queenston, 13 October 1812. On 27 May 1813, Scott led an amphibious attack on Fort George. He was again engaged on the Niagara front during the battles of Chippawa and Lundy's Lane, July 1814.

Roger Hale Shaeffe. Major general, British Army. The American-born Shaeffe, in command of Fort George, reinforced the forces of the slain Brock at Queenston (13 October 1812); he was awarded a baronetcy for the victory. He commanded forces at York against the successful American attack on 27 April 1813.

Sir John Coape Sherbrooke. Lieutenant general, British Army. Lieutenant governor of Nova Scotia, he sent a naval force and five hundred troops to occupy Castine, Maine, in September 1814.

Moses Smith. Crewman aboard *Constitution* and *John Adams*. His memoirs of his service during the war, *Naval Scenes in the Last War* (1846), is one of the few detailed eyewitness accounts of the life aboard an American frigate during the War of 1812.

Samuel Smith. Major general, Maryland militia. In command of Fort McHenry, Baltimore, during the British attack in September 1814.

Charles Stewart. Captain, USN. Morris, then a lieutenant, commanded the operation that led to Decatur's recapture of the *Philadelphia*. During the War of 1812, Stewart was captain of *Constellation* at Norfolk, under a British blockade. He later commanded *Constitution* on its final voyage of the war, during which she fought *Cyane* and *Levant*, 20 February 1815.

Zachary Taylor. Captain, USA. Defended Fort Harrison on the Wabash, Vincennes, Indiana, and Fort Madison and conducted numerous engagements with Indians and British forces in present-day Iowa and Wisconsin.

Tecumseh. Shawnee chief in the Indiana Territory and powerful advocate of a return to traditional customs and resistance to white encroachment. Supported by the British, Tecumseh incited the Creeks and other tribes in Alabama to resist white settlers. Slain (reputedly by Richard Mentor Johnson) while fighting with the British in the battle of Thames,Ontario, 5 October 1813.

Tenskwatawa (the "Prophet"). Brother and collaborator of Tecumseh. Fought William Henry Harrison at Tippecanoe, 7 November 1811.

John Vincent. Brigadier general, British Army. Commander of Fort George on Lake Ontario when Winfield Scott's amphibious force attacked on 27 May 1813.

Sir James Borlase Warren. Admiral, RN. Commander in chief on the North American Station, 1807–1810 and 1813–1814. Warren was replaced in March 1814 when the North American command was divided and Admiral Cochrane was appointed to succeed him.

Lewis Warrington. Master commandant, USN. Commanded *Peacock* in fight with *Epervier*, 18 April 1813, and fought the last naval battle of the war against *Nautilus*, 1 July 1815, in the Indian Ocean.

George Washington. President of the United States, 1789–1797. In March 1794 he signed into law a bill authorizing the construction of *Constitution* and five other frigates.

William Weatherford (Red Eagle). Son of a Scottish trader and Creek mother, Red Eagle became a leader of the Red Stick faction of the Creeks and led 750 warriors against Fort Mims in August 1813. He also led the Red Sticks in several other battles with Andrew Jackson and General John Floyd in Mississippi Territory (present-day Alabama) in 1813 and 1814.

James Wilkinson. Major general, USA. A veteran of the Revolutionary War and a controversial figure during the early nineteenth century, Wilkinson commanded the armies of the northeast. On 17 October 1813 he embarked from Sackets Harbor, New York, to attack Montreal.

James Winchester. Brigadier general, USA. Serving under Harrison in the Northwest, Winchester fought Procter's force at Frenchtown (Michigan) in January 1813.

William Winder. Brigadier general, USA. Organized and led the defense of Washington, D.C., in August 1814.

Sir James Lucas Yeo. Commodore, RN. Commanded forces on the Great Lakes from his base at Kingston, Ontario.

TIMELINE OF KEY EVENTS IN THE WAR OF 1812

August 1785: frigate *Alliance* sold to Philadelphia merchant; U.S. Navy and U.S. Marine Corps disbanded.

October–November 1793: Barbary pirates seize eleven U.S. merchant ships in the Mediterranean.

27 March 1794: President Washington signs bill authorizing the construction of six new frigates—*Constitution*, *United States*, *President*, *Congress*, *Constellation*, and *Chesapeake.*

10 May 1797: USS *United States* launched in Philadelphia.

7 September 1797: USS *Constellation* launched in Baltimore.

21 October 21 1797: USS *Constitution* launched in Boston.

1 August 1798: Battle of the Nile (Aboukir Bay)—British fleet under Nelson destroys French fleet off Egypt.

9 February 1799: Quasi-War with France intensifies when USS *Constellation* captures French frigate *L'Insurgent* in the Caribbean in first combat of the conflict.

10 August 1799: USS *Congress* launched in Portsmouth, New Hampshire.

30 September 1799: USS *Essex* launched at Salem, Massachusetts.

2 December 1799: USS *Chesapeake* launched at Gosport Shipyard, Portsmouth, Virginia.

10 April 1800: USS *President* launched in New York.

2 April 1801: Copenhagen Raid—British fleet under Nelson defeats Danish fleet.

31 October 1803: *Philadelphia* runs aground in Tripoli Harbor; Captain William Bainbridge and crew taken captive.

16 February 1804: Lieutenant Stephen Decatur of USS *Intrepid* recaptures and destroys the *Philadelphia.*

21 October 1805: Battle of Trafalgar—Nelson mortally wounded in victory over combined French and Spanish fleets.

25 April 1806: HMS *Leander* fires on the American merchant ship *Republic* off New York City, killing seaman John Pierce.

7 January 1807: Great Britain issues order in council against neutral trade with its enemies, notably France.

22 June 1807: HMS *Leopard* fires on *Chesapeake* off Virginia Capes and seizes four deserters from *Chesapeake.*

22 December 1807: Congress passes President Jefferson's proposed embargo.

16 May 1811: Confrontation between *President* and HMS *Little Belt* in the Atlantic.

7 November 1811: Battle of Tippecanoe and destruction of Prophet's Town, Indiana.

1 June 1812: President Madison asks Congress to declare war on Great Britain.

18 June 1812: Madison signs declaration of war following congressional approval.

5 July 1812: *Constitution* under Captain Isaac Hull departs Annapolis for New York; Hull's orders entitle him to attack, capture, and defend.

12 July 1812: U.S. forces under Brigadier General William Hull cross the Detroit River and attack British positions in Upper Canada.

15–19 July 1812: *Constitution* encounters squadron of five British warships—*Shannon*, *Africa*, *Aeolus*, *Guerriere*, and *Belvidera*—off New Jersey.

17 July 1812: British capture the American Fort Michilimackinac, Lake Huron.

13 August 1812: *Essex* under Captain David Porter captures HMS *Alert* in the Atlantic.

15 August 1812: Americans besieged by Potawatomi in Fort Dearborn (Chicago) evacuate on General Hull's orders; most are killed or captured within a few hours of leaving the fort.

16 August 1812: General Hull surrenders Fort Detroit to Major General Isaac Brock.

19 August 1812: *Constitution* sinks *Guerriere* in North Atlantic.

4 October 1812: British attack Ogdensburg, New York.

13 October 1812: Battle of Queenston (Niagara frontier); Brock is killed, Lieutenant Colonel Winfield Scott captured.

18 October 1812: USS *Wasp* under Master Commandant Jacob Jones defeats HMS *Frolic* in North Atlantic but is later captured by HMS *Poictiers*.

25 October 1812: *United States* under Commodore Stephen Decatur captures HMS *Macedonian* in the Atlantic off Africa.

8 December 1812: Midshipman Archibald Hamilton of the *United States* presents *Macedonian*'s flag to Dolley Madison at naval ball in Washington.

29 December 1812: *Constitution* under Bainbridge defeats HMS *Java* in the Atlantic off Brazil.

18–23 January 1813: Battles of Frenchtown and River Raisin (Michigan).

22 February 1813: USS *Hornet* under Master Commandant James Lawrence sinks HMS *Peacock* off northern coast of South America.

3 March 1813: British fleet under Rear Admiral George Cockburn enters Chesapeake Bay to disrupt commerce and raid coastal towns and fortifications.

4 March 1813: After an arduous journey around Cape Horn, *Essex* under Porter enters the Pacific Ocean.

26 March 1813: British squadron attacks and seizes four Baltimore Clippers in the Rappahannock River, Virginia.

27 April 1813: Combined U.S. sea and land force captures British provincial capital at York (Toronto) on Lake Ontario.

29 April 1813: Cockburn attacks Frenchtown, turned back at Elkton, Maryland.

3 May 1813: Cockburn attacks Havre de Grace, Maryland.

5 May 1813: British and Indian force under Major General Henry Procter attacks Fort Meigs, Ohio; Americans suffer heavy casualties but hold the fort.

6 May 1813: Cockburn attacks Fredericktown and Georgetown, Maryland.

27 May 1813: Combined U.S. sea and land force captures Fort George at mouth of Niagara River on Lake Ontario.

29 May 1813: British attack U.S. naval base at Sackets Harbor, New York, but are turned back.

5 June 1813: Americans turned back at Stoney Creek, Ontario.

22 June 1813: Battle of Craney Island, Virginia; British are turned back.

25 June 1813: Same British force attacks and loots Hampton, Virginia.

20 July–13 August 1813: USS *Argus* under Commander William Henry Allen enters British waters; eventually sinks or captures twenty-one British merchant ships.

21 July 1813: Procter lays siege to Fort Meigs; held off again by General William Henry Harrison.

1 August 1813: Procter attacks Fort Stephenson, Ohio; turned back after two-day siege by U.S. force under Lieutenant George Croghan.

10 August 1813: Cockburn's force attacks St. Michaels, Maryland.

14 August 1813: *Argus* is defeated by HMS *Pelican* in Irish Sea; Allen is killed.

30 August 1813: Massacre at Fort Mims, Alabama, by Creek Indians (Red Stick faction) under William Weatherford ("Red Eagle").

10 September 1813: American squadron on Lake Erie under Master Commandant Oliver Hazard Perry captures an entire British squadron at Put-in-Bay, Ohio.

27 September 1813: British under Procter and their Indian allies under Tecumseh abandon Fort Detroit and Fort Amherstburg and retreat east to Burlington, Ontario.

5 October 1813: American force of regulars and militia under Harrison defeat Procter's combined force at the Thames River, Ontario; Tecumseh is killed, Procter escapes.

17 October 1813: U.S. force led by Major General James Wilkinson departs Sackets Harbor for voyage down St. Lawrence River to attack Montreal.

October 1813: Porter and the *Essex*, accompanied by captured vessels, sail west across the Pacific to the Marquesas for repairs, rest, and recreation.

9 November 1813: Major General Andrew Jackson leads regulars and Tennessee militia against the Creeks at Talladega, Alabama.

11 November 1813: Wilkinson's force battles British at Crysler's Farm, Ontario, on way to Montreal.

December 1813: Americans evacuate Niagara frontier; British reclaim lost land, occupy Fort Niagara, attack Buffalo and Black Rock, New York.

13 December 1813: *Essex* departs the Marquesas for coast of South America.

23 December 1813: Jackson leads regulars and Tennessee militia against Creeks at Holy Ground, Alabama.

22 January 1814: Battle of Emuckfaw Creek, Alabama.

3 February 1814: *Essex* anchors in Valparaiso harbor, Chile.

7 February 1814: HMS *Phoebe* under Captain James Hillyar and HMS *Cherub* arrive at Valparaiso and attempt to blockade *Essex* in the harbor.

27–28 March 1814: Jackson's regulars and militia rout Creeks at Horseshoe Bend, Alabama.

28 March 1814: *Essex*'s attempted escape from Valparaiso foiled by a broken mast; Porter surrenders to Hillyar.

March–April 1814: Napoleon abdicates, is exiled to Elba; experienced British infantry and officers are freed up for redeployment to North American conflict.

20 April 1814: USS *Frolic* under Master Commandant Joseph Bainbridge (brother of William) surrenders to HMS *Orpheus* after long chase in the Caribbean.

29 April 1814: USS *Peacock* under Master Commandant Lewis Warrington captures HMS *Epervier* in the Caribbean.

28 June 1814: *Wasp* under Master Commandant Johnston Blakely sinks HMS *Reindeer* in the Atlantic.

5 July 1814: American regulars under Major General Jacob Brown and Brigadier General Winfield Scott defeat British under Major General Phineas Riall at Chippawa on the Canadian side of the Niagara River.

25 July 1814: An American attack force is turned back in an exceptionally bloody fight at Lundy's Lane on the Canadian side of the Niagara River.

4 August 1814: American attack on Fort Michilimackinac led by Croghan fails to dislodge British defenders.

15 August 1814: British under Major General Gordon Drummond attack Americans at Fort Erie; the attack fails, but the siege lasts until mid-September, when the British eventually give up.

16 August 1814: British fleet under Cochrane returns to the Chesapeake and conducts numerous raids on coastal towns, farms, and settlements in Maryland and Virginia through September.

19 August 1814: Large British force under Major General Robert Ross lands at Benedict, Maryland, near Washington.

24 August 1814: Ross's force overcomes combined American regulars and militia at Bladensburg, Maryland, on the outskirts of Washington and occupies the capital that evening.

25 August 1814: British burn the U.S. Capitol and the President's House (White House); they evacuate that evening and re-board their ships the next day.

1 September 1814: British force under Lieutenant General Sir John Coape Sherbrooke attacks and occupies Castine, Maine, gaining control of a substantial portion of the northern coast of Maine.

11 September 1814: Master Commandant Thomas Macdonough leads U.S. squadron to victory against the British squadron at Plattsburgh Bay, Lake Champlain.

———: Lieutenant General Sir George Prevost withdraws the British force from Plattsburgh and returns to Montreal.

12 September 1814: Ross's force disembarks at Long Point, Maryland; later that day it attacks and turns back the Americans' first line of defense.

———: Ross killed by American sniper; Colonel Arthur Brooke assumes command.

13 September 1814: British naval force begins the bombardment of Fort McHenry in Baltimore Harbor.

14 September 1814: British land force under Brooke declines to attack Baltimore fortifications and returns to ships; Francis Scott Key writes "The Star-Spangled Banner."

15 September 1814: British land and naval attack on Fort Boyer, Alabama, is repelled.

26 September 1814: British attack on American privateer *General Armstrong*, under Captain Samuel Chester Reid, at Fayal in the Azores delays arrival of British infantry for attack on New Orleans.

5 November 1814: Americans abandon Fort Erie and return to U.S. territory.

7 November 1814: American force under Andrew Jackson attacks and occupies Spanish-held Pensacola, Florida.

26–27 November 1814: British fleet leaves Negril, Jamaica, for the attack on New Orleans.

14 December 1814: Five gunboats under Lieutenant Thomas ap Catesby Jones stationed at the entrance to Lake Borgne, Louisiana, succumb to larger attacking British force.

21 December 1814: British land at Villiers Plantation, Louisiana, and establish camp.

23 December 1814: Jackson conducts a night attack on British encampment at Villiers Plantation.

24 December 1814: U.S. and British negotiators in Ghent, Flanders, sign peace treaty.

8 January 1815: Jackson's entrenched force turns back the British attack at Chalmette, Louisiana.

15 January 1815: Decatur surrenders frigate *President* to British squadron in the Atlantic.

27 January 1815: British evacuate Louisiana.

11 February 1815: HMS *Favorite* arrives in New York City with Treaty of Ghent and news of peace.

14 February 1815: Treaty reaches Washington.

16 February 1815: Senate approves treaty and President Madison signs it, ending the war.

20 February 1815: *Constitution* under Captain Charles Stewart captures HMS *Cyane* and HMS *Levant* off the coast of Africa near Madeira.

23 March 1815: *Hornet* under Captain James Biddle defeats HMS *Penguin* in South Atlantic.

18 June 1815: Duke of Wellington defeats Napoleon at Waterloo.

30 June 1815: *Peacock* under Warrington defeats HMS *Nautilus* in Indian Ocean.

INTRODUCTION

At the 1912 annual meeting of the American Historical Association, held that year in Boston, one of America's preeminent historians, Charles Francis Adams, the great-grandson of John Adams, gave the keynote address to an audience of distinguished academics and public officials, including former President Theodore Roosevelt, who was now president of the Association. Adams's theme was the widely discussed—and controversial—issue of whether the United States was a "world power" and, if so, when did she become one. He answered in the affirmative, and gave the moment of her rise to preeminence:

> I propose to specify the exact day of the year and month and week, the hour and almost the minute at which the United States blazed as an indisputable world power on the astonished, and, for some time yet, incredulous nations. To be specific, it was at thirty minutes after six o'clock of the afternoon of Wednesday, August 19, 1812. On that day and at that hour, just twenty weeks over a hundred

years ago, this country, I confidently submit, became a nationality to be reckoned with; and such it has ever since been.

Adams did not have to remind his audience what had happened at that specified moment. They all knew, as did every schoolboy in the nation. That was the moment when the American frigate *Constitution* shattered and sank the British frigate *Guerriere* in the first major sea battle of the War of 1812.

The significance of that victory—that the United States had achieved the rank of world power within a few decades of its birth—resonated with Americans for decades before and after Adams's address. A century after the war, the American intellectual elite were still thrilled by the U.S. military success against the imperial might of Great Britain.

But time has passed, and that battle and the war it inaugurated have slipped from our collective remembrance and from the pages of our history books.

It is said that the trouble with trying to learn history is that they keep adding to it. From the day our nation was founded, Americans have been making history at a heady pace. Finding space on the cluttered shelves of our memory for the new "stuff" forces us into periodic house cleanings to make way for it. In the process, events that no longer seem as important as they once did get condensed into smaller spaces, while others get carted off to the historical attic.

The War of 1812, in which a small, upstart country defied the world's most fearsome military power, is one of those events that has undergone vigorous historical condensation over the past several decades. Indeed, until quite recently, it looked like it was being packed up for attic storage. The title of a book published in 1990 might have astonished Charles Adams: *The War of 1812: A Forgotten Conflict.*

Trends in high school history textbooks, a handy benchmark of who's in and who's out, suggest that the War of 1812 is boxed and on its way up the stairs. L. D. Baldwin's and M. S. Warring's *History of Our Republic*, published in 1965, was typical of its time, devoting twelve of its eight hundred pages to the War of 1812 and containing three references to Commodore Stephen Decatur, including a brief sidebar biography, whom the authors praised as "one of the authentic heroes of the War of 1812."

A high school text book of similar sophistication, *Pathways to the Present*, published in 1998, gives only two pages to the War of 1812 and makes no mention of Decatur, in whose honor scores of American cities, counties, libraries, ships, and streets have been named since his tragic death in 1820.

A nine-month high school class attempting to cover four centuries of American history can spend only so much time on the War of 1812, of course. When *History of Our Republic* was published, the civil rights movement was just getting under way, the Vietnam War lay almost entirely in the future, the Cold War was far from settled, Islam was an inconsequential actor on the world stage, and no one could assume that America would close out the twentieth century as the transcendent military and economic power.

But for many of our ancestors, including some still living, the War of 1812 marked America's coming of age, when she took her rightful place among the leading nations of the world. It was in the years immediately after the war that the people of the United States began to think of themselves as "Americans," an appellation that had been mostly used by the British, and as a term of derision. Prior to the war, our ancestors thought of themselves as Pennsylvanians, New Yorkers, or Virginians—people identified by their state or region who had joined together in a whole that remained very much the sum of its parts.

Somewhere along the way, perhaps during the latter part of the twentieth century, the War of 1812—sometimes called the Second War of Independence—began to fade from memory and drift out of our curricula. Perhaps it was too identified with the heroic and the romantic at a time when the heroic and the romantic had fallen out of fashion among professional historians.

The heroic and the romantic have lived on, however, in popular fiction through the prodigious talent of a half-dozen or so bestselling British novelists who embraced "the age of fighting sail" as their theme. Though their stories deal primarily with Britain's naval conflict with Napoleon, several of these writers provide memorable accounts—thinly disguised as fiction—of some of the epochal sea battles of the War of 1812 through the eyes of their British protagonists.

For more than half a century, American readers have been devouring the books of these British authors, with their quasi-fictional adventures of British naval officers going to sea in mighty wooden sailing ships to battle England's enemies, including us! C. S. Forester created the genre in 1937 with his first Horatio Hornblower novel. In the 1970s C. Northcote Parkinson took time off from weightier endeavors like creating "Parkinson's Law" to write his Richard

Delancey series of Napoleonic nautical novels. Also widely read on both sides of the Atlantic are Dudley Pope's Nicholas Ramage series, Richard Woodman's Nathaniel Drinkwater series, and perhaps most popular of all, Patrick O'Brian's twenty-novel series featuring Jack Aubrey and Stephen Maturin, which has sold eight million copies since *Master and Commander* was published in 1970.

Although these books are largely devoted to England's struggle against the French and its shifting array of allies and conquests, several authors, notably O'Brian, occasionally venture across the North Atlantic to the renewed conflict with their former colonies. In *The Fortune of War*, Jack Aubrey witnesses the battles between *Java* and *Constitution* and between *Chesapeake* and *Shannon*, while *The Far Side of the World* follows Aubrey's voyage across the Pacific in search of USS *Norfolk*, a fictionalized version of the hunt for David Porter, whose USS *Essex* was devastating the British whaling fleet. In *The Reverse of the Medal*, *Letter of Marque*, and *Wine-Dark Sea*, Aubrey tangles with a couple of the five hundred or more American privateers who captured or sank an estimated 1,345 British merchant ships during the War of 1812.

And while C. S. Forester is famous for the Hornblower series and for his immensely readable *The Age of Fighting Sail* (1956), a historical account of America's naval actions against the British during the War of 1812, few know of *The Captain from Connecticut* (1941), his only fictional account of the war from an American perspective. The book's snowy opening scene in New York Harbor bears a striking resemblance to the launch of Decatur's ill-fated voyage in the *President*.

However compelling, dramatic, heroic, and wonderfully romantic these works of fiction are, few of their avid readers realize that the men who actually fought these battles were vastly more interesting than their fictional counterparts. There was a reason that Patrick O'Brian modeled Jack Aubrey and the *Sophie* after Sir Thomas Cochrane and his sloop of war *Speedy*. Aubrey's fictional taking of the Spanish xebec-frigate *Cacafuego* in *Master and Commander* is a close retelling of Cochrane's taking of *El Gamo*. As the ships closed for boarding, *Speedy*'s surgeon, Mr. Guthrie, took the helm of the vessel, much as Dr. Stephen Maturin does in *Master and Commander*, allowing Aubrey to lead his crew onto the enemy frigate. Indeed, in an Author's Note, O'Brian acknowledges his historical sources:

> When one is writing about the Royal Navy of the eighteenth and early nineteenth centuries it is difficult to do full justice to one's subject; for so very often the improbable reality outruns fiction. Even an uncommonly warm and industrious imagination could scarcely produce the frail shape of Commodore Nelson leaping from his battered seventy-four-gun *Captain* through the quarter-gallery window of the eighty-gun *San Nicholas*, taking her, and hurrying on across her deck to board the towering *San Josef* of a hundred and twelve guns.

Just as all the creative talent in the world could not invent a character like Nelson, no novelist could invent the ferocious and cunning Stephen Decatur, the firey David Porter, the bitter William Bainbridge in search of redemption, or the rough old salt Isaac Hull, on whose stout shoulders the hope of a young nation rested in the first month of war.

This is their story, and the story of the thousands of other American men and boys who stood behind the guns and gave better than they got.

CHAPTER ONE

AMERICA AND BRITAIN DRIFT TOWARD WAR

In his memoirs of his time as a sailor aboard the American frigates *Constitution* and *John Adams* during the War of 1812, Moses Smith recounts a tragic story about an American seaman's attempt to escape British impressment—a form of abduction and involuntary naval service practiced by recruiters for the Royal Navy in the early nineteenth century:

> About this time the *John Adams* arrived at Annapolis from a foreign cruise, and from her men we learned of a striking case of heroism, which is worthy to be told. A coloured seaman belonging to New York had been pressed into English service, and when the *Adams* was lying off their coast, he got an opportunity to come on board of her as one of a boat's crew, sent with an officer upon some errand. Thinking now his time had come to escape from the British, he determined if possible not to return. Accordingly, as he stood on the deck of the *Adams*, he suddenly seized a boarding axe, and in the presence of the crew, cut off the fingers of his right hand

> at a single blow. Then with his left hand holding up the bloody weapon, he exclaimed, "Now let the English take me if they want me." However disabled as he was, they took him back, our officers having no power to interfere. If patriotism be anything but a name, then surely this noble african deserved a better fate. There are exalted qualities often concealed beneath a darkened skin.[1]

Exactly how many Americans were impressed by the British is uncertain because of spotty record-keeping and limited reporting. Estimates range from a low of 2,500 to a high of 25,000 sailors. One source contends that about 2,400 seamen were impressed between 1792 and 1802.[2] When Captain Thomas Masterman Hardy sailed HMS *Victory* through the French line at Trafalgar and into *Redoubtable*'s port,[3] twenty-two impressed American sailors were serving aboard Nelson's flagship.[4] In 1805, British warships took up permanent station outside American ports to inspect American ships for British-born sailors, and the British consul in New York City as much as admitted that the port was effectively under blockade. Seizures of U.S. seamen resumed with vigor, and by the time America declared war in June 1812, impressments had tripled to about 7,500.

Britain's practice of impressment was driven by severe manpower shortages and the need to maintain a vast naval fleet and army to counter those of Napoleon. By 1812, Britain had been at war with France and its allies for all but a few of the past twenty years in a conflict that had been raging on and off for many decades before. The origins of the current conflict could be said to have stretched back to the Seven Years War, fought between 1754 and 1760, and known to Americans as the French and Indian War. That war led to the loss of French Canada to the British, and the pursuit of revenge led France to provide essential military support to the American colonies during their War of Independence. When Napoleon seized power in 1799, Anglo-French warfare resumed with a vengeance and continued at a high intensity until Napoleon was defeated at Waterloo in 1815.

This perpetual state of war stretched Britain's resources to the limits. Among the many problems she confronted were substantial and pervasive manpower shortages in the navy. With the work demanding, pay low, discipline severe, and risk of death high from disease, injury, and combat, the British fleet—which at times numbered as many as a thousand ships—struggled with a perennial shortage of seamen. During the Seven Years War the Royal Navy lost 133,700 men to disease and desertion alone.[5] When war with France flared up again in 1793 and continued largely unimpeded through the next several decades, the navy suffered an estimated additional 92,386 deaths from all sources, with deaths from combat accounting for the smallest number of all.[6] By 1812, most British ships were going to sea with less than a full complement, and many of those on board were inexperienced boys.

Such harsh and dangerous conditions deterred enlistment and encouraged desertions by those already in service. Desertions of able-bodied seamen ran high during these years, and many British deserters sought refuge in the American merchant fleet or navy, where the pay was higher, terms of enlistment shorter, and conditions better. One naval historian notes that "the problem was particularly acute for the detached squadrons operating in American waters, where individual desertions occurred daily, and where occasionally the entire crew of a small British naval vessel would mutiny, run the ship in to the American coast, and desert en masse."[7] Lord Nelson estimated that as many as 42,000 men had deserted between 1793 and 1802 and noted that "whenever a large convoy is assembled at Portsmouth and our fleet is in port, not less than 1,000 men desert from our navy."[8]

With the powerful navy essential to Britain's national defense and economic prosperity, British officers often went to extreme lengths to fill out their crews through impressment. Although the practice of impressment is often associated with wars of the late eighteenth and early nineteenth centuries, such abductions had been a staple of British recruiting practices well before then, as Falstaff observes in Shakespeare's *King Henry IV*:

> If I be not ashamed of my soldiers, I am a soused gurnet. I have misused the king's press damnably. I have got, in exchange of a hundred and fifty soldiers, three hundred and odd pounds. I press me none but good householders; yeoman's sons; inquire me out contracted bachelors....[9]

In the early years of the Napoleonic Wars, impressment was largely limited to the British Isles, where press gangs roamed the streets of coastal cities and abducted able-bodied males to serve aboard warships. As time passed, few able-bodied men were foolish enough to wander the streets of port cities at night, forcing the navy to extend its impressment activities farther afield. The ships of the neutral and militarily weak German seafaring states of Bremen and Hamburg were favorite targets of British officers for impressed sailors, as were those of the neutral United States, whose vast merchant fleet and naval ships often included among their crew many seamen who had emigrated, legally or illegally, from Britain and Ireland to America.

Because Britain did not recognize U.S. naturalization law, any British-born seaman working an American ship, even if he was a naturalized citizen and had the papers to prove it, was fair game for an English ship short of crewmen. The principle behind these seizures, regardless of naturalization, was the doctrine of inalienable allegiance, according to which anyone born a British subject remained a subject himself and could be seized long after he emigrated and acquired citizenship elsewhere.[10] Or as the *Times* noted, "The Americans cannot, by any verbal process whatever, rob England of her right to the services of English-born subjects. They cannot naturalize against nature."[11]

While American anger grew over the practice of impressment, the British ignored the complaints and justified the practice by noting that America's navy and the nation's vast merchant fleet had become welcome havens to British deserters. President Jefferson's Treasury secretary, Albert Gallatin, estimated that as many as five thousand British seamen were employed in the U.S. merchant fleet in 1803, but some later studies place this number as high as twenty thousand,[12] accounting for a substantial share of the estimated fifty thousand to one hundred thousand seamen serving on American merchant vessels at the time.[13] The historian Donald Hickey estimates that as many as ten thousand Americans may have been impressed into British service during the French Revolutionary and the Napoleonic Wars.[14] In part, the attraction of work aboard U.S. vessels may also have stemmed from the 1790 Act for the Government Regulation of Seamen, which established minimum standards of work and medical care on board U.S. ships.

British sailors also served aboard U.S. warships, sometimes in large numbers. In 1803, while struggling to raise a crew for the *Constitution*, Commodore Preble complained, "I don't believe I have 20 native American sailors on board" of the 165 or so present.[15] On one cruise during 1807, 149 of *Constitution*'s crew of 419 were said to be British subjects,[16] and even during the warfare that began in earnest in 1812, evidence suggests a continuing British presence on U.S. warships, though probably a fairly small one given that the death sentence would now apply to deserters to the enemy.

Many desertions occurred when British ships visited American and other foreign ports for repair and provisions, which in turn encouraged British officers to confine their sailors to the ship while in port, further adding to the misery of being a British sailor. One British seaman who escaped by jumping overboard in New York Harbor claimed he had not been off his ship in nine years. But even these extreme measures were sometimes overcome, as when in 1807 more than forty members of the crew of HMS *Jason* mutinied in New York Harbor in an attempt to flee British service.[17] Samuel Johnson once observed, "No man will be a sailor who has contrivance enough to get himself into jail; for being in a ship is being in a jail, with the chance of being drowned."[18]

Although by comparison with the American navy, life aboard a British warship was excessively harsh, such conditions largely mirrored those existing in England, where as many as two hundred separate offenses were punishable by hanging, and where public execution was a regular feature of town life.[19] Sometimes the punishment was worse, as when in March 1812 two British sailors who had earlier deserted to the French at the Isle of France (Mauritius) were sentenced to be hanged, drawn, and quartered at Horsemonger Lane in London.[20] Under some circumstances even officers were severely punished, as in October 1807 when Lieutenant William Berry of the *Hazard* was hanged for unclean sexual practices, which court documents describe as "the horrid and abominable crime which delicacy forbids us to name."[21]

In an effort to deter the impressments of American seamen by British officers, the U.S. Congress enacted in 1796 the Act for the Protection and Relief of American Seamen, which authorized the issuance of "Seaman's Protection Certificates."[22] But in fairness to Britain, many of the naturalizations claimed by her subjects, former or otherwise, were phony and often contrived for the convenience of avoiding hard duty at home. The certificates of citizenship the U.S. began issuing in 1796—called "protections" by sailors—were often of questionable origin. Some British seamen acquired such certificates by lying about their place of birth to compliant magistrates, while others simply bought them from "obliging" Americans, often for no more than a dollar.[23] Combined with Britain's contention that there existed an inalienable allegiance, such certificates—whether real or forged—were largely disregarded by British captains looking to fill out their crew from a waylaid American ship.

While most of the targets of these British search-and-abduct missions were American merchant vessels, and most American captains would peacefully, if reluctantly, comply with the demands, on a few occasions the British would insist upon searching U.S. warships for deserters. One such instance occurred in 1798 when the USS *Ganges*, a former merchantman recently converted to a lightly armed warship and sailing under the command of Captain Thomas Tingey, was accosted by the British frigate *Surprise* (formerly the French *Unité*)[24] as it returned home from a cruise of the Caribbean. According to what may have been an exaggerated report of the incident that appeared in the *Connecticut Courant*,

> an officer of the *Surprise*, an English frigate of 44 guns, boarded [the *Ganges*] … and demanded all the Englishmen on board, also to examine the protections of American seamen. Captain Tingey's answer was manly and noble. "A PUBLIC SHIP CARRIES NO PROTECTION BUT HER FLAG. I DO NOT EXPECT TO SUCCEED IN A CONTEST WITH YOU, BUT I WILL DIE AT MY QUARTERS BEFORE A MAN SHALL BE TAKEN FROM THE SHIP." The crew gave him three cheers, ran to quarters and called for *Yankee Doodle*. The *Surprise*, upon hearing of our determination, chose to leave us rather than to fight for dead men.[25]

While Britain claimed that its victims of impressment were limited to British-born seamen, in practice she impressed, intentionally or not, hundreds, if not thousands of American-born seamen into British crews. Reflecting the magnitude of such seizures, between 1802 and 1812 the British Admiralty voluntarily released about a third of the American seamen who were earlier impressed through the excessive zeal of some of its officers.

Most of the impressed American seamen were not so fortunate and spent many years aboard British warships, sometimes in combat against their own countrymen. Even less fortunate were the several thousand who were captured or impressed but sent to the prison camp at Dartmoor in southwest England or to the even more horrific British prison ships anchored at ports throughout the theater of war. At war's end, as many as 3,500 U.S. seamen, most taken from merchant ships and privateers, were held at Dartmoor, while thousands more were held in prison ships anchored off the English, American, or Jamaican coasts.

Britain's effort to bulk up its crews by abducting foreign sailors was accompanied by a more disturbing effort to find and punish deserters. The goal was not to bring strays back into the fold but to hang them from the yardarms as an example to any who might also be thinking about shortening their careers in the Royal Navy.

II

Britain eventually discovered the limits of America's patience with foreign interference with the rights of its sailors and ships. On a warm and sunny June day in 1807, the American frigate *Chesapeake,* commanded by Commodore James Barron, left her base in Norfolk, Virginia, for duty in the Mediterranean, where the U.S. Navy still patrolled to deter the Barbary pirates from seizing American merchant vessels and enslaving their crews. As the *Chesapeake* passed Lynnhaven Bay on her way to the Atlantic, her lookout sighted the British frigates *Melampus* and *Bellona*—the latter carrying fourteen impressed American crewmen—which were stationed off Lynnhaven to intercept the three French frigates under repair in Annapolis and Norfolk. History does not record the reaction to this sighting by three of *Chesapeake*'s new crewmen (one an African-American), William Ware, Daniel Martin, and John Strachan. Until their recent desertion from *Melampus,* the *Chesapeake*'s three new sailors had been involuntary members of the British crew as a result of their earlier impressment from an American ship.

From their spies in Norfolk, the British knew that the three Americans and another deserter were on board the *Chesapeake* and were intent upon getting them back. And as the *Chesapeake* rounded Cape Henry and entered the international waters of the Atlantic, she found herself pursued by the frigate *Leopard* under the command of Captain Salusbury Pryce Humphreys, son of a Shopshire clergyman and an *arriviste* to the minor gentry by way of marriage to an heiress. Late that afternoon the *Chesapeake* hove to in response to a signal from the *Leopard*, which sent a boarding party under the command of Lieutenant John Meade to the *Chesapeake*. Once on board, Meade asked Barron to muster his crew to be inspected for British deserters. Barron refused, Meade returned to his ship, and the *Leopard* soon fired several warning shots. Minutes later *Leopard* pulled alongside the American frigate and let go with several broadsides into the hull of the unprepared *Chesapeake*, killing four Americans and severely wounding eight.

Barron quickly struck his colors, but not before twenty-three-year-old Lieutenant William Henry Allen took a hot coal (legend has it that he carried the coal in his bare hands) from the galley and used it to ignite the fuse to fire one of *Chesapeake*'s cannons at the *Leopard*. The British reboarded the ship and removed the three *Melampus* deserters, as well as a fourth, a white sailor carried on the *Chesapeake*'s books as John Wilson (né Jenkin Ratford), who was also accused of deserting from British service. Alleged to be British by birth, Wilson/Ratford was later hanged from a ship's yardarm in Halifax, Nova Scotia, while the three other seamen were sentenced to five hundred lashes and then imprisoned in Halifax.

Viewed by most as responsible for not preparing *Chesapeake* for combat in an environment of threat and danger and for having surrendered his ship without firing a (authorized) shot, Barron was subjected to a court-martial headed by Captain Alexander Murray. Although acquitted on the charges of cowardice and unnecessary surrender of his ship, Barron was found guilty of neglecting to have his ship ready for battle and suspended from duty for five years without pay.[26] Although the case against Barron was strong, the circumstances surrounding the *Chesapeake*'s surrender and Barron's court-martial aroused strong and bitter feelings. Lieutenant Allen estimated that between 22 June 1807 and 27 August 1808, seven duels were fought between officers of the *Chesapeake*.[27] One naval historian puts the tally at nine.[28]

One duel between the ship's captain, Charles Gordon, and its doctor, Stark, degenerated to the point where the seconds were firing at each other as well. Alarmed by the growing violence among his officer corps, Secretary of the Navy Robert Smith ordered Captain Stephen Decatur to put an end to the dueling. Decatur, himself an active participant in duels during his naval career, responded to Smith, "I am happy to inform you that Captain Gordon has entirely recovered from his wounds—all differences between the officers & gentlemen at this place I am informed are adjusted."[29]

Upon his return to England, *Leopard*'s Captain Humphreys was also relieved of command and would never hold another, although this setback did not prevent his enjoying a rich and rewarding life. By the time war was finally declared in 1812, Humphreys had changed his name to Davenport and had married another, even wealthier, heiress following the untimely demise of his first wife in 1808.[30] British Vice Admiral George Cranfield Berkeley, who ran Britain's northern station from Halifax, Nova Scotia, and who ordered Humphreys to find and seize the hapless Ratford, was also relieved of command and called home. Britain's foreign secretary, George Canning, further admitted that his country had no right to search for deserters in American warships,[31] but such incidents continued until war was formally declared. Importantly, Canning's disclaimer did not apply to U.S. merchant ships, from which the vast majority of impressed American seamen were abducted.

The effects of the unprovoked attack on the *Chesapeake* were far-reaching and did as much as anything else to stoke the war fever slowly sweeping the American south and western frontier. At the port of Norfolk, Virginia, citizens attacked the British fleet's supply vessels and destroyed hundreds of water casks. Officials were forced to call up the militia when angry mobs isolated the British consul from the fleet. The *Washington Federalist* wrote, "We have never, on any occasion, witnessed the spirit of the people excited to so great a degree of indignation, or such a thirst for revenge." Soon after, the American poet William Ray published "War, Or a Prospect of It," which ended with the stanza,[32]

Remember Lexington
And Bunker's tragic hill;
The same who spilt your blood thereon,
Your blood again would spill.

President Jefferson responded to the spreading sense of outrage with the empty gesture of ordering British warships out of U.S. territorial waters, which did little to deter the marauding British warships. Just a few weeks later and close to where the *Leopard* attacked the *Chesapeake*, ships of the British fleet operating off the Virginia Capes fired on a federal revenue cutter carrying Vice President George Clinton and his sick daughter.[33] Ordered to stop by the British and then briefly pursued when it refused, the cutter's commander held his course and prepared the ship for combat. The British declined the offer, but not before firing several musket shots at the vice president's vessel.

The *Chesapeake-Leopard* engagement was by no means the first such affront to U.S. sensibilities, although it was the first involving a U.S. warship, making it particularly humiliating to Jefferson's government and his navy. More than a year earlier, in April 1806, the sixty-gun British frigate *Leander*, which often patrolled off New York City, intercepted the American merchant schooner *Republic* by firing a shot across its bow as it headed toward the entrance to New York Harbor. The schooner quickly complied, but the *Leander* inexplicably fired a second and a third shot, the last decapitating John Pierce, the *Republic*'s helmsman.[34]

Pierce's headless body was brought ashore and displayed at the Tontine Coffee House before being buried at public expense at the direction of

New York mayor DeWitt Clinton, nephew of Vice President Clinton. New Yorkers were outraged, and an angry mob set upon five of *Leander*'s supply boats, seizing their contents and distributing them to the city's poor. Another angry mob sailed out to retake two merchant ships that had earlier been seized by *Leander* and were waiting to be sold for prize money. Not to be outdone by an unruly mob seeking rough justice, President Jefferson ordered the arrest of the ship's captain, an order as empty as the later one banning British warships from American waters, and one that was never fulfilled.

The wanton nature of these acts undermined the influence of a substantial portion of the American public still opposed to war with Britain despite the indignities to which the nation was frequently treated. For them, the loss of a hapless sailor here and there was a small price to pay for the profitable commercial access to Britain and its hungry war machine. But the incident between the *Chesapeake* and *Leopard* began the shift in public sentiment and ultimately put America on the path to war.

III

Many Americans quickly resumed their efforts to profit from their antagonists' needs. Typical was the response in the Norfolk region where, just three weeks after the attack on the *Chesapeake*, Virginia farmers were meeting on the beach near Lynnhaven with the blockading British naval officers to sell them fresh beef. At the same time American merchant vessels laden with provisions left Norfolk to meet just outside the Virginia Capes with British supply tenders serving the squadron stationed at the mouth of the Chesapeake Bay to intercept American ships coming and going.

In the years leading up to the war, America was a major producer of raw materials and food stuffs for Britain and its Caribbean colonies and for the hungry French war machine that conquered most of continental Europe. The process benefited all sides. American grain, cotton, timber, tobacco, rum, and other products were shipped to Europe, and the proceeds of these exports financed imports of finished goods from Britain, including the British-made guns that armed several of the American warships. American food products also fed the vast slave economy of the French, British, and Dutch Caribbean colonies that grew the sugar that sweetened the tables of Europe and America.

American merchants also traded grain for sugar and turned the sugar into molasses, from which rum was produced by distillers in New York and New England for sale to Europe.

An economy dependent upon trade is also an economy dependent upon ocean transport, and American entrepreneurs and investors quickly turned this dependence into an opportunity to create one of the world's largest merchant fleets, supported by a vast shipbuilding and service industry employing tens of thousands of laborers, skilled tradesmen, and sailors. By 1810, more than 90 percent of America's exports and imports were carried in American ships, and this comparative advantage in seafaring led to America's dominance of the global whaling trade, which at this time was the only source of oil for household illumination. America's emphasis on shipping also encouraged the creation of domestic financial service industries such as insurance, stock-brokering, and banking to facilitate and protect the trade and the fleet that carried it.

Given America's comparative advantage in the production of raw materials, trade, and transport, the war in Europe was a boon to American industry. Businessmen, workers, and farmers found ready markets among the belligerent nations that had to maintain, equip, and feed vast armies and navies. Belonging to a neutral power, American merchants traded with England and France and the allies of both, profiting handsomely from the needs of all.

But as the Napoleonic Wars dragged on through their second decade, with no end in sight, the opposing powers looked for additional ways to undermine their enemy's ability to wage war, and the flow of supplies from neutral nations to the combatants became a choice target for interdiction.

In the early stages of its renewed war with France, Britain chose not to aggressively enforce its Rule of 1756, which limited trade by neutral countries with the nation's enemies. American merchant ships responded to the selective enforcement by pretending to honor these long-standing restrictions and adopting a process called the "broken voyage," by which products of, say, the West Indies destined for France were first taken to an American port, where they were "neutralized" for reshipment to Europe. Nonetheless, the process was not without tensions, and many American ships were still subject to search and seizure if it was believed they were headed to an enemy port under British blockade. Also during this early period in the conflict, Britain permitted the selective suspension of some of the provisions of the Navigation Acts to allow

American merchant ships to trade directly with British colonies in the West Indies. Such privileges did not sit well with British shipping interests, which opposed any relaxation of their legal monopoly on trade within the empire.

These accommodative trade practices began to unravel after 1803, when tensions between Britain and France worsened and a French invasion of the British Isles became a serious concern of the government. The first major blow to this liberalized system of trade came in May 1805 with the *Essex* (a U.S. merchant ship) decision, in which the Lords Commissioners of Appeals ruled that the "mere importation of goods into a neutral country was not enough to neutralize these goods unless a *bona fide* import duty was paid."[35] The ruling led to an increase in the number of American merchant ships seized in the Caribbean, English Channel, and North Sea and exacerbated the tensions between the two nations in an environment already simmering over the increase in the rate of impressment of American seamen.

Unwilling to let these restrictive acts go unanswered, Congress and the president began openly to discuss the possibility of retaliatory trade restrictions against Britain. In early 1806 they passed the Non-Importation Act, giving the president the power to prohibit the importation of a number of British products. Implemented in late 1807, the act was designed to threaten some British manufacturers with the loss of a major market in the hope that they would urge their government to loosen the new restrictions on American trade.

Also in 1806, during Charles James Fox's brief tenure as foreign secretary, Britain enacted the American Intercourse Bill to codify many of the informal liberalizations that had occurred over the past decade as well as those restrictions stemming from the *Essex* decision. But by attempting to clarify privileges and opportunities stemming from custom and lax enforcement, British maritime interests were mobilized to more aggressively defend and re-establish their privileges, including the monopoly they held on certain trade practices. In turn, the incitement of British shipping interests to more aggressively defend their interests would help foster the even more restrictive policies soon to emerge in a nation at war.

The first apparent blow to liberalization efforts occurred with the Orders in Council of 16 May 1806, proclaiming a blockade of a limited area of the French coastline but allowing neutral shipping outside the area, subject to certain restrictions. While Britain justified the new order as a further clarification of existing informal (and generous) concessions to neutral traders, the

Americans viewed the order as a formal codification of prohibitions that undermined the principles of free trade. With tensions further inflamed by *Leander*'s attack on an unarmed coaster outside New York City and an escalation in the rate of impressments, President Jefferson sent James Monroe and William Pinkney to London to negotiate a formal maritime treaty with Britain that would establish a new set of rules by which the Americans would respect Britain's compelling defense interests while Britain, in turn, would end impressment and permit a more open trade regime. But after months of negotiation, the treaty they brought back to Washington was unacceptable to both Congress and the president, in large part because it was silent on impressment. President Jefferson wrote to Monroe that "the British Commissioners appear to have screwed every article as far as it would bear, and yielded nothing."[36]

Seeing these worsening relations as an opportunity to exacerbate tensions between one of his enemies and a rich, productive neutral, Napoleon issued his Berlin Decree on 21 November 1806, putting Britain under blockade and prohibiting trade in British goods. While not a decree that the battered French navy could ever enforce on the high seas, it did allow Napoleon to exclude from French ports any ship that had previously visited a British port. Despite the decree's obviously undesirable consequences, American objections to it were rather tepid, focused as the country was on the bigger problems with Britain and its powerful navy and merchant fleet. Britain, consumed by the threat of Napoleon, saw it differently and responded to America's limited objection to the French decree by wondering whose side they were on in the conflict.

In response to the Berlin Decree, Britain issued a new order in council on 7 January 1807, which prohibited the ships of neutral nations from trading between ports under French control, further restricting opportunities for U.S. merchant vessels pursuing legitimate commercial interests on the European continent. Not surprisingly, the new order added fuel to the fire ignited by Britain's response to the Monroe-Pinkney mission. As these diplomatic tensions worsened, British shipping interests saw an opportunity, and the pressure they brought to bear on the government contributed to another order in council, issued on 11 November 1807, which prohibited any neutral ship from trading with France unless it first visited a British port and paid a duty.

Napoleon, in turn, responded with his Milan Decree of 7 December 1807, authorizing the seizure of any neutral ship that fulfilled the requirements of the new order in council. The historian Reginald Horsman observes, "The chains on America were complete. No American ship could sail to a European port under the control of Napoleon without being liable to seizure: by a British ship if she had not called at a British port, and by Napoleon's officials if she had."[37]

With diplomatic efforts yielding nothing, and with the threat of the Non-Importation Act doing little to soften Britain's hardening stance, Jefferson proposed the Embargo Act in early December 1807. Quickly passed by the House and Senate, the bill was signed into law three days before Christmas. The act placed a total embargo on all exports from and imports to the United States. A timid and wavering Jefferson justified it as an attempt to protect American ships, merchandise, and seamen, not an effort to retaliate against England and France for their many transgressions against American trade interests. Napoleon, perhaps wanting to demonstrate his understanding of these subtle nuances as well as his sense of humor, responded to Jefferson's new embargo with the Bayonne Decree of 17 April 1808, allowing French authorities to seize any and all American ships in French ports on the pretext that the Embargo Act had made such shipping illegal, and he was merely helping America enforce its laws.

The European powers quickly found alternatives to the embargoed American products—Britain, for example, began importing grain from Russia, often at lower prices. The only victim of the act was the American economy. Pundits described Jefferson's painful strategy as one of *O Grab Me* (embargo spelled backward). A political cartoonist sympathetic to the president's effort drew a snapping turtle labeled "Ograbme" holding onto the trousers of a British sailor while a caricature of Jefferson stands by saying "D—n it, how he nicks 'em."

Nick 'em he did, but the nicking was mostly at the flesh of American workers, farmers, seamen, and merchants, for whom the embargo was a catastrophe. In 1808 American exports fell to just $22 million, about a fifth of the $108 million of export business of the previous year, while imports that year declined to $58 million from 1807's $148 million. In New York City alone, 120 firms went out of business and 1,200 debtors were in custody, including 500 who owed ten dollars or less. The estimated number of destitute in New York rose ten-fold during 1808, and each week 6,000 lined up at the alms house for their daily distribution of food. Unemployed sailors paraded through town demanding bread or work, and hundreds of ships lay idle at the city's piers. Adding to the misery was an escalation in prices that put the basic necessities out of the reach of many.[38]

In Philadelphia, Mayor Robert Wharton wrote his brother, "Our city as to traffic is almost a desert, wharves crowded with empty vessels, the noise and buz of commerce not heard, whilst hundreds of labourers are ranging the streets without employ or the means of getting bread for their distressed Families."[39] Up until the embargo, the port of Philadelphia was visited by more than 3,500 merchant vessels a year, a level of business that it would never recover.

In Salem, Massachusetts, then a thriving port, only twenty-five of the town's 185 vessels remained active in trade. Unemployed mariners and shipbuilders flocked to soup kitchens, and in 1808 only three ships left Salem for a European port.[40] Altogether, an estimated 55,000 American seamen lost their jobs as well as another hundred thousand in related industries.[41]

Conditions for many workmen and merchants in Britain also became severe as Napoleon's conquest of continental Europe closed more and more ports to British trade, while America's Non-Intercourse Act, which replaced the disastrous Embargo Act, shut off the only important market—except for Russia—left open to British merchants. The winter of 1811–1812, moreover, was one of the bitterest in British history, as the Little Ice Age continued to ravage western Europe: "A crop failure drove up the price of wheat, warehouses were crammed with goods for which there was no market, factories were closing and workmen rioting."[42]

As British harassment continued, the American people were swept by waves of conflict and dissension, with the public mood swinging from anger at the British aggressor to anger at the Jefferson administration for its pointless Embargo Act, which hurt Americans far more than the British. Hostility toward Jefferson was at its most intense in New England, where dependence on maritime trade was greatest. Many northeastern leaders agitated for a regional convention to nullify the Embargo Act, while threats of secession were raised and debated in town meetings throughout the region. The intensity of feelings in Congress led to the first duel ever between members. New York Representative Barent Gardenier challenged Representative G. W. Campbell of Tennessee, a defender of Jefferson's policies. Gardenier was seriously wounded.[43]

IV

Still, the vast majority of Americans must have felt that a policy of vacillation was preferable to one of war or complete concession to British abuse. In November 1808 they elected James Madison, Jefferson's secretary of state, to the presidency by a comfortable margin on a "stay-the-course" strategy. Perhaps because he recognized that his efforts had done more harm than good, Jefferson's last act as president was to sign a bill replacing the Embargo Act with the Non-Intercourse Act, which would give American diplomats more flexibility in negotiating with Britain. Jefferson left Washington a few days later for Monticello, where he remained for the rest of his life, dividing his time between tending to his financially troubled plantation, complaining about the performance of American generals in the coming war, and corresponding with his friends and admirers throughout the world.

Madison quickly tried to reach a settlement with the European powers, promising both the British and French a restoration of commercial ties in return for the repeal of the decrees that harmed American trade and commerce. Directing his efforts first toward the British, he worked out a tentative agreement in Washington with Britain's minister to the United States, but it was rejected by Canning, the foreign minister. Napoleon took advantage of the breakdown in American negotiations with England, promising to respect American maritime trade if the British revoked their orders in council.

As was often the case, Napoleon failed to honor his promise and continued to seize American shipping, but his diplomatic gambit hastened the collapse of America's relations with Britain. In response to Napoleon's disingenuous concessions, President Madison advised the British in November 1810 that America would break off all trade if the orders in council were not repealed. Britain still refused, and the trade relations with America that had resumed with the enactment of the Non-Intercourse Act were promptly ended.

Although the U.S. sent numerous delegations to London in search of a diplomatic settlement of the frictions and confrontation that by now had become a regular feature of Anglo-American maritime and trade relations, the British government showed little interest in reaching an accommodation or in defusing the growing sentiment for war among the American people and their leaders. Indeed, Britain still maintained a de facto embargo of most American ports, boarding American ships in search of illegal cargo or to impress American sailors into British service.

Britain's intransigence changed the mood in America, and the U.S. Navy moved closer to a war footing. American naval officers received instructions that they were "to maintain and support at every risk & cost, the dignity of our Flag; And that offering yourself no unjust aggression, you are to submit to none."[44] In 1810, while in a convoy with a merchant ship near Charleston, South Carolina, Lieutenant Oliver Hazard Perry was confronted by a British warship whose captain demanded that Perry come on board to explain his activities. Perry refused and cleared his ship for action, explaining later that he had no intention of being "Leopardized."[45]

With tensions escalating and Americans demanding an end to the mistreatment of their ships and sailors, voters took their anger to the ballot box and turned out of office nearly half the members of the House of Representatives in the election of 1810. The new Congress was dominated by younger, more aggressive members—calling themselves the "young War Hawks"—among whom were Henry Clay and Richard Mentor Johnson of Kentucky, South Carolinians John Caldwell Calhoun and Langdon Cheves, Tennessean Felix Grundy, who resigned as chief justice of the Kentucky supreme court, moved to Tennessee, and ran for Congress so he could vote for war against England, and New York merchant Peter B. Porter.[46] Reflecting their stunning victory and influence, the newcomers elected freshman Henry Clay to be the speaker of the House. Among their demands of Madison was a harsher response to ongoing British aggression, particularly along the western frontier, where the British were inciting Indian tribes to violence against settlers moving into Ohio, Indiana, and the southeast territories that would later become the states of Alabama and Mississippi.

Although impressment and trade restrictions were the chief irritant driving both countries to the brink of war, another important source of concern was the belief among many Americans living on the frontier that British agents were inciting the western Indian tribes to strike out at the settlers who were moving into America's vast western territories. Although frontier settlement was formally discouraged by the federal government in Washington in recognition of the tribal claims to sovereignty over much of the land west of the Appalachians and in appreciation for the hideous violence that might occur as the two races came into conflict over the same piece of land, little was done to enforce the policy. As a result, settlers by the thousands crossed the Appalachian mountains to scratch out a life of independence and opportunity on hard-scrabble homesteads in the western states and in the territories of Mississippi, Illinois, Michigan, and Indiana. Between 1783 and 1812, the population of Kentucky increased from 12,000 to 400,000, and by 1810 the state of Ohio had a population of 230,000.[47] Farther west the settler populations were lower but growing. The population of the Indiana Territory was 24,500. The Missouri Territory had 20,000, and another 20,000 pioneer families were living in the territories of Michigan and Illinois.[48] A biographer of Andrew Jackson has captured the sheer power of this massive and relentless migration:

> The Americans of that time, especially frontiersmen, were feared and disdained by all who came up against them in North America. Like Goths and Vandals of old, like Arab horsemen sweeping across continents in the name of religion, like the Mongol Horde destroying Islamic cities that never recovered, like Zulu *impis* unleashing bloodbaths on fellow Africans, Americans were on their march of conquest. The Creeks called the Georgians *Ecunnaunuxulgee*—"people greedily grasping after the lands of the red people."[49]

In the late eighteenth century, the Spanish governor of Florida reported to his superiors that the American frontiersmen were as "nomadic as Arabs … and distinguished themselves from savages only in their color, language, and the superiority of their depraved cunning and untrustworthiness."[50]

Much of this settlement took place on Indian land that had been seized or "bought" under questionable circumstances, and the consequence of this massive encroachment and displacement was the inflaming of the Indian tribes and the encouragement of them to seek some remedy on their own. As time passed, their remedy of choice was to ally themselves with the British, who were equally alarmed by the incursion and its implications for their own control of under-populated British Canada. The British were also concerned about their lucrative fur trading business in the unsettled frontier lands around the Great Lakes, which legally belonged to the United States. By about 1810, the population of America was near 7.5 million people, compared to just about five hundred thousand in Canada. Of this number, many "Canadians" were settlers from the United States or descendants of the original French settlers and thus of suspect loyalty during a war with either country.[51]

Compounding the problem was Britain's reluctance to vacate America's Northwest Territories, which became the states of Indiana, Illinois, Michigan, and Wisconsin. Britain maintained seven outposts in U. S. territory to serve its economic interests in the region (mostly in the fur trade) and to cultivate its relationship with the many Indian tribes under pressure from U.S. settlers. At one point, Britain used Fort Niagara in New York as its capital of Upper Canada. Although the Treaty of Paris ceded these lands to the United States, it took the British nearly ten years to withdraw fully from the region. Their delayed departure initially stemmed from a reluctance to give up the lucrative fur trade in the region, but as the years passed their refusal to leave was based more on the desire to revisit the boundary issues and readjust them in Britain's favor. To this end, British Indian agents encouraged and abetted Indian resistance to the encroachment of Americans into the northwest.

Although the U.S. concluded more than three hundred treaties with the scattered tribes of the northwest beginning in June 1789, settlers in the region believed that the continuing British presence in the region was for the purpose of encouraging violence against American settlers. The historian Samuel Eliot Morison questions that belief but notes that "the British did supply the redskins with arms and ammunition for hunting 'game,' which could be and occasionally was human."[52] Despite these treaties, the British interference continued, escalating during the 1790s and into the new century.

In response to increased violence and the continued British presence in the Northwest Territories, President Washington in 1791 had ordered the Revolutionary War veteran General Arthur St. Clair—now serving as the governor of those territories—to lead an army of as many as two thousand men, including the entire regular army, from his headquarters in Cincinnati to build a fort at the Maumee (Miami) village of Kekionga (the site of present-day Fort Wayne, Indiana) on the Maumee River to counter British influence in the region. On 4 November 1791, about fifty miles short of his destination, St. Clair was attacked by a large force of Indians that included Tecumseh and was led by Miami chief Little Turtle and Shawnee chief Blue Jacket. St. Clair's force was soundly defeated and casualties were estimated to have been as high as nine hundred men, nearly half his force. With the additional loss of prisoners and deserters, the entire regular army was reduced to no more than three hundred men. Though victorious, Little Turtle recognized his vulnerability to the determined Americans and moved his people closer to a British post near what is now Toledo, Ohio.

It took several years for the American army to recover from the debacle, but a new army was raised, trained, and put under the command of another Revolutionary War veteran, General "Mad" Anthony Wayne, who in 1793 established his winter quarters at Greenville, Ohio, about ninety miles south-southwest of Little Turtle's camp. With the support, arms, and encouragement of the British in Upper Canada, the Indians attacked Wayne's force but were beaten back. Wayne continued north, pausing about thirty-five miles west-southwest of the British fort, where he constructed Fort Defiance and offered the Indians a peaceful settlement. They declined, and Wayne resumed the offensive. On 20 August 1794, his well-trained force attacked and beat Little Turtle and a combined Indian force of Miami, Shawnee, Ottawa, Chippewa, Potawatomi, Sauk, Fox, and Iroquois near present-day Toledo in a battle called Fallen Timbers. Indian villages and crops were destroyed in the aftermath, and in August 1795 the tribes agreed to Wayne's peace terms, ceding more land and privileges in the Northwest Territories to the Americans.

Some measure of peace was restored, and Jay's Treaty of 1794 led to the departure of the British from their outposts in U.S. territory, but tensions between Indians and settlers remained, and frequent acts of violence came to characterize life on the frontier. But given the opportunities and the population pressures in the coastal colonies, the threat of violence had little effect on the swelling tide of American settlers seeking new land.[53]

As tensions between the two countries soared following the unprovoked *Chesapeake-Leopard* confrontation in 1808, Britain grew increasingly concerned that American anger would exacerbate frictions in the northwest. These frictions, in turn, might encourage America to seize Canada and rid itself forever of a hostile British presence in North America. With much of Canada sparsely settled, Britain began to court and arm the northwest Indian tribes to serve as its first line of defense against its southern neighbor. The implementation of this western strategy fell to Matthew Elliot, Britain's Indian agent in the lake region of Canada. According to the Anglo-American historian Reginald Horsman, who has written extensively on the war and the conflicts leading up to it,

> Throughout these years British Indian agents advised and supplied Indians on the American side of the border. The Indians had ample reason to listen to the British, as their lands in the Old Northwest were under constant pressure from American settlers. Beginning in 1805 the Shawnee Tecumseh and his brother the Prophet were attempting to organize a general Indian confederacy to resist the American advance, and after 1807 they were aided by the British. Westerners argued that if war became necessary because of repeated British infringements of American neutral rights then the opportunity could be taken to smash the British-Indian alliance.[54]

With a more supportive Congress, Americans living on the frontier became emboldened by the angry expressions of support for their plight now emanating from Washington. The changing mood, in turn, stirred the more adventurous and aggressive among them to look for opportunities to test their strength, and to also test the degree to which Washington would support an attempt to strike a blow at the Indian tribes who were less willing to concede any more land to the settlers moving west.

Pressured by settlers encroaching on their lands, by 1811 many of the Indian tribes in the Northwest Territories had aligned themselves in a loose confederacy under the combined leadership the Shawnee chieftain Tecumseh and his one-eyed younger brother, Tenskwatawa, known as the Prophet. They were a formidable pair:

> [Tecumseh] was a man of intelligence, eloquence, courage, and character; a relentless enemy, but merciful to captives and respected by his opponents. His ugly, wry-witted brother Tenskwatawa ... was a shaman who reinforced Tecumseh's diplomacy by preaching a return to the Indians' ancestral way of life. The brothers had established a capital of sorts, called "Prophet's Town", at the junction of the Wabash and Tippecanoe Rivers in acknowledged Indian territory.[55]

As part of the return to ancestral ways of life, the two leaders urged Indians to reform, give up alcohol, stop selling their land to white settlers, avoid any trade or contact with whites, and unify the tribes to form a formidable block against settler encroachment. Tecumseh's proselytizing had the predictable result among the settlers in the west: "The entire frontier was alarmed; Indian prohibitionists were something new to backwoods experience."[56]

But it was Tecumseh's great misfortune that he had to vie for the control of what was then called the Indiana Territory with the territory's fierce and determined governor, William Henry Harrison. An "ardent expansionist," Harrison had succeeded in bribing, coercing, and cajoling the remnants of the many down-and-out Indian tribes in the area—a people he described as "the most depraved wretches on earth"[57] —to sell their land to settlers. Alarmed at Tecumseh's successful diplomacy among the otherwise disunited tribes and his creation of a Shawnee capital in the territory the governor nominally controlled, Harrison set in motion a process to ensure the safety of the settlers and secure his own expansionist plans.

In July 1811, he wrote to Madison's secretary of war, William Eustis, "If some decisive measures are not speedily adopted, we shall have a general combination of all of the tribes against us."[58] Madison reluctantly agreed to allow Harrison to deal with the matter as he saw fit, and the Fourth U.S. Infantry Regiment under Colonel John P. Boyd, an American who had served as a mercenary officer in the army of the Nizam of Hyderbad in India, was ordered to assist the governor. In the fall of 1811, Harrison had assembled an army of nine hundred to a thousand men drawn from regulars and militia and marched them north to dislodge the Shawnee from their fortified settlement at Prophet's Town.

When Harrison's army made camp outside Prophet's Town on 7 November 1811, the Shawnee and their allies prepared for war. Led by the "unstable Prophet"—now on his own because Tecumseh was away in the Mississippi Territory on a mission to bring the Creeks, Choctaws, and other tribes of the region into his confederacy—the warriors went into battle believing that their leader had "made medicine" that had rendered the Americans weak and their bullets as harmless as water. As the Americans slept with only a few sentries on duty, the Prophet led between six hundred and seven hundred warriors in a well-planned attack on the American camp in what would become known as the battle of Tippecanoe. It began around four o'clock in the morning when black-painted, hand-picked braves attempted to steal into the center of the camp and kill Harrison and his senior officers. But they were detected, and Harrison escaped—barely. As the two sides fought hand-to-hand in the center of camp, the Prophet's main body attacked the camp, and the Americans and Shawnee fought each other at point-blank range. The Indians finally turned back at dawn when the army's light dragoons were able to mount up and conduct a rare woodland charge that drove the last of the warriors into a swamp, where they were hunted down and killed. Reorganizing his surviving force, Harrison led an attack on Prophet's Town, seized its supplies, including many British muskets, and burned it to the ground.

The Prophet's defeat, combined with his false claim that he could make warriors immune to American bullets, undermined the brothers' credibility as leaders, and impaired their ability to form an effective Indian confederacy to counter the acquisitive settlers and the militias protecting them. Tecumseh had no choice but to throw in his lot with the British and become little more than a dependent mercenary leader of the auxiliary Indian regiments accompanying British regulars and Canadian militia in the upcoming military campaigns against the Americans. For Harrison, the victory would send him to the White House thirty years later, when he and his running mate, John Tyler of Virginia, would campaign as "Tippecanoe and Tyler too."

Although the victory at Tippecanoe prevented the creation of a formidable Indian confederacy, it did not end the raiding parties and the violence that often characterized life on America's frontier fringe. In May 1812, Harrison reported that "[m]ost Citizens in this Country have abandoned their farms and taken refuge in Such temporary forts as they have been able to construct."[59] These reports would further inflame public opinion against the British, whom most Americans by now viewed as the chief instigators of Indian depredations against settlers. "Republican newspapers carried accounts of the battle under such headings as 'ANGLO-SAVAGE WAR' or 'Anglo-Indian War'. '[T]he war on the Wabash is purely BRITISH' said the Lexington *Reporter*. '[T]he SCALPING KNIFE and TOMAHAWK of *British savages, is now again devastating our frontiers.' Niles Register* would proclaim 'We have had but one opinion as the cause of the depredations of the Indians ... they are instigated and supported by the British in Canada.'"[60]

Many Americans wanted to punish the British for encouraging the Indians to attack western settlers and arming them to do so. Others also wanted to drive them from Canada and add the rest of the North American continent to the United States. Congressman Henry Clay spoke for many on the western frontier when he exclaimed, "Is it nothing to us to extinguish the torch that lights up savage warfare? Is it nothing to acquire the entire fur trade connected with that country and to destroy the temptation and opportunity of violating your revenue and other laws?" And should any doubt his constituents' resolve, Clay later added that "the militia of Kentucky alone are competent to place Montreal and Upper Canada at your feet."[61]

Despite the vigorous efforts by some in the west to seize Canada for the United States, the majority of Americans were probably indifferent to the prospect of adding more land, and states, to the nation. The merchants of New England feared the disruption of their lucrative trading relations with their British counterparts. Others feared that the addition of more northern territories would upset the precarious balance of sectional interests between the north, south, and west. Congressman John Randolph of Roanoke, who claimed descent from Pocahontas, wore silver spurs, carried a riding crop, and quaffed porter in the House chambers with his favorite hound by his side,[62] was one of the most outspoken legislators against war with Britain because it would strengthen the north at the expense of the slave-holding planter class in the south. "Canada seems tempting in their sight," he argued. "That rich vein of Genesee land which is said to be even better on the other side of the lake than on this. Agrarian cupidity, not maritime right urges this war.... It is to acquire a preponderating northern interest that you are to launch into war."[63]

V

In May 1811, tensions were rising and patience was running low. British and French cruisers, including HMS *Guerriere*, were interrupting trade entering and leaving New York City, and Secretary of the Navy Paul Hamilton ordered Commodore John Rodgers and USS *President* to depart Annapolis and return immediately to station in the Atlantic. On May 1, the *Guerriere* had stopped the American brig *Spitfire* outside New York Harbor and had taken from her a seaman named John Diggio, a native of Maine.[64] With standing orders to protect American merchantmen operating within a league of the coast from harassment by British and French warships, Rodgers and the *President* sailed down the Chesapeake Bay and rounded Cape Henry on 14 May 1811 to offer whatever protection they could to the American merchant fleet.

Two days after departing, a lookout in *President*'s tops sighted a distant sail coming toward them, and Rodgers prepared the ship for battle. The sail belonged to the twenty-gun British sloop-of-war *Little Belt* (formerly the *Lille Belt*, as she was called prior to her capture from Denmark by the British), under the command of Captain Arthur Batt Bingham. At the time of the sighting, the *Little Belt* was sailing north under orders to join the *Guerriere*, by now an object of intense American ire because of her predations of American vessels. As Bingham closed on the *President* he realized that his quarry was an American frigate vastly more powerful than his own ship, and he quickly turned south toward Cape Hatteras to avoid a confrontation he had no chance of winning. The *President*, however, thinking that this might be the *Guerriere*,[65] followed and caught up to the *Little Belt* later that night. After a brief action, the British ship was badly damaged and thirty-two of its crew killed or wounded. The *President* was largely unscathed and suffered only one casualty.

Although both captains claimed the other fired first, and Rodgers insisted that darkness obscured his opponent's true size, both countries saw the incident as a justification of their own behavior in the tense days leading up to war. However uneven the match, Americans saw it as a payback for the cowardly *Chesapeake* incident and a worthy comeuppance for a warship and captain whose current career consisted largely of harassing unarmed merchant ships and abducting innocent American seamen. For the British, their opponent's pursuit of revenge through such an obvious mismatch confirmed their low opinion of America's naval capability.[66]

These conflicting views were reflected in the popular press, to which readers submitted celebratory poems and lyrics. In America, a song titled "Rodgers and Decatur; Tit for Tat" included the lines,[67]

> Our cannon roar'd and men huzza'd,
> And fir'd away so handy
> Till Bingham struck, he was so scared,
> At hearing doodle dandy.

Across the Atlantic in England, the amateur poets had a different view of the event, and in "Rodgers and the Little Belt" one wrote,

> When Rodgers fight notions felt,
> He grasped his sword in haste,
> But thought he'd better get a belt
> To hang it round his waist …
> I'll have it, cried the blust'ring Prig,
> And fierce his blade he drew,
> But found this Little Belt too big,
> It would not buckle too.

Several months later, in August 1811, Captain Isaac Hull and the *Constitution* conducted a series of diplomatic and other official visits to several European cities, including London, which would last into early January 1812. During that time Hull was subjected to relentless harassment from British ships at every point, including one incident in which a smaller British vessel, the brig *Redpole*, "accidentally" fired a few shots which struck the *Constitution* as she was sailing from Holland back to Cherbourg, where the British blockading fleet nearly succeeded in tricking the French shore batteries to fire at the *Constitution*.[68]

Nonetheless, after two decades of war and the closure of trade with much of Europe and now America, British merchants and workers were suffering, and representatives from manufacturing cities urged Parliament to repeal the Orders in Council. As support for peace grew in Britain, diplomacy might have avoided war. But in an era where more than a month was required to send a message from London to Washington, and another month required for a response, diplomacy did not keep up with events. The American historian Thomas Bailey describes the random occurrences that derailed whatever diplomatic progress was being made:

> In November, 1810, the aged George III went completely insane. A delay of several months was involved in establishing the regency, while American affairs received little attention. By May, 1812, increasing pressure from British manufacturing and mercantile groups was foreshadowing a repeal of the odious Orders in Council. Yet more confusion and delay were caused when Prime Minister Perceval was assassinated by a madman. It was not until June 16,

> 1812, that Lord Castlereagh, then Foreign Secretary, could announce in the House of Commons that the Orders in Council would be immediately suspended.[69]

British merchants quickly began to prepare their surplus goods for shipment to America, but by then events had moved too far and too fast, and America would not know of the repeal for another month. On 18 June 1812, two days after Britain's concession on the orders in council, the U. S. Congress declared war on Great Britain with a 79–49 vote in the House and a 19–13 vote in the Senate, the closest vote on any declaration of war in American history. Much of the opposition came from the northeastern states.

As the news of war spread west to a little frontier town eleven hundred miles away in Missouri Territory, seventy-eight-year-old Daniel Boone volunteered for the army. He was turned down for active duty for reasons of age but was allowed to serve, when and where he could, as a sentry and a frontier doctor.[70]

And so began an eminently avoidable war—a war caused by prickly sensitivities, relentless insults, and British refusal to take seriously American grievances over the long-standing policy of seizing American sailors to serve aboard British ships in her long war against France. There were no compelling issues of empire, plunder, revenge, ideology, religion, territorial integrity, or territorial gain. Instead, issues of grievance and insult drove the Americans to declare war on the world's greatest power. As the Anglo-American journalist Christopher Hitchens has observed, "People fight, as Kant and Hegel and Nietzsche have emphasized, for dignity and for 'recognition,' just as much for their 'real' interests."[71]

The warhawks from the west and south were probably driven more by these Hegelian forces than those in the north and along the coastal plain, whose economies and prosperity were dependent upon trade with Britain. But all Americans—north, west, and south—perceived a very "real" reason for war, one that turned more on issues of principle aroused by a long-simmering dispute over the rule of law and England's disregard for it. Whereas British ships went into battle with threats and boasts painted across their sails—such as the *Guerriere*'s "All who meet me have a care / I am England's Guerriere"—American warships painted their sails and pennants with principled declarations, of which the most popular was "Free Trade and Sailors' Rights."

America had no reason to believe, even in its most delusional of moments, that it had a chance of winning. When Congress acceded to President Madison's request and formally declared war, American land forces numbered no more than 6,750 out of the 10,000 authorized,[72] while the Marine Corps totaled 483, plus ten officers.[73] In contrast, Britain would field 84,000 infantry and cavalry at the battle of Waterloo three years later.

At sea, the odds against America were even worse because the British had largely destroyed the fleets of their European antagonists, and the vast and powerful British navy had little to do but protect troop ships and commercial vessels from marauding privateers or the stray warship of its diminished enemies. In June 1812, America's war fleet numbered sixteen vessels, of which only six (the frigates, each over a decade old) possessed more than thirty-eight guns; forty-four were the most that any U.S. frigate carried.

England, in contrast, had about five hundred warships in service, although the estimates vary widely among historians. One source estimates that as many as 245 were frigates or ships of similar size, compared with America's six. Another 191 or so were considered ships of the line—vessels armed with as few as fifty guns, the largest carrying a hundred or more cannons arrayed along four gun decks and serviced by a crew of more than a thousand men and boys. America had none of these. The rest of the fleets were filled out with smaller vessels—brigs, sloops, and schooners—several hundred for the British, ten for the Americans. A week before the declaration of war, the *Statesman* of London observed, "America certainly can not pretend to wage war with us; she has no navy to do it with."[74]

Masters of the ocean and all the world's seas, British ships sailed forth with breezy confidence and a majestic sense of place in the grand march of history. Indeed, the grandeur of their imperial might extended even to the names given their warships—*Victory*, *Revenge*, *Mars*, *Minotaur*, *Defiance*, *Colossus*, *Leviathan*, *Conqueror*, *Thunderer*, *Dreadnought*, and *Agamemnon*. Still obsessed with their newly won freedom and their novel form of government, the Americans named their ships in celebration of the institutions they were built to preserve. The mightiest frigates were christened the *President*, *Constitution*, *Congress*, and *United States*. In a few months the world would discover whether such names and the attitudes behind them made much difference when an American frigate named *Constitution* met up with a British frigate bearing the French name *Warrior*.

On 11 July 1812, three weeks after the declaration of war, four years of negotiation between the U.S. and Britain over the fate of the sailors abducted from the *Chesapeake* came to a close as the British schooner *Brim* delivered seamen John Strachan and Daniel Martin to Boston (William Ware had died in a Halifax hospital). The issue of repatriation and reparations had been settled earlier, but too late to ease the tensions between the countries. The Baltimore *Whig* sarcastically noted that it was "like restoring the hair after fracturing the skull."[75]

In a carefully choreographed reception, the two sailors were received in Boston Harbor on board the *Chesapeake*, now under the command of Captain William Bainbridge. The entire crew was turned out for the event, and Bainbridge made some brief welcoming remarks to the former captives:

> My Lads, I am glad to see you. From this Deck you were taken by British outrage. For your return to it you owe gratitude to the Government of your Country. Your Country now offers you, an opportunity to revenge your wrongs, and I cannot doubt but you will be desirous of doing so on board this very ship. I trust the Flag that flies on board of her, will gloriously defend you.[76]

Bainbridge noted in his letter to Secretary Paul Hamilton that the crew gave three cheers and added that the British officer who had delivered the captives had accepted his invitation to dine with him after the ceremony. As Bainbridge and his British counterpart took their meal in the captain's dining room below, the USS *Constitution*, commanded by Captain Isaac Hull and packed to the gunwales with a volunteer crew of 470 tough young men, slipped out of Hampton Roads and rounded the Virginia Capes in search of the enemy.

CHAPTER TWO

BACK ON LAND: THE FALL OF FORTS DETROIT AND DEARBORN

As Isaac Hull guided his ship into the Atlantic, four hundred miles to the west in Ohio his uncle, General William Hull—the fifty-nine-year-old governor of the Michigan Territory and a Revolutionary War hero—followed his orders to assemble an army of two thousand men to reinforce Fort Detroit in Michigan and defend the territory. Recently appointed to the rank of general in America's growing army, Hull and his troops were to protect the fort against an expected British attack across the river from Canada following America's declaration of war on Great Britain. Strategically located on the Detroit River—a strait linking Lake Huron with Lake Erie, and separating American territory from British Canada—control of the fort meant control of much of the water-borne commerce on the Great Lakes and the frontier territories of Indiana, Illinois, and Michigan.

Hull marched his army north from Urbana, Ohio, and arrived at Detroit on 5 July. Within a few days a small force of pro-American Canadians formed themselves into a cavalry unit and joined his force. Once the fort was secured, officers from the Ohio militia urged Hull to take advantage of Canada's weakened defenses and attack the British at Fort Malden on the Canadian side. Hull agreed and a week later crossed the Detroit River and marched seventeen miles south through enemy territory to lay siege to Malden, then defended by a smaller British force of three hundred regulars, four hundred Indians, and several hundred local militiamen.[1]

Although everything went smoothly during the first few weeks of an operation that kept the undermanned British forces on the defensive, General Hull was a cautious leader and worried about the security of his vulnerable supply line from Ohio, which could be difficult to defend from Indian attack or from the British who controlled Lake Erie. And Hull had good reason to be concerned: despite an escort of two hundred men from the Ohio militia, the first supply train—comprising three hundred head of cattle and seventy packhorses carrying flour—stopped about forty miles south of Detroit near the Raisin River to await an armed escort from the fort. But the 150 men Hull sent out under Major Thomas Van Horne were attacked by British Captain Adam Muir's force, which included Indians led by Tecumseh. Van Horne's men beat them back, but then returned to Detroit, deciding not to rescue the supply convoy halted further to the south.[2]

Casualties occurred on both sides, but two of Van Horne's men captured by the Indians were chopped to death to avenge the killing of a chief during the clash.[3] Desperate for supplies and anxious to get them through enemy lines before the British could reinforce their position, Hull sent a relief force of six hundred men to the stranded supply train. But this one too was pinned down by Indians and was soon forced to return to Fort Detroit. As Hull struggled to supply his men against a noose tightening around his vulnerable position, more bad news arrived, this time from the north where the small American force holding Fort Michilimackinac (on Mackinac Island), off the northern-most tip of Michigan, had surrendered to a much larger British force that took them by surprise.

And the bad news only got worse. In a pincer movement planned by Secretary of War William Eustis, Hull was to attack the British from the west, while General Henry Dearborn, who had once served as President Jefferson's secretary of war, was to attack the British from New York in the east across the Niagara River. But Dearborn was unable to raise the force he deemed necessary, and instead took it upon himself to negotiate a truce with General George Prevost on the Niagara frontier. Momentarily free of any American threat from the east, General Isaac Brock assembled all of the available forces in Upper Canada and sailed them west along the coast of Lake Erie to Malden to reinforce the troops facing Dearborn's Americans.

Hearing the news of Dearborn's truce informally from officers of the New York militia, and fearing that he would soon be cut off from his supply lines and surrounded by a larger force of Indians and British troops, Hull broke off his siege of Malden and retreated to Fort Detroit. Hull's hasty retreat in the face of little more than rumors of an impending attack, while opposed by a much smaller enemy force at Fort Malden, left many of his men questioning his leadership. One of his officers wrote, "This fatal and unaccountable step dispirited the troops" and "left to the tender mercy of the enemy the miserable Canadians, who had joined us."[4]

Some militia officers discussed plans to replace Hull, but a lack of support from the ranking officer of the regulars ended the effort before it began. Morale among the troops—now hunkered down behind the walls of Fort Detroit—was further undermined when a third attempt to break through to the supplies trapped at the *Raisin* failed to find the supply train's encampment. When Hull ordered the relief force to return to Detroit, many of the men refused to come back, so diminished was their confidence in his leadership.

The British took advantage of Hull's delay to bring in more troops and artillery and surround the American force entrenched in Fort Detroit. It was Hull's misfortune that the gathering British forces were led by General Isaac Brock, one of the most talented commanding officers the British had in Canada. And as Brock strengthened his forces and planned his attack, Britain's influential Indian agent Matthew Elliott organized the region's native warriors to join with Brock to expel the American invaders for good.

Preying on what he suspected was Hull's fear of a massacre from Britain's Indian allies, Brock tried to create the impression that many more Indian warriors were on their way and that the British might not be able to control them. On 16 August, while the British were still in the process of assembling their forces in preparation for an attack, a discombobulated General William Hull, without consulting any of his officers, raised the white flag over the fort and surrendered his command,[5] as well as his army, cannons, muskets, and five thousand pounds of gunpowder. The American Colonel Lewis Cass said that "even the women were indignant at so shameful a degradation of the American character."[6]

Ever the pessimist, Hull managed to spread his gloom and despair to others before being carted off as a prisoner of war. Several days before surrendering Fort Detroit, Hull sent a message to Captain Nathan Heald, commander of the sixty-five regulars and twenty civilians at Fort Dearborn (at what is now the intersection of Michigan Avenue and Wabash Drive in Chicago), urging him to withdraw hundreds of miles east to Fort Wayne in Indiana Territory because Fort Dearborn's safety would be in grave jeopardy if Fort Detroit were to fall, a prediction Dearborn personally fulfilled within a few days. Also of consideration for Fort Dearborn's security was the earlier loss of Fort Mackinac, which had cut off Heald's only reliable supply line around the lakes.

Carrying Hull's message of despair from Fort Detroit across the northern plains of Indiana Territory to Fort Dearborn was a force of thirty Miami scouts led by a skilled frontiersman named William Wells. Wells had been captured by the Miami as a child, raised as a warrior, adopted by Miami chief Little Turtle, and married off to the chief's sister. In his youth Wells had often fought as a Miami warrior against whites but later attempted to straddle both worlds.[7] Although Heald and his troops were well stocked in a strong fort and confident they could prevail in any fight against the unfriendly Potawatomi Indians in the area, the fort's commander reluctantly did as Hull ordered and arranged for the evacuation of the fort under the promised protection of five hundred Potawatomi, who had been threatening Fort Dearborn in the months leading up to its ordered evacuation.

Having spent a good bit of his life living with the Indians of the Western Territories, William Wells had no illusions about a Potawatomi promise of safe passage and urged Heald to ignore Hull's order to evacuate the fort. But Heald would not disobey his superior and began the evacuation after destroying what gunpowder they could not carry with them and pouring the fort's whiskey supply into a nearby stream.[8] Wells rode out of the fort with black paint covering his face as a traditional Miami sign that he expected to be killed before sundown.[9] Wells's prescience was demonstrated a short time later as the retreating American force, which included nine women and eighteen children, marched south along the shore of Lake Michigan. The American soldiers and civilians and their Miami escorts had gone but a few miles when the five hundred Potawatomi, egged on by agents from Tecumseh and British traders and angry at the loss of the whiskey and gunpowder, attacked the retreating column.

The fort's soldiers and Miami scouts put up a vain defense in hand-to-hand fighting. A Canadian historian describes the butchery: "Within the wagons, where the young children are huddled, there is greater horror. One young Indian slips in and slaughters twelve single-handed, slicing their heads from their bodies in a fury of blood lust."[10]

Most of the Americans and their Miami escorts were killed, but a few were captured and many of those were tortured. It was rumored that twenty-nine soldiers, seven women, and six children survived as prisoners and were distributed among the surrounding villages, marching past "the naked and headless bodies of the women and children" on their way.[11] Canadian historian Pierre Berton writes, "The Potawatomi knocked the seriously wounded captives on the head; later they used others as centerpieces for happy evenings of torture. Hardship and abuse killed more: only eighteen seemed to have survived until war's end."[12] Pinned to the ground by his fallen horse, Wells was shot dead, beheaded, and his head hoisted on a stake. "Another cuts out the heart and divides it among the chiefs who eat it raw, hoping thereby to absorb some of Wells's courage."[13]

Much of the blame for this series of debacles was deservedly laid on the shoulders of William Hull, the American military commander for the region who lost his nerve before a smaller force. Former president Thomas Jefferson denounced the "'treason, or the cowardice, or both, of Hull,' demanding that he be hanged or shot."[14] When Hull was later paroled by the British and returned to the United States, a court-martial was held and he was convicted of cowardice and neglect of duty. Though sentenced to death, he was spared by President Madison because of his "revolutionary services and advanced age."

As troop movements slowed in the west with winter's approach, the only bright spot of the early days of the western campaign against Britain was Captain Zachary Taylor's defense of Fort Harrison on the Wabash River in the western part of the Indiana Territory, near the Illinois border. Defended by a tiny garrison that included many on the sick list, Fort Harrison was attacked on 4 September by a large band of warriors led by Tecumseh. The Indians scored early and succeeded in burning down one of the fort's blockhouses in a violent conflagration fueled by the casks of whiskey stored there.[15] But Taylor was able to rally his small force, and the garrison held off Tecumseh's assault until a column of Kentucky militiamen broke the siege on the 8th and drove the Indians into retreat. Explaining his success, Taylor later told his commander, General Harrison, that "my presence of mind did not for a moment forsake me."[16]

At exactly the same time Fort Harrison was attacked, American troops at Fort Madison, much farther to the west on the Iowa side of the Mississippi River, were also under attack by Indians. On the first day of the assault, and within hailing distance of one of the fort's sentries, a soldier was killed and scalped.[17] The next day the Indians placed his heart and head on stakes and displayed them to the troops guarding the fort to frighten them into retreat or surrender. Despite the horrifying mutilation of their fellow soldier, the troops inside remained resolute, and the isolated Fort Madison held on for another year. Fort Wayne, in the northeast corner of Indiana Territory, was also under siege by Indians in late August and early September 1812. General William Henry Harrison ordered nine hundred troops from Ohio to relieve it, and reinforced this vanguard with another thousand troops whom he himself led to Fort Wayne. Thanks to his swift and overwhelming response, the siege was broken and the fort secured for the winter.

As the autumn chill set in along America's distant frontier, much of the northwest had been lost to the Indians and the British. Within the space of half a year, the Americans had been pushed out of Michigan, Illinois, and most of northern Indiana. They were also harried by hostile forces in the northwest corner of Ohio, a state since 1803. But however bad the situation was on the western frontier during those first few months of war, General Harrison had managed to stabilize the front by winter, successfully holding a thin line of forts stretching from central Indiana to the northwest corner of Ohio.

Elsewhere in the world, on 23 June 1812, five days after America declared war on Britain, advance elements of Napoleon's 422,000-man Grande Armée crossed from Poland, near Nieman, into Russia. Battle casualties, disease, and desertion would reduce the army to no more than a hundred thousand soldiers when it entered Moscow almost three months later on 14 September, just a week after Zachary Taylor beat back Tecumseh at Fort Harrison. The Russian capital had already been abandoned and set to the torch before Napoleon's arrival. Finding no shelter, forage, or food, the Grande Armée began its retreat from Moscow on 19 October, just as the Russian winter settled in.

CHAPTER THREE

OLD IRONSIDES

As his uncle William Hull contemplated the surrender of Fort Detroit to the British, Captain Isaac Hull was sailing into the Atlantic against an enemy whose naval forces outnumbered the Americans by about forty to one. Nothing in the record suggests the least bit of reluctance or doubt on Isaac's part about fulfilling his orders. To the contrary, his letters and log indicate that he approached the assignment with a sense of glee and confidence, despite the overwhelming odds and the inexperience of the crew he had cobbled together in the spring and early summer of 1812. But for Captain Hull, none of that mattered because the ship he commanded was one of the finest in the world. Boasting technological innovations that originated with the American warships of an earlier generation, the *Constitution* was more than a match for any British ship serving on the Atlantic station, and Hull was certain she would prevail in any battle on this first voyage of the new war.

When Congress gave President Madison his declaration of war, the secretary of the navy, Paul Hamilton, a planter from South Carolina, wrote to all of his officers about the situation and what would be expected of them. To Isaac

Hull, who was staying in Washington while *Constitution* received a quick overhaul in Alexandria, Virginia, Hamilton wrote,

> … you are with the force under your command entitled to every belligerent right to attack and capture, and to defend—You will use the utmost dispatch to reach New York after you have made your complement of men &c. at Annapolis—In your way hence you will not fail to notice the British flag … but you are not to understand me as impelling you to battle, previously to your having confidence in your crew unless attacked, or with a reasonable prospect of success.[1]

Some historians have criticized Hamilton for being vague about what he expected Hull to do if he sighted a British ship, but his orders, and the choices he left to Hull, may have reflected a concern that Hull would be commanding America's most valuable—and irreplaceable—weapon with a novice crew. Many of the crew had just signed on for a two-year term of service, and few possessed any experience aboard a ship of war. But with a state of war now existing between America and Britain, Hull had little time to train his crew of well-meaning amateurs for the violent, close-order combat that *Constitution* would soon face from the most fearsome navy on earth.

Incredibly, Hull seems not to have had a worry in the world about how his hastily assembled band of volunteer novices, numbering about 450 men, would perform at sea or in combat. Two weeks after war was declared, and just a few days before he and his ship departed Annapolis to rendezvous with Rodgers in New York, Hull wrote to Hamilton,

> By Sunday next, the Ship will be in tolerable order for Sea but the Crew you will readily conceive, must yet be unacquainted with a Ship of War, as many of them have but lately joined us and were never in an armed ship before. We are doing all that we can to make them acquainted with the duty, and in a few days, we shall have nothing to fear from a single deck Ship; indeed; unacquainted as we now are, we should I hope give a good account of any Frigate the enemy have….[2]

Hull left Annapolis on 5 July, heading down the Chesapeake Bay to the Virginia Capes, all the while drilling his crew in the arts of war, including extensive gunnery practice that required gun crews to hit barrels floating hundreds of yards away while the ship tilted in the wind and plowed though rolling waves. Along the way, Hull stopped to pick up supplies at towns and villages along the Virginia and Maryland coasts. Seven days later, on the 12th, the *Constitution* rounded Cape Henry and turned north to New York City, where she would join Rodgers's fleet, or so Hull thought.

On the early afternoon of 17 July, off Little Egg Harbor (about fifteen miles north of Atlantic City and just east of Beach Haven), Hull spotted the sails of four ships north of him, laying close in to the New Jersey coast. Light winds and a strong southerly current kept him from getting closer "to ascertain whether they were Enemy Ships, or our Squadron having got out of New York waiting the arrival of the *Constitution*, the latter of which I had reason to believe was the case."[3] Later in the afternoon, around four o'clock, a fifth ship was seen coming toward him from the northeast, and by nightfall it had taken up a position within six or eight miles of the *Constitution*. Hull gave the coded night signal to the newcomer but did not receive the corresponding response. Since the new arrival was most likely British, Hull wondered whether the four other ships lying closer to the shore were British as well. Indeed they were, and for most of that night they were just as uncertain about him.

Alone and confronting a vastly more powerful force, Hull made all sail and set a course to the southeast, where he would lay up until daylight, at which time he could assess his predicament. Preparing for the worst, the crew spent a restless night asleep at their guns, ready for combat at a moment's notice.[4] Hull never had an opportunity for a more careful assessment: the late-arriving fifth ship, which had failed properly to answer Hull's signal, was the *Guerriere*, 36 (numbers following ship names refer to the number of guns on board), and her captain, Richard Dacres, knew he had stumbled upon an American and was eager to beat her.

Fortunately for the *Constitution*, the other four British ships were still uncertain who was who when Hull, and then the *Guerriere*, came upon the squadron commanded by Captain Sir Philip Vere Broke. Like Hull, Broke was in search of Rodgers's squadron, which had sailed from New York on 22 June. Broke's flagship was the frigate *Shannon*, 36. She was sailing with *Africa*, 64, *Belvidera*, 36, and *Aeolus*, 32. *Guerriere* was rejoining Broke's fleet after being separated from the others. Although Hull by now was fairly sure he had stumbled onto a British fleet, the British were less sure who he was; there was still the possibility that he was the lagging *Guerriere*. Compounding the confusion, when the *Guerriere*, tailing the *Constitution*, came within range and signaled her fleet, she received no reply, a lapse that inspired charges and countercharges for years to come. Nor did *Guerriere* receive the expected "one rocket, two gun" reply from the unidentified *Constitution*. Should the distant sails belong to Commodore Rodgers and not Broke's squadron, Dacres thought it prudent to draw off until daylight when better identification could be made.

By dawn there was no doubt about who was who. But just as the chase would have begun, the wind fell off, leaving *Constitution* to drift aimlessly in the current. Her bow turned around to face *Aeolus* and *Belvidera*, which still had some wind and were closing the distance. A little past five o'clock, Hull launched two cutters, whose crews, bending their backs to their oars, towed the frigate back around and pulled her away from the enemy. Hull also ordered the crew to bring up a twenty-four-pounder from the gun deck to fire off the stern from the quarter deck. Two other guns were pulled into his cabin and run out the stern windows to fire astern at the pursuing British.

Moses Smith, sponger to the number one gun, recorded the event in his *Naval Scenes in the Last War*:

> Captain Hull came aft, coolly surveyed the scene, took a match in his hand, and ordered the quarter-master to hoist the American flag. I stood within a few feet of Hull at the time. He clapped the fire to my gun, No. 1, and such a barking as sounded over the sea! It was worth hearing. No sooner had our iron dog opened his mouth in this manner, than the whole enemy opened the whole of theirs. Every one of the ships fired directly toward us ... not a shot reached us then, at the distance we were.[5]

By now all ships were dead in the water, and when the British realized that *Constitution*'s crew was towing it out of range, they ordered their boats into the water and began towing their ships in pursuit. A light breeze came up, and Hull set studding sails and stay sails and had the crew hoist buckets of water aloft to pour on the canvas and tighten the fibers to hold every ounce of wind that blew by. But the wind did not last, and by now the British had concentrated all of the squadron's cutters and launches to pull Broke's *Shannon* and Richard Byron's *Belvidera* in pursuit of the *Constitution*. The ploy worked, and the extra muscle power of the British crews allowed Broke's flagship to gain on the American.

As the British ships closed the distance during these desperate hours, Hull prepared *Constitution* to slug it out with the larger British force slowly gaining on him. As Moses Smith remembered, "Hull called Lieutenant Morris to him and said calmly: 'Let's lay broadside to them, Mr. Morris, and fight the whole! If they sink us, we'll go down like men!'"

> Mr. Morris now spoke to Captain Hull: "There is one thing, sir, I think we'd better try."
> "What's that?" replied Hull.
> "Try to kedge her off," said the Lieutenant.[6]

Morris, who had spent the few days prior to *Constitution*'s departure from Annapolis trying, without success, to obtain a transfer to a ship of his own command, the better to advance his career, saw an opportunity of escape in the shallow waters off the coast of New Jersey. With a sandy seabed not far below them, Morris proposed to propel the ship forward by kedging her rather than towing. By Morris's reasoning, kedging would give them more speed with their limited manpower and boats. Hull readily agreed, and the launch and cutter were redeployed for the new effort.

A kedge is a small anchor with sharply pointed flukes. It is tied to a long rope and rowed in a boat to a point well forward of the ship, where it is dropped. When the kedge is lodged in the seabed, the crew pulls on the line, walking from the bow aft in a continuous motion that steadily brings the half-mile of line on board as the ship is towed toward the sunken kedge. Though kedging was typically performed to maneuver an unwieldy sailing ship in a crowded harbor, Morris realized that the technique could be employed to escape the British on a windless sea.

Using two boats and two kedges,[7] the crew spliced together every suitable piece of rope on board the ship to create two hawsers, each about a half-mile in length. A kedge anchor was fastened to each line and was then rowed about a half-mile forward and dropped into the water. On board, crewmen assembled at the bow, grabbed the line, and hauled the rope in, walking aft. Reaching the stern, each man let go of the line, walked forward to the bow, grabbed the line, and pulled again. As the process was repeated again and again, the ship slowly moved forward until they were "overruning and tripping the kedge as she came up with the end of the line."[8] As the first kedge was being pulled in, the crew repeated the procedure with the second kedge, which the cutter had already dropped well forward, while a second cutter rowed the first kedge out in front. By this back-breaking work, repeated throughout the day, the *Constitution* made her escape.

As the distance widened, the British realized how Hull had increased his speed. Broke ordered his fleet to do the same and designated *Belvidera* as lead in the pursuit. Fortunately for Hull, who now had several long guns facing aft, a pursuer that is towed, whether by oars or kedging, exposes his small boats to the guns of his quarry. Hull saw to it that the British appreciated their disadvantage, firing the occasional well-aimed ball from the twenty-four-pounder through the cut away taffrail on his quarterdeck.

And so it went through the day of 18 July, into the night and the wee hours of the 19th. Crews on the cutter and launch were relieved, and seamen took turns at the exhausting work of hauling the ship forward with their bare hands. "Men not actively engaged dropped and napped where they could, rotating from boat crew to shipboard duty and back again, as if on some diabolical treadmill. It was a performance worthy of a seasoned crew, and exceptional for one so green. Hull's leadership must have been exemplary."[9]

Shortly after five o'clock on the morning of the 19th, the wind picked up, filling the sails. Hull pulled in his cutters, and the *Constitution* was carried forward by the breeze. All five frigates were now running on a starboard tack with every inch of canvas set to capture the light breeze blowing from the south by east.[10] But *Constitution* was faster, and the British slowly fell behind as the chase continued for a third day. In the afternoon, the threat of a squall let Hull show Broke that his bag of tricks was not yet empty. With clouds forming and a strong wind rolling the *Constitution*'s side well over into the water, Hull made the threat of bad weather seem worse than it was by hauling up his sails by the brails and clewlines just as the squall hit. The light canvas was furled, a second reef taken in the mizzen topsail, and the ship brought under short sail in preparation for the worst. Seeing this, and wanting to protect their own sail and rigging from the approaching squall, the British shorted their sail and went on a different tack. With the British now sailing on the defensive, Hull added sail, blew forward, and increased the distance between the *Constitution* and Broke's fleet.[11] Though reaching a speed of eleven knots, Hull was able to bring in every one of his kedging boats, whereas the British cut theirs loose so as not to lose any time in their pursuit of the fleeing American.

The chase continued through another night, but by six o'clock in the morning on the 20th, the *Constitution* was out of sight. At a quarter past eight, Broke ended the chase and turned back to retrieve his abandoned boats. Though no combat took place during the three-day confrontation, the Americans gave the British an early taste of the seamanship that would bedevil them in the years to follow. Theodore Roosevelt observed, "In this chase Captain Isaac Hull was matched against five British Captains, two of whom, Broke and Byron, were fully equal to any in their navy; and while the latter showed great perseverance, good seamanship, and ready imitation, there can be no doubt that the palm in every way belongs to the cool old Yankee."[12]

Assessing the chase from the British perspective, the Anglo-American writer and naval historian C. S. Forester was less generous in his assessment of Broke's performance: "He had gained no credit from the incident; even if—as seems certain—*Constitution* was superior to all the British ships at every point of sailing, there had been found nowhere in the British squadron any ingenuity or inventiveness or moral drive to overcome that handicap in the face of the very high standard of Hull's professional accomplishments and the seamanlike qualities of his crew—who it must be remembered, had had only five days at sea in their present enlistment."[13]

Broke would have his revenge, but for now his fleet headed east to protect the West Indian convoy that had recently left the Caribbean for England. Three weeks later and the convoy safely out of Rodgers's and Hull's reach, Broke returned his squadron to the American coast. First, though, he sent Dacres and the *Guerriere* to Halifax for repairs and supplies. Hull had assumed that Broke would head for New York to cut him off, so he sailed for Boston to replenish his supplies and to discharge—and, he hoped, replace—the twenty sick or disabled crewmen confined to their hammocks.[14]

II

By any standard, *Constitution* was a thoroughbred, and her pedigree could be traced back to the fast American frigates of the Revolutionary War—the *Alliance*, *Hancock*, and *Randolph*, to name just a few—and the brilliant men who designed and built them. But that tradition came to a temporary end in the early years of the nation. Pressed by debts incurred during the War of Independence and unable to raise much revenue from the thirteen fractious states of the postwar confederation, America's Continental Congress had to save money wherever it could. Even the tiny navy, reduced by combat from fifty-three commissioned ships to only two when independence was won in 1781, was still too heavy a burden for the bankrupt confederation. The *Hague* was sold first, in 1782, but Congress held onto the *Alliance*, a sentimental favorite because it was once commanded by John Paul Jones, until 1785, when it was sold to the Philadelphia merchant Robert Morris for twenty-six thousand dollars.[15] Upon its sale, the U.S. Navy and Marine Corps were effectively disbanded.

Although very little technical or descriptive detail about the *Alliance* exists today, what remains suggests that she was remarkably advanced for her day and that the innovative design and construction techniques she and her sister ships embodied later served as the foundation for the dominating frigates that President George Washington commissioned a decade later, among which was the *Constitution*. The available information is derived from the plans for the *Randolph*, a Revolutionary War frigate whose design and construction reflected a collaboration of the Philadelphia shipbuilders Joshua Humphreys, then just twenty-five years old, and John Wharton.[16]

Existing plans for the *Randolph*, built for thirty-two guns, show the frigate to be about 20 percent longer and 20 percent heavier than the British thirty-twos she was built to challenge. She was also faster, and a British officer who sailed the similarly designed frigate *Hancock* after her capture described the ship as "the finest and fastest frigate in the world."[17] The French, who in turn captured the *Hancock* from the British (and renamed her *Iris*) in 1781, held the ship in the same high esteem. During her postwar service as a merchant ship, the *Alliance* achieved a record-breaking speed on her passage from Philadelphia to Canton in 1787.[18]

Within weeks of *Alliance*'s sale, two American merchant ships were seized by Algerine pirates in the Mediterranean Sea off the North African coast near modern-day Libya. Such depredations would continue for more than a decade, kept in check only by the occasional payment of tribute by the American government to the pirates. But in 1793 Algerine interference with American shipping escalated beyond that of a distant nuisance when a treaty between Portugal and Algiers led the Portuguese to end their naval policing at the Straits of Gibraltar, allowing the pirates to roam more easily into the Atlantic in search of booty. In October and November 1793, eleven American ships were seized along with 110 American crewmen, who were captured and held for ransom in deplorable conditions.[19]

Samuel Calder of Colchester, Connecticut, the master aboard the schooner *Jay* when she was captured en route from Malaga to Boston, recorded, "[W]e was all stript of all our Cloaths some Came on Shore without even a shirt, and was immediately put into Chains and put to hard labour, with only the allowance of three small loaves of black bread pr. day & water ... its [*sic*] not possible to Live long in this situation...."[20] American ships were not the only ones seized and plundered by the pirates in a process of depredation that stretched back several centuries. The Spanish author Miguel Cervantes spent two years as a slave of the Algerines following his capture as a young man late in the sixteenth century and accused them of inflicting cruelty on their prisoners as an end in itself. In *Don Quixote*, Cervantes put his experience to the service of art by offering this description of an Algerine slave-owner: "Every day he hanged a slave, and cut the ears off another. He did it merely for the sake of doing it."[21] Indeed, so common was the threat from Islamic pirates prowling the Mediterranean that the English author Daniel Defoe had his seventeenth-century character Robinson Crusoe spend time as a slave in North Africa before becoming a castaway.[22]

The news of these seizures greeted the new American Congress in December 1793 as it convened in Philadelphia, then the capital. In January 1794 the House voted to create and fund a naval force, and established a select committee to determine its size and cost. The committee recommended the construction of four ships of forty-four guns and two of twenty guns and authorized the expenditure of six hundred thousand dollars to build them. By March 1794 both the House and Senate passed the legislation to build the ships, but in the process substituted two thirty-six-gun ships for the two twenty-gun ships recommended by the committee. President Washington signed the bill into law on 27 March 1794.[23] Although America's federal government was not yet five years old, its elected officials had already grasped the importance of getting their fair share of any federal building projects, and the construction of the six new warships was distributed around the new country to ensure that everybody got a piece of the action. Boston, Philadelphia, and New York would each build a forty-four-gun frigate, while Baltimore, Portsmouth (New Hampshire), and Gosport (Portsmouth-Norfolk, Virginia) would build the thirty-sixes.[24]

Three months later, Joshua Humphreys was appointed to be the first "naval constructor" of the United States, and was allowed to extend the advanced designs he developed earlier for the *Randolph* into an entirely new type of frigate that he believed would be the most formidable warship of its class in the world. Humphreys knew that the United States had neither the resources nor the inclination to attempt to match the size of the fleets that its sometime adversaries could put to sea. As America was embarking upon a six-ship navy, the British fleet numbered in the many hundreds and grew larger by the month as the nation armed itself for war with France. But while quantity would be severely limited, quality would not, and Humphreys proceeded to design a ship that would be more than a match for any it would confront and nimble enough to escape those more powerful. He explained his strategy: "By building your ships of war larger and more powerful than they are in Europe you take a lead in two classes of ships ... which will in a degree render the Ships of Europe of the same class in a very great degree useless, but if you build of a same size & and construction you will allways be behind. It is only by taking a bold lead you have any chance of succeeding...."[25]

By "a bold lead," Humphreys meant ships that were faster and more powerful than those of America's adversaries. Humphreys borrowed from the concepts he first advanced in the *Randolph* by designing frigates that were both longer and wider than those of Britain and France. They would also be of a much stronger construction to give them both a sailing advantage and allow them to carry more guns of a larger caliber.

In a 1794 letter to Secretary of War Henry Knox, Humphreys described the qualities he hoped his frigates would possess and why such qualities were essential:

> [A]s our navy must for a considerable time be inferior in numbers, we are to consider what size ships will be most formidable and be an overmatch for those of an enemy; such Frigates as in blowing weather would be an overmatch for double deck ships, and in light

> winds to evade coming to action, or double deck ships as would be an overmatch for common double deck ships, and in blowing weather superior to ships of three decks, or in calm weather or light winds to outsail them. Ships built on these principles will render those of an enemy in a degree useless, or require a greater number before they dare attack our ships.[26]

Humphreys's proposal—that the United States Navy rely on a type of ship, the frigate, that saw only limited combat duty in most navies of that era—was bold, visionary, and risky. Derived from the French *fregate* and the Italian *fregatta*, frigates are thought to have made their appearance in the Mediterranean several centuries earlier as a small ship—about 250 tons—powered by both oars and sails. The first British ship to carry the designation was the 380-ton *Constant Warwick*, launched in 1646. The design and function of these ships evolved, and by the late eighteenth century frigates were expected to fight nothing larger than another frigate and were used mainly as advance scouts for a lumbering line of battleships in search of the enemy. The typical frigate carried proportionately more sail for the hull size than did the larger ships of the line.[27]

Serving as the eyes and ears of a larger fleet which could see no farther than the horizon and then only during the day, frigates served an essential reconnaissance role for an effective fighting force, and their absence could greatly diminish the effectiveness of fleet operations. At sea without frigates as he searched in vain for a French fleet bound for Egypt, Nelson is said to have cried out, "Frigates! Were I to die this moment, want of frigates would be found engraved on my heart."[28] Frigates also conveyed signals and carried messages from ship to ship and ship to shore. During battles they generally stood away from the fighting, entering the fray to assist disabled men-of-war or to rescue the crew of a sinking ship. The etiquette of the day considered it bad form for a battleship to fire on a frigate unless fired upon first.

But Humphreys was about to change all of this. Each of his big frigates—the *Constitution*, the *President*, and the *United States*—was 175 feet long to the perpendiculars, and forty-four feet wide at her stoutest—twenty feet longer and two to three feet wider than British frigates and about thirteen feet longer than those of the French.[29] Indeed, the *Constitution* was just ten feet shorter than Nelson's *Victory*, his hundred-gun flagship at Trafalgar, but had just one gun deck to *Victory*'s three. In size and armament, the American super frigates would be a good match even for the seventy-fours that filled out the British fleet as third-raters. Because of their greater length, some thought Humphreys's ships the fastest frigates in the world.[30]

Humphreys began with the basic frigate structure, which called for a single gun deck. With a number of innovations to that structure, particularly in the framing, he was able to make his frigates bigger and stronger. Humphreys's design called for no more than two inches of space—the standard was four to eight inches—between each of the ribs (called futtocks) that formed the frame, on which the hull planking and scantlings were nailed. Humphreys also required that the futtocks be hewn from live oak, making his frigates substantially stronger than any built by the British or French.

Adding to the ships' muscle was Humphreys's design masterstroke, described by some as an inverted cantilever system built into the hull, consisting of a dozen transverse riders of live oak that extended diagonally along the hull up from the keel to the berth deck beams, yielding a more rigid ship and a gun deck of exceptional strength, capable of carrying the heavier cannons that Humphreys envisioned while enhancing the sailing qualities of the ship.[31] The British were also experimenting with the development of more muscular frigates, but they were doing it on the cheap. Their plan was to cut down a sixty-four-gun ship to a single-deck frigate and arm her with twenty-four-pounders instead of the more conventional, and lighter, eighteen-pounders that most British frigates carried. These were called "razees" after the French *vaisseaux rasés* (razed ships). Also at about the same time, Britain captured the French large frigate *Pomone*, and used her design for the construction of the large British frigates *Endymion*, *Cambria*, *Acasta*, and *Lavinia*. Like the *Constitution*, then under construction in Boston, these frigates would also carry twenty-four-pounders.[32]

But unlike the *Constitution*, whose structure was strengthened by Humphreys's invention of the transverse riders, the big British frigates were built with conventional framing, and the weight of the heavier cannons proved to be a problem.

> They were, however, very big by British standards and did not give an entirely satisfactory return on the substantial investment in their construction. The 24 pounder frigates in particular were vulnerable to structural problems, and soon they were all reduced to 18-pounders. Not only did the heavier 24-pounders rack the hull,

> but they were found difficult to handle on a frigate's relatively lively deck and rate of fire and accuracy suffered as a result.[33]

These transverse riders, however, were not Humphreys's only innovation. His other major contribution was to strengthen and widen the spar decks to create what was nearly a continuous deck connecting the forecastle with the quarterdeck, in contrast to conventional frigate design, which called for a huge rectangular gap in the middle of the top deck for ventilation and supplies. From Humphreys's perspective, this gap diminished the ship's structural integrity and limited the size and number of spar deck armaments. Humphreys's deck design not only allowed for more and heavier armaments on the spar deck—the *Constitution*'s carried twenty-two thirty-two-pound carronades plus one long eighteen-pounder and two long twenty-fours as bowchasers[34]—but further strengthened the rest of the ship and improved its handling. With these design innovations, Humphreys's frigates were powerful, fast, and maneuverable. Watching the *Constitution* clear Gibraltar one day in 1803, Lord Nelson is said to have remarked, "I see trouble for Britain in those big frigates from across the sea."[35]

Seven months after Washington signed the bill authorizing the construction of the new frigates, eighty-one lumberjacks and carpenters set out from New London, Connecticut, to St. Simons Island, off the coast of Georgia, to harvest and shape the many tons of live oak that Humphreys specified for all of the framing that carried the weight of the guns and was exposed to the weather. Found only in the coastal swamps and marshes of the American south, live oak is the evergreen cousin of the more familiar deciduous red oak, common to most of North America and Europe. It possesses immense strength—twice as strong as white oak and three times as strong as pine[36]—and resists the rot that destroyed more wooden ships than storms or battles.

The gnarled shape of the live oak tree—it has a short, stocky trunk supporting dozens of thick branches spreading out at many angles to form its majestic crown—made it unsuitable for many parts of a ship but ideal for certain structural components. The dozens of twisted and curving branches that each tree offered could be easily fashioned into the one-piece angular deck supports called hanging knees and lodge knees or shaped into the futtocks that would form the frame of the frigate's hull.

Assisted by scores of slaves from nearby plantations, the woodsmen worked in the humid, bug-infested swamps to chop down the trees selected by the

Midship section of the USS *Constitution*

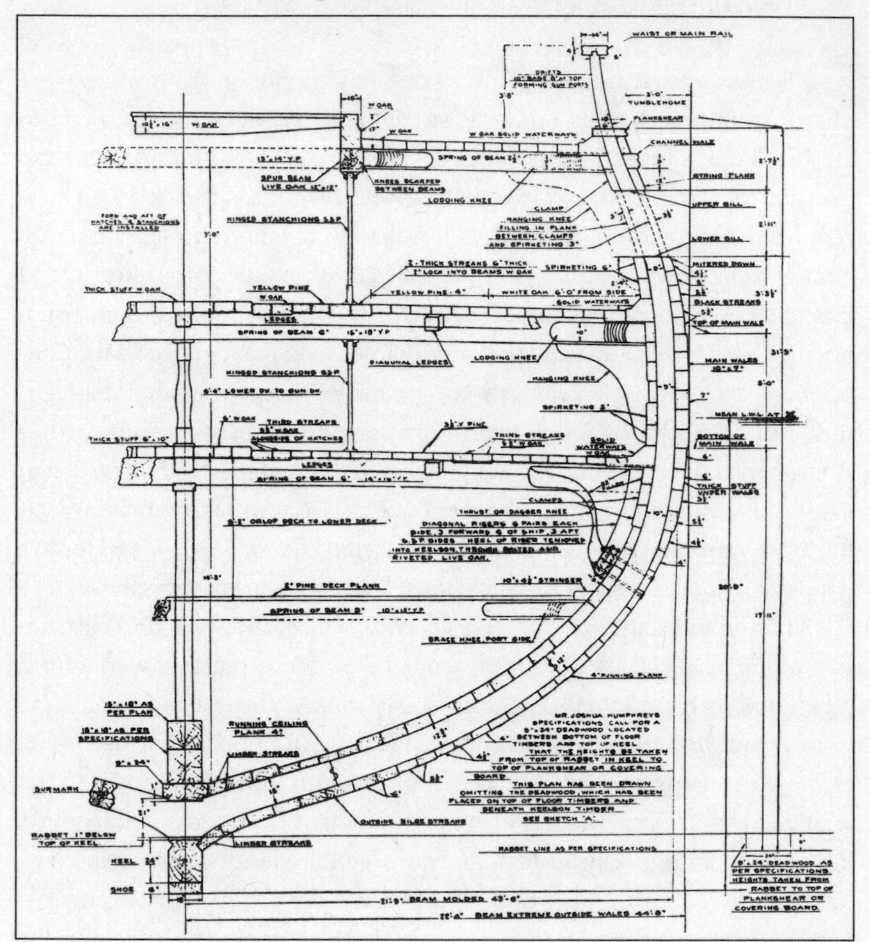

Courtesy of *The Frigate Constitution and Other Historic Ships*, Dover Publications, Inc.

shipwrights sent from northern ports to oversee the process. Carpenters hewed and sawed the wood into the dozens of different shapes that matched the molds and patterns sent from the shipyards. Humphreys had estimated that fifty-five men working twenty-four days a month could produce the timber for one frigate in two months,[37] but disease and hardship took their toll on both the men and on the oxen that dragged the felled trees from the forest. As the New England axmen grew sick and weary, slaves assumed more of the work, proving adept at the carpentry skills needed to cut and shape the nearly one thousand pieces of live oak that each of Humphreys's frigates required.

A year later, as construction progressed in each of the shipyards, Secretary of State Thomas Pickering gave President Washington a list of ten names proposed for the ships, "such as have occurred in my conversation with gentleman on the subject." Washington chose the first five that Pickering offered: *United States*, *President*, *Constitution*, *Congress*, and *Constellation*, the last referring to the circular array of fifteen stars on America's flag.[38] The sixth ship, the thirty-eight-gun *Chesapeake*, was not named until later, although that name appeared neither on Pickering's list nor among the forty names that Humphreys submitted.

Humphreys's own Federal Street shipyard in the Southwark section of Philadelphia[39] built the *United States*, but he directed that the *Constitution* be the work of Edmund Hartt's shipyard in Boston.[40] By late 1795, the *Constitution*'s long oak keel had been laid and many of the component structures, such as the stern frame and the live oak supports, had been cut and assembled. These were hoisted onto the keel by teams of oxen, whose brute strength powered the rudimentary cranes that moved the heavy timbers and frames from one place to another.[41] By September 1797, the hull was completed, caulked, painted, and sheathed in copper sheet provided by Paul Revere's metal shop.

The hull was watertight and ready for launching on the 20th when the tide in Boston Harbor reached its peak. Colonel Claghorn, who supervised construction, ordered the blocks that held the *Constitution* in place to be knocked out to allow the finished hull to slide down the ways and into the water. But the ship failed to move. Large screw jacks were employed to give the reluctant ship a powerful nudge, but they moved her only twenty-seven feet, well short of the water. Further efforts the next day moved her another thirty-one feet, still shy of the water. It was not until October 27 that improvements to the ways allowed the *Constitution* to slip into the water after Captain James Sever smashed a bottle of Madeira on the heel of her bowsprit.[42]

During the frigate's early years, many thought the twice-failed launch had been a bad omen, and the quality of the ship's first set of officers seemed to confirm their fears. In June 1798 Steven Higginson, the navy's agent in Boston, wrote to Secretary of War Timothy Pickering that the *Constitution*'s officers had joined the navy only because they were "incapable of getting their living in the common pursuits of life."[43] One of those officers was the twenty-five-year-old Isaac Hull, who in March 1798 was appointed Captain Samuel Nicholson's fourth lieutenant on the *Constitution*. Hull's short career at sea seemed to confirm Higginson's low opinion. Obtaining his commission through political preferment—Hull's Republican uncle William was a friend of Captain Nicholson—his earlier career in command of several merchant ships, though brief, was nothing short of disastrous. Two of his ships were captured by the French during the Quasi-War, while the third was a financial failure. With little likelihood of getting another merchant commission, Hull used his connections to get into the navy, where he managed to survive and then thrive. In 1799 the troublesome Nicholson was replaced by the more competent Captain Silas Talbot, who soon promoted Hull to first lieutenant.[44]

From its launch in 1798 until 1801, when Congress passed the Peace Establishment Act,[45] *Constitution* was engaged along the east coast and in the Caribbean protecting American merchantmen from French privateers during the Quasi-War with France, during which time she captured numerous prizes. In her first few years at sea, there were questions about her sailing abilities, which led to modifications and re-riggings as subsequent captains attempted to fulfill the ship's fearsome potential. Despite unhappiness over her handling, she was acknowledged to be fast, and during one stormy twenty-one-hour period recorded a sustained speed of between ten and twelve knots, making her one of the fastest ships afloat. The same qualities were soon recognized in all of America's big frigates, as the British naval historian James Henderson confirms: "With their great length and sail-power, they were the fastest warships in the world."[46] Indeed, as late as the 1840s, when *Constitution*'s sister ship the *United States* was approaching the ancient age of fifty, the old frigate was still considered the fastest ship in the U.S. Navy.[47]

III

Hull arrived at Boston on Sunday, 27 July 1812, after his harrowing chase. He stayed only a week to bring on board food, water, and new crewmen, shipping out on Sunday, 2 August. Some historians, beginning with Henry Adams, contend that Hull's stay was so brief, and confined to the outer harbor, because he believed that Navy Secretary Hamilton had dispatched orders relieving him of his command in favor of the more senior William Bainbridge.[48] Others, however, argue that Hull left quickly because he feared that a timid Hamilton might order the *Constitution* confined to Boston until a larger and stronger fleet could be assembled around her.[49]

Once out of Boston Harbor and well into the North Atlantic, a southerly breeze carried Hull north past Halifax, Nova Scotia, and into the Gulf of St. Lawrence, where he intended to raid British shipping. At one point he gave chase to the British brig *Ranger*, which, when night fell, cleverly deceived Hull by dropping into the water a float carrying a lantern that drifted one way while the darkened *Ranger* sailed off in another.[50] In the week following the *Constitution*'s departure from Boston, Hull continued to train his crew, prepare for battle, and make repairs on the ship, including the restoration of the taffrail that had been cut away during the chase off New Jersey. Cruising off Newfoundland, Hull took a few British prizes, met a Baltimore privateer that claimed it had been chased the whole day by the *Guerriere*,[51] and picked up rumors that elements of Broke's fleet were in the area to protect British merchantmen. On 17 August, Hull turned the *Constitution* on a southerly course. He was south of Halifax at about two o'clock on the 19th when, as Moses Smith recounts, a lookout in the tops spotted a hull down on the southeastern horizon:[52]

> "Where away?" inquired the Lieutenant in command.
> "Two points off the larboard bow, sir."
>
> Hull came on deck and ordered a midshipman into the top for a better look. "Mr. German! take the glass and go aloft. See if you can make out what she is."
>
> Once aloft, Midshipman German inspected the distant sail and cried down to Hull. "She's a great vessel sir. Tremendous sails."

Most of the crew had by now come up from below to see what was happening and to catch a glimpse of the unknown ship lurking to the south. Hull ordered a course set for the stranger, and with a light wind abeam, studding sails were set fore and aft to speed the *Constitution* on her way. Smith recalls, "The noble frigate fairly bounded over the billows, as we gave her a rap full, and spread her broad and tall wings to the gale."[53]

Headed northwest to Halifax with the wind in her face, *Guerriere* was standing by the wind on a starboard tack when lookouts on the British ship sighted the *Constitution* coming toward them from the north. As Dacres turned his ship to gain a favorable wind and tactical advantage, he had little reason to worry about the outcome. It had been nearly ten years since Britain had lost a ship-to-ship engagement. The preservation of this remarkable record, he thought, would be a fitting honor for the scion of one of the Royal Navy's most distinguished dynasties.

At sea since age eight, Dacres was the son of Vice Admiral James Richard Dacres, who took Curacao from the French and, in America's War of Independence, demolished Benedict Arnold's squadron of gunboats on Lake Champlain at the battle of Valcour Island.[54] An uncle, Sir Richard Dacres, helped open the Dardanelles in an assault on the pro-French Ottoman Empire. Now strutting the *Guerriere*'s quarterdeck as the American came closer, the twenty-eight-year-old Captain Dacres (a future vice admiral himself) must have tingled at the prospect of national glory.

So eager was Dacres to prove his mettle in this new war with America that three days earlier he sent a written challenge to John Rodgers, commodore of the American fleet, by way of a note written in the log of a passing merchant vessel headed to an American port: "Captain Dacres, Commander of his Britannic Majesty's *Guerriere* of 44 guns, presents his compliments to Commodore Rodgers of the United States frigate *President*, and will be very happy to meet him or any other American frigate of equal force to the *President* off Sandy Hook, for the purpose of having a few minutes tête-à-tête."[55]

Dacres singled out Rodgers because of the *President*'s now notorious nighttime encounter a year earlier with the smaller HMS *Little Belt*. Obsessed with avenging the thirteen British sailors who perished in that fight, the cocky Dacres had emblazoned his topsail with the taunt "Not the Little Belt."[56]

Positioning his ship for combat, Dacres had her course hauled up, took in her top-gallant sails, and backed her main topsail to slow the ship—steering "rap full"[57]—for the *Constitution*'s pending arrival. Hull responded by shortening sail, taking in topgallant sails and flying jib, sending down the royal yards, and putting another reef in the topsails. As the ships slowly closed, Dacres offered formal identification by hoisting three ensigns, and Hull responded by setting his colors to the two mastheads and one to the mizzen peak. The marine drummer beat to quarters while sand as well as ashes from the cook stove were strewn about the spar and gun decks to give firm footing and absorb the slippery blood that would flow in the impending battle.

When the *Constitution*'s identity was confirmed, the ten impressed American crewmen aboard the *Guerriere* petitioned Dacres that they not be forced to fight against their countrymen. Although Dacres's crew was already under strength, he graciously conceded, sending the Americans below to the cockpit, where they were expected to assist the ship's surgeon in caring for the wounded.[58]

Dacres took advantage of the lee gauge he was on to wear ship every now and again and offer the American his broadside. The first blast from *Guerriere* fell well short of the *Constitution*, and none of Dacres's subsequent cannonades did much damage. Nonetheless, as the pursuer on the weather gauge with the wind abaft, Hull had the disadvantage of being able to bring to bear only a few guns from his bow, while Dacres could tack and wear, leveling a broadside of fifteen eighteen-pound long guns at the American's vulnerable bow whenever he pleased. These maneuvers continued through the next hour as the *Guerriere* wore around to fire ineffectual broadsides from alternate sides while Hull yawed the *Constitution* in response to each to keep from getting raked across his bow.

On the *Guerriere*, both captain and crew were feeling cocky. From one of her masts hung a small barrel of molasses, a mocking gesture indicating the crew's intention to accommodate their Yankee prisoners' penchant for a drink called "switchel," a mixture of rum, molasses, sugar, and citrus juice.[59] And as the ships were closing, a confident Dacres brought his prisoner Captain William B. Orne, the master of the recently captured American merchantman *Betsey*, onto the quarterdeck. Dacres pointed to the *Constitution* and noted tartly that the ship bearing down upon him was "rather too bold to be an American." Still, he added, "the better he behaves the more honor we shall gain by taking him."[60]

Moses Smith recalls the minutes leading up to the confrontation:

> As we came up she began to fire. They were evidently trying to rake us. But we continued on our course tacking and half tacking, taking good care to avoid being raked. We came so near on one tack, that an eighteen pound shot came through us under the larboard knight-head, striking just abaft the breech of the gun to which I belonged. The splinters flew in all directions; but no one was hurt. We immediately picked up the shot, and put it in long Tom, a large gun loose on deck—and sent it home again, with our respects.[61]

By six o'clock, the *Constitution* was within fifty yards of the *Guerriere*, which was firing broadside after broadside at the American frigate. It was probably about this time that Hull gave what Moses Smith remembers as his final encouragement to the crew: "Men, now do your duty. Your officers cannot have entire command over you now. Each man must do all in his power for his country." As Hull shouted his encouragement, shots ripped through sail and rigging, and one snapped an iron hoop that held the mast together. Two Americans were killed and several wounded. Lieutenant Charles Morris is said to have asked for permission to open fire. "Not yet, sir," Hull replied.

Morris is said to have repeated the request three more times, and three times Hull gave the same answer: "Not yet." At a distance of half a pistol shot—less than twenty-five yards—Hull finally gave the order—"Now, boys, pour it into them!" [62] The gun captains of the *Constitution* touched match to cannon and let loose a ferocious broadside from double-shotted guns. As his cannons roared at the enemy, the portly Hull was said to have jumped up and down in such excitement that he split his trousers.[63]

Constitution's first broadside inflicted catastrophic damage. Nearly seven hundred pounds of cast iron shot crashed into *Guerriere*'s side and shredded her rigging. Oak and pine splinters flew as high as the mizzen top, and guns weighing a ton and a half were blown off their carriages as the devastating iron balls blasted through wooden scantlings. The American Orne wrote of that first broadside, "I heard a tremendous explosion from the opposing frigate. The effect of her shot seemed to make the *Guerriere* reel, and tremble as though she had received the shock of an earthquake."[64] The American gunners reloaded and continued a murderous bombardment from the twenty-four-pounders below and the thirty-two-pound carronades above.

Guerriere returned fire, but much of her shot flew high and through the rigging, where it did little damage. One shot, however, did shred enough halyards and braces to tangle up the American flag flying on the foremast in the debris. To the cheers of the crew, Smith recalls, "a little Irish chap (Dan Hogan) brimfull of courage" climbed up and secured the flag to the mast.[65]

Packed tightly below in the smoky and noisy gun deck, hundreds of crewmen worked like a well-oiled machine to pull the heavy guns in, clean and load them, run them out, and fire at the *Guerriere* in a sequence of elaborately coordinated actions taking less than two minutes. Among the hundreds serving *Constitution*'s guns were black crewmen, some of them freed slaves, others born free in the north where slavery had been abolished by the war's outbreak. Years later, dining in Boston with Josiah Quincy, Hull paid tribute, coarsely but with genuine admiration, to their performance that day: "I never had any better fighters than those niggers—they stripped to the waist, and fought like devils, sir, seeming to be utterly insensible to danger, and to be possessed with a determination to outfight the white sailors."[66] A century after the battle, the historian Charles Francis Adams added, "The cry that day was 'Remember the *Chesapeake*!' and perhaps those Maryland negroes, 'stripped to the waist', had it on their lips as well as in their hearts, as they worked the *Constitution*'s guns."[67]

Moments after combat commenced, *Guerriere*'s shattered mizzenmast fell over the starboard quarter and the main yard crashed into its slings. Moses Smith quotes an American gunner's reaction to the fallen mast: "By God we've made a brig of her! Next time we'll make her a sloop!"[68] Carrying more sail, the *Constitution* gained on the wounded *Guerriere*, whose bow was now twisting into the wind from the dragging mast. Hull luffed short around the enemy's bow and delivered another broadside from her starboard guns.

Constitution's maneuverability may have suffered from her loss of rigging and sails. She passed too close to the floundering *Guerriere*, whose bowsprit got tangled in *Constitution*'s starboard mizzen rigging. Dacres shot into *Constitution*'s stern with his bow guns, setting fire to Hull's cabin. Boarding parties on both sides were now organized and rushed to the rails. Dacres leaped onto the hammock nettings, waving his sword to rally his crew to board the enemy across the bridge made by *Guerriere*'s bowsprit, but a mizzen top man fired his musket and hit Dacres in the back, knocking him to the deck. On *Constitution*, Marine Lieutenant Bush leaped to the railing and called to Hull, "Shall I board her?" but a shot fired by a British marine crashed through his cheek bone and out the back of his head,[69] killing him instantly. Bush thus became the first U.S. Marine officer to die in combat.[70]

Lieutenant Morris and Mr. Alwyn, master, leaped on to the taffrail in an attempt to lash *Guerriere* to *Constitution* and hold her securely for boarding, but they too were hit by musket fire and were seriously wounded. In Morris's case it was a musket ball that entered his chest and passed completely through him. Despite the wound, Morris remained on duty until the end, finally collapsing in pain when the battle was over. He spent the next two weeks recuperating in bed, and would recover and be given his own ship in recognition of his courage. Two lieutenants on the *Guerriere* were also hit and killed, and the musket fire of the American marksmen stationed in the tops and the grape

U.S.S. *Constitution* vs. H.M.S. *Guerriere*
Off Georges Bank, August 19, 1812

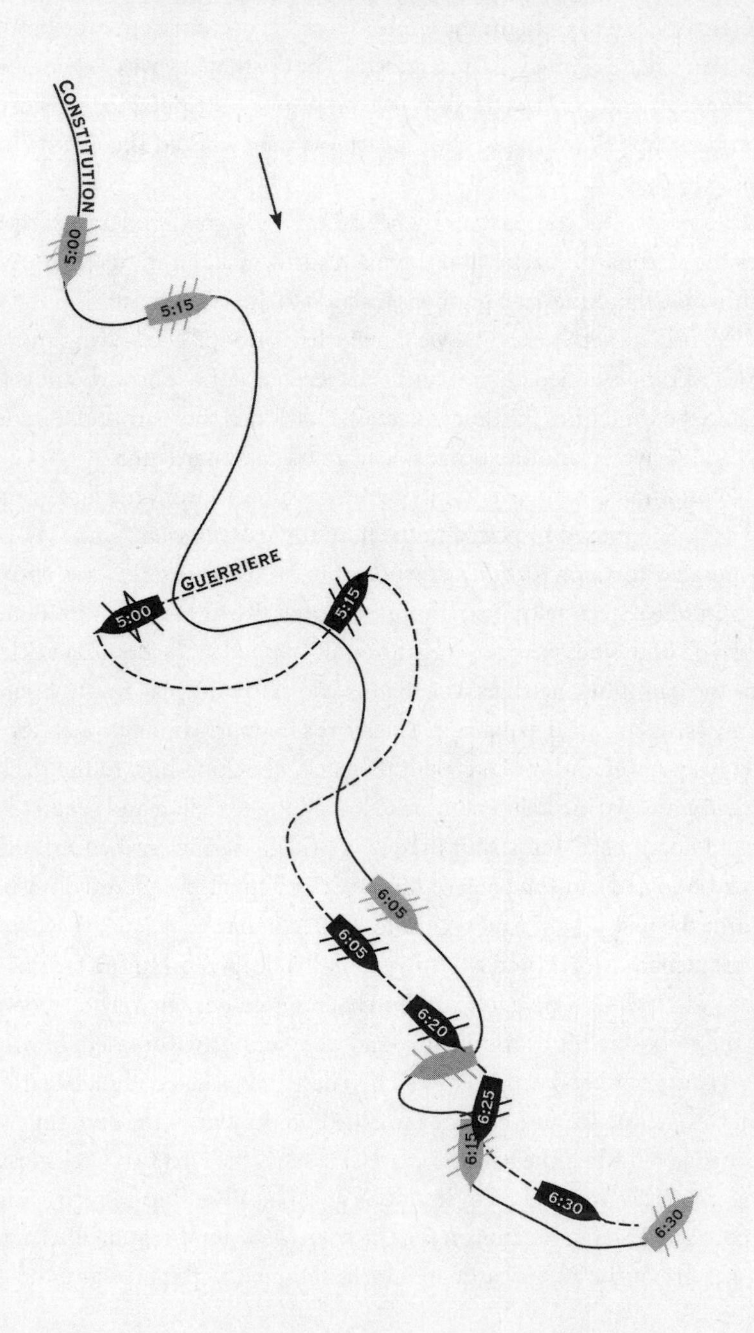

fired by the carronades picked off most of the British crew attempting to board from the forecastle.[71]

As the wind twisted the entangled ships around, they gradually parted before either side could board the other, and once away, the *Guerriere*'s foremast and mainmast toppled over the side, leaving her a defenseless hulk, pitching to and fro in the rolling waves, and dipping her guns into the water. Hull took *Constitution* out of cannon range to make a few repairs while the dismasted *Guerriere* wallowed helplessly. Orne described the scene on *Guerriere*:

> At about half past six o'clock in the evening, after the firing had ceased, I went on deck, and there beheld a scene which it would be difficult to describe. All the *Guerriere*'s masts were shot away, and she lay rolling like a log in the trough of the sea. Many of her men were employed in throwing the dead overboard. The decks were covered with blood, and had the appearance of a butcher's slaughterhouse ... and what with the groans of the wounded, the noise and confusion of the enraged survivors of the ill-fated ship rendered the whole scene a perfect hell.[72]

Also covering the *Guerriere*'s deck was a splattering of dark brown goo from the puncheon of molasses, which American shot had blown to pieces. Moses Smith was pleased to observe that "the yankee shot tasted the English molasses, not the yankee lips. We made the decks of the *Guerriere* so slippery, that her men could hardly stand! They had more switchel prepared for them than they knew what to do with."[73] *Constitution* received no serious damage, and when some of its sailors said they saw British cannon balls bounce off her thick oak scantlings, the crew awarded her the nickname *Old Ironsides*.

With the minor repairs completed, Hull returned to *Guerriere* as night fell and saw that a flag still flew from a stump of a mast that had been jury rigged to help stabilize the floundering ship. Unsure as to what Dacres intended, Hull sent Lieutenant Read and a boarding party in small boat to the *Guerriere* to inquire as to whether the British ship had surrendered.

According to Charles Lee Lewis, a prominent naval historian in the first half of the last century, when Read asked whether the British had struck, a wounded and disoriented Dacres is said to have replied, "I don't know that it would be prudent to continue the engagement any longer."

> "Do I understand you to say that you have struck?" asked Read.
>
> "Not precisely" replied Dacres, "... but I don't know that it will be worth while to fight any longer."
>
> "If you cannot decide, I will return aboard my ship and we will resume the engagement," answered Read.
>
> "Why, I am pretty much *hors de combat* already. I have hardly men enough left to work a single gun, and my ship is in a sinking condition."
>
> "I wish to know sir," demanded Read, "... whether I am to consider you a prisoner of war or an enemy? I have no time for further parley."
>
> At this Dacres conceded. "I believe now there is no alternative. If I could fight longer, I would with pleasure; but I ... must surrender."[74]

And with that Read took possession of the *Guerriere*. Midshipman Henry Gilliam was with Read. In a letter to his uncle, he described a deck covered in "pieces of skulls, brains, legs, arms and blood ... in every direction and groanes of the wounded were almost enough to make me curse the war."[75] Read offered Dacres the *Constitution*'s surgeon to help care for the wounded and dying. Dacres accepted gratefully, though perhaps a little surprised that the American surgeon—having only seven wounded to tend—was free of his own duties so soon after battle. The *Guerriere,* by contrast, suffered 101 casualties—more than a third of her crew—and the American and British surgeons labored through the night to save as many of the English wounded as they could. "One poor fellow had his jaw shot off; and while we were watching him he bled to death. Others deprived of arms and legs lingered in the greatest torture, until death put an end to their pains."[76]

Dacres was taken back to the *Constitution*, where he formally surrendered to Captain Hull. Hull refused Dacres's tender of his sword and replied, "No, no, I will not take the sword from one who knows so well how to use it,"[77] according to one of several versions of the capitulation. Other eyewitness accounts of the exchange vary somewhat from this description. Smith remembers the sword being offered, and apparently accepted. As Dacres placed the hilt of his sword in Hull's hand, Smith says he asked:[78]

> "Captain Hull, what have you got for men?"
>
> "Oh", replied Hull with a sly smile, "only a parcel of green bush-whackers, Captain Dacres."
>
> "Bush-whackers! They are more like tigers than men. I never saw men fight so. They fairly drove us from our quarters."

Smith says nothing about the return of the sword. It is said that in later years, while dining with Josiah Quincy in Boston, Hull recited another version of the exchange. According to Quincy's son Edmund, Hull said that he greeted Dacres as he came on board the *Constitution*, "'Sir, I am happy to see you,' whereupon Dacres, thinking he's being insulted, offers the 'surly reply of John Bull,' 'Ugh, damn you. I suppose you are.'"[79]

Whatever passed between the two captains, once the formalities of surrender were completed, much work remained. Though *Guerriere* was badly battered and filling with water from the thirty or so holes that *Constitution*'s guns had punched below her waterline, Hull wanted to bring her back as a prize. As carpenters and crew from both ships worked to repair the damage, a hawser was connected in an effort to take the prize in tow to Boston. But after several hours it became apparent that the damage was too severe and *Guerriere* was still taking on water despite the best efforts of both ships' carpenters.

As the wounded and the remaining crewmen were rowed to *Constitution*, Hull, according to one account, asked Dacres if there was anything of particular value he would want from the *Guerriere* before she was sunk. "Yes, there is," he replied, "my mother's Bible."[80] It was retrieved, and Read and a demolition crew returned to set the fires that would explode the shattered hulk. From a safe distance and with the British sailors securely imprisoned below in the hold, the crew of the *Constitution* watched as Read's fires spread through the ship, inching their way to the magazine and the barrels of black powder it held below. Moses Smith recalls, "The first intimation we had that the fire was at work was the discharge of the guns. One after another, as the flame advanced, they came booming towards us. Roar followed roar, flash followed flash, until the whole mass was enveloped in clouds of smoke."[81] The ghostly guns soon fell silent, and after a brief pause while the fire ate through the walls of the magazine, *Constitution*'s crew watched as *Guerriere* exploded, broke in half, and sank to her grave not far from where RMS *Titanic* would come to rest four months shy of a century later.

Eleven days after leaving the battleground, Hull approached Boston and anchored in the outer harbor in preparation for bringing his ship and her many prisoners to the city. Hull was asleep in his cabin on the morning of the 31st when he was awakened and warned of the presence of five ships headed toward them from the northeast. With the breeze blowing from a direction precluding escape to the sea, Hull ordered the anchor cable cut and took the ship into the safety of Boston's inner harbor. It turned out that the five ships were Commodore Rodgers's fleet, with Rodgers commanding the *President* and Stephen Decatur the *United States*, all returning from an unproductive cruise to the English Channel.

Word quickly spread though Boston, and to the rest of the country, that the first major naval victory of the war had gone to the underdog Americans, not the mighty British. As Hull eased the massive frigate into Boston Harbor, pleasure boats set out to escort her in, church bells pealed, and hundreds crowded to the dock to greet the ship and crew.

Great Britain, by contrast, was stunned. When the news of the defeat reached England, the *Times* spoke for many when it observed:

> It is not merely that an English frigate has been taken, after, what we are free to confess, may be called a brave resistance, but that it has been taken by a new enemy, an enemy unaccustomed to such triumphs, and likely to be rendered insolent and confident by them. He must be a weak politician who does not see how important the first triumph is in giving tone and character to the war. Never before in the history of the world did an English frigate strike to an American.[82]

Hull was outwardly modest in victory, and his several reports of the engagement to Navy Secretary Hamilton praised his crew: "From the smallest boy in the ship to the oldest Seaman, not a look of fear was seen. They all went into action, giving three cheers and requesting to be laid along side the enemy."[83] Hull also heaped praise on his fellow officers, especially Bush of the marines and Morris.[84]

Within a few days of his arrival to an ecstatic Boston, Hull joined Stephen Decatur at a breakfast in their honor at Quincy, Massachusetts. Elizabeth Susan Morton Quincy, the wife of Josiah Quincy, remembered the impression the two heroes made on her that morning: "These naval officers formed a striking contrast. Hull was easy and prepossessing in his manners, but looked accustomed to face the 'battle and the breeze.' Decatur was uncommonly handsome, and remarkable for the delicacy and refinement of his appearance."[85]

On 5 September, Boston honored Hull and his crew with a banquet at Faneuil Hall. Rewards and tokens of gratitude were provided by the federal government, the cities of New York, Philadelphia, Charleston, and his native state of Connecticut. Poems and songs were written and published, and paintings and prints of the engagement were made and circulated throughout the country. One popular tune titled "The Constitution and the Guerriere"[86] opened,

> It oft-times has been told,
> That the British seamen bold
> Could flog the tars of France
> So neat and handy, Oh!
> But they never met their match,
> Till the Yankees did them catch
> Oh, the Yankee boys for fighting
> Are the dandy, Oh!

Eight stanzas later, the song concludes with a rousing finale suited for a song to be sung in America's taverns:

> Now, fill your glasses full,
> And we'll drink to Captain Hull
> And so merrily we'll push
> Around the brandy, Oh!
> Johnny Bull may boast his fill,
> Let the world say what it will,
> The Yankee boys for fighting
> Are the dandy, Oh!

In early December, capping off a joyous victory tour through the country, Hull and other naval heroes were fêted at a ball in Washington attended by First Lady Dolley Madison. But as the honors rolled in, so too did a host of family problems that developed while Isaac Hull was at sea. Just three days before defeating *Guerriere*, his uncle, General William Hull, had surrendered Fort

Detroit to a greatly inferior British force without firing a shot. The luster added to the Hull name by the captain of the *Constitution* was dimmed by the uncle's disgrace at Fort Detroit and his pending court-martial. Another misfortune for the family was the death of Isaac Hull's brother, who left a widow and children whom Hull was duty-bound to support. Having spent many of his thirty-nine years at sea and now confronted with a host of family problems, Hull married for the first time four months later.

Seeking a commission that would better accommodate his new domestic responsibilities, Hull asked Navy Secretary Hamilton if he could exchange commands with Captain William Bainbridge, with whom he had served under Preble during the Barbary Wars and who was then commandant of the Boston Navy Yard. Hamilton agreed, and on 15 September 1812, Hull took over the navy yard and Bainbridge the *Constitution*.[87]

Hull never again commanded a ship during the war, but those who served under him during his brief cruise would never forget the leadership and patience he showed toward his untrained crew. The crew's affection toward Hull was not without reason. In the years that followed, he often looked after the families of those who died or were injured in his service. One seaman, Richard Dunn, who lost a leg in the fight with the *Guerriere*, received expedited pension approval from the secretary of the navy. Such pensions were modest, however, and the beneficiary was forbidden to receive any other income. Hull thought this unfair and compensated for the deficiency by hiring the disabled Dunn "off the books" at the several navy yards he commanded over the next decade.[88]

Even the defeated Dacres was generous in his praise of the American captain. In his 7 September report to his superior in Halifax, Vice Admiral Herbert Sawyer, Dacres wrote, "I feel it my duty to state that the conduct of Captain Hull and his Officers to our Men has been that of a brave Enemy, the greatest care being taken to prevent our Men losing the smallest trifle, and the great attention being paid to the wounded who through the attention and skill of Mr. [John] Irvine, [*Constitution*'s] Surgeon, I hope will do well."[89]

Dacres was soon exchanged for several Americans held by the British and stood for court-martial in Halifax on 2 October 1812. He defended his performance by noting the deteriorated condition of his ship, the vastly superior size of the American vessel, and simple bad luck. "The success of my opponent was owing to fortune," Dacres told the court. "It is my earnest wish, and would be the happiest period of my life, to be once more opposed to the *Constitution* … in a frigate of similar force to the *Guerriere*." Dacres added, by way of explanation for the defeat, "I felt much shocked, when on board the *Constitution*, to find a large proportion of the ship's company British seamen, and many of whom I recognized as having been foremost in the attempt to board."[90]

Attributing America's victories to British crewmen serving aboard her ships was a common theme of many British naval historians in the nineteenth century. Many decades later, Theodore Roosevelt, who began writing *The Naval War of 1812* (still in print) while a senior at Harvard College, commended Dacres's generous concession to the ten impressed Americans aboard the *Guerriere* who would not fight against their countrymen; but went on to observe that "we reach the somewhat remarkable conclusion, that the British ship was defeated because the Americans on board would *not* fight against their country, and that the American was victorious because the British on board *would*."[91]

Dacres was honorably acquitted on 2 October 1812—the "lamentable" condition of his ship was cited as the cause of his defeat[92]—but did not see action again during the war. Six days later, almost five hundred miles west and south across the Gulf of Maine in Boston Harbor, Commodore Rodgers's squadron of the *President*, *United States*, *Congress*, and *Argus* left Boston in search of British ships. Four days out of Boston, the *United States*, under the command of Commodore Stephen Decatur, separated from the fleet to hunt on his own. Three weeks later, on 29 October, the *Constitution*, under William Bainbridge, sailed from Boston with the brig *Hornet*, planning to rendezvous with the frigate *Essex*, under David Porter, just then leaving its mooring on the Delaware River near Chester, Pennsylvania. Decatur and Bainbridge, both veterans of the Barbary Wars and both sailing Joshua Humphreys's great ships of war, were about to shatter forever Britain's blind sense of naval superiority.

IV

Coming early in the war, and having important, but opposite, emotional effects on the adversaries, the fight between *Constitution* and *Guerriere* is often assumed to have been the first meeting of British and American warships during the war. In fact it was the fourth. The first occurred on 23 June, when the

President, 44, leading *Congress*, *Hornet*, and *Argus* on patrol, chased and exchanged fire with HMS *Belvidera*. *President*, under Rodgers, was in the lead and closing on *Belvidera*. The American's first volley did serious damage, and a second one might have won the day, but one of *President*'s long guns exploded, inflicting sixteen casualties, one of whom was Rodgers, who suffered a broken leg. The chase continued, more volleys were exchanged, and casualties were sustained, but by the end of the day *Belvidera* had managed to escape. Several weeks later, on 16 July, the American brig *Nautilus*, 14, was overtaken and captured off the coast of New Jersey by the same squadron that a few days later found *Constitution* in its midst.

In mid-July, near Bermuda, Captain David Porter of USS *Essex*, 32, came upon a British convoy of seven ships bound from Barbados to Quebec. Porter struck during the night and captured the troopship *Samuel and Sarah*, which was carrying 197 British soldiers to their new duty in Canada. Although the soldiers were allowed to continue on to Halifax under the code of honor of the time, they were still technically Porter's prisoners when released under "parole" and were honor-bound not to fight again until they were later "exchanged" for American prisoners of war. Over the next two weeks, the *Essex* took another six British prizes in the waters north of Bermuda before stumbling upon the sixteen-gun British sloop of war *Alert* on 13 August 1812.

To lure the smaller ship within range of his guns, Porter rigged the *Essex* to appear as a lumbering American merchantman that would make a profitable prize. Gun ports were closed, the ship's speed slowed, and men were sent aloft to set sails as if trying to escape. The rest of the crew cleared for action and waited patiently as the British ship closed to take the bait. As the *Alert* neared and fired a warning shot, *Essex* hove to and then let loose with a broadside of grape and canister as the *Alert* passed under her stern. The distance was too great for the carronades and little harm was done, but Porter put up his helm and opened another broadside as soon as the guns could bear. *Alert*, realizing the trap, tried to flee, but the *Essex* was soon alongside, and the British sloop struck her colors. The battle lasted eight minutes, wounding three British sailors.

CHAPTER FOUR

BACK ON LAND: FAILURE ON THE NIAGARA

As the autumn chill settled over the eastern United States, the land campaign against the British along the New York–Canada border fared no better than the one in the west. The commander of the campaign was Major General Stephen Van Rensselaer, "an estimable and honest old gentleman and worthy citizen," in Theodore Roosevelt's opinion, but "who knew nothing of military matters." He was to be supported by Brigadier General Alexander Smyth of the regular army, a political appointee who also had no military experience, and whose attitude was markedly uncooperative. Roosevelt observed that Smyth "issued proclamations so bombastic that they really must have come from an unsound mind."[1] The historian Alan Taylor's assessment of Smyth is no more flattering:

> General Alexander Smyth arrived to compound the divisions in the Niagara army. Irish-born, Virginian and Republican, Smyth was a stark contrast to Van Rensselaer, the Federalist grandee from New York.... Although subordinate in rank to Van Rensselaer,

> Smyth disdained the Federalist general as a military amateur. Rather than submit to his command at Lewiston, Smyth set up his own headquarters upriver at Buffalo.... Instead of combining and cooperating, the divided army worked at cross purposes.[2]

The purpose of the campaign in western New York was to seize the portage in the Niagara River region and thus cut off the enemy's communications and troop movements between western and eastern Canada by way of the Great Lakes. An estimated six thousand Americans attacked two thousand British troops and Indian warriors across the Niagara River on 12 October 1812, but Smyth's lack of cooperation reduced the Americans' strength, and robbed them of the better trained and motivated regulars. Several hundred Americans crossed the river on the night of the 12th in small boats below the falls and attacked the British settlement of Queenston. By the next morning, some six hundred U.S. troops under the command of twenty-six-year-old Lieutenant Colonel Winfield Scott controlled the high ground at Queenston and began to fortify their position against an expected counter-attack.[3]

The Americans held on through the day, but, having fought since midnight, they were weary, low on ammunition, and desperate for reinforcements. As the Americans strengthened their position, British reinforcements moved south from Fort George for the counter-attack. Under the command of American-born[4] Major General Roger H. Sheaffe, this force was made up of regulars, several companies of Canadian militia, a hundred or so Mohawk Indians, and "black pioneers," a company of about twenty-five fugitive slaves eager to remain free in British Canada. As Sheaffe marched south, Van Rensselaer attempted to bring reinforcements across the river to support the beleaguered Scott, but "[o]n his return to the east bank, [he] found that much of his militia army had dissolved into a crowd of spectators, watching the distant battle as if it were waged solely for their entertainment."[5]

When the militia refused to cross, Van Rensselaer offered the desperate American troops on the Canadian side of the river the opportunity to retreat and ordered boats sent across to accommodate them. But in this too he failed—the boatmen refused to put themselves at risk by crossing the river while the battle raged up above on the bluff. After repulsing several early attacks by Sheaffe's force, Scott realized that his isolated position was untenable and ordered a retreat to the river. The retreat quickly became disorderly, however,

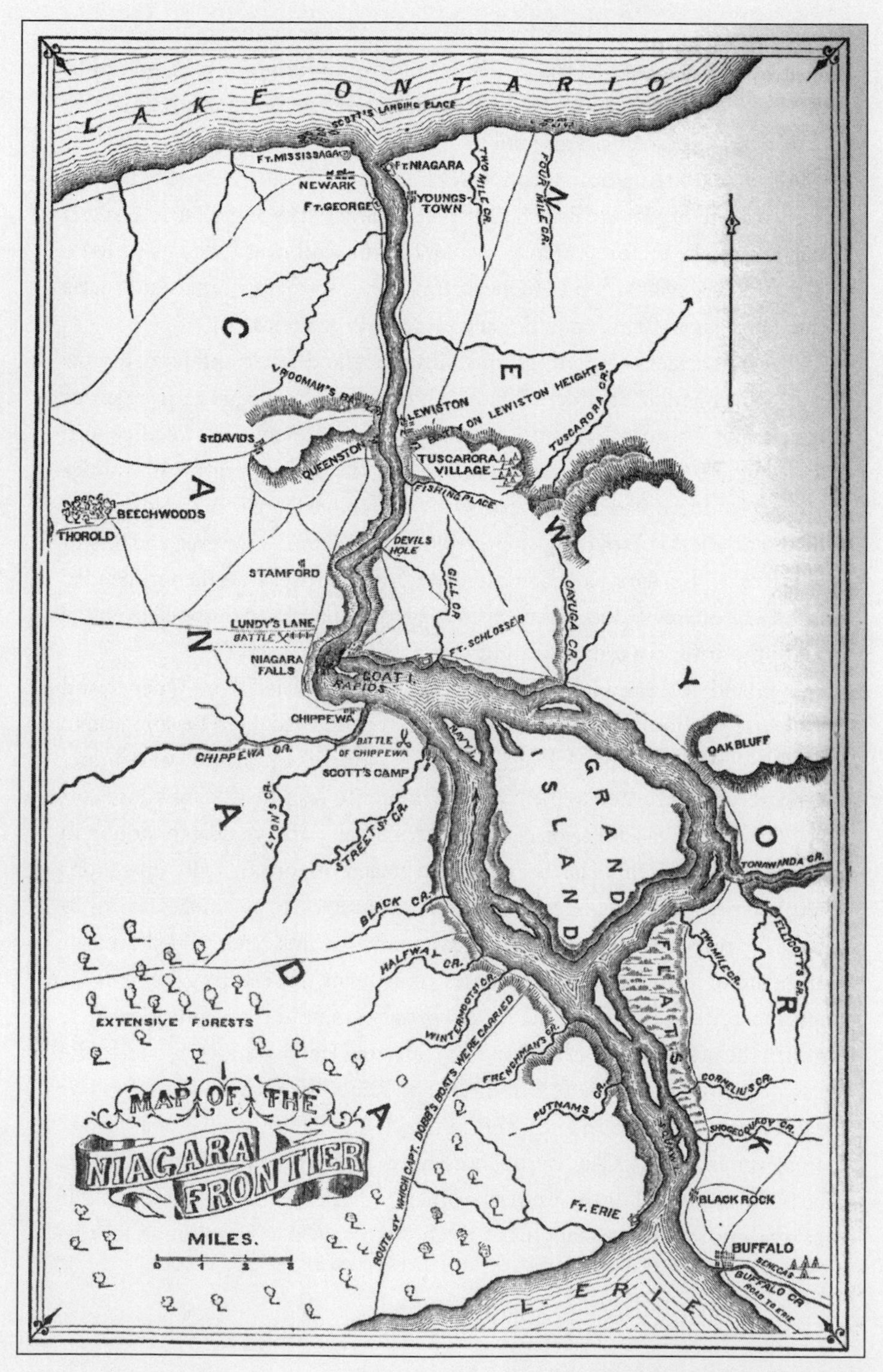

Courtesy of *Lossing's Pictorial Field Book of the War of 1812*

and the Americans panicked when they reached the river and found no boats. With his troops exhausted and nearly out of ammunition, and with no way to pull back to the American side, Scott surrendered his force, now numbering nearly a thousand regulars and militia.

Although the American forces were driven out of British territory, it was a bittersweet victory for the British. During the early stages of the battle, General Isaac Brock, the victor at Detroit over William Hull, was killed as he led a counter-attack against Scott at Queenston. It was soon apparent that Brock's death left a gap in British military talent in North America.

Van Rensselaer accepted responsibility for the debacle and tendered his resignation, which President Madison accepted. From his retirement at Monticello, Thomas Jefferson decried Van Rensselaer's "cowardice and incapacity."[6] Van Rensselaer was replaced by the uncooperative Alexander Smyth, who attempted another crossing with a larger force on 28 November. This attack was thwarted by a better prepared British force, however, and Smyth called it off within days. Hostilities along the Niagara River were then suspended for the winter. Smyth, too, was relieved of his command and dropped from the rolls of the army in a reorganization mandated by Congress.[7]

Winfield Scott and his fellow prisoners were paroled from Quebec and transported to Boston in late November. Scott continued on to Washington to give the secretary of war, William Eustis, his thoughts on the proper conduct of the war, and returned to the Niagara frontier to resume waging it. As Scott regrouped in the east for a spring offensive, similar plans were set in motion in the west. William Henry Harrison assumed greater responsibility for operations there and received enough resources from Washington to assemble an army to retake Detroit and attack Canada. Harrison had at first been passed over for command of the west in favor of James Winchester, a brigadier general in the regular army and veteran of the Revolutionary War, but the Kentuckians preempted the officials in Washington by promoting Harrison, an Ohioan, to the rank of major general in their militia. The Kentuckians, who were a major component of the western forces and could rely on their influential "War Hawk" congressman, Henry Clay, were successful in pressuring Washington to give Harrison command of the western armies. Winchester was offered a similar post in the east as a consolation, but he chose to stay on as Harrison's subordinate, a decision that many, especially those serving under him, would come to regret.

Rounding out this miserable year of defeat was General Henry Dearborn's timid thrust at Montreal, forced on him by the frustrated secretary of war. Sixty-one years old and no more suited to military command than William Hull, Smyth, or Van Rensselaer, Dearborn reluctantly marched his troops from Albany to Plattsburgh on Lake Champlain. From there, a small detachment marched north and crossed over into Canada to attack Montreal, but after several hours of confused and inclusive fighting, in which the New York militia again simply refused to follow across the border, the force withdrew. A contemporary dismissed Dearborn's failure as a "miscarriage, without even [the] heroism of disaster."[8]

As the year 1812 came to a close, Albert Gallatin, Madison's secretary of the Treasury, lamented, "The series of misfortunes exceeds all anticipations even by those who had the least confidence in our inexperienced officers and undisciplined men."[9] It was a discouraging year for the disorganized army of the United States. Elsewhere in the world, on 14 December 1812, the remnants of Napoleon's Grande Armée, now numbering about ten thousand, or one-fortieth of its original size, crossed the Neman back into Poland where his ill-fated invasion of Russia had begun less than six months before.

CHAPTER FIVE

STEPHEN DECATUR FINDS THE *MACEDONIAN*

It was the morning of the Sabbath, 25 October 1812, and a stiff breeze carried HMS *Macedonian* swiftly along a northwest-by-west course on her way to reinforce the British fleet on the West Indies station. Less than three years old and just refitted, the *Macedonian* was considered one of the best frigates in the British fleet. A carved statue of Alexander the Great was mounted under her bowsprit.

She had just fulfilled her escort duty for an East Indiaman bound for the Cape of Good Hope. As the merchant vessel continued alone to the south, now safely out of range of England's prowling enemies, the *Macedonian* made a brief stop at the Portuguese island of Madeira, where the officers restocked their supply of wine and fresh food and received reports of an American frigate in the area, rumored to be the thirty-two-gun *Essex*. Back at sea, *Macedonian*'s captain, John Surman Carden, ordered lookouts to the very top yards of the main and foremasts, where a sharp-eyed seaman could see as far as sixteen miles to the horizon. A young seaman aboard the *Macedonian* remembered that Carden seemed overly worried:

> Our Captain appeared more anxious than usual; he was on deck almost all of the time; the "look-out aloft" was more rigidly observed; and every little while the cry of "Mast-head there!" arrested our attention.... Thus we passed several days; the captain running up and down, and constantly hailing the man at the mast-head.... Indeed he seemed almost crazy with some pressing anxiety.[1]

But if Carden had an uneasy feeling about the Americans, it was not shared by his colleagues aboard *Macedonian*. His officers and crew were spoiling for a fight with the American navy, recently described by the *Times* of London as "a few fir built frigates with stripes of bunting manned by sons of bitches and outlaws."[2] As the officers took their Madeira and port in the ship's wardroom after dinner, the toast of preference was "To an American frigate."[3] Word had not yet reached Carden and his officers that the "sons of bitches" had already captured or sunk England's *Guerriere*, *Frolic*, and *Alert* in the first months of war.

Born of the minor Irish gentry and left fatherless at an early age when his soldier father died of wounds received during the American Revolution, Carden was anxious to advance his reputation and fortune in a navy becoming crowded with officers. He was relatively old for a frigate captain, and had seen little combat in his twenty-four years of service. Carden had been promoted to captain fourteen years earlier when the *Fisgard* (formerly the French *Resistance*[4]), on which he served as first lieutenant during the failed French invasion of Ireland, captured the *Immortalitie*. Although better liked than his predecessor, Carden was a strict disciplinarian and used the whip freely to shape the crew to his will and to train them for the combat soon to come.[5] His aggressive lieutenant, David Hope, claimed "the state of discipline on board was excellent; in no British ship was more attention paid to gunnery.... [T]he crew were constantly exercised at the great guns."[6]

Heading west from Madeira with studding sails set to capture the favorable breeze and speed them to the Caribbean, the crew sat down for the breakfast that would begin their day of rest. Boiled oatmeal was most likely on the menu for the crew, or *burgoo* if there was enough butter and sugar to add to it. Officers would eat much better: bacon and eggs from the hens kept below, or maybe some "pig's fry," a concoction made from a pig's lungs, heart, liver, and pancreas—chopped, seasoned, breaded, and fried, and probably similar to the "scrapple" served today in America's eastern states.

It was the practice aboard British war ships to reserve the morning of the Sabbath for worship, with some rest and recreation later in the day. For the lucky crew of the *Macedonian*, this would also include musical entertainment provided by an eight-man orchestra. The musicians had been taken by a Portuguese warship from a captured French prize. Carden had recently purchased the orchestra, which comprised German, Italian, and French musicians, and paid them from his own funds. He hoped the orchestra would add a touch of class to his ship and distinguish the *Macedonian* from the other vessels in the vast British fleet. Carden had promised the musicians they would not be subject to flogging and would be excused from any fighting. In return for these concessions, the musicians agreed not to play any French songs.[7]

As the men ate, they awaited the captain's command as to the required dress code when they were mustered on the spar deck for the brief Sabbath sermon. These sermons, mandated by the Admiralty, seldom conveyed a religious message. Captains sometimes used them as an opportunity to read the Articles of War, which contained a detailed enumeration of shipboard crimes and punishments, to the assembled crew.[8] Seamen were reminded, for example, that such offenses as "yielding and crying for quarter" or "failing to pursue the enemy" were among the half-dozen crimes punishable by death.[9]

In his novel *Master and Commander*, Patrick O'Brian describes a reading of the Articles:

> Death rang through and through the Articles; and even where the words were utterly incomprehensible the death had a fine, comminatory, Leviticus ring, and the crew took a grave pleasure in it all; it was what they were used to—it was what they heard the first Sunday in every month and upon all extraordinary occasions.... They found it comfortable to their spirits, and when the watch below was dismissed the men looked far more settled.[10]

Whatever the sermon, if any, the crew would, of course, be expected to turn out in their blue jackets with glistening gold anchor buttons, and their black tarpaulin hats trimmed in black ribbon with the ship's name painted in white on the crown. But what would not be known until the captain so ordered was whether they would wear their white trousers or blue ones, and if they would be required to wear the scarlet vest under the blue jacket. These questions briefly occupied fourteen-year-old Samuel Leech of Wanstead in Essex as he finished his oatmeal, and perhaps Captain Carden as well, but these sartorial issues were quickly forgotten when a lookout at the top most yard shouted "Sail Ho!"

> Carden rushed to the deck. "Where away is the sail? What does she look like?"
>
> "A large ship standing toward us sir," replied the lookout. As the distance closed, the young topman could take better stock of the stranger: "A large frigate bearing down upon us, sir." [11]

At the captain's signal the boatswain piped the crew to their duties with "All hands clear the ship for action," while the marine drum and fife beat to quarters, sending the three hundred men and boys of the *Macedonian* scrambling to their stations to prepare for battle. Deep below in the ship, standing outside the magazine, Samuel Leech, who served as powder monkey to gun number five on the main deck, waited in line with his wooden case for the linen cartridge stuffed with black powder that he would carry to the gun crews above, again and again, as the battle raged. As preparations neared completion and a nervous silence settled among the men standing ready at their stations, Lieutenant Bulford loudly ordered a few of the young midshipmen to stand guard at the bottom of the ladders leading to the berthing deck below and commanded them to shoot any crewmen seeking refuge from the battle that would soon rage above. [12]

As the *Macedonian* made ready for war, Carden was approached by his bandmaster who, in halting English, reminded the captain of the contractual conditions of the orchestra's service, including the exclusion from combat. Already short-handed, Carden began to protest, but quickly conceded and allowed the eight members of the band to seek refuge below in the cable tier. Less fortunate was seaman John Card, one of eight impressed American sailors forced to serve aboard the *Macedonian*. At his request, Card was granted permission to address the captain on the quarter-deck. Knuckling his forehead in respect, Card asked to be relieved of duty and treated as a prisoner of war because he should not be made to fight his countrymen. Perhaps still angered over having to grant a reprieve to his musicians, Carden refused, and ordered Card back to his station. He told Card he would have him shot if he made the request again.[13]

Twelve miles distant from the *Macedonian*, Captain Stephen Decatur of the frigate *United States* may have greeted the pleasant morning weather in his uniform of choice. A captured British seaman said Decatur looked more like a farmer than a Naval commander.[14] At about the time Carden's lookout found Decatur, a sailor on the *United States*' foremast head hailed the deck with the cry "Sail Ho!" as Decatur and his first lieutenant, Henry Allen, were going over the orders for the day.[15]

"Where away?" Decatur called out, and the lookout pointed forward on the starboard bow. Decatur ordered Allen into the rigging to confirm the sighting and make sure there was not more than one vessel in a part of the ocean often crowded with British shipping.

"Masthead. Can you make her out?" Decatur yelled to the lookouts.

"A squared rigged vessel, sir."

As the crew murmured with growing excitement, Decatur ordered them to keep quiet so he could hear and be heard. "What does she look like?"

"A large frigate bearing down upon us, sir."

The historian Alexander Slidell Mackenzie, a Naval officer and contemporary of Decatur, recorded that, as the commodore gave the order to clear the deck for action, a ten-year-old powder monkey named Jack Creamer approached and, touching his hat, asked, "Commodore, will you please have my name put down on the muster roll?"[16]

Creamer was one of about thirty "boys" aboard the *United States*, a number typical for a frigate of that size, although the smaller *Macedonian* carried about the same amount because of a shortage of able-bodied seamen. Not officially part of the crew, the boys received no pay and no regular rations. For the most part, they lived off the scraps and generosity of the individual crew members and officers they directly served. Nor did the boys receive a share of any prize money, and it was this particular disadvantage that the confident young Creamer, the son of a crewman who had died earlier in the year, wanted to discuss with his commodore.

"Why, my lad?" Decatur replied.

"So that I can draw my share of the prize money, Sir." Apparently impressed by something in the boy's straightforward approach, Decatur gave the order to add Creamer to the roll of eligible crewmen, and the youngster returned below decks to the gun he served as powder boy.

II

Stephen Decatur was born to the sea. Grandson of the French naval officer Étienne Decatur from the Huguenot enclave of La Rochelle, Decatur could trace his lineage through France to the de Katers of Holland, where conquest of the sea was a national obsession. Étienne ended up in Philadelphia, where he married an American girl of Celtic stock who soon bore him a son, Stephen. The son followed his father in a seafaring career and eventually embraced the American revolutionary cause, serving as a naval captain during the War of Independence. Stephen and his wife, Ann, had to flee from their home in Philadelphia when the British under Sir William Howe captured the city in August 1777. The Decaturs spent the next three years hiding in the village of Sinepuxent, in Worcester County, Maryland, where their son, another Stephen, was born on 5 January 1779.

After the American victory, Ann and Stephen returned to Philadelphia with their infant son, and the father resumed his career as a sea captain in America's burgeoning merchant fleet. Despite the family's maritime tradition, the Decaturs wanted their son to pursue the life of a gentleman and merchant in what was then America's most important city. They enrolled him in the Reverend Dr. James Abercrombie's Protestant Episcopal Academy[17] and then at the University of Pennsylvania, where he would study for a year before joining the Philadelphia merchant firm of Gurney and Smith as a clerk.

Based in America's busiest seaport, Gurney and Smith was active in trade, transportation, and shipbuilding and employed Stephen Sr. as a captain plying the trade route between Philadelphia and Bordeaux. Stephen Jr.'s responsibilities as a clerk included helping to oversee the building of one of America's three super frigates, USS *United States*, whose construction was authorized by President Washington in March 1794[18] and completed in 1797 for the sum of $299,336.[19] Gurney and Smith acted as agents for the U.S. Navy, handling the business arrangements for the construction of the frigate then being built in the Southwark shipyard of Joshua Humphreys.

Less than a year later, parental hopes for a career as a gentleman merchant gave way to the family's salty heritage when young Stephen, rather old at nineteen to start a Naval career, received his parents' reluctant permission to join the American Navy and sailed as a midshipman aboard the ship he had helped to build, the *United States*. With him on the voyage were two former classmates from the Episcopal Academy, Charles Stewart, a lieutenant who would one day command the *Constitution*, and Midshipman Richard Somers, who would die a hero during the Barbary Wars. Soon to follow this path to the sea was Stephen's younger brother James.

In the early nineteenth century, the life of a naval officer was vastly more demanding and physically challenging than it is today. They were expected to be able seamen, top-notch navigators, shrewd tacticians, and brave commanders who would calmly stroll the decks amidst a raging battle as the men around them were cut down by flying wood and iron. When the ships closed for boarding, the captain was expected to lead his crew, cutlass in hand, over the rail and onto the enemy's deck in hand-to-hand combat, much as Nelson had led his men onto the Spanish *San Nicolas* in the battle of St. Vincent. The attitude and training needed to prepare young men to survive and thrive in such a demanding profession fostered a heady sense of honor and a measure of personal courage blind to death and danger. In periods of idleness, when prickly standards of honor and courage demanded satisfaction and validation, these men engaged in numerous duels.

Dueling, though nominally illegal, experienced a revival in popularity among those who fancied themselves gentlemen subject to a higher code of honor. While the defense of honor was a powerful motive to dueling, so too was the belief that a duel would right wrongs and achieve justice in a decision from which there was no appeal. "God was supposed to nerve the arm of the combatant whose cause was just, and to grant him the victory over his opponent" observes one historian of the time. The French philosopher Montesquieu thought that such beliefs were not unnatural among a people just emerging from barbarism.[20]

According to Decatur's biographer Irwin Anthony, while dining aboard the *United States*, Decatur's good friend Midshipman Richard Somers had made some kidding reference to Decatur's careless dress. Decatur, in jest, called Somers a fool in front of their messmates.[21] The other midshipmen apparently mistook Decatur's joke for an insult to Somers's character, and several days later, when Somers offered a toast at dinner, they refused to join until Somers challenged Decatur's "familiarity." Somers, who knew Decatur's name-calling was in jest, took deep offense at his colleagues' refusal to join his toast and challenged all to a duel, scheduling each to meet him at the dueling grounds the next day at hourly intervals. He asked Decatur to serve as his second, a role that entailed certain administrative functions as well as the responsibility to take Somers's place under certain circumstances.

Decatur failed to talk Somers out of the duel, and on the appointed day he joined Somers at the dueling ground to await the adversaries at their hourly appointments. The first to arrive fired, wounded Somers in his right arm, and then departed. An hour later, the second challenger sustained his honor by further wounding Somers in his thigh. When the third challenger arrived, Decatur, as second, offered to take the place of the twice-wounded Somers, who was now slipping in and out of consciousness from the loss of blood. Somers refused, and insisted he be allowed to fire from where he sat. With Decatur holding Somers's elbow steady, the young midshipman got off a shot that wounded his third opponent. Sufficiently impressed by Somers's self-destructive bravery, the remaining opponents acknowledged the young officer's courage and withdrew.

A few years later, while at port in Malta, Decatur was involved in another duel, this time as second to sixteen-year-old Midshipman James Bainbridge (younger brother of Captain William Bainbridge), who had been challenged by a British officer then serving as secretary to Sir Alexander Ball, the British governor of Malta. The challenge stemmed from a series of insults exchanged between British and American officers at a theater in Valetta. In the jostling that followed, the British officer was knocked to the ground by young Bainbridge.

This British officer had a reputation as the island's most dangerous duelist, and the inexperienced Bainbridge had the good sense to ask his immediate superior, Lieutenant Decatur, to serve as his second. Recognizing his subordinate's profound disadvantage in the coming fight, Decatur cleverly managed to neutralize the Englishman's skill by insisting they fire at each other from four paces. Realizing Decatur's intentions, the challenger's second objected, arguing that is would not be a duel, but murder. "No sir," Decatur replied, "this looks like death but not murder. Your friend is a duelist, mine is wholly inexperienced. I am no duelist but I am acquainted with the use of a pistol. If you insist upon ten paces, I will fight your friend at that distance."[22] Confronted with Decatur's challenge, the British officers reluctantly agreed to his terms. Despite the close range, the first exchange of shots missed. In the exchange that followed, Bainbridge shot his opponent dead in the face.

Decatur and Bainbridge were ordered off the island by an angry Governor Ball and sent back to America by the navy (where both received promotions!). Less than two years later, Decatur returned to Malta in the *Constitution* for repairs, and Governor Ball, apparently not one to hold a grudge, invited him to dinner at his mansion. There Decatur met and befriended the dead officer's replacement, Samuel Taylor Coleridge, who had come to Malta to improve his health in the island's mild climate.[23] Many years later, Coleridge remembered how impressed he had been by the geo-political vision of the young American officer.[24]

On 13 May 1801 Decatur was ordered to the Mediterranean as first lieutenant of the frigate *Essex* under Captain William Bainbridge.[25] They were part of the fleet commanded by Commodore Richard Dale, which had been sent to the North African coast to counter threats to the American merchant vessels from the bashaw of Tunis, the dey of Algiers, the bey of Tripoli, the emperor of Morocco,[26] and other Turkish governors who oversaw these outposts of the Ottoman Empire, ruler of much of the southern and eastern Mediterranean coast.

The American government had been paying tribute to the Barbary States since 1795 to ensure that its merchant vessels remained unmolested by the Ottoman potentates who ruled the port cities of Tunis, Tripoli, Morocco, and Algiers. But in May 1801, the Americans refused the demand of Yusuf Karamanli, pashaw of Tripoli, for the same tribute in weapons and money as Algiers received. Karamanli declared war on America by sending a delegation to chop down the U.S. consulate's flag pole.[27]

Jefferson responded by sending the fleet, acting on a sentiment he expressed a decade earlier in a letter to Thomas Barclay: "We prefer war in all cases to tribute under any form, and to any people whatever." By the time Jefferson had taken office, the United States had paid the various Barbary states about two million dollars in tribute, an amount equal to one-fifth the annual federal revenues of the time.[28]

Despite the bluster and saber-rattling, Jefferson was at first reluctant to confront the Barbary States head on. Hostilities flared periodically, and little more than occasional sparring matches characterized the combat between adversaries during the first few years of the century. American officers probably saw more action on the dueling fields around the Mediterranean than they did at sea. But the situation changed in 1803, when, under Commodore Preble, the American fleet blockaded the port of Tripoli. Preble's fleet included the sixteen-gun brig *Argus* under Decatur's command.

But Preble's mission suffered an early setback that October when the frigate *Philadelphia*, under William Bainbridge, ran aground on a rocky shoal near the entrance to the city's harbor. The crew lightened the ship by throwing cannons, anchors, and supplies overboard, but they were unable to free her. Bainbridge soon surrendered the ship and his crew of 307 men to the pirates who swarmed around them. Fearful that the pirates, who successfully refloated the *Philadelphia*, would rearm her and turn the powerful frigate against the American blockading fleet, Preble ordered Decatur to destroy her. On the night of February 16, 1804, Lieutenant Decatur, leading eighty volunteers in the ketch *Intrepid*, secretly entered the harbor, boarded the *Philadelphia*, and set her afire. Decatur's crew included Lieutenants James Lawrence and Joseph Bainbridge and Midshipmen Thomas Macdonough and Charles Morris,[29] whose exploits would loom large in the coming war with England. The Americans suffered only one wounded; but left an estimated twenty to thirty Tripolitans dead.

Horatio Nelson called it "the most bold and daring act of its age,"[30] and Pope Pius VII said, "The United States, though in their infancy, have done more to humble the anti-Christian barbarians on the African coast than all the European states had done...."[31] An appreciative Congress awarded Decatur a ceremonial sword and all of the officers with him a bonus of two months pay. In August, Decatur was promoted to captain, retroactive to February 16. At age twenty-five, Stephen Decatur of Philadelphia became the youngest captain in the U.S. Navy.

Hostilities between the American fleet and the Tripolitans heated up that summer, and Preble again resumed his blockade of the port. During one engagement in early August, Decatur led a squadron of small gunboats—borrowed from the kingdom of Naples—against a Tripolitan fleet of similar vessels. Commanding one of the gunboats in Decatur's squadron was his younger brother James, now a lieutenant. After a brief exchange of cannon fire, the American gunboats closed for the attack and boarded the enemy ships, fighting hand to hand with cutlass, axe, and pike. Stephen Decatur and his crew quickly overwhelmed their adversary, while James induced another Tripolitan captain to surrender merely by threatening to board. But as James climbed aboard his prize to take formal possession, the enemy captain shot him through the head. Shocked at the deceit, the American gun boat pulled away as her crewmen gave what comfort could be offered to the dying James Decatur. Midshipman Brown, now in command of James's vessel, reported the treachery to Stephen as their gunboats passed in the sea.

Enraged, Decatur left half his crew with the Tripolitan prize and with just eleven American seamen (and a crew of Neapolitan sailors who operated the boat) took off in gunboat Number 4 in pursuit of the perfidious Tripolitan captain, whom they soon found and attacked. Led by Decatur and Midshipman Thomas Macdonough, the American seamen boarded the enemy's boat, and a violent struggle ensued between the two heavily armed crews. The Americans were outnumbered two to one. As knives stabbed and cutlasses slashed, Decatur made his way through the melee to his brother's murderer, and within minutes the two were rolling around on the deck in a deadly embrace that soon attracted members of both crews to their aid. As Decatur struggled to stay on top of the enemy captain, a Tripolitan seaman attempted to save his leader by aiming a savage blow of his scimitar at Decatur's exposed head. But before the blow fell, one of the wounded American crewman—Reuben James in one account, but Daniel Frazier according to another telling—threw himself under the pirate's sword, took the blow, and, amazingly, lived to tell about it. Decatur was saved, and with his hand briefly freed as others tumbled upon him and the enemy captain, he slipped his hand into his pocket, cocked the hammer of his pistol, and through his pantaloons shot the pirate dead. Several months later, in a letter to the father of one of his midshipmen (Robert Spence), Decatur glibly revealed his contempt for his brother's murderers by noting, "Some of the Turks died like men, but much the greater number like women." His thoughts on the performance of the Italian seamen who helped sail the gunboat were nearly as harsh.[32]

Several years later Decatur assumed command of the U.S. Navy Yard in Norfolk, Virginia. There he would have the opportunity to meet and dine with his British counterparts as they came in to port to resupply their ships. According to the historian Ira Dye, one of Decatur's guests at Norfolk was Captain John Surman Carden—then on a mission of suspect legality to bring back gold to England—who was proud to show off his newly-built *Macedonian* to his American counterpart. Over dinner Carden told Decatur he was unimpressed by the heavy twenty-four-pounders on the American frigates, thinking them unwieldy compared with the more maneuverable eighteen-pounders that British frigates carried. Armament was rated by the weight of the iron shot fired, and the gun that threw it was sized accordingly. A twenty-four-pound gun weighed about two and a half tons, while an eighteen-pounder weighed about two tons. Decatur, of course, disagreed, and bet Carden a beaver hat on the outcome of such a battle.[33]

III

Less than a year later, off the west coast of Madeira, as the *United States* and the *Macedonian* closed for battle, hundreds of crewmen aboard the two frigates worked furiously in dark and crowded decks to prepare their weapons for the showdown that would test Carden's judgment on the relative merits of the guns.

On board each ship, a marine drummer at the center of the deck played a distinctive drum roll called "the beat to quarters." As the drum beat reverberated through the ship, every member of the crew knew his duty of the moment, and he also knew that his performance of it could affect the day's outcome. Above deck, young, nimble seamen headed high into the swaying masts and rigging to prepare for battle. Mainsails would be brailed up to open the main deck for combat and visibility and to avoid the hazard of the big sails' catching fire. High above the main deck, t'gallats, studding sails, and royals earlier raised for speed would be dismantled, along with their rigging, masts, and spars, and stored below to reduce the amount of dangerous debris that could fall upon the deck and crew.

As unneeded sails were brought down and stored below, dozens of other crewmen dismantled the bulkheads at the stern of the gun deck separating the officers' quarters from the crew. The captain's personal belongings, plate, and cutlery were packed into wooden chests and barrels. When the dismantling was complete, the *United States*' gun deck would be a vast open space, more than 44 feet wide and stretching 170 feet from stem to stern, giving the crew and officers uninterrupted access to the thirty twenty-four-pound long guns that lined both sides of the ship. And with both decks now cleared and open, sand and ashes were spread upon them to give traction and absorb the slippery blood that would soon spill on the wooden decks by the gallon.

One deck below in the galley, the cook doused the stove's fire and secured his pots and pans, utensils, and food stores against the coming violence. If a meal had not been served within the last few hours, the cook assembled bread and other cold food stuffs, perhaps crocks of potted meat that hungry crewmen might later eat uncooked during a break in the battle. One deck below the galley, the surgeon and his two mates unpacked their instruments—bone saws and knives, bandages, and brandy—and set up the operating tables with strong leather straps in preparation for the amputation of shattered limbs. And below the surgeon, deep in the ship's stern, in a secure room shrouded with sheets of copper to keep out any moisture, flame, or sparks, the gunner unpacked his cartridges of black powder. Adolescent powder monkeys lined up on the other side of a dampened wool curtain to take the cartridges (made of cloth on British ships, lead sheet on American) in wood or leather cases to the guns above.

With the bulkheads down and main sails brailed, the ship's marines—there were about fifty of them on the *United States*—loaded their muskets and climbed the shrouds and ratlines to the fighting tops, where their marksmanship would be tested against the enemy. Several marines set and loaded a coehorn or two, a small swiveling howitzer with which they would clear the enemy's spar deck and tops of crew and combatants as the ships closed for boarding.

Nearly two hundred of the crewmen, trained and led by Lieutenant Henry Allen, took their stations on the gun deck below to prepare the massive twenty-four-pounders for war. Each gun was served by a crew of six to eleven men and was secured by thick hemp rope run through irons rings nailed to the deck and gunwales and attached to the sides and back of the gun carriage. In single-ship combat, only the guns on one side of the ship would be in use. If the enemy moved to the other side during the battle, the gun crews would simply shift to the guns on the other side and prepare them to fire as the enemy came in range.

The twenty-four-pound guns aboard the *United States* were a little more than ten feet in length, weighed almost five thousand pounds, and could fire a six-inch diameter, twenty-four-pound solid iron shot more than a mile and a half. Their point-blank, or un-elevated, range was about a thousand feet, and when fired at close range the guns could pierce two and a half feet of ship's timber. A well trained crew could get off about one shot a minute in a complicated drill that required close coordination by the men manning each gun.[34]

Long Twenty-Four-Pounder

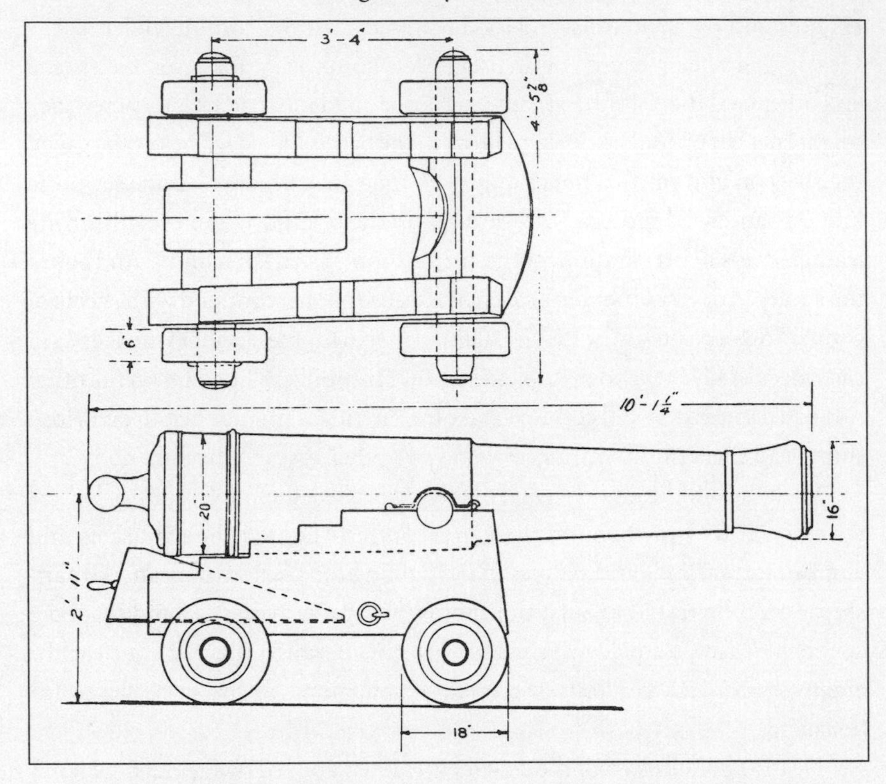

Courtesy of *The Frigate Constitution and Other Historic Ships*, Dover Publications, Inc.

The typical frigate of the time—whether British, French, or American—mounted as many as two dozen carronades on the quarter-deck, forecastle, and sometimes on the spar deck itself, which on an American frigate constituted nearly a continuous open deck stretching from bow to stern. Whereas the long guns below were designed to throw a twenty-four-pound shot over a long distance with some measure of accuracy, the shorter and lighter carronades, reserved for close-range combat, functioned more as heavy-duty shotguns. The carronades aboard the *United States* were some of the biggest, throwing forty-two-pound balls or a similar weight of grape shot at oak-crushing velocities.

In 1812 the carronade was a relatively new type of armament, but the typical frigate already mounted almost as many carronades as long guns, the exceptions being the American *Essex* and the British *Glatton*, built in the late eighteenth century and equipped almost exclusively with short-range carronades.[35] First cast at the Carron Iron Works in Stirlingshire, Scotland, in 1779,[36]

Carronade

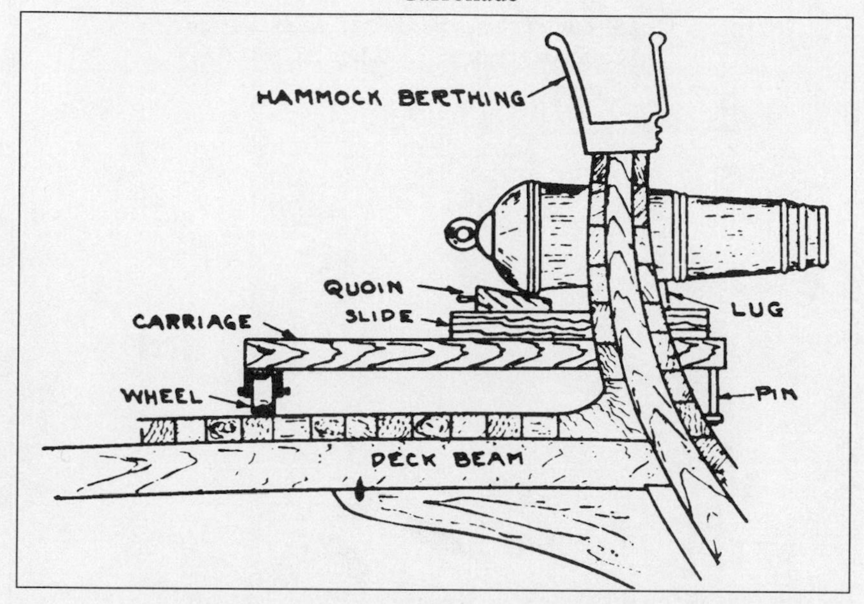

Courtesy of *The Frigate Constitution and Other Historic Ships*, Dover Publications, Inc.

the carronade was initially, and aptly, named the "smasher," but it soon became known by its place of origin. Not very accurate or lethal at long distances, the carronade could throw shot as heavy as sixty-eight pounds, relying upon weight rather than velocity to inflict damage.

The carronade used a smaller charge than a long gun did, so its barrel could be thinner and shorter, giving it exceptional power for its weight. An important complement to the traditional long gun that most warships carried, the carronade could be placed on the top-most decks without destabilizing the ship. A thirty-two-pound carronade, for example, weighed much less than a twenty-four-pound long gun, but it could send a thirty-two-pound shot or an equivalent volume of grape or canister as far as a half-mile. Fired at close range, carronades could inflict devastating damage on a wooden ship and its crew. A young seaman named Herman Melville, who served aboard the *United States* in the early 1840s, dubbed the ship's carronades "Iron Atillas" in recognition of their fearsome potential.[37]

As the *Macedonian* closed with *United States*, neither ship was quite sure who the other was, for it was the custom to maintain a measure of anonymity and deception as long as possible to gain whatever advantage uncertainty and surprise might offer. Carden was the first to reveal his nationality, running up

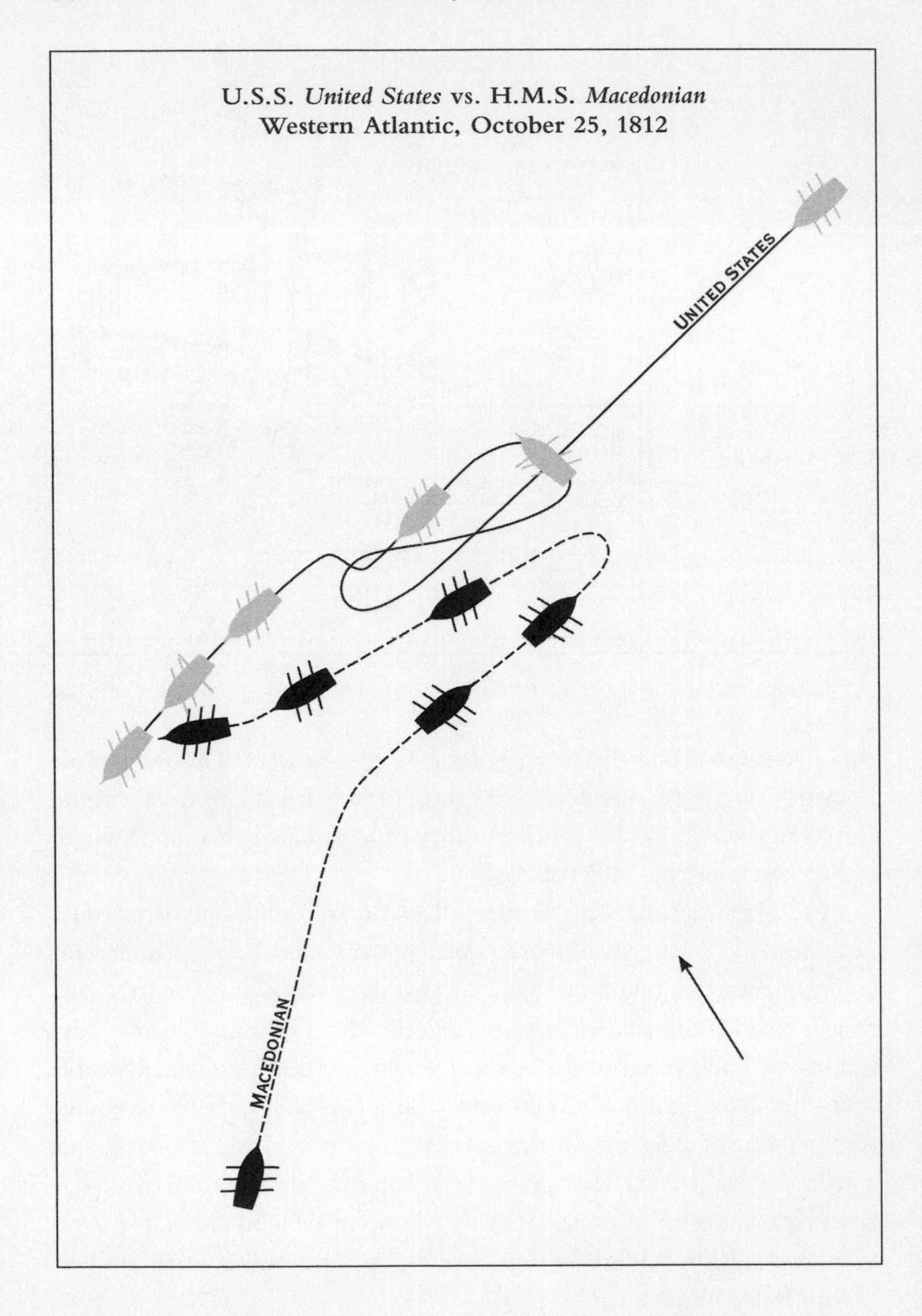

U.S.S. *United States* vs. H.M.S. *Macedonian*
Western Atlantic, October 25, 1812

the British colors at about half past eight in the morning, as well as a series of signal flags that spelled out Britain's secret recognition code in case his presumed adversary was actually a British ship. But there was no need for the query. Decatur responded by sending up to the three mastheads and the tip of the spanker gaff the red and white pennants of the U.S. Navy. Despite reports of his anxious state in the days leading up to the battle, Carden was ecstatic at the revelation and would later write: "I hailed it as the happiest hour of my life when we described the stranger to be an enemy, and in the excess of feeling could not help saying so to those around me."[38]

Perhaps from the reports he received in Madeira, Carden assumed that the American ship was the *Essex*.[39] Since that vessel was one of a very few to be armed entirely with short-range carronades, Carden intended to pummel the *Essex* from a distance with his eighteen-pounders, rendering the Americans' short-range guns ineffective. But the *Macedonian*'s first lieutenant, David Hope, objected vigorously, arguing instead that *Macedonian* should maintain its direct course for the enemy and close for combat by crossing its bow or stern and raking it with devastating broadsides. Hope was following Nelson's dictum, "Never mind manoeuvres, always go at them."[40] Carden, however, adhered to the Admiralty dictum that a captain in combat should always strive to maintain the weather gauge. One British naval historian has noted:

> In the Royal Navy it had become standard practice to try and maintain the weather gage: that is, to keep to windward of an opponent, as the windward ship has more control over when and how to come to close action. The leeward ship, in this case the *United States*, has to close against the wind, a much more difficult task. Furthermore, the leeward ship stands more chance of her broadside going over the enemy, whereas the broadside of the windward ship, if fired low when the ship is heeling towards the enemy, may just ricochet off the sea into the opponent's hull. These were standard tactics, but completely wrong in this situation.[41]

As the ships closed to within the range of their long guns, Decatur, who was on a close hauled port tack that would take him across the *Macedonian*'s bow, also ignored Nelson's dictum by ordering his crew to wear ship, and he sent *United States* sailing in the opposite direction. As the helm was put hard over to turn the ship away from the wind, dozens of young topmen scrambled through the rigging and spars to execute the complicated maneuver that began by brailing up the main course and gaff mizzen sail, taking in the mizzen stay sails, and shivering the topsail to keep its yard always pointing into the wind so it would have no effect, leaving the foresails to provide most of the drive and bring the ship around on a new course. With the wind now astern, the mizzen topsail was refilled, and as the *United States* came around further toward the wind on the other tack, the yards were braced around to take the wind, and the mizzen sails and staysails were reset.

Carden was stunned by the maneuver, thinking at first that the *United States* was attempting to flee when it turned its stern to him. But as the American came around on the new tack, Carden realized that his adversary had cleverly neutralized the *Macedonian*'s windward advantage. Carden had no choice but to follow and wear the *Macedonian* around on a starboard tack to run parallel with the *United States*. Closing within range, both ships fired broadsides that fell short of each other, but the volley from the *United States* carried far enough to show the British that she was not the *Essex*. Decatur wore again to the southwest on a port tack, and *Macedonian* again had no choice but to follow. Forced by Decatur to change direction again, Carden had now lost the considerable strategic advantage his original course had offered.

Despite the loss of favorable position, Carden and Hope never questioned the prospect of a swift and decisive victory and enough prize money to make them wealthy men. They were, after all, in command of one of the newest and fastest frigates of the Royal Navy, and their crew, guns, and tactics were superior in every way to those of the hapless Americans coming into range of the *Macedonian*'s eighteen-pounders, now primed and ready to roar. Carden reminded his crew of Nelson's immortal signal to the fleet at Trafalgar—"England expects every man will do his duty."[42]

Although the *United States* was larger and more powerful than the *Essex*, she had a reputation for being clumsy and difficult to handle, earning the nickname "Old Wagon." But in the hands of a skilled captain like Decatur, her speed, size, and weaponry could be effectively used to dominate a more nimble opponent. Decades later, Midshipman Samuel Franklin, a contemporary of Melville's aboard the *United States* in the 1840s, opined, "She was, properly sailed, the fastest vessel in the navy, and, some sailors thought, the fastest in the world. Sailors on the *United States* could feel the yaw, but they knew that the awkwardness was a constitutional condition of the 'greyhound' of the fleet ... and regarded her with reverence."[43]

Twenty minutes after the first broadside was fired to test the distance, both ships fired another in an attempt to disable their opponent's sails and ability to maneuver. Both broadsides found their targets—the *Macedonian* lost her mizzen-topmast and gaff-halyards, while the mizzen-topgallant-mast of the *United States* was shot away. With the *Macedonian* still on a parallel course, but astern the *United States*, both ships continued to fire at each other with their heavy guns, muscled into position by pike and crowbar to point in diagonal directions—the *Macedonian*'s slightly forward, the *United States*' slightly aft. The artillery duel continued for nearly another hour, the ships nicking each other with as many as a hundred broadsides.

Young Samuel Leech, responsible for bringing powder to gun number five on the *Macedonian*, remembered the early minutes of the battle:

> A strange noise such as I never heard before.... It sounded like the tearing of sails, just over our heads. This I soon ascertained to be the wind of the enemy's shot. The firing, after a few minutes cessation, recommenced. The roaring of the cannon could now be heard from all parts of our trembling ship, and, mingling as it did with that of our foes, it made a most hideous noise.[44]

Proceeding on a parallel course with the *Macedonian* to the southwest, Decatur was satisfied that his cannon fire had been far more effective than Carden's and ordered the sailing master to back the main topsail. In response, seamen pulled or loosened the running rigging to twist its yard around. By taking the wind from an obverse angle, the backed topsail redirected some of the wind's pressure back against the force filling the other sails and reduced the ship's speed. Having decided it was time to escalate the fight, Decatur slowed his ship to let the *Macedonian* catch up so he could unleash the combined might of his larger guns. Carden, not yet aware that he was the mouse to Decatur's cat, and failing to realize that the American was at a distinct advantage in any artillery duel, cooperated by bringing his ship closer to Decatur's.

Theodore Roosevelt, who was highly critical of Carden's tactics, was especially harsh in his judgment of this maneuver: "[H]aving already erred either from timidity or bad judgment, Captain Carden decided to add rashness to his catalogue of virtues. Accordingly, he bore up, and came down end on toward his adversary, with the wind on his port quarter."[45]

Both ships now fired broadside after broadside. So fierce and rapid was the *United States*' cannon fire—she is estimated to have fired two broadsides for every one from the *Macedonian*—that the British sailors briefly mistook the smoke and flame enveloping her hull for damage they had inflicted. The growing horror aboard their own ship soon disabused them of any such notion, however. Recalling Lieutenant Hope's boasts about the frequent drills and practice aboard *Macedonian*, Theodore Roosevelt sarcastically mused, "How they could have practiced so much and learned so little is certainly marvelous."[46]

Thirty minutes later the *Macedonian* lost her mizzenmast to the relentless pounding of Lieutenant Henry Allen's gunners. Mackenzie says that as the mast toppled, taking several topmen with it, the gun captain of a carronade on the quarter-deck of the *United States* quipped to his mates—echoing a similar jest supposedly made on the *Constitution* as she closed with *Guerriere*—"Ay ay Jack, we have made a brig of her." Decatur is said to have joined in, "Take good aim, my lad, and she will soon be a sloop." Turning to a nearby gun captain, Decatur ordered, "Aim at the yellow streak; her spars and rigging are going fast enough; she must have a little more hulling."[47]

On the gun deck of the *Macedonian*, Leech saw firsthand the result of Decatur's order:

> By and by I heard the shot strike the sides of our ship; the whole scene grew indescribably confused and horrible; it was like some awfully tremendous thunder-storm, whose deafening roar is attended by incessant streaks of lightening, carrying death in every flash, and strewing the ground with victims of its wrath: only, in our case, the scene was rendered more horrible than that by the presence of torrents of blood which dyed our decks."[48]

Leech was now supplying powder for four guns because their boys were dead or wounded. One of the boys was struck in the leg; he later lost it through amputation. Another boy lost his foot. On the quarter-deck, two more of Leech's young comrades—Portuguese boys serving the carronades—were killed. One had the flesh burnt off his face when the powder cartridge he carried to his gun took a spark and roared up into a fiery and sulfurous fury. As the burning boy lifted his arms in agony, a passing shot from the *United States* cut him in two.[49]

Throughout the next hour, as the two ships continued on a parallel course, Decatur used his speed, power, and sailing skills to reduce the *Macedonian* to a helpless wreck. Roosevelt describes the battering: "The *States* now laid her main topsail aback and made heavy play with her long guns, and, as her adversary came nearer, with her carronades also. The British ship would reply with her starboard guns, hauling up close to do so; as she came down, the American would ease off, run a little way and again come to, keeping up a terrific fire."[50]

On *Macedonian*'s gun deck, a crewman named Aldrich had both hands shot off, and then his bowels cut open by a second shot. Dying, he was thrown over the rail and into the sea. A goat kept below to provide milk for the officers had her hind legs blown away and was thrown overboard. And still, in the midst of this hideous carnage, *Macedonian*'s crew fought on. Among the killed were two of the impressed Americans, James Card, who had begged Carden to be imprisoned rather than made to fight his countrymen, and John Wallis.

Observing that most of the carronades on the *Macedonian*'s quarter-deck and forecastle were disabled, Decatur moved the *United States* to within fifty yards of her to batter her with the fearsome fire of his own forty-two-pound carronades. Firing now from two decks, Decatur pummeled his opponent until her main-topmast came crashing down onto the foretopmast, cluttering the deck with debris and leaving the ship unsailable.

Splinters from *Macedonian*'s shattered scantlings and timbers became lethal projectiles, maiming as many crewmen as did the iron shot from the American guns. Once or twice iron shot from the *United States* smashed into the muzzle of a British gun, ripping it from its tackle and sending the two-ton weapon careening around the deck while fragments of metal from the shattered muzzle tore into the flesh of nearby gun crews.

Hope received a nasty, though not fatal, head wound from an iron grommet that a cannon ball smashed loose from a hammock stored on the rail. As he was carried below, Hope shouted to the men to fight on. And they did, with the diminishing number of guns, and with whatever crewmen were not yet dead or disabled. The young Leech tried to describe what it was that drove his mates to keep fighting in such circumstances:

> That men are without thought when they stand amid the dying and the dead, is too absurd to be entertained a moment. We all appeared cheerful, but I know that many a serious thought ran through my mind: still, what could we do but keep up a semblance, at least, of animation. To run from our quarters would have been

> certain death from our own officers; to give way to gloom, or to show fear, would do no good, and might brand us with the name of cowards, and ensure certain defeat. Our only true philosophy, therefore, was to make the best of our situation, by fighting bravely and cheerfully.[51]

The *Macedonian*'s decimated crew fought on, and the guns of the *United States* rained death and destruction upon the shattered hulk. "Grape and canister shot were pouring through our portholes like leaden rain, carrying death in their trail. The large shot came against the ship's side like iron hail, shaking her to the very keel, or passing through her timbers, and scattering terrific splinters, which did more appalling work."[52]

Nan Kivell, a well-liked officer on the British frigate, took a canister shot in the chest near his heart, and shouting "Oh my God!" soon died of his wound. The school master received a fatal wound, while the boatswain, who was already wounded and getting treatment in sick bay, had his head smashed to pieces as he attempted to fasten a stopper on a back-stay that had been shot away. The damage to the ship was equally severe, as Carden described to the Admiralty in a letter shortly after the battle.

> I continued the battle to two hours and ten minutes, when, having the mizen mast shot away by the board, topmasts shot away by the caps, Main Yard shot in pieces, lower Masts badly wounded, lower Rigging all cut to pieces, a small proportion only of the Foresail left to the Fore Yard, all the Guns on the Quarter Deck and Forecastle disabled but two, and filled with wreck, two also on the Main Deck disabled, and several shot between wind and water.... being a perfect wreck and unmanageable Log.[53]

As the *Macedonian* struggled to maintain speed, Decatur let the *United States* fly well ahead of her, cross her path, and come around behind her on a larboard tack that would allow her to rake *Macedonian*'s stern. But Decatur held his fire as he passed menacingly behind the ship. Sensing that the wounds he had inflicted on his enemy were fatal, Decatur abruptly stopped firing and pulled away. Carden and Hope, as well as many of their crew, were still not prepared to believe that an American ship could defeat them, and they took Decatur's withdrawal as a sign that the *United States* had suffered even worse damage. The distance and the smoke from hundreds of black powder broadsides made it difficult to judge an opponent's condition. Carden seems to have believed that he had given as good as he got.

The *United States*, however, was largely undamaged. Decatur had broken off merely to replenish his cartridges, repair some rigging, and allow the British captain to contemplate the carnage about him. For a moment, perhaps encouraged by Hope, Carden missed the point of the opportunity Decatur was offering, and he prepared his ship and crew to board the *United States* when it returned. But when Decatur returned, he offered Carden a clearer indication of his intentions and of the *Macedonian*'s precarious situation. Wearing round and tacking toward the *Macedonian*, the *United States* took a raking position off Carden's starboard bow, and then hauled off and took a raking position off his stern, ready to blow the British frigate to splinters with a broadside from the guns of both decks.

Everyone except Hope got the point of Decatur's maneuver and threatening posture, and in a brief council with his officers and over the objections of Hope, who preferred death before dishonor, Carden ordered the colors struck, dumped the secret codes over the side in a lead-weighted case, and changed into a clean dress uniform for the surrender. Mackenzie writes that the first American officer to board the *Macedonian* was appalled by what he saw. "Fragments of the dead were distributed in every direction, the decks covered in blood, one continued agonizing yell of the unhappy wounded; a scene so horrible of my fellow creatures, I assure you, deprived me very much of the pleasure of victory."[54]

Dressed in his best and carrying his sword, Carden was rowed to the *United States* for the formal surrender and the shocking discovery of how little damage he had inflicted. Stunned by the sight of the unscathed decks of the *United States*, Carden presented his sword, and said to the Commodore: "I am an undone man. I am the first British naval officer that has struck his flag to an American."[55] But Decatur refused the sword, replying: "I could never accept the sword of a man who had so nobly defended the honor of it." He added, "You are mistaken, sir; your *Guerriere* has been taken by us and the flag of a frigate was struck before yours."[56]

The *Macedonian* had suffered 104 casualties—thirty-six dead and sixty-eight wounded, a number of whom soon died. About a hundred shots had pierced her hull, several below the water line, leaving the ship slowly sinking. Two of the masts were shot away, and much of the rigging lay in heaps on the deck or hanging overboard. The *United States*, by contrast, suffered just thirteen casualties, including seven dead, and little damage to the ship herself.

If he could not be the first American to defeat a British frigate, Decatur could at least be the first to bring one home, but the *Macedonian* had to be quickly repaired to prevent her from sinking, and before another British warship came along to take up the fight. Lieutenant Allen was dispatched to take command of the captive along with a crew to make the necessary repairs. Decatur also sent over his surgeon and assistants to help care for the many wounded. Magnanimous in victory, Decatur also paid Carden eight hundred dollars for the orchestra and for his ample wine stock and other stores, which were transferred to the *United States*. "The band now gladly changed their allegiance to a flag, under which they could once more play their own national airs."[57] Thirty years later, Herman Melville wrote that some original members of the band were still playing aboard the *United States*.[58]

A few days later, still at sea, Decatur wrote his wife, "One half the satisfaction arising from this victory is destroyed in seeing the mortification of poor Carden who deserved success as much as we did, who had the good fortune to obtain it. I do all I can to console him."[59] Months later when they parted, Carden wrote to Decatur, "I have much gratitude to express to you, my dear Sir, for all your kindnesses, and all my officers feel equally with myself. If ever we should turn the tables, we will endeavor, if possible, to improve on your unusual goodness."

Less generous in their view of the event were the editorial writers of the *Times*. On 26 December 1812, they picked up rumors in England that the *Macedonian* had been lost to Decatur:

> There is a report that another English frigate, the *Macedonian*, has been captured by an American. We shall certainly be very backward in believing a second recurrence of such a national disgrace. Certainly there was a time when it would not have been believed

> that the American navy could have appeared upon the seas after a six month's war with England; much less that it could, within that period, have been twice victorious.[60]

Once *Macedonian* had been stabilized and the ships had made their way back to the United States, Decatur is said to have sent for Jack Creamer, the young powder monkey who wanted his name entered on the ship's muster roll.

> "Well, Jack, we have taken her and your share of the prize, if we get her safe in, may be two hundred dollars: what will you do with it?"
>
> "I will send half to my mother, Sir, and the other half shall pay for my schooling."
>
> "That is noble" Decatur is said to have replied, and subsequently obtained for young Creamer a midshipman's warrant, and Jack would serve Decatur in three other actions.[61]

IV

It took two weeks to repair *Macedonian* for the voyage to America, and nearly a month to make the trip. The two ships passed Long Island's Montauk Point on 3 December 1812, but a thickening fog and the *Macedonian*'s limited sailing ability forced them to separate. Allen took the British prize northeast to Newport, Rhode Island, while Decatur took the *United States* west into Long Island Sound to New London, Connecticut, docking there on 4 December. Within hours of his arrival, he was told that in four days, on 8 December, in Washington, D.C., a great naval ball would be held to celebrate the recent victories of Captains Hull and Porter and to present the captured flag of the *Guerriere* to President Madison's wife, Dolley.

With his exquisite sense of glory and opportunity, Decatur ordered the young midshipman Archibald Hamilton, son of the secretary of the navy, Paul Hamilton, to leave immediately for Washington with the *Macedonian*'s colors. Decatur may have bristled that the first victory belonged to Hull and not to himself, but, by God, all America would know whom to honor for bringing home the first big prize and would learn about it in a suitable setting.

As Hamilton made his way to Washington, Mrs. B. H. Latrobe, wife of a Navy Department official, was at home preparing for the ball. At about five o'clock in the evening her husband came home and told her to illuminate the house, "as the account of a victory gained by Commodore Decatur had just arrived."[62] That evening as Latrobe and his wife made their way by carriage to the ball at Tomlinson's Hotel on Capitol Hill (on the site now occupied by the Supreme Court building[63]), the windows of the homes and businesses along Pennsylvania Avenue were brilliantly lit with candles and whale oil lamps to honor the heroes of the American navy.

Mrs. Latrobe later told a friend, "It is not likely I shall ever witness such another scene." Washington's newspaper, the *National Intelligencer*, reported, "Such a scene, as this occasion exhibited we have never before witnessed; and never, never so long as memory holds her seat, shall we forget it."[64] President Madison was not in attendance, but the First Lady represented him at the ball, which was also attended by the entire cabinet, most of Congress, and members of the Supreme Court. Hanging from the walls were the flags of the *Guerriere* and the *Alert*, the latter captured by Captain David Porter and the *Essex* in the first engagement of the war. At around nine o'clock rumors spread through the ballroom that Secretary Hamilton's son would soon arrive with stunning news of conquest, and about ten o'clock there was a commotion at the entrance of the hotel. Captain Stewart was called to the door, and he quickly returned to beckon Hull to join him. Hamilton then walked in through the curious and excited crowd, surrounded by his fellow naval officers. Unbuttoning his doublet to reveal his naval jacket, he was embraced by his parents and sisters and then strode toward Mrs. Madison, who sat in a place of honor in the center of the ballroom.

The crowd parted as Hamilton, carrying a bundle and accompanied by Hull and Stewart, approached the First Lady. Hull and Stewart pulled from the bundle the colors of the *Macedonian*, and others held it aloft above the heads of the three naval heroes. The crowd erupted in joy and the band played "Hail Columbia" as Midshipman Hamilton bowed and laid the *Macedonian*'s colors at Mrs. Madison's feet. A later historian wrote, "The navy's stock at that delirious moment could not have been higher. Nor could that of Stephen Decatur."[65]

V

The *United States* and the *Macedonian* were repaired and supplied at New London and Newport, respectively. They sailed together in mid-December for New York City, where another major celebration had been prepared for their arrival. After more than a week's struggle to get the two ships though the nasty currents of Hell Gate on the East River between Manhattan and Brooklyn, Decatur finally conceded to the impatient New York leaders, anchored the ships in Long Island Sound, and took his officers overland to the waiting city.

Hosted by Mayor DeWitt Clinton, the nephew of Jefferson's vice president, George Clinton, the celebration was scheduled for December 29 at the City Hotel on the west side of Broadway, just north of Trinity Church. The event was in honor of Decatur, Hull, and Jacob Jones, the commander of USS *Wasp*, which had captured HMS *Frolic*. Jones, unfortunately, could not attend, as he was in Washington explaining to a naval court of inquiry why, after taking the eighteen-gun brig *Frolic* with his eighteen-gun sloop of war *Wasp*, he did not attempt to capture the seventy-four-gun HMS *Poitiers*, which showed up shortly after *Frolic* surrendered.

As Mackenzie describes it, five hundred of New York City's leading citizens crowded into the packed hall decorated by colonnades representing ships' masts, entwined with flags and laurel. Each table had as its centerpiece a miniature frigate bearing the American flag. The head table, where Clinton, Decatur, and Hull sat with the city's leaders, featured a pool of water landscaped with real grass, upon which floated a frigate at its moorings. Behind the head table hung a ship's sail bearing an eagle holding a scroll proclaiming the elder Decatur's celebration of the Spartan oath: "Our children are the property of their country."

Following a toast to "Our Navy," the sail behind the head table was brailed up to reveal an illuminated, translucent painting depicting the *Constitution* taking *Guerriere*, *United States* taking *Macedonian*, and *Wasp* taking *Frolic*. The crowd rose and roared with tumultuous cheers. Toast after toast was offered to the navy as other decorative sails were clewed up around the hall to reveal more illuminated paintings with patriotic themes.

A little more than a week later, on January 7, the 450 ordinary seamen and marines of the *United States*, along with the young prisoner Samuel Leech, formerly of gun number 5 on the *Macedonian*, landed on the New York docks. Dressed in blue jackets and trousers with red vests and topped with glazed tarpaulin hats with ribbon streamers, the crewmen, led by Decatur and Allen and followed by the ship's marines, marched in procession along Pearl Street to Wall Street and then up Broadway to the City Hotel,[66] where the celebration was repeated for the crewmen. As they marched though lower Manhattan to the "inspiring airs" played by the orchestra acquired from the *Macedonian*, the sailors were greeted by the enthusiastic citizens of New York and "followed by crowds of urchins, emulous of one day imitating the heroism that excited their admiration."[67]

New York City alderman Cornelius Vanderbilt[68] welcomed them, and as the feast came to an end, Commodore Decatur and Lieutenant Allen entered the room to a roar of applause. Decatur gave a brief speech, commending his men for their gallantry and reminding them that the war had been undertaken for "Free Trade and no impressments." Decatur closed with the announcement that all the crew was invited to attend a play at the theater after the feast and that the entire pit had been reserved for their accommodation. In closing, he urged them to "maintain the same order in the midst of amusements, as you have done when sailing upon the ocean and conquering the enemy."[69]

Days after the New York City feast, sailors of *United States* discovered that one of their mates killed in the fight with *Macedonian* had left a widow and three children now facing destitution. They raised nearly a thousand dollars for the family's support and education and entrusted the sum to Decatur to invest on the family's behalf.[70]

A few weeks before the New York dinner and just after the ball at Tomlinson's Hotel in Washington, the *National Intelligencer* of Washington published a poem capturing America's heady mood:[71]

> Britannia sick of many an ill
> Sees various plagues await her
> Now finds another bitter pill
> Prescribed by one Decatur
> Let her go on and still continue
> To make the world all hate her
> Her venom we shall still survive

While we have one Decatur
Then let's maintain the sailor's right
and not one inch abate her
We need not dread her force or spite
With Hull and with Decatur

For a brief moment, America was joyous beyond reason. Its little navy had four times met the warships of the world's greatest sea power and, against all odds, four times sailed away the victor. Relying on the skill of her shipwrights, the pluck of her crews, and the cunning of her commanders, America's navy had turned the world on its head, or so it seemed. Shortly after the emotional celebration at Tomlinson's Hotel, however, Mrs. Latrobe wrote her friend Mrs. Juliana Miller:

> The aforesaid colors were then laid at the feet of Mrs Madison. Oh tempora. Oh mores. This was rather overdoing the affair.... Now, between ourselves, I think it was wrong to exalt [*sic*] so outrageously over our enemies. We may have reason to laugh on the other side of our mouths some of these days; and, as the English are so much stronger than we are with their Navy, there are ten chances to one that we are beaten. Therefore it is best to act moderately when we take a vessel; and I could not look at these colors with pleasure, the taking of which had made so many widows and orphans.[72]

CHAPTER SIX

BACK ON LAND: HARRISON ON THE MAUMEE

William Henry Harrison, given command of the northwestern front, had done what he could to stabilize the collapsing frontier. In early September 1812 he was under pressure from Secretary of War William Eustis—who himself was under pressure from the press and Congress—to go on the offensive in Michigan and retake lost territory. Flush with resources from Washington and commanding an army of nine thousand men, Harrison embarked on a campaign to retake Fort Detroit before winter set in.[1] He organized his force into four separate columns, planning to converge on British-held Detroit from the west and south. Before attacking the British, though, the four columns cleared out all the Indian villages in the Ohio and Indiana region, including a rebuilt Prophet's Town, which Harrison's force burned in November 1812 on its march north to Detroit.

As Harrison moved into Michigan, Colonel Henry Procter, who had assumed command of the British force after Brock's death at Queenston, went on the offensive. Anticipating Harrison's advance, he moved his force south from Detroit and occupied the American settlement of Frenchtown on the

Raisin River. He ordered a larger force of regulars and Indians under Major A. C. Muir to march southwest to meet Brigadier General James Winchester's force, which was moving east from Fort Wayne (in Indiana Territory) to join Harrison on the Maumee River in northwest Ohio.

The first contact between Muir's Indian scouts and the five frontiersmen scouting ahead of Winchester's column was on 25 September. Believing the Indians to be friendly, the Americans gave them details on the size and location of Winchester's column and were promptly killed and scalped.[2] Fortunately, the vanguard of the American column came upon the mutilated remains of their comrades before stumbling upon Muir's main force, and took up a strong defensive position in anticipation of an attack. Muir, running low on supplies, far from base, and having lost the element of surprise to an American force outnumbering his more than two to one, retired to Fort Malden on the Canadian side of the Detroit River.

Pushing on with his vastly larger force, Harrison was foiled not by the British, but by the weather. Weeks of relentless rain soaked his troops, turned primitive roads into impassable quagmires, and turned the rivers into deep, raging obstacles that spilled over their banks. The late autumn cold and the bad weather disrupted the delivery of rations to Harrison's scattered troops, and he lost many to illness or desertion.

Eustis, meanwhile, had grown tired of being browbeaten by Congress and the press[3] and resigned as secretary of war. James Monroe, the secretary of state, temporarily assumed leadership of the War Department. Within days, Monroe was confronted by a 12 December 1812 letter from Harrison urging a delay in the advance on Fort Detroit. The sub-freezing temperatures of the northwestern winter would make the rivers and muddy roads passable and would permit a time-saving march across frozen Lake Erie. President Madison and Monroe were reluctant to anger the western congressmen who supported Harrison, so they left the decision of when to attack Detroit up to the general.

With Washington's reluctant endorsement, Harrison began consolidating his forces for a mid-winter campaign. In late December, he again ordered Winchester to advance east from Fort Wayne down the Maumee River through Indiana and into Ohio to the Rapids near present day Toledo. There he was to establish a secure camp and build sleds for the coming attack on Malden. Harrison expected that his own force would arrive there in late January 1813, when the wet ground would have frozen deep enough to support his troops, horses, sleds, and wagons. But time was not on Harrison's side. Disease and desertion had reduced his force from about nine thousand to six thousand men, and Winchester's force suffered similar losses as it moved east.

When Winchester made camp at the Rapids of the Maumee River, several settlers from Frenchtown—thirty miles to the north on the River Raisin in Michigan—told him of the British occupation of their town and asked his help in pushing them out and back to Detroit.[4] Eager for a victory and facing a much smaller force, Winchester and his officers disregarded Harrison's orders to remain on the Maumee and agreed to attack the British and free the town. On 18 January an advance party of Kentuckians reached Frenchtown and in deep snow swiftly routed the British and their Indian allies, scalping about a dozen of the latter in the process.

Bouyed by their easy rout with few casualties, the Kentuckians pursued the enemy into the nearby woods. But the British had expected their pursuit and had established a makeshift defensive line in the thick trees and brush, from which they fired on the exposed pursuers. Although casualties ran high, the Kentuckians prevailed, and the British withdrew under the cover of darkness. On learning of the victory, Winchester further violated Harrison's orders by leading reinforcements north to Frenchtown, which offered little security in the event of a British counter-attack. And a counter-attack was precisely what Procter was contemplating. He quickly mobilized his forces at Malden and marched south on or about the same day that Winchester marched into Frenchtown.

Under Winchester's dilatory command, little was done to strengthen the town's defenses, despite credible warnings about Procter's movements. Fearing the worst, some of the soldiers found reasons to be elsewhere. Colonel Samuel Wells of the Seventeenth U.S. Infantry thought it a good time to get ordered back to the Rapids to help expedite the delivery of supplies north to Frenchtown. Harrison himself visited Winchester's new position, and having little choice but to grudgingly acknowledge the unauthorized victory, returned south to muster reinforcements to help hold the town.

Procter arrived the next day with a somewhat larger force than Winchester's—roughly 1,100 regulars, Indians, and militia against about 850 Americans holding the town. But Procter's attack was so slow getting underway and so poorly conceived that U.S. riflemen easily beat it back with deadly accuracy from the town's palisades. Badly shot up, the British troops retreated into the woods. But all was not well with the American position: the U.S. Seventeenth Infantry, encamped in the open on the left flank of Winchester's line, was exposed to withering fire from the British as well as from Indians under the Wyandot chiefs Roundhead and Walk-in-the-Water,[5] who had crossed the River Raisin and were encroaching on Frenchtown from the flank.

Lieutenant Colonel John Allen led two companies of Ohio militiamen from the security of the town to aid the Seventeenth but could not hold the line against the attacking enemy. Their failed effort soon turned into a disorganized retreat. "In Indian fighting, this was fatal," observes John Elting; "floundering in deep snow, the Americans were run down and butchered."[6] Another historian writes, "Before anything could be done, [the Indians] got to the rear and literally hacked the Americans to pieces." At least a hundred Kentuckians were scalped within a few minutes.[7] Allen was killed and scalped, while General Winchester, caught outside the gates of Frenchtown, was captured by Roundhead, who stripped him of most of his clothes before turning him over to Procter."[8]

Although nearly four hundred American troops still held the town from relatively secure positions, Procter urged the captured Winchester to order them to surrender, and allowed his Indian allies to conduct some violent demonstrations to encourage capitulation. Forced by Roundhead to witness a series of atrocities against captured Americans,[9] Winchester did as the British asked, perhaps out of fear that an Indian massacre would be carried out against the prisoners and those that remained in the fort, as Procter is alleged to have hinted. In response, an obedient Major George Madison, commanding the Kentucky Rifle Regiment inside the town, complied and surrendered his force to the British.

British Major Richardson was appalled at the condition of the remaining American force that surrendered:

> Their appearance was miserable to the last degree. They had the air of men to whom cleanliness was a virtue unknown, and their squalid bodies were covered by habiliments that had evidently undergone every change of season, and were arrived at the last stage of repair.... It was the depth of winter; but scarcely an individual was in possession of a great coat or cloak, and few of them warm garments of wool of any description.... They were covered with

> slouched hats, worn bare by constant use, beneath which their long hair fell matted and uncombed over their cheeks....[10]

Altogether about five hundred Americans were taken prisoner and marched north to Malden. Although the battle of Frenchtown was an important defeat for the American forces in the west, the British had paid heavily for their victory. Suffering casualties to a third of his force, Procter concluded it was too risky to hold Frenchtown with the remnants of a force that was small to begin with and vulnerable to the larger army he knew Harrison had assembled nearby. In the winter cold, Procter marched his prisoners, captured supplies, and wounded back to the security of Malden.

For the wounded American prisoners left at Frenchtown, Procter's decision to return to Canadian territory was a catastrophe. Between sixty and eighty badly wounded American soldiers were left behind in the care of Frenchtown's civilians. But on 23 January 1813, a group of Indians, drunk and eager for revenge and the spoils of war, broke off from the march north and returned to Frenchtown, which they ravaged. Houses were robbed and set on fire, and many of the wounded soldiers were killed and scalped. Others burned to death, too ill or injured to flee the burning buildings. As many as thirty were murdered and scalped or burned alive, while other Americans were marched away for ransom and torture.[11] Several American officers recalled that "the savages were suffered to commit every depredation upon our wounded.... many were tomahawked, and many were burned in the houses."[12] Another thirty or so escaped to the Rapids, where Harrison was encamped with a force that had now shrunk to about nine hundred men. When told of the loss of Frenchtown and the total destruction of Winchester's army, Harrison had little choice but to abandon the Rapids. Within days he marched the remnants of his force a short distance to the more secure Fort Meigs near where the Maumee enters Lake Erie.

The total number of U.S. troops killed at Frenchtown is estimated at about four hundred, and five hundred or so captured and marched off to prison. The battle at the River Raisin was a major disaster, comparable in magnitude to Detroit, Dearborn, and Queenston. Despite the ignominious loss, General Winchester was quick to reassure his superiors in Washington that the fault certainly did not lie with him. Writing to Secretary of War Monroe from captivity at Malden, he conceded that his defeat was regrettable but maintained that he was "flattered by the belief that no material error is chargeable upon myself."[13]

Nevertheless, General Harrison had managed to stabilize the front by holding a thin line of forts running from central Indiana through the northwest corner of Ohio. From this precarious base, in the midst of the punishing northwestern winter, Harrison prepared to retake Detroit. On 11 February he attempted to march his army from Ohio across a frozen Lake Erie to seize Fort Malden. But the lake was not frozen hard enough for a safe crossing, and Harrison was forced to return to Fort Meigs on the Maumee River, where he quartered his men for the winter.

And so 1812's string of military disasters on land extended into 1813. Poor training, amateurish tactics, and shockingly incompetent leadership combined to undermine every American military operation along the northern border. Theodore Roosevelt summed up the situation with admirable brevity: "While our navy had been successful, the war on land had been for us full of humiliation."[14]

CHAPTER SEVEN

BAINBRIDGE FINDS REDEMPTION

The transfer of *Constitution*'s command from Isaac Hull to Commodore William S. Bainbridge was not well received by the ship's crew. Some of the disappointment stemmed from the crew's affection for the affable Captain Hull. But a larger reason was Bainbridge's reputation as a jinxed commander whose career was marred by several failures in engagements with America's enemies. Indeed, Bainbridge had the distinction of being both the first and the second U.S. commanding officer to surrender his warship to an enemy, and the first, second, and third commander to lower the American flag in favor of another. He also had a reputation as a stern disciplinarian.

Moving directly from a career in the merchant fleet to command in the fledging American navy, Bainbridge was commissioned as a lieutenant in August 1798 and given the command of the small, lightly armed schooner *Retaliation*, a vessel Stephen Decatur (senior) had captured six months earlier, in the opening days of the Quasi-War, when she was the French privateer *Croyable*.[1] Operating with two other U.S. ships in a squadron stationed in the Caribbean, Bainbridge was to protect American merchant vessels from roving

French privateers. He became separated from the others and stumbled upon two French frigates—the *Insurgente* and *Volontaire*—each more powerful than his own small schooner.

Mistaking them for British or American ships, Bainbridge at first made no effort to keep his distance. By the time he realized his mistake, the French were close enough to fire a broadside at *Retaliation*. Resistance to the powerful opponents would have been futile, and Bainbridge had no choice but to surrender. Thus did Bainbridge become "the first U.S. naval officer to strike his flag to an enemy."[2] Even more embarrassing, Bainbridge's *Retaliation* was the only American ship lost in a conflict that cost the French eighty-five ships.[3]

Later cleared of any fault by the navy, Bainbridge was promoted and given command of the frigate *George Washington*. In May 1800 he was ordered to deliver America's annual tribute to Dey Bobba Mustapha in the city of Algiers. Bainbridge reluctantly agreed, contrary to his orders, to the Algerine request to deliver the dey's own tribute of tigers, lions, antelopes, parrots, ostriches, and more than a hundred black slaves across the Mediterranean to his suzerain in Constantinople, Selem III, grand seignor of the Ottoman Empire. After Bainbridge was underway, the dey's delegation demanded that Bainbridge fly the Algerine standard in place of the Stars and Stripes on the grounds that they were on an Algerine mission, not an American one. Bainbridge acceded to this demand as well, and the ship's log for that day reports that "some tears fell at this instance of national Humility."[4] Bainbridge did, however, manage to retaliate quietly by tacking to and fro so as to confuse his Muslim passengers as they attempted to pray in the direction of Mecca.

The errand to Constantinople, unfortunately, was not Bainbridge's last regrettable encounter with the Barbary pirates. Within a year he was back as part of a large American fleet that President Jefferson dispatched to accomplish through intimidation what the United States had failed to achieve through obsequious annual payments of tribute. Initially in command of the small frigate *Essex*, Bainbridge eventually commanded the thirty-six-gun frigate *Philadelphia*, a ship in Commodore Edward Preble's squadron blockading the city of Tripoli.

On 31 October 1803, sailing alone, Bainbridge entered the harbor in pursuit of two Tripolitan blockade runners but broke off the chase when he got too close to the shallow water near the shore. As he beat to windward to get back out to sea and deeper water, Bainbridge ran aground on an uncharted reef from which he found it impossible to dislodge his vessel.

Tripolitan gunboats soon surrounded *Philadelphia*. Having heaved most of his cannon overboard in a vain effort to lighten the frigate, Bainbridge became the second U.S. naval officer to surrender his ship to the enemy. Captured and held for ransom, Bainbridge defended his actions in a letter his captors allowed him to send to Preble:

> Some Fanatics may say that blowing the ship up would have been the proper result. I thought such conduct would not stand acquitted before God or Man, and I never presumed to think I had the liberty of putting to death the lives of 306 souls because they were placed under my command.[5]

These sentiments, however, were not shared by Commodore Preble, who wrote to the secretary of the navy, Benjamin Stoddert, "Would to God, that the Officers and crew of the *Philadelphia*, had one and all determined to prefer death to slavery; it is possible such a determination might [have] save[d] them from either."[6] Bainbridge and his 306 fellow officers, crewmen, and marines were held captive in Triopli for twenty months. In June 1805, Pasha Youssef Karamanli consented to a peace treaty and released the prisoners in return for a payment of sixty thousand dollars.[7]

When the crewmen of the *Constitution* learned in 1812 that the unlucky Bainbridge was to be their new commander, they were not shy about voicing their concerns. Shaken by their reaction, Bainbridge is reported to have offered Commodore Rodgers five thousand dollars to trade command of the *Constitution* for that of the *President*. Rodgers declined, leaving Bainbridge to confront the crew directly with the issue of his reputation and to hope for the best.[8]

Seaman Moses Smith, who served on the *Constitution* under Hull and was still on board when the transfer of command occurred, chose not to ship out with Bainbridge. According to Smith, the first encounter between the crew and their new captain was not a warm one. Addressing the assembled crewmen, Bainbridge asked, "My men, what do you know about me?"

> Perhaps speaking for all, several responded with the same concern, "We were with you sir, at the capture of the *Philadelphia* at Tripoli."
>
> "Well," continued the Captain, "go with me now, and I will do by you all that the service allows."[9]

Many members of the crew, like Moses Smith, chose not to go, and several of those without the option of transferring attempted to desert. Those caught were punished, and by the time *Constitution* left Boston in late October, the sullen crew became absorbed in the relentless drills and practices that would mold them into the same fierce fighting force that had shattered *Guerriere*.

On 9 September 1812, the secretary of the navy, Paul Hamilton, ordered Bainbridge to lead his squadron south "to annoy the enemy and to afford protection to our commerce, pursuing that course, which to your best judgment may ... appear to be best."[10] Accompanying him out of Boston was the smaller eighteen-gun brig *Hornet*, sailing under Master Commandant James Lawrence. Captain David Porter and the frigate *Essex* were expected to join them at sea. Porter would be leaving from his mooring on the Delaware River off Chester, Pennsylvania, where he had been paying a brief visit to his wife at their river-front mansion—a gift from Porter's wealthy father-in-law. Because of the difficulty of finding another ship at sea in an age of limited communications, Bainbridge established a series of rendezvous points at various locations along the coast of Brazil and sent the proposed meeting places to Porter at Chester. Once they met up, the three-ship squadron would attack and seize whatever British shipping they could find in the South Atlantic.

II

A ship of *Constitution*'s size usually sailed with a crew of four hundred or more, including officers and marines. Their ranks and numbers would have been similar to those that Theodore Roosevelt detailed as typical for a frigate in the War of 1812:[11]

1 captain	1 purser
4 lieutenants	1 surgeon
2 lieutenants of marines	2 surgeon's mates
2 sailing-masters	1 clerk
2 master's mates	1 carpenter
7 midshipmen	2 carpenter's mates
1 boatswain	1 cook
2 boatswain's mates	1 chaplain

1 yeoman of gun room	1 gunner
11 quarter gunners	120 able seaman
1 coxswain	150 ordinary seaman
1 sailmaker	30 boys
1 cooper	50 marines
1 steward	1 armorer
1 master of arms	400 in all

Every member of the crew knew exactly where he was supposed to be at any given time and what was expected of him under every set of circumstances the ship would confront. Moses Smith, for example, was assigned to the larboard foreyard arm while the ship was under sail during his watch, but he also served as the sponger on the number one gun during a battle. In a seven-man gun crew, one served as gun captain while each of the others had a specific duty to perform in operating the gun. Each man had other responsibilities, and depending upon the size of the overall shipboard complement, a gun crew could number as few as six or as many as fourteen men.[12]

"The captain of the gun crew points and elevates, primes, cocks and fires, stops vent, pricks cartridge." The next most important function was that of the first loader, "who sponges, rams home and runs out," followed by the third ranking member who "trims with handspike and runs out, while the next three members help run out the two to three ton gun when ready to fire."[13] As the crewmen worked in a coordinated frenzy, "powder monkeys"—the ship's boys, some not yet in their teens—brought them cartridges of gunpowder one by one from a secure magazine deep in the hold.

Each member of a gun crew had subsidiary duties that he was expected to perform during a battle. These tasks were usually designated by a letter next to his name in the ship's quarter bill. On a seven-man gun crew, two men's names were labeled "B" for "boarders." They were expected to come up to the deck when called and clamber over the sides and onto the enemy ship to attack its crew in hand-to-hand combat. In preparation for the call, boarders had cutlasses, pikes, axes, and other weapons with them at the gun. Two others were labeled "S" for sail trimmer. They helped with the ship's maneuvers when needed. Two others were labeled "P" for pump duty when the ship was taking on water. The man labeled "F" was assigned to the fire party. Another was labeled "L." He was responsible for fetching and maintaining a lantern in case the battle action continued into the night.

When not in battle or preparing for it, sailors were assigned to specific tasks at specific places to help sail the ship. Smith's designation at the larboard fore-yard arm would place him on the eighty-one-foot spar that held the foresail (lower sail) of the foremast of the ship. The designation "larboard" referred to his "watch" or period of duty, of which there were two on every ship—a larboard and starboard watch, a designation that continues to this day on ships of the U.S. Navy. Each watch served four hours on and four hours off, twenty-four hours a day, except during battles and rough weather, when everyone worked as long as was necessary to secure the safety of the ship. In turn, each of these watches was divided in half into quarter watches, where the men would relieve each other more frequently in the demanding tasks, such as working the tops while underway.

One of the best contemporary accounts of these duties and how they were organized is from Herman Melville. He served as a seaman aboard the frigate *United States* as a young man in the early 1830s and recorded his experiences in *White Jackets; or, The World in a Man-of-War*:

> ... in all men-of-war, besides this division [the two watches] there are others, rendered indispensable from the great number of men, and the necessity of precision discipline. Not only are particular bands assigned to the three *tops*, but in getting under weigh, or any other proceeding requiring all hands, particular men of these bands are assigned to each yard of the tops. Thus when the order is given to loose the main-royal, White-Jacket flies to obey it; and no one but him.
>
> And not only are particular bands stationed on the three decks of the ship at such times, but particular men of those bands are assigned to particular duties. Also, in tacking a ship, reefing top-sails, or "coming to", every man of a frigate's five-hundred-strong, knows his own special place, and is infallibly found there. He sees nothing else, attends to nothing else, and will stay there until grim death or an epaulette orders him away.[14]

For the most part, the men who worked the tops were the youngest, nimblest, and most skilled of the crew. Duties down on the deck or below it were the responsibility of the less skilled seamen and the older crewmen who no longer had the strength, endurance, or coordination to climb high and scurry safely among the swaying yards, spars, and rigging. One such group of veteran sailors, called the Sheet-Anchor-men, was stationed in the forecastle and had responsibility for the anchors, foreyard, and all the sails of the bowsprit. On his cruise aboard the *United States* two decades after the war, Melville wrote touchingly of these grizzled old salts:

> These are the fellows, who spin interminable yarns about Decatur, Hull and Bainbridge; and carry about their persons bits of "Old Ironsides", as Catholics do the wood of the true cross. These are the fellows, that some officers never pretend to damn, however much they may anathematize others. These are the fellows, that it does your soul good to look at;—hearty old members of the Old Guard; grim sea grenadiers, who, in tempest time, have lost many a tarpaulin overboard. These are the fellows, whose society some of the youngest midshipmen much affect; from whom they learn their best seamanship; and to whom they look up as veterans; if so be, that they have any reverence in their souls.[15]

The strict discipline and long hours of hard and dangerous work make shipboard duty seem extraordinarily harsh. Why, we wonder today, would any sensible young man volunteer to serve aboard these warships? Yet despite these apparent hardships, young and not-so-young men did volunteer, and in great numbers. They served on board the dozens of warships, and many more served on the hundreds of privateers, that went to sea during the war. An even greater number served on board the thousands of merchant and whaling vessels, where the conditions were often just as harsh and dangerous and where a single voyage might be measured in years rather than months. While some sought adventure and the camaraderie of a tight-knit crew, most did it out of necessity. They had to make a living and this was as good as any in a world where opportunities for the low born and uneducated were limited.

For the majority of ordinary Americans and Europeans in the early nineteenth century, life ashore was often just as harsh and unforgiving as at sea. The work day and work week were long, and muscle power was all they could offer an employer. With the exception of the tiny slice of America's prosperous professional, entrepreneurial, and land-holding elite, staying alive and reasonably healthy was a daily struggle, and self-reliance was vastly more important than it is today. In 1820, the average life expectancy at birth was only thirty-nine years in the United States, forty years in Britain, and just twenty-eight in Spain.[16]

The life of a sailor in America's young navy, then, had certain attractions. The pay was fairly good—more than the Royal Navy offered, which is why so many British sailors deserted in U.S. ports—and certainly more regular than one could expect from many occupations on land. As important as the pay were the benefits the navy provided—food, a secure place to sleep, a ration of beer or whiskey, a clothing allowance, and medical care. And while medical science back then left much to be desired, free, daily access to a medical professional was more than civilian laborers enjoyed.

By today's standards, the food at sea was unappealing, but so too were the eating choices ashore for a member of the semi-skilled working class. There was no refrigeration—except for what cooling was available in the spring houses of the well-to-do—and very little affordable canning either. Access to fresh vegetables and fruits was seasonal and only within the local community, and fresh meat was a luxury for all but the few who were members of the middle and upper classes. Other than in summer and fall, flour, root vegetables, and whatever poor cuts of meat or bone could be obtained—washed down by whiskey distilled by enterprising farmers—was the diet for the ordinary American. In early-nineteenth-century New York City, for instance, an urban family of modest circumstances faced culinary choices more limited than those of a seaman:

> Women worked hard to supplement a diet that consisted largely of bread and potatoes, corn and pease, beans and cabbage, and milk from cows fed on "swill". In good times, they might add salt meat and cheese, a little butter, some sugar, coffee, and tea. But meat and poultry, though widely available in city markets, were expensive, even when purchased for a reduced price at the end of the market day.[17]

When in port, and during the first week or two of a voyage, the sailor's diet would contain some fresh and perishable foods including eggs, butter, fruit, and vegetables. But once at sea for any length of time, the need to "safely" store food for as long as six months in a cramped and damp environment limited the culinary choices to those few products that could survive the mold, weevils, rats, and rot.

For most sailors the main meal was salted meat, usually pork or beef, which was provided by dockside suppliers under contract with the navy. The salting process began with slabs of fresh pork or beef cut into two- to four-pound slices. It was salted with rock salt, which extracted the meat's moisture and suppressed the growth of bacteria and mold. Cured to a leathery consistency, the rigid slabs were sealed in wooden casks and stored in the ship's hold. A sailor's bread came in the form of pre-cooked "biscuits," akin to big, dense crackers, which were stored in wooden casks. Cheese, rice, dried beans, butter, and whiskey rounded out the diet of the ordinary seaman. The officers dined on better fare but generally at their own expense. Pickled meats like tongue and corned beef—packed in brine and stored in clay crocks or wooden casks—were the tastier alternatives sometimes served in the officers' mess. Also available to officers who could afford the extra cost were fresh meat, eggs, and milk, provided by a small flock of livestock caged below in the hold.

Every crew was organized around the "mess," a more or less permanent group of eight sailors with its own dining service and cutlery. The jobs of food preparation, service, and clean-up rotated among the members. Each mess was identified by its own number. A metal tag with that number was affixed to its slab of meat when it was soaked in cold water overnight and then cooked for five or so hours the next day in a huge vat of hot water. Only one meal—dinner, served at midday—was cooked. Biscuits and cold leftovers constituted the other two daily meals.

In 1801, Congress specified the rations for enlisted men in the navy, including which meal would be served on which day of the week. While these regulations ensured that seamen received a minimally acceptable diet, the chief reason for the regulation may have been to fix an upper limit on how much the federal government would have to spend to feed them. As the table below reveals, the congressionally established ration for enlisted men was a grim and plain affair.[18]

Day	Meat	Bread	Suet	Cheese, etc.	Vegetable	Spirits
Sunday	1-1/4 lb beef	14 oz	1/4 lb	1/2 lb flour	—	1/2 pint
Monday	1 lb pork	14 oz	—	—	1/2 pint peas	1/2 pint
Tuesday	1 lb beef	14 oz	—	2 oz chs.	—	1/2 pint
Wednesday	1 lb pork	14 oz	—	—	1/2 pint rice	1/2 pint
Thursday	1-1/4 beef	14 oz	1/4 lb	1/2 lb flour	—	1/2 pint
Friday	molasses	14 oz	2 oz butter	4 oz chs.	1/2 pint rice	1/2 pint
Saturday	1 lb pork	14 oz	—	1 pint vinegar	1/2 pint peas	1/2 pint

The diet for a British sailor was similar, but a little leaner. Whereas the American tar had but one meatless day a week, his British counterpart had three, called "banyan days" after the Banyans of western India, a Hindu sect that practiced vegetarianism. When the beer ran out early in the voyage, corn whiskey or rum took its place—or wine, if available at port. Sugar and oatmeal were also available, but every other day.

Until 1805, the spirit of choice in the U.S. Navy was the same as in the Royal Navy—rum. But then politics intervened. Most of America's rum was distilled in New England, a stronghold of President Jefferson's Federalist opponents. The molasses from which it was made, in turn, came from sugar grown on British plantations in the Caribbean. Whiskey, in contrast, was distilled in the countryside from corn and grain grown by Jefferson's beloved yeoman farmer in his Republican strongholds of the south and west. Jefferson's secretary of the navy, Robert Smith, ordered American ships to be stocked with "pure rye whiskey of the 3rd or 2nd proof, and one year old," justifying the change on the grounds that it was "cheaper and more wholesome."[19]

Although the British tar at first glance seems to have enjoyed a more generous ration of alcohol than his American counterpart, the half pint of spirits available each day to U.S. sailors had a much higher alcohol content than the whiskeys and rums sold today and would have been enough to get drunk on if consumed at one sitting. Because not all sailors cared for drink or drunkenness, many would trade or sell all or part of their daily drink ration, and many of the sailors who acquired the extra rations would end each day in an alcoholic stupor. In an effort to limit the drunkenness that such a daily volume of alcohol could cause, the spirits were usually mixed with two to three parts water—a concoction called grog—before being given to the crew.

Accounts of the colorful life of the sailors of the time can create the impression that such indulgent and destructive drinking behavior was unique to life aboard ships. Quite the contrary: drinking habits at sea differed little from those on land; heavy drinking of strong spirits, and the accompanying epidemic of drunkenness, was a common characteristic of American life in the early nineteenth century. According to one historian, "More liquor was drunk in the early nineteenth century than ever before or since. The annual per capita consumption of spirits by those fifteen or older in 1820 was four times that of today."[20] At a time when the quality of water was suspect and other beverages like milk or fruit juice were expensive and subject to swift spoilage, alcoholic drinks had a hygienic advantage over other beverages. Alcohol was also thought to possess healthful attributes, and most medicinal products of the time were little more than flavored alcohol. Strong drink was a regular part of children's diets as well, and this in turn led to severe dependence and alcoholism later as adults, and the drunkenness that would lead to debilitating or fatal accidents. Indeed, the heavy drinking of strong spirits during those early decades may be one reason why, "for those who survived until age ten, life expectancy declined from fifty-seven to forty-eight years in the early nineteenth century."[21]

For most adult Americans in the early nineteenth century, the consumption of alcoholic beverages was not limited to after-hours leisure but was also a critical component of the workday for farmers, apprentices, builders, tradesmen, and of course, sailors. The typical workday allowed for an alcoholic beverage break at about eleven o'clock in the morning and another at two or four in the afternoon, when workers would either head off to a tavern, or some member of the crew, usually an adolescent, was sent to a tavern or general store for several bottles or a jug.[22]

Life at sea was not very different. Moses Smith's reminiscences of service aboard the *Constitution*, written thirty-four years later, are replete with references to his own degrading and dangerous drunkenness during those days, and to the redemption he would later find through abstinence. Indeed, so great was the drinking problem in those early years of the republic that it spawned a vigorous temperance movement (and religious revival), which succeeded in cutting America's consumption of alcohol in half between 1830 and 1845.[23]

Where life at sea did differ markedly from life on land (at least in America) was in the severity of the punishments for infractions to the law and the multitude of laws that could be broken. Although the discipline on American ships was not as harsh as that on British ships, it was, by today's standards, rigid and severe. Harsh whippings and chained confinement were meted out for what today seem minor infractions. But aboard a naval vessel in the early nineteenth century, modest mistakes or acts of carelessness in tending the sails in the rigging could put the ship and crew at great risk during a storm or battle. On a warship carrying more than four hundred high-spirited young men from America's rougher neighborhoods, confined to small spaces for long stretches of time with few diversions, a system of rigid rules and harsh punishment, and a police force of fifty or so well-armed marines, was essential.

For the most part, punishment involved a specified number of lashes on the bare back with a cat-o-nine-tails or confinement in the hold with feet and hands shackled in irons, or both. A typical punishment for a minor infraction was a dozen lashes, enough to break the skin and leave a painful reminder that lingered for weeks. Fighting, drunkenness, shirking duty, and disobedience were all subject to punishment. The harshest punishments were reserved for stealing from the ship or from a fellow crewman, and the more severe the crime, the greater the number of lashes. Corporal punishment could also be imposed when officers thought work was poorly done or not done swiftly enough. Moses Smith tells of an incident from his service on the *Constitution* under Hull. He and the other members of his fore top gang were reefing the sails at the lieutenant's orders, but one of them bungled his job and left part of the sail looser than good seamanship required. Seeing the clumsy work, the lieutenant ordered them down and demanded to know who failed to perform his task properly. But no one confessed, and the others refused to reveal the perpetrator. "This was too much for the Lieutenant," Smith wrote. "His wrath rose at once, and considering it as a conspiracy to defeat the discipline of the ship, he dealt alike with all. The whole gang of us took a flogging for our supper."[24]

Although American officers were perceived as less harsh than their British counterparts, all, including the well-liked Isaac Hull, were quick to sentence the guilty to a whipping when laws were broken. Most punishments were limited to one or two dozen lashes; more than that could inflict severe injury and result in a lengthy recuperation under the surgeon's care, depriving the ship of an able-bodied crewman. Nonetheless, some whippings were severe enough to jeopardize the life of the guilty party, and the purpose of these harsh punishments was more to set an example to others than to guide the guilty to better behavior in the future. One seaman remembers his whipping thus:

> I felt an astounding sensation between the shoulders under my neck, which went to my toe-nails in one direction, and my finger-nails in another, and stung me to the heart, as if a knife had gone through my body.... He [the boatswain's mate] came on a second time a few inches lower, and then I thought the former stroke was sweet and agreeable compared to that one.... I put my tongue between my teeth, held it there, and bit it almost in two pieces.[25]

Of all the whipping punishments, the most severe was to be "flogged through the fleet," a sentence generally imposed on those guilty of striking an officer or attempting to escape and was more common in the British navy. A court-martial imposed a punishment of between a hundred and a thousand lashes, a portion of which were to be inflicted in the presence of the crew of every ship in port. The offender was placed in a small boat and rowed from ship to ship, and at each stop he received twenty-five to fifty lashes. Before long, his back resembled "so much putrefied liver."[26] Few survived the ordeal, and those who did never really recovered, physically or mentally.[27] One witness remembers a particularly brutal incident in which the offender died midway through the punishment: "Joshua Davis tells us of a corpse being brought alongside, with the head hanging down and the bones laid bare from the neck to the waist. There were still fifty lashes due the man, so they were given to the corpse, at the captain's order."[28]

It was the rare enlisted man who left a memoir of any sort, so we have little information about those who served aboard the American ships during the War of 1812. In some cases we know their names and ranks and how much each was paid from the ships' logs that have survived the years and the perils of their environment. We know little about their ages, where they were from, or what they did before they joined the U.S. Navy. Their enlistments may have run for no more than two years, in contrast to the much longer obligations demanded by the short-handed British navy. Many of the enlistees were probably experienced sailors drawn from the major ports of Boston, New York, New London, Philadelphia, and Baltimore.

We also know little about the racial composition of the crews of the *Constitution*, the *United States*, or the dozen or more other warships of the young American navy. Ships' logs recorded a sailor's name, his signature (if he was literate), and his rating, and not much else, including race or citizenship. And while we might guess at ethnicity from family names, the names preserved in the logs from the War of 1812 are nearly all Anglo-Saxon, with a few scattered Celtic entries (Irishmen seem to have accounted for no more than about 10 percent of the *Constitution*'s later crews). But hiding among names like Moses Smith, Thomas Butler, Gideon Chauncey, and Elisha Newcomb are the many African-American seamen bearing the same Anglo-Saxon names as their white comrades.

The race of sailors seems never to have been part of the records kept on members of the crew, and very few of the written recollections have much to say on the subject apart from the occasional anecdote, usually singling out someone for a heroic, humorous, or otherwise memorable act. By 1812 many states—all in the north—had abolished slavery, and a large number of free blacks lived and worked in port cities. Many also served in the merchant and whaling fleets that employed American seamen by the tens of thousands. According to one analysis, free African-American sailors accounted for about 20 percent of the crews on merchant vessels shipping out of Providence, New York, and Philadelphia in the decade prior to the war.[29] Many were left unemployed by the embargo and war-related trade disruptions and were as eager as their white counterparts to obtain gainful employment and avenge the insults to their country.

In general orders of 1798, Secretary of the Navy Benjamin Stoddert prohibited the navy from enlisting black or mulatto seamen, but the prohibition appears not to have been enforced, and the many captains who selected and hired crewmen ignored it.[30] While some captains deliberately maintained all white ships, many did not, and the best guess of the historians who have researched the issue is that during the War of 1812 as much as 20 percent of the U.S. fleet may have been African-American seamen. In some of the crews of the much larger fleet of American privateers, the percentage might have been considerably higher. There are indications that some captains—both British and American—actually preferred blacks to whites. Britain Rear Admiral George Cockburn wrote to his superior in June 1814 that:

> I do not think we want recruiting Parties from the West India Regiments, as I much prefer your Idea of forming a Corps of Colonial Marines [all black] the Name by which they are now known and I assure you I should be most happy to have a Proportion of

> them embarked in the *Albion* in lieu of our own Marines, they are stronger Men and more trust worthy for we are sure they will not desert whereas I am sorry to say we have Many Instances of our Marines walking over to the Enemy.[31]

As the war drew to a close in early 1815, a British spy sent to scout Commodore Chauncey's fleet at Sackets Harbor reported:

> The sailors live on board their ships day & night—Most of the seamen have six months pay due them—They were bringing provisions into the harbor—a few naval stores arriving daily—a great many sleigh loads of lignum vitae in bulk had arrived—The great mass of the seaman appear to be coloured people.[32]

There appears to have been no explicit segregation of the crews, though it would have been difficult to achieve, in any case, in the confined quarters of a nineteenth-century warship, where all the crewmen slept and ate together on a single deck, and where hammocks were hung just eighteen inches apart to accommodate over four hundred seamen aboard the big frigates.[33] Nonetheless, black seamen were likely confined to the lower ranks and unlikely to rise to the level of noncommissioned officer.

We know from Hull's postwar recollections that African-Americans served with distinction aboard the *Constitution* when he fought the *Guerriere*, and they were probably still serving aboard the frigate a few months later when Captain Bainbridge sailed her out of Boston. More intriguing are the hints that come down to us about the racial composition of the eighteen-gun brig *Hornet* under Master Commandant David Lawrence, which accompanied Bainbridge and *Constitution* on that voyage. The *Hornet*'s crew, numbering about 150 men, may have been as much as 50 percent black, to judge from eyewitness accounts of its landing in New York City. One observer of a dinner and stage entertainment in honor of the *Hornet*'s victory over HMS *Peacock* remarked:

> The manager of the Park Theater in New York City, in testimony of the bravery of the lamented Captain Lawrence and his crew, manifested in the brilliant action with the British sloop of war *Peacock*, invited him and them to a play in honor of the victory

> achieved on that occasion. The crew marched together into the pit, and nearly one half of them were negroes.[34]

III

The *Constitution* and the *Hornet* left Boston Harbor on 27 October 1812 on a southerly course to meet *Essex*, leaving her anchorage in the Delaware River on the 28th.[35] Decatur had requested that the speedy *Essex* and its fiery captain, David Porter, be assigned to his squadron, but Bainbridge took advantage of his seniority to attach Porter to his own squadron.[36] The ships were to attempt to rendezvous at a series of predetermined locations along the South American coast. Porter's orders provided that, should he fail to find the *Constitution* and the *Hornet*, he should "act according to [his] best judgment."[37] That was an option he ultimately exercised, taking *Essex* around the treacherous Cape Horn and into the Pacific, where he harassed the British whaling fleet in the rich hunting grounds off the coast of Peru.

After a few stormy days in the North Atlantic, the weather turned mild as the *Constitution* followed a southeasterly course toward the Cape Verde Islands off West Africa in the hope of capturing British merchantmen in one of the many sea lanes *Constitution* would cross. All prizes had eluded them, however, when an overeager Bainbridge encountered the American merchantman *South Carolina*, which had sailed from Glasgow with a British license to trade. He seized the ship on grounds of disloyalty. Putting a prize crew on the *South Carolina*, Bainbridge sent her back to the United States for adjudication and reward. The commodore's streak of bad luck continued, however—the prize court eventually ruled against him and ordered him to pay damages to the *South Carolina*'s owner.[38]

Finding little else of interest or reward off the Cape Verde Islands, Bainbridge turned to the southwest and the coast of Portuguese Brazil, an ally against Napoleon with which Britain maintained extensive commercial ties. First landfall was made just south of the equator at the penal colony of Ilha Fernando de Noronha, where Bainbridge topped off his water casks and left word for Porter that the *Constitution* would spend the next two months off the coast of Brazil in search of British prizes. Heading west and south toward the Brazilian port of São Salvador, Bainbridge continued Hull's practice of

James Madison
Courtesy of the Library of Congress

Dolley Madison
Courtesy of the Library of Congress

Tecumseh
Courtesy of Lossing's Pictorial Field Book of the War of 1812

James Monroe
Courtesy of the Library of Congress

Isaac Hull
Courtesy of the Library of Congress

James Richard Dacres
© National Maritime Museum, Greenwich, London

Winfield Scott
Courtesy of the Library of Congress

William Henry Harrison
Courtesy of the Library of Congress

Stephen Decatur
Courtesy of the Library of Congress

William Bainbridge
Courtesy of the Library of Congress

War of 1812 American Generals
Top Row: Andrew Jackson;
Second Row: Henry Dearborn, Jacob Brown;
Third Row: William Henry Harrison;
Fourth Row: Winfield Scott, Zebulon Pike
Courtesy of the Library of Congress

John Borlase Warren

Alexander Cochrane

George Cockburn

David Porter
The Granger Collection, New York

James Hillyar
© National Maritime Museum, Greenwich, London

Henry Allen
Courtesy of Lossing's Pictorial Field Book of the War of 1812

David Lawrence
Courtesy of Lossing's Pictorial Field Book of the War of 1812

Philip Broke
© *National Maritime Museum, Greenwich, London*

Oliver Hazard Perry
Courtesy of the Library of Congress

Thomas Macdonough
Courtesy of the Library of Congress

Andrew Jackson
Courtesy of the Library of Congress

Charles Stewart
Courtesy of Lossing's Pictorial Field Book of the War of 1812

Samuel Reid
Courtesy of Lossing's Pictorial Field Book of the War of 1812

frequently drilling the two ships' crews in seamanship, gunnery, musketry, repelling boarders, and shortening the response time to a beat to quarters.

When Bainbridge arrived off São Salvador on 13 December 1812, the *Essex* was nowhere to be found, so he sent Lawrence and the *Hornet* into the harbor to make contact with the U.S. consul, Henry Hill, and pick up any pertinent news and intelligence about any British naval presence. The *Constitution*, meanwhile, stayed well out to sea in order to deceive any British ships calling at the port about the true strength of the American presence.

Lawrence found the eighteen-gun British war sloop *Bonne Citoyenne* undergoing minor repairs for a leak before heading back to Britain. Lawrence wanted to seize her in port, but Bainbridge refused out of respect for Portugal's nominal neutrality. Lawrence instead formally challenged *Bonne Citoyenne*'s captain, Pitt Barnaby Greene, to a single-ship combat with his equally matched vessel out on the ocean. Though Bainbridge assured Greene that *Constitution* would stay out of the fight, the British commander declined the duel. He was disinclined to accept the challenge largely because he was transporting a cargo of specie (gold and silver coin and plate) valued at half a million pounds and stood to receive a personal reward of five thousand pounds for its safe delivery to Britain. Duty and prudence overcame the thirst for valor, and Greene refused to budge. He remained in port despite the stream of insults from a frustrated Lawrence and Bainbridge.[39]

With little to show for his two months at sea in America's mightiest ship, Bainbridge left the *Hornet* outside São Salvador to intercept Greene if he tried to escape and turned *Constitution* east into the Atlantic in search of British warships and prizes. It was not long before one sailed within his range. In his journal entry for 29 December 1812, Bainbridge wrote that: "At 9 AM, discovered two Strange Sails on the weather bow, at 10 AM discovered strange sails to be Ships, one of them stood in for the land, and the other steered off shore in a direction toward us."[40] The two strange sails were the *Java*, forty-six days out of Spithead, and its prize, the American merchantman *William*, captured a few days earlier.

Under the command of Captain Henry Lambert, *Java* was stopping in Brazil to replenish her water supply. She was on the first leg of a lengthy voyage around the Cape of Good Hope to Bombay, where she would deliver copper sheet and some of her crew for several men-of-war being built by the British at the Wadia shipyard. As Britain's supply of home-grown oak diminished, the colony of India offered an attractive place for the construction of warships because of its abundant supplies of teak, an Asian wood stronger and more resistant to rot than oak.[41] *Java* was also transporting the newly appointed governor of India, Lieutenant General Sir Thomas Hislop, his entourage, and a detachment of troops to his new post in Bombay.

Originally built by the French as the *Renommée*, she was captured by the British in the Indian Ocean, renamed the *Java*, and put under the command of Lambert. Months earlier Lambert had brought her home to Britain from an engagement with the French off Mauritius in the Indian Ocean. While the *Java* was being refitted in Britain, Lambert was confronted by Britain's serious manpower shortage as he struggled to assemble a new crew for the voyage back to India. Using every recruiting trick he knew, Lambert finally pulled together the three hundred men and boys—many from questionable sources—needed to man the *Java*. According to one British naval historian, "It was found necessary to enlist sixty Irish landsmen, fifty rebellious seamen from the sloop *Coquette*, several drafts of pressed men, some 'volunteers' from prison ships, and a disproportionate number of boys from the Marine Society" (a training program to prepare young boys—mostly orphans—for a career at sea).[42]

Lambert, moreover, was apparently lax in preparing his ship for battle. One British historian notes that for many of *Java*'s crew, it was the first time they had ever manned a gun.[43] Perhaps because British officers were overconfident early in the conflict with America, Lambert had made little effort to train his crew for the eventuality of combat. Whereas Bainbridge continued to drill his increasingly seasoned crew, Lambert, by contrast, had conducted just one gunnery practice—and then only with unshotted cartridges—before stumbling upon *Constitution*.

By early afternoon both ships were close enough to exchange recognition codes by flag, and neither received a return signal indicating friend. Preparing for combat by taking up his mainsail and royals and shortening his canvas to topsails, top gallants, jib, and spanker,[44] Bainbridge tacked toward the enemy—whose speed, he surmised, indicated a frigate—and wore again to the southeast to avoid being raked. With the *Java* now trailing him but closing the distance, Bainbridge realized that his opponent's ship was faster than his and ordered several broadsides of canister and grape[45] aimed at *Java*'s rigging and sail when the distance between them closed to about a thousand yards. Most shots missed their mark and *Java* suffered little or no damage, nor was her pace of attack slowed.

At about two o'clock PM the ships were close enough to begin combat in earnest, and the first salvos were more damaging to *Constitution* than to *Java*. The American's rigging and sails were mauled and several crewmen killed or injured. Among the wounded was Bainbridge himself, hit in the thigh by musket fire. Commanding the faster and more maneuverable ship, Lambert several times raced ahead, intending to wear his ship across *Constitution*'s bow and rake her with a devastating broadside, but Bainbridge anticipated each attempt and wore *Constitution* in the same direction to keep the ships on a parallel course as gunners fired broadside after broadside into each other's hulls and rigging. Recognizing that Bainbridge was anticipating his efforts to cross *Constitution*'s bow, Lambert faked a third attempt to race ahead then quickly wore ship and came in under Bainbridge's larboard quarter, firing a savage broadside into *Constitution*'s vulnerable stern.

The effect was devastating. Four helmsmen were killed or wounded, the wheel was shot away, and nearly a dozen of the quarter-deck's carronade crews were dead or wounded. Bainbridge received a second wound in his thigh when a copper bolt—perhaps one forged by Paul Revere—flew across the deck at a deadly speed after being dislodged by a cannon ball that ripped into the ship's frame.[46] Lambert, however, did not realize how much damage he had done with his raking fire or how vulnerable *Constitution* was at this moment. Rather than quickly returning to pummel the momentarily floundering frigate, Lambert kept on a defensive parallel course, expecting an aggressive response from Bainbridge. That response did not come, however, and Lambert, presuming that the American was fleeing, took up the chase.

Lambert attempted to regain his lost advantage of time and position by tacking under *Constitution*'s stern and firing another raking broadside, but by now the distance was too great for much damage to be done, and the brief respite in the fight allowed Bainbridge to improvise a rudder-control system operated manually from below decks in response to verbal orders from the quarter-deck relayed by midshipmen running up and down the ladders.

As the wounded Bainbridge steadied himself by leaning on a midshipman for support, the Americans knew that their only hope was to pound out a

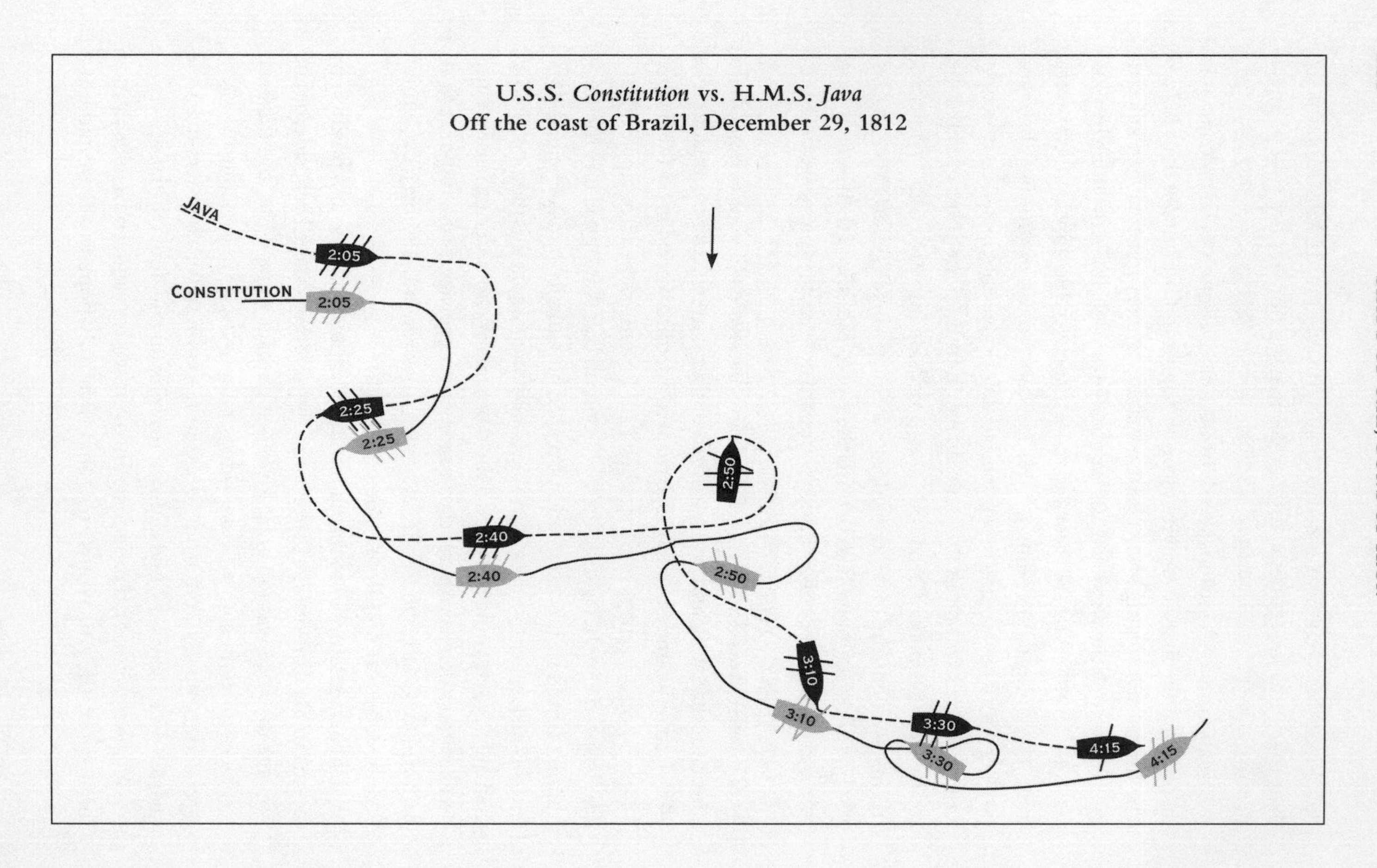
U.S.S. *Constitution* vs. H.M.S. *Java*
Off the coast of Brazil, December 29, 1812
JAVA
CONSTITUTION
2:05
2:05
2:25
2:25
2:40
2:40
2:50
2:50
3:10
3:10
3:30
3:30
4:15
4:15

victory close in, where the *Constitution*'s bigger and more numerous guns could prevail. Lambert unwittingly assisted Bainbridge's strategy. Suspecting that his opponent was badly damaged, Lambert closed the distance and took up a parallel course on *Constitution*'s weather gauge, setting up the only kind of battle that Bainbridge had any chance of winning.

The subsequent exchange of broadsides was everything Bainbridge could have hoped for. He set fore and main top courses and steered close to the wind to bring *Constitution*'s carronades and sharp-shooting marines into play. Lambert cooperated by keeping *Java* within range. In minutes *Java*'s bow-sprit cap, jib boom, and head sails were all shot away. When Bainbridge wore *Constitution* in an attempt to get around behind *Java* and rake her stern, the British frigate could not maneuver out of danger. Lambert wore his ship into the wind, using his spanker to drive the stern around. But with most of his steering sails destroyed, the maneuver failed. *Java* was now pointed helplessly dead into the wind, offering an easy target for a destructive broadside from *Constitution.* Wearing his ship around and reversing course to avoid being in "irons" like *Java*, Bainbridge had *Constitution* nicely positioned when *Java* maneuvered out of her trap. As *Java* finally came around, both ships were again on a parallel course with the wind off the larboard quarter. The advantage was now slowly but inexorably shifting to the Americans. As one British writer described the final few hours,

> It was *Constitution*'s guns which were now dealing death and destruction as Bainbridge steadied her deck with a backed mizzen topsail. Bainbridge was plying grape from his carronades and his sharpshooters in the tops were picking off men on *Java*'s upper decks. Despite this galling fire, Lambert's ill-assorted company stuck to their guns as their captain saw his sails shot away, his rigging flying loose, his men falling like corn stalks under the scythe as *Java*'s hull shuddered to the impact of round shot.[47]

Nine of Lambert's midshipmen were dead or wounded, leaving many of the gun crews without leadership or direction.[48] His rigging damaged, his maneuverability limited, and outgunned by his adversary, Lambert knew that his only chance, however slim, for victory lay in bringing his ship alongside the American, boarding her, and fighting it out hand to hand with axe, pike, and cutlass. But Lambert did not have enough control over his floundering ship to execute the maneuver at precisely the right spot, and *Java* tangled her damaged bowsprit in *Constitution*'s mizzen rigging. The ship was now locked in a position where it could bring only one gun to bear, while being exposed to the full weight of *Constitution*'s twenty-seven-gun broadside and well-aimed muskets fired from *Constitution*'s tops. A storm of lead and iron deterred Lambert's boarders from attempting to climb onto the American's deck from the entangled bow sprit.

The entanglement was devastating for the British. *Constitution*'s grape, round shot, and heavy lead musket balls ripped through *Java* and her crew. In his journal Bainbridge coldly and concisely sketched out the progress of destruction that he and his crew wreaked upon *Java* during the second hour of combat:[49]

> At 3 [PM] The Enemies Jib boom got foul of our Mizen Rigging
> At 3.05 Shot away the enemies foremast by the board
> At 3.15 Shot away The enemies Main Top mast just above the cap
> At 3.40 Shot away Gafft and Spunker boom
> At 3.55 Shot his mizen mast nearly by the board

The falling foremast crashed through two decks, and along with all of the other broken masts and rigging, left the decks of the *Java* in a state of confusion that obstructed any attempt by its inexperienced crew to organize an effective defense. But still she did not surrender, and as the *Java* broke free, the two ships resumed their eastward progress on a parallel course. This time *Constitution* took the weather gauge and used it to devastating effect. At about four o'clock PM, Bainbridge sailed ahead of Lambert and wore ship on a southerly course, crossing *Java*'s bow and raking her with his starboard twenty-four-pound long guns and forty-two-pound carronades as each came to bear on the enemy's vulnerable bow.

As his crew reloaded their starboard guns while *Constitution* sailed south, Bainbridge wore again to the north, crossed under *Java*'s stern, and let go with another raking fire that sent hundreds of pounds of cast iron shot racing from stern to bow through *Java*'s open decks. *Constitution*'s gun crews crossed the deck to the already loaded larboard guns as Bainbridge wore the ship around on a larboard tack and re-crossed his path in a rare double raking action to bring her guns to bear again on *Java*'s damaged stern. "The slaughter had been terrible," writes Theodore Roosevelt, "yet the British fought on with stubborn resolution, cheering lustily. But success was now hopeless, for nothing could stand against the cool precision of the Yankee fire."[50]

With many of her sails shot away and spars, rigging, and masts dragging in the water, *Java*'s progress slowed. She fired her few remaining operational guns until the Americans set more sail and pulled out of range. The firing from both sides continued, but by five o'clock PM *Java* was finished. Two of her masts were completely gone, her mainmast was but a stump, and her guns at last fell silent. Bainbridge took the *Constitution* a short distance away to make minor repairs before returning to close and accept *Java*'s expected surrender.

But surrender was not forthcoming. Captain Lambert had been seriously wounded, and the transfer of command produced temporary indecision. A musket ball fired from the tops by an American marine had hit Lambert in the chest, coming to rest near his spine.[51] *Java*'s surgeon, Dr. Thomas Cook Jones, later wrote of his examination of Lambert's wounds: "I saw him almost immediately afterward and found that the ball had entered his left side under the clavicle, fracturing the first rib, the splinters of which had severely lacerated the lungs. I put my finger in the wound, detached and extricated several pieces of the bone. He said he felt no annoyance from the wound in his breast, but complained of pain extending the whole length of his spine."[52]

Java's first lieutenant, Henry Ducie Chads, himself suffering from painful wounds, was now in command, and he recoiled from making his first act as commander the surrender of his ship to an American. As Chads recounted in his report to the Admiralty: "We still waited the attack of the Enemy, he now standing toward us for that purpose. On his coming nearly within hail of us & from his manoeuvre perceiving he intended a position a head where he could rake us without our possibility of our returning a shot."[53]

Chads had quickly rigged sails to the remaining stumps of masts and spars in an effort to get before the wind, gain maneuver, and defend England's honor. But the remains of the mainmast fell over within minutes, and the debris covered most of the guns on the starboard side. With his ship now helplessly rolling in the seas, and with *Constitution* prepared to pound her into splinters, Chads thought it might be time to reconsider his decision:

> I then consulted the Officers who agreed with myself that on having a great part of our Crew killed & wounded our Bowsprit and three masts gone, several guns useless, we should not be justified in waisting the lives of more of those remaining whom I hope their Lordships & Country will think have bravely defended His Majestys ship.[54]

Java surrendered at about 5:30 PM, and shortly after six Bainbridge sent First Lieutenant George Parker across in one of his few undamaged boats to take possession of the defeated frigate. Bainbridge reported nine crewmen dead and twenty-seven wounded, compared with *Java*'s fifty-seven dead and eighty-three wounded, (Some British historians put Java's casualties at twenty-two dead and 102 wounded,[55] a long-standing point of dispute with American historians.) Chads's report is silent on the number of casualties, but the difference in physical devastation to the two ships seems to support Bainbridge's higher figure.[56]

It quickly became apparent that *Java* required extensive repairs to be seaworthy enough to take home as a prize. But *Constitution* herself needed extensive repairs to her spars and rigging. Alone in the south Atlantic and far from home, they faced the risk that a larger British squadron might stumble upon them as they attempted to salvage their damaged prize. Bainbridge reluctantly decided, therefore, to sink the *Java*. With only two usable boats, it took two days to transfer the British prisoners, many of whom were badly wounded, to the *Constitution*. Before destroying the *Java*, Bainbridge took her wheel to replace his own, which had been shattered in the battle.[57] At three o'clock PM on New Year's Eve day, after the removal of the British officers' baggage, *Java* was set on fire. When the flames reached her magazine, the frigate exploded, though the blast was not as spectacular as the final explosion of *Guerriere*, according to *Constitution*'s surgeon, Amos Evans, who witnessed both.[58]

Writing twenty-seven years later, James Fenimore Cooper delighted in telling the story about "a British officer, visiting on board some years after the war, who commented that the steering wheel was the only thing aboard [the *Constitution*] whose workmanship failed to measure up to the high standard of the rest of the frigate—and was told, with the smugness exhibited by some of our people of that day, that the wheel was a trophy of the victory over the *Java*."[59]

IV

Constitution's victory over *Java* provoked the same reaction from the defeated British officers as had the victory over *Guerriere*. *Constitution* owed their victory, they said, to the presence of a large number of English sailors among her crew. An account of 26 January 1813 by one of *Java*'s lieutenants, printed in the *Naval Chronicle*, offered this excuse:

> Most of the crew of the *Constitution* were known to be English, and many of them our prime sailors; some had belonged to the *Iphigenia*, others to the *Guerriere*; and, I am sorry to say, three of the *Java*'s entered when prisoners. The surgeon of the *Constitution* was an Irishman, and lately an assistant surgeon in our navy.[60]

That surgeon, Amos A. Evans, may have been of Irish ancestry, but he was born in Maryland and, according to Roosevelt, had never served in the Royal Navy.[61]

Not everyone in England was persuaded by such rationalizations, which implied that English sailors were inclined to desertion and treason and that crews of English runaways under the command of American officers habitually prevailed in battle against English crews with English officers. In any case, the defeat stung. In late March 1813, when news of *Java*'s loss reached Britain, the *Times* ruefully observed:

> The public will learn with sentiments which we will not presume to anticipate that a third British frigate has struck to an American. Any one who would have predicted such a result of an American war this time last year would have been treated as a madman or a traitor. Yet down to this moment, not a single American frigate has struck her flag.[62]

The *Naval Chronicle* echoed the *Times*' concern: "We have still, however, to regret the disastrous progress of the naval war between this country and

America. Another frigate has fallen into the hands of the enemy!—The subject is too painful for us to dwell upon."[63] The same dismay was felt in Parliament, where in early 1813 the marquis of Lansdowne expressed his disbelief at the fortunes of the Royal Navy against the Americans:

> Some time ago it was imagined that in the event of war with America the first operation would be the destruction of her navy. What the fact has turned out to be, I am almost ashamed to mention. If anyone were asked what had been the services of our navy in this war, he would unfortunately find some difficulty in giving an answer.[64]

The former prime minister George Canning echoed these concerns when he declared, "It cannot be too deeply felt that the sacred spell of the invincibility of the British Navy was broken by these unfortunate captures."[65]

The Admiralty was probably as shocked as anyone in the kingdom. After five losses at sea in only six months of war against an inferior foe, Britain temporarily resolved the problem by taking the humiliating step of ordering her captains to avoid single-ship combat with the Americans. On 10 July 1813, First Secretary to the Admiralty John Wilson Croker issued "secret & confidential" orders to his officers:

> I have their Lordships Commands to acquaint you therewith, and they do not conceive that any of His Majestys Frigates should attempt to engage, single handed, the larger Class of American Ships.... In the event of one of His Majestys Frigates under your orders falling in with one of these Ships, her Captain should endeavour, in the first instance, to secure the retreat of His Majestys Ship, but if he finds he has advantage in sailing, he should endeavour to manoeuvre, and keep company with her, without coming to action, in the hope of falling in with some other of His Majestys Ships with whose assistance the Enemy might be attacked with reasonable hope of success.[66]

Croker's orders reflected growing unease within the Admiralty and within the officer corps itself. David Milne, the captain of a British frigate, expressed the thoughts of many when he wrote the next April to a colleague that "I cannot help feeling some anxiety as an officer where I am liable to meet with an enemy so superior in size of ship, weight of metal, and number and quality of men."[67] Fifteen years after she was awkwardly launched in Boston, *Constitution* and her big frigate sisters were proving the brilliance of Joshua Humphreys's concept and design.

Counting prisoners, the *Constitution*'s complement of men now numbered between eight and nine hundred men, of whom more than a hundred were wounded, many seriously, including Captain Lambert. The ship was short of space and it was summer in the southern hemisphere, so many of the enlisted men from the *Java* were allowed to remain in the open air of the upper deck or in the better ventilated gun deck, though in manacles to prevent an uprising. Bainbridge intended to take them to São Salvador in pro-British Brazil, where Lawrence was still waiting with the *Hornet*. There the prisoners could be turned over to the British consul for care (and the costly feeding and medical treatment) before being shipped back to England.

Approaching São Salvador, Bainbridge mistook the sails of the *Hornet* and her prizes—the recaptured American *William* and the British merchant vessel *Eleanor* (or *Ellen*)—for British warships. *Constitution* beat to quarters and Bainbridge ordered the British prisoners on the decks to be taken into the dark and fetid hold to prevent any trouble if combat were to resume with their brethren on the approaching ships. Bainbridge soon realized his mistake and had the prisoners returned to the deck, but he has been criticized for his treatment of his British prisoners. The prisoners who were seriously wounded must have suffered badly as they were hustled down the steep and narrow ladders and kept out of the way in the foul confines of the hold.

Both American and British critics see in Bainbridge's conduct a pattern of contempt for ordinary seamen that contrasts with his courtly behavior toward the officers of the enemy, who were provided every comfort and courtesy during their brief captivity. Other historians are less censorious. One acknowledged that "[t]his Act was to bring the wrath of some British observers down on Bainbridge's head, with charges of cruelty and malice, despite the obvious military requirement to ready his ship for battle that the situation generated."[68] Not long after these events, Bainbridge raised eyebrows with a letter to Congress requesting prize money for himself and his crew, even though *Java* had been destroyed and nothing of value recovered. "It is prize money that stimulates the sailor; patriotism and fame guide the officer."[69]

The voyage to São Salvador took but a day. The prisoners were released on 2 January 1813 while *Constitution* was resupplied and repaired. Lambert, dying and in severe pain, had been kept as comfortable as possible on a couch placed on *Constitution*'s quarter-deck, shaded from the blazing tropical sun by an awning. Wounded in both legs and struggling to walk with the help of two officers, Bainbridge came to Lambert and gave him back the sword with which he had surrendered his ship a few days earlier. "I return your sword, my dear sir, with the sincere wish that you recover, and wear it as you have hitherto done, with honor to yourself and your country."[70] Lambert died the next day and was buried in the Portuguese citadel of Fort San Pedro in São Salvador.[71]

Bainbridge negotiated a parole of the captured officers with Lieutenant General Hislop and Lieutenant Chads, whereby the officers promised to return to England and not fight again in the war until a formal exchange took place. Chads wrote in his initial report that "I cannot conclude this letter without expressing my grateful acknowledgement thus publicly for the generous treatment Captain Lambert and his Officers have experienced from our Gallant Enemy Commodore Bainbridge and his Officers."[72] The gratitude must have been sincere because Hislop, shortly after capture, gave Bainbridge a sword as a token of his respect and esteem,[73] and the two would go on to become "corresponding friends to the end of their days."[74]

Fearful that the British fleet in the area, led by the *Montagu*, 74, would soon attack, Bainbridge and the *Constitution* left for home on 5 January 1813. He was accompanied by *Hornet*'s two prizes, which included *Java*'s former prize, *William*. Bainbridge ordered Lawrence to continue watching over *Bonne Citoyenne* until no later than 25 January and then return home. Lawrence stayed on until 24 January, when the *Montagu* finally showed up and forced him to flee. As Bainbridge had done, he worked his way back to North America but at a leisurely pace that would allow him a thorough search for prizes. Much farther south, Porter and the *Essex* were still looking for *Constitution* at their scheduled rendezvous site, off Cabo Frio, a little east of Rio de Janeiro and well south of São Salvador.

Bainbridge arrived in Boston on 15 February 1813. Because of previous dispatches sent ashore at ports along the way, news of his victory had arrived almost a week earlier and was first announced at a performance of *Hamlet* in

Boston Theatre. Commodores Rodgers and Hull were in the audience. Adverse winds kept the *Constitution* from docking until the 18th, while the citizens of the city eagerly waited to welcome another conquering hero. According to one account of his delayed arrival:

> The route to the Exchange Coffee House was decorated with flags and streamers. A procession was formed at Faneuil Hall that included the Ancient and Honorable Artillery Company, the Boston Light Infantry, and the Wilson Blues. The tall commodore was escorted by Rodgers and the stumpy Hull, as well as other notables. Two bands played. And for the next two months Boston and the country gave themselves up to honoring the latest naval heroes.[75]

Another account of Bainbridge's joyous arrival notes the occurrence of the now obligatory public dinner and naval ball, followed by

> an outpouring of official appreciation. Massachusetts and New York passed legislative thanks, President Madison sent his own congratulations, and Congress voted to strike a gold medal to Bainbridge which he later helped design. Perhaps the most useful thanks was the fifty thousand dollars of prize money voted by Congress to award the officers and men of the *Constitution*. Bainbridge's share was seven thousand dollars—a fortune equal to what he had earned as a merchant trader in five years of peace.[76]

Silver medals were cast for the junior officers, and the average seaman and ship's boy received about sixty dollars in prize money,[77] although if Bainbridge had his way they might not have received even this. So contemptuous was he of their performance during a fight that produced more American casualties than any previous sea battle that he continued to complain about them in the months that followed. In a letter to the naval agent in New York, Bainbridge confided: "My crew owing to the constant Exercise we give them, are very active & clever at their Guns. But in all other respects they are inferior to any Crew I ever had."[78]

Bainbridge did not command another ship during the war. He was reappointed naval commandant of the Charlestown Navy Yard at Boston Harbor, the position he held before taking over the command of the *Constitution* from Hull. Bainbridge had been scheduled to assume command of the massive *Independence*, America's first ship of the line, but *Independence* was still under construction when the war ended a year later.

On 23 April 1813, a court-martial aboard *Gladiator* at Portsmouth, England, honorably acquitted Lieutenant Henry Ducie Chads. The court based its verdict on the ship's brave resistance and the damage *Java* inflicted on *Constitution*. The court was persuaded that *Java*'s stubborn defense had forced *Constitution* abruptly to end a voyage that had been scheduled to last until spring, and instead return to Boston for repairs.[79] "[H]e was made a commander shortly afterward, a captain two years later, and died in 1868 a full admiral and a Knight Grand Cross of the Order of the Bath."[80]

CHAPTER EIGHT

BACK ON LAND: HOLDING THE LINE

As 1813 unfolded in the east, the misfortune and lack of preparation hampering ground efforts in 1812 began infecting those of the new year as well. In early February, from his position at Ogdensburg, New York—a trading town on the south shore of the now frozen St. Lawrence River—Major Benjamin Forsyth crossed the ice and launched a quick strike against the nearby Elizabethtown in Canada, in response to an earlier British attack on Ogdensburg, during which a number of American prisoners were taken. Forsythe freed the captured Americans and rubbed salt in British wounds by taking fifty-two Canadians prisoner and seizing their supplies.[1] British Lieutenant Colonel "Red George" MacDonnell, commanding five hundred troops across the river in Prescott, Ontario, wanted revenge.

On 22 February, Prescott led his troops out onto the frozen St. Lawrence River in an exercise that seemed to be nothing more than a series of drills and training, or so it was made to appear for the benefit of the American troops watching from their limited defensive positions in Ogdensburg. But on a command from MacDonnell, the mock drill quickly turned into an attack that overwhelmed the unsuspecting Americans, who nonetheless did manage to inflict about seventy casualties on MacDonnell's men during the skirmish.[2] After brief resistance, Forsyth knew he was badly outnumbered, and ordered his troops out of the town as fast as they could leave. Though the American forces escaped without incurring significant casualties or capture, they did lose a substantial cache of weapons and supplies, as well as two ships and numerous buildings, to the British. The townspeople fared little better, as they were systematically looted by the enemy soldiers, and then by the enterprising citizens of the Canadian town of Prescott who followed the troops across the ice in search of whatever booty was left.

Forsyth immediately set in motion plans to retake the town, but the citizens of Ogdensburg beseeched him to find another place for his quarters, arguing that the presence of American soldiers so close to the border would leave them vulnerable to endless British attack and looting. Forsyth reluctantly conceded to their wish and moved his army southwest to Sackets Harbor, New York, near where Lake Ontario spills into the St. Lawrence River. No longer burdened by the presence of American troops, the citizens of Ogdensburg demonstrated their entrepreneurial acumen and ambidextrous loyalties by turning their town into a major supply depot for the British.[3]

Fortunately, the withdrawal from Ogdensburg did not portend another year of defeat and despair. Indeed, within a few months, as winter turned to spring, American troops would be on the move along many northern fronts, and the army's performance would sometimes resemble that of their brothers at sea, as ineffective commanders were replaced by smart young officers ready to prove their mettle.

One young American warrior brimming with promise was Brigadier General Zebulon Montgomery Pike, the thirty-four-year-old frontier explorer who had been sent out shortly after the return of Lewis and Clark's Corps of Discovery in command of a twenty-man exploring party to find the headwaters of the Mississippi and to negotiate treaties with the Indian tribes he encountered. In 1806 he led another, longer expedition to the southwest, where he was briefly detained by Spanish officials in what is now northern New Mexico. On the way back to St. Louis, he passed through Colorado where he attempted, without success, to climb the Rocky Mountain peak now named after him.

Now serving under the command of the lethargic General Henry Dearborn, Pike and his army of 1,600 sailed from Sackets Harbor on 22 April 1813 aboard the ships of Commodore Isaac Chauncey's Lake Ontario fleet. A voyage of 160 miles would take them to Britain's capital of Upper Canada, York (now called Toronto) on the lake's northwest shore, where they would launch an amphibious attack.

With the first wave ashore led by Benjamin Forsyth, Pike landed his men just west of town and out of range of the harbor's cannon. As Chauncey's fleet bombarded York from the water, Pike's troops attacked the town from the west. Outnumbered British troops and Canadian militia under Major General Sheaffe launched a counter-attack, but were quickly cut down in successive waves by the attacking American infantry. Seeing his position as hopeless, and with his Indian allies fleeing to the woods as Pike's men attacked— accompanied by fifes and drums playing "Yankee Doodle"[4]—Sheaffe ordered the destruction of York's supplies and ships, before retreating into the interior.

Among the supplies readied for destruction were the several hundred barrels of gun powder stored in the garrison's thick stone magazine. Rigged with fuses, it soon exploded with tremendous force, killing scores of American troops who were in the town mopping up the last bits of resistance. Ned Myers, a seaman from Chauncey's fleet said, "It was a dreadful sight; the dead being so mutilated that it was scarcely possible to tell their colour. I saw gun-barrels bent nearly double."[5] Army doctors "waded in blood, cutting off arms, legs & trepanning heads." One army surgeon remembers that he "cut & slashed for 48 hours without food or sleep."[6] Among the mortally wounded was General Pike, who was sitting on a log several hundred yards away questioning British prisoners when the magazine blew and sent rock shrapnel flying throughout the town. A fellow officer said that "a large Stone Struck him in the forehead and Stamped him for the Grave."[7] Other reports have him struck on the back. Badly wounded, he was evacuated to a ship, and lived long enough to receive the British flag from his troops.[8]

Angry American troops, now leaderless, claimed they found a scalp tacked onto a government building, and went on a rampage of looting and burning, in which many of the locals are also said to have participated. Among the buildings burnt to the ground was the provincial legislative building, an act of arson the British would later argue established a precedent for their own behavior in Washington a year and a half later.[9]

II

In the west at Malden, General Procter worried that the same fate would soon befall his limited forces as winter turned to spring and the weather became more conducive to marching and warfare. To the southeast across Lake Erie at Presque Isle (now Erie, Pennsylvania), Oliver Hazard Perry was building a fleet of war ships to challenge British superiority in the lake and isolate Malden from its supply lines running from Lake Ontario through Lake Erie. Added to Procter's problems was the American force entrenched to his south. At Fort Meigs in northwest Ohio, General William Henry Harrison would soon be massing troops for the attack on Canada that Perry's ships would support. With few options left, Procter had no choice but to take preemptive action.

With Harrison still wintering in Cincinnati, Procter was informed by his Indian scouts that Fort Meigs on the Maumee River in Ohio was undermanned because the Pennsylvania and Virginia militiamen had left for home and spring planting. When the weather finally cleared in late April, Procter assembled a force of nearly 2,200, including about 1,200 Indians led by Tecumseh and other chiefs, and sailed south across the western tip of Lake Erie to the mouth of the Maumee River near Fort Meigs.[10] Rumors of the attack arrived at Harrison's Cincinnati headquarters in late March. Alarmed at the prospect of again being attacked by the British while he was still well short of his objective in Michigan, Harrison immediately marched north to the fort with whatever men he could cobble together on a few days' notice. Along the way he gathered more men, and ordered Brigadier General Green Clay to follow as quickly as he could with a force of Kentucky militia.

The reinforcements arrived at Fort Meigs on 12 April, more than two weeks before Procter reached the Maumee, and the men began preparing it for the expected siege. Fort Meigs, constructed mostly of logs and thick earthen walls, and built under the supervision of Eleazer Wood, one of the first graduates of America's new military college at West Point,[11] held a commanding position in the region it defended. On the north it was protected by the Maumee River, deep ravines secured it on east and west sides, and a clear field of fire opened to the south. And with Harrison's reinforcements, it now bristled with rifle and cannon and defiant American troops. When the British force arrived on 28 April and took up positions on the opposite bank, Harrison, never at a loss for words, published the following general orders to stir his troops to noble resistance:

> Can the citizens of a free country ... think of submitting to an army composed of mercenary soldiers, reluctant Canadians goaded to the field by the bayonet, and of wretched, naked savages? Can the breast of an American soldier, when he casts his eyes to the opposite shore, the scene of his country's triumphs over the same foe, be influenced by any other feelings than hope of glory? ... To your posts fellow-citizens, and remember that the eyes of your country are upon you.[12]

Seeing the fort for the first time, Procter quickly recognized the tough challenge facing his army, and delayed his attack for several days to allow his force to dig in and his gun boats time to work their way up the Maumee River where they would support his attack. Finally ready on 1 May, British artillery and gunboats opened up on the fort as Tecumseh led a contingent of his warriors across the river to encircle the fort from the south. But the British barrage had little effect against an earthen fort that simply swallowed up the artillery shells heaved against its soft, thick walls of damp earth and logs. Because the Americans were low on ammunition, they did not at first return fire, and Harrison offered a *gill* of whiskey (four ounces) to any man who recovered a British shell. This produced more than 1,000 rounds that American artillerists fired back at the enemy.[13] As the British guns pounded away, Harrison sent a messenger to the approaching force of Kentuckians led by General Clay, ordering him to split his force and use the larger to attack the British position to the north across the river and spike the guns. In the meantime, Procter demanded the fort's surrender, but Harrison mockingly replied that "the British would gain more glory if they took the fort by fighting."[14]

On 5 May, eight hundred Kentuckians led by Colonel William Dudley floated down the Maumee River on flat boats and attacked the British force on the north bank. As they had a year earlier at Frenchtown, the Kentucky troops quickly routed the British and their Indian allies, and captured all of the artillery, which the Americans spiked by hammering nails into the guns' touch holes. At about the same time Dudley was attacking the British on the north bank, troops stationed in the fort sallied out under Colonel Miller and successfully attacked Procter's artillery position on the south bank, taking forty prisoners. But with a stunning victory in their grasp, Colonel Dudley's conquering Kentuckians lost all sense of discipline and took off into the woods in pursuit of the fleeing Indians, seeking scalps and revenge for last year's massacre at River Raisin. As the leaderless Kentuckians scattered through woods and fields, Procter regrouped for a counter-attack and ordered Tecumseh back across the river to join it. A savage battle ensued, and as the day came to a close, Dudley's force suffered a massive defeat. He and as many as two hundred of his men were killed, and about 500 were captured.[15] But the slaughter, unfortunately, did not end there.

The Indians, high on adrenalin from their victory over Dudley's force, wanted more, and the American prisoners—under the guard of British soldiers—offered an attractive opportunity. Several dozen or so of the Americans were taken from the British and forced to run through a gauntlet of armed warriors where they were beaten to death by clubs, tomahawks, and gun butts before being scalped. As many as twenty Americans are believed to have died in this way. For reasons never explained, Procter chose not to interfere with the torture, but when Tecumseh heard about it he rushed to the site, demanding that it end, and threatened a swift death to any of his warriors who refused his order. Indeed, so appalled was Tecumseh by the slaughter and the British failure to stop it that he is said to have called Procter a squaw[16] and told him to "Begone. You are not fit to command. Go and put on petticoats."[17]

The battle at Fort Meigs should have been another stunning British victory. The Americans had lost about 1,000 men, or nearly half their force, through death, wounds or capture. The British, in contrast, had fifteen dead, forty-six wounded, and forty-one taken prisoner. Indian casualties are unknown, as was usually the case.

With more than a thousand Americans still holding the fort—including the 170 of Dudley's surviving force that made it back behind the walls, as well as the remainder of the Kentucky militia under General Clay—Procter knew his chances for conquest were slim. Many in his army knew this as well. The Indians, having had their fill of victory, torture, and scalps, and unwilling to become cannon fodder in a frontal assault against an impregnable fort, began drifting away. The four hundred or so members of the Canadian militia were also eager to leave and get back home for the spring planting. With his army dissolving before the muddy walls of Fort Meigs, Procter abandoned the siege, and on 9 May marched his shrinking force back to Malden. Although the American force suffered horribly in the battle, Fort Meigs held, and it was only a matter of time, and not much at that, before Procter would find himself on the defensive.

III

In New York, the American offensive was already underway and showing more success than the year before. As winter gave way to spring, the Americans remained in possession of the land east of the Niagara River, while the British occupied the west. On the American side, Fort Niagara guarded the entrance to the river from the lake, while the western side of the river was secured by Britain's Fort George, now under the command of Brigadier General John Vincent—a veteran of action in the West Indies, Holland, and Denmark.

But the Americans were intent on changing this balance of power which had survived their ill-fated attack on Queenston nine months earlier. As before, the Americans would be under the command of the now *Colonel* Winfield Scott, who at the tender age of twenty-seven was about to prove himself one of the most adept tacticians and leaders of the war. What Scott intended, and what he worked diligently to plan and organize over the winter, was a well-coordinated amphibious assault on the British position. Helping to organize and lead the assault was Lieutenant Oliver Hazard Perry, who had weeks earlier been called up by Chauncey from his station on Lake Erie to participate in the operation. Perry would later write that on the day of the attack:

> The ship [*Madison*] was under way, with a light breeze from the eastward, quite fair for us; a thick mist hanging over Newark and Fort George, the sun breaking forth in the east, the vessels all under way, the lake covered with several hundred large boats, filled with soldiers, horses and artillery, advancing toward the enemy, altogether formed one of the grandest spectacles I ever beheld.[18]

With Isaac Chauncey in command of the naval forces, Scott's plan was to land the American assault force on a Lake Ontario beach just west of Fort George. Three waves of infantry would assault the beach from boats towed by, or embarking from, Chauncey's fleet, and seize the fort. As the troops landed and fought, the guns of the American fleet would provide cover for the landing party and fire on any British troops that came out to fight. To further confuse the British as to the American's precise intentions, Scott had American forces feint attacks all along the Niagara River south to Lake Erie.

Scott's plan worked perfectly. As the bombardment got underway along the entire line, American infantry hit the beach at 4:00 AM on 26 May 1813. Scott led the first wave of Benjamin Forsyth's riflemen ashore and went on the attack while Chauncey's guns shelled the land approaches to the beach. At the same time, Colonel James Burn took two mounted companies of light dragoons across the Niagara River north of the British position to cut off any retreat from Fort George. Surprised at the attack, General Vincent responded by ordering more than a hundred or so Glengarries down to the beach just as Scott's first wave was landing. One of the highlanders nearly bayoneted Scott, but within minutes more than half the Scots lay dead or wounded, a fate that awaited the company of Newfoundlanders who immediately followed them.[19]

The British counter-attacked again and again, but each time Winfield Scott and his troops beat them back. And as the hours rolled by, a second and third wave of American troops came ashore, stacking the odds against Vincent's defending force who were being cut up on the beach by American muskets and Chauncey's big guns. By midday, Vincent decided his situation was hopeless and attempted to save his force for another battle by abandoning Fort George.

As he retreated, Vincent ordered both magazines at the fort mined to keep the powder from the Americans. But Scott had no intention of letting the valuable supply of powder go up in smoke, or seeing a repeat of the horrendous casualties caused by last month's explosion at York. Leading two companies of soldiers on a borrowed horse, Scott rushed to the fort, but the first magazine blew up before he could reach it, knocking him off his horse and breaking his collar bone.[20] Nonetheless, Scott pressed on and led his troops to a successful rescue of the gun powder stored in the second magazine. With the powder secured, Scott rejoined his troops and led an attack on the retreating British troops who were now pulling back from their fortified positions on the lake and the river. But just as Scott stood on the brink of the complete destruction and capture of all of the British troops in the region, his commanding officer, Major General Morgan Lewis, ordered him to call off the attack. Reluctantly, Scott complied, and Vincent safely withdrew most of his remaining force, amounting to about 1,600 troops, and began marching them to Burlington at the western edge of Lake Ontario.

Realizing that the Americans had probably used most of their available troops in the region to raid Fort George, the British quickly retaliated by launching an attack the next day on the key American base on Lake Ontario—Sackets Harbor at the eastern end of the lake. Loading Lieutenant General Sir George Prevost and 800 British regulars on to his ships at Kingston, Ontario, Commodore Sir James Yeo sailed east across the lake from his base in Kingston to attack the thinly defended American base.

Commanding what forces were left in the town was the inexperienced but pugnacious Quaker and former school teacher, Jacob Brown, now a Brigadier General in the New York militia and in charge of about 650 regulars and militia. Brown's good fortune, and Yeo's bad luck, was an unexpected calm that settled over the lake just off Sackets Harbor, leaving the British fleet becalmed in the lake in full view of the town's defenders. With the dead wind giving Brown an extra day to fortify his positions and get his men in place, the British compounded their problems by landing their troops in the dark and at the wrong place in the early morning hours of the next day.

Though confusion reigned on both sides, the British assault under Colonel Edward Baynes scattered the militia holding the front line in Brown's defensive scheme. But as Baynes's men advanced into town, they came upon the regulars who held the next line around the fort, and who battered the British assault force into halting their attack. "I don't exaggerate when I tell you that shot, both grape and musket, flew like hail," remembered one British officer.[21] Fearing that the American militia would reorganize and outflank his now stalled smaller force, Baynes gave up the attack and retreated to Yeo's ships. What limited success the British did achieve was purely accidental, and was largely attributable to U.S. Navy Lieutenant Chauncey Wolcott, who set fire to much of the American naval supplies stored at Sackets Harbor when he mistakenly believed that defeat was imminent. All in all, the British incurred 260 casualties while the Americans had about a hundred.[22]

Back at the Niagara River, Dearborn and Lewis realized their mistake in calling off the action against Vincent so early, and attempted to rectify it by sending an army west from Fort George to finish off the retreating British force. But by now Vincent had been resupplied from the lake by Yeo and had reorganized his men as an effective fighting force in a safe position at Beaver Dam.

As the American force approached, and operating now without the benefit of Scott's leadership, Vincent launched a surprise attack and defeated the American force. The timid Dearborn decided to leave well enough alone and withdrew his army, leaving the British still in control of the supply lines to the beleaguered forces in the west. Dearborn's retreat also left intact a British army of sufficient size and skill to continue to harass the American forces trying to gain control over the Niagara region.

Although the British troops were pushed out of the area, their continued presence at Burlington on the western edge of Lake Ontario allowed Procter at Malden to maintain his precarious link to supplies and reinforcements from Upper Canada. Had Vincent's force been defeated and captured, Procter would have been isolated and might have more quickly abandoned his tenuous hold on Detroit, thereby allowing Harrison to recapture American territory without a fight. But it was not to be, and through happenstance and more bad luck, the British and their Indian allies would ultimately be the ones to pay the greater price for Lewis and Dearborn's reluctance to press the attack when Winfield Scott had them on the run.

As the first half of 1813 came to an end, America's ground forces were recovering from their setbacks of late 1812, and beginning to mount a credible offensive strategy. In every case where conflict occurred, the British were pushed back from points of strategic importance, while in every instance where they had attempted to gain it—such as at Fort Meigs or Sackets Harbor—American troops surrendered many lives but no ground, and the British were forced to abandon the effort. Having held the line through spring, the Americans were now prepared to push forward into Canada as summer began to unfold across the still chilly and damp northern border.

In a move that would soon add another talented leader to America's struggling land forces, in October 1812, the federal government ordered the Governor of Tennessee to muster 1,500 troops and march them south to fulfill President Madison's longstanding desire to take Florida from the Spanish. Governor Blount put a Nashville lawyer named Andrew Jackson in charge of the force. Although only 1,500 volunteers were sought, 2,100 showed up, and Jackson divided the men between his newly appointed officer corps of Thomas Hart Benton, William Hall, and John Coffee. In early January 1813 they marched to Natchez, Mississippi, where they awaited orders to proceed to New Orleans from where they would raid the territory of Florida. But in February

1813, Madison's new secretary of war, John Armstrong, instead ordered Jackson's army and command dissolved. The fiery Jackson flew into a rage, but there was little he could do. Congress had refused to approve Madison's plan for Florida, so neither Jackson nor his army was needed.[23] Jackson was ordered to disband his army where they were when the command was received—in Natchez, Mississippi—and each soldier was expected to get back to Tennessee on his own and at his expense. But Jackson ignored the order, and instead led his men back to Nashville in the same orderly formation that brought them to Natchez. "From the march back and for his unswerving determination to take care of his men, Jackson earned the nickname of *Old Hickory*."[24]

CHAPTER NINE

INTO THE PACIFIC

As Bainbridge turned north for home in early January 1813, David Porter and the *Essex* were still cruising off the coast of Brazil trying to find the American squadron. Their attempts to find Bainbridge at the pre-arranged meeting places and message drops had come to naught. The first rendezvous point, at Porto Praya in the Cape Verde Islands off West Africa, yielded no information on Bainbridge's whereabouts, but the *Essex* was able to stock up on citrus fruits to prevent an outbreak of scurvy among the crew. In addition to food, Porter records in his journal, "many of the seamen also furnished themselves with monkeys and young goats, as pets; and when we sailed from thence the ship bore no slight resemblance, as respected the different animals on board her, to Noah's Ark."[1]

The *Essex* crossed the equator on 23 November 1812 en route to the next rendezvous point off Brazil. The seamen making their first crossing were subjected to a humiliating ritual still practiced today by the crews of the world's navies. Midshipman William W. Feltus recorded that a small boat appeared on the lee bow bearing Neptune and his train and requesting permission to come aboard. According to Feltus,

> [A]s soon as it was granted one of the B mates with some others being in the fore chains, came over the Bows and mounted their carriage (made of some boards lashed together on an old gun carriage having two chairs lashed there on for Neptune & his wife) this carriage was drawn by 4 men some with their shirts off & their Bodies painted & others with their trowsers cut above their knee & their legs painted & their faces painted in this manner accompanied by his Barbers with their razors made of an iron hoop & constables & Band of music they marched on the quarter deck where he dismounted with his wife and spoke to the Captain for permission to shave such as had not crossed the line before[,] officers excepted....[2]

With a large fraction of the crew now bald, *Essex* resumed its southerly course to the Portuguese penal island of Fernando de Noronha. There Porter found a coded message from Bainbridge, written in lemon juice, instructing him to look for the *Constitution* off Cape Frio near Rio de Janeiro, almost at the Tropic of Capricorn. Porter set a course for the cape, but Bainbridge was now farther north off São Salvador and busy with the British. When Bainbridge failed to appear, Porter set the *Essex* on a course to the last planned meeting place: the Brazilian island of St. Catherine, five hundred miles south of Rio.[3]

Porter arrived on 19 January and cruised the nearby waters for a few days. Finding no sign of the *Constitution*, he continued south. A week later he fell in with a Portuguese merchant ship that told him a great battle had occurred weeks earlier in which an American ship had sunk a British one. Presuming that *Constitution* was the American ship in question, Porter reckoned that even if she were victorious she might have to return home for repairs, resupply, and prisoner disposition. Alone in the South Atlantic, Porter decided to exercise the option afforded him by Secretary of the Navy Hamilton to "lurk off St. Helena to harry British traffic to and from the Cape of Good Hope, or [to] round Cape Horn, to burst into the Pacific on a commerce destroying mission there."[4]

Porter was only the second American captain to take a United States warship into another ocean (Edward Preble was the first, also in the *Essex*), where he spent the next thirteen months harassing the British whaling fleet, seizing their valuable cargos of oil and ambergris, and engaging in an exotic tropical shore leave that would become a staple of U.S. naval recruiting for years to come.

II

Born in Boston 1780 and commissioned a midshipman in 1798, Porter shared with Stephen Decatur an illustrious naval lineage. Like Decatur, Porter was the son of a Revolutionary War naval captain and had spent much of his youth at sea or in the company of sailors and officers. And also like Decatur, he possessed the fierce and sometimes reckless courage often seen among British and American naval officers in the early nineteenth century. Porter, however, lacked Decatur's reasoned judgment to temper his ferocity, and he was not blessed with Decatur's good luck, so he sometimes landed in the kind of trouble that Decatur usually managed to avoid.

Porter seems to have harbored a bitter dislike for the British, an antipathy perhaps fueled by stories of his father, who was held captive during the War of Independence aboard the British prison ship *Jersey* with Porter's uncle (who did not survive). "Is it any wonder, then, that he swore Punic hatred against the British," observed an earlier U.S. naval historian, "and that years afterwards he carried at the masthead of the *Essex* the motto, 'Free Trade and Sailors' Rights,' as he swept British commerce from the Pacific."[5]

Porter's first service was aboard the *Constellation*, 38, commanded by the Revolutionary War hero Captain Thomas Truxtun. The ship's first lieutenant, to whom Porter reported, was John Rodgers, who later became the navy's senior officer during the War of 1812. Ten months later, *Constellation* captured the French frigate *L'Insurgente*, which three months earlier, with *Volontaire*, had captured Bainbridge and the *Retaliation*. Porter displayed characteristic courage when he cut down a damaged yard that threatened to bring down one of *Constellation*'s masts. A day later, as part of the crew sailing the captured *L'Insurgente*—and outnumbered 13 to 173 by their French captives[6]—Porter helped suppress an uprising by the French sailors when a storm separated them from *Constellation*.

Nine months later, as a lieutenant on the schooner *Experiment*, Porter revealed a cavalier attitude toward rules and orders while escorting U.S. merchant vessels through the pirate-infested Caribbean. Their convoy was attacked off the coast of Haiti by ten barges, each manned by about forty pirates. When Porter's superior, Lieutenant Commander Maley, announced that he would surrender in the face of such overwhelming odds, Porter, in an act bordering on mutiny, seized command of the *Experiment* and prepared her for combat. In a battle lasting seven hours, Porter fought off the pirates and managed to save two of the four merchant ships.[7] Lieutenant Charles Stewart soon took over Maley's command, and he and Porter began a notable series of Caribbean cruises ravaging French privateers and Haitian pirates.

America's concern about pirates soon shifted to the other side of the world when on 2 June 1801 a U.S. naval fleet sailed from Hampton Roads for the Mediterranean Sea to protect American merchant vessels and sailors from the worsening depredations of the Barbary pirates operating out of several ports on the North African coast. Porter was aboard the twelve-gun schooner *Enterprise* under Lieutenant Andrew Sterret, which took the pirate warship *Tripoli* off the coast of Malta in the first sea action of the war. In a three-hour battle between evenly matched ships at point-blank range, the defeated Algerine suffered thirty killed or wounded, while no American received so much as a scratch. The pirates' treachery—three times the Algerine commander Reis Mahomet Sous pretended to surrender the *Tripoli*, only to resume combat when the *Enterprise* came close enough to board—provoked their American opponents to inflict on them a particularly savage beating. In response to this first victory of the war, the Washington *Daily National Intelligencer* giddily observed, "We are lost in surprise."[8]

Returning to Baltimore for a brief respite from duty at sea, Porter's temper nearly got him killed in a bar fight. When Porter searched the harbor-side saloons for deserters, an angry bar keeper knocked him to the floor and kicked him several times before Porter drew his sword and ran it through his assailant. Barely escaping a lynch mob of the dead man's angry friends and patrons, Porter was later exonerated on grounds of self-defense.

Back on the Mediterranean, Porter was assigned to the frigate *Philadelphia*, now under the command of Captain William Bainbridge and taking part in the blockade of Tripoli. After the *Philadelphia* became stuck on a sandbar in the harbor and Bainbridge surrendered to the pirates, Porter and his crewmates endured nineteen months of captivity. With books and materials provide by the Danish consul, Porter kept himself busy teaching the imprisoned midshipmen sailing, navigation, and gunnery. When he was not teaching the young officers, Porter studied mathematics, French, and history, and consoled the disconsolate Bainbridge, who wondered whether this, his second loss of a ship, spelled the end of his naval career.[9]

Porter was finally released in June 1805, shortly after a small band of U.S. Marines, in a daring act now commemorated in their Corps' hymn, led a band of Greek and Egyptian mercenaries across the desert from Alexandria and threatened Derna, a city near Tripoli. Besieged on land and by sea, the dey was compelled to ransom the Americans for the equivalent of two hundred dollars a head and sign a peace treaty with the United States. After his release, Porter was promoted to master commandant and put in command of his old ship *Enterprise*. On Commodore John Rodgers's orders, Porter cruised the Mediterranean for two years, an assignment intended to help the young officer recover from his long captivity.

Porter soon recovered his health and his fiery temper. On the streets of Valetta, the capital of British-controlled Malta, at a time when tensions between the U.S. and Britain were growing because of British impressments of American seamen, Porter received what he claimed was an insult from a British sailor. Not one to leave well enough alone, Porter had the sailor dragged on board the *Enterprise* and flogged. The British responded by threatening to fire upon the *Enterprise* if he attempted to leave port before the issue was settled by Malta's governor. Porter left anyway, and in the process established the important precedent that a U.S. warship would not submit to local authority while in a foreign port.[10]

Released from European duty in 1807 and on leave in America, the feisty Porter, now a dashing twenty-seven-year-old naval officer, headed for New York City, where he fell in with the Lads of Kilkenny, a "loosely knit pack of literary-minded young blades out for a good time."[11] The Lads were led by Washington Irving, who called Porter "Sinbad" for his exploits in the Mediterranean.[12] Porter likely spent several months "haunting the Park Theater, Dyde's London Hotel (which stood next to the theater and advertised hospitality in the 'true Old English Style'), and Thomas Hodgkinson's Shakespeare Tavern ... at the corner of Nassau and Fulton Streets."[13]

After two months as a "minor social lion in Manhattan," Porter was called back to duty and headed south to Norfolk. A little later he courted and married the fifteen-year-old Evalina Anderson, daughter of the Pennsylvania innkeeper and congressman William Anderson, though not before having a nasty row with her brother, who described Porter as "piratical." After service in Norfolk, Porter was ordered to New Orleans to assume command of the U.S. naval station recently established there to protect American shipping in the Gulf. Under control of the United States for only four years—Jefferson had acquired the city in 1803 as part of the Louisiana Purchase—New Orleans had become an unruly city of French and Spanish adventurers, freed slaves, and scheming American dissidents, constantly threatened by, and accommodative to, pirates and privateers, for whom the city had been home base during the Quasi-War with France less than a decade earlier.

Porter took his new wife and joined his elderly father, who had been stationed in New Orleans a few months earlier as the city's sailing master. Since arriving, the ailing David Porter senior had become friends with George Farragut, New Orleans' previous sailing master and a former major in the American cavalry. George lived with his wife and five children outside the city on the shore of Lake Pontchartrain, and George and the elder Porter often went fishing together on the lake. On one of these trips Porter fell ill and was taken to Farragut's nearby home for care. George's wife, Elizabeth, nursed the old man as best she could, but in a few days he died, followed shortly by Elizabeth herself, who succumbed to yellow fever.[14]

Wanting to show gratitude for the kindness and sacrifice made by George Farragut—now the widowed father of five—the younger Porter offered to ease the family's burden by adopting George's nine-year-old son, David Glasgow Farragut, and raise him as an officer and a gentleman. George Farragut consented, and young David left with Porter to begin a new life. True to his promise, Porter had David Farragut appointed to a midshipman's berth in December 1810. Farragut was nine and a half at the time, and would go on to serve in that capacity under Porter aboard the *Essex* during the coming war with Britain. A half-century later, David Glasgow Farragut became the first American naval officer promoted to the rank of admiral. David Dixon Porter, Porter's own son, became the second.

After two years of miserable and frustrating duty in New Orleans, with a hot, humid climate that Porter believed was undermining his health, the young officer submitted his resignation to Secretary of the Navy Hamilton in July

1810. But Hamilton refused to accept it. With America and Britain drifting toward war, the secretary knew he would need every experienced officer for the country's ships, and sent back to Porter a complimentary letter urging him to stay on. Porter consented, and in return for his remaining in the navy, Hamilton transferred him to more agreeable duty on the east coast. Porter was soon given command of the thirty-two-gun frigate *Essex*.

Smaller than the super frigate *Constitution* and her two sister ships, the *Essex* was close in size and armament to the British frigates *Macedonian* and *Java*. Built in 1799 in Salem, Massachusetts, *Essex* was one of ten "subscription" warships, whose construction was financed by contributions from the citizens of the participating communities and which were given to the navy for service during the Quasi-War with France.[15] Designed by William Hackett, famed for several ships he built during the Revolutionary War, the *Essex*, when armed, as Hackett intended, with twenty-six long guns on her main deck and sixteen carronades above, was one of the finest ships in the navy.

By the time Porter took command, the *Essex*'s armament had been reconfigured by a previous captain in ways that seriously undermined her ability to sail and fight effectively. In 1810, most of the heavier long guns on the main deck were replaced by lighter carronades at the order of John Smith, her commander at the time. Smith was of the older, Nelsonian school of naval warfare, advocating that ships close quickly and batter it out toe-to-toe as armed boarders swarmed onto the enemy's deck with pikes and cutlasses, in the style of Trafalgar. By 1811, this doctrine was falling out of favor in the U.S. Navy because its powerful and more nimble frigates encouraged tactics and maneuver over the traditional naval slug fest. Indeed, Smith's notions were becoming the minority view worldwide, and only one other frigate, Britain's *Glatton*, was armed only with carronades, according to "the specification of her carronade-crazy captain, Henry Trollope."[16]

While boasting lethal firepower up close, a carronade-dependent ship like the *Essex* or *Glatton* was helpless at a distance and could find herself at a fatal disadvantage against a clever opponent who stood just outside the carronade's short range and pummeled her from a safe distance with well-aimed long guns. Porter had no use for such a strategy, and once in command of *Essex* he requested in a letter to Hamilton that the ship's original armament be restored, noting:

> Considering as I do that Carronades are merely an experiment in modern warfare and that their character is by no means established I do not conceive it proper to entrust the honor of the flag entirely to them.... Long guns are well known to be effective and management of them familiar to seamen. I have therefore required ... four long eighteen pounders to mount on gundeck and shall on receipt of them send on shore some defective Carronades. I hope, Sir, reasons I have given will in your opinion justify change.[17]

Hamilton, unmoved, responded, "It is not adjudged advisable to change armament of the *Essex*. If any carronades are defective, they are to be replaced by good ones, and not changed by long guns." His reasons for rejecting Porter's request may have had more to do with a national shortage of such long guns rather than any affection for carronades. The limited industrial capacity of America in 1810 could produce only a small number of naval guns of sufficient quality, and many U.S. ships of that time, such as the *Constitution*, were equipped with guns imported earlier from England or France.

The other serious problem with Smith's change to carronades was its effect on *Essex*'s sailing ability. Hackett's design presumed a gun deck carrying the much heavier long guns near the water line, and the lighter carronades above on the spar deck. Because the guns are so much heavier than anything else aboard the ship—long guns weighed as much as two to three tons, while carronades of equal throw weight were less than half that—their placement on board had a profound influence on the ship's balance and sailing capability. Replacing the heavier guns with lighter ones disturbed Hackett's careful balance of weight, length, beam, and height.

Despite these problems, Porter was intent on making the best of what he had, and he spent much of the next year rigorously training his crew for the war most expected to break out soon. As David Farragut would later remember from his service on the *Essex*,

> Every day the crew were exercised at the great guns, small arms and single stick. And I may here mention the fact that I have never been on a ship where the crew of the old *Essex* was represented that I have not found them to be the best swordsmen on board. They had

> been so thoroughly trained as boarders that every man was prepared for such emergency, with his cutlass as sharp as a razor, a dirk made by the ship's armorer out of a file, and a pistol.[18]

On 13 June 1812, with war looming, Hamilton ordered Porter to get *Essex* ready for extended sea duty, so Porter took *Essex* into the Brooklyn navy yard for a quick overhaul and a new foremast. War was declared on 18 June, and the *Essex* was afloat again in New York Harbor shortly before the 26th. An incident aboard the ship that day tells us something about Porter's reckless temper, but the reaction to it of ordinary Americans and of Washington officials tells us even more about their uncommon appreciation for the rights of an individual, even if he was a prospective enemy.

That morning, Porter mustered the crew at quarters to administer an oath of allegiance to the United States. One crewman, a sail maker named John Erving who carried papers, probably false, claiming he was born in Massachusetts, declined on the grounds that he was an Englishman, and asked to be dismissed from the crew. While these false papers may have saved him from impressment during peacetime, Erving had a legitimate concern that if captured in battle, he would likely be hanged by the British as a traitor. Erving was not alone in making such a request during the weeks leading up to open warfare, and many other U.S. commanders, notably Isaac Hull, allowed their British crewmen to leave or to serve on shore. But not Porter.

According to Porter's letter to Secretary Hamilton, "The crew requested me to permit them to tar & feather him, and turn him out of the ship with appropriate labels on him. I consented."[19] After Erving was tarred and feathered, the crew rowed him to the shore of Manhattan Island and left him there. The police report describes what followed:

> [D]eponent went from Street to Street naked from the waist up, smeare'd with Tar & feathers not knowing where to go, when a man (Benjamin Ford) told him to go into his shop from the mob, or crow'd of people then around him, that he staid in said Shop until the Police Magistrate took him from thence and put him in the City Prison for protection, where he has been cleansed and got a Shirt & Trowsers. The deponent further swears that none of the

> citizens or inhabitants of the City of New York done him any manner of injury, or insulted him, but that he has been assisted and protected by the civil authority thereof.[20]

The next day, a city official, Charles Christian, sent a letter to Porter stating that Erving "is in care of the Police of this City who have given him a Shirt & Trowsers. If you judge proper to give his chest and clothes to the bearer, Mr. Raynor, Police Officer, he will receive them. Erving says the Armourer of the *Essex* can inform you where his clothes is placed."[21]

Porter was unmoved by Erving's plight, and replied to Christian, "John Erving is an American Citizen, I herewith enclose a copy of his protection. His clothes cannot be delivered until I am furnished by the Purser with a statement of his accounts, should he not be indebted to the United States they shall be delivered to your order."[22] Meanwhile in Washington, Hamilton receved Porter's letter about two weeks later, the 30th, describing the tarring and feathering. He was not amused or sympathetic with Porter's dilemma:

> It is much to be regretted that you gave sanction to the proceedings on the part of your crew in the case of John Irving [*sic*].... Mobs will in Spite of all Law, sometimes Act licentiously, but Mobs should never be suffered to exist on board a Man of War.... Tyrany [*sic*] in whatever Shape it may appear, ought to be resisted by all men. I do exceedingly regret, that an officer of your rank & intelligence should have permitted the proceedings in question.[23]

The *New York Post* expressed the same views on 27 June:

> The story shall be closed by asking the reader a simple question; suppose the captain of an English frigate should suffer his men to tar and feather an American sailor in the port of London, because he would not join in a cruise to fight against his own country; what would you think of such an action?[24]

Less measured in his response was Captain Sir James Lucas Yeo of the British frigate *Southampton*, who sent his message to Porter by way of a letter published in a Philadelphia newspaper:

> Captain Sir James Yeo ... would be glad to have a tete a tete anywhere between the Capes of Delaware and Havana, where he would have the pleasure to break his own sword over his [Porter's] damned head, and put him down forward in irons.[25]

Porter, of course, accepted the challenge, and in his reply seems to show an inkling of remorse. Porter concluded his acceptance of Yeo's challenge with instructions for how to recognize him on the high seas:

> The *Essex* may be known by a flag bearing the motto "Free Trade and Sailors Rights;" and when it is struck to the *Southampton* Capt. P. will deserve the treatment promised by Sir James.[26]

They never met, but three days after Hamilton wrote his chilly reprimand, the *Essex* left New York Harbor and sailed off to attain the distinction of drawing first blood at the beginning of half a year of naval combat that would leave the Royal Navy deeply embarrassed by a string of ship-to-ship defeats. Repeating his success from the Barbary War, Porter captured the first British ship of the War of 1812 on 13 August.

Eight days out of New York, Porter found a convoy of seven British ships off Bermuda. Porter attacked at night, capturing the troopship *Samuel and Sarah*, transporting 197 British soldiers from Barbados to Canada, without the escorting frigate *Minerva*'s realizing what had happened. With no space to imprison the captives, Porter let them go "under parole," but not before taking fourteen thousand dollars from the captain's strong box.[27] Although the British soldiers were allowed to continue on to Halifax, they were still considered Porter's prisoners and were honor-bound not to fight again until they were later "exchanged" for American prisoners of war.

Over the next two weeks, the *Essex* took another six British prizes in the waters north of Bermuda before stumbling upon the sixteen-gun sloop of war *Alert* on 13 August 1812. Taking care not to frighten away the smaller ship, Porter rigged the *Essex* to look like a lumbering merchantman. Gun ports were kept closed, a drag was let out to slow the ship, and men were sent aloft to shake out the reefs and make sail as if she were trying to escape. The rest of Porter's crew cleared for action and waited patiently as the sloop closed to take the bait. As the *Alert* neared and fired a warning shot, *Essex* hove to and then fired a broadside of grape and canister. The distance was too great for the carronades and little harm was done, but Porter put up his helm and opened another broadside as soon as the guns could bear. *Alert*, realizing the trap, tried to flee, but the *Essex* was soon alongside her, and the sloop struck her colors. The battle lasted eight minutes, and three British sailors were wounded.

Again invoking the code of honor for prisoners, Porter allowed Captain Thomas Laugharne to take the *Alert* to St. Johns, New Brunswick, "in cartel." There he disembarked most of his crew and, with the few men who remained, sailed to New York, where he surrendered his ship to U.S. authorities.[28] *Alert* was condemned and sold for $13,416, and the proceeds were distributed to Porter and his crew; Commodore Rodgers also received a share of all prizes captured by a ship in his fleet. Porter's prize money for the two-month cruise was $1,570, equal to about a year's pay.[29] Still holding a number of prisoners from some of the nine ships he had captured, Porter headed back to port, but during the voyage some of the prisoners attempted to escape and seize the ship. Twelve-year-old Midshipman Farragut discovered the plot, fortunately, and alerted Porter in time to squelch it.

The success of this first cruise and of a subsequent cruise off the coast of Brazil gave Porter more British prizes in 1812—eleven—than any other American. *Constitution*, with nine, ranked second that year.[30] Although he later exaggerated the losses he inflicted on the British merchant fleet, Porter nonetheless struck a pose of some modesty in regard to his swift defeat of the *Alert*. In his letter to Secretary Hamilton he wrote, "I have the honor to inform you that on the 13th his Britannic Majesty's Sloop of War *Alert*, Captain T. L. P. Laugharne, ran down on our weather quarter, gave three cheers, and commenced an action (if so trifling a skirmish deserves a name) and after eight minutes firing struck her colors."[31]

III

Back at sea in January 1813, unable to find Bainbridge and the *Constitution*, and running low on food, Porter decided it was time to accept Secretary Hamilton's option and round Cape Horn for the Pacific, where he intended to resupply *Essex* at the first available South American port. Porter arrived at the Cape on 13 February 1813 and opted for the safer but longer open-ocean crossing rather than the dangerous inside passage through the Strait of Magellan.

Nonetheless, fierce head winds thwarted *Essex*'s progress, and huge rolling breakers battered in the gun ports and flooded the ship. Many crewmen feared they would die, several suffered frostbite, and some dropped to their knees in prayer. At one point a dazed and exhausted Porter had to be carried to his cabin to recover his wits. *Essex* finally made it round the Horn about 4 March, the first time an American warship had entered the Pacific by way of the Cape. Ten days later Porter sailed *Essex* into the harbor of Valparaiso, Chile, where she remained almost two weeks for repairs, resupply, and some rest and recreation for the crew before heading out to sea to raid the British whaling fleet.

In early 1813, Chile was a breakaway Spanish colony fighting for its independence. Although nominally neutral in the conflict between America and Britain and nominally in control of Chile, Spain leaned toward the British in their war against France and Napoleon and therefore leaned against America. Complicating relations between Britain and Spain (and its colony of Chile) was a growing revolutionary movement among Spain's colonies. Chile was by now in open revolt, but its independence was still tenuous, so the Chileans warmly received the American crew and officers. Reenforcing the pro-American feelings were emissaries from the United States, who were encouraging the revolt in order to rid the new world of the corrupting influence of European monarchies. The U.S. envoy to Chile, Joel R. Poinsett (now primarily remembered for introducing to his home country the familiar bright red tropical Christmas flower from Mexico), had openly sided with the revolutionaries, and he helped Porter weave his way through the political thicket to get *Essex* safely re-provisioned in what was technically a neutral port.

Reflecting Spanish concern over this unprecedented visit by a warship from the United States—an enemy of Spain's friend—two Spanish ships slipped out of Valparaiso shortly after Porter arrived and set a course due north to Lima, Peru, the base from which Spain attempted to rule her South American colonies. They warned the Viceroy of the unexpected presence of the American warship in what had been British-controlled waters. Taking note of the Spanish ships' departure, Porter observed: "It seemed beyond a doubt that they would conjecture my designs were not confined to doubling Cape Horn merely for the pleasure of visiting Valparaiso."[32]

During *Essex*'s brief stay in Valparaiso, her crew presumably explored the port's seamier quarters in search of diversion and relief, while her officers were fêted by the governor with a ball. Porter enjoyed himself but was unimpressed with the style of dancing and had mixed views on the female component of Chilean high society. The local dance, he observed,

> consisted of the most graceless and at the same time fatiguing movements of the body and limbs, accompanied by the most lascivious motions, gradually increasing in energy and violence until the fair one, apparently overcome with passion and exhausted with fatigue, was compelled to retire to her seat.... They [the women] disfigure themselves most lavishly with paint, but their features are agreeable, and their large dark eyes are remarkably brilliant and expressive. Were it not for their bad teeth ... they would be thought handsome.[33]

Porter left Valparaiso on 23 March, setting a course north-northwest to the Galapagos Islands, five hundred miles away, which once served as a hideaway for the pirates and privateers who preyed on the Spanish coastal and Pacific trade. In the early nineteenth century it served as a base for many of the whalers—both British and American—working the Pacific.

On the second day out, *Essex* came upon an American whaler, the *Charles*, whose captain warned him of the presence of a Peruvian privateer, the *Nereyda*, that had recently attacked him; the privateer had also captured two other American whalers, *Walker* and the *Barclay*. Porter found *Nereyda* the next day. Flying British colors to misrepresent his origin and purpose, *Essex* approached the Peruvian ship in the pose of a friend and ally. The deception worked, and a lieutenant from *Nereyda* was rowed over to the *Essex* to inform the British ship that the Peruvians had captured several American whalers, which they had sent on to Lima with prize crews, and had imprisoned the American crews in their hold.

Porter, who the Peruvians still thought was a British officer, asked if he could question the two American captains. The lieutenant complied and had them rowed over to the *Essex*, where Porter discretely informed the captives of the real situation. He then conveyed the same message to the *Nereyda* by hoisting the American colors, running out the guns, and firing a couple warning shots over the Peruvian's deck. The *Nereyda* quickly surrendered, and once the American captives were safely aboard the *Essex*, Porter had all of the *Nereyda*'s guns and arms thrown overboard and sent her back to Callao (Lima's port) with a note to the Viceroy labeling the *Nereyda*'s attack on American whalers "piratical."

Pleased with the success of his deception but not sure that British whalers would so easily mistake a falsely flagged American ship for one of their own, Porter had the *Essex* painted to look like a Spanish vessel. The ruse appears to have worked better than he expected, because a few days later he came across the captured *Barclay* headed in to port with her Spanish prize crew and a hold full of valuable whale oil. Because *Barclay*'s American captain did not want to risk recapture in the increasingly hostile waters, he elected to stay with the *Essex*, and from then on the *Barclay* would serve as a scout for *Essex* as the two ships searched the Pacific for British prizes.

Porter captured his first British ship, the whaler *Montezuma*, by posing as a Spanish ship and inviting *Montezuma*'s captain aboard for a meeting. Porter informed him of his captive status, and the ship was quickly surrendered. Two more British whalers, the *Georgiana* and the *Policy*, were captured in a similar fashion, and Porter had the guns taken from the whalers mounted on the larger *Georgiana*, which joined his growing squadron as an auxiliary warship. Lieutenant Downes was given command of *Georgiana* with forty-one sailors from the *Essex* and a half-dozen American crewmen from the British whalers. She was commissioned as an American ship and sailed off on her own to attack the British. Over the next five months, Porter and his fleet captured another nine British whalers off the Galapagos, putting a considerable dent in British commercial interests.

When word of Porter's exploits in the Pacific spread to the United States, his old drinking companion Washington Irving wrote,

> It occasioned great uneasiness in Great Britain. The merchants who had any property afloat in this quarter trembled with apprehension for its fate; the underwriters groaned at the catalog of captures, while the pride of the nation was sorely incensed at beholding a single frigate lording it over the Pacific, in saucy defiance of their thousand ships.[34]

A newspaper in British Canada offered a similar assessment of the damage, dourly noting that the *Essex* "had annihilated our commerce in the South Seas" and had harmed the Empire more "than all the rest of the American Navy."[35] There was also anger in Britain, and one member of Parliament, noting the shortage of whale oil for English lamps, observed that London "burnt dark for a year."[36]

Britain's worries in the Pacific were not limited to the whaling waters off South America. In what are now Washington and Oregon, American fur trappers and traders—notably those working for New York City's John Jacob Astor, America's first "millionaire"[37]—were also a threat to the British and their claims to that rich territory. The border between the United States and British Canada in the Pacific Northwest, disputed throughout the first half of the nineteenth century, was not settled until 1846, when the British agreed to a border along the forty-ninth parallel (three weeks, perhaps not coincidentally, after a resounding U.S. victory over Mexico in a similar dispute). Even so, friction between the two powers in the border region persisted until the Civil War.

The merchant ship *Columbia* claimed the Oregon territory for the United States in 1790 when she sailed up the river that would subsequently bear her name, although Spain and Britain had competing claims to the same territory (Captain George Vancouver of Britain had explored the area in 1792). A new threat to British interests appeared in 1811 when John Jacob Astor built Fort Astoria at the mouth of the Columbia River, not far from where Lewis and Clark had built Fort Clatsop as their winter quarters in 1805. He intended to use the fort as a base for his trapping operations and for processing furs for the lucrative trade with China, where North American furs were exchanged for silk, tea, and fine porcelain.

In response to the threat of commercial encroachment, the British mounted an armed naval expedition to the region to enforce their claim. In March 1813, at about the time Porter was dancing his way through Valparaiso, the British government dispatched the fur trading vessel *Isaac Todd* and the thirty-six-gun frigate *Phoebe,* under Captain James Hillyar, to sail around Cape Horn to the mouth of the Columbia River. Hillyar's orders were to destroy Fort Astoria and install a British operation in its place.

Like Porter, Hillyar was from a naval family and had been taken to sea as a young child by his father, a surgeon in the Royal Navy. In 1800, at the age of thirty-one, Hillyar was given command of the frigate *Niger* and served under Nelson, whose support and intervention led to Hillyar's promotion to post captain a few years later. In 1809 Hillyar was given command of the *Phoebe,* which since its launch in 1795 had served the Royal Navy with distinction and earned a series of victories against the French.[38] While under the earlier command of another Nelson favorite, Captain Thomas Bladen Capel, *Phoebe* was present at Trafalgar, where frigates served as scouts and messengers.[39]

In May 1813, on his way to Oregon, Hillyar stopped at Rio de Janeiro. There his squadron was expanded, and his orders were somewhat modified by Rear Admiral Sir Manley Dixon, commander of Britain's South American Station. Dixon revised Hillyar's orders in response to the reports he had received overland from Peru and Chile about the *Essex*'s activity in the Pacific, including the capture of three British whalers in April alone. Although Hillyar's original orders to sail to Oregon were unchanged, he was now to look out for the *Essex* while on the way, and to sink or capture her as the opportunity arose. The twenty-six-gun *Raccoon* and the eighteen-gun *Cherub* were added to Hillyar's squadron because of the growing British reluctance to engage American frigates in single-ship combat.[40] After leaving Rio, the squadron stopped briefly in Buenos Aires to top off its water casks and add supplies before the treacherous passage around Cape Horn. As the squadron headed south, messengers on horseback rode west across the pampas from Buenos Aires to Valparaiso to warn of the British approach.[41]

Porter meanwhile continued his plunder of the British whaling fleet, not yet aware that the enemy had sent armed vessels in pursuit of his makeshift squadron. In May the *Essex* took two more British whalers—the *Greenwich* and the *Atlantic*—and Porter found himself overwhelmed by the burden of the many British captives he had to feed and confine. He also had to accommodate the headstrong whaling captains in a style befitting their rank aboard the increasingly crowded *Essex*. In his journal, Porter recorded an incident involving two of these uncooperative captains. His discretion leaves us ignorant of the remedy he applied, but it appears to have been successful:

> They gave full vent to their anger ... and lavished on me, in particular, the most scurrilous epithets, giving me appellations that would have suited a buccaneer.... I determined next day to make them sensible of the impropriety of their conduct and did so without violating the principles of humanity or the rules of war. I let them feel that they were dependent entirely on my generosity [and they] were now so humbled by a sense of their own conduct that

> they would have licked the dust from my feet had it been required of them to do so.[42]

With more captives and prize ships than he could handle at sea, and running short of supplies, Porter sailed east from the Galapagos to Peru and docked at the small provincial port of Tumbes, near the border with Ecuador. There, on the fringe of the Spanish Empire, he was less likely to attract the notice of the more powerful authorities at Lima's port Callao, farther down the coast. Arriving on 19 June, Porter and his fleet of six ships, now probably one the largest to sail the Pacific in many years, were entertained by the governor of the region. Less than a week later, on the 24th, Porter's fleet grew to ten ships when Downes, sailing the converted whaler *Georgiana*, pulled into Tumbes with his three prizes: *Hector*, *Rose*, and *Catherine*.

Porter now faced a severe shortage of American naval officers to command the prizes. To make matters worse, Lieutenant Wilson's excessive drinking rendered him unfit for duty, and Lieutenant Cowan was killed in a duel on the beaches of the Galapagos. Even before meeting up with Downes and his prizes, Porter was so short-handed that he had to put his chaplain, David Adams, in command of *Atlantic*, and Marine Lieutenant John Gamble in charge of the *Greenwich*, accompanied by two of the *Essex*'s best seamen to compensate for Gamble's lack of sailing experience. Weeks later, when Downes, in command of the *Atlantic* (renamed the *Essex Junior*), set sail for Valparaiso with four of the prizes in the hope of selling them, Porter sent the drunken Wilson back to the U.S. in the *Georgiana*, which now carried one hundred thousand dollars' worth of captured spermaceti.[43]

Sailing with the *Essex Junior* was the recaptured American whaler *Barclay*. Reflecting the severe shortage of officers, the *Barclay* was under the nominal command of thirteen-year-old Midshipman David Farragut, reluctantly assisted by its former American captain, and several American sailors. At one point on the voyage south, the former captain, threatening to seize the ship and sail off to New Zealand, went below to get his pistols. Aided by loyal members of his prize crew, young Farragut is said to have "shouted in his boyish voice down the cabin ladder to the whaler that he was under arrest and that, if he came on the deck with his pistols, he would have the seamen throw him overboard."[44] The threat worked, and the *Barclay* made it to Valparaiso under Farragut's command.

As Downes led his fleet of prizes south to Valparaiso, Porter headed west back to the Galapagos, where in late July he captured the British whalers *Charlton*, *New Zealander*, and *Seringapatam*, the last of which resisted but surrendered when Marine Lieutenant Gamble fired a few broadsides from the *Greenwich*. In September, the *Essex* captured its last prize of the voyage, the *Sir Andrew Hammond*. Downes, meanwhile, had reached Valparaiso, but after two weeks in port he failed to sell any of his prizes, largely because the Chileans, whose financial resources were absorbed by the revolt against Spain, had no money to buy either the ships or the whale oil. While there, however, Downes received word from the messengers riding in from Buenos Aires that Hillyar's squadron of four ships had stopped at the Argentine capital and were now on their way to Cape Horn and the Pacific in pursuit of the *Essex*.[45]

Downes left immediately on a course north to warn Porter, whom he found on 30 September still cruising off the Galapagos. Downes also carried news of the American victories over the *Macedonian*, *Java*, and *Frolic*. Having been at sea for nearly a year, his crew weary and his ships in need of repair, resupply, and the extermination of the vermin thriving within the crowded decks and hold, Porter viewed the impending British threat as an occasion to find a safe harbor to recover and prepare. His choice of haven was the Marquesas, a string of ten little islands in the middle of the Pacific, 2,500 miles due west and a little south of the Galapagos. From there the Americans could at their leisure prepare for the coming battle with Hillyar, the outcome of which would add his name, Porter expected, to the list of frigate-killing American captains.

As Porter sailed west to the Marquesas, Hillyar's *Phoebe* entered the Pacific with *Raccoon* and *Cherub*—the *Isaac Todd* and her crew had been lost to the violent seas around the Horn. Once in contact with Spanish authorities, Hillyar discovered that Porter's depredations against the British whaling fleet had been far more severe than his superiors in Buenos Aires had realized. In response, Hillyar took the liberty of interpreting his orders to focus more closely on the *Essex* and ordered *Raccoon* to sail on alone to handle the problem with the American fur traders on the Columbia River. As *Phoebe* and *Cherub* cruised off the coast of South America in search of the *Essex*, the *Raccoon* continued north along the west coast of the Americas. On 30 November 1813, the British ship entered the mouth of the Columbia River only to discover that a month earlier—in response to rumors of the approaching British squadron—Astor's fur traders had called it quits and, in an act that denied *Raccoon*'s crew any prize money, sold their operation at Fort Astoria to members of the British-owned North West Company which, incidentally, had been their employer before they went to work for Astor.[46]

Porter 's squadron of five prizes, including *Essex Junior*, along with numerous English prisoners, arrived at the Marquesas in late October. The crews quickly set to work building a settlement on the island of Nuku Hiva that Porter named Madisonville, after the American president. Madisonville included huts for dwelling, a bakery, a sail loft, a sick house, and a cooper's shop. Porter's crew also constructed a defensive work called "Fort Madison."[47] Communication with natives in the immediate surroundings—one of the thirty-one tribes inhabiting the little island—was helped along by an Englishman named Wilson, a man "with a strong attachment to rum,"[48] who had been living among the islanders for several years and spoke their language. Once the settlement and fortification were complete, the crew and officers began the process of cleaning and repairing the *Essex* and the other ships as needed.

One of the first tasks was to rid the ships of the large and aggressive rat population that had been gnawing its way into the food supplies, the spare sails, and even into the cartridges loaded with gun powder. Sealing the gun ports and hatches, charcoal fires were started in various parts of the ships to suck out the oxygen and replace it with deadly carbon monoxide. The primitive fumigation worked, and Porter noted that somewhere between 1,200 and 1,500 rat carcasses were found and disposed of. Unfortunately, without the predatory rats, the ship was quickly infested with tropical insects, including huge roaches.

With the *Essex* beached in shallow water and careened over on her side, Porter put his crew and willing natives to work in cleaning and overhauling the ship. Using coconut shells, natives scraped barnacles and other debris, living and dead, clinging to the hull, and any deteriorated copper sheets were replaced with new ones taken from the supplies on the captured whalers. Worn and weather-beaten decks were rubbed down with a treatment the natives made from nuts and whale oil, rigging was replaced with rope made ashore, and the damaged main top mast was rebuilt.

Although the Marquesas were discovered in 1596 by the Spanish explorer Álvaro de Mendaña y Castro and were visited by the British circumnavigator James Cook in 1774, it was not apparent whether either explorer had claimed the islands for his country. Porter therefore took the opportunity to claim them for the United States, an act that few Americans supported when they learned of it. The *Salem Gazette* probably spoke for many when it condemned him for his conquest of "these simple and unoffending children of nature."[49] Anti-Madison federalist newspapers took another approach. One mused that the only good that might come of the annexation was that the "feeble and pusillanimous Madison" might be sent there to preside over their many tribes.[50]

In the end, Washington took no action on Porter's claim to the islands—probably because the British were torching the capital just as the news arrived. As one of Madison's biographers observed, "Having trouble nearer at home, Chief Madison of the Attakakahaneuahs and thirty other tribes did not ask Congress to accept the island."[51]

But the islanders certainly accepted Porter and his crew, and when the work day ended each afternoon at four o'clock, Porter allowed one-quarter of the crew to stay ashore until daybreak to enjoy the society of the compliant women of Nuku Hiva.[52] Porter himself, not immune to their charms, admired an eighteen-year-old island girl who was "of fair complexion and neatly attired, her skin and glossy black hair anointed with cocoa nut oil, her carriage majestic; and her whole appearance striking in the extreme." The venereal pleasures of the Nuku Hiva were not restricted to the enlisted men. When Porter's *Journal of a Cruise Made in the Pacific Ocean* was published in 1815, his account of life on the island scandalized reviewers:

> During the Marquesan visit, any vestiges of sexual repression were promptly put in abeyance. Porter, his officers and his men reveled with the "young girls" who were "handsome and well-formed; their skins were remarkably soft and smooth, and their complexions no darker than many brunett[e]s in America." Indeed, it was soon "helter-skelter and promiscuous intercourse, every girl the wife of every man." Such comments in his *Journal* were, of course, grist for the mills of English reviewers (one of whom called Porter a "hoary proficient in swinish sensualism") and domestic enemies alike. Significantly, some of the steamier passages in his 1815 edition were considerably watered down in that of 1822.[53]

The later edits to Porter's *Journal* in the interest of discretion do not appear to have been the work of the author.[54] Indeed, Porter was remarkably candid with the American public—and, by implication, with the young wife waiting his return to their home in Pennsylvania—about the diversions enjoyed during the Marquesan interlude of his cruise.

> [I] am well satisfied that an intercourse with strangers is not considered by them criminal; but on the contrary, attaches to them respect and consideration. Whether the two females, of which I am now speaking, would have carried their complaisance so far, I had not an opportunity at that time of knowing, but circumstances afterwards, which gave me further knowledge of the females of the Group, gave me no reason to doubt a willingness on their part to gratify every wish; but if there was a crime, the offense was ours, not theirs; they acted in compliance with the custom of their ancestors; we departed from the principles of virtue and morality which are so highly esteemed in civilization.[55]

Although Porter's book appears to have been well received in America, the British, who probably disliked Porter even more than he disliked them, disapproved. William Grifford, editor of the distinguished *Quarterly Review* observed:

> We cannot pollute our pages with the description which Captain Porter gives of his transactions with these people. His language and his ideas are so gross and indelicate, so utterly unfit for this hemisphere, that we must leave the undivided enjoyment of this part of the book to his own countrymen.[56]

Having claimed sovereignty over the islands, Porter also could not resist involvement in their political disputes. The Americans had settled among the Taiis, one of thirty-one tribes on the island, who were feuding with their neighbors, the Happahs. Downes subdued the Happahs with forty marines, but not before they "scoffed at our men, and exposed their posteriors to them with utmost contempt and derision." The Americans next joined a fight against the Taipis (Typees). Tougher fighters than the Happahs, the Taipis required two campaigns, during which Downes suffered a broken leg.

By December 1813, the repairs to the *Essex* neared completion. As the time for the squadron's departure approached, a number of the crewmen and the English prisoners grew reluctant to leave the idyllic island, with its abundant food and compliant women, and return to the harsh and dangerous life aboard a ship of war. Men began deserting, so Porter confined the crew and prisoners to their ships. In response, the native girls lined "the beach from morning until night" and "laughingly dipped their fingers into the sea and touched their eyes so as to let the salt water trickle down their cheeks" as a sign of sorrow for the loss of their lovers.[57] Confronting near mutinous conditions, Porter hastily set sail on 13 December while the ship's band played "The Girl I left Behind."

Porter also left behind four of the prizes under Marine Lieutenant Gamble and Midshipman Feltus, along with twenty-two crewmen and six prisoners, to establish a permanent base for the United States. They were also to provide him with a defensible refuge for repair and escape should he have a violent confrontation with the British warships that were searching the Pacific for him. By April 1814, Gamble and Feltus had received no further communication from Porter. During those four months, tensions had arisen among those left behind, and the small American presence on Nuku Hiva was in jeopardy. Tribal warfare resumed, and Feltus was murdered in early May. Several Americans mutinied and escaped with the British prisoners to New Zealand in the *Seringapatam*. Gamble finally left for the U.S. in the *Greenwich* with only four able-bodied sailors, but they were captured by the British near Hawaii. He and his crew of seven remained as prisoners until mid-1815, when the British freed them at Rio de Janeiro. From there Gamble took passage to New York, and arrived home in August 1815.[58]

During the weeks that Porter had rested and repaired his ship in the Marquesas, Hillyar had searched far and wide for him. In October, he stopped at Juan Fernandez and then Guayaquil on the coast of Ecuador, but there was no word of Porter or the *Essex*. In the seas around the Galapagos, he learned that Porter had been there until October, but was now gone. With no hint as to where to search, Hillyar took his small squadron to Lima, where he would wait the next few months for any word of the American.[59]

On 3 February 1814, about seven weeks after leaving the Marquesas, Porter returned to the harbor of Valparaiso, leaving the *Essex Junior* under Downes to keep watch offshore for Hillyar. The *Phoebe* and the *Cherub* appeared four days later. Since Chile was nominally Spanish, and Spain was nominally neutral, the harbor was off-limits to combat.

Although Porter and Hillyar had become acquainted years earlier when both were stationed in the Mediterranean, they were now professional adversaries who respected each other's skill and courage but were not above a little bravado in anticipation of their inevitable combat. As *Phoebe* entered the harbor, she sailed directly for the *Essex*, which, in response, beat to quarters and ran out her guns as crews stood ready with smoldering matches. *Phoebe*'s vulnerable bow was briefly exposed to a broadside from the *Essex*, but Hillyar regained control of his ship in time to avert a battle or collision. He brought her up close enough for the two captains to shout their greetings and threats. Porter wrote in his *Journal*:

> I told him again, if he did fall on board of me, there would be much bloodshed. He repeated his assurances, with the same nonchalance, that such was not his intention. Finding, however, that he luffed up so as to cause his ship to take aback, whereby her jib-boom came across my forecastle, I immediately called all hands to board the enemy, directing them, if the hulls touched, to spring upon the deck of the *Phoebe*.[60]

But the hulls never touched, and combat was avoided for the time being, for both captains respected the neutrality of the Chilean waters. Hillyar moored the *Phoebe* and the *Cherub* within shouting distance of the *Essex*, and over the next several days the British and American crews exchanged insults and challenges. The crew of the *Essex* sent a banner aloft proclaiming "Free Trade and Sailors' Rights"; *Phoebe* responded with her own banner—"God and Country: British sailors best rights: traitors offend both." At night the Americans loudly sang sarcastic songs of their own composing, often to the tune of "Yankee Doodle," and the British replied with a rousing "The Sweet Little Cherub that Sits up Aloft." The British, Porter noted in his *Journal*, sang better.[61]

On 9 March 1814, *Essex*'s crew sent a challenge to *Phoebe*'s, reading in part:

> The sons of liberty and commerce, on board the saucy *Essex*, whose motto is "Free Trade and Sailors' Rights," present their compliments to their oppressed brother tars, on board the ship whose motto is

> too tedious to mention, and hope they will put an end to all this nonsense of singing, sporting, hunting, and writing, which we know less about than the use of our guns—Send the Cherub, we will meet your frigate and fight you, then shake hands and be friends ... hail you as brethren whom we have liberated from slavery, and place you in future beyond the reach of a press gang.[62]

The British responded with a twenty-eight-line poem, written by a midshipman, which began,

> To you, Americans, who seek redress,
> For fancied wrongs from Britons you've sustained,
> Hear what we Britons now to you address,
> From malice free, from blasphemy unstain'd

It ended,

> When honor calls, we'll glory in his name,
> Acquit like men and hope you'll do the same.[63]

The officers, in contrast, had more serious business at hand, and over the next several weeks Hillyar and Porter met at the home of the American envoy, Joel Poinsett, in an attempt to establish the rules governing the ensuing combat and to resolve other matters, including the release of prisoners. In a letter to the Admiralty dated 28 February 1814, Hillyar noted, "I had interviews with him when in port, respecting the liberation of some British Seamen, his Prisoners. He has at last landed them and I have pledged myself that they shall not serve onboard any Ship under my orders, and that the British Government will immediately on hearing from me, restore an equal number of Americans."[64] But as for the larger issue, no agreement was possible: Porter wanted a set piece ship-to-ship fight and a guarantee that *Cherub* would stay out of it. Hillyar refused, arguing that the converted whaler *Essex Junior* was an even match for *Cherub*.

But Hillyar's real reason for refusing Porter's challenge was his belief that both his orders and the professional requirements of a British naval officer discouraged him from taking unnecessary risks when safer alternatives were available. As David Farragut's son Loyall wrote in his memoir of his father:

> [Hillyar] had gained his reputation by several single-ship combats, and only expected to retain it on the present occasion by an implicit obedience to his orders, viz., to capture the Essex with the least possible risk to his vessel and crew; and, as he had a superior force, he had determined not to leave anything to chance, believing any other course would call down on him the disapprobation of his government.[65]

With no likelihood of an agreement, Porter remained in the harbor, while Hillyar spent the time patrolling offshore to close off any opportunity for escape. At one point Porter attempted to goad Hillyar into a fight by taking two of his prizes out to sea and burning them in front of the British, but Hillyar refused to take the bait, confident that time was on his side and that he had the superior squadron. During this waiting game, Hillyar wrote his superiors, "I expect an awful combat if the two ships meet."[66]

That meeting finally occurred quite by accident when a strong wind broke *Essex*'s port anchor cable. The one remaining anchor was insufficient for the strength of the wind, and the *Essex* began to drag it as the wind blew her out of the harbor and in the direction of *Phoebe* and *Cherub*. Attempting to turn disaster into opportunity, Porter raised the anchor and set his sails. He would try to use the powerful winds to escape the unequal combat for which Hillyar was patiently waiting.

Essex was probably the fastest of the three ships, so Porter's hasty gamble might have paid off. But the strong wind became a fierce squall just as the American frigate was rounding the outermost point of the harbor, the Punta del Angeles. Unprepared for the blow, *Essex* tipped over nearly to her gunwales, and the main top mast, which had been repaired in the Marquesas, was ripped off, spilling four or five sailors into the water. Porter tried to bring his crippled ship back into the protection of the harbor, but a shift in the wind and *Essex*'s limited maneuverability made that impossible. He then headed for a small bay three miles away in the hope that he might be considered to be within Chile's neutral waters.

Hillyar was not so scrupulous, however. *Phoebe* and *Cherub* took up positions just beyond the range of *Essex*'s carronades, and *Phoebe* began firing her long eighteen-pounders. Porter attempted to swing his ship around to offer Hillyar his broadside, but every time he attempted the maneuver the springs were shot away, and the *Essex* suffered several casualties in these early exchanges. Firing the pair of long twelve-pounders mounted in his stern, Porter damaged the enemy's rigging and briefly drove them back. But when the repairs were completed thirty minutes later, *Cherub* and *Phoebe* returned and took up positions beyond the carronades' range and out of the stern guns' fire. From this position, they battered the *Essex*, taking a heavy toll on her masts and rigging.

With nothing left to lose, Porter put up all the sail he could on his remaining masts and spars and drove the *Essex* toward his opponents. He managed to get off a few broadsides with his carronades before both *Cherub* and *Phoebe* moved out of range. Her sails and rigging shot to pieces, *Essex* was wallowing helplessly in the swells, and the British resumed their devastating attack from a safe distance.

Years later Farragut recalled *Essex*'s last, desperate hours, though his memory may have embellished some of the details. One of the few guns that *Essex* could bear on the British became a prime target for the enemy, and three gun crews—fifteen men—fell victim to *Phoebe*'s long eighteen-pounders. At one of *Essex*'s bow guns a young Scot named Bissly had his leg shot off near the groin. Stanching the blood with a tourniquet made from his handkerchief, he told his shipmates, according to Farragut's recollection, that "I left my own country and adopted the United States, to fight for her. I hope I have this day proved myself worthy of my adoption. I am no longer of any use to you or to her, so good-by." At that he leaned on the rail and tipped himself over into the water. Bissly was one of about 120 Americans killed or wounded in the relentless attack. Let Theodore Roosevelt describe the ensuing devastation as he retells it from Farragut's memoirs:

> The ship caught fire, and the flames came bursting up the hatchway, and a quantity of powder exploded below. Many of the crew were knocked overboard by shot, and drowned; others leaped into the water thinking the ship was about to blow up, and tried to swim to land. Some succeeded; among them was one man who had sixteen

> or eighteen pieces of iron in his leg, scales from the muzzle of his gun.... The carpenter reported that he alone of his crew was fit for duty; the others were dead or disabled. Lieutenant Wilmer was knocked overboard by a splinter, and drowned; his little negro boy "[R]uff", came up on deck, and, hearing of the disaster, deliberately leaped into the sea and shared his master's fate. Lieutenant Odenheimer was also knocked overboard, but afterward regained the ship. A shot, glancing upward, killed four of the men standing by a gun, striking the last one and scattering his brains over his comrades.... The sailing master, Barnwell, when terribly wounded, remained at his post till he fainted from the loss of blood.... Porter himself was knocked down by the windage of a passing shot. While the young midshipman Farragut, was on the ward-room ladder, going below for gun primers, the captain of the gun directly opposite the hatchway was struck full in the face by an 18-pound shot, and tumbled back on him.... Later while standing by the man at the wheel, an old quartermaster named Francis Bland, a shot coming over the fore-yard took off the quartermaster's right leg, carrying away at the same time one of Farragut's coat tails.[67]

Bland died from the loss of blood before the surgeon could attend his wounds. Farragut also remembers how Porter remained intensely focused on the fight despite the slaughter around him. Finding the midshipman under the body of the mutilated gun captain, Porter was unmoved by the youngster's plight: "The Captain seeing me covered with blood asked if I was wounded, to which I replied 'I believe not sir'. 'Then', he said, 'where are the primers?'"[68]

Sensing the scale of the slaughter on board the *Essex*, *Phoebe*'s Lieutenant William Ingram urged Hillyar to close and board *Essex* to end the "deliberate murder." Hillyar, however, had no interest in risking his men as long as the Americans continued their fire. Minutes after he counseled Hillyar to show mercy to the Americans, Ingram was killed by a large splinter of wood which, dislodged from *Phoebe*'s rail by a shot from the *Essex*, pierced his head.[69]

Not every American sailor remained at his station as the battle wore on. One who fled was the aptly named William Roach, whom Porter sent Farragut to hunt down and kill—"Do your duty sir," Porter ordered. Farragut never found Roach and believed that he might have fled *Essex* on a small boat with other deserters.[70] In his pursuit of Roach, Farragut was helped by a seaman named William Call, whose leg had been nearly severed by British cannon shot and hung from the stump by a piece of skin. Nonetheless, with pistol in hand, Call dragged his bloody leg around the deck trying to get a shot at the deserter, also without success. Call's wounds were so severe that he was one of only two crewmen who had to be left behind in Valparaiso's hospital. He survived and ultimately made his way back to the United States.[71]

Essex's Lieutenant Cowell had his leg nearly shot off above the knee and was taken to the surgeons who, as custom required, offered to treat him ahead of the wounded enlisted men already waiting. Farragut says that Cowell replied: "No, doctor, none of that; fair play's a jewel. One man's life is as dear as another's; I would not cheat any poor fellow out of his turn."[72] Cowell died twenty-one days later from loss of blood and a wound that would not heal.

Recognizing the hopelessness of his position, Porter attempted to run the *Essex* onto the beach and burn her, but the wind again shifted unfavorably and blew her out to sea. Downes, commanding the *Essex Junior* nearby, rowed over with several men who gave up their places on the boat to their badly wounded comrades. At 5:45 PM, one of *Essex*'s magazines exploded, sending flames and smoke throughout the ship. Porter gave his men permission to escape by swimming ashore, and at about 6:20 struck his colors. One of the first British officers to take possession is said to have fainted from the sight of the carnage.[73] A midshipman from *Phoebe* remembered,

> I was in the 1st boat that boarded her. Nothing was to be seen all over her decks but dead, wounded and dying—we threw 63 overboard that were dead and there were several wounded that it would have been a mercy to do the same to.... One poor fellow, who had his thigh shot off, managed to crawl to a port and tumble himself into the water which put an end to his misery. There were 44 amputations performed that night.... Captain Porter was in tears when he went on board the Phoebe to give up his sword and he told Captain Hillyard that there were 15 of his brave fellows killed after she struck.[74]

One of the officers who boarded *Essex* demanded Porter's sword to confirm the surrender, but Porter refused: "That sir, is reserved for your master."[75] Of the 255 men aboard the *Essex* when the fight began, it is estimated that fifty-eight had been killed, sixty-six wounded, thirty-three were missing and presumed drowned, while twenty-four had swum to shore. *Phoebe* lost only four, including Lieutenant Ingram, while *Cherub* lost one. One reason for the disproportionate casualties is that the British had been able to fire ten shots to every one fired by Porter, and were outside the range of most of *Essex*'s guns.

After most ship-to-ship fights of the era, a chivalric generosity of spirit prevailed among the victors and the vanquished, but only bitterness followed this battle. On the surface, Hillyar was noble in victory, helping to bury the dead and care for the wounded, and in his official report he commended Porter:

> The defence of the *Essex*, taking into account our superiority of force, and the very discouraging circumstances of her having lost her main top-mast did honor to her brave defenders, and most fully evinced the courage of Captain Porter and those under his command. Her colours were not struck until the loss in killed and wounded was so awfully great, and her shattered condition so seriously bad, as to render further assistance unavailing.[76]

Hillyar, however, later complained about those seamen who swam to shore with Porter's urging, depriving him of prisoners. He wrote to the Admiralty that he was

> much hurt on hearing that [the men of the *Essex*] had been encouraged, when the result of the action was evidently decided, some to take to their boats, and others to swim to shore; many were drowned in the attempt; 16 were saved by the exertions of my people, and others, I believe between 30 and 40, effected their escape. I informed Captain Porter, that I considered the latter, in point of honor, as my prisoners; he said the encouragement was given when the ship was in danger from fire, and I have not pressed the point.[77]

The *Times*, however, did press the point: "The conduct of Captain Porter, however, on conniving at the escape of some of his men after surrender, agrees pretty well with the character we have before given of him, and shows that his sentiments of honor are but American."[78] One British naval historian offers another explanation for this unusual event: "These were the British seamen who had been induced to join the *Essex* out of the captured whalers, and who now realised the full meaning of the word 'traitors' on the flag the *Phoebe* was still flying."[79]

Porter, for his part, had his own grievances. Chief among them was that Hillyar, who had refused to fight him one-on-one, finally engaged him only when Porter's ship was damaged and Hillyar had a two-to-one advantage. Porter was also bitter about what he contended was a violation of Chilean neutrality. He was well within the three-mile limit of Chile's territorial waters, as some British writers concede,[80] though most dismiss the point as a technicality. Another complaint was that Hillyar deliberately continued to bombard the *Essex* for several minutes after her colors were struck. "I now believe he intended showing us no quarter, and that it would be just as well to die with my flag flying as struck, and was on the point of hoisting it, when ten minutes after hauling the colors down, he ceased firing."[81] But Porter did acknowledge Hillyar's kindness once the battle ended: "He has since our capture, shown the greatest humanity to my wounded … and the most generous and delicate deportment towards myself, my officers and crew."[82]

Midshipman Farragut might have taken issue with Porter's generous assessment of their captors, particularly in light of the efforts of the British crewmen to take his pet pig, "Master Murphy." While the British claimed Murphy as a captive, the thirteen-year-old Farragut claimed the animal to be the American crew's private property, and thus entitled to protection. Hoping to defuse a nasty fight, the British consented that the matter should be settled by a boxing match between Farragut and a young "reefer" from *Phoebe*'s crew. Farragut later described the bout:

> I knew there were few of any boys my age that could master me. So a Ring was formed and in the Open space, at it we went. I soon found, his pugilistic education did not equal mine, and that he was

> no match for me, and as he made the discovery as soon as I did, he yielded the Pig, and I took Master Murphy under my arm, feeling I had in some degree wiped off the disgrace of our capture.[83]

Despite the bitterness of battle, Hillyar paroled Porter and his crew and let them return on their own to America in the *Essex Junior*, provided they agreed not to take up arms until they were formally exchanged for British prisoners. On 27 April, Porter and his surviving crewmen left Valparaiso aboard the *Essex Junior* with papers provided by Hillyar granting them safe passage back to the United States. On 7 July 1814 they arrived at Sandy Hook, New Jersey, just outside New York's harbor, but were stopped from entering by the blockading British razee *Saturn*, commanded by Captain James Nash, who asked them to show their papers. Porter did so, and was allowed to proceed, but *Saturn* followed closely, and two hours later reboarded the *Essex Junior* claiming that Hillyar had no authority to offer safe passage and that Porter was instead Nash's prisoner.

Not knowing what would happen next, the angry Porter gave Downes a letter stating that "Captain Porter was now satisfied, that most British officers were not only destitute in honor, but regardless of the honor of each other,"[84] and then fled in an armed boat with several crewmen. *Saturn* gave chase, but Porter was saved by a fog that rolled in and hid them from the British. After a voyage of sixty miles, Porter came ashore on Long Island at the town of Babylon, where he was briefly detained by suspicious townsmen who thought he was a British spy.

The rest of his crew and officers, still in the hands of the *Saturn*, fared less well. The men were "mustered on deck with the pretence of detecting deserters; her officers insulted and treated with shameful outrage." They were soon released and with their captain, who had made his way to the city from Babylon, were honored with a dinner at Tammany Hall. Another dinner was held in Philadelphia, where the crew unhitched the horses from Porter's carriage and honored him by pulling it themselves through the city. The next stop was Washington, where Porter dined with President Madison. Porter's crew stayed on in Washington, where they took part in the city's inept defense against the attacking British. Porter returned to Chester, Pennsylvania, to be with his wife and son after an absence of more than a year and a half.

Elsewhere in America, ordinary people focused on the valor of the *Essex*'s captain and crew, not their defeat. A self-published poem circulated in Boston:[85]

> The Phoebe Frigate then was seen,
> Just lying off and on Sirs,
> The Cherub-Sloop of War I ween,
> Just made a Pair of Monsters!

And several lines later, when events turned darkly against the Americans ...

> The Essex sorely raked and gall'd;
> While able to defend her,
> The Essex crew are not appall'd
> They DIE but don't SURRENDER!

But they ultimately do, of course, and the poet continues,

> Our tears are render'd to the brave,
> Our hearts applause is given:
> Their names, In Memory we engrave,
> Their spirits rest in heaven

Theodore Roosevelt was as impressed as that poet when he wrote of the voyage's success:

> By this year's campaign in the Pacific, Captain Porter had saved all of our ships in those waters, had not cost the government a dollar, living purely on the enemy, and had taken from him nearly 4,000 tons of shipping and 400 men, completely breaking up his whaling trade in the South Pacific. The cruise was something *sui generis* in modern warfare, recalling to mind the cruises of the early English and Dutch navigators. An American ship was at a serious disadvantage in having no harbor of refuge away from home; while on almost every sea there were British, French and Spanish ports into which vessels of those nations could run for safety. It was an

> unprecedented thing for a small frigate to cruise a year and a half in enemy's waters, and to supply herself during the time purely through captured vessels with everything—cordage, sails, guns, anchors, provisions, and medicines, and even money to pay the officers and men! Porter's cruise was the very model of what such an expedition should be harassing the enemy most effectually at no cost whatever.[86]

The British were not as impressed by the feat. When news of Porter's defeat reached England in July 1814, the *Times*, nursing long-remembered grievances, reveled in the comeuppance of one of Britain's most detested opponents:

> It was yesterday reported with great confidence that the American frigate *Essex*, which has been so long blockaded on the coast of South America, by the *Phoebe*, Captain Hillyar, was captured by the latter in attempting to escape. We have great satisfaction in learning a confirmation of this intelligence. Porter was the fellow who in 1805 enticed a man on board his ship in the harbour of Malta for the purpose of causing him to be flogged; a circumstance which excited much indignation on the part of the British there; that Mr. Porter was obliged to weigh anchor, and make his escape in a few hours to avoid the consequences with which he was threatened.[87]

The *Essex*, though badly battered, did not sink. *Phoebe* escorted her around the treacherous Horn and back to England, where she was repaired and rechristened HMS *Essex*.

CHAPTER TEN

BACK ON LAND: HARRISON ON THE MAUMEE LINE

Back at Malden, having failed to dislodge William Henry Harrison from Fort Meigs, General Henry Procter knew that time was not on his side. Harrison's force would become stronger and more numerous as the year passed. His, in contrast, would only become weaker. Procter commanded the far western tip of a sparsely populated frontier empire under siege at dozens of points along its several-thousand-mile border with the United States. His distant force, he knew, had become a lower priority to the British command, which allocated its limited resources to securing its more important holdings in the east. Procter's immediate superior, Major General Francis de Rottenburg, had recently informed him of a contingency plan to evacuate his troops and withdraw entirely from the west if the British lost control of Lake Ontario. Though the chance of such an evacuation seemed slim—Commodore Isaac Chauncey had not been very aggressive in driving Captain Sir James Yeo to the decisive battle that America's leaders hoped would sweep the British from the lake—Rottenburg confirmed to Procter the diminished importance of his western outpost.

Not only were Procter's requests for more troops and supplies rejected, but some of his troops were shifted east to help secure the more essential Ontario and Niagara regions. Procter's supplies were running so low that he was hard pressed to feed the many thousands of Indian allies and dependents living in encampments near Malden.[1] Nevertheless, Procter remained confident that his troops would prevail in any combat with the Americans, and in early July 1813 he sailed his troops across Lake Erie and up the Maumee River in a campaign that he hoped would finally dislodge the Americans from Fort Meigs in northwest Ohio. By destroying the fort, Procter believed he could secure Malden by pushing the Americans farther south and east, leaving more of the overland access to Malden in the hands of the British and their Indian allies. And by plundering the countryside around Fort Meigs and its depot on the Sandusky River, Procter could also replenish his dwindling supplies.

British regulars and Canadian militiamen in Procter's force numbered about five hundred, while the Indians led by Tecumseh totaled about a thousand. Hoping to repeat the only successful part of their earlier siege of Fort Meigs, Procter agreed to Tecumseh's plan to stage a mock battle near the fort to trick the Americans into thinking that a supply column approaching the fort was under attack.[2] Hearing the battle, the Americans, according to the plan, would be drawn out of the fort in force. When they emerged, the waiting British and Indians would attack and annihilate them, much as they had done in May.

But the fort's commander, Brigadier General Green Clay of Kentucky, knew that no supply train was expected and refused the bait. So while Procter's troops shot blanks in the air and whooped and yelled through the woods and meadows with their Indian allies, the Americans, undeceived, kept to the safety of their fort. With no reasonable prospect of taking the fort by direct assault, Procter withdrew some days later, taking his troops by ship down the Maumee to Lake Erie and then up the Sandusky River to seize the supplies Harrison was collecting at his thinly defended depots.

The defense of the American depots rested entirely on tiny Fort Stephenson, which occupied no more than an acre near the mouth of the Sandusky. Its 160 men were under the command of twenty-one-year-old Major George Croghan. Believing that the small force had no chance against Procter and Tecumseh, Harrison wrote to Croghan, "Immediately on receiving this letter, you will abandon Ft. Stephenson, set it on fire, and repair with your command this night to Headquarters." Croghan was to join Harrison upriver, where they would retreat to the security of Fort Seneca, a few miles upriver from Fort Stephenson.[3]

Delaying his response by a day, Croghan replied to Harrison, "I have just received yours of yesterday, 10:00 PM, ordering me to destroy this place and make good my retreat, which was received too late to be carried into execution. We have determined to maintain this place, and by heavens we can." Harrison would have none of it and swiftly replied, "An officer who presumes to aver that he has made his resolution and that he will act in direct opposition to the orders of his General, can no longer be entrusted with a separate command."[4]

Harrison ordered Croghan removed, but shortly after the order arrived, Procter's force encircled the fort and began the siege. Although Procter later argued that he was not convinced it was wise to try to take the fort, he claimed that officials from Britain's Indian Department, who led his Indian auxiliaries during these campaigns, insisted that if he did not immediately attack and take Fort Stephenson, it would be difficult to motivate their increasingly demoralized Indian allies in the future.

Procter first tried to scare the Americans. "He attempted to persuade the defenders to surrender using the method employed effectively by Brock at Detroit [a year earlier]," writes Horsman. "He sent word that unless the Americans surrendered he could not guarantee them safety from the Indians."[5] Croghan refused the offer and prepared his men for battle, leaving Procter with little choice but to attack with his superior force. But Procter's siege, characteristically, was poorly conceived and the troops poorly prepared. On the afternoon of 2 August, Procter ordered his men to advance without ladders, fascines, or axes against a walled fort surrounded by a deep trench. Croghan ordered his troops to hold their fire until the British were within fifty yards. When the enemy had come within that range, the Americans let loose a barrage of musket fire and grape shot from "Old Betsy," the fort's lone piece of artillery. The cannon fire sent the Indians running, but the British regulars kept coming—and dying—cut down in their repeated attempts to cross the field and the ditch.

When Procter finally called off the attack hours later, the British had suffered thirty missing, twenty-six dead, and forty-one wounded, plus an unknown number of Indian casualties during the first few minutes of the fight. Croghan's force suffered one dead and seven wounded.[6] The next day Procter evacuated his remaining force and sailed back to Malden. The assault on Fort Stephenson would be the last British land attack in the western theater of the war.

Croghan's victory against such odds put General Harrison in a rather awkward position, for his shaky command had little to show for its year-long efforts. The historian John K. Mahon describes Harrison's dilemma:

> ... General Harrison found himself in the embarrassing position of relieving an officer who had just won a victory against five times his numbers. Moreover, Croghan added to his embarrassment by explaining his insubordination. By the time he had received Harrison's order, he said, it was more dangerous to carry it out than to stay and fight. His officers concurred in that. He had then written his reply in strong terms because he expected that it would fall into enemy hands, and he wanted it to impress them. There was little Harrison could do but reinstate the major, who at twenty-one was a national hero."[7]

As Procter returned his demoralized force to Malden, Harrison was in the final stages of organizing his army for the thrust into western Canada. If successful, the campaign would end British influence in the region forever. Harrison had reason for optimism, because joining him was one of the more fearsome fighters to take the field during the war.

Richard Mentor Johnson, a colonel in the Kentucky militia, had trained and now led a force of a thousand mounted infantrymen that would play a decisive role in Harrison's assault on British power in the west. Elected to the House of Representatives in 1806 and a member of the young War Hawks, Johnson was the popular scion of a powerful Kentucky family that had never lost touch with its humble origins. Trained as a lawyer, Johnson often waived fees for indigent clients and was generous to those in need. "[H]is home was a mecca for disabled veterans, widows and orphans seeking assistance. No one was refused hospitality at Blue Spring Farm, his estate near Great Crossings. An acquaintance 'heard men say they were treated so well by Col. Johnson when they went out there, they loved to go.'"[8]

Johnson's approach to western warfare was to raise and train a regiment of mounted infantry who could fight in the woods and rough terrain with a musket, as opposed to traditional cavalry tactics emphasizing support of infantry with lance and saber on an open field. An influential politician who did not want "to be idle during the recess of Congress,"[9] Johnson asked Secretary of War Armstrong for permission to raise and train such a force. He got it on 26 February 1813. Well liked and respected in Kentucky, Johnson easily raised the thousand men and officers authorized—"hardy, keen, daring and ruthless" men—and set about training them for a new kind of warfare.

Harrison initially opposed the creation of this new mounted regiment, as did other Kentucky leaders, on the grounds that Congress had repealed the Volunteer Acts a month earlier. Johnson got his way, however, and the governor of Kentucky, who had the authority to appoint officers in the state militia, followed his suggestions.

Johnson's men provided their own horses, weapons, stripped-down equipment, and uniforms—a red-fringed black leather hunting shirt and trousers with a bright head kerchief.[10] Marked by tight discipline and fierce determination, Johnson's mounted infantry was trained to attack in all terrain, fire on the enemy at a full gallop, dismount, reload, and fire again. Each man was armed with a tomahawk, scalping knife, and rifle. Mahon describes the qualities that distinguished this extraordinary regiment:

> Johnson trained them far beyond the level usually attained by citizen soldiers. He prescribed a battle formation and practiced it so often that men and horses fell automatically into their places. He made them charge into lines of infantrymen who actually fired, until they learned to carry a charge straight into the hostile line.[11]

Johnson's mounted shock troops arrived in the northwest theater in early June 1813 and honed their skills and tactics by attacking all the Indian warriors they encountered on a seven-hundred-mile ride through hostile territory, from River Raisin to Fort Wayne. British infantry and their Indian allies holding on in Upper Canada were about to meet a fighting force at the top of its game.

CHAPTER ELEVEN

THE TIDE TURNS IN THE ATLANTIC

At the beginning of 1813, leaders of both nations adopted major changes in war policy in response to early British losses and American victories. Neither Washington nor London was yet aware of Bainbridge's recent defeat of the *Java* or of David Porter's assault on Britain's whaling fleet—just then getting underway in the Pacific—but the early American victories over *Guerriere*, *Alert*, *Frolic*, and *Macedonian* were more than enough to galvanize opinion on both sides of the Atlantic and set in motion major changes in naval strategy.

In Washington, the view was that if the United States could humble the world's largest navy with a fleet of just sixteen ships, imagine what it could do with more and bigger ships. On 2 January 1813, Congress authorized the construction of four ships of at least seventy-four guns and six ships of at least forty-four. Measuring force by the number of guns, James Fenimore Cooper observed, "This was at once multiplying the force of the navy tenfold, and it may be esteemed the first step that was ever actually put in execution, towards establishing a marine that might prove of material moment, in influencing the results of a war."[1] Perhaps in response to naval victories in the early months of 1813, Congress on 3 March further authorized the construction of six sloops of war and "as many vessels on the lakes as public service required."[2]

Across the Atlantic in London, the same events evoked different emotions but a similar response—more ships were needed. "By the beginning of the year 1813 the British had been thoroughly aroused by the American successes," writes Theodore Roosevelt, "and active measures were at once taken to counteract them. The naval force on the American station was substantially increased, and a strict blockade put in place to keep the big American frigates in port. The British frigates now cruised in couples, and orders had been issued by the Board of Admiralty that a British frigate armed with 18-pounders was not to engage an American twenty-four-pounder."[3]

By February, Britain had assembled a vast fleet of warships to contain and exclude the American Navy from the entire eastern edge of the western hemisphere. Leading the force was Admiral Sir John Borlase Warren, who personally commanded fifteen seventy-fours, a fifty-gun ship, fifteen frigates, and twenty sloops and brigs. Holding the Jamaica station was Vice Admiral Charles Stirling, with four frigates and twelve sloops and brigs. Rear Admiral Sir Francis Laforey led the Leeward Islands with a seventy-four, four frigates, and sixteen smaller ships. Off Newfoundland cruised Vice Admiral Edmund Nagle's squadron, a fifty-gun ship, two frigates, and six smaller vessels. And off the Brazilian coast, Rear Admiral Manley Dixon commanded a seventy-four, two frigates, and six smaller ships. The empire was striking back, and as C. S. Forester observed, "It was an astonishing exertion; Nelson had won the victory of the Nile with not much more than half this strength."[4]

As the politicians debated and devised their response to unexpected events, Master Commandant James Lawrence and his brig *Hornet* were still off the coast of São Salvador waiting for the specie-laden *Bonne Citoyenne* to make a break for the sea and Britain. William Bainbridge had ordered Lawrence, who had been blocking the harbor since 13 December 1812, to remain there until as late as April.

Those orders, of course, were subject to contingencies, exceptions, and discretion, and one such contingency occurred on 24 January when Britain's seventy-four-gun *Montagu* showed up and chased the much smaller eighteen-gun *Hornet* into the port of São Salvador. When night fell, Lawrence escaped by slipping the *Hornet* out to sea and well past the grasp of the slower *Montagu*.

After escaping the harbor, Lawrence continued north along the Brazilian coast, where in the middle of February he captured the brig *Resolution* and its twenty-four thousand dollars in specie. Denied the riches of the *Bonne Citoyenne* after a month of waiting, Lawrence intended to head home by way of a leisurely route that would offer him and his crew the opportunity to earn the esteem of their nation and plenty of prize money.

Lawrence was born in Burlington, New Jersey, in 1781 to John Lawrence, a loyalist in the American Revolution. The father's politics made for an uncomfortable boyhood growing up in a small town in the immediate aftermath of a bitter war, but James's situation improved when he moved in with his half-sister in Perth Amboy, and she provided him with the best tutors. That education, in turn, allowed him to enter the navy as a midshipman. He served in the West Indies on the *Ganges*, *New York*, and *Adams*, where he found the duty to be tedious but managed to impress enough of his superiors to merit promotion to lieutenant before age twenty.[5]

Lawrence's career took a more interesting turn when he was assigned to the *Enterprise* under then Lieutenant Isaac Hull and sent to the Mediterranean as part of Preble's fleet. Not too long after arriving at the Tripolitan station, Hull took command of the larger *Argus* and Lawrence came under Decatur's command. During his service off Tripoli, Lawrence served directly under Decatur, assuming command of the squadron's flagship *Enterprise* when Decatur and others took off after the Barbary pirates in little gunboats. He also served as Decatur's second in command aboard the *Intrepid* during the daring raid to recapture and burn the *Philadelphia* at Tripoli in 1804.

Lawrence seems to have been held in high esteem by his fellow officers and by those who served under him. The historian Henry Gruppe recounts a revealing episode from Lawrence's duty off the coast of North Africa:

> On one occasion in the Mediterranean, the beggar-poor midshipmen, intent on honoring Commodore John Rodgers with a party, concluded that their meager allowances would not permit invitations to the commodore's lieutenants. But when they realized that to omit all the lieutenants would mean the absence of Mr. Lawrence, every purse was emptied on the table. Amid wild cheering, it was found that the small coins just added up to a sum that would permit the inclusion of Lawrence, the only lieutenant so honored.[6]

Reassigned to the states in 1811 and now a master commandant, Lawrence was given command of the *Hornet,* a super brig of eighteen guns, sixteen of them thirty-two-pound carronades, eight to a side. In October 1813, Lawrence and the *Hornet* were assigned to Bainbridge's squadron, and it was in pursuit of that duty that he now found himself off the northern coast of South America.[7]

Almost two weeks after taking the *Resolution* off the coast of Brazil, Lawrence was cruising farther north and west off British Guyana near the mouth of the Demerara River when he came upon a British brig and chased her into the shallows. He cut off his pursuit for fear that *Hornet* might become lodged on an unseen sandbar or in a shallow mud flat. As he pulled up short, Lawrence discovered another brig, HMS *Espiegle,* 18, under the command of Captain John Taylor, lying behind the protection of a sand bar. As Lawrence beat around the bank to get at the *Espiegle, Hornet*'s lookouts discovered another brig off the ship's weather quarter, farther out to sea. It was HMS *Peacock,* 18, under the command of Captain William Peake, which that morning had left its anchorage near the *Espiegle* in the Demerara to patrol the coast line against American and French raiders.

Peacock offered a better opportunity for attack than *Espiegle,* Lawrence had the crew beat to quarters and the ship cleared for action while keeping the *Hornet* close by the wind to get the weather gauge. Once he had it, he tacked and raised his colors. Both ships were now coming at each other on parallel courses, both on the wind, with *Hornet* on a starboard and the *Peacock* on a port tack. Both ships were of similar size, but the advantage in armament went to *Hornet,* which carried thirty-two-pound carronades to the *Peacock*'s twenty-four pounders. The Americans also had a slight advantage in crew. Not counting the prisoners from *Resolution, Hornet* had about 140 men (half of whom were probably black sailors), while *Peacock* carried about 130.[8]

Peake had a reputation as a stickler for a smart and tidy ship. The British naval historian Richard Woodman observes,

> His ship was aptly named, and as aptly nick-named "the yacht", for the fastidious attention paid to the order and brilliance of her decks, the polish of her brass, and the neatness of her ropes. As for her guns, her carronade breechings were parcelled in canvas and the elevating screws gleamed with polish—so unused had small

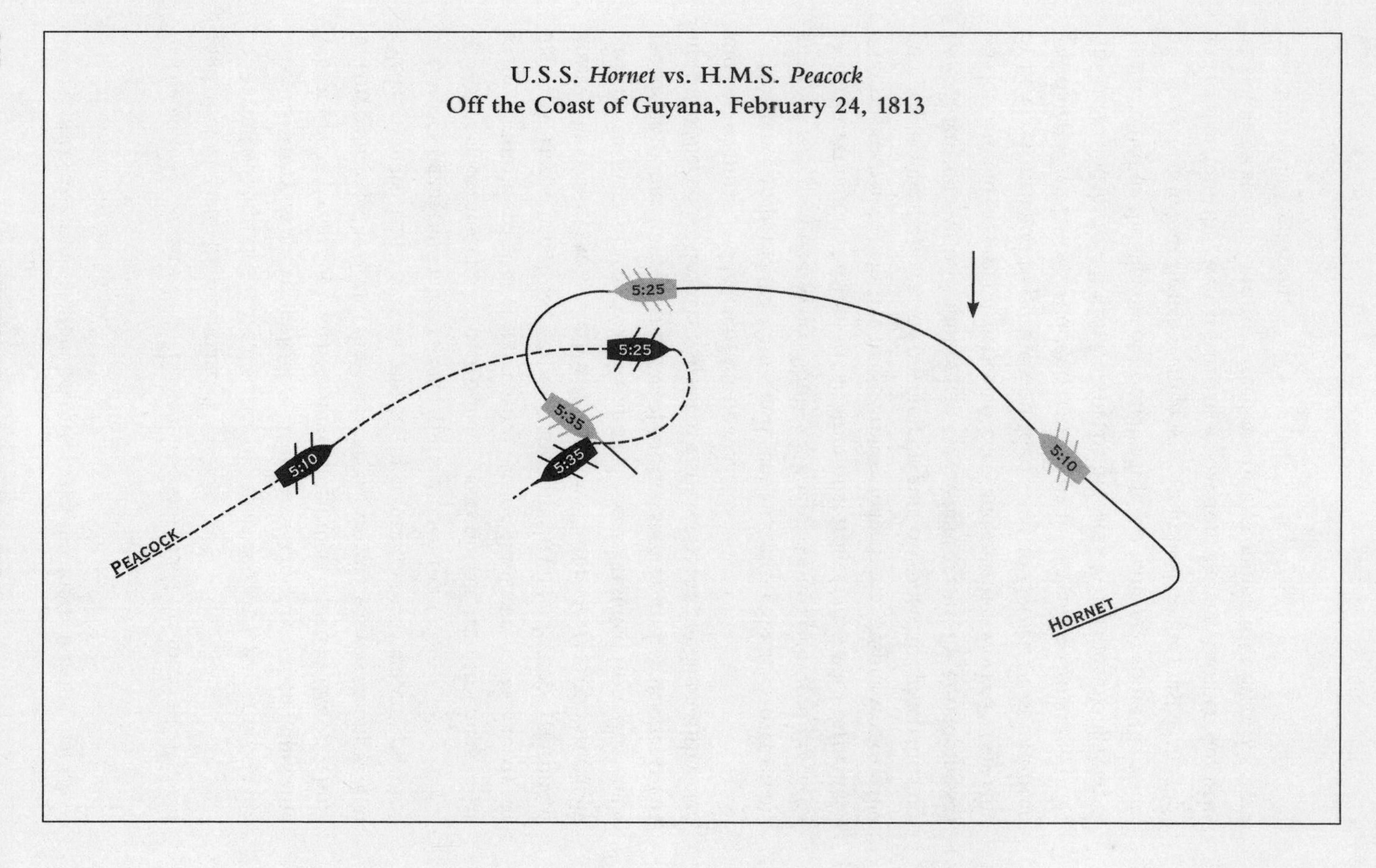
U.S.S. *Hornet* vs. H.M.S. *Peacock*
Off the Coast of Guyana, February 24, 1813
PEACOCK
HORNET
5:10
5:35
5:25
5:35
5:25
5:10

> cruisers on remote stations become to fighting for their living that they had lost the knack.[9]

In Theodore Roosevelt's view, "Peake had confounded the mere incidents of good discipline with the essentials."[10]

As the two ships closed at a distance of half a pistol shot, gun crews on the larboard battery on both ships let loose their destructive fire as their guns came to bear on the passing opponent. American gunners aimed at *Peacock*'s hull, and the damage to the British ship was severe. Peake himself was among several killed early in the fight. *Peacock*'s gunners, by contrast, aimed high, cutting some of *Hornet*'s rigging and killing a man in the mizzen-top.

As the ships came clear of each other, *Peacock* put her helm around in order to fire her starboard guns at the passing *Hornet*. But Lawrence was ready for the move; *Hornet* herself wore around and came in under *Peacock*'s starboard quarter, raking her exposed stern with her heavy carronades from devastatingly close range. Many of the casualties aboard *Peacock* resulted from this single broadside. Within fourteen minutes of the first shot, *Peacock* struck her colors and pulled her ensign down as a signal of distress. She was fast filling with water, and her mainmast had fallen by the board.[11]

Lawrence anchored the *Hornet* and sent Lieutenant Shubrick over on his cutter to take the prize. When Shubrick boarded and discovered *Peacock*'s precarious condition, he sent for another boat from *Hornet* with carpenters, officers, and crew to help save the severely damaged ship. Despite working the pumps, plugging the holes, and pitching the guns overboard to lighten the ship, *Peacock* settled lower, and Shubrick knew the fight against the enveloping sea was lost. He and the other American officers and crewmen worked to save the British crewmen and to get the wounded safely to *Hornet*. Most had been evacuated when *Peacock* suddenly sank early that evening, drowning three Americans and thirteen British working below decks. When the sinking *Peacock* finally settled on the shallow bottom, her fore top remained above the water, offering refuge to four British seamen who scrambled up the mast to the tops and held on until they were rescued by a boat from *Hornet*. Another four British sailors escaped to land, and freedom, by absconding with *Peacock*'s stern boat during the confusion.

Far from home and with almost as many prisoners as crew crammed into his small ship, Lawrence was particularly concerned about an attack by *Peacock*'s companion, *Espiegle*, still anchored in the Demerara only four miles away. Surely *Espiegle*'s Captain Taylor had heard the sounds of gunfire and would be coming to the aid of his countrymen. Lawrence had nothing to fear, however, for Taylor never budged from the safety of his anchorage behind the bar. Later, in a court-martial assembled to investigate his failure to act, Taylor claimed not to have been aware of the fight, but the court did not believe him, and he was dismissed from service. He appealed, and since the evidence against him was inconclusive, he was reinstated but with a "heavy loss of seniority."[12]

With his prisoners securely stowed, the wounded cared for, and the necessary repairs made to *Hornet*, Lawrence got underway at two o'clock the next morning, sailing back to the United States with about 277 men on board the small brig. Water rations were reduced to three pints per day, and on 19 March 1813, a little more than three weeks after the battle, *Hornet* anchored at Holmes Hole on Martha's Vineyard to take on fresh water and supplies. From there she sailed down Long Island Sound to New York City, where the officers and crew were fêted by the town fathers.

Lawrence and his crew also received accolades from their British captives. Some accounts of the aftermath tell that a "British sailor, requiring an amputation, would not submit to the surgeon's saw until Lawrence sat beside him, held his hand and promised to adopt his son should the sailor not survive."[13] His small son had been with him on the *Peacock*, and was now a popular prisoner on board the *Hornet*. It was the father's second amputation, and he survived. Back in New York, the British officers of the *Peacock* published a card (presented a certificate), signed by the first and second lieutenants, the master, surgeon, and purser, claiming:

> We ceased to consider ourselves prisoners; and everything that friendship could dictate was adopted by you and the officers of the *Hornet* to remedy the inconvenience we would otherwise have experienced from the unavoidable loss of the whole of our property and clothes owing to the sudden sinking of the *Peacock*.[14]

Though his British captives were generous in their praise, their nation was not, and the news of the loss of the *Peacock* in a one-on-one fight arrived a few months after the bad news about *Java*. C. S. Forester summed up the mood in both countries in early 1813:

> The public in America and England could only be aware that once more comparatively equal forces had met and once more a crushing, a preposterously one-sided victory had been won by the Americans. Not one such victory, or two, but five.[15]

Of deeper concern to the Admiralty was the fear that the American victories would stiffen the resolve of the French navy, which heretofore had not distinguished itself in combat. On 7 March 1813, off the coast of Africa at Sierra Leone, the British frigate *Amelia* met the French frigate *Arethuse* in one of the bloodiest fights of the war. The *Arethuse* succeeded in beating off the *Amelia*, who lost half her crew and more than half her officers. The *Naval Chronicle* lamented in late March 1813:

> It is long since anything like this persevering effort has been witnessed on the part of the French. Is it not obvious they are stimulated by American triumphs? Does the Admiralty now believe we were wrong in foreseeing a train of ills from the surrender of the *Guerriere*? ... The French sailor who went into battle, with a persuasion, founded on long experience, that his antagonist must be victorious, was already half conquered. How different when he learns that his dreaded opponent has been beaten, yea, thrice beaten, by a new and inexperienced enemy. Not only does this cure him of superstitious terror, but it substitutes a spirit of emulation, and national rivalry.[16]

The *Naval Chronicle* concluded, "The Americans ought to be made to feel the real weight of the British trident, when properly wielded; and not be allowed to skulk from their challenge for mastery of the ocean, under the shelter of some compromising special-pleading treaty, till not only our losses have been indemnified, our defeats avenged, but the spell be restored."[17] Forester wrote that the duke of Wellington came to a similar conclusion: "I have been very uneasy about the American naval success. I think we should have peace with America before the season for opening the campaign in Canada, if we could take one or two of these damned frigates."[18]

II

For thirty-one-year-old Master Commandant James Lawrence, the swift victory over *Peacock* was the accomplishment he needed to secure his promotion to the rank of captain and to a more prestigious command, a promotion he believed was overdue. Lawrence was one of the many deserving master commandants who resented the earlier promotion of Lieutenant Charles Morris directly to the rank of captain after he was seriously wounded in the *Constitution*'s fight with *Guerriere*, the first such promotion since Decatur's in the Barbary Wars. Indeed, Lawrence was so disturbed by the Morris promotion that he had complained directly to the secretary of the navy:

> After devoting nearly fifteen years of the prime of my life faithfully to the service of my country, without a furlough ... you must not think hard of my remonstrating thus plainly on Lt. Morris's promotion over me. I assure you I should regret extremely leaving the Service at any period, particularly at this, but if outranked by an officer who has no greater claim than myself to promotion, I have no alternative.[19]

Secretary Hamilton's swift reply to Lawrence made clear his views on veiled threats from junior officers: "[I]f (without cause) you leave the service of your country, there will still remain heroes and patriots to support the honor of its flag."[20] After due deliberation, Lawrence chose to remain on the side of heroes and patriots.

With Lawrence's promotion to captain came a new assignment, thanks to William Bainbridge, who was very much impressed with his performance on the long voyage south, and who had considerable influence within the navy. On 4 May, the new secretary of the navy, William Jones, offered Lawrence the *Constitution*—Bainbridge was giving it up to take command of the Boston navy yard. But no sooner had the offer been made than Jones was informed that Captain Samuel Evans, suffering from some illness, had resigned his command of the frigate *Chesapeake*, now docked in Boston after a lengthy cruise in which she had secured several prizes. While *Constitution* was still laid up for repairs, *Chesapeake* was in good enough condition to quickly return to sea. A man of Lawrence's talents, Jones decided, should be back at war, and two days later Lawrence was appointed to the command of *Chesapeake*. *Constitution* went to Captain Charles Stewart, who had distinguished himself in Hampton Roads by keeping the frigate *Constellation* safe from British attackers.[21]

Lawrence might have preferred to stay with the *Hornet* and the enthusiastic crew he had trained to fighting perfection, but the navy insisted: his talents were needed on the *Chesapeake*, and Jones ignored his four letters of protest.[22] A loyal officer with no other option but to quit the service, Lawrence did as he was told. He soon left New York City for Boston, arriving in mid-May to assume command of what some contend was a troubled ship.

One of the problems he confronted was a number of vacancies in the crew and officer corps. During *Chesapeake*'s previous voyage, some of the crewmen's two-year enlistments had expired, and a dispute over prize money and back pay (precipitated by an inept navy paymaster at Boston) left many sailors disgruntled. Lawrence had to search for new crewmen in the seedy taverns and inns that served the sea trade, and from other ships docked, or blockaded, in the harbor.

If recruiting a new crew were not problem enough, the *Chesapeake* was also deficient in her officer corps, forcing Lawrence to scramble around the port in search of qualified leaders. *Chesapeake*'s first lieutenant, O. A. Paige, took ill while ashore and soon died. His acting replacement, Lieutenant Pierce, had his own problems, chiefly his inability to maintain civil relations with any of the other officers on board. Apparently the personality problems were severe enough to encourage the short-handed Lawrence to allow Pierce to quit the ship.

Paige's, and then Pierce's, replacement, Augustus Ludlow, twenty-one years old and a man of limited experience, had formerly served as third lieutenant on *Chesapeake*. Backing him up were two midshipmen, also young and with limited experience, who had been hastily appointed second and third lieutenants for the coming voyage. One was William Cox, who had served as midshipman on *Hornet* and had followed Lawrence to the *Chesapeake*; he now found himself the frigate's third lieutenant.[23] Bit by bit in the few days available to him, Lawrence cobbled together a serviceable crew and an adequate officer corps.

Many crewmen stayed on from the previous voyage, and some others were enlisted from *Constitution*, still undergoing repairs. But others contend that the new crew included dozens of inexperienced landsmen plus a number of less than enthusiastic foreigners—including English (some say as many as forty) and Portuguese, among whom were said to be several troublemakers. Although some American historians emphasize the inexperience of *Chesapeake*'s crew, other British and American historians claim that the facts indicate otherwise. The naval historian Peter Padfield argues, "The men were not raw: of the 388 officers, men and marines on *Chesapeake*'s pay list on 1st June, 279, or nearly three-quarters, had served in the previous cruise under Captain Evans."[24] Lieutenant Ludlow seems not to have been concerned about the readiness of *Chesapeake* when he wrote to his brother the day before sailing, "There is a report we shall go to sea on Sunday, but I cannot believe it. I hardly think we shall go out in such fine weather when there are three frigates off. The ship is in better order for battle than ever I saw before."[25]

If Lawrence went to sea with a crew of novices, he was by no means the first captain of an American frigate to do so. When Hull left Annapolis in the *Constitution* just days after war was declared, many of his crewmen were without experience on a warship. Similarly, when Bainbridge took over the *Constitution* from Hull after her return to Boston following the defeat of *Guerriere*, some of her crew were unwilling to stay on, for they viewed Bainbridge as an unlucky commander and a harsh disciplinarian. Nonetheless, both captains had the luxury of several uninterrupted weeks at sea to train their crews and hone their skills before having to meet an enemy, and both had the benefit of an experienced corps of officers to train and lead the crew. Lawrence, in contrast, had only a few days to train his crew, and none of that training occurred at sea. The naval officer and historian Captain Edward L. Beach Jr. sums up the conflicting views about Lawrence's new crew quite well:

> Lawrence had no opportunity to shake his men down into a smoothly functioning man-of-war's crew. History commonly says that his defeat came about because his crew was not well trained,

> yet there is much more to this than simple training in handling guns or sails. His men had done this all their adult lives, but they had never done it together. To function at its best, a team, or crew, must live together and work together. They must come to know one another, respect one another, and support one another. Books have been written about the intangibles of how teams work, how the invisible tendons of morale hold them together during difficulty, how the strength of the whole is greater than the sum of its parts. No one really knows how this works, but all athletic coaches, and all sports fans, recognize its importance.[26]

While Lawrence tried to ready his crew, Captain Philip Veres Broke of the British frigate *Shannon*, 38, maintained the blockade at the mouth of Boston Harbor with the frigate *Tenedos*, 38. Whereas most British captains had become complacent after years of easy success against the French, Broke worked his crew relentlessly in gunnery and hand-to-hand combat. Theodore Roosevelt thought him the best of those who fought against the Americans, and in a rare instance of agreement with the British naval historian William James, he concurred with the latter's view that "in the course of a year or two, by the paternal care and excellent regulations of Captain Broke, the ship's company became as pleasant to command as it was dangerous to meet."[27] Roosevelt again admiringly quotes James's description of the training regimen:

> Every day, for about an hour and a half in the forenoon, when not prevented by chase or the state of the weather, the men were exercised at training the guns, and for the same time in the afternoon in the use of the broadsword, pike, musket, etc. Twice a week the crew fired at targets, both with great guns and musketry; and Captain Broke, as an additional stimulus beyond the emulation excited, gave a pound of tobacco to every man that put a shot through the bulls-eye.[28]

Though his men were highly trained and eager to fight, Broke had not yet put them to the test. Earlier in the war, he and *Shannon* were part of the British fleet off New Jersey that nearly captured the *Constitution*, but the wily Isaac Hull escaped unscathed. Broke's failure to catch Hull allowed the American to go on to sink *Guerriere* a month later, the first of several stinging losses that Broke longed to avenge. Woodman describes the captain's attitude: "As an officer and a gentleman of honour, Broke smarted under the humiliation the Americans' parvenu navy had inflicted upon his own service, and he was not averse to a trial of strength."[29]

Broke bristled at the *Guerriere*'s loss but saw a silver lining:

> We are all very angry at hearing that the American frigate *Constitution*, whom our squadron hunted so lately has taken one of our frigates and burned her. However this will all forward the chance of *Shannon*'s making an honorable gamer of it as the enemy will be saucy now.[30]

Broke had been *Shannon*'s Captain since she was launched seven years earlier, and his frustration with his lack of opportunity to distinguish himself in combat began long before this new war with the Americans. While on duty against the French, Broke wrote to his wife in frustration:

> I would give any of the French frigate Captains all the prize money I should obtain by taking him if he would only come out voluntarily to give me an opportunity of going home with honor ... but I must stay by old *Shannon* so long as she will bear me and perhaps she may be gracious enough to make me some return for my constancy—either in laurels or lucre.[31]

But still, the disappointment continued, and the trial of strength for which he hoped remained beyond his grasp. Earlier that spring, Commodore Rodgers and his squadron sailed out of Boston Harbor unmolested,[32] perhaps because Broke's new orders from Admiralty prohibited him from taking on the big frigates one-on-one, or maybe because Rodgers simply out-sailed Broke and got away clean. In either case, Broke was eager for a fight and was already drafting a formal challenge that he would soon send to Lawrence. As an inducement for Lawrence to accept his challenge, on 25 May Broke ordered *Tenedos* to cruise farther north, nearer Cape Sable on the western tip of Nova Scotia, for the next three weeks, leaving only *Shannon* offshore of Boston Harbor.

III

Built in the Gosport Shipyard (now the Norfolk Naval Shipyard) at Portsmouth, Virginia, in 1799 for the sum of $220,677, (largely with slave labor, claim some British historians),[33] *Chesapeake* was one of three smaller thirty-eight-gun frigates that supplemented the three super frigates of the forty-four-gun *Constitution* class. She was originally planned as a forty-four, but her designer, Josiah Fox, thought Humphreys's super frigates too large. Fox was also short of molded timbers and got permission from Secretary of Navy Robert Smith to construct a frigate of more modest dimensions.[34] At a length of 151 feet, she was smaller than the big frigates but nearly an even match for British frigates like *Macedonian* and *Shannon*. Her fifty guns—twenty-eight eighteen-pound long guns, eighteen thirty-eight-pound carronades, a couple long twelve-pounders, a long eighteen, and a twelve-pound carronade—could throw 550 pounds of iron in a single broadside. Her spirited crew and officers had given each of *Chesapeake*'s guns a patriotic name. Engraved in copper and affixed to the guns' wooden carriages, the names included Brother Jonathan, True Blue, Yankee Protection, Putnam, Raging Eagle, Viper, General Warren, Mad Anthony, America, Washington, Liberty for Ever, Dreadnought, Defiance, and Liberty or Death.[35]

Chesapeake's launch, like the *Constitution*'s, was not auspicious. She got stuck twice in the stays, and a workman died during her launch, rendering her an unlucky ship in the eyes of many a superstitious tar. *Constitution* may have defied the ill omens of her launch, but *Chesapeake*'s captains and crew seemed to sail under a curse. The savage and unprovoked attack by HMS *Leopard* in 1807 left twenty men dead or wounded and provoked many duels among its officers. And on the voyage preceding Lawrence's appointment, *Chesapeake*'s commander, Captain Samuel Evans, took seriously ill and had to retire from the service.

Nor did *Chesapeake* sail particularly well. Stephen Decatur, who commanded her after the *Leopard* affair, complained that "*Chesapeake* as a Vessel of War Sails uncommonly dull."[36] The prize captain who brought her to Britain from Halifax was not impressed by her handling and "felt there was no argument for copying her hull form."[37] But she was powerfully built, like most American frigates, and sheathed in scantlings of thick live oak. Because of the shortage of oak in the British Isles, the *Shannon* was built of fir. Though essentially of the same size and armament as *Chesapeake*, she was not nearly as strong.

Chesapeake's standing orders from the secretary of the navy were to get underway as quickly as possible and sail northeast to intercept store ships and troopships crossing the Atlantic to resupply and reinforce the British army in Canada. She was also ordered to attack the British whaling fleet off the coast of Greenland. The *Hornet*, under the command of Captain Biddle, would accompany him. By late May it was no secret that *Chesapeake* would soon head to sea. Broke had been informed and was prepared for her departure. Closely matched with *Shannon* in armament, size, and crew, *Chesapeake* offered Broke and the Royal Navy their best chance to vindicate their tarnished reputations and end the unrelieved record of defeat against the Americans.

On 1 June 1813, just eleven days after assuming command of *Chesapeake*, Lawrence weighed anchor and sailed out of Boston Harbor with what some contend was an unhappy crew and with a hastily assembled novice corps of officers. Lawrence hoped that their spirit would compensate for their lack of training. He mustered the crew on deck as *Chesapeake* sailed by Boston Lighthouse and urged them to "Peacock" the enemy. Unimpressed, the men used the assembly to complain about their missing prize money. Lawrence was taken aback by such surliness on the eve of battle, says James Fenimore Cooper, and he ordered the purser to issue prize money chits as the men headed back to their duties.[38]

Broke had gone to unusual lengths to devise and execute a detailed battle plan, which took into account the respective strengths and weaknesses of the opposing forces and drew heavily on lessons from past confrontations with American ships. Where the Americans had superior strength, he would challenge with cunning surprise, and his marines would play a key role in the battle plan: "[D]rilled into the marines who manned his fighting tops, was that every man at the helm, and every officer, not to mention anyone else identifiable as holding a critically important position, was to be shot as quickly as possible.... 'Kill them,' he said time after time, 'and the ship is ours.'"[39]

Relying on the marksmanship of his marines in the tops, Broke's strategy entailed considerable, though calculated, risk in positioning his ship so as to give them a clear field of fire. The necessity of seizing the weather gauge—putting your ship downwind of an opponent to gain maximum freedom of maneuver—was a fundamental principle of naval warfare, but Broke was prepared to surrender that advantage to the *Chesapeake*. The wind from behind the American ship would blow the smoke from her broadsides toward the *Shannon*. The visibility from Broke's deck would be impaired, but the marines aloft would have a clear view of *Chesapeake*'s deck and of every officer standing upon it.[40] At the same time, officers on *Shannon* would be hidden from the marines on *Chesapeake*.

Finally, Broke intended to compensate for the *Cheapeake*'s superior durability by diminishing her maneuverability, preventing her from bringing her guns to bear against the much less sturdy *Shannon*. Captain Beach describes how Broke accomplished this by the clever rearrangement of his guns:

> Two cannon had been carefully placed on *Shannon*'s forecastle, one a thirty-two pound carronade loaded with anti-personnel grape and canister to sweep the enemy ship's forecastle, the other a long 9 pounder on a raised swivel that could be elevated to the unusual angle of thirty-three degrees—and loaded with dismantling shot to knock down *Chesapeake*'s headsail. A similar huge improvised shotgun was located on *Shannon*'s quarterdeck, as was another elevated long 9 with dismantling shot intended for the enemy's spanker, her main steering sail.[41]

As he waited for *Chesapeake* to leave the harbor, Broke fell in with a Liverpool privateer, *Sir John Sherbrooke*, which was in possession of an American privateer, *General Plumer*. The American's hold was filled with booty and fifty-four prisoners, including forty Irish passengers who had been seized from the British merchant ship *Duck* while on their way from Waterford to Canada to take up work as servants. Expecting a nasty fight and needing as large a crew as he could get, Broke asked for volunteers. Of the Irishmen who stepped forward, he picked twenty-two of the youngest and toughest to serve as boarders.[42]

Broke then took care that Lawrence would not avoid the challenge—and the trap. Knowing of Lawrence's heady sense of honor from the taunts and insults he had earlier hurled at Captain Pitt Barnaby Greene of *Bonne Citoyenne* for refusing to come out and fight at São Salvador, Broke turned the tables by sending a written challenge to Lawrence by way of an American fisherman, Eben Slocum, captured a few days earlier.

"[F]or courteousness, manliness, and candor," Broke's letter of challenge, in Roosevelt's view, was "the very model of what an epistle should be."[43] But even by the standards of the time, it was windy and officious, reading as if drafted by the Admiralty's legal team. The American naval historian and strategist Admiral Alfred Thayer Mahan may have been closer to the mark when he likened it to a challenge "of a French duelist, nervously anxious lest he should misplace an accent in the name of a man whom he intended to force into a fight and kill."[44] The letter was almost a thousand words long, including a postscript, and the envelope bore a clarifying addendum written, apparently, after it had been sealed. There are none of the stirring phrases one would expect to find in such a challenge. Unlike the short and pointed threats that Yeo and Dacres sent to their antagonists, Broke's missive wanders into verbosity: "Be assured, Sir, that it is not from any doubt I can entertain of your wishing to close with my proposals; but merely to provide an answer to any objection which might be made, and very reasonably, upon the chance of our receiving unfair support."[45] And so on.

But Lawrence never received that challenge, having already weighed anchor and moved his ship farther out into the harbor on the day Broke dispatched the letter. Indeed, there was no reason to offer a written invitation; *Shannon* had been sailing provocatively close to the mouth of the harbor, alone, for several days, and the invitation was unmistakable. All Boston knew of it, and as Lawrence headed out, Broke noted in his log that the American was flying three ensigns and a white flag on the foremast proclaiming "Free Trade and Seamen's Rights."[46] Lawrence sailed *Chesapeake* to the outer harbor, where he anchored in full sight of *Shannon*. Broke took *Shannon* toward the lighthouse and close hauled to a light breeze from the west, luffed up, and fired a single, teasing shot.[47] *I am here. I am ready. Chesapeake* fired a single gun in acceptance of the offer.

Lawrence and his crew made final preparations for the fight and for the cruise to follow. The captain wrote a note to the secretary of the navy to explain why he was taking the liberty of modifying his orders to make way to the north and intercept British ships entering the Gulf of St. Lawrence: "Since I had the honor of addressing you last ... I am now getting under way to carry into execution the instructions you have honoured me with. An English frigate is now in plain sight from my deck ... & should she be alone I am in hopes to give a good account of her before night. My crew appear to be in fine spirits, & I trust will do their duty."[48]

By early afternoon, Lawrence was ready and gave the order to get under way. A breeze blew from the southwest, and both ships headed out to sea.

Shannon put about her helm to wear ship, set her jib, and when round on a southeasterly course the top gallants and fore course were dropped and sheeted home. "The *Chesapeake*, meanwhile, set all her studding sails aloft and walked out after them, a splendid, tapering mass of white sunlit and shadowed canvas against the green land."[49] Behind *Chesapeake* was a small fleet of private pleasure craft and small commercial vessels sailing out to watch an American beat up on the British again. Among the spectator craft was a large private schooner said to have been bearing Captains Hull and Bainbridge, coming out to watch their young protégé perform.[50]

Sailing out to the battleground, both ships beat to quarters. Gear was stowed and carried below as the carpenters knocked down the walls of the wardroom and officers quarters to provide an unobstructed gun deck stretching from bow to stern. With the wardroom gone, British historian Peter Padfield writes, Broke had the carpenters erect a table on the quarterdeck, surrounded it with a canvas screen to shield it from the men's gaze, and invited his officers to dine with him.

> They gathered around the white cloth agleam with his silver service and glassware, claret in decanters making a splash of colour between their shadows—[First Lieutenant George Thomas] Watt, and [Second Lieutenant Provo] Wallis, [Third Lieutenant Charles Leslie] Falkiner and two Marine officers, [Lieutenant James] Johns and [Lieutenant John] Law, each backed by his own servant, each a little constrained by the occasion and by an effort at unconcern. And whenever they stood to glance over the starboard-quarter hammocks, there, like fate itself, was the towering spread of the *Chesapeake*'s canvas, always just a fraction closer, the sun moulding white highlights on the starboard side of her studding sails, and the ripple at her bow.[51]

They were well out to sea when Lawrence, concerned about a trap, rounded to, pointed his ship toward Salem, and fired a gun. Broke followed suit, pointed in the same direction, backed his sails, and fired a single gun in return. Apparently satisfied by Broke's response, Lawrence returned *Chesapeake* to a seaward course, and Broke followed suit. By four that afternoon,

Broke felt he was far enough from Boston to risk a fight and the damage it might cause to his vessel even if he won. Slowing to allow *Chesapeake*, now about four miles back, to close, Broke ordered the top gallants taken in and the staysails lowered. The table on the quarterdeck was cleared away, the men were piped for a serving of grog, and the kids tethered in the manger on the gun deck below were carried up and thrown overboard to keep them from getting in the way of the gun crews. "[Broke] watched the poor things struggling as they drifted astern."[52]

On the *Chesapeake*, Lawrence ordered his lieutenants to add canister and bar shot to the one round of grape already in the guns. He had earlier taken in his royals and topgallant sails and was now closing the distance. Her sails shortened to fighting canvas, *Chesapeake* was coming on to *Shannon* under full topsails, foretopmast staysail and jib alone.[53] Standing high on a gun slide in cocked hat, his hair braided in a queue and tied behind in a black ribbon, sporting heavy gold epaulettes on his best blue coat laced with gold and buttoned across his chest and snowy white shirt, Lawrence urged his men on as the ships came in range of each other: "*Peacock* her, my lads, *Peacock* her," he urged his crew. Several hundred yards ahead, wearing a top hat, which offered better protection to his head than his uniform cocked hat would do, Broke assembled his own crew. He reminded them of the recent defeats and of how the newspapers claimed that the "English have forgotten how to fight." He closed his brief exhortation by reminding them, "Kill the men and the ship is yours."[54]

As *Chesapeake* shortened to fighting canvas, Broke responded by shortening to single reefed topsails and jib, laying *Shannon* to with the wind just forward of her starboard beam. Several sails were then shivered, and *Shannon* slowed to receive her opponent. *Chesapeake*, running on full topsails, came up fast behind and closed the distance on the weather gauge, as Broke hoped she would do. It was a risky tactic that could easily turn to disaster. As the British crewmen watched *Chesapeake* close behind them, it looked as if the American would use the advantage of position, wind, and speed to cut in under *Shannon*'s stern quarter and rake her as she passed by.

But Lawrence pulled up alongside *Shannon*, about forty yards away, shivered his sails to reduce his speed, and took a position fairly alongside of *Shannon*, yard-arm to yard-arm. We can only speculate why Lawrence gave up

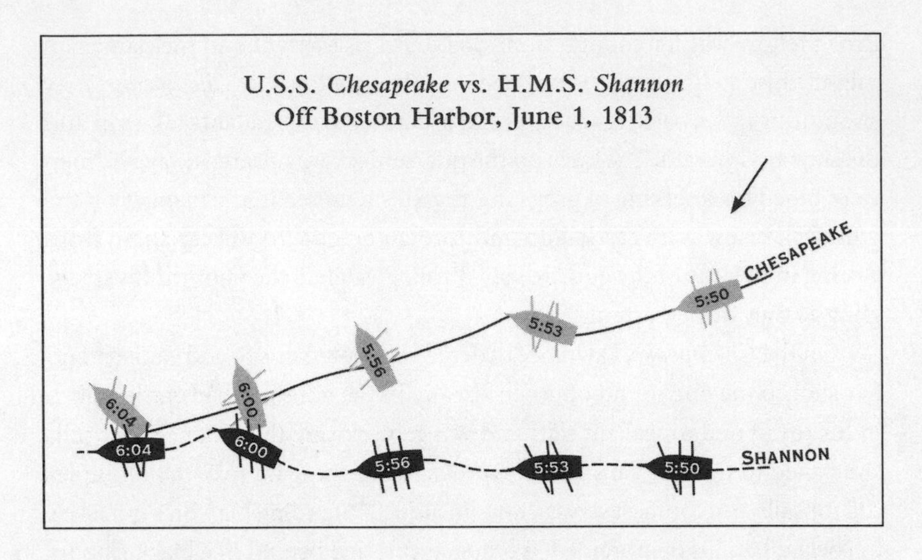

a potential advantage of position simply to slug it out ship to ship. Some historians suggest that he was motivated by a misplaced sense of chivalry that demanded an even playing field, while others wonder whether it was a case of overconfidence stemming from a string of easy American ship-to-ship victories, including his own over *Peacock*. Whatever the reason, Lawrence seems to have gone to a great deal of trouble to give Broke advantages he had no reason to expect.

Broke had *Shannon*'s guns loaded alternately with two round shot and a keg of musket balls, and one round shot and one double-headed shot. *Shannon*'s guns fired as they bore. The captain of the fourteenth gun, William Mindham, was the first to pull the lanyard to let loose the hammer and flint, fire the powder, and send his shot flying toward *Chesapeake*.[55] As *Shannon*'s guns fired singly, Lawrence waited until he was exactly abeam before he let roar his full broadside. As the two ships continued on parallel courses, cannon fire continued back and forth for eight or so short minutes, during which Broke's strategy played out exactly as he had planned. *Chesapeake*'s foretopsail tie and jib sheet were shot away. Farther back, her spanker-brails were loosened, and the sail blew out.[56]

Below decks, *Shannon*'s well-aimed shot took a swift and heavy toll on *Cheseapeake*'s gun crews. After the first few volleys, Second Lieutenant George Budd, commanding the guns, was horrified to discover that only a portion of the 150 or so crewmen stationed on the gun deck remained on their feet and continued to work their guns. Still, *Chesapeake*'s faltering return fire left a trail of devastation across the decks of *Shannon*. "Thomas Selby, able seaman on the fo'c'sle, had his head smashed from his body, Neil Gilchrist was cut in two by a 32 pound ball, Thomas Barry, a young lad, was taken off by a star shot across his middle."[57] Broke narrowly escaped injury himself when shot from *Chesapeake* shattered one of the guns on the quarterdeck and hurled shrapnel between his legs. The captain of the gun, Driscoll, was not so lucky: the same shot fractured both his knee caps, while the gun's loader took a shot of grape in his stomach. Falling to the deck in bloody agony, he begged those near him to put a hand into his wound and remove the shot. "I shall do well enough if you only do that." He did not live through the day.[58]

But *Chesapeake* was getting the worst of it. Casualties ran high as *Shannon*'s carefully placed carronades swept *Chesapeake*'s top decks like giant shotguns with canister and musket balls. In *Shannon*'s tops, Midshipmen William Smith and Philip Cosnahan led the fore and main top men in clearing *Chesapeake*'s decks and rigging of seamen and marines. Smith commanded those in foretops, while Cosnahan, sitting astride the starboard main yardarm, fired the muskets that sailors behind him loaded and passed up.[59] British marines, sailors, and officers fired toward *Chesapeake*'s decks, taking careful aim at anyone acting as if he were in command or trying to steer the ship from the double wheel mounted on the quarterdeck.

For *Chesapeake*'s officer corps, Broke's battle plan was catastrophic. Captain Lawrence took a musket ball in his leg, and as he struggled to get up, Royal Marine Lieutenant John Law shot him through his gut. Newly promoted Lieutenant Ludlow lay mortally wounded, shot twice by grape and muskets. Bleeding severely, he dragged himself below to safety. Also mortally wounded were Lieutenant Broom, the marine officer, Mr. Ballard, a recent midshipman now acting as fourth lieutenant, and the boatswain. Mr. White, the ship's sailing master, died immediately from his wounds. With one exception, each of *Chesapeake*'s officers had been shot at least twice. Most of those stationed on the quarterdeck were dead or dying, and the untended wheel spun crazily as *Chesapeake*, without stay sails, jib, or spanker, floundered out of control. Anyone who tried to steady the wheel and regain control was quickly picked off by *Shannon*'s marines and top men. Casualties among the American marines, who stood at their stations as others panicked and ran, were horrific. Of the forty-four on board, fourteen were killed, including Lieutenant Broom and Corporal

Dixon. Another twenty were wounded, including Sergeants Twin and Harris. Only nine marines, now led by a corporal, were left to defend the decks as the ships closed for boarding.[60]

Severely wounded and seeing his ship drifting uncontrollably toward *Shannon*, Lawrence ordered the bugler to call up the crew from below decks for boarding, but seeing that cannon shot and musket balls still flew thick across the deck, the bugler refused to budge from his hiding place under the launch. Verbal orders were finally shouted to the gun crews stationed below. Among those responding was Third Lieutenant William Cox, who had been commanding the gun crews. Shocked at the carnage and by his captain's severe wounds, Cox helped the semiconscious Lawrence below to the surgeon. As he was taken below, Lawrence kept repeating, "Don't give up the ship." Cox was unaware that he was one of only two officers above the rank of midshipman left standing.

Chesapeake wallowed uncontrollably. Her stern drifted toward Shannon's bow, and her mizzen rigging became foul of her enemy's fore chains, or according to another account, an anchor fluke. *Shannon* took advantage of her plight and raked her quarter, wreaking more havoc on *Chesapeake*'s bloody deck with canister fired from her fore- and aft-mounted carronades. "Seeing that the enemy were flinching from his guns,"[61] Broke gave the order to secure the ships and board. Despite the carnage and absence of officers, *Chesapeake*'s remaining crew mounted a stiff resistance. Attempting to lash the ships together in preparation for boarding, *Shannon*'s boatswain, William Stevens, had his arm hacked off by a cutlass and was riddled with musket balls. Remarkably, Stevens survived.[62]

Broke led his boarders onto *Chesapeake*'s decks; some Americans ran below for safety, but many stayed to fight. *Chesapeake*'s chaplain, Samuel Livermore, charged at the British boarders, fired a pistol at one of them, and then came at Broke with his cutlass. But Broke was the better swordsman and hacked at Livermore's arm. The U.S. Marines still in the tops fired at the British assault force below, hitting Lieutenant Watt in the foot and wounding Midshipman Samwell, but they were soon blown out of the masts and spars by a well aimed shot of langridge (a load of irregularly shaped shot, used to damage rigging) fired from one of the two nine-pounders Broke had mounted fore and aft on the *Shannon*. In *Shannon*'s rigging, British topmen continued to fire at anything that moved on *Chesapeake*'s deck or in her rigging. As the ships lay together, British Midshipman Smith, commanding the musketry in the foretop, led five men across *Shannon*'s foreyard and onto *Chesapeake*'s main yard, where they could better pick off the Americans scrambling around on the deck below them.

As Broke's force fought for control of *Chesapeake*'s deck, Lieutenant Budd, who had been commanding the gun batteries below, led the dozen or so men he could muster up the companionway and assaulted Broke and his force. In the early minutes of the counter-attack, *Shannon*'s purser, Aldham, and Broke's clerk, Dunn, were mortally wounded by a blast of grape from one of *Chesapeake*'s carronades. Budd took a bad blow from a cutlass and tumbled back down the gangway. Already mortally wounded, Ludlow dragged himself up from below to join Budd's force and help in the counter-attack, but he and his followers were routed by cutlass-wielding British boarders.[63]

Resistance was fading, but a few Americans fought on. One attacked Broke with a pike, which Broke parried. Broke then ran his attacker through with his sword, only to be clubbed with the butt of a musket. The blow knocked the top hat from Broke's head and struck him on his shoulder. Within seconds, another American slashed at Broke's head with a saber, cutting through his skull and exposing part of his brain. Broke collapsed, bleeding profusely, and was protected by his gun captain, William Mindham. As the American swordsman prepared to strike again, John Hill, a British marine, impaled him on his bayonet. John Collier and the coxswain William Stack chased down Broke's other assailants and hacked them to death.

As the deck was slowly cleared of American resistance, the boarders fired down the gangways to discourage those below at the guns from coming on deck, and they fired into the rigging to clear out any remaining riflemen. Fifteen minutes after the battled had begun, Watt, who had come back on board from the *Shannon*, where he had tended to his injured foot, struck *Chesapeake*'s colors. He called for a British ensign to raise in its place, but in the confusion the American flag flew above the British ensign when they were raised. Seeing the British ensign coming down and believing that the Americans had regained their ship, the crew of *Shannon*'s number seven main deck gun fired a blast of grape at those lowering the flag. The top of Watt's head was shot off and several others near him were killed before the friendly fire could be halted.

The carnage aboard both ships was horrific but much worse on *Chesapeake*. Midshipman Smith was one of the first British officers to venture below decks after the surrender, and a British historian describes what greeted the young officer:

> Below the scuppers were dark with blood; patches and spurts of blood stained the deck and even the beams overhead, and fragments of flesh, scalp skin with pigtails, unrecognizable pieces of gore, slivers of moments-ago living tissue were plastered loosely about the timbers. On the starboard side forward the fingers of a dismembered hand were sticking above a port as if their owner had pushed them through from outboard. Pieces of limb still covered with clothing, stained deep red through and through were scattered among the wreck and loose ropes on deck as if kicked out of the way, and among them the still forms of those who had been killed in the rush of boarders, and others lying, moving faintly.[64]

IV

Though brief, the duel between *Shannon* and *Chesapeake* was the bloodiest of the war. Roosevelt provides the grim tally:

> Of [*Chesapeake*'s] crew of 379 men, 61 were killed, or mortally wounded, including her captain, her first and fourth lieutenants, the lieutenant of marines, the master (White), boatswain (Adams) and three midshipmen, and 85 severely and slightly wounded, including both her other lieutenants, five midshipmen, and the chaplain; total, 148; the loss falling almost entirely upon the American portion of the crew. Of the *Shannon*'s men, 33 were killed outright or died of their wounds, including the first lieutenant, purser, captain's clerk, and one midshipman, and 50 wounded, including the captain himself and the boatswain; total 88.[65]

Although British marksmen in the tops were an important part of the swift victory, *Shannon*'s gunnery was just as devastating to the Americans, landing more than two shots for every one landed by *Chesapeake*'s gunners. So swift was the victory and so disorganized was the Americans' brief defense that *Chesapeake*'s signal book containing secret recognition codes was captured by the British before it could be thrown overboard in a lead-weighted sack.

In a tribute to Broke's intense training of his crew in gunnery and boarding, Roosevelt puts this disparity into perspective, noting that despite its deficiency in shots scored, "*Chesapeake* battered the *Shannon*'s hull far more than either *Java*, *Guerriere*, or *Macedonian* did the hulls of their opponents, and that she suffered less in return ... than they did."[66] Perhaps reflecting the intensity of the *Chesapeake*'s brief but fierce resistance to the boarding, *Shannon* also suffered a high death toll compared with the British frigates that had *lost* to the Americans earlier—thirty-three dead on the *Shannon*, fifteen on the *Guerriere*, thirty-six on the *Macedonian*, and twenty-two on the *Java*. In his report on 6 June 1813 to his commanding officer, Captain Thomas Bladen Capel, Broke observed, "The enemy made a desperate, but disorderly resistance."[67]

Because the damage to *Chesapeake* was not severe, and because the two wounded ships lay very near Boston Harbor, the British quickly put the American prisoners under guard and made ready to sail the captured *Chesapeake* to Halifax with a prize crew under Lieutenant Falkiner. Lieutenant Wallis assumed command of the *Shannon*.

As the severely wounded Broke slipped in and out of consciousness in his quarters on *Shannon*, Lawrence, shot through the abdomen with a musket ball, lay dying aboard the *Chesapeake*. Peritonitis set in, and Lawrence spent the four remaining days of his life in delirious agony, still urging his crew, "Don't give up the ship."[68] With Broke incapacitated, Falkiner seems to have taken advantage of the opportunity to exact revenge for Britain's past humiliations, and charges of mistreatment and murder by both sides have dogged the battle's aftermath ever since.

While it was common to confine the captured crew in a secure place below decks, enemy officers were generally held captive under the conventions of a chivalric honor system that allowed them to roam more or less freely, socialize with their victorious counterparts, and keep their property. Not so under Falkiner and Wallis. U.S. Midshipman William Berry says he was beaten shortly after his capture and that the British midshipmen took their American counterparts' clothes and weapons. He also claimed that the American midshipmen were imprisoned below: "Eleven of our midshipmen were confined in a small place, nine feet by six, with an old sail to lie on, and a guard at the door, until a day or two before our arrival at Halifax; and likewise eleven of us upon five rations, and some days only one meal."[69] Some reports have the mortally wounded Captain Lawrence faring not much better than his crew. Beach charges:

> Lawrence was given medical care but scant courtesy while he lay dying aboard the frigate he commanded such a short time. His captors had taken over everything aboard ship, and even refused to return his wife's letters to him. By account of the officers and crew of the beaten ship, the British lieutenants in charge, and their prize crew, "behaved with brutality."[70]

The American crew and officers were not the only captives at risk of ill treatment. Shortly after surrender, the *Shannon*'s officers went on a hunt among the *Chesapeake*'s crew for British deserters. Estimates placed the number of Englishmen in *Chesapeake*'s crew at about forty, and identifying them kept the British busy on the voyage to Halifax. The punishment for service aboard an American warship was death by hanging, but British naval authorities, desperate for crewmen, were often willing to accept all manner of excuses in return for enlistment in the Royal Navy. Thomas Jones, age twenty-three, said the Americans threatened to put him in irons if he did not serve on *Chesapeake*. Henry Simpson, twenty-seven, claimed he was made drunk in New York and taken on board. John Bell, thirty-five, said he was forced into service when *Chesapeake* captured the merchant ship *Volunteer*, on which he served. Bell agreed to help identify other British seamen on *Chesapeake* who were not as forthcoming as he was.[71] Not so lucky was the captured *Chesapeake* crewman J. Warburton, an Englishman sailing under the name of Parker. Warburton was found among the wounded and identified as a former crewman of the *Eolus* who had mutinied against the British prize-master and sailed the recaptured vessel into Salem, Massachusetts. Later in the year he was tried, convicted, and hanged on HMS *Prince* while it lay at anchor at Spithead.[72]

Lawrence died on 4 June, as the two ships were off Sambro Light at the entrance to Halifax. His body was moved to *Chesapeake*'s quarter deck and wrapped in the American flag. A British civilian who managed to get on board the ship shortly after it arrived in Halifax described the same horrific scene that had confronted Midshipman Smith immediately after the battle:

> The deck was not cleaned ... and the coils and folds of rope were steeped in gore as if in a slaughter house.... Pieces of skin, with pendant hair, were adhering to the sides of the ship, and in one place I noticed portions of finger protruding, as if thrust through the outer wall of the frigate.... [I]t was a scene of devastation as difficult to forget as to describe. It is one of the most painful reminiscences of my youth ... and it made upon me a mournful impression that, even now, remains as vivid as ever.[73]

Though Lieutenants Falkiner and Wallis may have been lacking in the courtesies then common among naval adversaries, their superiors at Halifax were not. Henry Gruppe describes the hero's funeral given Captain Lawrence:

> Six Royal Navy captains served as his pall bearers while a band and 300 members of the British 64th Regiment of Foot rendered honors. The procession of mourners to the cemetery was long, with officers and men from both the *Chesapeake* and *Shannon* joining in poignant tribute to a gallant captain. Wrote one of the American officers at the funeral "I can truly say that all appeared to lament his death, and I heard several say that they considered the blood which had been shed on the *Chesapeake*'s deck as being as dear to them as that of their own countrymen.[74]

Lieutenant Ludlow, suffering a severe head wound from a saber slash, was recuperating in Watt's old cabin on *Shannon*. He was expected to pull through, and on the voyage to Halifax had engaged Lieutenant Wallis in many spirited "what if" conversations about the battle. But once in Halifax, his condition deteriorated and he soon died and was buried with Lawrence. As he lay dying, he asked the *Shannon*'s fifer to play him "Yankee Doodle"—"I think nothing will cheer me up as much as that tune." Apparently, the young man played it with such vigor that the imprisoned Americans in the hold below briefly thought they were about to be recaptured, while the *Shannon*'s crewmen scrambled onto the deck in alarm.[75]

Six weeks later, under a flag of truce, the officers' bodies were returned to the United States and buried in Salem. Lawrence was later reburied in Trinity churchyard in New York. Wallis and Falkiner were promoted to commanders, and Lieutenant William Cox—the only American officer not wounded—was subjected to a court-martial. The wounded Lieutenant Budd filed charges against Cox, claiming he should have taken charge of the fighting deck instead of carrying Lawrence below.[76] Some claimed Lawrence ordered him to do it, but whatever the facts, a scapegoat was needed to bear the brunt of America's first significant naval loss, and the acting lieutenant was the nearest suspect. Cox was tried by general court-martial, found guilty, and sentenced "to be cashiered with a perpetual incapacity to serve in the Navy of the United States." (Congress exonerated Cox in 1952, and his rank of Third Lieutenant was posthumously restored.[77])

The news of the loss reached Boston within hours of the battle, and the rest of America soon after. "The whole town became one scene of silence and mourning. The grand celebration supper was cancelled, the silent tables cleared."[78] For the British in Canada, however, the victory was bracing. Years later a resident of Halifax, Thomas Haliburton, remembered the Sunday morning when the news of *Shannon*'s victory arrived:

> I was attending divine service in St. Paul's Church at that time, when a person was seen to enter hurriedly, whisper something to a friend in the garrison pew, and then as hastily withdraw. The effect was electrical, for whatever the news was, it flew from pew to pew, and one by one the congregation left the church.... I, too, left the building to enquire into the cause of the commotion. I was informed by a person in the crowd that an English man-of-war was coming up the harbour with an American frigate as her prize! By that time, the ships were in full view, near St. George Island, and slowly moving through the water. Every housetop and every wharf was crowded with groups of excited people, and, as ships successively passed, they were greeted by vociferous cheers.[79]

In Great Britain, cannons were fired from the Tower of London in celebration of a long overdue victory. Banquets were held, and illuminations performed throughout the capital. The *Naval Chronicle* reflected the national jubilation in a fulsome tribute: "The brilliant style in which the business was done, may perhaps be equaled, but we are sure will never be excelled, by any incident that can be quoted from British history."[80]

Laudatory poems were quickly composed and rushed into print. Among the poets was Lieutenant Edward Stewart of HMS *Royal Oak*, who wrote:[81]

> Three fatal fights Britannia saw with mixed surprise and woe,
> For thrice she saw the Union Flag by hostile hands laid low.
> Then casting around an anxious eye amongst her naval men,
> Her choice she made, that choice was Broke to raise her flag again …
> Hail Suffolk's pride! Such fame may I, a son of Suffolk share,
> Or if I fall, like glorious Watt, to fall what hour so fair.
> And prove tho' thrice superior force might transient trophies gain,
> Britannia rules the wat'ry world, sole Empress of the Main.

Less elegant, but cleverly to the point was the last stanza in a poem titled "Impromptu":[82]

> Quite sure of the game
> As from harbour they came
> A dinner and wine they bespoke;
> But for meat they got balls
> From our stout wooden walls
> And the dinner engagement was *Broke*.

Despite his wounds, Broke was able to record for his superior officer in Halifax some details of the stirring victory. In his letter to Captain Thomas Bladen Capel, Broke eschewed the modest, business-like tone typical of such reports. Neglecting to mention the confusion that led to the avoidable death of Lieutenant Watt, Broke wrote, "The American flag was hauled down, and the proud old British Union floated triumphant over it." Describing the boarding that carried the day, he recorded, "Our gallant bands appointed to that service immediately rushed in, under their respective officers, upon the enemy's deck, driving everything before them with irresistible fury."[83] But not everyone in Britain was so impressed. At a dinner at the duke of Wellington's table, Admiral Sir Isaac Coffin is said to have observed tartly (in one of several, though similar, variations of his alleged remarks), "It was well Broke met Lawrence and *Chesapeake*, and not Hull and *Constitution*."[84] Though Coffin's remarks are widely quoted by both American and British historians, in fairness to Broke it must be acknowledged that Admiral Coffin's own lackluster career left him in no position to pass judgment on a fellow officer.[85]

Broke remained unconscious for most of the voyage back to Halifax, and as the *Shannon* sailed into the harbor amid raucous cheers from the shore, his crewmen remained silent in consideration for their captain's fragile health. Returning to Britain as one of the great heroes of the war, he was awarded a baronetcy in 1813, one of just two frigate captains to be so honored for single-ship actions during the long years of warfare against France and America.[86] The citizens of his home county of Suffolk presented Broke with an elaborate silver salver depicting the battle. In 1815 he was made a knight commander of the Order of the Bath.[87]

The accolades were well deserved. Broke was one of the best the British had, and his gunnery techniques and innovations were incorporated into British naval manuals in the early nineteenth century. But Broke would never command again. His injuries were severe and he never fully recovered from them. He turned down the command of a new super frigate in 1814 on the urging of his wife, Louisa. Broke lived for another twenty-seven years as an invalid, often suffering from severe headaches. In 1841, in response to worsening pain, he traveled to London for an operation on his brain that he hoped would alleviate the suffering. While there, he received news that his son George had been promoted from lieutenant to commander, and in his letter of congratulations Broke added,

> I hear all is well at home today, and they are to send us a little turkey from the old farm for our Christmas dinner, my doctor giving me no hopes of getting home for several weeks yet.[88]

Ten days later Broke was dead.

CHAPTER TWELVE

BACK ON LAND: BRITISH ON THE CHESAPEAKE, 1813

As Admiral Sir James Borlase Warren tightened his blockade on the American coast, intercepting cargo ships big and small and seizing their goods, much of the country's trade with the rest of the world, as well as the coastal trade among the states, came to a standstill. Only New England escaped the full rigor of the blockade, partly because of its difficult weather but also for strategic reasons. Although he would later be criticized for laxness, Warren appreciated the region's opposition to the war and the essential supplies that New England farmers and merchants smuggled to British forces in Canada.[1] As Sir George Prevost wrote to the secretary of war, Lord Bathurst:

> Two thirds of the army in Canada are at this moment eating beef provided by American contractors, drawn principally from the states of Vermont and New York. This circumstance, as well as the introduction of large sums of specie into this province, being notorious in the United States, it is to be expected Congress will take steps to deprive us of those resources, and under that

> apprehension large droves are daily crossing the lines coming into Lower Canada.[2]

So serious was the smuggling of supplies from New England to the British that the already overcommitted U.S. Navy stationed the sloop of war *Enterprise* off the coast of Maine to discourage trade with the enemy.[3] But despite the economic hardships of the blockade, the nation's resolve to sustain the war remained strong, and the growing American military presence along the Canadian border posed a serious threat to Britain's last remaining North American colony.

With the colony of Canada at risk and no apparent weakening of America's resolve, Warren was compelled in early 1813 to take the war more directly to the civilian population, and the prosperous communities along the coasts of the Chesapeake and Delaware bays were his targets. Leading the assault would be Admiral Sir George Cockburn, recently assigned to Warren by the Admiralty. Now forty-one years old, Cockburn had been at sea since the age of ten, and his distinguished naval career had earned him rapid promotion to rear admiral in 1812. A favorite of one of his commanders, the influential Admiral Lord Hood, Cockburn gained the rank of post captain at twenty-one. Two years later he had the good fortune of catching the attention of Horatio Nelson, who was aboard Cockburn's frigate *Minerve* when it captured the Spanish frigate *Santa Sabina*, commanded by Captain Don Jacobo Stuart, the great-grandson of England's King James II, whom William of Orange had deposed in the Glorious Revolution of 1688.[4]

Cockburn was in command of British naval forces off the coast of Spain in late October 1812 when he was ordered to wind up his affairs in Europe and report to Warren in Bermuda, where he would take command of the Chesapeake campaign. Evidence suggests that the earl of Bathurst's appointment of Cockburn to the North American station reflected the government's waning confidence in Warren's leadership and a desire to prosecute the war more aggressively than had been done during the first few months of conflict. During Warren's hesitant command of the North American station, American privateers ravaged British commerce, Canada was threatened by America's growing military presence along the border, and American warships moved in and out of Boston Harbor despite the blockade. The nineteenth-century British naval historian William James argued:

> [I]nstead of one of the ten or twelve dashing flag-officers ... being sent out to fight the Americans into compliance, a superannuated admiral, whose services, such as they were, bore a very old date, arrived, early in March 1813, in Chesapeake Bay, to try the effect of diplomacy and procrastination. Had not Sir John Warren's second in command, Rear-Admiral Cockburn, been of a more active turn, the inhabitants of that very exposed part of the American sea-frontier ... would scarcely have known, except by hearsay, that war existed.[5]

Arriving in Bermuda in mid-January 1813, Cockburn formed a squadron under his flagship *Marlborough*, 74, and on 3 March brought it into Lynnhaven Bay near the mouth of the Chesapeake. Within a week, Cockburn sent Warren a sixteen-point memo outlining his early intentions and pressing the admiral for more resources and a bolder effort.[6] Taking command of England's Chesapeake fleet—which with four ships of the line, six frigates, and a number of smaller vessels possessed more fire power than all the vessels of America's small navy combined—Cockburn moved aggressively to stamp his mark upon the powerful British naval squadron that had little to show for its might and the time spent on the bay. "His orders to his subordinates were to be prepared to chase at a moment's notice, and his officers and men understood that failure to obey orders could bring disgrace and professional ruin to an officer, or as many as 350 lashes to an enlisted sailor."[7]

Beginning in early 1813, the British squadron in the Chesapeake embarked upon a more aggressive campaign of chasing and capturing American privateers coming down the bay from Baltimore on their way into the Atlantic and British shipping lanes. The privateers *Lottery* and *Cora* were taken in February, but not before the former had put up stiff and costly resistance against the more powerful British ships. The American government responded to the growing British presence by hiring into naval service several privateers to patrol the Chesapeake. Cockburn responded by sending three ships under Captain Burnett up the York, Rappahannock, and Potomac Rivers in search of the schooners. In early April 1813, part way up the Rappahannock toward Fredericksburg, Virginia, Burnett caught and captured the four speedy Baltimore Clippers—the *Lynx, Arab, Racer*, and *Dolphin*[8]—and added them to Cockburn's fleet. The lesson learned, fewer American ships ventured out into the bay, allowing Warren to turn his attention to the next stage of his assault.

Believing that their force was still too small for a direct attack on the major cities of Washington, Baltimore, Norfolk, and Annapolis, Warren and Cockburn targeted the smaller towns and villages tucked away among the many rivers, inlets, and creeks along the Chesapeake coast. In his report to John Wilson Croker, the secretary of the Admiralty, Warren described his latest intentions:

> Being of the opinion that a light flotilla of small vessels would be of essential use in cutting off the enemies [*sic*] supplies, and destroying their foundries, stores and public works, by penetrating the rivers at the head of the Chesapeake; I directed Rear-admiral Cockburn to take under his orders the *Maidstone, Fantome, Mohawk, Highflyer* and three of the captured prize armed schooners; and the rear-admiral having selected a detachment, composed of one hundred and eighty seaman, and two hundred marines from the naval brigade of the squadron, together with lieutenant Robertson, of the Royal Artillery, and a small detachment of that corps ..., the whole proceeded upon the above-mentioned service.[9]

Warren's choice of the upper Chesapeake was strategically wise. With the British blockade ending much of America's city-to-city coastal trade, shipments of food and other goods now traversed the rough roads connecting the major cities and towns of the east coast. The main road connecting Baltimore to Philadelphia passed through the area, and French Town on the Elk River was one of the way stations on the route.

After plundering the inhabitants of Poole's, Sharp's, Tilghman's, and Poplar Islands, on 28 April Cockburn moved his force up the Elk River, and with 150 marines attacked French Town, whose militia, before retreating, offered scattered resistance from a gun battery of Revolutionary War–era four-pounders that had most recently served as ballast in a fishing vessel.[10] Cockburn took the town without much resistance, and as he later reported to Warren, destroyed whatever useful supplies he found:

> Its depots of stores; the whole of the latter, therefore, consisting of much flour, a large quantity of army clothing, of saddles and bri-

> dles, and other equipment for cavalry, &c. &c. together with various merchandise, were immediately set fire to, and entirely consumed, as were five vessels lying near the place; and the guns of the battery, being too heavy to bring away, were disabled as effectually as possible, by Lieutenant Robertson and his artillerymen.[11]

Having taken French Town and destroyed the homes and buildings that it comprised, Cockburn's force moved upriver to Elkton. Stiff resistance from the militia manning Fort Defiance—protecting thirty vessels seeking refuge at the port—turned back Cockburn's marines. Among the militia defending Elkton during this period were two companies from Lancaster County, Pennsylvania, whose farmers depended on the mills of Elkton to grind their wheat into flour and ship it to market. Among those serving in the Lancaster militia was a young officer named James Buchanan, the future president.

Three days after taking French Town, Cockburn's squadron crossed the bay and took a position off the port of Harvre de Grace, a small settlement at the mouth of the Susquehanna River. The British attacked the town on the morning of 3 May, firing Congreve rockets in advance of the troops' landing. Although the damage was light, the rockets terrified the defenders.[12]

After minor resistance—which some accounts attribute to an Irishman named John O'Neill, then a prosperous merchant, who claimed to have been the only one manning one of the gun batteries protecting the town[13]—Cockburn's marines quickly overran Havre de Grace. Only one townsman, a Mr. Webster, died in the attack, hit on the head by one of the Congreve rockets in the first hours of the assault. Although the British continued to use Congreve rockets in most of their major combined land-sea assaults in the bay, Webster is believed to have been the only rocket casualty of the war.

After the town's artillery battery was overrun, scattered house-to-house resistance confronted the British force until the local militia fled to the countryside. As they did at French Town, the British destroyed or seized whatever stores they found, including 130 small arms stored there. They also seized whatever they found of value among the property of the citizens.

> Their manner was, on entering a house, to plunder it of such articles as could be of any service to them … and convey them to their barges. Every man had his hatchet in his girdle, and when

> wardrobes and bureaus happened to be locked, they were made to yield with the force of the instrument. This was not a work of much time, and as soon as it was accomplished, they set fire to the house and entered another for the same purposes.[14]

After looting the town, Cockburn decided that his assault on Havre de Grace should become an example to other stubborn towns that might be tempted to resist his force. Expressing concern about the American militia hiding in the nearby woods, Cockburn reported to Warren,

> I did not judge it prudent to allow of their being further followed with our small numbers, therefore after setting fire to some of the houses, to cause the proprietors (who had deserted them, and formed a part of the militia who had fled to the woods,) to understand and feel what they were liable to bring upon themselves, by building batteries and acting towards us with so much useless rancour, I embarked in the boats....[15]

In reporting to have burned "some of the houses," Cockburn was too modest. In fact he burned forty of the sixty houses in Havre de Grace, including that of Commodore Rodgers, who was then at sea on the *President*.[16] Those not burned were plundered and vandalized. According to one source, "horses were killed in their stables, and troops 'cut hogs through the back, and some partly through, and then left them to run'. More houses would have been torched except for the pleas of several women to spare a portion of the town. A British officer was persuaded not to burn St. John's Episcopal Church, although the pews, pulpit, and all of the windows were destroyed." According to William Marine's account of the battle,

> General orders had been given to burn every house, and these were rigorously executed, till they were at length countermanded by the admiral. Immediately after he came on shore ... two or three ladies, who had courageously remained in their houses, during the whole commotion, endeavored by all the powers of female eloquence to dissuade him from his rash purposes. He was unmoved at first; but when they represented to him the misery he was causing, and

> pointed to the smoking ruins under which was buried all that could keep their proprietors from want and wretchedness, he relented and countermanded his original orders.[17]

The destruction and plunder of the town reverberated throughout the country. Inflammatory poems circulated to a wide audience eager to believe the worst of British behavior. A student at Princeton, hearing news of the burning, is believed to have written "The Lay of the Scottish Fiddle, A Tale of Havre De Grace,"[18] which includes the lines

> Seem'd Susquehanna's wave on fire,
> And red with conflagration dire.
> The spreading bays ensanguined flood
> Seem'd stained with hint of human blood

Although the capture and destruction of the town was of little military consequence, Cockburn did learn from a local snitch that the Principio foundry, an important manufacturer of cannon for the American forces, lay just across the Susquehanna. That afternoon, Cockburn sent a small force across the river to destroy the foundry, including twenty-eight long thirty-two-pounders waiting to be shipped, and several more in the process of being fabricated.

Two days later, Cockburn re-crossed the bay to the eastern side and sailed up the Sassafras River to the towns of Fredericktown and Georgetown. As his force moved up the Sassafras, the local militia blasted away at his boats from both banks of the river, wounding five of his men, one seriously. In retaliation, Cockburn put both towns to the torch, but not before his troops pilfered and plundered their way through the stores, farms, and houses. According to one contemporary account, the British "'so far descended in petty pilfering as to rob the black ferry-man, Friday, of his all and his pig, which lived with him in his hut.' They even went so far as to take the ear-rings from the ears of one of the ladies in Georgetown, and to rob others of their clothing."[19]

To his modest credit, Cockburn, in the end, did spare two houses in Fredericktown, "defended vigorously by a local maiden lady of means, named Miss Kitty Knight, who was caring for an elderly shut-in in a neighboring farm house." After less than two weeks of burning and looting, a delegation from Charleston, Maryland, a small port town at the far north of the bay,[20] assured

Cockburn that the town would offer no resistance and invited him to inspect it. With that concession, Cockburn believed he had made his point upon the civilian population living in the bay's coastal cities. Reassembling his force, the rear-admiral sailed south and rejoined Warren at Lynnhaven Bay.

Beyond raw terror and the acquisition through seizure and purchase of an ample supply of food for the invading force, Cockburn achieved little of strategic value from his raids. In Henry Adams's view, "The people, harassed by this warfare, remembered with extreme bitterness the marauding of Cockburn and his sailors."[21] Several months later, when rumors abounded that Cockburn had returned briefly to Britain, the *Boston Gazette* wrote:

> It is stated as a fact that the notorious barbarian Admiral Cockburn has gone to England in the *Cressy*, British ship of war. We know not for what purpose he has gone home; but this we do know, that there breathes not in any quarter of the globe a more savage monster than this British Admiral. He is a disgrace to England and human nature; and we do not hesitate to say that, by his profligate and barbarous conduct to the Americans, he has forfeited the right to be treated as other prisoners of war, should he ever chance to be taken.[22]

At a banquet in Annapolis at around the same time, a toast was "'drunk with great enthusiasm': Admirals Warren and Cockburn; may the eternal vengeance of Heaven hurl them to some station that will terminate their inhuman butcheries and savage cruelties—they disgrace human nature."[23]

Cockburn's depredations may have contributed to the unity of the still divided American people over a costly war that not all supported. Choosing largely civilian targets and avoiding well-fortified positions, Cockburn appeared more a marauder than a soldier, and his open effort to encourage slaves to flee their masters and seek freedom with his army may have strengthened southern support for the war. Indeed, the British continued to experience considerable resistance on the bay, and American intransigence led to serious and costly defeats for British forces stationed there. British efforts to replicate in Delaware Bay Cockburn's destructive foray into the upper Chesapeake came to naught when a British naval force under Captain John P. Beresford was repulsed at

Lewes, Delaware, after lobbing about a thousand shells into the town with little effect.

However brief and destructive the raids in the upper Chesapeake, they were just the beginning of a major British effort in this prosperous area to subdue the Americans and to take the pressure off the Canadian front, where sustained American victories along the poorly defended border could lead to the loss of Britain's remaining presence on the North American continent.

II

As Cockburn readied his force in Lynnhaven Bay for its first raids on the Chesapeake towns, Bathurst ordered Colonel Sir Thomas Sidney Beckwith, a distinguished veteran of campaigns in India and Spain, to lead a newly formed expeditionary force numbering 2,400, then being assembled in Bermuda.

Composed largely of two battalions of royal marines, Beckwith's force also included three hundred French chasseurs—misleadingly named the "Canadian Chasseurs" in the hope that the promise of resettlement in Canada after the war would improve their behavior. They were in fact French deserters and prisoners from the war in Europe who were offered an opportunity to fight Americans rather than to languish in prisons.[24] As if the chasseurs did not reveal the extent to which recruits of questionable quality were welcomed into the British forces in North America, Beckwith's expeditionary force included three hundred British infantry organized as the 102nd regiment of the line under Lieutenant Colonel Charles James Napier. One American historian observes, "Napier's 102nd Foot also was a hard lot, originally the New South Wales (or 'Rum') Corps, formed from military criminals and deserters for service in Australia, and apparently including some Australians."[25] In 1808, officers of the corps had led the so-called "Rum Rebellion" against the governor of New South Wales, William Bligh, one-time captain of HMS *Bounty*.[26] At that time, Australia served as a penal colony for the British Empire.

Bathurst's orders to Beckwith made it clear that his primary mission was to harass the Americans, not to seize territory, which might provoke their retaliation along the under-defended Canadian border. Within a week of returning to Lynnhaven from his attacks on the northern Chesapeake, Warren sailed to Bermuda to pick up Beckwith's force. He did not arrive at the island until 3 June 1813, but by mid-June he was back in the Chesapeake with a force numbering five thousand men. Commanding what was probably the most powerful force on the North American continent, Warren first targeted the U.S. frigate *Constellation*, securely anchored just a few miles up the Elizabeth River at Norfolk and recently placed under the command of Captain Joseph Tarbell.

At thirty-eight guns and nearly 1,300 tons, *Constellation* was closer in size and arms to the typical British frigate and smaller than America's three super frigates. About the size of the *Chesapeake*, she was built in Baltimore in 1797 and named for the new American flag, whose thirteen stars in a blue field represented a "new constellation." She had seen service in the Quasi-War with France and the Barbary Wars in the Mediterranean and was under the command of thirty-five-year-old Captain Charles Stewart when the British forced *Constellation* to seek refuge at Norfolk.

A red-headed Philadelphian of Scotch-Irish stock and at sea since the age of thirteen, Stewart was given his first command of an armed schooner in the Quasi-War. He proceeded to capture two French war ships, thus assuring himself of rapid advancement in the young American navy. One of "Preble's Boys"—he served as the commodore's second in command during the Barbary Wars—Stewart took command of the newly refitted *Constellation* in early 1813 when Captain William Bainbridge transferred to the *Constitution*. Stewart was about to leave the Chesapeake in February to cruise the Atlantic when the British blockade at the Virginia Capes forced him back into the bay.

Facing a nearby British naval force that would soon increase to a number greater than the entire U.S. Navy, Stewart had no illusions about getting out to sea any time soon. He protected the ship by having it kedged up the Elizabeth River in the dark of night. On 5 February, Stewart wrote to Secretary of the Navy Jones:

> At seven P.M. … by placing our boats with lights along the narrows, the pilot, Mr. James Thomas brought her up in Safety to fort Norfolk. The object of the Enemy appeared to be this Ship, as they got underway … on the evenings flood with a leading breeze and run up the roads. Finding us gone they went down again and anchored in Lynnhaven Bay. As they are in force, it is very probable some attempt may be made at Norfolk.[27]

News of Cockburn's depredations on the north shore of the bay had spread to the American forces assembled near Norfolk. Inflamed by reports of burning and looting, they were intent on defending themselves and their communities from attack. Adding to the anger was a report in *Niles' Register* that quoted Cockburn as promising his men, "We will storm Ft. Nelson and be in Norfolk to supper. There you will find two banks ... and for your exertions and bravery you will have three days' plunder and the free use of a number of fine women."[28] The British indignantly denied the report, but as events would prove, the little town of Hampton would soon discover that Niles was wrong only about the target city.

Expecting an attack at any time, Stewart, the commandant of the Gosport (Norfolk) Navy Yard, Captain John Cassin, and Brigadier General Robert B. Taylor began to secure the area leading up to the *Constellation*'s anchorage off Norfolk in the shallow waters of the Elizabeth River. By June 1813, men of the U.S. Navy and Army and of the Virginia militia had established a substantial defense against the more formidable force that Warren had assembled just a few miles away in Lynnhaven. Cockburn, however, was unimpressed by the Americans' defensive efforts, and he looked forward to an easy sweep of the river by his more numerous and better trained force.

By attacking the island which he said was only protected by a "tolerably numerous" force of four hundred to five hundred men, he said the Americans would be forced to retreat toward Richmond. He added sarcastically, "From what I have lately seen and know of them, I have no doubt a larger proportion of their now Heroes will be inclined to take advantage of such a circumstance." In regard to Norfolk commander Robert B. Taylor, he added contemptuously that he believed the general "never saw a shot fired."[29]

Not much more than a mile down the Elizabeth River at Norfolk, *Constellation* was anchored just below the shore of the batteries of Fort Nelson on the west bank and Fort Norfolk on the east. As a last line of defense, four hulks were sunk in the mouth of the harbor in front of the frigate to block any British ship that made it past the impressive gauntlet the Americans had assembled between Hampton Roads and *Constellation*.

As impressive as these fortifications and obstacles were, the most important part of the defense of *Constellation* began about a mile down the Elizabeth River, where it flowed into Hampton Roads, the southernmost part of the

Chesapeake Bay, before spilling into the Atlantic. There lay Craney Island, a small, flat piece of land just off the east bank of the Elizabeth River, surrounded by hundreds of yards of muddy shoals, which Stewart and Cassin made the first line of *Constellation*'s defense.

Under the command of General Taylor of the Virginia militia, the Craney Island force numbered 737 men, drawn from regulars, marines, and sailors from *Constellation*, and local militia. At the north end of the island facing the east bank and the mouth of the river, Taylor erected a battery of seven cannon of varying caliber. Stretching across the mouth of the Elizabeth from Craney Island to Lamberts Point on the west bank of the river, Stewart stationed a dense line of fifteen to twenty small armed vessels—sloops, gunboats, and schooners—to block the way. Another gun battery was erected on Lamberts Point to cover the river's entrance from the west. If the British broke through these defenses and those of Forts Nelson and Norfolk, the last line of defense would be the thirty-eight long guns of the *Constellation*, whose decks were surrounded by pitch-soaked netting to a height of twenty feet to deter a surprise boarding by a British assault force.[30]

As spring turned to summer, the Americans at Norfolk were ready for a British assault. It came on the morning of 22 June 1813, when Warren sent a combined force of as many as 4,000 men in a two-pronged attack on Craney Island.[31] Colonel Beckwith landed 2,500 royal marines and regulars (Adams says 800) at Pig's Point on the mainland, just north of the island. At the same time, Captain Samuel J. Pechell and Captain John M. Hanchett led an amphibious attack with 1,500 men in fifty or so barges,[32] attacking Taylor's men while Beckwith's flanking force waded over from the mainland.

The shallow shoals and mud flats surrounding Craney Island prevented Warren from bringing any of his ships close enough to provide artillery support for the attack. But given his enormous advantage in manpower, that hardly seemed to matter—or so Warren thought. He also counted on the element of surprise, but the Americans had been apprised of the attack from several sources, notably a Portuguese merchant ship that had arrived at Norfolk the night before and had seen the British force massing for the attack.

As dawn broke on the 22nd, the British assault force moved in for the attack. Following a successful landing at Pig's Point, Beckwith's marines and chasseurs struggled along the riverbank through deep water, muddy swamps, and thick brush toward the shallows they would wade through to Craney Island.

After hours of struggle and the desertion of many of the chasseurs, Beckwith's force reached a point directly across the narrow stretch of water from the island. There they were spotted by the Americans, who raised their flag in challenge. Concerned that his men would be too exposed to the American guns while wading through the open shallows, Beckwith ordered the marines to fire a barrage of Congreve rockets to distract the defenders from Pechell's amphibious force approaching from the north.

Napier's brigade of chasseurs was in the lead and well within the range of the Americans' small artillery battery when he ordered his men to take cover in the woods away from the river. But his order came just as the island's defenders launched a withering barrage of fire into the retreating British ranks. Napier later reported, "The marines could not do it before the battery threw three rounds into the thick of them." He stated that eight or nine marines were killed or wounded, along with two sergeants of the 102nd. One sergeant recovered, but "the other was killed, both his legs being shot off close to his body. Good God! What a horrid site it was!"[33]

After floundering in the swampy muck for several hours and finding no way to assault the island without taking heavy casualties in a doomed attack, Beckwith ordered a retreat, re-embarked his force, and returned to the fleet without having inflicted any damage on the American force. Napier is reported to have challenged the order to return to the ships, but to no avail. With Beckwith's decision to withdraw, the smaller American force could now turn its full attention to the amphibious attack from the bay.

By late morning, the amphibious assault force, consisting of two columns of barges, came into range of Taylor's remaining guns as it approached the island from the north. Hanchett chose to command his column from a comfortable seat in the stern of the *Centipede*, Admiral Warren's fifty-two-foot green barge.[34] Exhibiting the same overconfidence as Cockburn, Hanchett made a show of his disdain for the Yankee defenders by holding an open umbrella over his head as the barge approached Craney Island.

Major James Faulkner commanded the American battery, which had by now lost three of its eight cannons, including the twenty-four-pounder that had scattered Beckwith's men. The Americans loaded their cannons with grape and canister and waited. "Are they close enough for our fire?" Captain Arthur Emmerson asked Faulkner. "No Sir," he replied, "Let them approach a little nearer."[35] As the barges came near the shore, Faulkner finally gave the order to fire, and five well-aimed guns let loose a violent spray of iron shot into the packed British boats just as the lead barge got stuck in the mud about three hundred yards from the shore. The American battery switched to solid shot and within minutes had disabled three of the barges. As the shallow water filled with desperate soldiers struggling through deep mud to whatever safety they could find, a round shot pierced the *Centipede*'s stern, killing several chasseurs, cutting both legs off another, and giving Hanchett a bad wound in his thigh.

As the British soldiers floundered in the water, American infantrymen waded in, firing their muskets at the boats and the men in them, taking prisoners, and inflicting further losses on the attackers. By the afternoon, with his amphibious assault force stuck in the mud and under fire, Warren called off the attack and ordered them back to the fleet. Casualty estimates vary, but it seems that few of the combatants on either side came to much harm, thanks largely to the inaccuracy of their guns at long range. One source[36] counts three British dead and sixteen wounded; Beckwith reported the same number of deaths, but with eight wounded and fifty-two missing. Napier reported seventy-one casualties.[37] Twenty-two members of the amphibious force waded ashore and were taken prisoner, while forty men were said to have deserted from Beckwith's land force. Another forty or so of Hanchett's force were reported missing, perhaps through drowning or desertion. The Americans suffered no casualties.

III

Constellation and Norfolk were safe, but not so the little town of Hampton, ten miles across the bay on the tip of the neck formed by the James and York Rivers. In the words of a contemporary, "The British again turned their attention to the easier duties of laying waste to unprotected villages."[38] Four days after the failed attack on Craney Island, Warren's force crossed the bay, and Beckwith landed 2,000 sullen and beaten men near Hampton and began the attack. The town was defended by about 450 Virginia militiamen, who put up enough resistance to inflict forty to fifty casualties. Beckwith's men soon put the militia to flight, however, and moved into the now undefended town. The British looting was not notable given the nature and purpose of Warren's

Chesapeake campaign. What makes the attack on Hampton memorable was the campaign of rape on which some of Beckwith's men embarked, a rare occurrence in a war that usually left civilians, though not their property, unharmed. In the delicately oblique language of a more reticent age, the Americans complained, "The sex hitherto guarded by the soldier's honor escaped not the rude assault of superior force."[39]

Women were not the only victims of the attack on Hampton. Blaming the French chasseurs, Napier wrote in his diary:

> They really murdered without object but the pleasure of murdering. One robbed a poor Yankee and pretended all sorts of anxiety for him; it was the custom of war he said to rob a prisoner, but he was sorry for him. When he had thus coaxed the man into confidence he told him to walk on before, as he must go to the general; the poor wretch obeyed, and when his back was turned the musket was fired into his brains.... I would rather see ten of them shot than one American. It is quite shocking to have men who speak your own language brought in wounded; one feels as if they were English peasants and that we are killing our own people.[40]

Napier also recorded in his diary that Beckwith "ought to have hanged several villains at Little Hampton; but every horror was perpetrated with impunity—rape, murder, pillage—and not a man was punished."[41] The British at first refused to acknowledge the barbaric acts that took place at Hampton. Writing on 28 June, just a few days after the battle, Beckwith's report to Warren bordered on the delusional when he observed, in what might have been the first attempt at a whitewash, "The gallantry of Captn. Smith the officers and men of the two Companies Canadian Chasseurs who led the attack were highly conspicuous and praiseworthy; as well as the steadiness and good conduct of the officers...."[42]

As word of the rape and pillage spread among the Americans and through the British fleet, Beckwith wrote a revised account of the attack on Hampton, including a series of recriminations that he had apparently omitted from his first report. A week later, on 5 July, Beckwith wrote to Warren:

> It is with great Regret I am obliged to entreat your Attention to the Situation & Conduct of the Two Independent Companies of Foreigners embarked on this service.... Their Behaviour on the recent Landing at Hampton, has already been reported to You, together with the circumstances of their dispersing to plunder in every direction; their brutal Treatment of several Peaceable Inhabitants, whose Age or Infirmities rendered them unable to get out of their Way, the necessity of sending them in from the Outposts; and upon the Representation of their Officers, who found it impossible to check them, and whose lives they threatened, the subsequent Necessity of re-embarking & sending them off to their ship.[43]

In response to the growing anger and concern over the chasseurs' behavior at Hampton, Warren felt obliged to write to General Taylor that future "military operations should be carried on with all the liberality and humanity that becomes the respective nations. Any infringement of the established usage of war will instantly be noticed and punished."[44]

The British blamed the crime on the *Chasseurs Britannique*, the three hundred French prisoners and deserters who had joined the British army in lieu of imprisonment. Napier later acknowledged, however, that the British troops themselves could barely be restrained from joining in, and none of the British officers seems to have tried to stop the rampaging Frenchmen.[45] "Well! whatever horrible acts were done at Hampton, they were not done by the 102nd, for they were never let to quit their ranks, and they almost mutinied at my preventing them joining in the sack of that unfortunate town."[46] Recognizing that the chasseurs' uncivilized behavior would only reinforce the Americans' determination to resist, Warren soon shipped them off to Nova Scotia, where they continued to misbehave, terrorizing the inhabitants of Halifax.[47]

Later in July, Cockburn led a small force out through the Virginia Capes to attack the settlements of coastal North Carolina, including the town of Portsmouth on Ocracoke Island. Napier accompanied him with the rowdy 102nd Regiment and later wrote of this and the other similar assaults on the civilian population:

> Strong is my dislike to what is perhaps a necessary part of our job, viz. plundering and ruining the peasantry. We drive all their cattle

> and of course ruin them; my hands are clean, but it is hateful to see the poor Yankees robbed, and to be the robber. If we should take fairly it would not be so bad, but the rich escape; for the loss of a few cows and oxen is nothing to a rich man, while you ruin a poor peasant if you take his only cow.[48]

While Cockburn raided coastal Carolina in mid-July 1813, Warren sailed the rest of the fleet north in the bay to the mouth of the Potomac, where he launched five vessels and six hundred men to attack Washington. The difficulty of navigating the river forced him to abandon the effort and to call the force back. Warren then sailed north, contemplating an attack on Annapolis or Baltimore, but abandoned that effort as well when he became convinced that both cities were defended by thousands of troops. Turning his attention to low-risk targets, Warren sailed his considerable force to the small towns on the eastern shore of the bay, attacking Kent Island, then the little town of St. Michaels.

The townsmen of St. Michaels were aware of the atrocities committed two months earlier in Hampton and had no intention of giving up without a fight. As Cockburn's force neared, they prepared a series of obstacles and artillery batteries to challenge the British as they inched their way up the narrow Miles River. Landing three hundred troops transported on barges, the British soon came under attack from a battery manned by Lieutenants William Dodson and Richard Kennemont and by a slave named John Stevens. (Other accounts describe an American battery force of sixteen men.)[49] Firing a barrage of canister and scrap metal at the landing force, the defenders killed nineteen of the enemy before escaping to safety.

Undeterred, the British turned the newly captured battery on St. Michaels, while the barges continued up the river until they were blocked by a log-and-chain boom stretched across the entrance to the town's harbor. A second American battery on the riverbank, commanded by Captain Vickers of the Easton Artillery, fired on the stalled barges and the captured nine-pounders. Well-directed fire hit several barges, forcing the abandonment of the nine-pounders. Cockburn gave up the attack and settled for an artillery barrage as he withdrew.

After six months of campaigning in the Chesapeake with an enormously powerful force, Warren had accomplished little beyond the destruction of civilian property in a few small towns, which probably strengthened American resistance. One early-twentieth-century historian of the campaign concludes, "[Cockburn] failed of his purpose, for every act of barbarity caused the war to become more popular, and induced the people to make greater sacrifices for its support."[50] Napier had recorded the same judgment in his memoirs: "We were five months cruising along that hostile coast, acting with so much absurdity, and so like buccaneers ... that we did no good to English fame, no real injury to America."[51]

By late summer, confronting high rates of desertion and widespread illness, Warren departed for Halifax and the cooler climate of Canada, leaving behind only a small squadron under Captain Robert Barrie and the *Dragon* to continue the blockade. For the moment, the Chesapeake would be at peace.

CHAPTER THIRTEEN

HENRY ALLEN RAVAGES THE ENGLISH

Just weeks after Lawrence was buried in Halifax, Lieutenant Henry Allen was in New York City completing preparations for the first voyage of his first command, the *Argus*, an eighteen-gun, two-masted brig sloop. At about two-thirds the displacement of *Hornet*, she was one of the smallest warships in the navy. Built in New York in 1803 for the princely sum of $37,000, she served the young republic as a speedy commerce raider. During the first six months of the war, *Argus* captured six prizes, the best performance of the smaller ships and nearly equal to what *President* accomplished under Commodore Rodgers. But that was less than what had been hoped for, and her captain, Arthur Sinclair, thought the voyage "long, unpleasant and … unsuccessful."[1] Near Bermuda on the return home, *Argus* had stumbled into a six-ship British squadron that chased her for several days across the tempestuous winter Atlantic.

Bringing her into New York on 2 January 1813, Sinclair had had as much of the *Argus* as he cared for. He allowed his command to lapse by simply not returning after a three-week leave of absence. After 70 days at sea, with every sail, mast, plank, line, and yard strained by her stormy flight from the British, *Argus* was in need of repairs. The responsibility fell to Henry Allen, who had returned to port a few months earlier after serving as Decatur's first lieutenant on board the *United States* during the capture of the *Macedonian*. By tradition, first lieutenants of victorious ships received their own command at the first opportunity, and in mid-February, when Sinclair's default left the speedy *Argus* available, Allen was awarded her command.

Under standing orders to get *Argus* back out to sea, Allen soon discovered the precariousness of the ship's condition, and he embarked on an ambitious program of repairs, which he and Decatur thought could be completed in less than a month. But the work proved more extensive than expected, and was hobbled by a shortage of crewmen. The *Argus*'s full complement was 125 officers and men, but when Allen took over, desertions, sickness, and the expiration of enlistments had left her with only a hundred.

The British blockade had left ports like New York with a surfeit of able-bodied seamen, so finding another twenty-five for the *Argus* should have been an easy task. But just as Allen began his search for men, the Department of the Navy launched an effort to build and man a fleet on the Great Lakes in support of the faltering border war with Canada. The navy ordered *Argus* to send a lieutenant and fifty men, including two midshipmen and a sailing master, to the Great Lakes by early March, reducing Allen's already short-handed crew to less than half its full strength. Meanwhile, death, desertion, and expiring enlistments continued to rob him of men. By the time he set sail in June 1813, only twenty-three members of the original crew were left.[2]

The shrinking of the crew also disrupted and delayed the ship's repairs and refitting. To speed the process, Decatur detailed crewmen from other warships in the harbor to the work on the *Argus*. In late March, seventy men from the *John Adams* came on board for five days to lend a hand, and after they left about twenty-five seamen from the *United States* arrived for several days' work. While the repairs were made, Allen searched New York's waterfront for a crew. Some came from the gunboat flotilla stationed in the harbor; some recently discharged from the *Chesapeake* signed on, and others came from idle merchant ships rotting at the docks because of the blockade.

Even as Allen added men to the crew, several of those he had already signed on were drifting away for one reason or another. Midshipman Ben Eames was arrested by the New York police, reason unknown. Marine private Daniel

Stickee died, and Midshipman Yates was coughing up blood. Others were discharged for various reasons of unfitness, while Midshipman Jameson, "wounded by Venus," entered the sick list for two months with a bad case of syphilis. In the end, it took seventy-five volunteers from the *Hornet*, which was not yet ready for sea, to enable *Argus* to embark on a short training mission in Long Island Sound to protect the coasting trade from the British blockading force that had bottled up both escape routes from New York.

Heading up the East River, *Argus* passed easily through the usually treacherous Hell Gate, thanks to a favorable wind from the southeast, and entered the sound for an uneventful cruise mostly devoted to training and drills. Less than two weeks later, she was back in New York, and Allen immediately began making preparations for a much longer cruise of commerce raiding off the coasts of England and France. In order for Allen to be able to provide prize crews for the expected captures, Decatur ordered him to add thirty or so more men to his existing crew. So once again Allen and his officers had to prowl the docks for qualified crewmen, whom they successfully assembled one by one over the next several weeks, crowding them into what little space was left in the ship. Like most American crews during the war, the men of the *Argus* reflected the mix of races in America's polyglot population. Excluding officers and passengers, the crew now numbered about 126, of whom nineteen—or about 15 percent—were black. Allen's servant, Appene, was Chinese. Most of the crewmen were native-born Americans, or so they claimed if they had lost or could hide their British and Irish accents.

The squadron was finally ready for sea on 9 May 1813, and the *Argus* and the *United States*, commanded by Commodore Decatur, sailed south through the narrows and anchored off Sandy Hook, where they would await an opportunity to slip past the British blockade. *Macedonian*, under command of Captain Jacob Jones, soon joined them, and the small squadron remained there for the next five days under the wary eye of HMS *Valiant* and HMS *Acasta*.

As *Argus* lay at anchor off Sandy Hook, a small boat sailed out from the New Jersey shore with a twenty-three-year-old man wishing to volunteer as an officer. He had heard about the voyage and the shortage of crewmen and thought that his experience as captain of his own merchant vessel would be of value to Allen. It was, and although Allen had no authority to grant commissions, he allowed Uriah Phillips Levy to sign on as a sailing master with the understanding that he would fulfill the duties of a lieutenant. Levy—who would live and dine with the other officers, including the commissioned lieutenants William Henry Watson and William Howard Allen (no relation to Henry Allen)—thus became one of a handful of Jews then serving in America's fledgling navy.

While they waited for a break in the blockade, confidential orders arrived from Washington instructing Decatur to separate the *Argus* from his squadron for a special mission. Secretary of the Navy Jones advised the commodore, "The President of the United States having in view a special service for the United States Brig *Argus*, you will direct Lieutenant Allen to await the further orders from this Department with the *Argus*, in a perfect state of efficiency in preparation for departure at a moment's notice." Three weeks later, on 2 June 1813, those further orders arrived, advising Allen that "the service destined the Argus is that of conveying our Minister, the Honorable Mr. Crawford, to France, and from thence immediately on a cruise, for which you will receive orders ... in due time."[3]

William Harris Crawford, a U.S. senator from Georgia, had just been appointed minister to France. His predecessor, Joel Barlow, had been stationed in Paris until the duke of Bassano, the foreign minister, summoned him to Vilna (Vilnius), Lithuania, Napoleon's ancillary capital during his invasion of Russia. After the repeal of Britain's orders in council, Bassano was eager to resolve outstanding disputes with the Americans and to negotiate a new commercial treaty. But by the time Barlow arrived in Vilna after a damp and chilly journey of 1,400 miles, the French were in full retreat from Russia. They abandoned Vilna as the pursuing Russian army closed in.

Barlow was one of the many diplomats who set out for the safety of Paris. The bitter weather and the unheated coaches wrecked his health, however, and he died of pneumonia in a Polish village on the day after Christmas. President Madison selected Crawford to assume Barlow's critical mission, and Allen and the *Argus* were ordered to transport him to France as quickly as possible.

Accompanied by his new secretary of legation, Dr. Henry Jackson, a professor of "chymistry" at the University of Georgia, Crawford arrived in New York in the second week of June and boarded the *Argus* for the Atlantic crossing. A few days earlier, Allen had received the remainder of his orders: get to sea and "without deviating for any other object" safely deliver Crawford to the first French port he could reach. From there, Allen was to "proceed on a cruise against the commerce and light cruisers of the enemy," with the qualification that he destroy his captures and not return them as prizes unless they were extremely valuable and he was "morally certain" that they could safely reach a friendly port. According to the naval historian Ira Dye,

> Allen was told that "the enemy should be made to feel the effects of our hostility" and that the best way to do this was to destroy British commerce, fisheries and coastal trade right in their own home waters. Secretary Jones was drawing on his own experience as a merchant and shipowner and was perceptive in telling Allen what to pursue. Convoys were continually entering or leaving British home waters, the coasting trades employed a large number of ships, and the herring fisheries off the northwestern coast of Scotland alone amounted to three hundred to four hundred vessels. All of this shipping was surprisingly vulnerable, and its owners were politically powerful men who, along with the insurance syndicates, would be hit in the pocketbooks. This, Secretary Jones predicted correctly, would "produce an astonishing sensation."[4]

After a swift but sometimes stormy crossing of just twenty-four days, during which they took one prize, Allen safely delivered Crawford and Jackson to the French port of L'Orient on the southern coast of the Finistère peninsula on 11 July 1813. After an unpleasant inspection by the French police and customs officials and a day of quarantine, *Argus* was allowed to proceed into the harbor.

II

With Crawford and Jackson on their way to Paris and *Argus* moored in the harbor, Allen spent the next week making minor repairs, adding supplies, and topping off his water. Nine days later, in the early evening of 20 July, he headed due west into the Atlantic. Once *Argus* cleared Finistère, Allen turned her north across the English Channel, past Land's End, and through St. George's Channel. In the target-rich waters between England and Ireland, Allen would pursue the second half of his orders. Over the next three and a half weeks, the *Argus* and its cobbled-together crew would capture more British vessels than any other

American warship in the conflict. James Fenimore Cooper claimed that her exploits would "revive the recollections of those of Captain Jones, Wickes, and Conyngham, during the Revolution."[5]

Late in the afternoon three days out of L'Orient, while still in the English Channel, Allen caught sight of a distant sail and gave chase. The sail belonged to the schooner *Matilda*, an American privateer that the British had captured and sold into the merchant fleet. By early evening the speedy *Argus* had caught up with her. After a few warning shots, *Matilda* surrendered. Allen determined that the schooner qualified for the exception to his general orders to destroy what he captured. He installed a prize crew to sail her to France and sell her valuable cargo. The proceeds would be distributed to *Argus*'s officers and crew.

Matilda stayed with *Argus* through the night. Early the next morning, *Argus*'s lookouts sighted the brig *Susannah* off the Scilly Islands. Allen took off in pursuit, and *Matilda* broke off for the closest French port. Out of Madeira with a cargo of wine destined for London and the cellars of the countess of Shaftesbury, *Susannah* quickly surrendered when *Argus* caught up with her. Allen's order required him to imprison the crew and destroy the ship and its cargo, since wine did not meet the test of extreme value. But *Susannah* carried two female passengers, and a harmful or inconvenient act against women of high birth was considered barbaric by the chivalric standards of naval officers in the early nineteenth century. Determined not to break that code of honor, Allen reluctantly let the *Susannah* go, but not before taking "a few" half pipes (sixty-gallon casks) of her best wine,[6] as well as six hundred dollars in coin that a British merchant in Madeira was sending to his wife in London. Most of the remaining wine was poured out into the bilge. With a few surviving casks, the *Susannah* sailed on to England, soon landing at the Cornish fishing village of Penzance.

Allen had little enough to show for his capture of *Susannah*, but the more substantial gains from the *Matilda* would soon be lost as well. The British frigate *Revolutionnaire* overtook *Matilda* and her American prize crew before they could get to a safe port in France. Allen, of course, knew nothing of the loss. Three days later, still cruising the entrance of the English Channel between Land's End and Brest, *Argus* went after the English brig *Richard*, which surrendered after a chase of a few hours and several warning shots. The *Richard* was returning from Gibraltar to London in ballast (empty of cargo). Given his orders, Allen had little choice but to imprison *Richard*'s crew and set the ship afire.

Sailing alone in enemy waters, Allen might have been more cautious had he known that British warships in the home waters were already in a state of high alert for American marauders. Weeks before *Argus* arrived at L'Orient, rumors had swept through Britain that an American privateer was cruising off the north of Ireland, seizing ships and cargo, and disrupting the herring fleet. These reports soon found their way to the Cove of Cork, where Vice Admiral Edward Thornbrough commanded the Irish Station from the stern cabin of HMS *Trent.* Thornbrough responded to the threat by sending ships to assigned sections of the Irish coast, including HMS *Helena* and *Pelican*, which were to protect British commerce along the west coast of Ireland.

So urgent were Thornbrough's orders that the *Pelican*, which had just arrived in the cove from the West Indies, had barely enough time to bring on essential supplies before departing the next morning with *Helena*. Similar to *Argus* but newer, the *Pelican* was a two-masted brig-of-war armed with sixteen thirty-two-pound carronades and a few smaller guns mounted in her stern and bow. She was also a little bigger than *Argus* and more strongly built. Thornbrough put *Pelican* and her captain, forty-three-year-old John Fordyce Maples, under the command of Captain Montressor of the *Helena*, which was of the same class and design as *Pelican* but a little bigger still.

Any change in orders or new information for the two ships would be relayed overland from Cork to the coastal villages of Buncrana and Killybegs. *Pelican* and *Helena* were expected to check in periodically at either place. On 12 July 1813, three days out of Cork and now off the west coast of Ireland, the two ships lost contact with one another when a thick fog settled in. When the fog lifted several hours later, Maples found that *Helena* had drifted out of range and was nowhere to be seen.

As *Pelican* and *Helena* searched for each other as well as for American privateers, Thornbrough received word on 19 July from two of his other ships that the waters around Ireland were free of privateers and that the earlier rumors of American pillage were unfounded. He began recalling and reassigning his ships, and messages for Captain Montressor were sent to Buncrana and Killybegs. Maples anchored *Pelican* off Killybegs in Donegal Bay a week later and received Thornbrough's order to return immediately to Cork.

Less than a week after Thornbrough recalled his ships, the *Susannah* arrived at Penzance with the alarming news that an American warship, swifter and vastly more destructive than any privateer, was prowling the home waters and capturing British ships at will. When the news reached London, the Admiralty began the slow and tedious process of transmitting the information by messenger and ship to its various commands. Another week passed before Thornbrough in Cork learned of the *Argus*'s predations.

Allen knew that the British would strengthen their defensive forces once *Susannah* reached land, and he began to take protective measures of his own. First, he moved from the mouth of the English Channel to the west coast of Ireland, where *Pelican* had been searching for the nonexistent privateer. Then he changed the appearance of his ship. The white stripe around her gun ports made *Argus* easily recognizable as an American warship. Allen's men repainted it to match the pale yellow of the British navy. The next morning, the *Argus* spied a sail off Cape Clear on the southwest tip of Ireland, and Allen thought he had his chance to test the deception. He gave chase, but as the *Argus* closed on her quarry, lookouts in the tops saw a second sail and then a third. As the distance narrowed, the lookouts discovered that the three sets of sails belonged to British warships, and Allen wasted no time getting away.

Four days later, on 1 August 1813, *Argus* lay in the mouth of the River Shannon, ready to pounce on any of the promising targets sailing to or from the port of Limerick, sixty miles upriver. Seeing her British flag and yellow stripe, the commander of the Kerry Head signal station, Lieutenant Fricker, took the *Argus* to be "one of His Majesty's Brigs on the largest scale with a bright yellow side and nine ports...."[7] Poor Fricker discovered his error a few hours later, when *Argus* hoisted the American colors and fired several warning shots at an English merchant brig sailing downriver from Limerick. The *Fowey*, out of Dartmouth with a cargo of 85,000 pounds of pork intended for the British naval base at Portsmouth, quickly surrendered. Once again obeying his orders to seize only cargo of exceptional value, Allen took the *Fowey*'s crew of four prisoner and set fire to the meat-laden ship, which burnt down to the water line as it drifted to shore.[8]

Fricker sent news of the threat to Cork. Thornbrough, who had not yet heard from London that the *Argus* was on the loose in British waters, thought he was contending with a marauding privateer rather than a well-armed warship and dispatched the twenty-two-gun sloop *Jalouse* to deal with the menace.

Jalouse, however, was stranded by unfavorable winds in Cork Harbor for the next three days. While *Jalouse* struggled with gale winds, *Argus* remained off the Shannon, and on 2 August captured the *Lady Frances* on her way from Limerick to Liverpool with a cargo of butter, flour, and hides. Allen confiscated some of the butter and took the crew prisoner, replacing them with an American crew under Lieutenant Howard Allen. That night, when the storm that kept *Jalouse* at Cork and *Pelican* in Donegal Bay swept into the mouth of the Shannon, the *Argus* and the *Lady Frances* struggled to stay together. By 4 August, they had been blown nearly fifty miles north to Galway Bay. When the storm finally broke, Henry Allen relieved the exhausted Howard Allen and his crew with replacements under Sailing Master Uriah Levy.

The same break in the weather that let Allen replace the crew on *Lady Frances* allowed *Jalouse* to break free on 4 August and *Pelican* two days later. On the 7th, Allen ordered the *Lady Frances* put to the torch, took Levy and his crew back on board, and turned south to Cape Clear and away from seas to which he knew angry British warships would soon be swarming. Passing the cape on Sunday, 8 August, Allen turned east toward the Channel, had brief contact with a British frigate, and reached the seas off Cork by nightfall before turning back around to the west.

As dawn broke off Kinsale on 9 August, *Argus* caught up with four ships and boarded the largest, *Jason*, as the other three fled. It turned out to be a Russian ship out of Cork, whose crew told Allen of the *Jalouse*'s recent departure from the harbor. Allen let *Jason* continue and went after the other three ships. He soon caught two of them, the *Barbados* and the *Alliance*, both British and both in ballast. Allen imprisoned both crews and torched the ships, whose flames could be seen from the British signal station on Clear Island just off the cape. Allen now had forty-nine prisoners on board, including a woman taken from the *Richard*.

The next morning Allen found himself in the middle of a ninety-ship guarded convoy from the Leeward Islands laden with valuable cargo on its way to British ports. A frigate spotted *Argus* and took after her, but Allen had already gained the weather gauge and took advantage of *Argus*'s speed to slip away before the frigate could take any action. He then got past the brig *Frolic* (briefly captured, then lost, by the Americans in October 1812) to take the schooner *Cordelia* at the tail end of the convoy. Allen ordered his crew to destroy the cargo of molasses and sugar, but not the ship. He transferred his crowd of prisoners to *Cordelia* and allowed her to proceed to Bristol, her original destination.[9] As she passed Cork, three of the released merchant captains disembarked to report their losses to an embarrassed Vice Admiral Thornbrough, who sat helplessly in his cabin in Cork Harbor as *Argus* flitted in and out of a well-guarded convoy just off the coast where he had established his command.

By now Maples and the *Pelican* were out of Donegal Bay and heading down the west coast of Ireland. He learned about the *Argus* from another ship's report of the boarding of the *Jason*. At the Cape Clear signal station Maples got news of the burning of *Barbados* and *Alliance*. Sailing east toward Cork later that day, *Pelican* found a cutter off Dundeady Island trying to salvage one of the burnt hulks. Anchoring in Cork Harbor on the morning of 12 August, Maples sent crewmen into town for supplies and had himself rowed to the *Trent* to receive new orders from Thornbrough. Concerned about the safety of the Leeward convoy, now making its way from the southern coast of Ireland to ports in the west of England, Thornbrough assigned Maples to search for *Argus* in St. George's Channel. An hour later, *Pelican* was back at sea, trailing the Leeward convoy as it sailed east under the protection of the frigate *Leonidas*.[10]

As Maples set out to protect the convoy's northern flank, Allen continued to plunder it. Protected by fog in Bristol Channel, he captured the *Mariner*, a large merchant vessel out of St. Croix loaded with sugar. He replaced her crew with men from the *Argus*. Howard Allen and the two ships, both flying British colors, pursued a dozen ships sighted to the leeward. After another long chase ending in early evening, the *Argus* captured the *Betsey*, loaded with rum and sugar from St. Vincent.

Judging *Betsey*'s cargo to be of some value, Allen put Levy in charge of a prize crew made up of nine men from *Argus* and some Swedes from *Betsey*'s original crew and ordered him to sail to the nearest French port. After Levy departed, *Argus* proceeded to capture the cutter *Jane*, the brig *Eleano*, and the cutter-sloop *John and Thomas*. All the prisoners were put on the *Eleanor* and sent to Bristol. Howard Allen and his prize crew on *Mariner* were ordered back to *Argus*, and both *Mariner* and *John and Thomas* were torched and sunk. Allen had no sooner finished this extraordinary assault on British merchant shipping than he set off after another cutter-sloop, the *Dinah and Betty*, loaded with cattle. Allen butchered two of the animals for *Argus*'s hungry crew and set fire to the *Dinah and Betty*, apparently burning to death the remaining cattle.[11]

Rather than press his extraordinary luck, Allen left the richly rewarding Bristol Channel and set a course to the northwest to the Irish side of St. George's Channel. Levy and the *Betsey* went in the opposite direction, sailing south around Land's End, then across the English Channel to France. But Levy never made it.

Less than a day after Levy separated from *Argus*, the *Leonidas* recaptured *Betsey* and her American prize crew, along with the Swedes. Levy had recognized the perils of trying to reach France in a lumbering merchant vessel through tightly patrolled waters. He had drilled holes through *Betsey*'s hull and plugged them with wooden dowels. If the British recaptured the ship, Levy could scuttle her by pulling the plugs and thus deprive the enemy of her cargo. But as the captured crew came on board *Leonidas*, one of the Swedes informed the British of the holes. Captain Seymour got his carpenters onto the *Betsey* in time to save her.

His captors charged Levy with illegally attempting to destroy a prize that the British had justly earned, much as the Americans had earned it the day before. Levy responded he was acting under orders. Ira Dye relates:

> The question of whether Levy's action was legal was put to the law officers at the Admiralty, whose opinion was that while it was "irregular and attended with inconvenience" it was not a breach of any law, and that Levy couldn't be punished for it, whether or not he was acting under orders.[12]

While Levy was confined on the *Leonidas*, Allen settled in off the southeast coast of Ireland and waited to see what promising targets would sail by. The brig *Ann*, carrying slate and woolens from Cardigan to London, was the first to fall. *Ann*'s crew was brought on board the *Argus* and its bulky cargo was sunk. A short time later, Allen stopped a Portuguese brig on her way to Cork and loaded her with his prisoners from *Ann* and *Dinah and Betty*.

As soon as Allen was relieved of his prisoners, three sails appeared on the horizon. Allen chased two of them, well-armed merchantmen whose refusal to surrender forced him to fire two broadsides at the larger vessel, the *Defiance*, before she struck her flag. Her crew now imprisoned on *Argus* and replaced by an American prize crew, *Defiance* sailed with *Argus* as she searched the crowded channel for prey. At two o'clock the next morning, *Argus* seized the *Baltic* near the end of her journey transporting sugar from Barbados to Dublin. Three hours later, *Argus* overtook a sloop loaded with lumber. After dumping the boards into the sea, Allen loaded the sloop with his prisoners and sent her into port as his men set fire to *Baltic* and *Defiance*.

The thirteenth of August brought a break for *Argus*'s exhausted crew, who had been sustaining intense operations around the clock. Several days of chasing, capturing, imprisoning, guarding, unloading cargo, manning prizes, and destroying prizes in enemy waters must have taxed the crew and officers, even though they were accustomed to twelve to sixteen hours a day of rough and risky work on a crowded ship. What little rest they got came to an end at nine o'clock that night when *Argus* stumbled across the *Belford*, carrying wine and linen from Dublin to London. Allen took some silver and imprisoned the crew and around midnight set the ship afire.

III

On patrol in St. George's Channel, Captain Maples and the *Pelican* heard much about the *Argus*. Waylaying and boarding merchant ships he thought might be *Argus* prizes, Maples learned about the most recent attack from the crew of *Mary*, who the night before had witnessed the burning of *Baltic* and *Defiance*. Maples knew he was getting close to his quarry. Just after midnight, Maples saw a ship aflame off to the northeast. It was the *Belford*, and Maples set the *Pelican* on a course for it. A few hours later, at 3:45 AM on 14 August 1813, *Pelican* found the *Argus* and closed for action in the dim light of dawn.

It had been a busy night for Allen's crew. What valuable cargo could be taken from *Belford* had to be unloaded and rowed back to *Argus*. Likewise the prisoners, who had to be secured below. These tasks were not completed until very early in the morning, when the crew of one of the watches was at last allowed to turn in. They had been in their hammocks no more than ten minutes before the beat to quarters summoned them to their stations at about four o'clock. Groggy and bleary-eyed, the crewmen stumbled up the ladders from the berth deck to take their positions at the guns or the sails.

Some historians have criticized Allen for choosing to stand and fight when his crew was not ready, jeopardizing a stunning string of successes that had created "the greatest consternation among the London merchants," in the words of Theodore Roosevelt.[13] In Henry Adams's view, "the labor of such a service falling on a brig of three hundred tons and a crew of a hundred men, and the impunity with which he defied danger seemed to make Allen reckless."[14] The British-American novelist C. S. Forester offered a more practical cost-benefit analysis:

> If he had put his helm up and fled before the wind as soon as he had identified the *Pelican* there might have been some small jeers in the British press, some small disappointment in the United States; but if, after having run his enemy below the horizon, he had then appeared to harass the Liverpool shipping, vanished again to raid the Nore, shown up later in the western approaches, the jeers would have been speedily drowned in consternation. His appearance in Irish waters had already sent up insurance rates; a phantom raider, flitting from one area to another, would have sent them higher still. Rising insurance rates would be more likely to achieve the object of the war—to cause Great Britain to moderate her demands at sea—than would the capture or destruction of a single brig of war.[15]

This is the effect that Secretary of the Navy Jones had hoped to achieve, but naval officers in the early nineteenth century were made of different stuff; they sometimes cared little about the larger picture when the issue of honor was at stake. Ira Dye, who as a young naval officer commanded a submarine during World War II, may have captured best the conflict confronting Henry Allen that dawn off St. David's Head in Wales:

> [C]ommanders of detached ships were, in those days, expected to use wisdom and initiative and to disregard parts of their orders if such disregard better served their mission. But Henry Allen's highly developed sense of personal honor plus all of the experiences of his professional life had pointed him toward just this moment, when he would command a ship in action against a roughly equal British ship of war. He would finally erase in his mind the little humiliations handed to the infant U.S. Navy during his service in the Mediterranean, expunge the disgrace of the *Chesapeake* and

> *Leopard* encounter, and wipe clean the memory of the arrogant British first lieutenant after the victory of the frigate *United States* over the *Macedonian*. There was probably never any real doubt in his mind that he should fight the *Pelican,* and he was fully confident—indeed overconfident—of winning. He had "made up his mind not to run away from any two-masted enemy ship" and had told his crew that the *Argus* could whip any English ... sloop-of-war in ten minutes.[16]

The two ships were closely matched, but the advantage in size and armament tilted to the *Pelican.* She mounted sixteen thirty-two-pound carronades, while *Argus* had eighteen twenty-four-pound carronades with the extra two pushing out of her bridal ports. And thanks to aggressive impressments as he cruised the waters off Ireland, Maples had a larger crew than the prize crew–depleted *Argus*. And at that moment, *Pelican* also had the advantage of the weather gauge as she bore down on *Argus* "under a cloud of canvass."[17]

Eager for an important victory and anxious that his much faster quarry might flee, Maples came in from the southwest with every sail set. Allen responded by trying to seize the weather gauge for *Argus*, but Maples anticipated the move and cut him off. Allen could then have used his speed to get away or stayed and fought. He chose to stay, shortened sail, and waited for *Pelican* to come in range. She did so at six o'clock. Minutes after both ships hoisted their colors, Allen wore to the west and let fly a broadside from his port guns. Maples immediately responded with a broadside from his starboard battery, and the two ships battered away at each other with their carronades.

Though Henry Allen owed his high standing in the navy in part to his crews' training in gunnery, such training was not in evidence that day. Indeed, from the beginning of the voyage in New York in June through its rampage in the British waters, Allen had little time to train his new crew in the finer points of naval warfare. Few of *Argus*'s shots hit their mark with any effect that morning, while *Pelican*'s return fire was devastatingly fierce and accurate. Within the first few exchanges, one of *Pelican's* six-inch shots smashed through Allen's thigh, nearly severing his leg.

Allen was knocked to the deck, and though in pain and bleeding profusely, he attempted to maintain command while propped up on one elbow. He soon lost consciousness, however, and was carried to the hold where surgeon

U.S.S. *Argus* vs. H.M.S. *Pelican*
St. Georges Channel, August 14, 1813

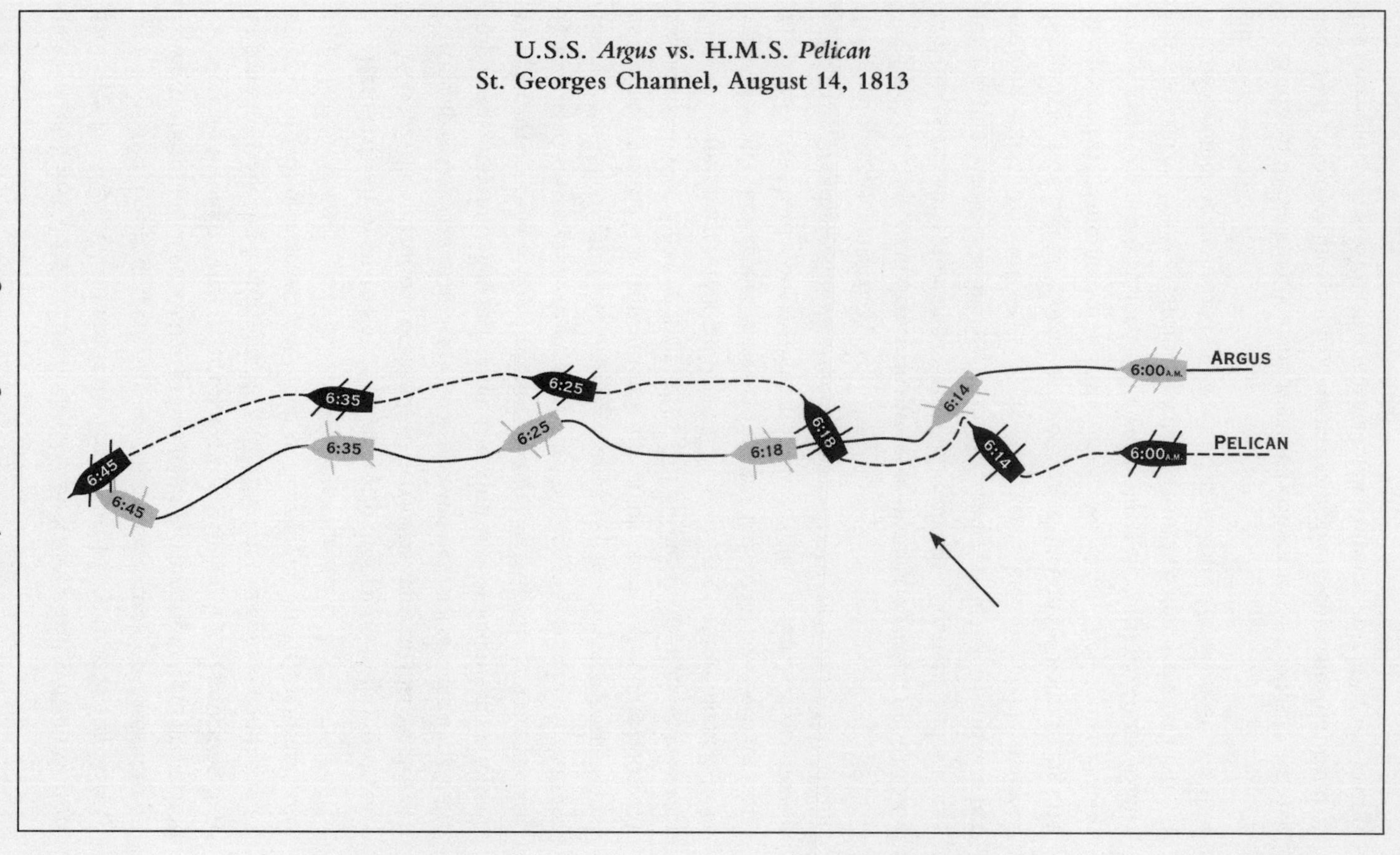

Inderwick labored in a rising sea of carnage. First Lieutenant William Watson took over for Allen in the midst of a relentless broadside from *Pelican*. Heavy iron balls and deadly grape flying across the deck took off Midshipman Edwards's head and killed seaman Joshua Jones. A whizzing piece of grape shot cut a crease through Watson's scalp, exposing his skull and knocking him unconscious. Second Lieutenant Howard Allen now assumed command as another broadside tore away at much of the rigging on the mainmast and ripped off the larboard shrouds supporting the foremast.

Despite the chaos on deck and the damage to the rigging, twenty-two-year-old Howard Allen performed brilliantly. When it was apparent that Maples was bearing up to take *Pelican* under *Argus*'s stern and deliver a savage raking at the ship's weakest point, Allen luffed into the wind and backed his main topsail, bringing *Argus* to a near stop. Instead of coming in under the American's stern, *Pelican* headed straight to *Argus*'s larboard battery, exposing her bow to the raking fire of Allen's ready and waiting carronades. The American gunners fired as they bore but did little damage to the vulnerable enemy. Theodore Roosevelt would write regretfully that "had the men at the guns done their duty as well as those on the quarter-deck did theirs, the issue of the fight would have been very different."[18] Dye echoed these sentiments: "This could have been the turning point of the battle: single-ship actions were often decided on one hugely destructive broadside. But the *Argus*'s broadside was ineffectual and left the *Pelican* almost undamaged."[19]

There are few second chances in mortal combat. As *Argus* lost more rigging and braces, her ability to maneuver was seriously compromised, and within a few minutes Maples was finally able to cross under *Argus*'s stern and rake her with impunity. *Argus* was dead in the water, her rudder inoperable, many of her guns knocked off their slides. Maples ranged around the floundering brig and poured in the fire. According to the surgeon's journal, Midshipman Delphy, whose legs were nearly severed at the knees, survived for three hours. Joshua Jones was killed. George Gardiner lived for about half an hour after his thigh was taken off close to the body by a round shot. John Finlay's head was shot off.[20]

Below in the sickbay, Watson regained consciousness. After Inderwick sewed his scalp back into place, he came above and resumed his command of the floundering ship. With *Pelican* firing freely, Watson's only hope was to drift toward *Pelican* and defeat her in hand-to-hand combat. But when the two ships finally came together, the British seamen swarmed over the gunwales and through frayed netting to seize the American ship. As many of *Argus*'s exhausted and demoralized crew fled below, Watson remained on deck to bring down the colors.

It was as lopsided a fight as one would see in this war. *Pelican* suffered two deaths—an Englishman and one of the impressed Americans serving with Maples—and five wounded, all of whom recovered. There was little damage to her hull or rigging. *Argus* suffered twelve dead, including the mortally wounded, and seven wounded who recovered. Dye describes the toll as "the highest per capita battle casualty rate of any American navy ship during the War of 1812."[21] Later that day, Maples wrote to Thornbrough:

> No eulogium I could use would do sufficient justice to the merits of my gallant officers and crew, which consisted of 116; the cool courage they displayed, and the precision of their fire, could only be equalled by their zeal to distinguish themselves....[22]

IV

What went wrong that day has been a source of speculation among many historians, mostly Americans, because *Argus*'s performance in that final fight was unlike that of any other U.S. ship during the war and it was in marked contrast to her performance theretofore during the voyage. Her commander was thought to be one of the best, and his reputation for superior gunnery is at variance with the deficiencies that contributed to *Argus*'s failure that day. In the fight between the *Shannon* and the *Chesapeake*, which ended in an even quicker defeat for the Americans, the Yankee crew at least inflicted heavy casualties on the British victor.

The navy's investigation after the war attributed the loss to fatigue among the crew and to the sudden incapacity of her top two officers. James Fenimore Cooper, in his *History of the Navy of the United States of America* (1846), appears to have been one of the first to speculate in print on the reasons for defeat, suggesting two. He cited the improper loading of the guns, suggesting that this may have been why *Argus* did so little damage to *Pelican*:

> It is one tradition of the service that the *Argus* was lost by double shotting the carronades. It is certain that a carronade will not bear two shot to advantage. In her first cruise, the *Essex*, which vessel had an armament of carronades, took a merchant-brig, on which Captain Porter determined to try the effect of his broadside. The frigate ranged fairly alongside her prize, and fired a whole broadside into her, each gun being double-shotted. Nearly every shot struck, and but two or three, with the exception of those from the long twelves, penetrated the brig's sides.[23]

The more important reason, Cooper suggested (and he was one of the first to do so), was drunkenness among *Argus*'s crew. According to Cooper,

> On the night of the 13th of August, the *Argus* fell in with a vessel from Oporto, loaded with wine. It has been said, apparently on authority entitled to credit, that a good deal of the liquor was brought on board the brig clandestinely, as the boats passed to and fro, and that many of the people, who had been over-worked and kept from their rest, partook of the refreshment it afforded too freely.[24]

Theodore Roosevelt repeated this story.[25] Several years later, so did Henry Adams.[26] The problem with these retellings is that it's not clear that a ship from Oporto (a port city in northern Portugal, now called Porto) was captured that night or any other night during *Argus*'s voyage. The ship captured on 13 August was out of Dublin and carried wine, but none of the records of the voyage or of the subsequent official inquiry into the defeat indicates that any wine was taken on board. *Argus*'s surgeon records in his journal for the 13th, "At 9 PM fired a gun and brought too a large Brig the Belford—which nearly ran aboard of us—She proved to be from Dublin bound to London laden with linen Wine &c worth £100,000—Took out of her a box of Plate [silver] and at 12oClk burnt her."[27]

None of these records, of course, proves that the exhausted crewmen, or enough of them, were not drunk. Some wine may have been secreted on board after the capture of the *Belford*, and the crew may have imbibed a few too many rounds in celebration before they took to their hammocks for some badly needed sleep. The officers were as tired and overworked as the crew, so their attentiveness to minor indiscipline might have been less than the dangerous circumstances under which *Argus* sailed required. The crew might have gotten into some of the wine taken earlier from the *Susannah*. Whatever the case, the crew appears not to have been in top form that night. They were outperformed by their adversary at deadly cost.

Neither crew behaved well in the immediate aftermath of the battle. British boarders looted the *Argus*, trampling some of the wounded lying on the deck. In the absence of their officers, who were removed to the *Pelican*, the American crewmen remaining on the *Argus* behaved no better. Maples kindly allowed the two ships to "lie to" while Inderwick amputated Henry Allen's shattered leg at mid-thigh. When finished with Allen, Inderwick kept busy caring for and comforting his other ravaged charges. He later recalled:

> Owing to the disordered state of the vessel the wounded have wretched accommodation—if that term may be used—I endeavoured to make their condition as comfortable as possible—Divided, those of our people who remained on board, and were well into watches—in different parts of the vessel—Mr. Hudson, Mr. Dennisson & myself sitting up with the Captain—Directed Lemonade & Tamarind water be kept made and served to the Wounded.[28]

As her captors sailed the *Argus* to Plymouth, Allen showed signs of recovery and was transferred to the Mill Prison Hospital several days after they arrived on 16 August. But his recovery was short-lived. The severe wound was healing poorly and becoming gangrenous, while fever and nausea swept through Allen's weakened body. On 18 August, he slipped into a coma and died late that night. *Argus*'s officers and the American consul, John Hawker, pooled their money to buy a coffin inscribed with Allen's name and rank, while Rear Admiral Thomas Byam Martin, the commanding officer at Plymouth, ordered that Allen be buried with full military honors. Inderwick described the solemnities:

> On the coffin was a velvet pall, over which was spread the American ensign, and on it were laid his hat and sword. As the coffin was being removed to the hearse, the guard saluted; when deposited, the procession moved forward, the band playing the "Dead March

> in Saul." [Handel] Upon arrival near the church, the guard halted and clubbed arms, single files inward, through which the procession passed to the church, into which the corpse was carried and deposited in the center aisle.[29]

On 28 August 1813, the *Times* reported that the procession assembled for Allen's funeral included a guard of honor, the lieutenant-colonel of the Royal Marines and two companies of that corps, marine captains, subalterns, and the Royal Marine band. The hearse was attended by eight seamen from the *Argus*, and eight captains of the Royal Navy served as pall bearers. The hearse was followed by Allen's servants, the remaining officers of the *Argus*, the American vice-consul, more captains of the Royal Navy, and a bevy of officers of the British army and the Royal Marines. Last in line were "a very numerous and respectable retinue of Inhabitants." Allen was interred in the yard of St. Andrew's next to Midshipman Richard Delphy, "who had both legs shot off at the knees, and whose internment had taken place only the preceding evening."[30]

Shortly after the funeral, *Argus*'s officers were moved to the village of Ashburton, where they lived comfortably as prisoners on parole with hundreds of French officers in similar straits. Less fortunate was the crew of the *Argus*, including the noncommissioned officer Uriah Levy, who were incarcerated at Dartmoor prison. They remained there in misery many months after peace was concluded in early 1815.

With back-to-back victories over the Americans within the space of three summer months, British confidence began to heal, as the *Naval Chronicle* noted with a restored, though still cautious, bravado:

> The Americans told us, that we were not to reckon upon our superior valour by sea, till we could boast of more than one instance—that of the *Shannon* and *Chesapeake*. Here, then, is another in point; and we doubt not of giving them yet as many more as they give us opportunities.[31]

CHAPTER FOURTEEN

BACK ON LAND: ALABAMA BURNING

Among the many northern Indian tribes in the path of the American expansion were the Shawnee, now living in scattered settlements in South Carolina, Tennessee, Ohio, Missouri, and Indiana. They originally inhabited the Ohio River Valley of western Pennsylvania and Ohio, but unsuccessful warfare against the powerful Iroquois in the 1660s forced them to flee south. As Iroquois power waned, the Shawnee returned to their ancestral lands of western Pennsylvania in the early eighteenth century, only to be pushed west into Ohio and Indiana by American settlers coming over the Allegheny Mountains in search of fertile land.

By the early nineteenth century the Shawnee were again under pressure, this time from the south as American settlers moved north from Kentucky across the Ohio River into the territories of Ohio and Indiana. Tired of retreating and surrendering land, the remnants of the Shawnee nation—led by Tenskwatawa (the Prophet) and his brother Tecumseh—decided to make their stand in the Indiana territory, and they rallied to their cause, as did many of the threatened tribes that would join them. Though the majority of Shawnee tribesmen declined the invitation, the Prophet moved with his supporters to a site on Tippecanoe Creek in western Indiana territory, where they joined with the Kickapoo and Potawatomi in a formidable force of about three thousand warriors at their new capital, called Prophet's Town.

William Henry Harrison, the territorial governor, recognized the threat that the Shawnee entrenchment at Tippecanoe posed to the white settlement in Indiana, and his attack on the town in November 1811 effectively ended the Prophet's Town alliance and the organized Indian resistance to America's westward expansion in that region. But the spirit of the uprising lived on thanks to Tecumseh. He was absent when Harrison attacked, having traveled to the Mississippi Territory to preach his vision of resistance and traditional values to the beleaguered tribes there.

Tecumseh's mission "was arguably the most impressive journey ever made on behalf of Indian unity," according to his British biographer John Sugden. "With him went a handpicked party, six Shawnees, six Kickapoos, six Winnebagos and two Creek guides."[1]

They left Prophet's Town in July 1811, traveling south by the Wabash River to the Ohio, and then on foot across Kentucky and Tennessee into the Mississippi Territory. There, in a land of mostly uninhabited wilderness, lived about two thousand Cherokee warriors and their families, and about half as many Chickasaw. South of the Cherokee lived about six thousand Choctaw warriors. To the east, in what is now Alabama and western Georgia, lived members of the Creek Confederacy, a loose association of several tribes with a common culture. The Creeks—numbering about eighteen thousand all together, and able to field about five thousand warriors—were settled in about forty separate villages dotting the banks of the Alabama, Talapoosa, Coosa, Chattahoochee, and Flint Rivers. A splinter of the Creek nation had earlier moved south and east into what was then Spanish Florida and became known as the Seminoles.[2]

With President Jefferson's purchase of the Louisiana Territory in 1803 and Louisiana's admission to the Union as a state in 1812, American interest in the area increased. When a federal road was cut through the region to connect Georgia and Louisiana, small groups of settlers began to enter Mississippi Territory from Tennessee and Georgia, and in February 1813 the United States seized the fledging settlement at Mobile from the Spanish. With the advent of the War of 1812, agents from Spain, America, and England took a heightened interest in the Creeks' territorial concerns, and each attempted to influence the

Indians to act against the others. But none of the emissaries succeeded as much as Tecumseh, who urged the Creeks to stand up for themselves.

The Indians of the south were ripe for exploitation by a charismatic leader who promised to restore their land, dignity, independence, and culture, all of which were slipping away under the relentless pressure of the U.S. government and the white settlers drifting in from all sides. At the same time, the southern tribes were incurring burdensome trade debts with the United States in exchange for manufactured goods and food, and land concessions had become a common mechanism to extinguish the debt. Sugden observes:

> In 1805 the Choctaws had ceded four million acres for less than two cents an acre, nearly all of it to offset debts. The Chickasaws lost land northeast of the Tennessee, also for a derisory pittance. Between 1801 and 1823, the Cherokees relinquished ten million acres in nine cessions.[3]

At the same time the Indians were losing land to the whites, they were also undergoing a profound social disruption as alien cultural and modern economic practices crept into societies that had been little changed for centuries. Many Cherokees, in particular, embraced commercial trade and European-style farmsteads, and several became slave owners. Contributing to the pace and scope of the Westernization of the Indian tribes of the southeast were deliberate policies of the federal government to make them more like the white settlers and to integrate them more closely into American society.

In 1796, President George Washington appointed Benjamin Hawkins as U.S. Indian agent to the Creeks. From his base in Coweta, Georgia (near present-day Atlanta), at the eastern edge of Creek territory, Hawkins attempted to keep the peace, and he encouraged the tribes to adopt a Western system of farming and crafts, though with mixed results. Henry Adams argued in the late nineteenth century that the "success of these experiments was not at first great, for the larger number of Indians saw no advantage to becoming laborers, and preferred sitting in the squares of the towns, or hunting; but here and there chiefs or half-breeds had farms, slaves, stock, orchards and spinning wheels."[4]

As the Indians slowly absorbed white culture, they increasingly intermarried with whites in the southeast. By the time war broke out between Britain and America, a number of southern tribal leaders were of mixed blood, as were many of the Americanized settlers who encroached on tribal lands. One of the most famous Creek leaders, Alexander McGillivray, was only one-quarter Indian. John Ross, a prominent Cherokee, was one-eighth Indian, and the five sons of the Scottish trader James Colbert and his Chickasaw wife became leading figures in the Chickasaw Nation. To the east, the warrior Peter McQueen, who would lead one of the Creeks' first violent uprisings, was a wealthy slave-owning mestizo, while William Weatherford, another Creek leader, was only one quarter Indian.[5]

Into this swirling mix of cultural and territorial tension Tecumseh and his party entered with their message of redemption. Arriving late in the summer of 1811 at the western edge of the Mississippi Territory, Tecumseh and his followers sought allies and converts to his cause among the Choctaws. At assemblies in towns and villages in east-central Mississippi, the Shawnee chieftain performed dances and made speeches, encouraging an uprising and the Indians' return to traditional ways. Among the Choctaws, however, he found little interest in going to war against the powerful United States, which, simultaneously, was making every effort to ensure his failure. From the the time of his arrival, Tecumseh was dogged by the Indian agent Hawkins, who attended most of Tecumseh's presentations and discouraged the tribal leaders from joining the Shawnee. Failing to gain many followers in the western Mississippi Territory, Tecumseh traveled east into Alabama, where his case for war and traditional values found a more receptive audience among the Creeks.

Forty-three years old and described by witnesses as tall and handsome, Tecumseh could use his striking presence to great effect in speech and dance. Still trailed by the energetic Hawkins, Tecumseh made his presentation to a Creek council in Tuckabatchee (near present-day Montgomery) in September 1811. "Stripped to their breech-cloths, moccasins, and ornaments," wrote one witness, Tecumseh and his followers "had placed eagle feathers on their heads and painted their faces black, while buffalo tails hung behind from their belts. Other tails were attached to their arms, ingeniously made to stand out, by means of bands."[6] When Hawkins and his party finally left the village to return to their base at Coweta, Tecumseh was free to speak more candidly to the assembled Indian leaders. A nineteenth-century historian offered the following account, based on contemporary sources, of Tecumseh's speech:

> He exhorted them to return to their primitive customs; to throw aside the plow and loom, and to abandon an agricultural life, which was unbecoming to Indian warriors. He told them that after the whites had possessed the greater part of their country, turned its beautiful forests into large fields and stained their clear rivers with the washings of the soil, they would then subject them to African servitude. He exhorted them to assimilate in no way with the grasping, unprincipled race; to use none of their arms and wear none of their clothes, but dress in the skins of beasts, which the great spirit had given his children for food and raiment, and to use the war club, scalping-knife and the bow. He concluded by announcing that the British, their former friends, had sent him from the Big Lakes to procure their services in expelling the Americans from all Indian soil; that the King of England was ready handsomely to reward all who would fight for his cause.[7]

An Osage who heard a similar speech by Tecumseh several months later in Missouri describes his reaction to the Shawnee chieftain's address: "I wish it was in my power to do justice to the eloquence of this distinguished man, but it is utterly impossible. The richest colors, shaded with a master's pencil, would fall infinitely short of the glowing finish of the original.... It was a simple but vehement narrative of the wrongs imposed by the white people on the Indians, and an exhortation for the latter to resist them."[8]

Though Tecumseh never received much support from the elders of the Creek tribes and towns, many younger warriors were stirred by his call to commit themselves to a different vision of the future. One group of Creek converts who displayed their commitment to the cause by defiantly brandishing red clubs soon became known as the "Red Sticks." That commitment deepened with the appearance of a comet that autumn, followed by a series of earthquakes in December and January. These omens moved many undecided warriors to join Tecumseh.

In January 1812, four months after Tecumseh's visit to Alabama, two hundred Creeks were reported to be on the Wabash River in Indiana, and one year later Little Warrior, from the village of Wewocau, on the Coosa took part with six other Creeks in the battle of River Raisin. On their way home to Alabama—allegedly carrying messages from the British at Malden to the Spaniards in Pensacola asking the Spaniards to provide weapons and powder to the Creeks—Little Warrior and his band murdered members of two white families living along the Ohio River in Indiana.[9]

Hawkins demanded that the culprits be turned over to him for trial and punishment, but the leaders of the Creeks refused. They held their own trial instead, found Little Warrior guilty, tracked him down at Hickory Ground on the Coosa, and killed him and most of his followers in late March or early April. Incensed at the capitulation to white demands, and the execution of their heroes, some of the younger Creek warriors rose up in revolt, forcing the tribal leaders to flee to Coweta and seek Hawkins's protection. Over the next several months, the Red Sticks tracked down and killed most of the Creek leaders responsible for Little Warrior's death.

America's war with Britain was well underway when violence flared within the Creek nation. The British tried to capitalize on the conflict in the Mississippi Territory by inciting the Creeks to rise up against the Americans, who were also pressing against Britain's ally Spain in Florida. Spanish officials in Florida were not sure which way to turn, but after some prodding by the British emissaries, they decided that it was in their interest to arm the Creeks and invited Peter McQueen, a mixed-race Creek leader of the Red Sticks, to come to Pensacola for ammunition.[10]

In July 1813, McQueen, Josiah Francis, and High-Headed Jim (also known as Tustennuggee Emathla and Jim Boy) led about three hundred Creek warriors to Pensacola for the promised weapons. American settlers along the Tombigbee and Tensaw north of Mobile got wind of the mission, however, and appealed to the territory's governor for protection. General Flournoy, the American commander at Mobile, refused to send regular troops or volunteers. Left to themselves and fearing annihilation, the settlers answered the call of the local militia leader Colonel James Caller for volunteers. A number of mixed-race soldiers and officers from other towns and settlements, including Captain Dixon Bailey and Major Daniel Beasley, joined Caller. With about 180 men under his command, and "wearing a calico hunting shirt, a high bell-crowned hat and top boots, and riding a large fine bay horse,"[11] Caller marched his force east to intercept McQueenon on his return from Pensacola. On 27 July 1813,

Caller's scouts found the Creeks encamped nearby, cooking their midday meal on the banks of Burnt Corn Creek, about eighty miles due north of Pensacola.

Caller ordered an attack on the enemy encampment, routing the Creeks and capturing much of their supplies. But the Creeks, led by High-Headed Jim, soon rallied, counter-attacked, and drove the disorganized militia into the woods. American casualties were light—only two dead—and nothing is known of the Creek casualties. The Creeks had lost most of their supplies to the Americans, but they returned to Pensacola, where the Spanish replaced what was lost. However indecisive the results, the battle at Burnt Corn was the first act of organized warfare between the whites and Indians in the Mississippi Territory. The tensions soon escalated into a bloody conflagration. Sensing the danger, General Ferdinand Leigh Claiborne, newly installed as the commander of Fort Stoddert, thirty miles north of Mobile, began to prepare his seven hundred regulars and militia for the worst … and the worst arrived within a month.

II

Panicked by the news of armed Indians routing their militia, settlers throughout southern Alabama began to fortify their villages and build stockades, to which they flocked for security and strength. Worried settlers—whites, Indians, and mixed-race—gathered at the house of a wealthy farmer, Samuel Mims, forty miles north of Mobile and just a few miles east of where the Alabama River joins the Tombigbee before spilling into Lake Tensaw. Supported by militia, the settlers built a stockade around Mims's house, enclosing about an acre of land and filling the space with temporary shelters. They cut port holes built into the timber pickets for the rifles and built gates in the east and the west walls of their fort.

As more settlers sought refuge within the fort, they built rude dwellings wherever space allowed and planted crops outside the stockade. The black slaves who belonged to the white and Indian settlers built their shelters outside the walls of what was now known as Fort Mims. By late August 1813, seventeen structures had been built within the walls, and the population of the tiny fort, including the militia under Major Daniel Beasley, a regular U.S. Army officer of mixed race,[12] numbered 553 men, women, and children of a variety of races, including several Spanish deserters from Pensacola.[13]

With the arms supplied by the Spanish, a thousand Creek warriors[14] under William Weatherford—the son of a white Georgian frontiersman and an Indian mother and known to the Creeks as Red Eagle—marched south to the Lake Tensaw region. Henry Adams believed that Weatherford and McQueen picked Fort Mims as their target because of the mixed-race officers Beasley and Bailey, both of whom helped lead the attack on McQueen's column at Burnt Corn.[15]

Along the way, Weatherford's force attacked the plantation of Zachariah McGirth on 20 August, capturing several slaves who gave Weatherford information about Fort Mims. One of the slaves, named Joe, escaped from Weatherford and fled to Fort Mims, where he warned the settlers of the impending attack. They tightened security for a day or two, but when nothing happened—Weatherford had halted his force to give them a rest in the humid heat of Alabama's late summer—they let down their guard.

On 29 August, two slaves tending the cattle in a pasture near the fort spotted a hundred or so warriors hiding in the woods. They reported the news to the fort's command, and a squad of mounted soldiers searched the area but found nothing. Believing that the slaves had lied, Beasley had one of them flogged. The next morning, the beaten slave again spotted an Indian force approaching the fort. To avoid another beating by the soldiers and massacre by the Indian warriors, the slave fled to nearby Fort Pierce.[16] At about noon, as the drum roll announced the soldiers' midday meal, Weatherford's force—"Every man painted red or black and stripped to the buff"[17]—attacked the fort, whose gates were wide open and walls unguarded.

Major Beasley ran to shut the eastern gate, but it was obstructed, and he fell under a swarm of Creek warriors. Though they enjoyed the advantage of surprise, the Creeks were hindered by a bevy of "prophets," who believed themselves immune to the white man's bullets. Five of the leading prophets were "immediately shot down, while engaged in dancing and incantations. This greatly abated the ardor of the enemy, many of whom retreated through the gate for the moment."[18]

But only for a moment. The Creek attack quickly resumed, and the outnumbered defenders struggled to mount an effective resistance. In the confined acre of the fort, men, women, and children fell as the Creek warriors hacked and shot their way into the ill-prepared citadel. Ordered to defend the northern wall, Captain Bailey soon found himself the sole surviving officer and tried to rally his troops as the Creeks poured in. As Bailey's men fought for their lives, women urged them on, loaded their rifles, and brought them water.

As settlers fled into the fort's buildings, the Creeks set them afire. "The shrieks of the women and children went up to high heaven," reported one witness.[19] Bailey and his remaining men turned the loom house into a bastion and poured what fire they could into the attackers. Samuel Mims's brother David took a musket ball in his neck and shouted "Oh God, I'm a dead man!" as he fell. An Indian leaped upon him, took off his scalp, and waved it triumphantly.[20]

The dwindling number of defenders crowded into Mims's farm house in the middle of the enclosure, but that too was soon set afire, and several of the soldiers who fought from holes punched in the roof burned to death as the fire swept into the attic. By late afternoon, most of the resistance had ended, and the victorious Creeks embarked upon a gruesome mopping up operation. The nineteenth-century historian Albert Pickett, who interviewed a few of the survivors, wrote:

> The bastion was broken down, and the helpless inmates were butchered in the quickest manner, and blood and brains bespattered the whole earth. The children were seized by their legs and killed by beating their heads against the stockading. The women were scalped, and those who were pregnant were opened, while they were alive, and the embryo infants let out of the womb.... The British at Pensacola had offered a reward of five dollars for every American scalp. The Indians jerked the skin from the whole head, and, collecting all the effects which the fire had not consumed, retired to the east, one mile from the ruins, where they smoked their pipes and trimmed and dried their scalps.[21]

Few of Fort Mims's inhabitants survived. Some mixed-race captives were allowed to live, and the blacks who remained alive were taken as slaves by the Creek victors. Fifteen others—whites, blacks, mixed-race, and Indians—managed to escape. The number of settlers and soldiers killed was originally reckoned at four to five hundred. More recent estimates put it at fewer than 250, still a horrific figure.[22] The Creeks paid a heavy price for their victory. Three to four hundred warriors fell, but they were only a part of the Creek Confederacy's losses. As the Indians withdrew with their scalps and booty, word of the Fort Mims massacre spread quickly across the American frontier, and the forces of vengeance were set in motion.

III

Sent by General Claiborne to bury the dead, Major Joseph P. Kennedy found his way to Fort Mims by following the circling buzzards. He directed his men to dig two pits, and prepared a grim report for Claiborne,

> Indians, Negroes, white men, women and children, lay in promiscuous ruin. All were scalped, and the females, of every age were butchered in a manner which neither decency nor language will permit me to describe. The main building was burned to ashes, which were filled with bones. The plains and woods around were covered with dead bodies. All the houses were consumed by fire, except the block-house and part of the pickets. The soldiers and officers with one voice, called on Divine Providence to revenge the death of our murdered friends.[23]

And revenge they would get. Secretary of War John Armstrong Jr. called upon the western governors to suppress the Creeks. On 20 September 1813, the Tennessee legislature took up a proposal to send 3,500 troops to Alabama to preserve order and punish the enemy. But the obvious choice to lead those troops, Andrew Jackson, general of the Western Tennessee militia, was in bed recovering from a wound received in a duel seventeen days earlier.

Earlier that summer, Jackson had served as second to Billy Carroll in his duel with Jesse Benton, the hot-tempered brother of Thomas Hart Benton, a prominent political figure in frontier Tennessee and a future U.S. senator. Billy received a slight wound to his thumb, but Jesse suffered a nasty wound in his buttocks, making him the laughing stock of the state. The Benton brothers held Jackson responsible for the embarrassing outcome, and on 3 September 1813—two and a half months after the duel, and three days after the massacre at Fort Mims—they exacted their revenge.

Walking across Nashville's town square to the post office with his close friend and ally John Coffee, Jackson spotted the Bentons in the doorway of the City Hotel. Turning toward Thomas Hart Benton, Jackson pulled out his whip and proclaimed, "Now you damned rascal, I'm going to punish you. Defend yourself."[24] Both drew pistols, and Jackson backed Tom Benton into the hotel and down the corridor. The aggrieved Jesse, meanwhile, circled behind Jackson and shot the general in the back, shattering his shoulder and sending another ball into his arm. As he fell, Jackson fired at Tom Benton but missed. Tom fired twice at Jackson, now lying on the floor in a pool of blood, and he missed too. John Coffee arrived and fired at Tom Benton to avenge the wounding of his friend. His shot missed as well, and the Bentons fled while Coffee carried Jackson to a doctor.

As the doctors struggled to save Jackson's life, the Bentons strutted around the town square proclaiming their victory. But Jackson was the more popular figure, and Tom Benton soon realized that he and his brother had tangled with the wrong man. Days later, the Bentons left Nashville for their hometown of Franklin. Tom soon enlisted in the army and served during the War of 1812. After his discharge, he moved to Missouri, got involved in politics, and became the state's first U.S. senator, serving with Jackson in the eighteenth Congress.

Andrew Jackson, meanwhile, suffered badly from his wounds, but when the legislature authorized raising an army to send to Alabama, Jackson insisted on taking the command. Governor Blount conceded, and a few weeks later Jackson's men mustered in Fayetteville, Tennessee, to march against the Creeks. Jackson's orders to his officers and men left no doubt about their duty:

> Brave Tennesseans! Your frontier is threatened with invasion by the savage foe! Already do they advance towards your frontier with their scalping knives unsheathed, to butcher your wives, your children, and your helpless babes. Time is not to be lost. We must hasten to the frontier, or we will find it drenched in the blood of our fellow-citizens.[25]

For General Andrew Jackson, these orders were remarkably restrained. As America's many enemies would soon discover, Jackson was a man of towering rage, unyielding determination, and majestic ferocity. A recent biographer describes the power of the avenging forces that gathered in Nashville:

> Divine Providence was waiting, but not in godly form. It was off to the north, in the Cumberland country, in the guise of a tall, fierce man whose eyes could blaze with fury, racked now with terrible wounds, his body thin to the point of emaciation. Andrew Jackson well understood the word revenge, and he thirsted for it.[26]

For the Indians of the southeast and their British and Spanish allies seeking advantage along the Gulf Coast, Andrew Jackson would be the fourth horseman of the Apocalypse:

> And when he had opened the fourth seal, I heard the voice of the fourth beast say, Come and See.
>
> And I looked, and behold a pale horse: and his name that sat upon him was Death, and Hell followed with him. And power was given unto them over the fourth part of the earth, to kill with sword, and with hunger, and with death, and with the beasts of the earth. (Revelation 6: 6–7)

CHAPTER FIFTEEN

"WE HAVE MET THE ENEMY AND THEY ARE OURS"

Very early in the war both sides realized that much of the armed conflict would take place along the five-thousand-mile border between the United States and British North America. And with much of the eastern portion of that border defined by lakes, rivers, or straits, the importance of an effective naval presence was obvious.

Many thousands of miles away at his headquarters at the base of the Pyrenees, Field Marshall the Marquis of Wellington took time out from fighting the French to respond to a letter from Lord Bathurst, the secretary of state for war and the colonies, seeking his advice on the conduct of the war with the United States. "Any offensive operation founded upon Canada," Wellington wrote, "must be preceded by the establishment of a naval superiority on the Lakes.... The defence of Canada and the cooperation of the Indians depends on the navigation of the Lakes."[1]

President Madison received similar advice within months of his declaration of war, though from a humbler source. Daniel Dobbins, an American trader who plied both sides of Lake Erie for customers and supplies, found himself on the Canadian coast of the lake when war was declared and was imprisoned for refusing an oath not to take up arms against the British. Dobbins escaped—with his boat—and sailed east to Fort Detroit, which General Hull had just reinforced in anticipation of a British attack. Letting the U.S. Army take his ship for supply use, Dobbins joined one of the fort's scouting units. When Hull surrendered the fort, Dobbins was again made prisoner. This time, however, there would be no chance of parole, and Dobbins faced the death penalty as a result of his earlier escape from the British and his refusal to take the oath.[2]

But again Daniel Dobbins managed to escape. Pursued by Indians, Dobbins found an abandoned canoe on the Lake Erie shore and paddled across sixty miles of open water to Sandusky, Ohio. From there he took a horse to the village of Cleveland, acquired another canoe, and paddled east along the coast of Lake Erie for another 150 miles until he reached Pennsylvania's militia general, David Mead, at Presque Isle (now Erie, Pennsylvania). Dobbins brought the first report of the loss of Fort Detroit to American authorities.

Mead sent Dobbins on to Washington, where in September 1812 he gave his eye-witness account of the surrender of Fort Detroit to the president and other senior officials and urged them to put a flotilla of warships on Lake Erie. The best place to build and station such a fleet, he argued, was the protected harbor of Presque Isle. Madison concurred, commissioned Dobbins as a sailing master, and sent him back to Lake Erie with two thousand dollars to get the ships built. Dobbins returned to Presque Isle in November 1812 to create America's newest naval base.

Meanwhile Lieutenant Jesse D. Elliott of the navy was dispatched to the Black Rock naval base, near Buffalo on the east bank of the Niagara River, downstream from Lake Erie and across the lake from Presque Isle, to organize a fleet to challenge the British and protect the border. On 8 October 1813, Elliott led about a hundred American soldiers and sailors on a night raid across the Niagara River and captured two British brigs, the *Detroit* and the *Caledonia*, anchored off Britain's Fort Erie. With too little wind to escape into the lake, Elliott drifted down the Niagara to Black Rock as the British fired at him from the fort. The *Detroit* ran aground and had to be destroyed, but *Caledonia* was brought safely into American possession. Over the next several months, Elliott purchased four merchant ships for the squadron and refitted them for combat.

Commodore Isaac Chauncey, America's naval commander of the Great Lakes, visited Dobbins at Presque Isle on New Year's Day, 1814. Surveying

Dobbins's work in the bitter cold, Chauncey thought the four gunboats then under construction were too small, and he had Dobbins lengthen two of them by ten feet or more. Chauncey then traveled to Black Rock, where several more warships were under construction, to be ready by spring.[3]

While Dobbins and his workmen labored through the winter, twenty-seven-year-old Master Commandant Oliver Hazard Perry was becoming bored with his command of the gunboat squadron at Newport, Rhode Island. He requested a transfer to a sea-going warship, hoping to bask in the kind of glory that Hull, Porter, and Decatur had won in their early victories over the British. No ship was available, however, so he requested and received a transfer to the Lakes, where fighting was soon expected. When Chauncey heard of Perry's interest, he wrote to him, "You are the very person that I want for a particular service, in which you may gain reputation for Yourself and honour for your country."[4] On 8 February 1813, Secretary of the Navy William Jones ordered Perry and 150 of his gunboat sailors from Newport to join Chauncey on the Lakes.

Like Decatur and Porter, Perry was born into a naval family of warrior lineage, but his was tempered by a dose of pacifism. On his mother's side he was descended from the Scottish hero William Wallace, while a paternal great-grandfather, Edmund Perry, was an influential Quaker who fled England for tolerant Rhode Island to escape persecution during the rule of Oliver Cromwell.[5] Closer to home, Perry's father, five brothers, and two brothers-in-law were naval officers.[6] His father, Christopher Perry, fought the British during the Revolutionary War with the Kingston Reds and later as a privateer until captured. Jailed in the notorious British prison ship *Jersey*, he was one of the lucky ones who managed to escape, and the experience left him with resentment for the British. During the Quasi-War with France, Christopher served as a captain in the navy, commanding the *General Greene*, on which the fourteen-year-old Oliver served as a midshipman. Perry distinguished himself during the Barbary Wars and at seventeen was commissioned a lieutenant.[7]

Years later, while in command of the schooner *Revenge*, Perry ran aground in a heavy fog near New London, Connecticut, and lost the ship. Though exonerated in the subsequent inquiry—the loss was blamed on the pilot—some historians[8] speculate that the incident, along with frequent health problems, may have tarnished Perry's reputation and cost him the sea-going post he sought in the early days of the War of 1812. Perry complained to the secretary of the navy when the less senior Lieutenant Henry Allen received the command of the *Argus*, which Perry thought had been promised to him.[9]

Perry leaped at the opportunity of an active command on the Great Lakes, and on 28 February 1813 met with Chauncey at Albany, New York, where the commodore was conferring with General Dearborn about expediting the army's lagging supplies. Chauncey, short of men himself, pulled rank and took about fifty of Perry's Rhode Islanders. With the details worked out and orders conveyed, Master Commandant Perry and the remaining hundred or so of his men marched west to Presque Isle to build the fleet and take control of Lake Erie from the British. Perry crossed the frozen lake on a horse-drawn sled and arrived in late March.

II

The Lake strategy that Dearborn and Chauncey were developing called for combined land and sea operations to seize strategic British bases while protecting American bases from British attack. The first major effort in this strategy was the successful attack on York (present-day Toronto), Ontario, the capital of Upper Canada, in April 1813. Chauncey's fleet landed General Zebulon Pike and his 1,700 soldiers just west of York. As Pike's army moved east toward the city, Chauncey's fleet bombarded the defenders from positions just off shore, forcing the British and their Indian allies to flee into the interior. Though the Americans abandoned York shortly after its capture, the attack was a major setback for the British. Supplies destined for Procter's army and the fleet at Fort Malden in the west were lost and could not be replaced for the foreseeable future. And the loss of the thirty-gun frigate *Sir Isaac Brock*, then under construction at York, prevented Commodore James Lucas Yeo from reaching rough parity with Chauncey's bigger fleet on Lake Ontario.[10]

A month later, Chauncey teamed up with Colonel Winfield Scott for an amphibious assault on Fort George, at the mouth of the Niagara River where it spills into Lake Ontario. Perry, briefly taking leave of his duties at Presque Isle, helped coordinate the naval bombardment of the fort and then led about five men ashore for the attack.[11] With another successful attack under his belt, Chauncey planned to repeat the amphibious attacks on Lake Erie. In particular, he intended for Perry's fleet to take Harrison's Ohio-based army across the lake, recapture Fort Detroit, and drive the British and their menacing Indian allies out of Upper Canada. Circumstances on Lake Erie were more challenging for the Americans than on Lake Ontario, however, and tactics had to be adjusted.

In contrast to the aggressive and creative use by both the British and the Americans of combined sea-and-land operations, neither of the squadrons on Lake Ontario was interested in provoking a decisive battle for control of the lake. The commander of the British squadrons was Sir James Lucas Yeo, who had been appointed to that position in May 1813 by Admiral John Borlase Warren, who then was in command of all British naval activity in the Americas. Some think Yeo was not the best choice for an important position where the British were already at a numerical and logistical disadvantage. In the view of C. S. Forester, "The appointment of a commander in chief whose principal qualification was the fact that he had just lost his ship constitutes a great part of the explanation of subsequent events on the Lakes."[12]

Chauncey, too, was not without his critics. Though he planned and executed a number of successful amphibious operations against British land bases in Canada, many historians believe he purposely avoided direct confrontation with Yeo's squadron despite his numerical superiority. By the spring of 1813, the British had eight ships on Lake Ontario, with two under construction, while the American squadron numbered eleven, with five under construction. Forester was harshly critical of both leaders:

> [T]here were repeated skirmishes but never a pitched battle. Yeo and Chauncey were men of similar temperament regarding decisive action. Each of them had material viewpoint; each was anxious to conserve his strength and dreaded the future. Conditions never suited the commander who had the initiative.... The one who had the superiority in long guns thought his adversary would benefit from his superiority in carronades; each ... complained about the sailing qualities or the handiness of the vessels under his command; the wind was unfavorable, or the military situation on land called for restraint afloat.[13]

Another Anglo-American historian assesses the timidity of both sides:

> The inability of either side to win a decisive victory on Lake Ontario was of most benefit to the British. Their aims in the war were essentially defensive. The United States hoped to capture Canada and force Britain to change her maritime policies.... American rewards in this area were simply not commensurate with the efforts expended.[14]

There is probably a good deal of truth in these charges, for Chauncey was certainly not overly aggressive in the pursuit and destruction of Yeo's squadron. But to his credit, he does seem to have been a good strategist and an excellent judge of character in the subordinates he selected and to whom he gave great responsibility: Oliver Hazard Perry, Winfield Scott, Thomas Macdonough, and Zebulon Pike.

The British recognized America's increasingly formidable naval presence on Lake Erie as the serious threat it was to their undermanned positions at Malden and Detroit, and they took counter-actions of their own. Docked just south of Malden at Amherstburg on the Detroit River, the British squadron amounted to six ships of varying sizes, arms, and states of completion. In February 1813, as Perry was on his way to Presque Isle, British Admiral Warren appointed Captain Robert Heriot Barclay, a veteran of Trafalgar who had lost an arm in a later frigate engagement with the French, to take command of Britain's precarious naval presence on the Lakes. Bad weather, however, delayed his arrival at Kingston, Ontario, until early May. In the meantime Warren seems to have changed his mind and given the Lake command to Yeo, who in turn offered the Erie command to Captain W. H. Mulcaster. When Mulcaster turned it down, Yeo offered it to the recently arrived Barclay, who accepted. As a result of these repeated delays in assigning responsibility, British naval preparations on Lake Erie were well behind those of the Americans. Barclay did not arrive at his squadron's Amherstburg base until early June, just as Perry was readying his larger fleet at Presque Isle for battle.

Barclay's delay gave Perry a two-month advantage in preparation, which he would use to great effect as ice on the lake thawed, allowing passage and combat. Warm weather also allowed him to speed up construction, and the four ships of various sizes advanced under Dobbins's direction. Surrounded by Pennsylvania's forests of pine for the decks and a variety of hard woods for the hull, the shipwrights and laborers who struggled through the winter enjoyed an abundance of materials. But while the frontier offered cheap and ready wood, manufactured goods—ropes and sails, cannon, shot and other metal goods, and gun powder—were difficult to come by. For these goods, Perry had to turn to the booming manufacturing town of Pittsburgh, whose population had doubled between 1810 and 1815, or to Philadelphia and Washington, D.C., further to the east.[15] Despite its booming population, however, Pittsburgh was short of skilled workers, so blacksmiths and carpenters had to be brought in from Pennsylvania's other cities, hundreds of miles away. It took one group of carpenters four weeks to make the journey from Philadelphia.

Perry himself went to Pittsburgh in April to hurry along the supplies and inspect their quality, but two months later he was complaining about delays. Although Pittsburgh was only about 127 miles away, there were no roads of any use, and goods had to be shipped upstream on the Allegheny River and then up the French Creek, both swollen by spring rains and melting snow. The cost was substantial—a thousand dollars to ship a single cannon from Albany, for example, and a hundred dollars for a barrel of flour. The secretary of the navy complained about the excessive spending and was especially critical of Perry's decision to buy lead for ballast when there were plenty of perfectly good rocks scattered around Presque Isle. Perry retorted that the rocks were not appropriate ballast for his shallow draft ships and that in any event the lead could be resold for the price he paid for it and the money returned to the U.S. Treasury.[16]

Manufactured goods were not the only necessities in short supply at the distant post. As much as Perry complained about the lack of goods, he was even more vociferous about the shortage of manpower and what he believed was Chauncey's lack of interest in resolving it. All crewmen and workers sent to the Lakes from eastern cities and blockaded ports arrived first at Chauncey's headquarters at Sackets Harbor, New York, whence they were assigned to the various posts in the theater. Perry was convinced that Chauncey was keeping the best for himself and that whenever men from Chauncey's fleet were ordered west to join Perry, he received the least capable men and the worst troublemakers.

As the Presque Isle ships neared completion, Perry had only 120 sailors to man a squadron that would require 700. Giving up on Chauncey, Perry circumvented his superior officers and took his complaint directly to the Navy Department. When Chauncey discovered Perry's violation of the chain of command, an angry series of letters were exchanged, and from then on neither man trusted the other. Nonetheless, Chauncey did conduct two drafts of men from his Ontario station and sent 150 of them to Perry. But Perry was less than satisfied with what showed up at Presque Isle, and in a letter he told Chauncey exactly what he thought of the men sent:

> The men that came ... are a motley set, blacks, Soldiers, and boys, I cannot think that you saw them after they were selected. I am, however, pleased to see anything in the shape of a man.[17]

Chauncey's sharp response offers insight into the complicated race relations of the time, or any time for that matter. In his famous reply, Chauncey wrote:

> I regret that you are not pleased with the men sent you ... for to my knowledge a part of them are not surpassed by any seaman we have on the fleet, and I have yet to learn that the Colour of the skin, or cut and trimmings of the coat, can effect a man's qualifications or usefulness. I have nearly 50 Blacks on board of this ship, and many of them are amongst my best men.[18]

Chauncey added, "As you have assured the secretary that you should conceive yourself equal or superior to the enemy, with a force of men so much less than I had deemed necessary, there will be a great deal expected from you by your country...."

Unconsoled, the prickly Perry offered his resignation, complaining again to Secretary Jones that "... they may sir, be as good as they are on the other Lake, but if so, that squadron must be poorly manned indeed."[19] In Perry's defense, one historian of the Lakes campaign notes that of the fifty black crewmen whom Chauncey had among his "best men," he provided not a one to Perry. There were also reports circulating that Chauncey kept twice as many crewmen on the *General Pike* as he needed. Samuel Hambleton, Perry's purser, wrote in his journal:

> Several weeks ago, the Secretary of the navy informed Captain Perry that a sufficient number for both lakes had been forwarded. This is true; but, unfortunately, they were all sent to Lake Ontario, where our portion was detained without necessity. For instance,

> the Pike, with a single deck and twenty six guns, had four hundred men, most of them prime seamen, mustering in all four hundred and seventy; and even now he has not sent a single officer of rank or experience except Captain Elliott.[20]

In light of Perry's repeated efforts to circumvent the chain of command, Chauncey's response was surprisingly temperate, and he discouraged Perry's resignation:

> I regret your determination for various reasons; the first and most important is, that the public service would suffer from a change, and your removal might in some degree defeat the objects of the campaign. Although I conceive that you have treated me with less candour than I was entitled to, considering the warm interest that I have always taken in your behalf, yet my confidence in your zeal and ability has been undiminished, and I should really regret that any circumstance should remove you from your present command before you have accomplished the objects for which you were sent to Erie.... You ought also to consider that the first duty of an officer is to sacrifice all personal feelings to his public duties.[21]

Secretary Jones took a similar approach in his response, reminding Perry that it "is the duty of an officer, and in none does his character shine more conspicuous, to sacrifice all personal motives and feelings when in collision with the public good. This sacrifice you are called to make...."[22] The letters had the desired effect, and Perry remained at his post as the two opposing squadrons readied for battle.

For the British on Lake Erie, and most other places in the Canadian interior, the supply and manpower problems were even more severe than those confronting the Americans. In contrast to the United States, with its rapidly developing trade and manufacturing, Canada remained sparsely populated and possessed no centers of industry or manufacture of any consequence. The finished goods needed for warfare, such as tools, cannon, rope, sails, gun powder, and rifles, had to be shipped across the Atlantic and down the St. Lawrence River to Montreal during the summer months, when the river was free of ice, and then sent west over land and lakes to the empire's isolated outposts. Britain's lengthy supply lines and depots were vulnerable to American attack, and the capture of Fort George and York in April and May 1813 denied the British desperately needed supplies to fit out their Erie and Ontario fleets. Also in short supply were food for the army and its restive Indian allies and money to pay the dispirited troops. Procter also knew that once Perry had his fleet on the lake, all British shipping west from Long Point, Ontario, would be halted, and his army and Barclay's fleet would be isolated and starved.

After helping in the American victory at Fort George, Perry traveled to Black Rock, seizing the opportunity to join the five ships that had been refitted there over the winter with the rest of his squadron at Presque Isle. With the British now on the run from the eastern end of the Niagara peninsula and Fort Erie abandoned, the five small vessels would be able to make the difficult journey up the churning Niagara River to Lake Erie unmolested.

The journey from Black Rock to Presque Isle was not without difficulty or danger, however. The rough current in the river that drained Lake Erie into Ontario made it impossible to sail the ships south to the lake, so the ships had to be warped upstream by teams of sailors and oxen. Helped by two hundred soldiers sent by General Dearborn, man and beast were yoked to tow lines and dragged the ships against a strong current. It took nearly two weeks to accomplish the task, and Perry wrote to Chauncey that the fatigue was "almost incredible."[23]

Somewhere between the Niagara and Presque Isle, Barclay's few ships searched for the little squadron on its way from Black Rock. The American ships slipped by his patrol—aided, Barclay complained, by a heavy fog—and by 20 June Perry had muscled all of the Black Rock fleet over the sand bar and into the harbor at Presque Isle.

Perry now pressed the workers to finish construction of the new ships, and by 10 July, the new squadron was launched and anchored in the bay. With the ships from Black Rock, Perry's fleet numbered nine vessels. The two largest—the two-masted brigs *Lawrence* and *Niagara*—were 141 feet long and armed with twenty guns, mostly short-range carronades. Seven smaller ships rounded out the total: The captured *Caledonia*, 3; schooners *Scorpion*, 2, *Tigress*, 1, *Somers*, 2, *Porcupine*,1, *Ariel*, 4; *Ohio*, 1; and the sloop *Trippe*, 1.[24] Hastily constructed in an isolated frontier ship yard with few supplies and a shortage of skilled workmen, these were far from the best ships the navy had afloat. As one historian records: "Noah Brown, who supervised building the two [brigs], said that they were good for one battle, no more. Constructed as they were of green wood, a musket ball could penetrate their two inches of planking."[25]

There is disagreement about how the brig *Lawrence* acquired its name. Many historians of the era attribute the name to Perry, who wanted to honor the sacrifice of his good friend Captain James Lawrence, who was killed on the *Chesapeake* in its fight with the *Shannon* off Boston. Others contend that *Lawrence* was not the ship's original name, but that the navy ordered that one of the new brigs be named after the fallen hero. Perry bestowed the name on the brig that he had selected as his own.[26]

Lawrence's battle flag—a black banner emblazoned with the eponymous hero's dying words, "Don't give up the ship"—is one of the most famous in American history. Its origins, however, are the subject of dispute. The older histories of the war say that Perry ordered it sewn by Hambleton the purser and the ship's sail maker. But historians at Erie's Maritime Museum note that local legend attributes the flag to Margaret Forster Steuart, sister of Colonel Thomas Steuart, a friend of Perry's. Margaret, according to this account, asked Perry how the women of Erie could help him. He responded by asking her to make a flag bearing Lawrence's words, and she promptly produced the eight-foot-by-nine-foot banner with the help of her two daughters, three nieces, and a cousin.[27]

With his ships largely finished, Perry turned to the problem that had dogged him from the beginning—how to man them. The ten ships normally would have required a combined crew of 740 men for combat operations, but by mid-July Perry had fewer than a hundred ready for duty. With the 120 men sent by Chauncey (the men Perry had found so unsatisfactory) and more from General Harrison's army, Perry had 490 men by the end of July—still short of the 740 he wanted but enough to get underway.

III

Getting underway from Presque Isle, however, posed a greater challenge than bringing the Black Rock fleet up the Niagara River against a strong current. Across the narrow mouth of the bay separating the thin peninsula from the mainland was a sand bar and shoal that the two large brigs could not clear.

Adding to the difficulty, Barclay's fleet was on constant patrol outside the harbor. The Americans would be especially vulnerable to attack as they struggled to move their ships over the shallow bar. But for reasons now unknown, Barclay's fleet disappeared on the last day of July. Perry took advantage of his adversary's absence and began the process of getting his ships out of the harbor.

The first to go over the bar were the smaller ships from Black Rock, which set up a protective ring outside the mouth. For the heavier ships, whose draft exceeded by several feet the depth of the shallows, Perry's men had constructed devices called "camels," invented by the Dutch, which were watertight boxes fastened to the hull just below water level that added buoyancy when filled with air. Each brig was lightened by the removal of cannon and anything else not needed for the passage and air was pumped into the camels, lifting the vessels three feet in the water. The brig was still several inches short of clearing the bar and shoals, and it took scores of seamen and local militiamen a night and a day to drag *Lawrence* across the mile of shallow water to the lake, as one of the smaller ships rode beside her to offer whatever protection she could in the event that Barclay's ships returned.

Once *Lawrence* was free of the shallows, though not yet rearmed, Perry's men began the same process with her sister ship *Niagara*.[28] The second brig, however, got stuck in the sand just as the British fleet returned. Though Barclay had come upon the American ships at the hour of their greatest disadvantage, Perry concealed their vulnerability by ordering *Ariel* and *Scorpion*, with their combined six guns, to attack Barclay's small fleet. Barclay knew that the American fleet outnumbered his, and Perry's audacity fooled him into thinking that the Americans were over the bar and on the attack. As *Ariel* and *Scorpion* closed, firing their long twenty-four pounders, Barclay chose caution over combat and fled. At Malden, he reported to General Procter that he had seen "the whole of the enemies force over the bar and in a most formidable state of preparation," then sailed back to Amherstburg, where his small fleet could be strengthened by the twenty-gun *Detroit*, now nearing completion.[29]

With the British gone and his squadron over the bar, Perry spent the next few days anchored off shore as the brigs' forty heavy guns were rowed out and placed in their carriages on the ships. Perry also used the time to add to his still woefully short-handed crews, a task made easier when Lieutenant Jesse Elliott arrived from Chauncey's headquarters with the hundred or so seamen. One of

Perry's subordinates later complained that Elliott kept the best men for himself when he took command of the *Niagara*.[30]

On 12 August, Perry's squadron finally weighed anchor and sailed west on Lake Erie to Sandusky Bay, where General Harrison had assembled his army in preparation for the invasion of Canada and the recapture of Detroit. He took on military supplies for Harrison near Buffalo and arrived at Sandusky on the 16th. Harrison provided Perry, still desperately short-handed, with a hundred Kentucky riflemen. The elite fighters in the northwestern conflicts, the Kentuckians had developed a breezy self-confidence and independence that at first conflicted with the tight discipline of the navy. Once on board, they wandered all over in uncontrolled curiosity, dressed in their frontier militia uniforms.

In an effort to undermine the Indians' wavering confidence in the ability of the British to maintain control in the western reaches of the frontier, Harrison engaged in a clever bit of diplomacy, inviting twenty-six leaders of the Wyandot, Shawnee, and Delaware tribes, "among whom were three highly influential ones, Crane, Black Hoof and Captain Tommy by name,"[31] to visit Perry's fleet at Sandusky and watch a demonstration of the Americans' superior naval firepower.

> The object of the General in bringing the Indians was, that they might inform their friends then with the enemy of our force, with the hope of detaching them. They were, of course, filled with wonder at the spectacle of our "big canoes."[32]

Having impressed the Indians, Harrison and Perry cruised the area in search of a secure place to anchor and establish their headquarters. They finally settled on the sheltered harbor of Put-in-Bay, off the eastern shore of the Bass Islands, a chain of small islands just north of the peninsula that sheltered Sandusky. There Perry's fleet would have a secure anchorage to keep a close watch on Barclay's fleet in the lake.

As Perry prepared for battle, fever returned to the fleet, striking officers and crew as it had done earlier at Presque Isle and again as he reconnoitered the eastern edges of the lake. It has been called the "bilious fever," "lake fever," and "cholera morbus and dysentery." The disease was rampant, and most of the medical personnel struggled with their own illness as they cared for the sick.[33]

Fortunately, good health soon returned to the fleet. Eager to establish control of Lake Erie, Perry taunted Barclay by provocatively sailing his squadron into the mouth of the Detroit River, reconnoitering the coast line for a suitable site to land Harrison's army. Barclay, however, left the challenge unanswered, as he still suffered from much the same problems as Perry did: He was woefully short of experienced crewmen, and his largest ship, the *Detroit*, was not yet complete. Pike's capture of York that spring and Perry's control of shipping on Lake Erie, moreover, ensured that when the *Detroit* was ready for launch, she would have no cannon. What little supplies the British had were bottled up in Long Point.

Though Perry's taunts failed to dislodge Barclay from his base, they did exacerbate the growing frictions between the British and their Indian allies under Tecumseh and the other supportive chiefs assembled from the angry tribes of the northwest. Adding to Britain's Indian problem was the arrival of the Wyandot leaders—perhaps the same ones hosted by Harrison at Sandusky—who came with news of the Americans' growing force and their intention to attack.[34] As the summer of 1813 was coming to a close, General Procter was responsible for between fourteen and twenty thousand soldiers and Indians, many of whom were dependents of warriors allied with the British. With supplies cut off, food was running short, and the troops had not been paid in months. Tecumseh grew restive and irritated at the lack of any military action by his British leaders. Some Indians openly accused the British of cowardice.[35] Procter bore the brunt of Tecumseh's complaints, and he in turn urged Barclay to attack the menacing American navy.

Barclay was no coward, but neither was he a fool. He refused to send his small and undermanned fleet to certain defeat. Procter responded by giving him 250 redcoats from his already depleted army and eighteen guns (of four different calibers) from Fort Malden to arm *Detroit*. Malden was cut off from the east, and its situation had become desperate. Barclay wrote, "So perfectly destitute was the port, that there was not a day's flour in store, and the crews of the squadron under my command were on half allowances of many things, and when that was done there was no more."[36] Time was on the enemy's side, and Barclay now had little choice but to seek the decisive battle against the Americans. On 9 September he sailed out of Amherstburg in pursuit of Perry's larger fleet, now anchored thirty-five miles to the south at Put-in-Bay.

Thanks to three Americans who had just come from Malden, Perry knew exactly what Barclay's situation was and that an attack was imminent. On 6 September he cruised off Malden and Amherstberg to see for himself what state of readiness Barclay was in. Upon his return to Put-in-Bay, Perry posted lookout ships at the tiny Sister Islands off to the west and called his officers to the *Lawrence* to plan the expected battle. Orders were given, signals confirmed, contingencies established. The signal for action would be the hoisting of the *Lawrence*'s enormous battle flag.[37]

The next morning at five o'clock, lookouts sighted the British fleet nine miles west of Put-in-Bay. As the enemy approached, Perry struggled against an unfavorable wind to get his fleet out of the harbor. A fortunate shift of nearly ninety degrees, however, soon gave the Americans the favorable weather gauge for the attack. The two fleets, sailing slowly in the same direction, formed their lines of battle. Perry's fleet outnumbered Barclay's nine ships to six. And while the British had more guns—sixty-three to the Americans' fifty-four—the American guns were larger and combined could throw almost twice as much metal as those of the British. Longer guns gave the British the advantage in range, which would put the American ships at grave risk during the early hours of the battle. Joseph Icenhower describes the danger: "Very simply put, Barclay could annihilate the Americans at long range; Perry could blast the British out of the water at short range with his thirty-nine 32-pound carronades, larger guns than any in the opposing fleet. Perry therefore determined to lay his vessels alongside the enemy ... and so instructed his captains."[38] Aboard each fleet, sailors and officers scrambled to prepare their ships for combat.

Perry's plan was for the twenty-gun *Lawrence* to seek out the nineteen-gun *Detroit*, while Elliott, commanding the twenty-gun *Niagara*, would engage the seventeen-gun *Queen Charlotte*, the second-largest ship in Barclay's fleet. The seven smaller American ships would either support the two brigs or seek out the four smaller British ships. It was a fine plan under the circumstances and should have led to a swift American victory if all the officers had followed it. But some did not, putting their fleet in considerable jeopardy.

Several miles across Lake Erie, Barclay prepared his smaller, cobbled-together squadron. Though short of supplies and trained seamen, he was filled with determination and "had a quartermaster nail his colors to the mast so they could not be lowered in surrender."[39] Just prior to firing the first shot at the *Lawrence*,

Barclay ordered the bugle sounded and had the musicians play *Rule Britannia* to inspire the crew.[40] As the fleets closed, both sides tested the range with cannon fire, and Barclay soon found that his guns could reach Perry long before Perry's carronades could reach him. According to Roosevelt, "At 11:45 AM the *Detroit* opened the action by a shot from her long 24, which fell short. At 11:50 she fired a second shot which went crashing through *Lawrence*." By 12:30, when most of the ships of both squadrons were now within range of each other, "the action was going on with great fury."[41]

But not all ships were yet within range. For some reason, Lieutenant Jesse Elliott held *Niagara* back from action while Perry and *Lawrence* plowed ahead, with the schooners *Ariel* and *Scorpion* in the lead. As the *Lawrence* closed with the *Detroit* in the van of the British fleet, Barclay began scoring hits well before Perry's carronades were within range. And with *Niagara* lagging far behind and out of the action, the well-armed *Queen Charlotte* joined in the bombardment of the *Lawrence* as Barclay directed thirty-five of his squadron's sixty-three guns at Perry's flagship. With British shot crashing through his bulkheads and hull, ripping away his spars and rigging, Perry managed to bring the battered *Lawrence* within three hundred yards of the British line, where he could finally let fly with his powerful carronades in a ship-to-ships slugfest that would last the next two and a half hours. *Lawrence*'s sailing master, William Taylor, wrote in his log that by 1:30 his ship was "[s]o entirely disabled that we could work the brig no longer. Called the men from the tops and the marines to work the guns. At this time our braces, bowlines, sheets, and in fact, almost every strand of rigging cut off. Mast and Spars cut through in various places."[42]

Though his face was covered with blood from wounds to his forehead and neck, Lieutenant Yarnall stayed at his post on the *Lawrence*. His nose had swollen to a "portentous size" after being struck by a flying splinter blown from the bulkhead. Covering the sticky blood on Yarnall's face was a thin layer of feathery cat-tail down blown out of the mattresses hung in the netting above the bulkheads. Dr. Parsons thought Yarnall looked like a "huge owl," and "even the wounded were moved to merriment by his ludicrous appearance."[43] Treated for his wounds, Yarnall reported to Perry that everyone in his division was dead or incapacitated. Perry shifted some men to him, but the replacements were soon killed or wounded.

As Perry helped the short-handed crew of one of the few guns still in operation, a twenty-four-pound shot struck the gun captain as he prepared to

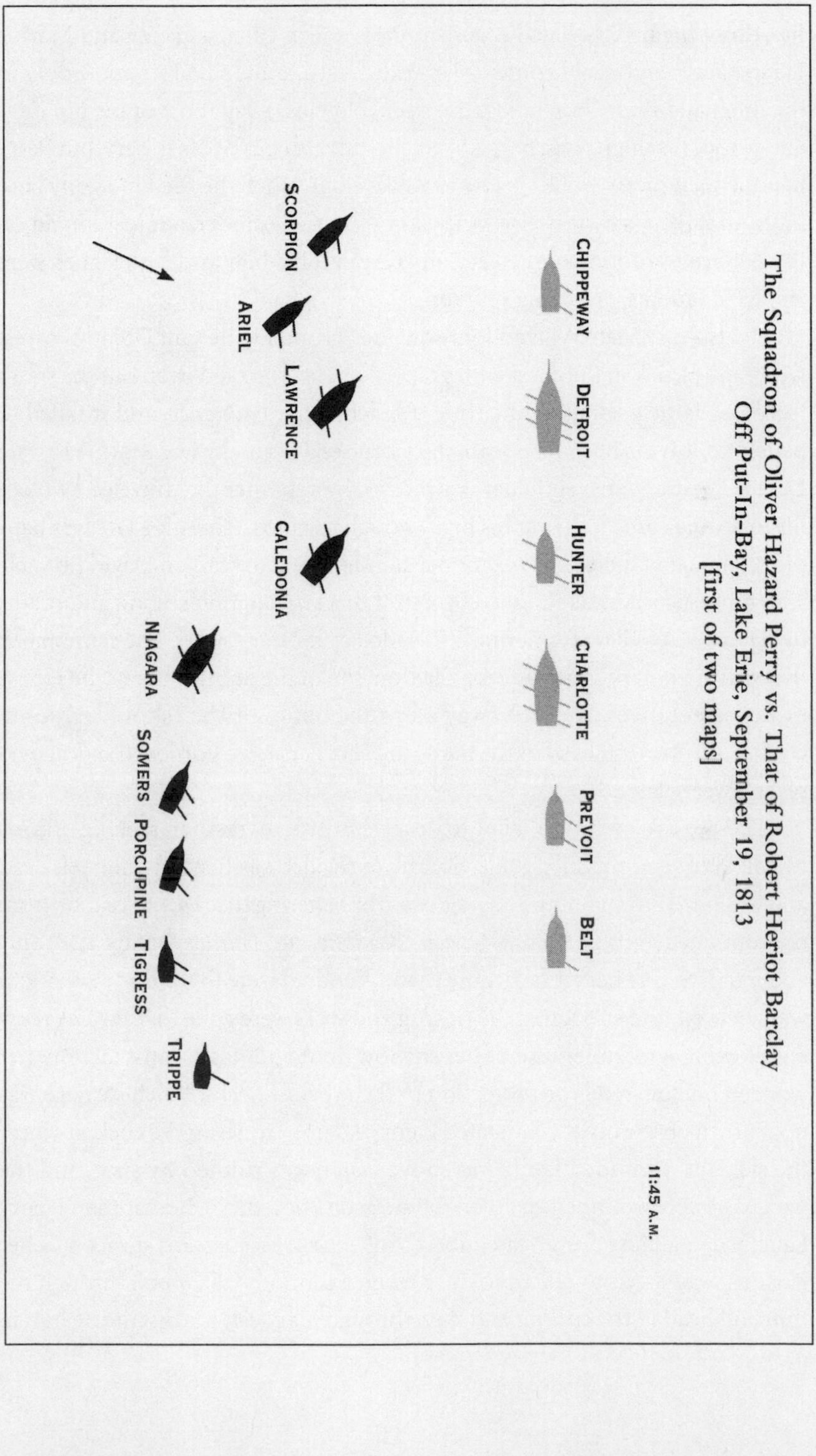

The Squadron of Oliver Hazard Perry vs. That of Robert Heriot Barclay
Off Put-In-Bay, Lake Erie, September 19, 1813
[first of two maps]

11:45 A.M.

CHIPPEWAY
DETROIT
HUNTER
CHARLOTTE
PREVOIT
BELT

SCORPION
ARIEL
LAWRENCE
CALEDONIA
NIAGARA
SOMERS
PORCUPINE
TIGRESS
TRIPPE

fire, dropping his mutilated corpse at Perry's feet. Later, as Perry and Marine Lieutenant John Brooks conferred on the deck, a cannon ball struck Brooks in the thigh and threw him across the deck, blowing away most of his hip joint and part of his thigh.[44] He begged Perry to put him out of his misery, but Perry had the men carry Brooks below to the cockpit, where he died in agony later in the day. Perry's own twelve-year-old brother, Alexander, a midshipman on the *Lawrence*, took two musket balls through his hat, and his clothes were ripped to tatters from flying splinters.[45]

Boatswain's Mate William Johnson and Second Lieutenant Dulany Forrest were both struck in the chest with grape shot and knocked over. But the shot's force was largely spent by the time it reached the *Lawrence*, and it failed to penetrate, leaving both men with nasty bruises. Less lucky was Marine Private David Christie, whose shoulder was pierced by a splinter that traveled through his torso and came to rest at his hip. Though disabled, Christie's fate was happier than that of the unknown gunner standing next to seaman David Bunnell. The gunner's head was smashed by a shot that sent so much blood and brains flying that Bunnell was temporarily blinded by the gory spray. The cannon ball that struck Masters Mate Thomas Claxton, son of the doorkeeper of the House of Representatives, "carried away all of the bones of the [shoulder] joint, clavicle, scapula and head of the humerus," Dr. Parsons recorded. Claxton died several weeks later.[46]

Dressed as a common sailor to deceive British marksman seeking officers to kill, Perry commanded the action from the deck as his crewmen fell dead and wounded around him. So savage was the battering that *Lawrence* took from the combined guns of *Detroit*, *Queen Charlotte*, and *Hunter* that by 1:30, only about nineteen of her crew of more than a hundred were fit for duty. Every gun was wrecked, and enough of the rigging and spars were gone to leave *Lawrence* a wallowing wreck. Because of her shallow draft and hasty construction, her wooden hull offered little protection to those below decks. "Such carnage was not known on the ocean," lamented Henry Adams, "for even the cockpit where the sick and wounded lay, being above water, was riddled by shot, and the wounded were wounded again on the surgeon's board."[47] Midshipman Henry Laub, who had just been treated for a broken arm by assistant surgeon Usher Parsons, was about to return to duty when a cannon ball ripped through the thin bulkhead of the cockpit and then through his chest, nearly cutting him in half. Charles Poughigh, a Naragansett Indian, was being treated for two broken arms when another iron ball ripped through the bulkhead and cut off both his legs. He died shortly thereafter.[48] With so few men left to operate the ship, several of the less seriously wounded were coaxed up from the cockpit to help the eighteen or so able crewmen to position the few guns that remained in action. "Perry himself fired the last effective heavy gun, assisted only by the purser and chaplain."[49]

By two o'clock, few of *Lawrence*'s guns remained operable. Sailing Master Taylor wrote cryptically in his log, "At 2 P.M. most of the guns dismounted, breaching gone, carriages knocked to pieces. Called the few surviving men from the first division to man the guns aft." *Lawrence*'s gunnery also suffered from the inexperience of her hastily assembled crew. Roosevelt explained that the "raw and inexperienced American crews committed the same fault the British so often fell into on the ocean, and overloaded their carronades. In consequence ... the sides of the *Detroit* were dotted by marks from shot that did not penetrate."[50] Though *Lawrence* got the worst of it, her carronades had almost two hours to batter the British ships before they fell silent. Barclay was wounded in the thigh, and his first lieutenant was killed. An early-twentieth-century Canadian history of the battle vividly describes one terrible blow to the British:

> Captain Finnis [of the *Queen Charlotte*] ... was killed by a round shot ... and the same ball carried off Lieutenant Garden [his second], a promising young officer of the Newfoundland Regiment, mingling the blood of one and the brains of the other, on the bulwark, in one melancholy and undistinguishable mass.[51]

With his situation hopeless and *Niagara* still inexplicably lying well back from the fight, Perry, with his brother Alexander, hauled down his pennant and the battle flag. In a gig rowed by four sailors, he abandoned the *Lawrence*, leaving the wounded Lieutenant Yarnall in command. Still dressed as an ordinary seaman, Perry stood up in the small boat, legend has it, but the sailors pulled him down when the fleeing gig attracted intense British fire. Some of the oars were splintered in the barrage, but the gig and her crew were miraculously untouched. Barclay suspected something was afoot but could do nothing to stop it: "The action continued with great fury until half-past two, when I perceived my opponent [the *Lawrence*] drop astern and a boat passing from him to the *Niagara*, which vessel was at this time perfectly fresh."[52]

Exactly what happened next is the subject of dispute, "lost in myth and polemics,"[53] but Perry was rowed to the lagging *Niagara* and took command. And while Elliott was rowed to the accompanying schooners, perhaps under Perry's orders to bring them forward into the fight, Perry raised his battle flag emblazoned with Lawrence's last words and "showed the signal from the *Niagara*, for close action, and immediately bore up, under his foresail, topsails, and topgallant sail. As the American vessels hoisted their answering flags, this order was received with three cheers, and it was obeyed with alacrity and spirit."[54] Still holding the favorable weather gauge, Perry brought *Niagara* into the battle before the British could take possession of the helpless *Lawrence*, whose colors had been struck shortly after Perry's departure. Though the British cheered at the surrender, Barclay was unable just then to take possession of *Lawrence* as all of his small boats had been shot to pieces.[55]

Making the most of a fully-crewed, fresh ship more powerfully armed than any other vessel still on the lake, Perry plunged *Niagara* into the British line and let rip with gunfire. Barclay, whose battered *Detroit* was a choice target for Perry, would recall, "The American commodore, seeing that as yet the day was against him ... made a noble and, alas! too successful an effort to regain it; for he bore up, and supported by his small vessels, passed within pistol shot and took up a raking position on our bow."[56]

Casualties on both sides were high as the ships battered each other at close range. Gerald Altoff describes the carnage on *Niagara* as it sailed through the British squadron:

> Iron, lead and wood splinters cut down more than 20 *Niagara* crewmen in the next few minutes. Private John Reems ... was struck either by musket balls or canister shot in the head and arm; the head wound sheared off a large piece of skull just under his hairline. Sergeant Sanford A. Mason ... was hit in the left hand and arm by wood splinters, and Private George McManomy ... was peppered in his arms and legs by at least a half dozen wood splinters. A British cannonball smashed through *Niagara*'s bulwark near

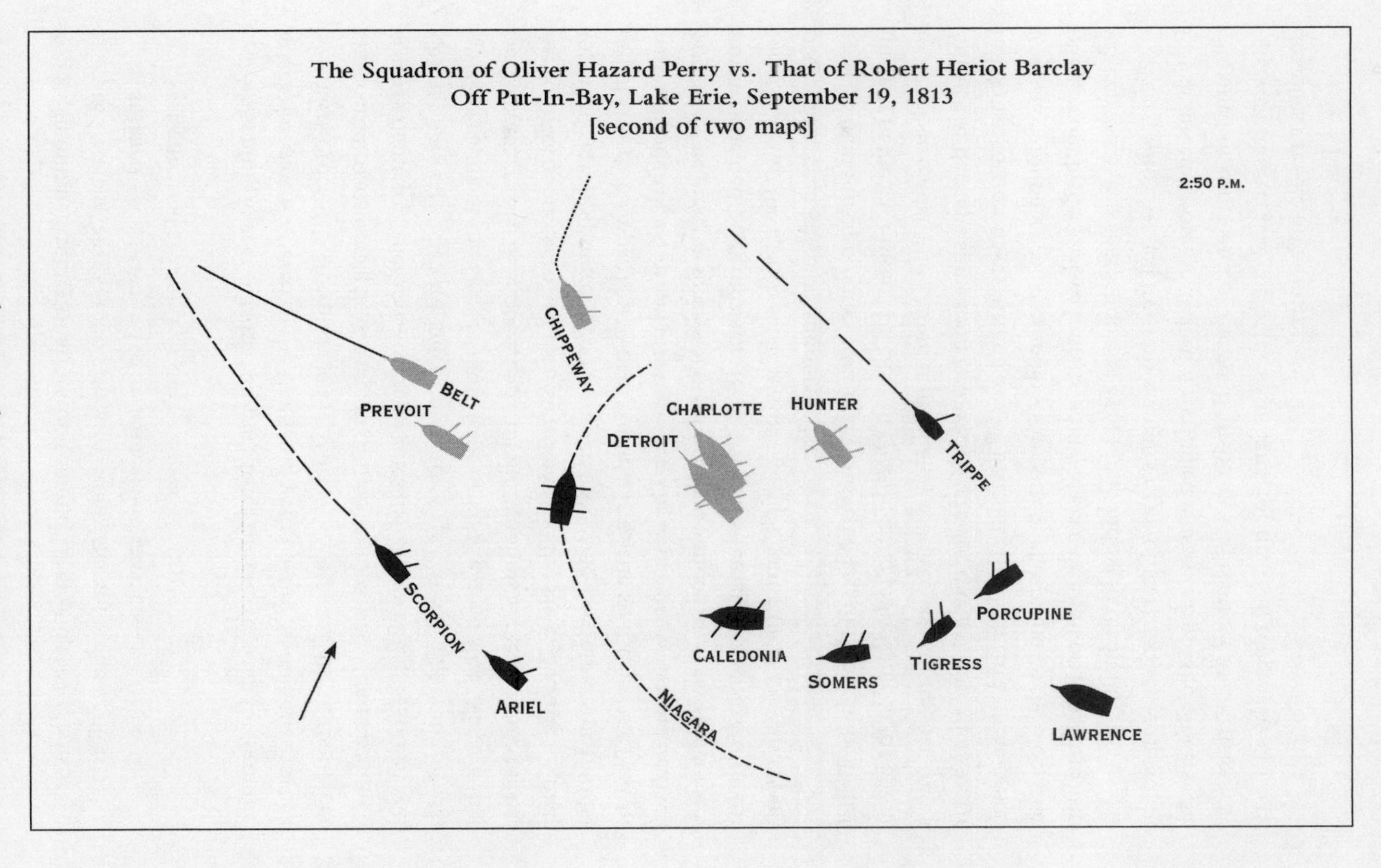

The Squadron of Oliver Hazard Perry vs. That of Robert Heriot Barclay
Off Put-In-Bay, Lake Erie, September 19, 1813
[second of two maps]

> gun number eight, driving a wood splinter deep into the right leg of Ordinary Seaman John Bellamy, while Seaman James Lanford suffered a severe wound to his left leg; both men crawled below to seek medical assistance.[57]

Attempting to get out from *Niagara*'s fierce fire and regroup for a counter attack, Barclay, wounded in the thigh and with his first lieutenant mortally wounded, ordered *Detroit* and *Queen Charlotte* to wear and bring about their starboard broadsides against *Niagara*. But both ships, badly damaged, were scarcely maneuverable, and within minutes the *Detroit*'s rigging fouled with *Queen Charlotte*'s when the latter ran her bow sprit and head booms into the mizzen rigging of the *Detroit*. Both ships came to a dead stop. *Niagara* then came about, crossed their bows, and shot the two ships to pieces, while the two American schooners crossed their sterns and did the same. Backing his main topsail to slow his progress, Perry poured broadside after broadside into the crippled British ships. Thirty-two-pound carronade shot from the *Niagara* passed through one ship and into the other. The damage to wood and flesh was horrific. "The piercing shrieks of the mortally wounded on every side showed how terrific had been the carnage."[58] "Barclay's remaining arm was hit and mangled.... In the British squadron, every ship's commander and his deputy had by now been killed or wounded."[59]

Less than fifteen minutes after Perry crashed *Niagara* through the British line, one of the few officers still alive on *Queen Charlotte* appeared at the taffrail to signal surrender, and *Detroit* immediately followed by striking her colors. The rest of Barclay's ships soon followed. "Here, for the first time in history, a full British squadron was surrendered."[60] Boarding the defeated *Detroit*, American sailors found a bear, presumably someone's pet, lapping up the blood that puddled on the decks. Two Indians, who had been brought on board the British ship to serve as sharpshooters, were found hiding in the hold.[61]

Perry, who changed from his seaman's to an officer's jacket, accepted the British surrender on the deck of the crippled *Lawrence* from the officers who remained in command of the six British ships. Alexander Mackenzie, who interviewed several of the battle's survivors for his 1840 biography of Perry, describes the solemn moment:

> [Perry,] standing on the after-part of the quarter deck, received the officers of the different captured vessels as they came to tender the surrender of their vessels and their own submission of prisoners. At the head of them was an officer of the forty-first regiment, who acted as marine officer on board the *Detroit*, and was charged by Commodore Barclay with the delivery of his sword; he was in full dress. When they had approached, picking their way among the wreck and carnage of the deck, they held their swords with hilts towards Perry, and tendered them to his acceptance. With a dignified and solemn air, the most remote possible from any betrayal of exultation, and in a low tone of voice, he requested them to retain their side-arms; inquired with deep concern for Commodore Barclay and the wounded officers, tendering to them every comfort his ship afforded, and expressing his regret that he had not a spare medical officer to send them.[62]

And indeed he did not. Usher Parsons was the only American surgeon available, the other three being incapacitated with fever. Barclay's wounds were serious but not mortal. Early in the battle he received a nasty grape wound in his thigh that forced him to sick bay. But when his second was mortally wounded, Barclay struggled back on deck to resume command, and in the subsequent fight with *Niagara*, another round of grape shot shattered the shoulder blade of his remaining arm.

From the deck of the *Lawrence*, Perry also penned brief reports to his superiors. To Navy Secretary Jones, Master and Commander Oliver Hazard Perry wrote, "It has pleased the Almighty to give to the arms of the United States a signal victory over their enemies on this Lake. The British squadron consisting of two ships, two brigs, one schooner and a sloop, have this moment surrendered to the force under my command after a sharp conflict." To General William Henry Harrison, waiting at Sandusky with an army of five thousand men ready to invade Canada, Perry wrote in pencil on the back of an old envelope: "We have met the enemy and they are ours—two ships, two brigs, one schooner and a sloop. Yours, with very great respect and esteem O. H. Perry."[63]

The hapless Barclay, however, sent a somber letter to his superiors on 12 September, noting his disadvantages on that fateful day. After describing the severe supply shortages that hobbled the command at Malden, Barclay continued, "Such were the motives which induced Major Genl. Procter to concur in the necessity of a battle being risqued under the many disadvantages which I laboured, and it now remains for me, the most melancholy task, to relate to you the unfortunate issue of that Battle, as well as the many untoward circumstances that led to that event."[64]

Henry Adams appreciated the magnitude of Perry's triumph that day:

> The luck which attended Perry's career on the Lake saved him from injury when every other officer on the two opposing flagships and four-fifths of his crew were killed or wounded, and enabled him to perform a feat almost without parallel in naval warfare, giving him a well-won immortality by means of the disaster unnecessarily incurred.... More than any other battle of the time, the victory on Lake Erie was won by the courage and obstinacy of a single man.[65]

Casualties on both sides were severe. According to Mahon, among the British, forty-four men died, while twenty-one Americans lost their lives, most of them on the *Lawrence*. Other historians, notably Henry Adams and Reginald Horsman, put the American death toll higher at twenty-seven, with the deaths on the *Lawrence* alone reaching twenty-two. Total wounded on both sides numbered more than 160 men, with the *Lawrence* again counting for most of America's share. Because of the large number of dead, the wounds of those still left alive, and the exhaustion of those still standing at the end of the battle, ordinary sailors were buried at sea in a nighttime service conducted by Chaplain Breese. In the presence of the few able-bodied seamen who could be assembled, the chaplain read the service for burial at sea of the Church of England as the bodies of the dead, sewn into their canvas hammocks and weighted with a thirty-two-pound iron shot, were slipped over the side and committed to the deep.

By contrast, the dead officers from both sides were taken to Bass Island to be buried near the shore of the lake. With both crews dressed in their best uniforms and flags at half mast, the bodies were taken ashore as the surviving musicians played a dirge. A procession was formed with the body of the youngest casualty carried in the lead, followed by the next higher in ranks, also ordered by age, and alternating by British and American dead. The body of Captain Finnis of *Queen Charlotte* was last in the solemn procession. Following the bodies was a procession of officers, also ordered by rank, marching two by two, Americans alternating with British, Perry closing the procession. Drums and fifes were played by men of both squadrons, and the ships anchored off shore fired their minute guns in honor of the dead.

Still to be attended were the many wounded, as well as those still suffering from fever and dysentery. The wounded were fortunate that the one surgeon not incapacitated by illness was the young and enlightened Parsons, as revealed in the Naval Historical Center's comments on the doctor's reports after the battle:

> Dr. Parsons had to treat about 100 sick and wounded on the day of the battle. He reported a remarkable rate of success in the treatment of the wounded. This was no doubt due in part to the doctor's insistence on boiling all drinking water, keeping hospital quarters clean and ventilated, and providing an adequate diet of fresh food for the injured. Moreover, there were so many wounded that Parsons had to delay a day or two before performing amputations, which allowed patients time to recover somewhat from the trauma of their injuries.[66]

In his own account of his effort, published in the *New England Journal of Medicine and Surgery* in October 1818, Parsons wrote:

> The wounded [arteries] occupied my first attention, all of which except where amputation was required, were rendered secure before dark. Having no assistant, I deemed it safer to defer amputating till morning in the meantime suffered the tourniquettes to remain on the [limbs]. Nothing more was done through the night than to administer opiates, and preserve shattered limbs in

> a uniform position. At day light a subject was on the table for amputation of the thigh, and at 11 o'clock all amputations were finished. . . . The compound and simple fractures were next attended to; then luxations [dislocated joints], lacerations, and contusions; all which occupied my time till 12 o'clock at night.[67]

In the same article, Parsons explained why he believed the recovery rate among his patients was so much higher than the norm:

> First, the purity of the air. The patients were ranged along on the upper deck, with no other shelter from the weather, than a high awning to shade them. They continued lying in this situation for a fortnight, and, when taken on shore, were placed in very spacious apartments well ventilated. Secondly, to the supply of food best adapted to their cases, as fowls, fresh meat, milk, eggs, and an abundance of vegetables. The second day after the action, the farmers on the Ohio shore brought along side every article of the above description that could be desired. Thirdly to the happy state of mind, which victory occasioned. The observations, which I have been enabled to make on the wounded of three engagements, have convinced me, that this state of mind has greater effect, than has generally been supposed; and that the surgeon of the conquering side will, *caeteris paribus*, always be more successful.[68]

Twelve days after the battle, Parsons wrote to his parents to tell them of the battle and of his success in treating the many wounded. Noting that the more senior surgeons were ill with fever, Usher told his parents that their absence

> has operated in my favour as I have had all the amputating to perform and it affords me the greatest pleasure to reflect that in no case have I failed of the best success. This has impressed the Commodore with so favourable an opinion toward me that I have not the least doubt of his rendering me assistance in a better situation. He is the first warm friend I have met with in the service capable of assisting me. I am now on my way in the *Lawrence* for Erie, having all the sick and the wounded on board and shall continue with

them in the hospital 'til the most of them recover, and then intend to shape my course for Cape Home.[69]

IV

As was often the case in the war's sea battles, victors were magnanimous to the vanquished. Shortly after the surrender, Perry visited the badly wounded Barclay aboard the *Detroit* and, seeing his suffering, promised that he would do whatever he could to arrange a swift parole so that he could return to England and continue his recovery in the company of his loved ones. Also at Barclay's request, Perry advanced a considerable sum of money to the British commodore and his officers to help them finance a more comfortable captivity and return trip home. A recent Canadian history of the war observes:

> Perry was as gallant in victory as he was determined in battle. He and his men gathered in the British and Canadian wounded and treated them with brotherly care and consideration. Perry personally tended Barclay, and supported him as both men stood at a burial of the dead of both sides ashore in the Bass Islands. It was a poignant moment of mutual respect and decency that said as much about the honour of the respective navies as it did about the character of the men involved.[70]

Shortly after the battle many of the British prisoners were taken to Presque Isle, where their wounds could be better tended to, and later to Pittsburgh, where, once healed, escape would be more difficult.

Britain's secretary of state for war and colonies, the earl Bathurst, first learned of the defeat in early November from American newspapers. Having been advised earlier by Wellington that the Lakes were key to the war, Bathurst was determined to hold them, though by the time he read of the news, British forces in Upper Canada were in full retreat. "He at once wrote to Prevost asking the governor to explain how the entire fleet could have been made to surrender. He ordered Prevost to bend every effort during the winter to re-establish a British force on Lake Erie in order to keep control of Upper Canada, and to maintain contact with the Indians."[71]

London's *Gentleman's Magazine* offered a somewhat different perspective when it reported that the "defeated fleet was not part of the British navy, but was a local organization."[72] Britain's *Naval Chronicle* adopted a similar excuse, but also questioned the propriety of a naval officer abandoning one ship only to command another to victory.

> We must now advert to a miscarriage, of minor importance, affecting our own interests. Nova Scotia and Boston papers have brought intelligence, that our flotilla on Lake Erie has been completely defeated by the American Commodore Perry. It may, however, serve to diminish our vexation at this occurrence, to learn, that the flotilla in question was not a branch of the British navy, but was solely manned, equipped, and managed by the public-spirited exertions of certain Canadians, who had formed themselves into a kind of Lake Fencibles. Yet this conflict, though it left Perry the conqueror of the day, exposes his conduct, and that of his squadron, to the most disgraceful suspicions.[73]

When Perry later recorded his own thoughts after the battle, he was generous in his praise of the black sailors who served on his ships. "They seemed to be absolutely insensible to danger. When Captain Barclay came on board the *Niagara*, and beheld the sickly and partly-colored beings around him, an expression of chagrin escaped him at having been conquered by such men."[74] As was always the case with lost ships and battles, Barclay was tried for the defeat at a court-martial, but was honorably acquitted in appreciation of the odds against him.

As news of the victory on the lake spread through the country, awards, prizes, and accolades were heaped upon Perry and his men. Both he and Elliott were awarded gold medals (carrying the legend *Oliverus H. Perry, Princeps stagno Eriensi, Classem Totam Condudit*) by Congress, all officers received three months' extra pay, swords were awarded to midshipmen and sailing masters, and the six ships captured yielded prize money aplenty. Congress in 1814 authorized the purchase of Barclay's captured fleet for $250,000, and the proceeds of the sale were distributed as prize money to the officers and the crew according to predetermined shares established by the navy. As the commander of the U.S. Navy on the Lakes, Chauncey received $12,750, while Perry and Elliott, who held the same rank, each received $7,140. Congress, however, awarded Perry an additional $5,000 in recognition of his extraordinary leadership. The remaining officers received smaller shares that declined in value with their rank, while the 596 ordinary seamen, soldiers, and marines split the remaining $95,625. At a time when ordinary seamen earned very little, a prize payment of $160 per crewman amounted to quite a bonus.[75]

Even Secretary Jones could not resist offering uncharacteristically enthusiastic compliments to the victorious Perry. In his letter to the master commandant of 21 September 1813, Jones gushed, "Every demonstration of joy and admiration, that a victory so transcendently brilliant, decisive and important in its consequences, could excite, was exhibited as far and as fast as a roar of cannon and the splendour of illumination could travel."[76]

Much further down the chain of command, Sailing Master William Taylor wrote a letter to his wife, Abby, on 15 September, five days after the battle, expressing gratitude that he came through it unhurt:

> Heaven has allow'd us, My dear Wife, to gain a most decisive victory & preserved your husband unhurt. I say unhurt because my wound was trifling, I scarcely felt it, a flesh wound in my thigh ... I expect to go to Erie today with the Lawrence & all the sick & wounded—where I will write you again—My love to our Dear Parents Brothers & Sisters—friends and acquaintances—kiss my little children—I felt perfectly cool in action—my prayers were for you and the children—God be praised that I was spared, to take care of you all—may I never lose that confidence which I placed in him on that day it animated me to exertion.—Heaven bless you.[77]

Less joyous were the letters Perry had to write to the families of those who died on the *Lawrence*. To John Brooks of Medford, Massachusetts, a retired general, Perry wrote:

> It is with heartfelt pain I am under the necessity of communicating to you the irreparable loss which you and our country have sustained in the death of your gallant and worthy son, Lieutenant John

> Brooks, who fell in action with the British squadron.... His friend Mr. Hambleton, who is severely wounded, will write you the moment he is able. I sympathize with you most deeply.[78]

Brooks responded to Perry with a profoundly moving statement of a father's love for son and country. After congratulating Perry on his great victory, Brooks asked,

> Should you have a few moments at your command, it would be laying me under lasting obligation to inform me of the most prominent circumstances as to the time and manner of his fall. It would also be gratifying to me to know what disposition has been made of his effects, and whether his arms of different kinds have been disposed of or are retained. If the latter, it would be particularly grateful to me to be in possession of his best sword and sash; the former as a relic, the latter on account of it being the sash I wore through the whole of the American Revolution.[79]

In late October 1813, Perry resigned his command of Lake Erie, and turned it over to Master Commandant Jesse Elliott. From Buffalo, where they parted company with Harrison and the recovering Barclay, Perry and a number of his crewmen embarked on their victory tour across New York to his home and new command in Newport, Rhode Island.

> Wherever Perry passed a night, illuminations, hastily-prepared festivities, and rude but hearty hospitality, conveyed to him a nation's gratitude. He was accompanied in his journey by Sailing-master Taylor, of the *Lawrence*; by his young brother James Alexander; by his boat's crew; and by a revolutionary fifer, Cyrus Tiffany by name, a sort of amphibious warrior, who having fought by land and by water, and being already stricken in years, allowed himself considerable license in speech, and, having wit at will, had been a source of great amusement to the crew of *Lawrence*.[80]

The bigger the town, the more impressive the victory celebration. Public events were held in Utica and Schenectady, and as his party neared Albany, Perry was met by the mayor, the recorder, and members of the common council, and all were escorted into the city by a volunteer cavalry and a parade of citizens mounted or in carriages. In the council hall of the state's capitol, the mayor gave him the "freedom of the city in a gold box" and a "costly sword which had been prepared in anticipation of his arrival." That night a ball was held in Perry's honor, "and the ladies had also an opportunity of seeing the youthful hero, and wondering that the individual who had been so terrible to his enemies on the deck of the *Lawrence* and *Niagara*, should be here only distinguished for the courteous grace and rare modesty of his demeanour."[81]

Americans not lucky enough to live in the path of Perry's home-bound victory tour participated in the joyous celebration through the songs and poems in Perry's honor that were quickly penned and published throughout the nation and sung in homes and taverns. One of the more popular songs was "Perry's Victory", written by Andrew C. Mitchell and set to an Irish jig called "St. Patrick's Day in the Morning":

> Now let us remember the tenth of September,
> When Yankees gave Britons a warming,
> When our foes on Lake Erie, were beaten and weary,
> So full of conceit in the morning;
> To the skillful, and brave, who our country did save,
> Our gratitude ought to be warming,
> So let us be merry, in toasting of Perry,
> September tenth in the morning.

Despite their opposition to the war, the citizens of Providence, Rhode Island, welcomed Perry with warmth and honor. The local paper observed that "however we may differ with respect to the cause in which his talents are employed, yet wherever valour and humanity, ability and modesty, are so happily blended as in Commodore Perry, adorning himself and his country, they justly receive the meed of universal praise."[82] From Providence, it was a short trip to his home in Newport, where again joyous crowds met Perry on 18 November and escorted him to his home, where he was greeted by his wife, his older son, and a second son born in his absence.

To his purser, Samuel Hambleton, still in Erie recovering from his nasty shoulder wound, Perry wrote, "I found on my arrival another noble boy, and Mrs. Perry in excellent health; my oldest [almost two years old] has grown finely, and is, in my opinion, charming. Many of your friends have made the most particular inquiries after you. They will rejoice if you again come to this place. I need not assure you how much it would add to my happiness to have so esteemed a friend with me."[83]

After spending some time with his family, Perry embarked on a victory tour of America's leading cities—among them Boston, Philadelphia, New York, and Washington—where he was fêted by the leading citizens with sumptuous banquets and lavish entertainment in honor of his victory. The ceremony held in late January 1814 in Baltimore may have been typical. The day after a visit to the circus, a dinner (arranged by a bipartisan committee) was given him by Baltimore's "most distinguished citizens of both parties":

> The spacious room in which it was given had been elaborately decorated by a distinguished artist. At one extremity was a large transparent painting of the battle of the tenth of September, representing the brilliant and decisive moment when Perry, having borne up in the *Niagara*, was passing through the midst of the enemy's squadron firing raking broadsides from both batteries; while at the opposite extremity, raised above the adjoining rows of tables, was the representation of the stern of a ship labeled *Niagara*, on the quarter-deck of which was seated the president of the day, with Perry and the invited guests. Behind them rose a mast, braced together with massive bands, on which were inscribed, in letters of gold, the names of Hull, Jones, Decatur, Bainbridge, Lawrence, Ludlow, Burrows, Allen and Perry, while from the masthead was suspended a banner, bearing the memorable despatch to General Harrison, "We have met the enemy, and they are ours."[84]

With the British navy now swept from Lake Erie and Procter isolated in Detroit with few supplies, General Harrison was free to move his troops north for the invasion. On or around 20 September 1813, no more than two weeks after Perry's capture of the British squadron, and after hasty repairs to his battered ships and those taken from the British, Perry and his sailors began to ferry the American army from Ohio across Lake Erie to Canada for a battle that General Harrison hoped would finally drive the British out of America's Northwest territories.

CHAPTER SIXTEEN

HARRISON TAKES DETROIT, JACKSON ALABAMA

As Perry battled Barclay off the Bass Islands on 10 September, the cannons' roar carried across the empty stretches of Lake Erie and could be heard as far away as Fort Malden, thirty miles to the north. In an era when a naval gun fight could last as little as ten or fifteen minutes and rarely lasted longer than an hour, the three hours of thunderous cannon fire that rolled across the water to the British base on the Detroit River was hard to interpret. No one knew whether it boded well or ill for their understrength fleet.

But as night fell and not a single ship returned to port, General Procter assumed the worst—that the entire British squadron was captured or destroyed, and that Harrison's army would soon be upon him. With food and arms in short supply, and with his diminished army further reduced by the two hundred men he lent to Barclay, Procter felt he had no choice but to abandon Upper Canada (Ontario) to the approaching Americans. But while Procter had every reason to be despondent about a decision that would probably wreck his career and leave him remembered as the British officer who lost half of Canada to the

Americans, he knew that his retreat would be absolutely disastrous for his ally Tecumseh. Tecumseh knew this as well, and he intended to make sure that the contemplated retreat never occurred.

Trusting that the British were in Upper Canada to stay, the Shawnee under Tecumseh and other chiefs had settled along the Michigan banks of the Detroit River. Tecumseh and about eighty warriors and their families lived on Grosse Isle in the middle of the river. As many as 14,000 Indians, including 2,000 warriors, may have been in the vicinity. A delegation of Wyandots had come through the region in late August with news of Perry's fleet and Harrison's army. Tecumseh and Roundhead, however, never saw the Americans as a serious threat. They were confident they and their British allies could defeat them again, as they did at River Raisin and outside the walls of Fort Meigs. Tecumseh boasted to the Wyandot delegation, "We are happy to learn your Father [Harrison] is coming out of his hole as he has been like a groundhog under the ground and [his coming] will save us much trouble in walking to meet him."[1] But not all of the Indians at Malden shared the Shawnee chieftain's confidence. Walk-in-the-Water, for one, made his own plans to get out of the way if Harrison came north.

Tecumseh's plans were frustrated in late August or early September when the distinguished but elderly Wyandot warrior chief Roundhead died of natural causes, leaving to Tecumseh the entire burden of keeping the Indian alliance together as danger approached. Procter sensed the danger and later wrote that "the Indian cause and ours experienced a serious loss in the death of Roundhead."[2] Without informing the Indians or his own general staff, Procter gave orders to dismantle the fort and pack up whatever supplies could be carried in the wagons.

Tecumseh discovered Procter's real intentions on 14 September, when several Indians told him that they saw Malden's walls being pulled down into the surrounding ditch. Procter's adjutant, Lieutenant Colonel Warburton, was equally astonished when he heard the same news from his own men. As accusations of treachery and cowardice flew through the Indian encampments and the British barracks, Tecumseh demanded that the British Indian agent Colonel Matthew Elliott bring Procter to a council of the tribes to explain himself.On 18 September, Procter reluctantly agreed to meet them at the council house at Fort Malden. John Richardson, a witness of the meeting, described Tecumseh rising to address the many chiefs, Indian and British:

> Habited in a close leather dress, his athletic proportions were admirably delineated, while a large plume of ostrich feathers, by which he was generally distinguished, overshadowing his brow, and contrasting with the darkness of his complexion and the brilliancy of his black and piercing eye, gave a singularly wild and terrific expression to his features. It was evident that he could be terrible.[3]

After reviewing the promises made to them and reminding Procter of the Indians' loyalty to the British in their wars with the Americans, Tecumseh spoke bluntly about the general:

> Father, we see you are drawing back, and we are sorry to see our Father doing so without seeing the enemy. We must compare our Father's conduct to a fat animal that carries its tail upon its back, but when affrighted, it drops it between its legs and runs off.[4]

Finally, reminding Procter that the Americans had never defeated them in an open battle and that there were enough men and ammunition to put up a fight, Tecumseh concluded his speech by proclaiming: "We are determined to defend our lands, and if it is [the Great Spirit's] will, we wish to leave our bones upon them."[5]

Though Tecumseh's bravado made a deep impression on his fellow Indians and on Procter's subordinates, Procter himself remained unmoved. With Perry in complete control of the lake, the Americans could land wherever they wanted and easily surround his exposed position at the tip of the giant peninsula that makes up much of what is now the province of Ontario. Procter's force, comprising Indian warriors, British regulars, and local militia, numbered nearly 2,500 men. Harrison, with an estimated 4,500 troops under his command, had the larger army, while Procter had the advantage of a defensive position. But with supplies dwindling and no likelihood of reinforcements, the British could easily be cut off and starved into submission. Procter's combined force, and their families, consumed fourteen head of cattle and seven thousand pounds of flour a day—well in excess of what could be provided locally—and by now all were on short rations. It was this kind of shortage that sent Barclay off to battle. With the navy's defeat, starvation loomed unless Procter's forces could march far enough inland to be supplied from Burlington at the western tip of Lake Ontario.

Procter was constrained by the fear that the abandoned and angry Indians would become violent and turn on the small British force or on the vulnerable civilians who remained after the soldiers retreated. He promised to return to the council in two days but instead returned to his headquarters to the north at Sandwich. He left his adjutant, Warburton, with the responsibility of providing the promised response to Tecumseh, but Warburton refused. As Fort Malden's supplies continued to be moved north to where the Thames River emptied into the Detroit, the Indians' anger grew, and Elliott, who worried that something violent and ugly would happen, urged Procter to meet with Tecumseh.

Procter agreed. Using a map, he appealed to Tecumseh's good strategic sense, describing their mutual vulnerabilities in the face of the attacking Americans and showing the chief where the two of them should together make their stand against Harrison. That place was called Chatham, up the Thames where the river forked. Procter promised to fortify the forks and wait for Harrison's army to attack. Tecumseh agreed, and within two hours he had brought most of the other chiefs and tribes on board with the plan. The retreat up the river would begin the next day as the Indians who had agreed to stay with the British moved their families and possessions across the Detroit River to the Canadian side in preparation for the march east.

About 1,200 warriors from thirteen tribes—Kickapoos, Winnegabos, Sacs, Shawnees, Wyandots, Miamis, Munsee, Delawares, Potawatomis, Ojibwas, Ottawas, Senecas, and twenty-five Creeks from Alabama—along with their families, marched east with the British. Many civilians, including several old Tories who had fled America during the War of Independence, joined in the column that would soon number in the many thousands.[6] As troops and Indians moved out, Malden and the public buildings in Amherstburg were put to the torch.

On 22 September, two days after the second council between Procter and Tecumseh, Harrison's army assembled on Bass Island for transport to the Middle Sister Island, and then to Canada on the 27th. As Perry's squadron transported the bulk of Harrison's army to a landing just east of Malden—and later at Amherstburg, once they discovered the British were gone—Colonel Robert Johnson, a congressman from Kentucky, raced his Kentucky cavalry north along the coast into Michigan to the banks of the Detroit River, where Perry's ships ferried man and beast to the Canadian side to join the rest of Harrison's force.

Ensign Benjamin Holmes of the Canadian Light Dragoons was left behind with a small force at Malden to watch for Harrison's arrival. He spotted Harrison's force out on the lake on the morning of the 27th and sent a messenger to alert Procter and the redcoats waiting at Sandwich, who then began their march up the Thames to cover the retreating civilians. Pulling down the bridge over the Aux Canard, which separated Malden from Sandwich in the north, Holmes joined the rest of the retreating army on its way to Chatham, where Procter had promised Tecumseh they would make their stand. Harrison's force included a few Pennsylvania militiamen willing to cross the border into Canada, but was mostly a mix of regulars, Kentucky volunteers, and Johnson's cavalry. The Kentuckians were under the command of seven generals, who in turn reported to their commander in chief, Governor Isaac Shelby, a hero of the Revolutionary War. Rounding out the leadership team was Oliver Hazard Perry.

Colonel Johnson's mounted Kentucky riflemen had been trained to attack on a gallop through the woods and fire a rifle with some accuracy while mounted and moving. Dressed in the uniforms of black buckskin trimmed with red fringe and armed with a rifle, a tomahawk, and a scalping knife, they were described as "hardy, keen, daring and ruthless."[7] Having recently completed a lengthy search-and-destroy mission through Indian country south of Lake Michigan, the mounted Kentuckians were ready and eager for battle. Johnson used his considerable influence in Washington to make sure they would get it.

II

Hauling tons of supplies and marching with thousands of civilians, Procter managed to cover no more than nine miles a day. He seemed in no hurry to get out of Harrison's way or to prepare a defensible position. Indeed, for much of the retreat, Procter rode well ahead of his force in a comfortable carriage. The military historian John Elting has remarked, "Fortunately, for the

Americans, Procter was even more incompetent at retreating than attacking."[8] With his force assembled and now numbering about 3,500—hundreds having been left behind to secure Malden and Detroit—Harrison turned east on 2 October in pursuit of the retreating British force.

The Thames in this region of Ontario is easily navigable. The Americans hauled supplies and artillery in barges protected by three gunboats provided by Oliver Hazard Perry, who had volunteered to accompany Harrison. On 4 October, Harrison's army reached the third and unfordable branch of the Thames, only to find that the Indians had destroyed the bridge and were waiting on the other side to attack the Americans as they struggled across. Harrison brought several cannon forward and sent Johnson's mounted riflemen across the water to drive the Indians back. In two hours the bridge was repaired, and the Americans were back on the march. Believing the enemy near, Harrison sent Johnson forward to reconnoiter. After a brief skirmish, Johnson's men seized Arnolds Mill near a ford across the river. With the Americans fast closing, the British set fire to their boats and to several barns where their supplies and equipment were stored.

Procter was far ahead, so it remained for Tecumseh and Warburton to lead the combined British and Indian force. Warburton was eager to turn and make a stand, but Tecumseh urged him to stick with the original plan and continue the march to Chatham, which Procter had promised to fortify. But when the retreating British finally arrived at Chatham, there were no fortifications and no General Procter. The dismayed but composed allies led their men in an orderly march a few more miles upriver to Moraviantown, where they hoped to find suitable ground to form a defensible line.

As dawn broke on 5 October, the Americans resumed their march, narrowing the distance between themselves and the British and occasionally overtaking a straggling wagon and driver, from whom they gained detailed information about Procter's fleeing army. Procter had to pick a place to make his stand, and a field near Moraviantown offered a defensible position. With the river to his left and a swamp to his right, Procter could not be outflanked, and his small force could be concentrated for maximum effect. An added advantage was a small swamp in the middle of the British line that would prevent the Americans from concentrating their superior force for a smashing attack on Procter's center. Harrison would have to split his force and attack both British lines separately, while Tecumseh's force flanked them from the swamp on the right.

Procter placed the bulk of his troops on the left side of his line, stretching 250 yards from the river to the small swamp in the middle, where the ground was more open and solid.[9] Their ranks were badly depleted from illness, desertion, and capture. Poor planning and bad luck, moreover, had forced the British soldiers to miss most of their meals on the ill-managed march, and they were hungry, exhausted, and demoralized as Harrison's much larger force closed in for the kill.

With the British regulars stretched across the open field, Tecumseh's warriors took up a position on the right where the woods were thicker and the ground a little swampy. It would be difficult for the enemy to assault them in force, and the terrain was well-suited to the hand-to-hand fighting at which the Indians were skilled. But like the shrinking British force, the Indian ranks suffered considerable attrition as their confidence in British leadership wavered. In the last few days of the march, Walk-in-the-Water took off with his Wyandots and a few Shawnees, and the Delawares also disappeared. Twelve hundred Indians had begun the march with Tecumseh, but no more than five hundred remained by the time he moved his warriors into line. As both sides prepared for the coming fight, Procter and Tecumseh were probably outnumbered two to one.

At eight o'clock in the morning, several hundred yards west of the British position, Harrison assembled his force in a line for the assault. The plan was for Johnson's mounted men directly to assault the thin British line on the Americans' right. The result was a stunning success for the Americans, as the British left line folded in a matter of minutes. Using only half the force of Kentuckians under the command of Johnson's brother James, the mounted infantry charged with fury, firing at the British line as they rode through it to take up a position at its rear. Quickly dismounting and reloading, Johnson's men now fired at the British from behind, and the fight on the British left was quickly over. Forty-three redcoats were dead or mortally wounded, and the rest surrendered or fled the field. Procter made a brief attempt to rally his retreating men, but quickly gave up and galloped away to safety. Of the Kentuckians, one was killed and three wounded. Matthew Elliott described the British effort as "shameful in the highest degree."[10]

While his brother successfully attacked Procter's left, Robert Johnson led the full force of mounted Kentuckians against the British right. He quickly saw, however, that the greater danger was on his left flank past the small swamp where Tecumseh's warriors lay hidden in the dense woods and brush. As his brother continued forward, Johnson wheeled half his force to the left[11] and charged through the swamp toward the Indian line. Forced to dismount by the thick brush and the swampy ground, Johnson's men soon found themselves in a crowded melee of hand-to-hand fighting.

Casualties mounted as the adversaries chopped, shot, and slashed at each other in the swampy forest. Johnson himself received five wounds as he and his men pushed the warriors back and to the left, where they would be exposed to the musket fire of Governor Shelby's infantry. Now under attack from two sides, the Indians retreated through the large swamp and into the woods, and the Battle of the River Thames was over. Fifteen Americans were killed and thirty wounded, says Henry Adams, and most of those casualties occurred during Johnson's assault on Tecumseh's line. Others put the American loss at half that number—seven killed, twenty-two wounded.[12] Adams assesses the outcome:

> The battle lasted, with sharpness, not more than twenty minutes; and none but the men under Johnson's command enjoyed opportunity to share in the first and most perilous assault. The British loss was only twelve men killed, and thirty-six wounded. The total number of British prisoners taken on the field and in the Moravian town, or elsewhere on the day of battle, was four hundred and seventy-seven; in the whole campaign, six hundred. All Procter's baggage, artillery, small arms, stores, and hospital were captured.... The Indians left thirty-three dead on the field, among them one reported to be Tecumthe.[13]

Adams is correct in noting that the body was *reported* to be Tecumseh's. Though it seems certain that Tecumseh died in the battle, historians have been divided over how he died and whether his body was ever found among the Indian dead. Years later, as his national political ambitions grew, Richard Johnson claimed that it was he who killed Tecumseh in hand-to-hand combat. When he pursued the presidency of the United States in 1836 and 1840, Johnson's supporters made a slogan of a line from a Richard Eammons poem: "Rumpsey, Dumpsey, Colonel Johnson killed Tecumseh."[14]

According to some accounts, captured members of Britain's Forty-first Foot identified Tecumseh's body for the Americans. Several Kentuckians were reported to have avenged the atrocities at River Raisin by making razor strops from the Indian's skin.[15] There is no clear evidence to support these claims, which have been debated ever since. Donald Hickey has recently argued that Tecumseh's body was most likely found and was mutilated for souvenirs by Kentucky militiamen.[16]

With Procter's defeat and flight, Tecumseh's death, and the capture of more than half the regulars and all of the army's supplies, ammunition, and arms, Britain's military presence in much of Upper Canada ceased. Harrison's force, well supplied and largely unbloodied, ruled the land, and nothing prevented him from marching on Burlington and then York, while Chauncey's fleet, augmented with men from Perry's victorious Erie fleet, bombarded the last remaining British outposts from off shore to prevent their resupply. Given the imbalance of forces and the decisive American victories on land and sea, all of Upper Canada could have been in American hands within a month or two.

Indeed, it appears that the British command expected as much and took steps to minimize their losses. One Canadian historian recently described the British response to Procter's defeat as panicked retrenchment:

> Sir George Prevost at Quebec now issued an order that would have capped Harrison's victory with a gift. He sent instructions to de Rottenburg to evacuate *all* of Upper Canada—Burlington, York, the Niagara frontier, all of it—and retire to Kingston. Prevost had convinced himself that prudence had required him to hand over virtually all of Canada but the St. Lawrence Valley to the United States. General John Vincent at Burlington considered the order ... [and] decided to remain at Burlington.... Vincent's disobedience ensured that some part of what [Tecumseh] had died for would survive.[17]

Vincent's insubordination did no such thing, actually, and in fact was largely irrelevant to Canada's future. Harrison had no orders to seize Burlington or any other part of Upper Canada because it was not the intention of Congress, the president, or the Department of War to conquer and claim any part of Britain's Canadian colony. Demonstrating America's limited aims in the operation, Harrison himself was back in Detroit on 7 October, two days after the battle, and three days later his army followed. On 14 October, the Kentucky volunteers, who had formed the vast majority of his force, were discharged and sent home. Two weeks later, only two brigades of the regular army were stationed north of the Maumee. Harrison's duty had been to end British encroachment into, and Indian attacks against, America's Northwest Territories. In this he succeeded. By late October, Harrison and the remainder of his army, accompanied by Perry, returned to Buffalo, New York.

III

As Tecumseh's force was routed in Canada, Andrew Jackson and a force of western Tennessee volunteers hunted for Tecumseh's followers in the eastern Mississippi Territory (now the state of Alabama). In response to the secretary of war's request for reinforcements, the western governors sent four armies of militiamen to attack the Creek Indians in their scattered settlements in Alabama.

Jackson and his volunteers were ready in early October to march south from Fayetteville, Tennessee. Among these men was a twenty-seven-year-old frontiersman and farmer from Franklin County named Davy Crockett, who kept "the camp alive with his quaint conceits and marvelous narratives."[18] Meanwhile an eastern Tennessee army under the command of General John Cocke assembled in Knoxville. Farther east, Major General Thomas Pinckney and Brigadier General John Floyd assembled a thousand-man force drawn from the Georgia militia and, together with about three hundred friendly Creek warriors, prepared to move west into Alabama. Farther south at Fort Stoddart, near Mobile, Brigadier General Thomas Flournoy would close the circle around the Creeks by marching north with his Mississippi volunteers, accompanied by U.S. Army regulars under Brigadier General Ferdinand Claiborne.

Jackson was the first to get his army in the field and the first to attack. By 10 October, Jackson's force reached Huntsville and from there moved another twenty miles south to a bend in the Tennessee where his troops built Fort Deposit (near modern-day Guntersville). There they awaited the promised supplies from Nashville and Cocke's force from eastern Tennessee—neither of which arrived.[19] Vowing to "live on acorns," Jackson pushed his troops over the mountains to the valley of the upper Coosa River, where he built Fort Strother to serve as his new base.

On 3 November, the Creek village of Tallassahatchee, east of the Coosa (near Jacksonville, Alabama) and home to fewer than three hundred warriors, was the first to feel Jackson's fury. With nine hundred cavalry and mounted infantry and a small force of friendly Cherokees, Major General John Coffee surrounded the village at sunrise and lured the warriors into attacking him. When they did, Coffee's surrounding force swarmed the Creeks from all sides and swiftly annihilated them. About two hundred of the estimated 284 warriors at the village were killed in the attack, along with a few women, while Coffee's force suffered only five dead and forty wounded.

Coffee later wrote that "the enemy fought with savage fury and met death with all its horrors, without shrinking or complaining: not one asked to be spared, but fought as long as they could stand or sit."[20] Less elegantly, but perhaps more accurately, Davy Crockett recalled, "We shot them like dogs."[21] Others were troubled by the slaughter. Lieutenant Richard Keith Call wrote, "Some of the cabins had taken fire, and half consumed human bodies were seen among the smoking ruin. In other instances, dogs had torn and feasted on mangled bodies of their masters. Heart sick, I turned from the revolting scene."[22] Jackson himself made a rare demonstration of pity amidst the carnage. An Indian boy, aged ten months, who "was lifted from the breast of his dead mother", was sent by Jackson to his wife Rachel in Tennessee to be brought up as their ward. Named Lyncoya, the boy lived with the Jacksons at Hermitage until he died of tuberculosis in his teens.[23]

Within a few days of the battle, Jackson received word that the small village of friendly Creeks at Talladega, about thirty miles southwest of Fort Strother, was besieged by hostile Creeks. Believing that General Cocke's force from eastern Tennessee was just behind him, Jackson left his supplies and his sick and wounded behind at the fort and marched to Talladega. About six miles from the village on the night of 7 November, Jackson gave his men a few hours to rest and then proceeded. According to the Anglo-American historian Reginald Horsman, Jackson

> marched at 4:00 a.m., with cavalry on his wings to encircle the enemy, his militia and volunteers in the center, and an advance to lure the enemy into an attack against the middle of the American

> line. When the Indians attacked, the advance retreated as planned. For a moment there was great danger when some of the militia broke and ran, but the Indians, about 1,000 strong, were held by the rest of the American infantry, encircled by the cavalry, and quickly forced to flee.[24]

Casualties among the Creeks were proportionately smaller than in the earlier battle because the break in Jackson's line allowed many to escape. Jackson claimed that nearly three hundred Creeks were found dead on the field. Among the U.S. force, about seventeen were killed and over eighty wounded. To his wife, Rachel, Jackson wrote that "we were out of provisions and half starved for many days, and to heighten my mortification when we returned here last evening had not one mouthfull to give the wounded or well; but that god that fed moses in the wilderness in the night brought us a partial Supply. A small quantity of meat and meal was brought in by the contractor."[25]

But this small shipment was hardly enough. Animals captured from the Creeks and purchased from the Cherokees were slaughtered, cooked, and distributed to the men. But there was not enough to go around, so Jackson limited himself and his staff to the offal, which had been discarded after the steers were butchered. Major John Reid wrote:

> Tripes, however hastily provided in a camp, without bread or seasoning, can only be palatable to an appetite very highly whetted; yet this constituted for several days, the only diet at headquarters, during which time the general seemed entirely satisfied with his fare.[26]

After several days, the beef ran out, and the men went back to short rations. "Racked by hunger and sickness—Jackson also suffered from acute dysentery—his men grew resentful."[27] Faced with hunger and a citizen army ready to mutiny, Jackson surrendered to the inevitable and ordered his force back to Fort Deposit, where they could be more easily supplied. On the way, however, the army's advance guard came across the long-awaited supply train headed toward the Coosa. The stubborn Jackson canceled the withdrawal and ordered his unhappy troops back to Strother, where a message of surrender soon arrived from the Creeks at Hillabee Town on the Tallapoosa. It was sent by Robert Grierson, a

Scotch trader who lived among the Creeks, and carried to Jackson by one of his slaves. The Hillabee Creeks, Grierson wrote, were:

> Begging me to offer to your Excellency terms of pacification with the United States. The glorious action you obtained [at Talladega] has such a good effect on their passions [that] the Hillabees from this day forever offer to lay down their arms, and to join in peace and amity with the United States.[28]

But Grierson wrote to the wrong general.[29] As the Hillabee Creeks attempted to surrender to Jackson, the sluggish Cocke had finally gone on the offensive. On 18 November, he sent a force of East Tennessee militiamen under General White to attack the unresisting Indians, who were waiting to surrender at Hillabee Town, killing sixty and imprisoning two hundred. With little appreciation for the divided and confused command of the American forces that confronted them, the Creeks in the region assumed treachery and hardened their resistance.

A week later, on 24 November, the Georgians encamped at Coweta finally joined the campaign, sending a force of almost a thousand to attack the Red Stick town of Autossee, on the Tallapoosa in west central Alabama. On the 28th, as White's force prepared to move on the town, the Creeks attacked first. White's force beat them off with artillery and bayonets, losing only eleven men. White claimed that about two hundred Creeks were killed, many by grapeshot as they charged the American line.

By now the Creeks were reeling from a series of devastating attacks that left as many as 750 warriors dead and others on the run.[30] They had entered the hostilities in Alabama with a force of only 2,500 to 4,000 warriors. The autumn attacks dealt a serious blow to their capacity to resist, and many of their main towns were now destroyed or abandoned. Jackson wanted to exploit the opportunity and finish them off, but with his volunteer troops grumbling about supplies, enlistments expiring, and Governor Blount wavering in his commitment to the effort, the general had little choice but to let his men return home on 12 December 1813. Undaunted and ready to resume the offensive, Jackson remained at Strother with a small force and awaited the replacements he had requested from Blount.

A day after Jackson released his men, Generals Flournoy and Claiborne finally moved north from Fort Stoddert on a hundred-mile trek to the Creek village of Econochaca near present-day Montgomery, where the Coosa and Tallapoosa meet. There were reports that the Red Stick chief William Weatherford (Red Eagle) and a group of warriors had gathered there, and Claiborne intended to destroy them. Econochaca was called the "Holy Ground" by whites because the town, which also served as a place of refuge and storage for food and arms, was believed to be the object of divine protection. Red Stick leader Josiah Francis told his warriors that it was protected by invisible "wizard circles" that would strike dead any white man who tried to cross them.[31] Leading a mixed force of about a thousand men, including regulars, militiamen, volunteers, and a band of friendly Choctaws, Flournoy attacked. When it became apparent to the defending warriors that the wizard circles were failing to deter the American infantry, many fled, including Weatherford, who is reported to have escaped by diving with his horse, Arrow, into the river.

Econochaca's capture and destruction and the failure of the wizard circles damaged the Prophet's reputation and Red Stick morale.[32] The Americans, however, found their thirst for revenge intensified by their victory. Claiborne had let his Choctaw allies sack the Holy Ground, but as his troops approached the center of the village, they encountered in the public square a tall poll from which hung "300 white and mixed blood scalps taken at Fort Mims. Men and women, infants, the old and the young." They also found a letter from the Spanish governor of Pensacola, Gonzalez Manrique, congratulating the chiefs of the Creek Nation on their victory at Fort Mims.[33]

Back at Fort Strother, Jackson held on with a force of a few hundred. Instead of reinforcements, he received a letter from Governor Blount urging his return to Tennessee. With the memory of Fort Mims fading and Tennessee's need for vengeance satisfied by Jackson's earlier victories, public interest in bearing further burdens of war was diminishing. Strongly objecting, Jackson replied that a loss of will would embolden all of the Indians to join with the Red Sticks, and Tennessee's borders would be "drenched with blood."[34]

As Jackson pleaded his case from Alabama, Blount was under pressure from Secretary of War Armstrong and General Pinckney to maintain a substantial military force in Alabama. In late December 1813, when Jackson's force at Strother had dwindled to no more than 130 men, Blount reluctantly sent Jackson 800 militiamen, whose term of enlistment ran for only sixty days. The men arrived on 14 January 1814. Notwithstanding their lack of training and experience, Jackson marched them out of Strother three days later for an attack

Impressment of an American seaman by British officers.
Courtesy of the Library of Congress

British squadron chases USS *Constitution* off New Jersey coast, 15–19 July 1812.
Courtesy of the Library of Congress

A Baltimore Clipper.
Courtesy of Lossing's Pictorial Field Book of the War of 1812

USS *Constitution* batters the HMS *Guerriere*, 19 August 1812.
Courtesy of the Library of Congress

USS *United States* shatters and captures the HMS *Macedonian*, 25 October 1812.
Courtesy of the Library of Congress

Battle of Lundy's Lane, 25 July 1814.
Courtesy of the Library of Congress

Battle of Lake Erie, 10 September 1813.
Courtesy of the Library of Congress

Perry transfers his command to the USS *Niagara*, 10 September 1813.
Courtesy of the Library of Congress

Perry writing a message to Harrison announcing the defeat of the British squadron on Lake Erie, 10 September 1813.
© Bettmann/CORBIS

We have met the enemy and they are ours:
Two Ships, two Brigs one
Schooner & one Sloop.
Yours, with great respect and esteem
O H Perry.

Facsimile of Perry's message to Harrison, 10 September 1813.
Courtesy of Lossing's Pictorial Field Book of the War of 1812

Macdonough on USS *Saratoga* at the battle of Lake Champlain, 11 September 1814.
The Granger Collection, New York

Battle of Lake Champlain (Plattsburgh), 11 September 1814.
Courtesy of the Library of Congress

British burning Washington, D.C., 24–25 August 1814.
The Granger Collection, New York

British sailors attacking *General Armstrong* in Fayal harbor, 26 September 1814.
Courtesy of the Library of Congress

Andrew Jackson commanding regulars at the battle of New Orleans, 8 January 1815.
Courtesy of the Library of Congress

American militia at the battle of New Orleans, 8 January 1815.
The Granger Collection, New York

on the Red Stick settlements along the upper Tallapoosa. It was a bold move. "Would one dare march them deep into hostile country? Yes, one would, if one's name was Andrew Jackson."[35]

With a force numbering about 930 men, plus about 200 to 300 friendly Creeks and Cherokees, Jackson's target was a hostile Creek settlement near where Emuckfaw Creek joined the Tallapoosa River. Arrayed against Jackson's inexperienced men was a large force of Creeks who had learned something from their earlier defeats, and this time were better prepared. On 22 January, Jackson's encampment near the Emuckfaw was attacked in the early hours, but he beat it back. Later that day the Red Sticks attacked again, and when General Coffee attempted to outflank the Indians, three-fourths of his men refused to follow. Coffee was badly wounded, and he and a few of his men were nearly cut off before being rescued by their Indian allies.[36]

Jackson recognized that it was only a matter of time before disaster befell his poorly trained force, so he began an orderly retreat back to Fort Strother. But on the 24th, under Red Stick harassment at the crossing of Enotachopco Creek, his force almost collapsed into panic. A few courageous officers maintained order, and the Creeks turned back. Indeed, the steadfast Coffee, suffering from wounds received the day before, rose from his litter and rode into action. Dr. John Shelby, the hospital surgeon, also joined the fight, and Jackson himself was in the thick of it. Major Reid wrote, "In a shower of balls, of which he seemed unmindful, [Jackson] was seen performing the duties of subordinate officers, rallying the alarmed, halting them in their flight, forming his columns, inspiring them by his example."[37]

While Jackson struggled with his raw recruits at Emuckfaw, the passive Georgia militia under General Floyd decided to return to the war they had largely watched from the safety of Georgia. On 18 January, Floyd marched from his base at Fort Mitchell on the Chattahoochee, intending to attack the Creek settlement of Tuckaubatchee on Tallapoosa, about fifty miles from Jackson's position. The Creeks had plenty of warning that the Georgians were coming and, perhaps emboldened by recent successes, opted for a night attack on the approaching militia. But not all of the Red Sticks were as bold as Red Eagle, who hatched the plan. The men selected to lead the "forlorn hope" into the heart of Floyd's camp, Paddy Walsh and High Hat Jim, objected, calling the plan a "measure of insanity and desperation, a sure and unnecessary sacrifice of three hundred men."[38] Debate continued, insults flew, and anger flared as the Indian leaders argued around the campfire. In the end, a discouraged Red Eagle mounted his horse and left the camp with his followers.

Even without Red Eagle, however, there were enough willing Creeks to attempt the attack, and during the night they slipped into the swamps surrounding the American camp. With a force of twelve hundred Georgia volunteers and four hundred friendly Creeks, Floyd was encamped about ten miles away from his target on the morning of 27 January 1814 when the Red Sticks attacked. After hours of bitter fighting, the Indians finally retreated, leaving behind thirty-seven dead. Floyd's Creek allies "committed the usual atrocities on the dead enemies—slicing them open, cutting off privates, ripping out a heart and parading it around. They had great sport with a corpse they kept putting on a horse. Every time it fell off they shouted 'Whiskey too much.'"[39] Floyd, who lost seventeen men, with 132 wounded, ended the campaign then and there and returned to Fort Mitchell.[40]

IV

Badgered by Jackson and under orders from Washington, Governor Blount finally summoned five thousand Tennessee militiamen for six months of service and sent them to Fort Strother to serve under Jackson. To his men's and officers' complaints about the hardships of duty, Jackson responded with tighter discipline, which was reinforced by the leadership of the regulars of the Thirty-ninth Regiment, recently assigned to Jackson by General Pinckney. Recruited in Knoxville and for the most part made up of native-born Americans of Scotch-Irish descent, the well-trained men of the Thirty-ninth, including a twenty-one-year-old third lieutenant named Sam Houston, would form the core of Jackson's new army.

Jackson intended to whip this new force into shape, whatever it took. When his second in command, the reluctant General John Cocke from east Tennessee, encouraged insubordination, Jackson had him arrested. He also arrested a brigadier general for similar failings and had a Tennessee militia private, John Woods, court-martialed for mutiny.

> The defendant was convicted and shot—the first execution of a militiaman since the Revolution. The sanguinary lesson was not

> lost on his men. In this campaign, as in others, Jackson got the most out of his men because they feared him more than the enemy.[41]

Training and preparation proceeded at Fort Strother through February and into March, when Jackson received word from friendly Indians that the Red Sticks were concentrating at a fortified position on the Tallapoosa. Perhaps over-confident from their recent successes against Jackson and Floyd, a large force of Red Sticks—whose numbers were estimated at between seven hundred and twelve hundred[42]—had gathered on a peninsula of some hundred acres formed by a bend in the Tallapoosa River (about ten miles west of modern Alexander City, Alabama). Near the tip of the peninsula, called Cholocco Litabixee ("horse's hoof") by the Creeks and Horseshoe Bend by the whites, the Creeks built the town of Tohopeka (meaning "fortified place"). About three hundred log huts sheltered several thousand warriors as well as women and children who sought refuge from the encroaching American armies.

The Red Sticks constructed a concave breastwork of large logs across the land side of the peninsula and cut into it a double level of loopholes through which they could direct their enfilade at the Americans. The night before the attack, in a ceremony at Tohopeka, three Red Stick "prophets, their gyrating bodies outlined by the campfire, danced the Dance of the Lakes, taught them by the Shawnees."[43]

Though the land side of the encampment was heavily fortified, the Indians built no defensive works at the end of the peninsula flanked by the river. The area was inadequately manned despite the proximity of the hundreds of lodges filled with women and children. Instead, the river bank was covered with beached canoes that the Indians could use for escape if Jackson's force breached the breastwork and overwhelmed the fort. With just over three thousand men, Jackson reached Horseshoe Bend on 28 March and, after a quick survey of the fortification, decided on a plan of attack that would have him leading the bulk of the infantry against the breastwork while General Coffee—leading a force of seven hundred mounted men assisted by Indian auxiliaries—would attack from the rear.

Dawn found the American army assembled on the field facing the breastwork. The three prophets resumed their performance, to the beat of drums, on the top of a knoll behind the wall, where they would be visible to both the Red

Sticks and Americans. "They shrieked as they danced, cursing the white enemy, calling upon the warriors to be brave. Their bodies were painted black. Each wore his badge of office, an entire cow's tail dyed bright red fastened to an arm, the thick end at shoulder height, tail end tied to the wrist, the long cow hairs dangling below the hand, waving in the morning air as they danced."[44] With only about a third of the warriors armed with muskets, the Red Sticks would need all the supernatural intervention they could get.

Jackson opened the battle with his two small artillery pieces, inflicting little damage on the massive log breastwork but making enough noise to distract the Red Sticks from Coffee's effort in the rear. As the cannon fired in the front, Jackson's Cherokee allies swam across the Tallapoosa and retrieved the canoes to ferry a combined force of about two hundred whites and friendly Indians to the Red Sticks' rear. Moving in from the river, the small force attacked Tohopeka, occupied the high ground behind the breastwork, and shot at the Creeks who manned it. With his enemy now distracted from behind, Jackson ordered the Thirty-ninth Regiment forward to storm the breastwork.

> Resistance was savage. Major Lemuel Montgomery, the first man onto the breastwork, was shot dead; Ensign Samuel Houston, the first across it was badly wounded; two lieutenants killed. But the regulars stormed across the logs, bayonets and musket butts clearing the way through war clubs and tomahawks until the Red Sticks broke and scattered—to rally, to fight to the death, to be hunted down in the gullies and thickets of the Horseshoe's interior.[45]

At six foot five, Houston offered an easy target as he leaped onto the breastwork brandishing his sword. A barbed arrow pierced his thigh just below his groin, and dropped him to the ground in pain and blood. Another officer pulled it out (Houston later claimed he had to force his colleague to do it[46]), and a surgeon stopped the bleeding well enough for Houston to continue the fight. Later in the day, as the Americans were driving the last pockets of resistance from the brush and brambles of the peninsula, a limping Houston led a volunteer platoon against an entrenched group of Red Sticks, receiving multiple gunshot wounds in his arm and shoulder. Jackson, who witnessed the performance, promoted the now badly wounded Houston to the rank of second lieutenant.[47]

The Indian dead on the field were numbered at 557, but other accounts put the total dead closer to 800. It is thought that 200 or so Red Sticks escaped by jumping into the river. Some took refuge in the thick brush of the peninsula, but the Americans set it on fire and shot the warriors as they escaped. Some 500 squaws and children were captured. On the American side, casualties were heaviest among the men of the Thirty-ninth, who charged the front of the breastwork and lost twenty killed. The Creek and Cherokee allies lost twenty-three of their warriors. About eighty of the American and allied Indian wounded later died in transport to hospitals in the rear. Instead of burying the American dead near the field of battle as was customary, Jackson had their bodies weighted down and sunk to the bottom of the Tallapoosa, since "after the fight at Emuckfa[w] the Red Sticks had dug up the American dead and scalped and stripped them. Some dead Indians at Horseshoe Bend were found in the clothing of those American dead."[48]

Six months of American attacks on the Red Sticks had taken a heavy toll on the Creek tribes in Alabama. Villages were destroyed, the economy disrupted, tribes displaced, and several thousand warriors were dead or maimed. Enough was enough, and those Red Sticks still in the field had to choose between surrender or flight. The Red Stick leader Red Eagle (William Weatherford) recognized the inevitability of their destruction and chose to give up the fight. Alone, he slipped through the American lines at Fort Jackson, recently built at the confluence of the Coosa and Tallapoosa Rivers, and rode directly to Jackson's tent, where he surrendered to the astonished general. Red Eagle said:

> I am in your power, do with me as you please. I am a soldier. I have done the white people all the harm I could; I have fought them, and fought them bravely: if I had an army I would yet fight, and contend to the last: but I have none; my people are all gone. I can do no more than weep over the misfortunes of my nation.[49]

Jackson judged him to be sincere and offered clemency. Others wanted Weatherford punished, but Jackson knew that a surrendered Red Eagle would cause other Red Sticks to give up their arms and return to peace. Red Eagle spent the rest of his life in prosperous retirement in Monroe County, Alabama, raising fine horses. Until his death in 1826, Weatherford often visited Jackson at Hermitage, and the two old warriors would sit together on the grand porch and talk about fast horses and the days when they were mortal enemies. But not all of the Red Stick leaders were ready to follow Red Eagle's example: Josiah Francis, Paddy Walsh, Peter McQueen, and High-Headed Jim fled to Pensacola for the protection the Spanish and their British allies would offer.[50]

Though generous to Weatherford, Jackson would exact a high price from the defeated Creeks and the other tribes in the region. Recently appointed brigadier general in the United States Army and commander of the Seventh Military District, based in Mobile, Jackson was authorized by Secretary of War Armstrong to negotiate the terms of peace. Despite the substantial support he received from friendly Creeks and Cherokees during the war, Jackson made no distinction between friends and enemies when he forced the tribes to surrender substantial portions of their land as a condition for peace:

> [O]n August 9, 1814, Jackson forced all the tribal leaders to sign the treaty of Fort Jackson, which stripped the Indians of more than 20,000,000 acres of land—over half of their territory. Such a massive land grab pleased Jackson's western supporters but left most government officials aghast.[51]

The British, still locked in a dangerous war, were not as ready as the Creeks to concede victory to the Americans. The harsh treaty imposed on the Indians offered the British fertile ground to incite insurrection. Operating out of Spanish Pensacola, the British began to furnish the refugee Red Sticks with food, clothing, and weapons. Admiral Cochrane ordered Captain Hugh Pigot and the frigate *Orpheus* to sail to the region and recruit an Indian force to retake Mobile and establish a stronger British presence in the Gulf. But as was often the case, the British underestimated Jackson. Horsman notes:

> It was well for the United States government that an efficient general had made his mark and had been placed in command of the Gulf coast in the Spring of 1814, for Britain was preparing a major effort in the region. Since the beginning of the war the British cabinet had well realized the vital importance of New Orleans and the mouth of the Mississippi to the whole Mississippi Valley. The power that dominated New Orleans controlled huge areas to the

> north, and could ruin the trade of America's rapidly expanding trans-Appalachian settlements.[52]

The British cabinet was correct in its assessment of the strategic value of New Orleans and in devoting resources to this vital theater. But the Americans were no less prescient than their British brethren, and the resource they would provide the region was the towering rage of Brigadier General Andrew Jackson. *Come and See.*

CHAPTER SEVENTEEN

LETTERS OF MARQUE AND REPRISAL

Three weeks after Congress declared war on Great Britain, Captain Joshua Barney sailed out of Baltimore in command of the fast schooner *Rossie*. With a crew of a hundred men and officers, she was armed with eleven twelve-pounders and a long nine.[1] Barney sailed down the Chesapeake Bay to Hampton Roads and into the Atlantic, only about a week behind Isaac Hull and the *Constitution*, who had embarked on his momentous voyage from Annapolis on 5 July 1812.

Like Hull, who captured the *Guerriere* five weeks later, Barney would enjoy a successful voyage, capturing fifteen British merchantmen and taking 166 prisoners over the next four and a half months. But the fifty-two-year-old Barney no longer held a commission in the United States Navy, and the *Rossie* was owned by an investment consortium of Baltimore merchants. These men supplied the ship and hired the crew with the expectation of great profits from the sale of the British ships and cargo—1.3 million dollars' worth, as it turned out—that *Rossie* would seize on her voyage. Barney was one of an estimated 150 armed "letter of marque" privateers who set sail against the British in the first two months of war. The strength of the U.S. Navy, by comparison, was sixteen warships, only eight of which were ready for sea when war was declared.[2] A British merchant vessel was ten times more likely to be attacked by a privateer than by a ship of the navy during much of the war.

Over the next two and a half years, more than 500 privateers would set sail from American coastal ports in pursuit of British shipping. Capturing an estimated 1,500 to 2,500 of the enemy's vessels, they prodded both nations toward peace talks. Although historians and naval experts continue to debate the value of the privateers' service during the war, Admiral Alfred Thayer Mahan, writing in the early twentieth century, grudgingly confirmed their contribution:

> The United States flooded the seas with privateers, producing an effect upon British commerce, which, though inconclusive singly, doubtless cooperated powerfully with other motives to dispose the enemy to liberal terms of peace. It was the reply, and the only reply, to commercial blockade.[3]

Certainly the British were annoyed by these swarms of entrepreneurial privateers and complained about their success from the beginning. In a story about the loss of the *Java* in December 1812, the *Times* of London lamented "that Lloyd's List contains notices of upwards of 500 British vessels captured in seven months time by the Americans.... Anyone who had predicted such a result of an American war this time last year would have been treated as a madman or traitor."[4]

The *Times* may have been surprised, but other British publications foresaw the success of the American marauders. The editors of the *Statesman*, drawing on the experience of the War of Independence, warned:

> America can certainly not pretend to wage a maritime war with us. She has no navy to do it with. But America has nearly 100,000 as good seamen as any in the world, all of whom would be actively employed against our trade on every part of the ocean in their fast-sailing ships-of-war, many of whom will be able to cope with our smaller cruisers; and they will be found to be sweeping in the West Indian seas, and even carrying desolation into the chops of the Channel. Everyone must recollect what they did in the latter

> part of the American war. The books at Lloyd's will recount it; and the rate of assurances at that time will clearly prove what their diminutive strength was able to effect in the face of our navy, and that when nearly one hundred pendants were flying on their coast. Were we then able to prevent their going in and going out, or stop them from taking our trade and our storeships, even in sight of our garrisons? ... The Americans will be found to be a different sort of enemy by sea than the French. They possess nautical knowledge, with equal enterprise to ourselves. They will be found attempting deeds which a Frenchman would never think of; and they will have all the ports of the enemy open, in which they can make their retreat and their booty.[5]

II

Privateers were commonplace throughout the centuries leading up to the War of 1812. Most countries supplemented their naval forces by granting letters of marque and reprisal to privately financed and operated ships, usually armed with cannon. The recipients of the letters—"privateers"—were permitted to raid the enemy's military and merchant shipping and to keep a portion of the proceeds of the sale of whatever they seized. While controversial even then—in 1785 Benjamin Franklin wrote, "It is high time, for the sake of humanity, to put a stop to this enormity"[6]—most countries reluctantly embraced the practice because it allowed them to mobilize a large fleet of armed ships during wartime at little or no cost to the treasury.

Privateers allowed the poorly funded U.S. government in the early 1800s to avoid the huge expense of a large standing navy. Indeed, Article I, Section 8, of the Constitution provides, "Congress shall have the power ... To declare War, grant Letters of Marque and Reprisal, and make rules concerning captures on Land and Water."

Despite its legal sanction, a number of historians have likened privateering to piracy. Both privateers and pirates preyed on merchant vessels, but privateers received official permission from the state and were limited to attacking ships under an enemy flag; pirates were indiscriminate in their choice of prey. Pirates also kept the booty for themselves, while privateers were generally required to turn their takings over to the state that issued their letters of marque, which then returned some portion to the privateers. Another important difference was that captured pirates were generally tried and hanged, while privateers were treated as prisoners of war and held for the duration or exchanged.

Among history's notable privateers were (for at least part of their careers) Sir Francis Drake, Henry Morgan, and William Kidd. The Barbary pirates, who preyed on Mediterranean shipping from their North African ports for many centuries, were in fact privateers, raiding European and American commerce with encouragement and permission from officials of the Ottoman Empire, which then ruled North Africa, the Balkans, and the Middle East. At one point or another in their professional careers, several leading U.S. naval officers were privateers.[7]

A case could also be made that the epic voyage of John Paul Jones aboard the *Bonhomme Richard* was a quasi-privateering venture. Stranded in France after turning over command of the *Ranger* to his lieutenant, Thomas Simpson, Jones waited for the Continental Congress to offer a command of suitable prestige. When none was forthcoming, Jones arranged with the French to refit the East India merchant ship *Duc de Duras* as a frigate (renamed the *Bonhomme Richard*) and give him the command. "She became a warship in the Continental Navy for her final hour," relates one naval historian, "under a kind of lend-lease charter arrangement which made the French regard her much as a privateer, as far as their own bookkeeping was concerned."[8]

Bonhomme Richard's officers and ship's boys were mostly Americans, but the rest of the crew was a polyglot mix of European nationalities. More than half the petty officers were English or Irish, as were the complements of able and ordinary seamen. The 140 marines on board were under the command of French officers and were serving in the French Regiment de Walsh-Serrant, made up mostly of Irish volunteers.[9] Only about a third of the crew was American, and more than a quarter was English![10] After settlement of the prize money with the French government, the share to the officers and crew of *Bonhomme Richard* amounted to $26,583 in gold, a tenth of which was Jones's.[11]

The system was often abused, of course. There were many marauders like the Lafitte brothers, Pierre and Jean, whose claim to privateer status was dubious. The Lafittes attacked and seized Spanish ships in the Caribbean from their base at Barataria Bay on the Louisiana coast, just south of New Orleans.[12] They claimed privateers' commissions from the Republic of Cartegena in South America, but that republic, though in revolt against Spain, was something of a legal fiction and enjoyed no international recognition.[13] Nonetheless, no one worried about the Lafittes' paperwork in 1815 when they helped Andrew Jackson fend off the British at New Orleans.

The legal foundations of privateering were elaborated by Hugo Grotius at the beginning of the seventeenth century. A merchant ship employed by the Dutch East India Company had seized a Portuguese vessel in the Singapore Strait. Since the Dutch were at war with Portugal, the company claimed the Portuguese cargo as a prize and engaged the twenty-year-old Grotius, who became one of the most influential jurists of all time, to write a brief in defense of its position. Citing Roman precedents and principles of natural law, Grotius argued that wartime booty belongs to the state whose subjects seized it. His position prevailed in the case at hand and became settled international law.[14]

In the rough-and-tumble world of early ocean commerce, most merchant ships were armed and assumed the right to defend themselves against attack. If they captured their attacker, they were absolved of criminal culpability, but any prizes and prisoners belonged to the captor's sovereign. This principle of self-defense evolved into the conventions of privateering, according to which a ship could obtain advance approval from its sovereign to attack vessels of a hostile power, even if unprovoked.

The privilege of taking prizes survived at sea long after it disappeared for armies on land. Until the mid-nineteenth century, both naval and merchant ships were entitled to seize prizes. The chief reason for the difference may be the international character of the high seas. One naval historian describes the oceanic free-for-all:

> The theory was that since the sea belonged to nobody it belonged to everybody, and since it was not ruled by any acknowledged state or sovereign power it had no laws at all. When there was war going on, as there usually was, private property that was three miles or more out had nothing sacred about it. It was free game. It could be legally seized.[15]

Letters of marque and reprisal and the laws that governed them were an attempt to impose some kind of order and civility in an otherwise lawless arena. Laws governing letters of marque typically required the privateer to provide for the fair and humane treatment of prisoners. Under U.S. law, all prisoners had to be treated well; if they were not, the privateer risked losing his license. Upon reaching port, prisoners were transferred to the custody of the federal government, which, during the War of 1812, would have attempted to exchange them for American prisoners. The number of prisoners taken by American privateers was in fact substantial. An 1830 State Department auditor's report, prepared for Secretary of State Martin Van Buren, reported that 4,812 of the 15,508 British seamen captured by the United States during the War of 1812 were taken by privateers.[16]

Before the Revolution, each American colony reserved for itself the right to issue letters of marque and reprisal. During the Revolutionary War, as a result, colonies controlled by the British, such as New York, issued such letters to pro-British privateers, who then preyed on shipping from other colonial ports.

In 1776, the Continental Congress also assumed the power to issue letters of marque.[17] Four years later, with an American navy now in existence, Congress defined by statute how the value of any prizes was to be distributed among the parties involved.[18] If a prize captured by a commissioned ship of the fledgling navy was of a force equal or superior to that of the captor, the entire value of the prize went to the officers and crew. If the prize was of lesser force (a problem confronting Stephen Decatur in his capture of *Macedonian*), then half the proceeds went to the government, and half went to officers and crew. Of the latter portion, 5 percent went to the squadron commander whether or not he participated in the capture; 10 percent went to the captain of the captor (plus the squadron commander's share if operating independently); 10 percent was shared by lieutenants, sailing masters, and captains of marines; 10 percent was shared by the upper-level professions, including surgeons, chaplains, and carpenters; 17.5 percent was shared by the midshipmen and the next level of professional staff, including schoolmasters, sail makers, armorers, and masters-at-arms; 21.5 percent was shared by the remaining noncommissioned officers; and the remaining 35 percent was shared by the seamen, marines, and boys.

Letters of marque and reprisal were not necessarily limited to the citizens or residents of the issuing country. After the French Revolution, the new republic replaced its former ambassador to the United States with the controversial Edmond Charles "Citizen" Genet, whom the Marquis de Lafayette called "a statue walking around looking for a pedestal to stand on."[19] Shortly after his arrival in the United States in 1793, Genet began issuing French letters of marque to privateers based in America to attack British shipping. Two French-commissioned privateers—the *Citoyen Genet* and the *Sans Coulotte*—were launched from Charleston, South Carolina, where many French refugees had landed following a slave uprising in Haiti. Adding to America's diplomatic difficulties was the *Citoyen Genet*'s subsequent capture of two British prizes, which she triumphantly brought into Philadelphia while Genet was visiting the city.[20] Some years later, during the War of 1812, Americans created a similar controversy by acquiring letters of marque from the United States government and launching privateers from Napoleon's France. The most fearsome of these was the sixteen-gun *True-Blooded Yankee*, which sailed from Brest in March 1813. She captured thirty-seven vessels off Ireland and Scotland and burned seven more.[21]

III

When the United States, with its meager navy, finally declared war on Great Britain on 18 June 1812, it turned to a fleet of privateers to attack the ocean-borne commerce on which the economy of the British Empire depended. Eight days after the declaration of war, Congress, pursuant to Article I, Section 8, of the Constitution, authorized the issuance of commissions to privateers and established the rules by which this newly-created private fleet would conduct its activities during the war. With this new law and its subsequent revisions,

> the government took upon itself the task of exercising greater control over the force. This control included centralizing issuance of commissions; specific admonitions regarding behavior at sea, backed up by the Navy itself; a provision for punishing offenders by naval court martial; the unique incentives of conditional pay status plus payment of one-half the estimated value of a *destroyed* enemy vessel, public or private; and the unheard of implementation of a pension system for privateersmen and their families.[22]

The new law seems to have achieved its purpose: Though the U.S. Navy had fewer than twenty ships, 150 privateer vessels were commissioned and set sail within two months of the declaration of war.

America's vast maritime industry—merchants, seamen, investors, insurers, ship owners, captains, suppliers, victuallers, ship builders—had suffered severely during the years of embargo and blockade and was expected to suffer further now that hostilities were declared between England and America. In the major port city of Baltimore, a thousand sailors had been idled. In 1805, goods worth seven and a half million dollars had been shipped from Baltimore; in 1808, the figure was under two million dollars.[23] Among the members of the city's maritime industry, there was little work, but there were plenty of idle resources ready to be redeployed in privateering. It is not surprising, then, that one of the first privateers of the war sailed from Baltimore, which produced a large share of the American privateering fleet.

Baltimore businessmen, sailors, shipbuilders, and ordinary citizens became enthusiastic and proud supporters of the privateering effort. The privateer *George Washington*, on her maiden voyage from Norfolk, Virginia, in July 1812, just weeks after war was declared, stopped at Baltimore before heading out to sea. One of her seamen, George Little, later wrote:

> When we arrived in Baltimore, I found the most active preparations were in progress to prosecute the war. A number of privateers were fitting out; and everywhere the American flag might be seen flying, denoting the places of rendezvous; in a word, the most intense excitement prevailed throughout the city.[24]

With few other maritime opportunities available, investors in port cities easily raised the money to fund hundreds of costly privateering voyages. While much of the money raised was devoted to acquiring a ship and outfitting it for war, a large crew was also needed, as well as the supplies to sustain it on voyages of up to four months. There had to be enough crewmen to man the guns, serve in the boarding crew when the ships closed, guard any prisoners, and man any prizes on their return to a U.S. port. While the typical merchant vessel of the day was crewed by no more than a dozen or two men, a privateer required more than a hundred.

Some privateers were funded by a wealthy individual, but most relied on consortiums of investors to organize, finance, and launch the vessels and crew that would seek a letter of marque and embark from eastern ports in search of prizes and profits. Although there was no organized stock market in the early nineteenth century, shares in privateer ventures had already assumed many of the attributes common to today's equity markets. As early as 1739, when colonial Americans joined Britain's war against Spain, investors rallied to the war effort and organized privateers to go after Spanish shipping—giving New Yorkers a preview, as one historian sees it, of the high-flying finance to come:

> Upon the outbreak of hostilities with the Spaniards in 1739, New York ran true to form and speculation in privateer's shares began before the end of the year. Prices rose and fell on the unsubstantiated rumors of rich captures and bad losses.... [T]he privateer's stock market flourished to the delight of the gambling financier of those days and contributed its bit to the financial experience of New York....[25]

These forms of investment re-emerged in the War of 1812. The *Baltimore American* reported on 25 June 1812, "a subscription paper was opened at the Merchant's Coffee House in Baltimore for equipping a Letter of Marque to the extent of $20,000 in shares of $500 each."[26]

IV

Like the naval crews of the day, most privateer crews were made up of merchant seamen left idle and impoverished by the embargo and blockade. They also included navy sailors looking for less demanding and more profitable work. Similarly, the officer corps was drawn from ex-navy men or from officers of the merchant fleet. Privateer crews were ethnically diverse. The race of crewmen was not recorded officially, but anecdotal evidence indicates that both American and British crews included a number of black sailors.

One such report comes from Captain Nathaniel Shaler of the privateer *Governor Tompkins*. On 1 January 1813, Shaler wrote to his agent about a confrontation he stumbled into with a bigger and better-armed British frigate:

> Her first broadside killed two men, and wounded six others.... The name of one of my poor fellows who was killed ought to be registered in the book of fame, and remembered with reverence as long as bravery is considered a virtue. He was a black man, by the name

> of John Johnson; and twenty-four pound shot struck him in the hip, and took away all the lower part of his body. In this state the poor, brave fellow lay on the deck and several times exclaimed to his shipmates, "fire away boys, neber haul de color down." The other [man killed] was also a black man, by the name of John Davis, and [he] was struck in much the same way: he fell near me, and several times requested to be thrown overboard, saying he was only in the way of others. While America has such sailors, she has little to fear from tyrants of the ocean.[27]

Eight months later, on 5 August 1813, the privateer *Decatur,* 7, out of Charleston, South Carolina, encountered the British war sloop *Dominica*, 14, and beat her in a savage battle. After the Americans boarded *Dominica* and "fought with unparalleled vigor and desperate courage," three out of four British seamen were dead or wounded. When the survivors were taken to port, Charles R. Simpson, a British agent for prisoners in the United States, described the *Decatur*'s crew:

> [It was] a very large Crew...who amounted in number I believe to be 93 chiefly if not all Blacks & Mulattoes. And in Ferocity and cruelty exceeded by none.... [A]fter a most desperate Discharge of Musketry [they] succeeded in Boarding when a Scene of Cruelty was exhibited which has perhaps never been equaled. The Boarders Killing in the most merciless manner all the Wounded on the Decks.[28]

The Americans denied the massacre, and South Carolina District Judge John Drayton reported to Secretary of State James Monroe that the *Decatur*'s crew "treated the prisoners with utmost humanity." Other British sources appear to support the American version. The *Naval Chronicle* reported that on *Dominica* "12 ... men were killed, and 44 wounded. Five of the latter have since died." This tally leaves thirty-nine surviving wounded from *Dominica*, not what one would expect from Simpson's "scene of cruelty."[29]

How the prize money earned on a voyage was distributed among the privateer's many interests—owners, investors, officers, and crew—was determined by formal contractual agreements that governed the venture.[30] For a successful raider, the profits and the individual rewards could be substantial. Sailing out of Bristol, Rhode Island, with a crew of about 120 men, the brig *Yankee* completed six successful voyages under three different captains and captured forty prizes. "In all, it was estimated, *Yankee* destroyed $5,000,000 worth of enemy shipping and supplies, and brought home or sent home booty worth more than $1,000,000." On *Yankee*'s fifth cruise, "the two Negro cabin boys got, respectively, $1,121.89 and $738.19."[31]

V

Beyond providing opportunities for seamen and investors, the boom in privateering spurred shipbuilders to develop new breeds of swift and nimble raiders. Among the finest of these was the schooner known as the Baltimore Clipper (or Baltimore Flyer, as it was called during the war). Henry Adams described its ingenious design:

> The private armed vessel was built rather to fly than to fight, and its value depended far more on its ability to escape than on its capacity to attack. If the privateer could sail close to the wind, and wear or tack in the twinkling of an eye; if she could spread an immense amount of canvas and run off as fast as a frigate before the wind; and if she had ... one long range gun pivoted amidships, with plenty of men in case boarding became necessary, she was perfect. To obtain these results the builders and sailors ran excessive risks. Too lightly built and too heavily sparred, the privateer was never a comfortable or a safe vessel. Beautiful beyond anything then known in naval construction, such vessels aroused boundless admiration, but defied imitators.[32]

Like the powerful super frigates designed by Joshua Humphrey of Philadelphia, the Baltimore Flyer was a uniquely American technological achievement. Historians of naval architecture debate its origins, but it is thought to have evolved from the sloop (from the Dutch *sloep* and Swedish *slup*), a single-masted fore-and-aft rigged vessel that was developed in the coastal regions of northern Europe. The naval architect Thomas C. Gillmer describes the sloop's advantages:

> Sometime in the mid-seventeenth century, smaller coastwise vessels began to appear whose sails hung no more from the long awkward sprits or square yards, but from gaffs pivoted aloft at the mast. This evolution of rig, probably born in Holland, became the true fore-and-aft sail. It was an invention of liberation.... Their quick maneuvering in going to windward must have attracted amazement and envy, and larger coastwise boats soon began to use the style of sail.[33]

With the addition of a second mast, the sloop became the schooner, which in turn became the ship of choice for American commerce. Its basic design could be endlessly adapted for specialized tasks—shipping, fishing, war, pilot-boat or customs duty—and particular environments—the bays and rivers of coastal trade or the oceans of international commerce. In the middle of the eighteenth century, a distinctive Chesapeake schooner emerged, whose speed and handling attracted the interest of European navies and merchants. The Royal Navy acquired many of these vessels as pilot boats and packets, and they were often delivered to Britain with a hold full of Maryland tobacco to maximize the transaction's revenue.

American sloops and schooners were used as privateers during the French and Indian War. In the Revolutionary War they served as privateers as well as commissioned vessels in the Continental Navy. The Revolution and the subsequent blockade created a demand for ships suited to smuggling and privateering, so Chesapeake builders began designing more for speed and handling than for durability and cargo capacity. The result was the "sharp-built" schooner—named for the sleek hull design, flush deck, low free board, and rakish tilt to the masts that gave the vessel its distinctive look and agility. As this design was exclusive to the ship yards of the upper Chesapeake Bay, sharp-built ships became known as Baltimore Flyers.

Many of these ships ultimately fell into British hands, but their captors were baffled by their difficult and mercurial sailing habits. One British captain is said to have admitted to a captured American privateer,

> You Americans are a singular people as it respects seamanship and enterprise. In England, we cannot build vessels as your Baltimore

> Clippers: we have no models. And even if we had them, they would be of no service to us, for we never would sail them as you do. We are afraid of their long masts and heavy spars and would soon cut down and reduce them to our standard. We strengthen them, put in bulkheads, after which they would lose their sailing qualities and would be of no further service as cruising vessels.[34]

Schooners and sloops dominated the privateer fleet. Of the 526 commissioned privateers that Robert Gardiner has counted, 364 were described as schooners and thirty-five as sloops.[35] The remaining vessels included twenty-six ships and sixty-seven brigs—both classes being "ship-rigged," i.e., carrying square sails—and thirty-four vessels of varying types, including one three-masted xebec.

Privateers' preference for schooners over ship-rigged vessels had more to do with handling than with speed. While the sleek Baltimore Clippers were certainly faster than the typical merchant ships of the day, they were no faster than smaller ship-rigged warships like brigs or frigates, and in some cases may have been slower, especially in rough seas, where a schooner's speed would suffer more than a frigate's. A ship's speed depends as much on the length of its hull (called hull speed) as on any other feature, and most brigs and frigates were longer and sleeker than other warships. Under ideal conditions, a frigate could reach a top speed of twelve knots or so, about the same as the better schooners. The British frigate *Solebay* was fast gaining on John Paul Jones's sloop *Providence* when Jones made his daring escape by relying on the sloop's superior handling. Privateer schooners in the War of 1812 used the same tricks to take a ship or two from a convoy escorted by a frigate or brig. A schooner's advantage in sailing close to the wind allowed many a privateer to snatch his prize from a protected convoy.

A common tactic was to approach the part of a convoy farthest from the armed escort—a frigate or brig—and make as much noise as possible with cannon and musket fire to attract the escort's attention. As the escort turned toward the intruder, the privateer would flee downwind (with the wind right aft, or blowing behind him). The escort would pursue, closing over the next several miles while it enjoyed the advantage of the wind. Once the hunter and the hunted were many miles from the convoy, the privateer's schooner, with the advantage of its gaff-rigged sails, would quickly tack and turn, and "with her great fore triangular sails and her tall gaff fore- and main-sails hauled sharply in," would turn back toward the now unprotected convoy on a close hauled course (sailing nearly into the wind). The ship-rigged escort, unable to sail as close to the wind as the schooner, would have to undertake the cumbersome process of "wearing" its way (zig-zagging like a switch-back road up a mountain) back to the convoy. As the escort struggled to return, "the privateer had time to cut out about two or three helpless merchant vessels, capture the crews, either destroy or put prize crews aboard, and depart. This tactic was practiced to create an organized confusion, often routinely predictable, among enemy vessels."[36]

Some of the finest fast schooners were built by Thomas Kemp. He began his apprenticeship at St. Michaels in Talbot County, but in 1805 he moved across the bay to Fells Point in Baltimore, where the skilled workmen and subcontractors were beginning to concentrate and where pay was higher. A year later, at age twenty-seven, Kemp started his own company. In 1806 he launched the *Lynx*. The *Rossie* and *Superior* followed in 1808 and the *Comet* in 1810. The *Chasseur*, a fast cargo vessel, was completed in 1813. *Rossie*, *Chasseur*, and *Comet*, converted to privateers in the war, enjoyed some of the most productive voyages of the war. The *Lynx*, purchased by the U.S. Navy in 1813, was captured on the Rappahannock River by Cockburn's forces and put into British service for the duration of the war.[37]

VI

Kemp's *Chasseur*, under Captain Thomas Boyle of Baltimore, made one of the most remarkable privateer voyages of the war. Originally launched as a blockade-running merchant ship, the timidity of her first captains confined the *Chasseur* to the Chesapeake for months at a time. After a year, the schooner was sold to New York investors who converted her to a privateer and put her under Boyle's command. During a five-and-a-half-month cruise in the waters around the British Isles, Boyle and *Chasseur* took an estimated forty-five prizes before returning to Baltimore.[38] On his arrival in British waters, Boyle dispatched a "proclamation" to London to be posted on the bulletin at Lloyds:

> Whereas, It has become customary with the admirals of Great Britain, commanding small forces on the coast of the United States,

> particularly with Sir John Borlaise Warren and Sir Alexander Cochrane, to declare all the coast of said United states in a state of strict and rigorous blockade without possessing the power to justify such a declaration or stationing an adequate force to maintain said blockade;
>
> I do, therefore, by virtue of the power and authority in me vested (possessing sufficient force), declare all the ports, harbors, bays, creeks, rivers, inlets, outlets, islands and seacoast of the United Kingdom of Great Britain and Ireland in a state of strict and rigorous blockade....[39]

Boyle's taunting attitude was typical of American privateers, who gave their ships such names as *Black Joke*, *Teazer*, *Orders in Council*, *Saucy Jack*, *Macaroni*, *Right of Search*, and *Impertinent*.

Baltimore seems to have launched more privateers than any other American seaport. According to one source,[40] Baltimore accounted for 130 privateers, with New York a distant second at forty-five. Another source, counting states rather than ports, puts Massachusetts at the top with 150 privateers commissioned, Maryland second at 112, and New York third with 102. This same source contends that New York City fitted out more privateers than any other city.[41]

Massachusetts's lead among the states may be a result of its large number of individual ports, including Boston, Salem, New Bedford, Marblehead, and Gloucester. Salem alone is said to have dispatched forty privateers during the conflict, including eight that set out within ten days of the declaration of war. Only thirty-six privateers sailed from southern ports—thirteen from Charleston alone. Charleston's *Saucy Jack* captured more British ships than all the privateers of Savannah and New Orleans combined.[42] In early 1814, a writer to the *Naval Chronicle* reported, "The *Saucy Jack*, that recently sailed from Charlestown upon her *sixth cruise*, is stated to have destroyed property on the sea to the amount of *a million of dollars*!"[43]

It is estimated that American privateers captured more than two thousand British ships during the War of 1812, arousing considerable anxiety among the influential commercial class, which bore most of the losses and the escalating cost of engaging in trade. The evidence suggests that the concerns of Britain's merchants and financiers pressured the government to bring the conflict to an end. The merchants of Glasgow, for example, adopted a resolution on

17 September 1814 that illustrates the "heat and alarm" with which they viewed the privateers' depredations:

> Resolved. That the number of American privateers with which our channels have been infested, the audacity with which they have approached our coasts, and the success with which their enterprise has been attended have proved injurious to our commerce, humbling to our pride, and discreditable to the directors of our naval power, whose flag till late waved over every sea and triumphed over every rival. That there is reason to believe that in a short space of less than 24 months above 800 vessels have been captured by that power whose maritime strength we have hitherto impolitically held in scorn.[44]

Earlier that year, correspondents to the *Naval Chronicle* expressed dismay at the apparent impotence of the Royal Navy:

> The insurance between Bristol and Waterford or Cork is now three times higher than it was when we were at war with all Europe! The admiralty lords have been overwhelmed with letters of complaint or remonstrance; public meetings have been held in Liverpool and Bristol, by the merchants and ship-owners, and many several strictures passed upon the public conduct of those at the head of the naval department.... But the truth is, that our navy contains scarcely a single sloop that is fairly a match for the weakest American built vessel of that class of ships of war. And most of them are so obviously deficient, that their commanders, whatever be their character for valour and skill, run the risk of compromising their reputations in the event of a battle with an American, almost without chance of victory.[45]

Two themes emerge in such complaints. Despite the substantial numerical advantage of the Royal Navy, privateers and the U.S. Navy were seriously disrupting British commerce and maritime trade, and their success is to be attributed to the unique skills of American seamen, officers, and ship-builders.

The grudging admiration that Americans won for their seamanship and warfare is revealed in the novel *Tom Cringle's Log*, originally serialized in *Blackwood's* magazine of London beginning in 1829. The author, Michael Scott, had been a merchant in Jamaica, and he wrote vividly from his own seafaring experiences during the war:

> I don't like Americans. I never did and never shall like them. I have seldom met an American gentleman in the large and complete sense of the term. I have no wish to eat with them, drink with them, deal with or consort with them in any way; but let me tell the whole truth—*nor* fight with them, were it not for the laurels to be acquired by overcoming an enemy so brave, determined and alert, and every way so worthy of one's steel as they have always proved. In gunnery and small-arm practice we were as thoroughly weathered on by the Americans as we overtopped them in the bull-dog courage with which our boarders handled those genuine English weapons—the cutlass and the pike. In the field, or grappling in mortal combat on the blood-slippery quarter-deck of an enemy's vessel, a British soldier or sailor is the bravest of the brave. No soldier or sailor of any country, saving and excepting those damned Yankees, can stand against them.[46]

Two decades after the war, the Frenchman Alexis de Toqueville admired the reckless daring of American seamen:

> The European sailor navigates with prudence; he only sets sail when the weather is favorable; if an unfortunate accident befalls him, he puts into port; at night he furls a portion of his canvas, and when a whitening billow intimates the vicinity of land, he checks his way and takes an observation of the sun. But the American neglects these precautions and braves these dangers. He weighs anchor in the midst of tempestuous gales; by night and day he spreads his sheets to the winds; he repairs as he goes along such damage as his vessel may have sustained in the storm; and when he at last approaches the term of his voyage, he darts onward to the

> shore as if he already descried a port. The Americans are often shipwrecked, but no trader crosses the sea so rapidly.[47]

The American reputation for ferocity in battle was won in encounters like that of three British warships with Captain Sam Reid of the privateer *General Armstrong*. In the waning days of the war, Reid and his small crew made a stand "as close to a 'Thermopylae' as any American fighting men have yet come."[48] On 26 September 1814 Captain Reid, looking for a safe place to restock his ship with fresh water, sailed the *General Armstrong* into the harbor of Fayal, one of the larger islands in the Portuguese Azores. Thirty-one years old and the son of a British naval officer who joined the American cause after being captured during the Revolutionary War, the Connecticut-born Reid had been at sea since age eleven and had served as a midshipman in the navy before joining the merchant fleet. Reid's ship has been described as a schooner (Roosevelt) and a brigantine (Stivers); she could have been either at one time or another, since the designation was determined mainly by the rigging and many smaller American ships could be rigged either way, depending upon the duty and the weather. A privateer sailing out of New York under a series of captains, the *General Armstrong* had had a remarkably successful career, capturing twenty-four British prizes.

A Portuguese port, Fayal was technically neutral, and Reid should have been safe from attack as long as he remained within the harbor. But the fine points of international law were sometimes ignored in the heat of a conflict, particularly with regard to privateers, whom British officers regarded as little more than pirates. Within several hours of the *General Armstrong*'s arrival in the Portuguese harbor, her lookout spotted a sail outside the harbor waiting for a pilot to bring her in.

The sail belonged to HMS *Carnation*, a brig of eighteen guns under the command of Captain George Bentham. As the *Carnation* drifted into the harbor, the cautious Reid ordered his men to put out the sweeps and row their ship closer to the shore, where she could dock under the guns of Fayal castle. While it was unlikely that the Portuguese gunners would come to the Americans' aid, the shallow waters in which the *General Armstrong* waited would prevent the larger *Carnation* from getting too close. Reid dropped his anchors and attached springs to the cables to allow him better to bring his guns to bear on any hostile ship that approached his vulnerable anchorage.

Carnation carried twice the firepower of the smaller *General Armstrong*, whose chief armament was a long twenty-four-pounder mounted on a pivot amidships, and six nine-pound long guns, mounted three to a side. The only weapons in which her ninety-man crew was not deficient were small arms—muskets and pistols—which they had seized from a multitude of British captives. Reid soon discovered that the British position was much stronger than he had realized. Toward sundown, the remaining ships of a British squadron—the seventy-four-gun *Plantagenet* under Captain Robert Floyd, and the thirty-eight-gun frigate *Rota*, under Captain Phillip Somerville—sailed into the harbor. Like the *Carnation*, they were carrying British troops to Jamaica for the planned invasion of New Orleans.

Vastly outnumbered and with no escape possible, Reid might honorably have evacuated his crew and sought safety in the town, where the American Consul, John B. Dabney, could have arranged for their protection. But Reid was made of sterner stuff, and he responded to the threat by preparing for battle:

> Reid ordered his men and boys to battle stations.... Every gunner, every layer, every powder monkey was at his post. Tubbed matches were lit. Swabs, wormers, linstocks, rammers, ball racks, bags of grape, all were set out in their proper places. Boarding nets were spread clear around the schooner—not past the shrouds, as would have been done if a boarding party were expected directly from another vessel, but below the gunnels outside; for if the British boarded at all it would have to be from small boats.[49]

Word spread quickly through city that a small American schooner was preparing to take on three British warships. By early evening, the entire dock area and every space in town that offered a view of the harbor was packed with eager spectators. They would not be disappointed: When darkness fell, several British boats—exactly how many is subject to dispute—carrying as many as thirty armed men began to row toward the *General Armstrong* in what may have been an attempt to provoke Reid into firing the first shot. The privateer, it seems, was happy to oblige, and fired a volley from his guns and muskets. The British boats hesitated then returned fire from their muskets and from guns mounted in their bows, killing a man on the *General Armstrong* and wounding another. Reid ordered a second broadside, and the British boats retreated.

The American consul protested the violation of Fayal's neutrality, and the Portuguese governor penned a letter of protest to Captain Floyd, who ignored it. He had induced Reid to fire first, and the necessary provocation was duly noted. As far as Floyd was concerned, Reid had violated Fayal's neutrality, and the British had no choice but to protect themselves from this American hothead.

An hour after the first hesitant attack, a much larger group of British boats was assembled behind *Carnation* and dispatched to the *General Armstrong*. Exactly how many boats and sailors were sent against the *General Armstrong* is also disputed. Estimates range from twenty boats with 400 men[50] to seven boats with 180 men.[51] The boats were under the command of Lieutenant William Matterface, and each carried a carronade in the bow. For the first part of the assault, the boats were accompanied by *Carnation*, which blocked the Americans' path to the open sea. *Carnation* approached as closely as the harbor's depth allowed, from which point the boats rowed behind a rocky reef near the privateer, where they remained until the attack began in earnest around midnight.

As the British moved in, the Americans opened up with the twenty-four-pound pivot gun and the long nines. The British returned fire with their carronades, one of which knocked the Americans' pivot gun off its mount. It was soon apparent that the British plan was to divide their force, half the men attacking the *General Armstrong*'s bow and half going after the starboard quarter. Reid split his force in two to meet them, assigning First Lieutenant Frederick Worth to lead the men at the bow, with Reid himself leading the aft division.

Both sides fired at each other with cannon and carronades until the British came alongside the privateer and secured their open boats below the angle at which the American guns could reach them. The fighting became savage as the British mounted the privateer's sides and cut through the heavy netting. As the British seamen struggled to climb the slippery hull, the Americans fired from point-blank range with muskets and pistols. When the protective netting gave way and the British clawed their way up to the bulkheads, the Americans speared them with pikes and hacked at them with cutlasses and hatchets.

There were reports that Americans poured boiling water and pitch onto the crowded open decks of the enemy boats. They also climbed out on the spars until they were over the British boats and dropped the heaviest cannon shot they could carry. Falling eighty feet or more, the shot smashed through the floor and sank the boat. As the attack at the stern began to waver under Reid's savage defense, American sailors counter-attacked by leaping into the assault boats, slashing and clubbing their way through any enemy seamen still on board.

> The slaughter among the English was appalling. Their boats floated free, filled with dead and dying. Many men panicked and jumped overboard to swim to shore, so that the stretch between *General Armstrong* and the beach below the castle was stippled with bobbing heads.[52]

After a half-hour of intense fighting, the boats still afloat at the aft quarter gave up the fight and retreated to *Carnation.* But in the bow, the American force was faltering, and the attackers were gaining the deck. Second Lieutenant Alexander O. Williams died when a musket ball pierced his forehead, and the other two lieutenants who led the forward division were wounded. Seeing the danger, Reid led his now victorious aft division into the melee at the *General Armstrong*'s bow. Hacking, stabbing, and shooting their way into the midst of the attackers, Reid's reinforcements quickly turned the tide. The remainder of the British assault force fell back into what boats were still afloat and either fled to shore or rowed back to the squadron. In forty minutes it was all over.

The casualty count among the Americans was light—two dead, seven wounded. The figures reported for the British vary greatly. Roosevelt quotes thirty-four killed and eighty-six wounded, including four officers, among whom was the brave Matterface, who led the attack. Two of the attacking British boats were sunk, two were captured, and three made it back to the squadron. The estimated total of 120 British casualties was one of the highest such figures for a sea battle during the war. The British were undaunted, however, and the next day, the dead buried and the wounded cared for, Floyd moved the *Carnation* closer to shore, intending to take apart the *General Armstrong* with his superior fire power.

But once again, the British underestimated Reid's determination and the resilience of his crew, which worked through the night to remount the long twenty-four. As she moved into range, *Carnation* opened up, but her first volley was high and flew into the town, shattering a woman's thigh, killing a boy, and maiming some livestock. Captain Bentham soon found his range, and he began to hull the privateer. But Reid's gunners found theirs as well, and though fighting back with fewer than half the guns of *Carnation*, *General Armstrong* managed to drive the brig back into the harbor, to the cheers of the crowds on shore, by scoring more deadly hits than her better-armed adversary.

Reid knew that time was not on his side, however. He and his crew had already gone well beyond what honor required, so, burying his few dead at sea and sending his wounded to shore, Reid nailed the American flag to the mast, threw his cannon overboard, and scuttled the ship. The captain was the last to leave, remaining on the deck of the sinking schooner until all of his crew was safely off. The *General Armstrong* did not have far to sink in the shallow water. Shortly after Reid abandoned ship, the British arrived, took possession of what remained above the water, and set it afire.

The confrontation, however, was not yet over. The British claimed that two of Reid's crewmen were deserters from their fleet and sent a force into town to capture them. Reid and his men moved into the hills, commandeered a monastery, and awaited the attack. The British found them but, having been bested by the privateers three times in three days, decided not to attack the well-defended fortification and returned to their ships.

After making repairs, burying their dead, and tending to the many wounded, Floyd's force finally sailed away on 4 October 1814. They had wasted eight days in a port they had entered earlier merely to replenish their fresh water. Those eight days were exceptionally costly to the British effort in North America. Reid's stubborn defense delayed the enemy squadron's arrival at New Orleans for the British assault, perhaps saving that city. Roosevelt's assessment that "[f]ew regular commanders could have done as well as Captain Reid"[53] conforms to Andrew Jackson's: "If there had been no battle of Fayal ... there would have been no battle of New Orleans."[54]

VII

Incidents like Reid's delay of Floyd's squadron and the damage inflicted on British commercial interests by the hundreds of privateers stalking the sea lanes suggest that privateers played an important role in forcing Britain to the peace table. Some historians have questioned whether privateering was a prudent use of American resources in the War of 1812, but the losses inflicted on the British by America's 526 or so commissioned privateers were unquestionably substantial. The most conservative estimate of 600 vessels lost would have been an economic blow, even for the world's leading maritime power.[55]

Whatever damage the American privateers inflicted on the enemy, only a fraction of them were financially successful, for the spoils were unequally distributed. As many as three hundred commissioned privateers made no captures at all during the war; those who did averaged more than ten apiece.[56] Even for the successful ships, profits were modest, and many failed to cover the considerable expenses of a cruise.[57] Most of the privateers' success came early in the war, as did the U.S. Navy's. As Britain tightened its blockade and increased the number of warships devoted to the North American station, privateering became more dangerous and less rewarding. Fewer privateers were launched with each passing year. In Baltimore, for example, forty-five privateers were built in 1812, twenty-three in 1813, and only eight in 1814. Word of a pending peace treaty reached America in the early months of 1815, and only one privateer was built in Baltimore that year.[58]

Astute investors seem to have appreciated, even early in the war, the difficulty of profiting from privateering. Adams describes one attempt to shift the risk to the government:

> In November 1812 the owners of twenty-four New York privateers sent to Congress a memorial declaring that the profits of private naval war were by no means equal to the hazards, and that the spirit of privateering stood in danger of extinction unless the government would consent in some manner to grant a bounty for the capture or destruction of the enemy's property.[59]

The secretary of the Treasury, Albert Gallatin, opposed the request, arguing that such concessions were unlikely to attract more privateers to the war effort. He was confident that privateering, like any other form of gambling, would attract more adventurers than it could support. Congress at first concurred with Gallatin and offered no support. As the war continued, however, and the British blockade tightened, Congress relented and in August 1813 enacted a series of subsidies, including a reduction by one-third of the federal duties (previously amounting to 40 percent of value) levied on prize goods. Congress also approved a twenty-five-dollar bounty for every British seaman captured or killed in combat, payment of half the estimated value of any enemy vessel destroyed,[60] and the provision of a pension for any privateer wounded or disabled in the line of duty, or to his dependents if he died in action.

Could the United States have achieved more at sea without the privateers? In his *History of the United States, 1801–1817*, published late in the nineteenth century, Henry Adams speculated that the money might have been better spent on the U.S. Navy. Evaluating the bounties and subsidies Congress provided to privateers in August 1813, Adams wrote,

> These complaints and palliations tended to show that the privateer cost the public more than the equivalent vessel would have cost. If instead of five hundred privateers of all sizes and efficiency, the government would have kept twenty-five sloops-of-war constantly at sea destroying the enemy's commerce, the result would have been about the same as far as concerned injury to the enemy, while in another respect the government would have escaped one of its chief difficulties. Nothing injured the Navy so much as privateering. Seamen commonly preferred the harder but more profitable and shorter cruise in a privateer, where fighting was not expected or wished, to the strict discipline and murderous battles of government ships, where wages were low and prize money scarce.[61]

The Massachusetts port of Marblehead provided 120 of its citizens to the navy, Adams observed, while 726 served on privateers. "[M]ore careful inquiry might show," he speculated, "that, valuable as privateers were, the government would have done better to retain all military in its own hands." A few years after Adams published his history, Admiral Alfred T. Mahan undertook a comparison of the navy's record with the privateers'. In *Seapower in Its Relation to the War of 1812*, he revealed that "the result showed itself in a fact which has never been appreciated, and perhaps never noted, that the national ships-of-war were far more effective as prize takers than were the privateers."[62] Mahan concluded that the U.S. Navy's twenty-two men-of-war averaged 7.5 prizes each, while the privateers averaged only 2.5 prizes per ship.[63] With navy ships deemed three times more effective than privateers, so the argument goes, national resources might have been more effectively devoted to public ships rather than to privateers.

The debate over alternative courses of action might be interesting to historians and military theorists, but the policy favored by Adams and Mahan never occurred to anyone in an official capacity at the time. This is not to say Adams and Mahan were wrong, only that the benefits of hindsight were not available to those directing the war. Most of the navy's successful men-of-war had been commissioned before the war by presidents who by 1812 were long dead (George Washington) or out of power (John Adams). In contrast, the men in power immediately before and during the war squandered public resources on ineffective naval strategies (Jefferson's hundreds of useless gunboats, for example, or Madison's unused double-decker behemoths) that yielded payoffs vastly smaller than the 2.5 prizes per privateer cited by Mahan. However inefficient the privateers were, they sailed at little or no public expense, effectively harassing the British, and their remuneration was based on their performance.

CHAPTER EIGHTEEN

MONTREAL, AND BACK TO THE NIAGARA

General William Henry Harrison's victory over General Henry Proctor at the Battle of the Thames in early October 1813 completed the sweep of the British and their Indian allies from the western states and territories and Upper Canada. Except for the isolated outpost on Mackinac Island off the northern tip of Michigan, the British presence in North America now extended no farther west than Burlington at the far edge of Lake Ontario. Following his joint victory with Perry, Harrison was ordered by Secretary of War John Armstrong to take his force of regulars to the American base at Sackets Harbor, New York, close to the border with Lower Canada, where it was expected that the land war with Great Britain would intensify. Perry moved his victorious American force across Lake Erie from Malden to Buffalo, where he and Harrison were fêted by the citizens. Soon afterward, Harrison took his troops to Sackets Harbor at the eastern reaches of Lake Ontario.

Granted a leave of absence, Harrison visited Washington, D.C., where he was celebrated as a conquering hero, and then returned to Ohio to command the American forces in the northwest. The conniving Armstrong, however, did not care for Harrison, one of the army's few competent generals at the time. Taking advantage of the arrival of peace in the northwestern states and territories, the secretary began to annoy and undermine Harrison at every opportunity, mostly by communicating directly with the general's subordinates rather than through the general himself, as protocol required. By May 1814, Harrison had had his fill of Armstrong's backstabbing. He submitted his "resignation" to the president while urging his supporters in Kentucky to appeal to Madison to reject it. The president was ill, however, and convalescing at Montpelier. Armstrong accepted Harrison's resignation and appointed Andrew Jackson to replace him. Thus ended William Henry Harrison's involvement in the War of 1812.

Armstrong's campaign to undermine a successful general was typical of the relations between American politicians and the leadership of the U.S. Army during much of the nineteenth century. While the navy managed to avoid political pressure and maintain a system of promotion based on merit and seniority, the general command of the army was heavily influenced by politics. Presidents Jefferson and Madison, in particular, used the power of appointment to ensure that the army's leadership was in the hands of reliable partisans, regardless of competence.

The appointment of Major General Henry Dearborn was typical of the partisanship that undermined the nation's ability to wage war against a more powerful enemy. Born in New Hampshire and trained as a physician, Dearborn embraced the revolutionary cause and served loyally and effectively in the War of Independence. A militia officer, he participated in the conflicts at Bunker Hill, Quebec, Freeman's Farm, Ticonderoga, Valley Forge, Monmouth, and Yorktown. Elected to the House of Representatives from Maine, Dearborn was a rare Republican (Jeffersonian) in Federalist New England, a distinction that led to his appointment as secretary of war in the Jefferson administration. President Madison replaced him with another loyal Republican, William Eustis of Massachusetts, and gave Dearborn the post of federal customs collector in Boston. When war was declared in 1812 and Madison needed politically reliable men to lead the army, he appointed Dearborn to the command of the critically important northeastern theater, despite his lack of experience commanding a large force.

Old, ill, and lacking energy, Dearborn was less than effective in that command. American forces in the northeast managed to do as well as they did in the first months of the war because of the skill and energy of younger officers like Jacob Brown, Winfield Scott, Oliver Hazard Perry, and Zebulon Pike, who led the men and did the fighting. On 8 June 1813, Dearborn wrote to Armstrong, "My ill state of health renders it extremely painful to attend to the current duties; and unless my health improves soon, I fear I shall be compelled to retire to someplace where my mind may be more at ease for a short time."[1] A week later, his subordinate Morgan Lewis wrote to Armstrong, "I have doubts whether he will ever again be fit for service.... [H]e has been repeatedly in a state of convalescence, but relapses on the least agitation of mind."[2]

By mid-1813, the British were back on the attack, raiding American towns and forts across the Niagara River. After Colonel Charles Boerstler's demoralizing defeat at Beaver Dams in June, Madison and Armstrong decided it was time for Dearborn to go. On 6 July 1813, Armstrong wrote to him, "I have the President's orders to express to you the decision that you retire from the command of District No. 9, and of the troops within the same, until your health be re-established and until further orders."[3]

A week later, on 15 July, Dearborn was replaced by his newly-appointed second in command, General James Wilkinson, one of the most sinister men ever to wear the uniform of a U.S. Army officer. One subordinate officer complained about the change in command, "age and fatuity were being replaced by age and imbecility."[4] Even Thomas Jefferson, whose intense partisanship forced these incompetents upon a young nation at risk, confided in early 1813 to Benjamin Rush, "So wretched a succession of generals never before destroyed the fairest expectations of a nation."[5]

Like Dearborn, Wilkinson had been an officer during the War of Independence. A Republican, he survived Jefferson's reduction in strength of the standing army and the partisan purge of one-third of the officer corps. When the United States acquired a new garrison at New Orleans with the Louisiana Purchase, Wilkinson received the appointment to its command.

During the Revolution, Wilkinson served with John Armstrong on the staff of General Horatio Gates, a vain and jealous man who spent much of the war trying to undermine the command of General Washington.[6] Here Wilkinson had cut his teeth as a conspirator against his country. His reputation for gossip and scheming brought his service on Gates's staff to an early end, and he became the clothier general for the army. Lingering allegations of corruption forced him to resign from the army in 1781. Later in that decade, Wilkinson worked as an intermediary between Spanish New Orleans and the western territories, notably Kentucky, and he is alleged to have sworn allegiance to the king of Spain.

Spain eventually lost confidence in Wilkinson, but the young American republic, apparently suffering from selective amnesia, did not. In 1791, Wilkinson received a commission in the U.S. Army and began his second military career. Jefferson appointed him the first governor of the Louisiana Territory in 1805, but his tenure was cut short by the numerous complaints about his conduct. In the waning days of the Jefferson administration, Wilkinson was given command of the troops protecting New Orleans from foreign incursions. Nine hundred soldiers died of disease in the pestilent swamps from which he refused to move them. Another 166 deserted, and forty officers died or resigned.[7]

Wilkinson's willingness to turn on colleagues and collaborators kept him in the good graces of the Republican administrations of the early nineteenth century despite his contemptible lack of integrity and neglect of duty. After conspiring with Jefferson's rival Aaron Burr to establish, with Spain's help, an independent nation out of a portion of the Louisiana Territory, he revealed the plot to Jefferson and testified against Burr at his trial. The great nineteenth-century historian Frederick Jackson Turner called Wilkinson "the most consummate artist in treason that the nation ever possessed."[8] More colorfully, Winfield Scott recalled that "Serving under Wilkinson was like being married to a prostitute."[9]

By 1811, President Madison had concluded that the cost of keeping Wilkinson in some official capacity vastly outweighed whatever benefit he brought to the party, and he ordered his court-martial on a number of charges. An inconclusive ruling on Christmas Day of that year left the final decision to Madison. Never decisive when it came to partisan issues, Madison left Wilkinson in an important command in America's deficient army.

> Madison's handling of the Wilkinson case was damaging to his presidency and was probably the worst mistake he made while in the White House.... [B]y dodging his responsibility, Madison

> harmed the war effort, hurt the army's morale, and in effect became a buck-passer instead of a courageous leader.[10]

Thus acquitted, Wilkinson resumed his command at New Orleans, where he continued to offend many of the leading citizens and federal officials. By 1813, his mismanagement was so notorious that many members of the Louisiana militia refused to serve under him and Louisiana's two senators told Madison they would go over to the opposition unless Wilkinson was removed.[11] In the perverse politics of the Madison administration, the solution was to promote Wilkinson to an even more important position: command of America's most troubled theater of war—the New York–Canadian border. In a letter dated 12 March, Armstrong offered encouragement to his friend:

> Why should you remain in your land of cypress when patriotism and ambition equally invite to one where grows the laurel? Again, the men of the North and East want you; those of the South and West are less sensible to your merits and less anxious to have you among them. I speak to you with a frankness due to you and to myself, and again advise, Come to the North, and come quickly! If our cards be well played, we may renew the scene at Saratoga.[12]

Wilkinson's immediate subordinate in his new command was the equally incompetent Major General Wade Hampton, who led several thousand troops in Vermont. A Virginian by birth, Hampton had served during the Revolutionary War before moving to South Carolina, where he became one of the state's wealthiest planters and a leader in the Republican Party. He joined the army in 1808 and by 1813 was in command of the Lake Champlain sector, nominally under General Dearborn. Although he had little military experience or knowledge, Hampton was, like Dearborn and Wilkinson, politically well-connected. He accepted the appointment to Vermont with the understanding that, as a very important person, he would report directly to the secretary of war. Given Hampton's character, it was not an auspicious appointment. "In an age of stiff-necked individualists he was conspicuous for his overweening pride, hair-trigger sensitivity, obstinacy, and rigid code of personal honor."[13]

Hampton also hated James Wilkinson with a passion, regarding him "as something too corrupt and beneath contempt for a general to deign to notice." Wilkinson's opinion of Hampton was no better, and "from 1808 onward, their feud had increasingly split the army's officers into hostile cliques."[14] Notwithstanding these explosive conflicts, Madison and Armstrong charged these two antagonists with working together to turn the tide against the British forces along the troubled northeastern border.

The partisanship that afflicted the army's general staff was also evident in the cabinet, where the incompetence of Madison's appointments rivaled that of his generals. Congressman John C. Calhoun lamented, "Our executive officers are most incompetent men. We are literally boren down under the effects of errors and mismanagement."[15] Madison's first secretary of war, William Eustis, had no talent for his position, and he was encouraged to resign in December 1812. His replacement, John Armstrong of New York, was a Republican partisan only slightly more competent.

> Although knowledgeable about military affairs, Armstrong was abrasive and indolent and a well known enemy of the Virginia dynasty. In 1783 he had written the Newburgh Letters inciting the Continental Army to mutiny.... He also had a reputation for intrigue, a reputation that was largely justified.[16]

The ambitious Armstrong had his eye on the presidency, and he appreciated the political utility of a little military glory.[17] Knowing that a productive relationship was unlikely to develop between two leaders as high-strung and incompetent as Wilkinson and Hampton, Armstrong traveled to the front in late summer, establishing his headquarters at Sackets Harbor on 5 September 1813. His purpose was to goad his generals, partly for the good of the country, but also for the good of his political career, which would benefit from a victory. After a series of meetings with the most senior military leaders in the northeastern theater—including the corrupt Wilkinson, the timid Chauncey, and the mediocre Morgan Lewis—Armstrong decided on a strategy that had no hope of succeeding.

II

It was Armstrong's intention to mount an amphibious attack against Kingston, right across the lake from Sackets Harbor, but Chauncey, horrified at the prospect of risking his ships and reputation in actual combat, argued that the better target was Montreal, 140 miles north east down the St. Lawrence River, where his ships would not have to be used because of rapids, rocks, and shallow water. Wilkinson, meanwhile, in an effort to delay and obfuscate, opposed whatever Armstrong wanted. When Armstrong came around to the Wilkinson view, the general's view was suddenly clouded with second thoughts.

The question of which way to attack was still unsettled by mid-October, when reports reached the American command that the British had used the delay to reinforce Kingston. Confronted with a better prepared opponent, Armstrong reluctantly agreed to an attack on Montreal following a plan that Wilkinson's council of war had formulated back in August: Wilkinson's force would move down the St. Lawrence, converging at Montreal with Hampton's force coming up from Vermont.

Charged with leading a poorly prepared army against a well-fortified target with harsh winter weather bearing down on them, Wilkinson opted for delay. He sailed west to Fort George at the mouth of the Niagara River, ostensibly to muster the troops left there under the command of Winfield Scott and personally lead them east to Sackets Harbor for the attack on Montreal. His real motive was probably to get away from Sackets Harbor and Armstrong's meddling. Wilkinson stayed at Fort George for nearly a month before returning to Sackets Harbor on 4 October, giving every appearance of being ill. He was taking laudanum (containing opium) as a cure, which gave him a "giddy head." According to one officer, during the journey down the river, "the general became very merry, and sung and repeated stories."[18] Despite his illness and the medication, the "scientific soldier" reassumed command of the force that Brigadier General Jacob Brown had been organizing in his absence in the vicinity of Sackets Harbor.

As Wilkinson assembled his force on Lake Ontario, his nominal subordinate, General Hampton, was readying the second prong of the attack at Burlington, Vermont. Because the two refused to communicate with each other,

Armstrong relayed Wilkinson's orders to Hampton to attack Montreal from the south as Wilkinson moved in from the west. As Wilkinson whiled away his time at Fort George, Hampton mobilized his poorly trained army and marched them toward Montreal on 19 September.

The army that Wilkinson led out of Sackets Harbor numbered about seven thousand men and was organized into four brigades under John Boyd, Leonard Covington, Robert Swartwout, and Jacob Brown. Despite Brown's efforts during Wilkinson's absence at Fort George, the short notice for a major operation against an entrenched enemy in hostile weather had left many gaps and deficiencies in the operation. Supplies were inadequate, there were not enough boats to carry the troops downriver, and Chauncey had exploited the confusion in command to further extract himself and his ships from the operation.

The attack was finally launched down the St. Lawrence in late October. British warships under Yeo came in behind them from Lake Ontario, meeting no resistance as they shot up the camps on Grenadier Island and destroyed some of the boats that were to carry the Americans down river. Despite these difficulties, by 6 November the American force had passed Ogdensburg, where a heavy fog had prevented the British batteries in Prescott from doing much damage. Colonel Alexander Macomb moved his force onto the north bank of the river to sweep away any British resistance and artillery that could damage the boats or attack the troops as they moved northeast down the river to Montreal.

But as the Americans focused on the British forces assembling downriver, Major General Francis de Rottenburg, following Prevost's instructions,[19] sent out a British force from Kingston to harass the Americans from the rear. On the north bank of the St. Lawrence, Lieutenant Colonel Joseph Morrison led about nine hundred men behind the advancing Americans, while his naval counterpart, Captain William Mulcaster—unsullied by Chauncey's diffident covering force—led a flotilla of gun boats down the river, attacking and harassing Wilkinson's force whenever the opportunity arose.

Wilkinson did not know as he moved his men toward Montreal that the supporting force under Hampton had already taken itself out of the campaign through incompetence and timidity. Concerned that what he believed was a large British force at Île aux Noix in the Richelieu River, near the north end of Lake Champlain, might attack his flank, Hampton, with Armstrong's approval, led his troops in mid-October forty miles due west from Odelltown on the U.S.-Canadian border to Four Corners, New York, on the Chateauguay River.

Hampton's force of four thousand men moved north from Four Corners on 21 October and made good progress until the 25th, when, north of the town of Spears, his advanced guard discovered a British-Canadian defensive work built of several lines of abatis with a light artillery emplacement covering the field in front of it.[20] Hampton did not realize that the fortification was defended by no more than eight hundred men, comprising militia, Canadian fencibles, French-Canadian Voltigeurs, and some Indians under the command of Lieutenant Colonel Charles-Michel d'Irumberry de Salaberry, a French-Canadian who had served with the British in Europe during the Napoleonic Wars.

Hampton began the attack by sending Colonel Robert Purdy and the fifteen hundred men of the First Infantry brigade on a night mission to flank the enemy. Purdy would attack from the rear the next day as Hampton's main force attacked from the front. But Purdy got lost in a heavy rain storm and, misled by his guides, stumbled into a Canadian force waiting for him on both banks of the Chateauguay.[21] As Hampton waited for his plan to unfold, a messenger arrived from Armstrong ordering him to construct winter quarters for ten thousand men. Unsure whether this order was an addition to his earlier orders to attack Montreal or a replacement of them, the prickly Hampton sent Armstrong his resignation. He would have marched his men back to Plattsburgh had not the sound of musket fire indicated that Purdy's force had made contact.

Despite his anger and the submission of his resignation, Hampton moved his force forward to attack the British and relieve Purdy. He did so, however, with timid parade-ground maneuvers conducted at a safe distance. The Canadian defenders responded with jeers and cat calls from behind their fortifications. Hampton interpreted the loud and boisterous cries from the enemy as proof they were more numerous than he had thought. Leaving Purdy to extract himself as best he could, Hampton withdrew from the attack and the next day, after a council of war with his officers, gave up the effort altogether. He marched back to Four Corners, leaving Wilkinson to attack Montreal on his own.[22]

Three weeks later, Hampton received orders from Wilkinson ordering him to meet him at St. Regis on the St. Lawrence and to bring with him thirty days' rations for the seven thousand or so men under Wilkinson's command. The orders were ludicrous—Hampton could barely provision his own force, and the absence of fodder had forced him to send his horses back to Plattsburgh. Even if such supplies were available, it was impossible to get them to Wilkinson over the primitive trails connecting Hampton to the St. Lawrence. In response, Hampton sent Colonel Henry Atkinson north to find Wilkinson and give him the bad news.

On the day that Hampton received his orders from Wilkinson, the American force on the St. Lawrence had advanced eighteen miles past Ogdensburg and was preparing to tackle the Long Sault—eight continuous miles of rough rapids that could be safely navigated only during daylight—as Canadian farmers took pot shots at them from the river bank.[23] To protect the vulnerable force, Jacob Brown assumed command of a combined force of 2,500 men on the north bank and moved north, sweeping away whatever resistance the British posed, while Brigadier General John Boyd's brigade followed as a rear guard to protect the Americans from Morrison's advancing force.

Brown's force, with Winfield Scott in the vanguard, reported on 11 November that the north bank of the river was swept clean of enemies as far as Cornwall. Wilkinson thereupon ordered his men into the boats for the long, arduous descent through the Long Sault. The night before, they had moored at Crysler Island, just off the north bank of John Crysler's farm. As the troops prepared for the run through the rapids in rain and sleet, Boyd reported to Wilkinson that Morrison and Mulcaster were poised to attack them from behind, and marched his 2,500 men upstream to confront the advancing British.

Boyd, unfortunately, was not a good choice to lead the troops against a fast-closing British force eager for a fight. As Boerstler's commanding officer, Boyd bore some responsibility for the disaster at Beaver Dams earlier in the year. His then commanding officer, Morgan Lewis, described Boyd as "A compound of ignorance, vanity and petulance, with nothing to recommend him but that species of bravery in the field which is vaporing, boisterous, stifling reflection, blinding observation, and better adapted to the bully than the sailor."[24] Boyd's fellow officers in the Montreal campaign held similar views. According to Adams, "[Jacob] Brown was said to have threatened to resign rather than serve under him, and Winfield Scott, who that day was with Macomb and Brown in the advance, described Boyd as amiable and respectable in a subordinate position, but 'vacillating and imbecile beyond all endurance as a chief under high responsibilities.'"[25]

Morrison, whose force numbered only about nine hundred, responded to the pending American assault by digging in on an open field at the western end of John Crysler's farm. The north end of his line was protected by a swampy forest, while the south end extended to the banks of the St. Lawrence, where Mulcaster covered the right flank and the field before it with artillery from his gunboats anchored off shore. Had Brown or Macomb commanded the rearguard, he hardly could have escaped destruction, but Boyd, instead of organizing a coordinated attack with artillery support, pitched his regiments into action as they came up. Struggling across rain-slick gullies and sodden plowed fields, the Americans stumbled into action piecemeal, never achieving any decisive numerical superiority on the firing line.

At the end of the day, the Americans had failed to dislodge Morrison's force and were beaten back repeatedly. Only the incessant attacks on Morrison's left flank by the Light Dragoons led Colonel John de Barth Walbach saved the Americans from a complete rout. Beaten and bloodied, Boyd's force assembled on the river bank, whence they were rowed to the safety on the southern side. Morrison's small force suffered twenty-three killed and 148 wounded—a fifth of his force—while Boyd's larger force lost 102 killed and 237 wounded.[26]

Despite their victory at Crysler's Farm, Morrison's depleted force returned to Kingston, thus ending any further threat to Wilkinson's rear, and the American force continued to Montreal. Steadily advancing in the rain and sleet, the Americans embarked down the treacherous rapids of the Long Sault on 12 November and days later met up with Jacob Brown's force at Cornwall, sixty miles upstream from Montreal. As Wilkinson and his command began to organize their force at Cornwall for the final thrust at Montreal, Colonel Atkinson caught up with them and gave Wilkinson the message that Hampton's force would not be joining them any time soon and that the requested supplies would not be arriving either. After a council of war, the officers all agreed that it was prudent to break off the campaign and seek secure winter quarters.

For Wilkinson, Hampton's letter offered a timely opportunity to shift the blame of any subsequent failure to his uncooperative subordinate. He wrote to Hampton, "such resolution defeats the grand objects of the campaign in this quarter, which, before the receipt of your letter, were thought to be completely in our power, no suspicion being entertained that you would decline the junction directed, it will oblige us to take post at French Mills, on Salmon River, or in their vicinity for the winter."[27]

Although safe from the British, the army spent a miserable winter confronting disease, deprivation, and desertion at French Mills. Hampton had, for all intents and purposes, abandoned Plattsburg for Washington, D.C., as did many of his officers. And absent any leadership, the supply system in northeast New York, such as it was, collapsed into corruption and incompetence until Major General George Izard, Macomb, and Atkinson could get it back in operation. In January, Armstrong ordered Wilkinson to abandon the camp and send Jacob Brown with two thousand men back to Sackets Harbor. Wilkinson and the rest of the force would shift to Plattsburgh, while the sick would be moved across the lake to Burlington, Vermont, where a new hospital had been built to accommodate soldiers suffering from "diarrhea, dysentery, pneumonia, typhus and frostbite."[28] As Armstrong contemplated ways to rid the army of the politically influential Wilkinson, Wilkinson looked for ways to polish his tarnished image and save his career. He decided, notwithstanding Armstrong's orders, that a successful offensive operation might do the trick.

On 27 March 1814, Wilkinson led four thousand men from Plattsburgh north through deep snow to re-engage the British along the Canadian border. The first obstacle as they crossed the border was a stone mill turned into a British outpost on the Lacolle River, defended by a mixed force of about 180 men. Wilkinson attacked, but the British and Canadians resisted stoutly. A relief force sent from the British base at Île aux Noir to the west was beaten back by Alexander Macomb's force. But as the sun set and dark shadows crossed the snowy fields surrounding the mill, whose defenders were nearly out of ammunition, Wilkinson lost what little courage he had and ordered a retreat back to Plattsburgh. Two weeks later, on 11 April, the politically ambitious Armstrong, in desperate need of a victory to advance his career ahead of the equally ambitious James Monroe, relieved Wilkinson of his command. He was replaced by George Izard on 1 May in what would be the beginning of a wholesale cleansing of the army's top command.

Wilkinson later whined that Armstrong had, through "artifice ... deprived me of my sword in the dawn of the campaign."[29] Hampton resigned, and Morgan Lewis and John Boyd were kicked upstairs to positions where they could do little harm. In their places, Armstrong promoted a younger and more energetic corps of officers who had demonstrated courage and success on the battlefield in the early days of this frustrating war. George Izard and Jacob Brown were both promoted to major general, while Alexander Macomb,

Winfield Scott, Eleazar Wheelock Ripley, Edmund Gaines, Daniel Bissell, and Thomas Smith were elevated from colonel to brigadier general. These changes, late in coming, probably did nothing more than allow the Americans to hold the line against the British. The opportunity to make major gains against the poorly led and undermanned British forces in Lower Canada, as Harrison had done in Upper Canada, had been lost.

III

Wilkinson's dismissal in April 1814 coincided with Napoleon's abdication at Fountainbleu, which led to his exile on Elba. With the European war winding down, some in Britain urged a more vigorous campaign against the United States. The *Times* reported on 15 April, "Now that the tyrant Bonaparte has been consigned to infamy, there is no public feeling in this country stronger than that of the indignation against the Americans."[30] Lord Bathurst wrote to Sir George Prevost that Napoleon's defeat would allow more troops and artillery to prosecute the war in North America. Although Wellington had a few months earlier expressed pessimism about Britain's campaign against the Americans, Bathurst was eager to achieve some territorial gains that might tip the balance in Britain's favor as it negotiated a settlement of the conflict.[31]

Bathurst's plan, which did not reach Prevost until the middle of July, had two main objectives: "The first was to guarantee the safety of Canada during the balance of the war. The second was to secure the basis of a satisfactory boundary rectification by enabling British peace commissioners to argue *uti possidetis* (or, for retention of conquered territory)."[32] To execute the plan, Prevost would soon receive another three thousand soldiers, with ten thousand more promised in the near future.

When news of Napoleon's abdication reached Washington, the implications for the war with Britain were not lost on Armstrong, whose northern armies struggled to contain the relatively small British force in Lower Canada. Armstrong was determined to preempt the expected build-up with a quick American offensive. His preferred target remained Kingston. The timid Chauncey, however, remained recalcitrant, so Armstrong instead proposed moving six to eight thousand men across the Niagara frontier for an attack on Burlington, the last British stronghold in Upper Canada, on the western edge of Lake Ontario. He hoped to drive the British out of Upper Canada and force them to shift troops from east to west, leaving Lower Canada vulnerable to attack by Izard, now in command at Sackets Harbor.

Madison's cabinet approved the plan for the assault, which would be led by Major General Brown, the new commander in the Niagara theater. Chauncey promised to arrive at the Niagara River by 1 July to transport Brown's force to Burlington. Armstrong urged Brown, in the meantime, to cross the Niagara and reclaim territory recently lost to the British. The Americans had captured Fort George and its vicinity in May 1813, but the defending troops had since been dispatched to support Wilkinson's ill-fated foray down the St. Lawrence. The British had taken advantage of the thinly stretched American forces along the Niagara front to regain Canadian territory and to cross the river and harass the few remaining American troops and the civilian population.

Under the command of the energetic but inexperienced Major General Phineas Riall, a British force of nearly 600 men crossed the river on 18 December 1813 and attacked the poorly prepared Fort Niagara, killing sixty-five Americans, mostly by bayonet, and capturing 344. Then with 500 regulars and an equal number of Indians, Riall swept through several towns, routing the civilian population and putting houses and farms to the torch, while the Indians took what scalps they could. Less than two weeks later, Riall returned with a larger force, vanquished the militia and took Black Rock and Buffalo. Both settlements and any dwellings that had survived the earlier assault were burned to the ground. "The number of civilians slaughtered was never accurately established," writes Elting. "American reinforcements coming into the area found hogs devouring the dead bodies of some of them amid the charred wreckage of their homes."[33]

By the spring of 1814, the American side of the river was secure again, and the U.S. Army turned its attention to training its soldiers. Recognizing the seriously unprepared condition of the American troops, Armstrong established a "camp of instruction" at Plattsburgh under Izard and another at Buffalo under Winfield Scott. The soldiers at Buffalo, under the direction of Winfield Scott, were trained with an intensity never before seen in an American army. Scott drilled his men up to ten hours a day. Deserters were apprehended, and some were shot. "To prove to his men he meant business, Scott made an example of five convicted deserters," one of Scott's biographer's reports. "He lined them up before a firing squad, all five standing before their newly dug graves. Four of the men met their doom. The fifth, a mere boy, was spared; Scott had directed that the muskets fired at him should be loaded with blanks."[34] Nonetheless, morale improved when the men realized that the object of these training exercises was their safety, health, and well-being.

"Scott knew that there was nothing wrong with the American soldier: given proper training and leadership he could trash redcoats and redskins alike. What he gave ... was intense uniform instruction, based on the excellent 1791 French drill regulations and designed to build a collection of individual regiments into an efficient, tightly coordinated fighting army."[35] He emphasized "daily routine matters such as outposting, night patrolling, guards, sentinels, camp sanitation, police, rules of civility, etiquette and courtesy—'the indispensable outworks of subordination.'"[36] Special attention was given to the camp's "police"—the sanitation and good order that kept troops healthy. Scott insisted that the camp be immaculately clean, and he oversaw the proper preparation of the men's rations.

After a year of hard campaigning in rough weather, the troops' uniforms were in deplorable condition. Blue jackets and light trousers had been shipped to Scott but had been mysteriously diverted to Plattsburgh and Sackets Harbor. Since no dark blue cloth was available in western New York, Scott had two thousand short jackets made from local gray homespun. Some historians have argued that these accidental uniforms were the model for what became the standard dress at West Point, though others attribute the similarity to mere coincidence.[37]

As July approached, the American military leadership in Washington and in the Niagara theater worried that Chauncey's ships would fail to show up as planned to transport Brown's troops across Lake Ontario for the assault on Burlington. In a sharply worded letter to the commodore, Brown demanded that he arrive no later than 10 July.[38] On 3 July, the American force moved across the Niagara River to begin the attack on the British fortifications. Scott, along with Brigadier General Eleazar Wheelock Ripley (the speaker of the Massachusetts house of representatives),[39] commanded a combined force of a little more than 2,700 regulars. They crossed the river in the dark and the two companies landed to the north and south, respectively, of Britain's Fort Erie, still under construction, where Lake Erie spills into the Niagara River. Former congressman Peter B. Porter followed Ripley across the river with a volunteer force of

753 Pennsylvanians and 600 Indians from the Iroquois federation, led by Hog-A-Hoa-Qua, who in turn was supported by the chiefs Red Jacket, Cornplanter, Two Guns, and I-Like-Her.[40] That night Fort Erie was held by only 137 British soldiers, who quickly surrendered to the much larger force after firing a few shots "for the honor of the flag."

The next morning, the Fourth of July, Brown marched his four thousand regulars, volunteers, and Indians north along the western bank of the Niagara toward Fort George on Lake Ontario, where he expected Chauncey's fleet to meet him a week later for the planned invasion. As Brown moved north, with Scott's troops in the van, Riall marched south from the fort to meet them, gathering along the way as many regulars, militiamen, and Indians as he could. He halted just north of the Chippawa River, where he formed his 2,100 men into a defensive line behind the river and dug in for the fight.

As Riall positioned his force, Lieutenant Colonel Thomas Pearson, who was already stationed on the Chippawa with a small force, moved south across the river to harry Scott's advance and destroy the bridges. Scott, however, had prepared for such an effort by placing a few light field guns with his advance guard, who blasted Pearson's force out of every position it attempted to hold. By the evening of the 4th, Scott camped just south of the Chippawa behind Street's Creek and waited for the forces under Ripley and Porter to catch up.

On 5 July, Scott paused to allow his men a belated Fourth of July dinner (the noon meal). They were concluding the festivities when Indians and Canadian militiamen moved into the cover of nearby woods and began to snipe at them. Brown ordered Porter to push them back, which he quickly did, but as he pursued the fleeing Canadians in the open near the Chippawa, Riall's regulars attacked. Porter's disorganized Pennsylvanians and their Indian allies fled to the rear with Riall's infantry behind them.

Recognizing the danger that this swift change of fortune posed for the entire campaign, Brown rode back to bring Scott's force up to meet the attack. Scott, apparently unaware of the danger, was fortuitously already moving his regiments forward to "top off the day with a dress parade in the open fields between Street's Creek and the Chippawa"[41] and "to keep his men in breath." Brown came upon them yelling, "You will have a battle."[42] Scott sent Towson's artillery forward and double-timed his men on to the field, where they came under immediate attack from Riall's artillery, which, along with his infantry, had already established their position in preparation for the attack south of the Chippawa.

Seeing that the American force was dressed in gray jackets, rather than the dark blue of the regulars, Riall assumed he was up against some New York militiamen sent over from Buffalo and that his own force of regulars would send them packing back across the river and end the American threat against British territory. But Riall was quickly disabused of that happy thought when he observed the precision and confidence with which Scott's force assembled on the field while British shells cut through its ranks. "Those are regulars, by God," Riall is reported to have said,[43] and shortly thereafter, Towson's artillery, now in place on Scott's right flank, began to take out their British counterparts with faster and more accurate fire.

Scott's force of 1,300 stood in a long line two men deep. Riall prepared his 1,500 men for a frontal assault in two columns, which he expected would muscle their way through the thin American line. But Scott was ready. As Riall's force came forward, Scott held his center in place and moved his two flanking regiments into position to receive Riall's advancing columns. As Riall's force marched into the line, the Americans opened fire, ripping the tight columns to pieces. Scott ordered his men to charge at the reeling British. The gray-clad Americans raced forward with bayonets leveled, and the enemy line broke and scrambled back across the Chippawa.

For Americans of the early nineteenth century, Scott's swift victory was enormously important. Henry Adams, writing at a time when Americans still relished a war that marked their coming of age, explained why the victory was so gratifying:

> For completeness, Scott's victory at Chippawa could be compared with that of Isaac Hull over the *Guerriere*; but in one respect Scott surpassed Hull. The *Constitution* was a much heavier ship than its enemy: but Scott's brigade was weaker, both in men and guns, than Riall's force.[44]

Brown wanted to follow up with an attack across the Chippawa on Riall's beaten but now securely entrenched force. His subordinates, however, persuaded him that his effort should be devoted to getting to Fort George, where they would meet Chauncey for the voyage to Burlington. So Brown's combined force of regulars marched north to Queenston. From there they sent out reconnaissance parties to secure the region and to provoke the British garrison at Fort George to come out and fight. The garrison would not be provoked, however. They too were looking for Chauncey's arrival. By 15 July, ten days after the victory at Chippawa, the fleet was nowhere to be seen, and Brown had received no word of a delay or change of plans. Brown had angrily written to Chauncey on the 13th:

> I have looked for your fleet with the greatest anxiety since the 10th. I do not doubt my ability to meet the enemy in the field, and to march in any direction over his country, your fleet carrying for me the necessary supplies.... There is not a doubt resting in my mind but that we have between us the command of sufficient means to conquer Upper Canada within two months, if there is a prompt and zealous co-operation and a vigorous application of these means.[45]

But while Brown waited and the British prepared, Chauncey had taken to his bed, ill—so he claimed—with fever. Despite the pleas of Brown at Niagara and Armstrong in Washington, Chauncey would not budge, nor would he allow his second in command to lead the fleet in his place. Meanwhile, with reinforcements coming in and the Canadian militiamen returning from planting their fields, Riall was back on the move and nipping at the edges of Brown's insecure position, attacking foraging parties and disrupting the Americans' lines of communication with New York.

Brown recognized that his already tenuous position in enemy territory was increasingly perilous as Lieutenant General Sir Gordon Drummond assembled a force larger than his, so he reluctantly gave up and moved his force south to a base camp along the Chippawa, where he would be closer to his supplies. When word of the American withdrawal spread, Riall moved a force of about 2,600 men to a slightly raised position on Lundy's Lane, several miles north of Brown's camp.

Drummond had landed a force at Fort Niagara on the east side of the river to distract Brown from Riall's movement. Unaware of Riall's approach, Brown decided to return to Queenston and meet Drummond head on, sending Scott's force of barely 1,100 men to blaze their way back north. No more than a mile or two from camp, Scott stumbled on a group of British dragoons drinking at a tavern. From the proprietor, Scott learned that Riall's force was just a few miles away, and as the late afternoon shadows lengthened over the field, he moved forward to attack.

Riall, seeing Scott moving in for the attack without a bit of hesitation, presumed that the American's confidence stemmed from possession of a superior force. With instructions from Drummond to avoid combat, Riall ordered his own force and another one camped a few miles north to retreat to Queenston. But halfway through Riall's evacuation of his position on Lundy's Lane, Drummond appeared with a battalion of regulars and ordered Riall to hold the position.

As Scott advanced and his skirmishers came under heavy fire, he realized he was outnumbered. Since an assault against a larger and entrenched enemy force would be suicidal, he drew his men into a defensive line and sent word to headquarters quickly to send up Brown's and Ripley's forces. Both sides were exchanging steady fire from a distance when Major T. S. Jesup, holding Scott's right flank, stumbled on a British force in the process of deploying to protect Drummond's flank. Jesup attacked and sent them flying back with heavy losses. In the process, he captured a badly wounded General Riall. Scott's force, however, continued to take the brunt of the fierce British counter-attack.

> From seven till nine o'clock Scott's brigade hung on the British left and centre, charging repeatedly close on the enemy's guns; and when at last with the darkness their firing ceased from sheer exhaustion, they were not yet beaten.... With a small and exhausted force that could not have numbered more than six hundred men, and which Drummond by a vigorous movement might have wholly destroyed, Scott clung to the enemy's flank until in the darkness Ripley's brigade came down on the run.[46]

Drummond, convinced by Scott's fierce resistance that he was outnumbered, chose not to counter-attack. As the dark of night finally settled on the confused battlefield, Brown arrived with 1,200 men to relieve Scott's battered force, which reformed behind Ripley's fresh troops.

The next morning the Americans attacked. They drove the British back in several places and gained the high ground just as Colonel Hercules Scott's force of 1,200 British troops and militiamen arrived. Stumbling into the heart of the American line, these reinforcements were caught in withering fire and quickly scattered in retreat. Drummond, wounded in the neck and knocked out of action for a brief period, rallied his men and made three desperate attempts to recover the high ground from Brown's force. Each time he was blasted back by intense fire from the American infantry.

The two sides battered each other for control of the hill as evening turned to night. Winfield Scott brought forward a new battalion that he had reorganized in the rear, throwing them into the fight between two of Ripley's regiments. Drummond's line broke under the unexpected assault and fell back as Scott's force rushed forward. But Scott had told no one of his plans. In the fading light, Ripley's beleaguered men mistook the attacking Americans on their flanks and in front for the enemy and fired into them. Under assault from the British in front and the Americans on either side, Scott's force was pummeled to pieces just as it was on the verge of victory and soon withdrew. "Scott had had two horses killed under him and been badly bruised by the glancing impact of an almost-spent cannonball. He rode across the field to Jesup's position where he soon was so badly wounded that he had to be carried off the field."[47] Brown was wounded in the thigh and collapsed from the loss of blood. Although the Americans still held the high ground, Brown, over the objection of several officers, ordered his men to abandon the position, and the army reformed at the Chippawa.

Lundy's Lane was one of the hardest fought battles of the war. Although the British entered the conflict nearly even with the Americans in strength, the arrival of Drummond and Hercules Scott brought their numbers to 2,900 regulars and about 600 militiamen. The Americans had 1,900 regulars and 300 militiamen. Casualties were severe on both sides: 81 British were killed, 562 wounded, and 233 missing or captured. The Americans suffered 171 killed, 573 wounded, and 117 missing or captured.[48] Late that night, perhaps delirious from loss of blood, Brown ordered Ripley to return to the battlefield and retrieve the abandoned guns. Ripley dutifully obeyed and with about 1,200 men returned to Lundy's Lane to confront Drummond's 2,200. The two sides considered each other from a distance, and Ripley soon withdrew without firing a shot. The American force retired south to the security of Fort Erie.

Brown, Scott, and the rest of the wounded, including the captured Riall, were ferried across the Niagara River to Buffalo for treatment. Scott's wounds were so severe and his recuperation so lengthy that he played no further role in the war.[49] "Veterans of Wellington's army reported that the recent fighting was rougher than anything they had seen against the French in Spain."[50] Henry Adams quotes one Canadian authority:

> The officers of the army from Spain who have been engaged in Upper Canada have acknowledged that they never saw such determined charges as were made by Americans in the late actions.... In the action of the 25th of July the Americans charged to the very muzzles of our cannon, and actually bayoneted the artillery men who were at their guns. Their charges were not once or twice only, but repeated and long, and the steadiness of British soldiers alone could have withstood them.[51]

IV

However mauled, the two armies quickly recovered and resumed the conflict. Brigadier General Edmund Gaines replaced Ripley in the command of Fort Erie and continued the work of repairing and reinforcing the fort against the expected attack. Built by the British on a point of strategic importance, the fort was protected on the land side by defensive walls and redoubts that stretched for seven hundred yards, ending at the water's edge at both ends, but was left open in the back to the Niagara River. The front wall was further protected by a ditch containing a strong palisade behind an abatis of felled trees. Three batteries of thirteen guns mounted in secure redoubts along the walls provided enfilade across the land side of the fortification. Inside, Gaines had about two thousand veterans of the recent campaign, all of them ready to continue the fierce resistance they had shown at Chippawa and Lundy's Lane.

Drummond was just as determined to expel this last remaining American incursion into British territory, and in early August he marched his rested and reinforced army south from Queenston to Fort Erie. On 13 August he opened fire on the fortifications with his siege guns, though with little effect. The same day, the British boldly captured two American gunboats stationed near the fort and turned their guns on its unprotected river side. The combined artillery of the British, however, was inadequate for a fort of such size and strength.

In the wee hours of 15 August, Drummond sent 1,300 men under Lieutenant Colonel Victor Fischer to attack the fort at what he believed was its weakest point—where the southern-most reach of the wall ended at the water. When the distracted Americans rushed south to repel Fischer's attack, Drummond would launch two attacks at the northern end of the fort—one under Colonel Hercules Scott, the other under the commander's nephew Lieutenant Colonel William Drummond of Kelty. To force his men to close quickly and rout the Americans with bayonet, Drummond had the flints removed from their muskets, leaving his soldiers armed with little more than cumbersome lances.

Gaines anticipated Drummond's move and was fully prepared for the attack. Once the British siege guns fell silent, the defenders moved back into position. American outposts found the British forces well before they reached the walls and opened fire to alert the fort. At the southern corner where the wall met the water, Fischer's force, bearing disarmed muskets, waded through the shallow water. The American reserve force, armed with fully operational muskets and backed up by artillery, was waiting. As the British floundered through the water, the Americans opened fire, driving Fischer's helpless men into a quick and panicked retreat. Towson's artillery did much the same to those of Fischer's force who tried to scale the nearby walls with ladders too short and too few. In his report of the fight, Fischer wrote that his men "found themselves entangled between the rocks and the water, and by the retreat of the flank companies were thrown in such confusion as to render it impossible to give them any kind of formation during the darkness of the night, at which time they were exposed to a most galling fire of the enemy's battery."[52] In minutes, the southern attack was over and in retreat.

To the north, Lieutenant Colonels Scott and Drummond advanced as soon as they heard the firing in the south. Once again the Americans were waiting, and the two attacking forces were caught in a withering fire of muskets and cannon. Scott was killed, and many of his men turned back. A few drifted westward, however, joining Drummond's renewed assault on the northern bastion, which soon fell. But once inside the bastion, Drummond's men were trapped. American infantrymen were at every exit. Several attempts to break out failed, and Drummond was killed.

The British refused to give up, however, and as the two sides struggled at Fort Erie's northern bastion, a British lieutenant of artillery turned a captured American gun around and began firing at the blocked exits. He got only two shots off before sparks from the muzzle blast ignited the bastion's magazine. A terrific explosion killed or maimed as many as 300 of the British attackers. As the few survivors fled from the fort, several were cut down in the open field by the Americans still firing from the walls. British losses included another 539 missing or captured. American casualties were estimated at 130.[53]

Despite the horrible setback, Lieutenant General Drummond would not lift the siege. Reinforcements brought his force up to three thousand men, and three heavy gun batteries were constructed 500 yards from the fort in the hope of blasting the Americans into surrender. A heavy rain turned the British camp into a cold swamp. By late August, Jacob Brown had recovered from his wounds and resumed command. Always aggressive and uncomfortable on the defense, Brown proposed an attack on the British camp from the fort to seize as much equipment as possible as the British fled in disarray. Most of his officers thought the plan too risky, but Brown ignored their concerns. On 17 September, 1,600 men under Brigadier General Peter B. Porter followed a trail through the woods that Brown's pioneers had secretly cleared and surprised the British batteries. Casualties were heavy on both sides, and more than 1,100 men were killed, wounded, or missing. Ripley and Porter were both badly wounded, and Drummond decided that enough was enough. Four days later, he gave up the siege and marched his men north to Chippawa.

Two weeks later, on 5 November, the Americans evacuated Fort Erie, blowing up its redoubts and walls to discourage a British reoccupation. After four months of bloody fighting, the boundary between the contending forces along the Niagara River was unchanged from where it stood in early summer. American soldiers had proved, at terrible cost, that they could handle British regulars in close combat, but the invasion of Upper Canada had been repelled.[54]

Drummond sought to shift the blame for the stalemate. He attributed his loss at Fort Erie to the ordinary soldier and the foreigners serving under him. In his official report he argued, "The main body of DeWatteville's regiment [assorted Europeans commanded by Fischer] retreated in such confusion that they carried the King's regiment before them in a torrent. Thus by the misconduct of this foreign corps has the opportunity been totally lost." As for the soldiers under him, who died by the hundreds in savage fights where neither side flinched, Drummond complained, "The agony of mind I suffer from the present disgraceful and unfortunate conduct of the troops committed to my superintendence, wounds me to the soul!"[55]

Chauncey, too, had some explaining to do. While Brown's foray along the Niagara River had little to show for the expenditure of material and men, it was intended as the first stage of a campaign to take Burlington and York with Chauncey's help. But Chauncey had never arrived, and as Brown waited day after day in Canadian territory, the British were able to bring in reinforcements and drive him out. Chauncey refused to acknowledge his fault. He had, after all, finally shown up off Fort George on Lake Ontario. But he was three weeks late. By then, the beleaguered Brown had already sought refuge in Fort Erie, at the opposite end of the river. In response to Brown's angry letter, Chauncey asked, "[Am I to] infer that I had pledged myself to meet you on a particular day at the head of the Lake, for the purpose of co-operation, and in case of disaster to your army, thus to turn their resentment from you, who are alone responsible, upon me, who could not by any possibility have prevented, or retarded even, your discomfiture?"[56]

Nonetheless, the stalemate that summer along the Niagara, combined with a series of victories elsewhere, stiffened American resolve and tilted the peace negotiations at Ghent in the Americans' favor.

CHAPTER NINETEEN

MACDONOUGH SINKS BRITAIN

Within weeks of America's declaration of war on Britain, officials on both sides sought to broker a peace settlement before the violence began, lest war drag on until one side capitulated or both were depleted of money and men. On 26 June 1812, a week after the declaration, Madison sent a note to America's *chargé d'affaires* in London, Jonathan Russell, authorizing him to negotiate an armistice based upon Britain's willingness to withdraw the Orders in Council and end impressments. In return, America would promise to bar all British subjects from working on U.S. ships. Lord Castlereagh demurred, arguing that the Orders had already been withdrawn and that Britain would never give up the right of impressment. Indeed, many in Britain believed that once word of the revocation of the Orders reached America, the state of war would end and an armistice would be signed. But that did not happen.[1]

The British attempted to revive the stalled peace discussions through the offices of Admiral Sir John Borlase Warren, recently sent to Halifax to assume command of the American station. Britain's minister to the United States,

Augustus J. Foster, urged officials in Canada to make peace overtures to the Americans, and General Henry Dearborn agreed to an unauthorized armistice on 8 August 1812.[2] The agreement was repudiated by officials in Washington, however, because it did not protect American seamen from impressment.[3]

In March 1813, the Russian government, eager to restore trade with America and anxious to keep Britain focused on the struggle against Napoleon, offered to sponsor negotiations in St. Petersburg. With the war along the Canadian border going worse than expected, the Americans were amenable to a settlement before things got any worse. The United States sent peace commissioners—John Quincy Adams, James A. Bayard, and Albert Gallatin—to Russia with Secretary of State James Monroe's instructions to urge the British to transfer Canada to the United States and end impressment. The British had told the Russians that they would not participate in talks, but the Russians, eager for a deal and ever optimistic that something could be achieved, withheld that information from the Americans. Adams, Bayard, and Gallatin waited in St. Petersburg for the British envoys for six months before giving up and returning to the United States in early 1814.

Though Britain refused to participate in discussions mediated by the Russians, they were open to direct discussions with the United States. In November 1813, Lord Castlereagh wrote to Monroe that Britain was prepared "to enter upon a direct negociation for the restoration of Peace."[4] Madison agreed, and he added Henry Clay and Jonathan Russell to the team of peace commissioners who had traveled to St. Petersburg. The negotiations were originally planned for Gothenburg, Sweden, but with the diminution of hostilities on the European continent, both sides agreed that Ghent, in Belgium, was the more convenient location.

A British team composed of mid-level officials was appointed by May, but the hope that a favorable turn of events in the North American campaign would make the Americans more receptive to British demands delayed the envoys' departure for Ghent. The Americans, of course, had similar thoughts, and Secretary of War Armstrong probably believed that a successful attack by Jacob Brown on the Niagara frontier and at Burlington, Vermont, would produce a more compliant British attitude.

The negotiations formally opened on 8 August 1814, and the British demands were extreme and punitive. In addition to refusing any compromise on impressment, an issue the Americans had dropped in June, they demanded the surrender to Britain and to the Indians of substantial territory in the Old Northwest, Maine, and Minnesota to create a buffer between the United States and Canada. The British also insisted on the removal of warships and fortifications from the Great Lakes and on major fishing concessions.[5]

The list of demands continued—British control of navigation on the Great Lakes, renunciation of American fishing rights off Newfoundland, and the restoration of Louisiana to Spain.[6] By any standard, Britain's terms were extreme, and the Americans, having prevented the British from occupying U.S. soil for more than a day or two, were unlikely to accept them. The British, however, were about to upset that calculation. Napoleon's abdication freed up men, materiel, and ships for the North American theater. Lord Bathurst was planning a series of major ground assaults to seize vast tracts of territory and to attack major centers of American government and commerce. It is unlikely that the British negotiators, junior as they were, knew about these plans. All they knew was to insist on the harsh terms they were instructed to offer.

Bathurst believed that a serious military defeat, perhaps with the loss of territory, would induce the anxious American negotiators to accept Britain's terms. By the spring of 1813, he was planning a three-pronged attack on the territory of the United States with tens of thousands of troops transported across the Atlantic from the momentarily peaceful European continent. First, an amphibious force sailing from Bermuda would attack the east coast. Second, a force from Halifax would invade and occupy northern Maine. Finally, Sir George Prevost and a large force would attack Sackets Harbor in New York and wipe out the American naval presence on Lake Erie and Lake Champlain.[7]

Not long after Bathurst's plan was set in motion, a fourth prong was added—an attack on New Orleans. The pecuniary incentives for this addition to the plan were as strong as the military rationale. After more than a year of blockade, New Orleans was crowded with products that had been shipped down the Mississippi from the frontier and stored in the city's warehouses and in the idled ships rotting alongside her docks. By 1814, the value of the accumulated goods was thought to be twenty million dollars. The prospect of looting a city so engorged with wealth was enormously appealing.

Vice Admiral Sir Alexander Cochrane, who in early 1814 had replaced Sir John Borlase Warren as commander in chief of the fleet on the North American Station, believed that the loss of such wealth would be a serious blow to the American economy and that the looting of New Orleans would leave him and his officers enormously enriched.[8] The attack on New Orleans was scheduled for 20 November 1814, three months after the attacks on Washington, Baltimore, Maine, and Plattsburgh were to take place.

Of the four prongs of Britain's 1814 campaign against the United States, Sir George Prevost's attack on Sackets Harbor and the American fleet on the Great Lakes received the most resources. From Montreal, Prevost would lead twelve thousand men and a naval squadron down the Richelieu River valley, across Lake Champlain, and down the Hudson to Albany and New York City.

By 1814, the corridor between Montreal and New York was the most fought over real estate on the North American continent,[9] though Lake Champlain itself had been undisturbed during this war. C. S. Forester observes:

> Lake Champlain had so far figured curiously little in the history of the war. In previous wars Montcalm and Abercromby and Amherst and Burgoyne, Ethan Allen and Benedict Arnold had all fought on its surface or around its shores. It offered one hundred and seven miles of navigable water in almost a direct line from Montreal to New York; on that route the Hudson River offered a somewhat longer stretch of navigable water....[10]

During the French and Indian War, which spanned more than a decade between 1754 and 1766, the river and lake valleys that stretched from New York City to Montreal were the scene of bloody battles between the British and French and their colonial and Indian allies. Peace was briefly restored to the wilderness when the French lost Canada to the British, but with the declaration of American independence, the valley corridor became a tempting target for British forces massing in Montreal.

In October 1776, off Valcour Island in Lake Champlain, just a few miles south of Plattsburgh, New York, a small fleet under the command of Benedict Arnold held off a larger British fleet sent to clear the way for an invasion south. So stiff was Arnold's resistance that the British postponed their invasion until the following spring, allowing the Americans an extra six months to prepare. When it finally came, the Americans were ready, and the British force under General Burgoyne was soundly defeated at Saratoga in October 1777, again thanks to the daring and courage of Benedict Arnold, who repeatedly rallied the American force to hold the line and beat back every attempt the British made on it.

Despite Britain's troubled history of conflict in the valley, the military benefits of seizing and holding the corridor were too great to ignore. Bathurst was determined to conquer the valley by assembling in Montreal the largest force that Britain had ever mustered in North America. Comprising as many as twelve thousand troops, many of them veterans of Wellington's Peninsular campaign, and operating under the direct command of General Prevost, the army was ordered south into New York to seize as much territory as possible and force the Americans to accept Britain's harsh terms for peace.

Although the region was mostly uninhabited wilderness, its attraction to attacking armies (and vulnerability for defenders) was its combination of rivers and lakes forming an uninterrupted waterway upon which men and supplies could be transported by flat-bottom boat almost the entire 380 miles from Montreal to New York City. From Montreal, a boat could float down the St. Lawrence to the mouth of the Richelieu River, where it would be rowed and towed south to Lake Champlain. From there it could be sailed south into Lake George. From Fort William Henry (site of the notorious Indian massacre depicted in *The Last of the Mohicans*), at the southern end of Lake George, the boat and supplies would have to be dragged about fifteen miles to Glenn Falls from which there was clear sailing on the Hudson all the way to New York City, 210 miles to the south. The military historian Donald Hickey concludes, "Whoever controlled these waters—particularly Lake Champlain—controlled the whole region."[11]

Recognizing the attraction of the corridor to an invading British army, the United States maintained both land and naval forces on and around Lake Champlain and the town of Plattsburg. Initially commanded by the less-than-competent General Wade Hampton, the Plattsburgh command transferred to General George Izard in the shake-up that sent Generals Wilkinson and Hampton and several other officers into retirement.

II

As Prevost assembled his vast force in Montreal in the summer of 1814, the U.S. naval command on Lake Chaplain was in the hands of thirty-year-old

Master Commandant Thomas Macdonough, born and raised at the Trap farm in central Delaware. The sixth of ten children born to the sometime medical doctor, sometime jurist, and onetime Revolutionary War officer Major Thomas McDonough Sr. and his wife Lydia, Macdonough (who later changed the spelling of his surname) was an orphan by the age of twelve. He and his older siblings, of whom four were sisters, inherited only the land and the house, as well as first-rate political connections from his father's war service.

To make ends meet, Thomas became a clerk in nearby Middleton, while his older brother James, taking advantage of the family's political connections, entered the navy as a midshipman. The sisters were married off and formed their own families in the region. Serving aboard the frigate *Constellation* under Captain Thomas Truxton and Lieutenant John Rodgers during the Quasi-War with France, James lost his foot in the fight with the French frigate *L'Insurgente*, and returned to Trap farm with a small pension and many stories of travel and adventure.

Inspired by his brother's tales about life in the navy, Thomas used the same family connections to secure a midshipman's appointment, and on 27 May 1800, at age sixteen he reported for duty aboard the USS *Ganges*, docked at New Castle, Delaware. A converted merchantman, the *Ganges* was a slow sailer, and one of the few things she captured during her Caribbean cruise was yellow fever, which sent Macdonough and many of his crew mates to a filthy hospital in Havana. He later recounted that "nearly all of the men and officers died and were taken out in carts as so many hogs would have been."[12] The *Ganges* had left port by the time Macdonough and a few of his mates recovered, so they booked passage on a merchant vessel bound for Philadelphia. Carrying Spanish cargo at a time Britain was at war with France and its vassal Spain, the merchantman was seized by the British off the Capes of Delaware. Macdonough, penniless by now, was let off in Norfolk before the ship was taken to Halifax.

At Norfolk, where the United States maintained a naval base at Gosport, the naval agent gave them food and clothing and enough money to get back to their homes. The U.S. Navy was reduced in size when hostilities with France ended, but Macdonough kept his commission and was assigned to the *Constellation* on her cruise of the Mediterranean in 1802. The Barbary pirates had been seizing American ships and enslaving their sailors or holding them for ransom, and the United States hoped that a show of force would deter them. After an uneventful cruise, Macdonough was assigned to the frigate *Philadelphia*, commanded by Captain William Bainbridge, and returned to the Mediterranean to patrol the Barbary coast.

The *Philadelphia* had no sooner cleared the Strait of Gibraltar than it took the Tripolitan ship *Meshoba* as she was towing a captured American brig back to port. With the good fortune that would continue to mark his career, Macdonough was assigned to the prize crew that took the *Meshoba* back to Gibraltar. The *Philadelphia* sailed on to Tripoli, where she ran aground in the harbor and her crew was captured and imprisoned. Macdonough was transferred to the *Enterprise*, then under the command of the fast-rising Lieutenant Stephen Decatur. The two quickly became fast friends. "As Decatur became Commodore Edward Preble's favorite lieutenant and star pupil," observes the historian Edward Eckert, "Macdonough would be Decatur's favorite midshipman and best student."[13] During his tour of duty in the Mediterranean with Decatur, Macdonough learned to appreciate the skill, courage, and leadership of Admiral Nelson, whose exploits in the region had made him a hero of the young officers of the English-speaking navies.

In the escalating conflict with the Barbary pirates, Macdonough and Decatur became a fearsome duo. Macdonough was with Decatur in February 1804 when he recaptured the *Philadelphia* and set her afire and six months later when he chased down the Tripolitan gunboat whose captain had murdered Decatur's brother James. The twenty-year-old Macdonough led one of the boarding parties that captured the ship, killed the offending captain, and killed or wounded more than twenty members of his crew. A month later, on 10 September, in recognition of his outstanding service, Preble gave Macdonough his own gunboat to command and a promotion to the rank of lieutenant. Macdonough spent another twenty-two months in the Mediterranean, part of that time in an Italian shipyard at Ancona overseeing the construction of four gunboats for the American fleet. The knowledge he gained during this assignment in Italy and his study of Nelson's leadership would serve him well a decade later when his country was in peril.

Returning to the U.S. in 1806, Macdonough enjoyed a long leave of absence with his family in Delaware before returning to duty under Isaac Hull, who was there supervising the construction at Middleton, Connecticut, of several gunboats that President Jefferson had commissioned to be the mainstay of America's naval defense. Though Hull was reassigned a few months later, bringing Macdonough's stay in Connecticut to an end, the young officer was there long enough to establish a tender friendship with seventeen-year-old Lucy Ann Shaler.

Over the next several years, Macdonough served in many capacities and on a number of ships. But the power of his leadership was perhaps most clearly demonstrated at the time of his departure from the frigate *Essex*, on which he briefly served in 1809. In a gesture that Fletcher Pratt called "one of those fascinating and fugitive glimpses of a man that come through the eyes of other people," the crew of the *Essex* presented Macdonough with a letter, signed by or on behalf of every man, which read in part:

> Permit us, Sir, before your departure to return you our most Sincere thanks and acknowledgements for your officer-like Conduct and Philanthropy during the time we have had the happiness of being under your command as Second officer. We don't Wish to trouble you with a great Harrangue. We can only assure you, Sir, that we all feel as one in the Cause of Regret at your about to leave the Ship....
>
> We have only to add, Sir, that we wish you all the happiness that man can enjoy, and may He who holds the Destiny of Mankind guide you Safe through life and Pilot you at last to the harbour of Rest is the Hearty prayer of the Subscribers.

Edward Eckert concludes from this unusual episode, "His men had shown that they not only respected him but liked him as well. Macdonough had the elusive gift of being able to make others do what he willed without forcing them to do so."[14]

By 1810, Macdonough was twenty-six and eager to marry and start a family. His meager lieutenant's pay, however, was incompatible with that aspiration, so he obtained a temporary furlough to serve as the captain of a merchant vessel in order to build up his financial resources. Thirteen months later, war with Britain seemed likely, and Secretary of the Navy Paul Hamilton recalled him to active duty. Macdonough appealed, citing the financial exigencies of "a domestic engagement."[15] Hamilton, moved by Macdonough's "high character," relented and extended his furlough for one more merchant cruise.[16]

That cruise, however, was suspended when Congress, responding to worsening relations with Britain, enacted a ninety-day embargo. Macdonough returned to Middleton, was confirmed in the Episcopal Church, and began the preparations for his marriage to Miss Shaler. On 17 July 1812, he was awarded the plum position of first lieutenant under Captain William Bainbridge on the *Constellation*. For reasons now unknown, however, he sought instead the less prestigious command of a gunboat squadron stationed in Portland, Maine. Perhaps he had second thoughts about serving again under a captain known for his harsh discipline and bad luck, but Bainbridge was certainly eager to have Macdonough. After the offer was turned down, Bainbridge wrote to him, "I shall lose an excellent first lieutenant, one in whom I have the highest confidence. But if *love* and the Gods have decreed it otherwise I must be satisfied, and wherever you go you carry my best wishes for your happiness."[17]

When Macdonough declined the appointment to the *Constellation*, luck was again with him. He had been in Maine only a few days when he was ordered to leave immediately for Lake Champlain to take over from Lieutenant Sidney Smith the command of the new squadron there. The prevailing view in the navy was that Smith was inadequate for this command on the critical invasion route between the Hudson and St. Lawrence Valleys, and he was demoted to Macdonough's second in command (in which position he would confirm the navy's assessment of his capabilities). At a cost of seventy-five dollars, Macdonough hired a horse and chaise for the four-day journey from Portland to Burlington, Vermont, where he assumed his new command in October 1812. A few months later, he returned to Middleton to marry Lucy. They spent their honeymoon riding back to Vergennes, Vermont, in the dead of winter, where they began their marriage in "primitive rented quarters."[18]

Macdonough was given two objectives in his new command. First, and more urgently, he was to deter as best he could the rampant smuggling of vital supplies from the farmers and Indians of Vermont to the British forces in Canada. The commander in chief of British forces in North America, Sir George Prevost, claimed that two-thirds of his army's beef came from Vermont and New York. General George Izard, commander of the American land forces protecting Lake Champlain, complained to the War Department,

> On the eastern side of Lake Champlain, the high roads are insufficient for the cattle pouring into Canada. Like herds of buffaloes they press through the forests, making paths for themselves. Were it not for these supplies, the British forces in Canada would soon be suffering from famine.[19]

Despite aggressive efforts to end the smuggling, the potential profits were so high that seized goods were sometime recaptured by their smugglers, who over-powered the customs officials and reshipped them to the enemy.

Macdonough's second objective was to build a naval force and work with the army to secure the corridor against an expected British invasion from Montreal. Given the difficulty of moving an army through the undeveloped wilderness of upstate New York, Lake Champlain offered the most efficient way of quickly moving a large force south or north. Upon his arrival, Macdonough discovered that the U.S. "fleet" on Lake Champlain consisted of two gunboats, one so leaky that it was beached most of the time to prevent it from sinking. The Americans were utterly unequipped to defend against an attack on Plattsburgh or Burlington by the small British squadron based at Île aux Noix, where Lake Champlain spills into the Richelieu River. Macdonough turned his attention to harvesting the vast natural resources that surrounded him to build a fleet that could control the lake.

The War Department had transferred to the Lake Champlain command six civilian sloops it had purchased as transports and supply vessels, including the sixty-five-foot *President*, the sixty-four-foot *Bulldog* (renamed *Eagle*), and the sixty-one-foot *Hunter*. These new acquisitions required considerable modification, a task that was the first order of business for the lieutenant and his men at their shipyard in Burlington.

As the lake's ice pack thawed in the spring of 1813, Macdonough launched his newly modified ships. With the three new sloops—*President*, *Growler*, and *Eagle*, each carrying eleven guns—and three new gunboats, the Americans now dominated the lake. Macdonough ordered Lieutenant Smith, commanding the *Eagle*, and sailing master Jarius Loomis, commanding the *Growler*, to keep the British out of the lake but to do so while remaining within the borders of the United States. They could block the entrance to the Richelieu River but not enter it.

Still smarting from his loss of command, Smith was eager to regain his reputation and attempted to do so by disregarding his orders.[20] On 3 June 1814, he added more than forty soldiers to his ships and sailed *Eagle* and *Growler* across the border and into the Richelieu, intending to capture three fleeing galleys and perhaps the British naval base at Île aux Noix. While it was certainly a bold move, the weather argued against it. With the current running north down the Richelieu and the wind blowing from the south, Smith's pilot warned that it might be very difficult to get out of the river once they had entered it. Smith ignored the warning and sailed into what was probably an ambush. As *Growler* and *Eagle* came down the river toward the shallow waters near Île aux Noix, British troops on both banks opened fire with muskets and artillery, and three British gunboats moved in for the attack. The fight lasted nearly four hours, but with both ships disabled and unable to retreat from the narrow river, Smith struck his flag and surrendered America's two new warships and 113 officers and men.

A winter's worth of ship construction thus changed hands in an afternoon, and the balance of power in the lake shifted decidedly to the British. President Madison lamented, "The loss of our command on Lake Champlain at so critical a moment is deeply to be regretted."[21] The British repaired the captured sloops and renamed them the *Broke* and the *Shannon* in honor of the victory over Lawrence and the *Chesapeake*.[22] Their names were later changed again, this time to the *Chubb* and the *Finch*. Under both sets of names, these ships played important roles in the coming British assaults on American positions.

That summer, Commander Thomas Everard of the Royal Navy arrived for a two week visit to Quebec. With the American presence on Lake Champlain now reduced to a single ship—the *President*—Everard was persuaded to lead an attack on American bases there.[23] Taking fifty men from his crew and thirty volunteers, and joined by Lieutenant Daniel Pring, the new commander at Île aux Noix, Everard headed up the Richelieu with about a thousand troops under the command of Lieutenant Colonel John Murray. Accompanied by the *Chubb* and *Finch*, Everard's force landed at Plattsburgh on 30 July, quickly routed the militia, and burned the blockhouse, barracks, and military storehouses. The force then sailed east over Lake Champlain and successfully attacked the small town of Swanton, Vermont. From there they headed south to Burlington, where they tried, without success, to draw Macdonough and the *President* onto the lake for a fight. Macdonough refused, and the three thousand regulars and volunteers defending the town forced Everard to turn back. With his two week visitation nearing its close, Everard ended the campaign and returned to his ship at Quebec.[24]

Fortunately for Macdonough, his superiors in Washington understood the grave risk that a poorly defended Lake Champlain posed for the United States and had every confidence in his abilities. Upon receiving word of the loss of the *Eagle* and *Growler*, the new secretary of the navy, William Jones, wrote to Macdonough on 17 June 1813:

> I have received your letter, announcing the unfortunate disaster and loss of the two Sloops under the command of Lieutenant Smith, as it would appear by the imprudence of that officer, of which, however, you will enquire into, and report to me the result.
>
> It now only remains, to regain by every possible exertion, the ascendancy which we have lost; for which purpose, you are authorized to purchase, arm and equip, in an efficient manner, two of the best sloops, or other vessels to be procured on the Lake...[25]

In a further sign of Washington's confidence in him, Macdonough was promoted to the rank of master commandant in late July. The confidence, it seems, was well placed: by late summer Macdonough had refitted the three sloops and converted the gunboats into more maneuverable row galleys. Though the squadron was small—the *President*, *Commodore Preble*, and *Montgomery*, plus four gunboats—it was enough to regain control of the lake and bottle up the British in the Richelieu River.

As winter closed in and ice formed on the lake, Macdonough moved his small fleet south from Burlington to Otter Creek and shifted his headquarters and ships seven miles up the creek to the falls at Vergennes, where the fledgling force was protected from British attack. Vergennes was also near the water-powered mills that included "eight forges, a blast furnace, an air furnace, a rolling mill, a wire factory and grist, saw and fulling mills." By the time hostilities resumed in early 1814, they had a thousand new thirty-two-pound cannon balls as Macdonough and his craftsmen went to work rebuilding the fleet to meet the coming challenge.[26]

Macdonough's spies were certain that the British intended to construct a brig at Île aux Noix, so he hired the shipbuilders Adam and Noah Brown of New York to build his own brig at Vergennes. Famous for the sloop of war *Peacock* and the privateer *Prince de Neufchatel*, the Brown brothers had also built the brigs *Lawrence* and *Niagara*, which led Perry's fleet to victory at Put-in-Bay. The Browns produced the warship in just forty days. The keel was laid on 7 March, and the finished hull slid down the ways into Otter Creek on 11 April. Masts, spars, and rigging were added over the next week and a half. A variation of the design of Perry's two brigs, the ship was 143 feet long with a beam of 36 feet, 6 inches, and was expected to carry eighteen carronades—twelve thirty-two-pounders and six forty-two-pounders, and eight twenty-four-pound long guns on her main deck. The brig was the most powerful ship on Lake Champlain. Macdonough named her, fittingly enough, the *Saratoga*, after the Revolutionary War battle in which the British were defeated in their last foray down the "Great Warpath" of the Lake Champlain–Hudson River corridor.

As Macdonough readied *Saratoga*, his new second in command, Lieutenant Stephen Cassin, urged him to take a look at a hull then under construction in Vergennes for the newly-formed Lake Champlain Steamboat Company. By 1814, steam-powered commercial vessels were in profitable service in major ports, harbors, and bays along the American seaboard, and Lake Champlain was just months away from having its own. According to one version of the story, the shipyard had not yet received the boiler, fire box, and drive train from New York. The equipment was not expected for another two months, by which time the Brown brothers could have built an entire sailing ship. (In Theodore Roosevelt's version, the steam equipment was already installed and operating, but Macdonough did not trust its reliability.[27]) In any case, Macdonough passed up the opportunity to commission the world's first steam-powered warship. With Secretary Jones's approval, he bought the 120-foot hull and had the Brown brothers refit it as a schooner. The *Ticonderoga*, as she was called, was launched in May 1814.

With the ships built and ready for war, Macdonough found himself in much the same situation as Perry had been in the year before—plenty of ships but not enough officers and crew to man them. Meanwhile, Lieutenant Pring, either ignorant of the expansion of Macdonough's fleet or aware of his shortage of manpower, left Île aux Noix in early May with *Linnet*, *Chubb*, *Finch*, seven gunboats, and any vessel they could seize along the way, and sailed for Otter Creek—a major river flowing into Lake Champlain from the south—where he intended to deny Macdonough access to the lake by sinking stone-laden ships in the river's narrow mouth.

But Pring's progress south was slowed by contrary winds, and he lost the element of surprise. Macdonough and Brigadier General Alexander Macomb were able to bolster their batteries at the mouth of the river with a larger force and several gunboats. When Pring arrived, it was apparent that the American force was large enough to beat off any attack. After less than an hour's exchange of gun fire, Pring withdrew his squadron. "Every Tree on the Lake shore seems to have a Jonathan [an American] stationed behind it," he wrote to a friend.[28]

By mid-March, Macdonough had raised a crew of 329 men and officers, only half the number he required. Desperate, he asked Macomb to loan him 250 soldiers, but General Izard intervened, complaining to Secretary of War Armstrong that Macdonough's effort was "'in every respect a very unpleasant one', which mortified their commanders and was unjust to the men who enlisted for ground duty."[29] Compounding Macdonough's recruiting problem, many of the men he had recruited, especially the young officers and midshipmen, were anxious to leave, concerned that the absence of saltwater service would hinder their careers.

Some of the seamen sent to Macdonough, as earlier to Perry, were black. Macdonough discouraged his sailing master, Henry Few, who was on a recruiting drive in Providence, Rhode Island, from sending any more, for reasons he never specified. An earlier shipment from Few included "four Collard men which were Recomd. as Smart Seamen," and Macdonough could have had another fifty. On 22 June, Macdonough wrote to his recruiting officers not to send more black tars, a request Few and New York recruiter C. B. Thompson found an imposition in their efforts.[30]

By late May Macdonough had enough men to leave Vergennes and enter the lake with his new ships. Now outgunned, Pring retreated down the Richelieu River to Île aux Noix, and Lake Champlain returned to American control. But Britain was determined to win the naval arms race on the lake. Pre-constructed frames for four vessels were shipped to Montreal from British shipyards, to be allotted evenly between Lakes Champlain and Ontario.

About the time that Macdonough learned about the construction of more British ships, he also learned that Britain was sending to North America thousands of hardened veterans from Wellington's army, who were no longer needed in Europe. In April 1814, Napoleon had abdicated and fled to Elba. With Europe at peace (for the time being), Britain planned to send as many as fifteen thousand men to Canada to seize as much territory as they could in New York, Vermont, and Maine before a peace treaty was signed in Ghent.

If history was any guide, the Richelieu River and Lake Champlain valleys were the logical route for a British force seeking to inflict the most damage possible and to sever disgruntled New England from the rest of the nation. In preparation for the invasion, two fifty-five-foot gunboats, the *Drummond* and the *Murray*, were towed up the Richelieu to bolster the small squadron at Île aux Noix, and the shipwright William Simmons was sent to the naval base to build the *Confiance*, a brig of 147 feet and thirty-seven guns, to challenge *Saratoga*.

Informed by British deserters of the heightened activity at Île aux Noix, Macdonough asked Jones for another ship or two, preferably a brig. Jones demurred, but President Madison recognized the growing threat and approved the request over Jones's objection. On 5 July 1814, the Brown brothers returned to Lake Champlain to construct a brig of eighteen guns. Adam Brown arrived in mid July with two hundred workers drawn from the New York shipyards. After conferring with Macdonough, he headed for Vergennes, where he had the keel laid for the new ship within five days. Using whatever unseasoned wood was handy and the skills acquired in building *Saratoga*, Brown finished the hull nineteen days later and slid it down the ways into Otter Creek, where it received its masts, spars, sails, rigging, and cannon. On 27 August, the new ship—the *Eagle*—floated down the river, entered the lake, and joined the squadron.

Over Macdonough's objections, command of the new brig was given to Master Commandant Robert Henley. Once senior to Macdonough, Henley had since built a rather mediocre record in the navy and lost ground in the seniority rankings. He had also engaged in a nasty quarrel with Captain John Cassin, the father of Macdonough's key subordinate, Lieutenant Stephen Cassin. Although Henley had been passed over for promotion on numerous occasions, recommendations by Perry and Porter swayed Jones, who awarded him command of the *Eagle* against his better judgment.

Shortly after *Eagle* joined the fleet, *Confiance* slid down the ways at Île aux Noix. Captain Peter Fisher had assumed command of the British squadron from Lieutenant Pring. The addition of *Confiance* and the gunboats brought the squadron to a size that required command by a post captain. Pring was downgraded to second in command, and the fleet, as it prepared for a battle that would determine control of Lake Champlain and upstate New York, was placed in the hands of a newcomer. Fisher, however, held the post for only two months. On 1 September 1814, Commodore Yeo further shook up the Lake Champlain chain of command by replacing the inexperienced and ill-tempered Fisher[31] with the more seasoned Captain George Downie.

III

Bathurst had conceived the campaign down the Hudson valley to New York City shortly after Napoleon's abdication on 11 April 1814. By June the plans were fleshed out, and Bathurst wrote to Prevost. He informed the general that he would soon receive ten thousand additional troops and continued with the orders for the offensive:

> When this force shall have been placed under your command, His Majesty's Government conceive that the Canadas will not only be protected for the time being against any attack which the enemy may have the means of making, but it will enable you to commence offensive operations on the Enemy's Frontier before the close of this Campaign.... The objects of your operation will be; first, to give immediate protection: secondly, to obtain if possible ultimate security to His Majesty's Possessions in America.
>
> The entire destruction of Sackets Harbour and the Naval Establishments on Lake Erie and Lake Champlain come under the first description ... and the occupation of Detroit and the Michigan Country come under the second.[32]

The first of the promised reinforcements arrived directly from Bordeaux on 29 July. By 17 August, the entire additional force, numbering more than thirteen thousand men and officers, had arrived in the vicinity of Montreal.

Altogether, the British force in Canada now numbered close to thirty thousand men, nearly half of them veterans of Wellington's campaign in Spain.

Sackets Harbor, close to the U.S.–Canadian border and no more than twenty-five miles as the crow flies across Lake Ontario from Yeo's fleet at Kingston, was the logical target. The capture and destruction of Commodore Isaac Chauncey's fleet at Sackets Harbor would be a major setback for the Americans. Prevost, however, believed that Chauncey had, with the launch of the sixty-two-gun frigate *Superior* in early August, regained control of Lake Ontario and that the transport of a large British force across the lake would entail substantial risk.[33] He therefore eliminated Detroit and Sackets Harbor as targets. Lake Champlain became Prevost's default target, the objective being to cut off New England from the rest of the United States.

An assault on Lake Champlain promised to secure for Prevost's now substantial army its supply lines to the farmers of Vermont, which Prevost knew the Americans were determined to shut down. After weighing all of his options, Prevost wrote back to Bathurst on 5 August:

> The state of Vermont having Shown a decided opposition to the War, and very large supplies of Specie coming in daily from thence, as well as the whole of the Cattle required for the use of the troops, I mean for the present to confine myself in any offensive operation to the Western side of Lake Champlain.[34]

Prevost's decision to conduct his offensive on the western (New York) side of the lake in order to preserve his supply lines on the eastern side put his offensive on less favorable terrain and ceded to Macdonough's fleet a more favorable position than it would have had if it were forced to defend Burlington, Vermont, across the lake.

Officials in Washington, however, would squander this advantage. Expecting the British to attack at Sackets Harbor or along the Niagara, Armstrong, in a letter of 27 July, ordered General Izard and his 5,500 regulars to move west. Izard himself had believed such a move to the west might be necessary, but by early August he had surmised from Prevost's preparations in the north that the Champlain region was the likely target.[35] By the time Izard received Armstrong's letter on 10 August, he had moved his force ten miles north of Plattsburgh to the village of Chazy, New York, where he intended to challenge Prevost's force as it marched south. Stunned by Armstrong's orders, Izard wrote back the next day:

> I will make the movement you direct, if possible; but I shall do it with the apprehension of risking the force under my command, and with the certainty that Cumberland Head will in less than three days after my departure be in the hands of the enemy. He is in force superior to mine in my front; he daily threatens an attack on my position at Champlain; we are in hourly expectation of a serious conflict.[36]

Irritated by Izard's objections, Armstrong reiterated his orders in a second letter, and on 29 August, just three days before Prevost moved his massive force across the border at Champlain, a small town just inside the U.S. border, Izard decamped from Chazy and marched four thousand of his men west to Sackets Harbor. Left behind to defend Plattsburgh against the ten thousand battle-hardened British regulars was Brigadier General Alexander Macomb, in command of only three thousand men, half of whom were new recruits or convalescing from wounds or illness.[37]

Macomb abandoned any attempt to hold the line at Chazy and pulled his force back through Plattsburgh to the redoubts and blockhouses that Izard had constructed on the south bank of the Saranac River, which flows through the town into Lake Champlain. Macomb's force was vastly inferior in numbers and experience to Prevost's, but he was of the new breed of officers recently promoted for their aggressiveness in battle, and he intended to harass the British as they moved south and to hold the line at Plattsburgh whatever the cost.

As Macomb arranged his forces to meet the British, the new brig *Eagle* arrived on the lake and was readied for action. Macdonough was still short of crewmen, but he knew through his intelligence sources that *Confiance* was still many days from being ready to sail. He used the few days available to train his officers and crewmen to work as a fleet in a coordinated defense against a British squadron that would soon arrive in the protected bay at Plattsburgh, where the American army and navy lay in wait.

But that confrontation was still a week or two away. Prevost had crossed the border on 1 September, his experienced force easily brushing aside the efforts of General Benjamin Mooer's New York militia to slow the march. As

Downie struggled to ready his naval force at Île aux Noix, Prevost was already well into U.S. territory, nearing the outskirts of Plattsburgh. Though formidable, Prevost's British-Canadian force nevertheless suffered some serious deficiencies, chief of which was its leader himself. The Canadian historian Suthren observes with regret,

> If Isaac Brock had lived for this moment, the prospect of what he ... might have done with such force invites speculation. But Sir George was venturing into waters in which he swam poorly. His personality and inclination had suited him to the careful husbandry of resources and extreme caution the precarious defense of the Canadas demanded—in some eyes; now he was called upon to lay aside the administrator's pen and take up the sword, and at Sackets Harbor and elsewhere Prevost had not shown the ability to distinguish between due prudence and a fatal reluctance to simply fight.[38]

Compounding Prevost's problems of leadership was the enormous difference in experience and attitude between him and the reinforcements from Bordeaux, especially the officers who had accompanied them to North America. Few if any of the veterans who crossed the Atlantic in cramped, rolling ships wanted to be in North America in an unpleasant conflict against the feisty Americans, who had already fought the British to a rare and unexpected defeat twenty years earlier. Having conquered Napoleon after more than a decade of bloody combat, they had expected easy garrison duty on the European continent or a return home to England. Instead, they were sent off to an unpopular war to serve under incompetent leadership.

In contrast to the generals recently arrived from France and serving as their subordinates, neither Prevost nor his adjutant general, Edward Baynes, had much combat experience.[39] A sensible leader would have realized that such disparities called for some delicacy in command, but Prevost instead relied on his substantially enhanced authority, falling back on his inner martinet and chastising his subordinates for trivial infractions.

A natural leader like Wellington cared little how his force suited up for battle, as long as they fought at the peak of their capabilities and carried the day. Wellington himself eschewed a formal uniform, preferring to command his vast force in a "blue frock-coat and pantaloons of a civilian cut."[40] But

Prevost seems to have resented that liberality of dress and personal affectation, and he was determined to impose a more stringent dress code upon the veteran force, including officers. On 23 August, a week before crossing the border into the United States, Prevost issued a general order concerning the proper dress:

> The Excellency deems it expedient to direct that the General Officers in Charge of Divisions & Brigades do uphold His Majesty's Commands in that respect, and only admit of such diversion from them as may be justified by particular causes of Service and Climate—and even then uniformity is to be retained.[41]

These orders did not sit well with the veterans, who did not want to be in North America whoever their commander was. Lieutenant William Grattan of the Eighty-eighth Regiment complained that Wellington had

> never harassed us with reviews, or petty annoyances, which, so far from promoting discipline, or doing good in any way, have a contrary effect.... Provided we brought our men into the field well appointed, and with sixty rounds of good ammunition each, he never looked to see whether their trowsers were black, blue or grey, and so to ourselves [i.e., officers], we might be rigged out in all colours of the rainbow if we fancied it.[42]

But not everyone turned against Prevost as he marched to Plattsburgh. On 30 August, two days before her father crossed the border with one of the largest armies ever amassed on the North American continent, Anne Prevost wrote in her journal:

> I was most sanguine that something very brilliant would be achieved. I had often thought with regret that my Father had never yet been engaged in any bright affair—he had considered it necessary to conduct the defence of the Canadas with much caution,—defence, not conquest, was necessarily his object. But now I thought the time had arrived when all murmurs would be silenced—I was delighted to think my Father was commanding some thousands of Wellington's soldiers!... Oh how high the pulse of hope beat at

> that moment. I do not recollect that I had any sort of fear as to the result of the Expedition. I looked forward to certain victory.[43]

Prevost's army made good time as it moved down the west bank of the lake. Henry Adams remarks, "So little did this army apprehend difficulty, that in advancing to Plattsburgh in the face of Macomb's skirmishers they did not once form in line, or pay attention to the troops and militia who obstructed the road." Macomb himself later reported, "So undaunted was the enemy that he never deployed in his whole march, always pressing on in column."[44]

On 6 September, Prevost entered the north side of Plattsburgh without meaningful resistance and prepared to attack south across the Saranac River and dislodge the small force that Macomb had dug in against him. The precise number of men in Prevost's force at this point is not known with certainty. Adams[45] says it probably numbered eighteen thousand plus Canadian militiamen, but others believe it was smaller. The Canadian historian J. Mackay Hitsman[46] says Prevost crossed the border with 10,351 officers and men. David Skaggs[47] believes Prevost left Montreal with fourteen thousand but left half of them behind as reserves along the way. Only about seven thousand British soldiers, says Skaggs, entered Plattsburgh in early September. Whatever the exact number, the British outnumbered Macomb's force by more than two to one, and the Prevost's soldiers were among the best in the world.

Prevost's initial plan was to attack Macomb's entrenched force the next day, but he called off the attack because of Macdonough's squadron anchored just off shore in Plattsburgh Bay. With Macomb's force dug in close to the shore, Prevost feared that Macdonough's eighty-six guns would rip into his flank if he attacked before Downie's squadron defeated Macdonough's.

IV

Macdonough had moved his squadron from the lake to the shelter of Plattsburgh Bay on 5 September in anticipation of Prevost's assault. He positioned his ships so that they could offer a stout defense against the expected British squadron while aiding Macomb's troops on shore. Macdonough's plan was to anchor his larger ships in a line just off the banks south of Plattsburgh, facing out toward the entrance of the bay. The *Eagle*, 20, commanded by Lieutenant Robert Henly, would be in the van and hold the northern flank of the line close to the shoals, limiting the ability of the British to maneuver around it. South of the *Eagle* was Macdonough's flagship, *Saratoga*, 26, followed by *Ticonderoga*, 17, under the command of Lieutenant Cassin, and *Preble*, 7, under Lieutenant Charles Budd. Macdonough positioned his line of ships so that the southern flank was "anchored" by tiny Crab Island, upon which he placed a long six-pounder manned by ambulatory invalids convalescing in the island's military hospital. Supporting the four larger ships were ten gunboats of various sizes armed with sixteen guns among them. The gunboats would lie behind the line, popping out between the bigger ships to fire at the British as opportunities emerged. The little gunboats were also expected to plug any gaps between the larger ships, thus preventing the British squadron from piercing the line—"crossing the T"—and raking the bow and stern of the anchored Americans with devastating broadsides.

Macdonough deeply admired Horatio Nelson and was familiar with his legendary career, yet he consciously embraced the strategy of the French fleet in the Battle of Nile, in which Nelson sank or captured eleven of thirteen French ships of the line, stranding Napoleon's army in Egypt and leaving Britain in control of the eastern Mediterranean.[48] But Macdonough improved on the French strategy, ensuring that his ships would have the advantage of maneuver while still holding a stationary line between the British squadron and the American coast behind them. Henry Adams describes in some detail the nautical "technology" Macdonough employed:

> As the battle was to be fought at anchor, both squadrons would as a matter of course be anchored with springs on their cables; but Macdonough took the additional precaution of laying a kedge off each buoy of the *Saratoga*, bringing their hawsers in on two quarters, and letting them hang in bights under water. This arrangement enabled him to wind his ship at any time without fear of having his cables cut by the enemy's shot, and to use his larboard broadside, if his starboard guns should be disabled. In effect, it doubled his fighting capacity.[49]

By keeping his ships stationary and using a complex system of "springs" and "kedges" to alter the direction in which a ship's broadside could be aimed, Macdonough achieved most of the benefits of maneuver while freeing himself

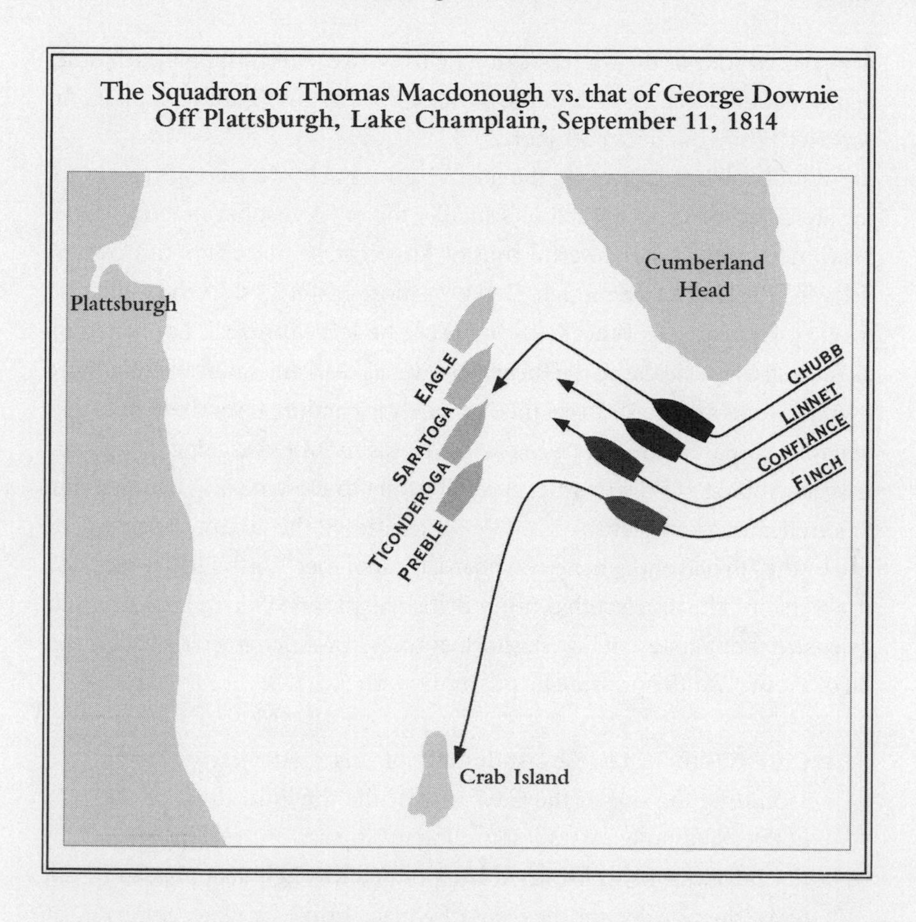

from the vagaries of the wind. This tactic also freed crewmen to man the guns instead of working the sails. More importantly, the British ships had a very limited range of maneuver once they passed Cumberland Head and entered the bay, where they were exposed to the broadsides Macdonough had arranged for them.

On land, Izard and Macomb had done their best during the summer to prepare a formidable defense. The steep banks of the Saranac where it emptied into the lake provided a natural defense against attackers attempting to cross the river and scale the slippery slopes while entrenched defenders fired down on them. Behind the riverbank, Izard had constructed three redoubts and two blockhouses on a small isthmus flanked by the river and lake, all designed by Major Joseph G. Totten, the tenth graduate of the recently established Military Academy at West Point. Named Forts Moreau, Brown, and Scott, the redoubts were placed so that their interlocking fields of fire could support each other and were built close enough to the bay to allow the land guns to support the American ships anchored off shore.[50]

With his army in place on the north bank of the Saranac and massed for the attack south against Macomb's smaller force, Prevost began to fret about his vulnerability to the powerful guns of American ships and about Downie's delay in attacking Macdonough. Downie's most powerful ship, the *Confiance*, was not yet ready, as Prevost knew before he left Montreal. Launched on 22 August, *Confiance* lay in the Richelieu River as workers frantically scrambled over her decks and masts to get the ship ready for action. Over the next couple of days, her masts were stepped, spars and guns mounted, rigging strung, and crew assembled as Prevost sent repeated letters to Downie importuning him to join the attack at Plattsburgh. *Confiance* entered the lake on 1 September, and by the 7th had enough men on board, most of them untrained, to function as a warship. The nineteenth century British historian William James, usually defensive about apparent British shortcomings, was uncharacteristically critical of Prevost for the pressure he put on Downie:

> On the 10th, just as the last draught of this motley crew ... was ascending the side of the *Confiance*, while the loud clank of the builder's hammer was still sounding in all parts of the ship, while the guns were being breeched and pointed through the ports, and while the powder, for the want of a place fitted for its reception, was lying in a boat alongside, an officer from Sir George Prevost came to solicit the instant co-operation of the British squadron.[51]

Finally, in the wee hours of 11 September, Downie left Île aux Noix, sailing south to join the *Linnet* and the several gunboats already near the bay in support of Prevost at Plattsburgh. The historian James observed that the British sailors were hardly prepared to do battle with their American counterparts, who had been training together for several weeks, if not longer: "[The] men of the *Confiance* ... were all strangers to each other and to their officers; and Captain Downie was acquainted with no officer on board his ship but his first lieutenant, and the latter with none of the officers."[52] If Downie was uncertain about the prospects, he was not about to let his men or fellow officers know it. At a mess hall in the border town of Odellton, Downie boasted that with the *Confiance* alone "he could lick the whole American squadron."[53]

Macdonough faced similar problems but had more time to deal with them. Perpetually short of crew, he pressed Izard and Macomb for soldiers to serve as sailors, and the equally shorthanded generals grudgingly provided a few. Seven members of Macomb's regimental band, and one of their wives, volunteered.[54] The *Eagle* had to accept forty-six soldiers who had been imprisoned for various crimes. Macomb, who was something of an expert on military justice, believed the assignment was cruel and unusual punishment.[55]

> "Some were chained in pairs, one with a ball & chain & some was shackled." Smith removed the irons from forty-six men and brought them to the ship, where he had them washed, barbered, fed and dressed in the last of the available slops. After a night's rest in hammocks made from sails, Smith "put them to the Guns & kept them at it constantly till the fight & they behaved well for greenhorns.[56]

Historians debate whether Macdonough was a man of deep religious conviction. There is some evidence that he was. A confirmed Episcopalian, he convened his officers on the deck of *Saratoga* just before the battle and read from the Book of Common Prayer, beseeching God (in the same words with which the British simultaneously prayed) to "take the cause into thine own hand, and judge between us and our enemies." Whether this prayer was an act of true devotion or merely part of the routinized preparation for battle we cannot say. Theodore Roosevelt assumed the sincerity of these men about to face the horrors of naval warfare:

> As the English squadron stood bravely in, young Macdonough, who feared his foes not at all, but his God a great deal, knelt for a moment, with his officers, on the quarter deck; and then ensued a few minutes of perfect quiet, the men waiting with grim expectancy for the start of the fight.[57]

In the early hours of 11 September, Downie halted his squadron behind Cumberland Head, "scaled" his guns (firing them without shot) to alert Prevost of his arrival, and lowered a gig to reconnoiter Macdonough's position. Aboard his flagship *Confiance*, Downie set the plan of battle and assigned to each of his ships its target for defeat. In size and guns, the fleets were closely matched, but the *Confiance* was easily the most powerful ship on the lake, closer in size to a frigate than to Macdonough's brigs. Armed with thirty-seven guns—thirty-one long twenty-four-pounders and six carronades—and rated at 1,200 tons with a crew of 325, *Confiance* easily outclassed Macdonough's largest, the *Saratoga*, which carried twenty-six guns, of which eighteen were short range carronades. With her crew of 240, *Saratoga*, displaced only 734 tons.[58] The odds were in Downie's favor, and he expected to make short work of the weaker *Saratoga* and quickly turn the day for the British.

Downie and *Confiance* rounded Cumberland Head at the north end of the bay at around seven o'clock in the morning. Behind him were the much smaller *Linnet*, 16, only 350 tons, commanded by Captain Thomas Pring, the even smaller *Chubb*, 11 (Lieutenant McGee) and *Finch*, 10 (Lieutenant William Hicks). Also with Downie were ten or twelve gunboats—the exact number is still in dispute. As Downie's squadron came into the tight waters of the bay, in honor of his hero Nelson, Macdonough conveyed by signal flags a message of encouragement to his fleet: *Impressed seamen call on every man to do his duty.*[59]

Downie's plan was to sail *Confiance* up the American line, fire a wood-splintering broadside at the smaller *Eagle*, and turn back to take up a position off *Saratoga*'s bow and rake her without mercy. *Finch*, with the help of the gunboats, would take on either *Ticonderoga* or *Preble*, while *Linnet* and *Chubb* would finish off *Eagle*, which would still be reeling from *Confiance*'s earlier broadside. The wind, however, failed to cooperate, and as Downie rounded the peninsula and entered the bay, it shifted against him.

Instead of blowing from the northeast and over what would have been the starboard quarters of the British ships, the wind now blew right into Downie's face from the northwest. Forced to claw his way into the bay on a close-hauled tack that slowed his speed, reduced his ability to maneuver, and kept him far south of his intended course, Downie could not get near the *Eagle* and was forced to sail directly into *Saratoga*'s waiting broadside. *Finch*, which had rounded Cumberland Head too far south, could now barely get near the American line, while *Linnet* and *Chubb* struggled to close with the much larger *Eagle*.

Eagle was the first to fire, aiming at *Confiance*, but her poorly-aimed broadside fell short of the British and did no damage. As *Confiance* struggled to close in the light winds, the brig *Linnet*, on course to *Eagle*, passed near *Saratoga* and fired a broadside from her eight long twelve-pounders. All the shots fell short of their target

> except one that struck a hen-coop which happened to be aboard the *Saratoga*. There was a game cock inside, and instead of being frightened at his sudden release, he jumped up on a gun-slide, clapped his wings, and crowed lustily. The men laughed and cheered; and immediately afterward Macdonough fired the first shot from one of the long guns.[60]

Macdonough put the smoldering match to the touch hole of the long twenty-four pounder, sending forty-eight pounds of iron shot in two grapefruit-sized balls across the placid waters of the bay nearly at the speed of sound. The well-aimed shot ripped through a hawse hole on *Confiance*'s bow, killing and maiming several sailors. The two iron balls crossed the open deck of the *Confiance* from stem to stern, destroying the ship's wheel. As Downie continued his labored course toward *Saratoga*, Macdonough's crew pounded at *Confiance*'s unarmed bow with shot after shot, while the gunboats stationed behind *Saratoga* popped in and out to fire their guns at the British flagship.

As the two flagships closed, *Linnet* and *Chubb* made their way to *Eagle*. But just as *Linnet* took her position abeam of *Eagle*, *Chubb* passed under *Linnet*'s stern and into the guns of *Eagle*. Seizing the opportunity, Lieutenant Henley fired two broadsides from his thirty-two-pound carronades and eighteen-pound long guns at the closing *Chubb*. Within minutes, he had shot away most of *Chubb*'s sails and rigging. Her captain was injured, and several of her crew and soldiers took refuge below as *Saratoga*'s marines fired from her fighting tops.

Command of the *Chubb* devolved to Midshipman Bodell, who attempted to maintain the attack by ordering out the sweeps and rowing the damaged vessel toward *Eagle*. But *Eagle*'s accurate fire shot away most of the oars, and with no means of control, *Chubb* drifted helplessly southward, floating between the closing *Confiance* and *Saratoga*. With the wounded captain's permission, Bodell lowered her colors, surrendering a fourth of the British fleet before *Confiance* had even fired her first broadside. Midshipman Platt of *Saratoga* took possession of *Chubb* and had her towed behind the American line to an anchorage at the mouth of the Saranac.[61] "Of the crew of forty-one, six were dead and sixteen were so badly wounded they could not serve: not a man was untouched. There were only six men on deck when *Chubb* was taken."[62]

With *Chubb* out of the way, *Confiance* gained the distance she needed, turned her starboard to *Saratoga*, and fired a double-shot broadside from the thirteen long twenty-four-pounders that faced the American brig. It took only a split second for the six hundred pounds of iron to fly across the lake and smash into *Saratoga*, shuddering her timbers so powerfully that nearly half her crew was knocked to the deck. When the smoke cleared, one in five of *Saratoga*'s men was wounded or killed, including Macdonough's first lieutenant, Peter Gamble, who died instantly at the gun he was sighting.[63] The two flagships were now abeam of each other, positioned for a classic broadside-to-broadside bout—Macdonough's nine heavy carronades, forty-two- and thirty-two-pounders, plus a couple of long guns, facing Downie's thirteen long twenty-four-pounders.

Downie fell in the first fifteen minutes by a shot that hit the mouth of one of his guns, knocking the two-and-a-half-ton barrel off its wooden carriage and into his chest, killing him instantly. Lieutenant Robertson assumed the command of *Confiance* and rallied his seamen to continue the fight as heavy metal shot flew from ship to ship, killing and maiming both men and officers.

Robertson was unable to locate *Confiance*'s signal book to advise the other ships of Downie's death and to inform Pring, now the senior officer, that command of the squadron had devolved to him. All of *Confiance*'s boats had been shattered to splinters in the early minutes of the fight, so the message could not be delivered to Pring by hand. The British therefore continued the increasingly uneven battle with no one in effective command. Just as the advantage shifted to the Americans, a shot from *Confiance* split *Saratoga*'s spanker boom. Half of the heavy pine spar fell on Macdonough's head as he bent down to sight his favorite gun on the quarterdeck. He fell to the deck and was feared dead, but in two or three minutes he recovered and resumed command. Minutes later, a shot ricocheted off a gun barrel, decapitating midshipman Bellamy.[64] The sailor's severed head flew through the air and struck Macdonough's own, splattering him with brains and blood and knocking him again into the scuppers. Macdonough recovered from this gruesome blow as well and rallied his men to stand by their guns, which one by one were being knocked out of action by *Confiance*'s deadly broadsides.

James Fenimore Cooper described the scene of mounting casualties on the *Saratoga*:

> Mr. Brum, the master, a venerable old seaman, while winding the ship, had a large splinter driven so near his body, as actually to strip off his clothes. For a minute he was thought to be dead, but, on gaining his feet, he made an apron of his pocket handkerchief, and coolly went to work again with the springs! A few months later this veteran died, as is thought of the injury. Mr. Lavallette had a shot box, on which he was standing, knocked from under his feet, and he too, was once knocked down by the head of a seaman.... In short, very few escaped altogether; and in this desperate fight, it appears to have been agreed to on both sides, to call no man wounded who could keep out of a hospital. Many who were not included among the wounded, feel the effects of their hurts to this day. It is said, that scarcely an individual escaped on board either the *Confiance* or *Saratoga*, without some injury.[65]

As Macdonough traded broadsides with *Confiance*, *Eagle* and *Linnet* continued their own fierce fight just to the north. *Eagle*'s springs were soon shot away, and as the ship twisted away and into the wind, she momentarily lost her ability to direct fire at *Linnet*, which continued to hammer her with relentless broadsides. Casualties ran high, especially among the prisoners. Three of the volunteer bandsmen were killed, including one who was found by his wife bringing powder to his gun.[66]

In a controversial move that angered Macdonough and led to bitter charges and counter-charges after the battle, Lieutenant Henley raised *Eagle*'s topsails, cut his cable, and ran down the line to take a position near *Saratoga*. *Linnet* briefly held her position in the north, directing her fire at the remaining American gunboats, but soon followed *Eagle* south and took up a raking position off *Saratoga*'s bow, forcing Macdonough simultaneously to fight the two largest ships in the British squadron.[67]

Farther down Macdonough's line, the *Finch* struggled upwind. Failing to reach her target (the schooner *Ticonderoga*), she went after the sloop *Commodore Preble*, anchored just north of Crab Island. Expecting *Finch*'s support, the lightly armed British gunboats went on the attack against *Ticonderoga*, which was armed with a dozen long guns of various weights. Her commander, Lieutenant Stephen Cassin, "walked the taffrail, where he could watch the movements of the enemy's galleys, amidst showers of canister and grape, directing discharges of musket-balls, and other light missiles, effectually keeping the British at bay."[68]

Once in range, Cassin let fly with a broadside or two of grape, which killed and wounded several on the British boats. Then, turning *Ticonderoga* on her springs, he fired at the approaching *Finch*, ripping up her rigging and sending a few balls through her hull. *Ticonderoga*'s lieutenant, John Stansbury, was cut in two by British shot. His fate was not known until his body parts floated to the surface of the bay two days later. Outgunned by the well-managed schooner, the British gunboats went into permanent retreat and were not heard from again. Lieutenant Budd was in command of the *Preble*, anchored a short distance to the south. Thinking that he was about to be overrun by the concentration of gunboats, Budd cut his cables and let *Preble* drift back and away to the Plattsburgh shore, leaving Cassin and *Ticonderoga* to hold the southern end of the line.

Seeing the *Preble* in flight, Lieutenant Hicks turned *Finch* toward *Ticonderoga*. It was an unequal match, however, and within minutes *Finch*'s sails and rigging were disabled, her rudder knocked out of action, and her hold filling with water. Unable to control her course, *Finch* went aground on the rocks off Crab Island. In an effort to lighten his ship, Hicks ordered the carronades dumped overboard, but the ship remained stuck on the rocks. With the few guns he had left to load and shoot, Hicks continued the fight while sustaining return fire from both the *Ticonderoga* and the six-pound long gun on Crab Island.

No longer threatened by *Finch*, Cassin turned *Ticonderoga* to direct her long guns at *Confiance*, which, with *Linnet*, continued to battle *Saratoga* and *Eagle* at the north end of the line. *Saratoga* and *Confiance* had been at each other for more than an hour, and all of Macdonough's starboard guns were out of action. Of the 250 crewmen who began the battle on *Saratoga*, only about a hundred were still in the fight.[69] When the last functioning carronade was knocked off its wooden slide, bounced across the bloody deck, and rolled down the hatch to the deck below, it was time to use the preset springs and cables to turn, or "wind" (as a clock), the *Saratoga* 180 degrees, bringing the carronades of her uninjured larboard side to bear on the enemy. Letting go with the stern and bow anchors, *Saratoga*'s crew pulled the hawser of the starboard kedge to the stern and then pulled the stern toward the kedge, which remained firmly anchored in the muddy floor of the bay. As *Saratoga* began to turn on her anchorage, Pring readied *Linnet* to rake the brig's exposed stern as it wound toward him. Expecting as much, Macdonough moved his crewmen to the forecastle, where they had some protection from *Linnet*'s raking fire, which hit *Saratoga* with diminished effect.

As each of *Saratoga*'s larboard guns came to bear on *Confiance*, gun captains touched match to powder, and sixty to eighty pounds of grape and shot flew across the water, further battering the flagship. In minutes, *Saratoga* had turned completely around, and her (new) full broadside of nine carronades and four long twenty-four-pounders blasted away at *Confiance*, killing or wounding half the remaining crew. With only four operable starboard guns, Lieutenant Robertson attempted the same turning maneuver but failed in the execution.[70] *Confiance* was stuck in a vulnerable position, largely because Macdonough had shot away her cables and anchors in the first minutes of the fight. As she wallowed helplessly, the target of the raging guns of *Saratoga*, *Eagle*, *Ticonderoga*, and several of the now emboldened American gunboats, her brave but inexperienced crew refused to continue a fight that would soon reduce their ship to splinters. Robertson struck his colors. Three days later, midshipman R. Lea, now imprisoned on *Confiance*, wrote to his mother in England that "the havoc on both sides is dreadful. I don't think there are more than five of our men, out of three hundred, but what are killed or wounded."[71]

Though on the fringe of the battle, the *Linnet* was badly damaged and taking on water. Despite the loss of *Chubb* and *Confiance* and the grounding of *Finch*, Pring was not ready to concede, even though he faced the Americans' three largest ships alone. Macdonough, respecting Pring's noble stand, turned *Saratoga* to face him and let fly with a broadside into the damaged *Linnet* for several more minutes. Having made his point and defended the honor of his country, Pring finally struck his colors. Off Crab Island, Hicks realized from the absence of gunfire in the north that the battle was over. With little hope of surviving in an unarmed ship stuck on the rocks, Hicks struck *Finch*'s colors and made the surrender complete. In her long and storied naval history before the War of 1812, Britain had never lost a squadron. Now, a year and a day after Perry's victory on Lake Erie, she had lost a second one to the Americans.

Early that evening, with the prisoners secured, prize crews aboard the captured vessels, and the wounded cared for to the extent possible, Thomas

Macdonough, following two of his naval heroes—Nelson at the Nile and Perry at Erie[72]—penned a note to Navy Secretary Jones: "The Almighty has been pleased to Grant us a Signal Victory on Lake Champlain in the Capture of one Frigate, one Brig, and two sloops of war of the enemy."

V

The timing of Prevost's attack against Macomb's growing force depended on the arrival of Downie's squadron, which would protect his left flank from Macdonough's guns. Without that protection, the skittish Prevost would retreat. His plan had been for Major General Brisbane to feint an attack on the plankless bridges crossing the Saranac at Plattsburgh, distracting the Americans from the real assault, which Major General Robinson would lead. Fording the Saranac three miles upriver, Robinson's much larger force would attack Macomb's unfortified left and rear and send the American fleeing south.

The British heard the scaling of Downie's guns shortly after sunrise on 11 September, but Prevost held back Robinson's assault until ten o'clock. The assault began as a fiasco, with the force losing its way, backtracking, and wasting another hour trying to find the river. Once they crossed the seventy yards of the shallow water, though, they easily fought off the light American defense at the distant end of their flank. Now on Macomb's exposed flank, Robinson prepared to move southeast for the final assault on the entrenched American line, confident he would swiftly prevail.

As soon as Robinson had organized his force on the American side of the Saranac, however, he received orders calling off the assault. Prevost, it seems, had been watching the naval battle from Plattsburgh's north shore. When he saw *Confiance*, *Linnet*, and *Finch* strike their colors to Macdonough, he lost his nerve. Through his adjutant, Major General Baynes, Prevost sent the following order to Robinson:

> I am directed to inform you that the "Confiance" and the Brig having struck her colours in consequence of the Frigate having grounded, it will no longer be prudent to persevere in the Service committed to your charge, and it is therefore the Orders of the

> Commander of the Forces that you immediately return with the Troops under your command.[73]

The astonished Robinson reluctantly obeyed. He returned his force to the north bank of the river, then, with the thousands of crack British troops held in reserve, began the long retreat north to Montreal. For the American defenders, the brief skirmishes left thirty-seven men dead and sixty-two wounded.[74] The British casualties were thirty-five dead, forty-seven wounded, and seventy-two taken prisoner. An even larger number of British infantrymen, estimated at 234, were reported missing, but they are believed to have taken advantage of the "fog of war" to desert in pursuit of prosperity in this new country so rich in land, resources, and opportunity.[75]

The two hours of battle on the lake were far more costly than skirmishes on shore. Theodore Roosevelt estimates that two hundred American and three hundred British seamen were killed. The British figure is only a rough estimate, as the defeated squadron had no opportunity formally to muster the captured crewmen.[76] The log books, moreover, had been thrown overboard to avoid capture, and many of the British dead had been tossed into the bay as the battle raged. The ships on each side fared as poorly as the men: "the *Saratoga* had 55 shot-holes in her hull, the *Confiance* 105, and the *Eagle* and *Linnet* suffered in proportion."[77] Indeed, the *Eagle* counted thirty-nine shots that pierced her hull. Many of the officers and men on both sides had little or no training for the tasks they were expected to perform, but they fought with uncommon valor. "In this battle," Roosevelt concludes, "the crews on both sides behaved with equal bravery, and left nothing to be desired in this respect."[78]

Macdonough's victory in Plattsburgh Bay was as close to a turning point as one can identify in this muddled conflict. The British negotiators at Ghent were intent on forcing a settlement on terms very much to Britain's advantage, but such a settlement required decisive victories on sea and land. Macdonough's plucky squadron and the citizens of Baltimore who manned the city's ramparts by the thousands forced the British to recognize that some version of the prewar *status quo ante* was as good as they would get. In a letter from Monticello to President Madison, Thomas Jefferson reflected that after "the defeat of a second hostile fleet on the lakes by McDonough," the British must "be stung to the soul by these repeated victories over them on that element on which they wish the world to think them invincible."[79]

Macdonough's achievement at Plattsburgh would receive the accolades of American and British historians over the remainder of the nineteenth century:

> On Lake Champlain Thomas Macdonough had done what no other naval commander was able to do in modern time. He had beaten the monarch of the seas at her own game with an inferior fleet.... The British naval historian William Laird Clowes has called Macdonough's victory, "a most notable feat, one which, on the whole, surpassed that of any other captain of either navy in this war." Alfred Thayer Mahan, the American naval strategist and historian, labeled the action the most "decisive" battle in the War of 1812, and Theodore Roosevelt wrote that at Lake Champlain Macdonough "won a higher fame than any other commander of the war, British or American." Novelist and historian James Fenimore Cooper felt that he had slighted the importance of the battle in his first edition of the *History of the Navy*, and he wrote a letter apologizing for his account to Captain Horace B. Sawyer. Cooper told Sawyer, "The Battle of Plattsburgh Bay is the most honorable affair, that has ever occurred to our arms. Hitherto it has not been sufficiently noticed, but I think it will henceforth take its proper place in our annals."[80]

The estimation of Macdonough's victory did not fade in the following century. C. S. Forester wrote in 1956, "Any invasion of the United States by the northern route was now impossible, at least until the Royal Navy, starting with nothing, could build up a superior fleet on Lake Champlain, and that would be never if the Americans knew their business as well as they appeared to know it."[81] The British naval historian G. J. Marcus echoed Forester a decade and a half later: "The action of Plattsburgh proved decisive in the war. The American squadrons were now in complete control of the Great Lakes, and a British invasion of the United States from Canada was clearly impossible."[82]

The reputation of Governor General Sir George Prevost, who led his vast and largely unused army of veterans back to Montreal, was ruined. The Canadian Hitsman writes of the anger among the officers who had served with Wellington in Spain:

> Naturally on their return to Lower Canada they associated with the English-speaking minority which had grown to hate Sir George Prevost and was actively campaigning for his replacement.... Correspondents at Quebec fed the London and Glasgow newspapers with tirades against the "timid, temporizing policy" of Sir George Prevost.[83]

Henry Adams quotes the shocked response of the editor of London's *Annual Register*: "It is scarcely possible to conceive the degree of mortification and disappointment which the intelligence of this defeat created in Great Britain."[84] Even Prevost's adoring daughter Anne did not hide her disappointment when she wrote in her journal on 12 September:

> The mortifying news arrived that our Squadron was defeated, captured and Captain Downie killed.... I was breathless till I heard what the Army was about; the loss of the Fleet seemed to me a secondary consideration, and when Mr. B went on to say the Army was in retreat, it seemed to me I heard a death's knell ringing in my ears.... I felt certain that ... it would bring the greatest Odium on my father....[85]

Her father, however, saw it differently, and ten days later he composed a report of the events for Lord Bathurst, blaming the debacle on the dead Captain Downie. "The disastrous and unlooked for result of the Naval Contest by depriving me of the only means by which I could avail myself of any advantage I might gain, rendered a perseverance of the attack of the Enemy's position highly imprudent, as well as hazardous."[86]

Commodore Yeo and the duke of Wellington eventually held contradictory views on the battle of Lake Plattsburgh, but they were both critical of Prevost's performance. To Admiralty Secretary Croker, Yeo wrote, "It appears to me, and I have good reason to believe, that Captain Downie was urged, and his ships hurried into action, before she was in a fit state to meet the enemy," and he ultimately brought official charges against Prevost.[87] Wellington wrote to Bathurst, "It is very obvious to me that you must remove Sir George Prevost."[88] Bathurst agreed, and Prevost was soon called back to England to face a naval court of inquiry, which found him responsible for the Plattsburgh defeat. Hoping to clear his name, he requested another hearing, but he died in 1816, before a new court of inquiry could convene.

Master Commandant Thomas Macdonough, by contrast, became a national hero, and, as a consequence, a very wealthy man. "The final tally of the value of the British squadron was $329,000, of which Macdonough was to receive $22,807—the largest single day's prize awarded during the War of 1812."[89] More would follow. "He received a gold medal from Congress, 1,000 acres of land in Cayuga County from New York, and 100 acres on Cumberland Head from Vermont. He was also given valuable keepsakes by other cities and states. In one month, he said, 'from a poor lieutenant I became a rich man.'"[90]

After the British surrender, Macdonough returned their swords to the surviving British officers. Captain Pring of *Linnet* wrote of the experience, "I have much satisfaction in making you acquainted with the humane treatment the wounded have received from Commodore Macdonough; they were immediately removed to his own hospital on Crab Island, and furnished with every requisite. His generous and polite attention to myself, the officers, and men, will hereafter be gratefully remembered."[91]

When news of the defeat reached England, a correspondent to the *Naval Chronicles* wrote, "These defeats and disasters in America excited the most rapturous applause from the friends of that people in Paris. In the theatres, coffee-houses, and places of public resort were heard the loudest acclamations and prognostics of our fall!"[92] But the greatest reverberations of the defeat were felt not in Paris or in London or in Washington but in Ghent, where British and American negotiators struggled to reach an agreement.

CHAPTER TWENTY

BACK ON LAND: WASHINGTON AND BALTIMORE

As the main prong of Great Britain's three-pronged attack on America faltered and failed at Plattsburgh, three hundred miles to the east, along the coast of Maine, prong number two was succeeding handsomely. One of Bathurst's objectives in the war was the cession by the U.S. of the disputed territory in Maine between the Penobscot River and the border with Lower Canada. Occupied by the Americans since the Treaty of Paris ended the Revolutionary War, Maine's northern protuberance—jutting 180 miles north into Canadian territory—greatly interfered with commerce and communication between Canada's three largest settlements, Montreal, Quebec, and Halifax. When the St. Lawrence River froze in the winter, British supplies and troops had to travel overland on a long and arduous loop around the American territory. But that problem could be remedied by war, and in March 1814 the legislature of New Brunswick petitioned the prince regent that,

> when a negotiation for Peace shall take place between Great Britain and the United States of America, His Royal Highness will be

> graciously pleased to direct such measures as he may think proper, to alter the boundary between those States and this Province, so that the important lines of communication between this and the neighboring Province of Lower Canada, by the River St. John may not be interrupted.[1]

Maine was still part of Massachusetts, and its citizens felt some dissatisfaction with their distant rulers in Boston. There were some who thought that a British takeover might be a welcome change. The occasional British raiding party along coastal Maine met little resistance from the local militia, and many of the area's residents conducted a lucrative trade in food and other goods with the enemy in New Brunswick.

Lieutenant General Sir John Sherbrooke, the governor of Nova Scotia, and Admiral Sir Thomas Hardy[2] led a substantial force against the coastal town of Eastport, Maine, just over the border from New Brunswick, on 11 July 1814. Access to Eastport was blocked by Fort Sullivan's eighty-six regulars and 250 militiamen led by Major Perly Putnam, but when Hardy landed 600 men from his squadron and threatened to destroy Eastport if Putnam resisted, the Americans withdrew, and Hardy took control of the town and surrounding countryside.

Hardy understood that land seized in Maine would formally revert to Great Britain when the war ended. Some accounts claim that the admiral gave the citizens of Eastport and its environs seven days to sign an oath of allegiance to Britain or get out of town. About a third of the citizens chose the latter course,[3] abandoning their homes and land in favor of their country. The rest stayed, took the loyalty oath, and continued their lucrative trade with the enemy, now without fear of harassment or loss of goods to the American warships patrolling Maine's coast in search of smugglers. Other historians dispute this account. Agreements, they say, were required only of those who wanted to conduct business with Britain, while other agreements and oaths were limited simply to a promise to keep the peace.[4]

Six weeks later, on 1 September, the same day Prevost crossed the Canada–New York border on his way to Plattsburgh, a substantial British force under Sherbrooke entered the mouth of the Penobscot River to seize the towns and villages along its banks, including Bangor. He was accompanied by a substantial force that included 2,500 veteran infantrymen from Gibraltar and a fleet comprising *Dragon*, 74, the frigates *Endymion* and *Bacchante*, the sloop *Sylph*, and ten transports.[5]

The Penobscot region was not Sherbrooke's first target—he was aiming for the town of Machias, just down the coast from Eastport—but while in transit he was told that the heavy corvette-light frigate *Adams*, 28, had just sailed up the Penobscot River to Hampden to repair damages incurred on a reef off the Maine coast. Commanded by Captain Charles Morris—now recovered from severe wounds received in the fight between *Constitution* and *Guerriere*—the *Adams* had just completed a successful voyage of commerce raiding and had taken or destroyed nine British vessels off Maine and New Brunswick. Given the opportunity to seize one of the few American warships still at sea, Sherbrooke moved his substantial force to the Penobscot and the lucrative prize it promised.

The American troops at the undermanned forts at the mouth of the river fired a few perfunctory shots at the British fleet before spiking their guns and retreating up river to safety. To lighten his ship for repairs, Morris had already unloaded his guns, which were now positioned along the river to challenge the British as they sailed up against the current. The militia was called out, but not all reported for duty. Many of the six hundred or so who did had no arms.[6] The British attacked on 2 September. Shots were exchanged, but a bayonet attack by the redcoats sent the militiamen flying. Morris spiked his guns and set his ship on fire before withdrawing inland. The British sacked Bangor, exacting a thirty-thousand-dollar bond to ensure the delivery to Sherbrooke of the seven vessels then under construction at the port. Hampden, too, was sacked and its meeting house burnt to the ground. Casualties were light for such a conquest—only one British death and thirteen among the Americans.

Having secured the Penobscot region, the British took Machias, achieving effective control of the northern half of Maine. Sherbrooke reorganized all of Maine north of the Penobscot into the province of New Brunswick and began to collect custom duties on products moving in and out of the Maine ports.

II

The third prong of Bathurst's American offensive, which was focused on the Chesapeake Bay, did not achieve the unequivocal success that the British enjoyed in Maine. Bathurst wrote to Admiralty Secretary Croker that the goal of the force being organized at Bermuda was "to effect a diversion on the coasts of the United States in favor of the armies employed in the defense of Upper and Lower Canada."[7] The British, however, overestimated the ability of America's leaders to recognize the seriousness of the northern threat. The United States actually reduced its military presence at Plattsburgh, not that it made much difference in the outcome of either campaign.

Vice Admiral Sir Alexander Forrester Inglis Cochrane, ninth son of the eighth earl of Dundonald, took over command of the Chesapeake force from Admiral Warren in January 1814, though Warren did not formally relinquish his North American command until 1 April.[8] Influential but ineffective, Warren had been removed through a clever bureaucratic ruse when the Admiralty separated the Jamaican and Leeward Island command from the rest of the North American waters, yielding two smaller posts instead of a large one. The more limited geographic scope and smaller fleet no longer justified a full admiral, so Warren was replaced by the lower-ranking Cochrane. The *Naval Chronicle*'s skepticism was typical of the British press: "[T]here is no foundation for the report of Lord Cochrane's being to have the command of a squadron of frigates. That would look like energy in the Admiralty Board."[9]

The Cochranes were a prominent family in the Royal Navy in the first decades of the nineteenth century. The vice admiral's son served with him in the Chesapeake as captain of the frigate *Surprise*, and his nephew, Sir Thomas Cochrane, the dashing captain of HMS *Speedy*, was the inspiration for Patrick O'Brian's fictional hero Jack Aubrey. Sir Alexander Cochrane, now fifty-five years old, had served in North America during the Revolutionary War, developing a dislike for Americans. In a letter to Bathurst of 14 July 1814, Cochrane wrote, "I have it much to heart to give them a complete drubbing before peace is made, when I trust their northern limits will be circumscribed and the command of the Mississippi wrested from them."[10] Cochrane's fleet captain, Edward Codrington, held similar views. "I do not believe there is anywhere a more detestable race of people," he confided to his wife.[11]

There were few limits to what Cochrane would do to weaken and defeat the Americans. Within days of assuming command, he played on one of the deepest fears of the southern states with a proclamation to the slaves in the Chesapeake region:

> All those who may be disposed to emigrate from the United States, will with their families, be received on board his Majesty's ships or vessels of war, or at military posts that may be established upon or near the coast of the United States, when they will have their choice of either entering into his Majesty's sea or land forces, or as being sent as FREE settlers, to the British possessions....[12]

The response was surprisingly limited—perhaps three hundred slaves fled to the British fleet. But the attempt to undermine the slave system was just one of several assaults that month on the inhabitants of the region. Elting quotes Cochrane's orders to his squadrons on blockade duty along the American coast "to destroy and lay waste such towns and districts ... as you may find assailable," while the vice admiral accused the Americans of inhumane treatment of Canadians.[13]

Cochrane was probably referring to the burning of the public buildings at York, Ontario, by U.S. troops on 27 April 1813 and Colonel John Campbell's raid across Lake Erie on 14 May 1814, which left Port Dover in ashes.[14] Though Campbell's raid took no civilian lives, the British quickly exacted harsh revenge; Major General Phineas Riall's raid on Black Rock and Buffalo in New York killed a number of civilians.

Napoleon's exile allowed Britain to provide Cochrane with a much larger force than Warren had received a year earlier. In early June, a force of about a thousand marines arrived in Bermuda from the Mediterranean, followed by as many as three thousand infantrymen from France[15] under the command of Major General Robert Ross. A forty-eight-year-old Irish country gentleman who had served competently under Wellington, Ross had fought Napoleon's armies in Egypt, Italy, Portugal, Spain, and France. Although a harsh disciplinarian, the affable Ross had the respect of his troops because his men understood that his discipline led to victory with fewer casualties and that the general was always in the thick of the fight with his troops. "He had been wounded twice, and at Pamplona had two horses shot out from under him. Sometimes he almost seemed to be daring death."[16]

Ross was subordinate to Cochrane, but Bathurst provided him with a generous measure of authority:

> The Admiral would pick the targets, but Ross should "freely express" his opinion from the military point of view. He also had veto power over the use of his troops, and once ashore had complete control over their operations.[17]

Cochrane was waiting for Ross at Bermuda when his fleet arrived on 24 July 1814. With Codrington, they discussed a number of possible targets for attack before settling on the Chesapeake region.

Numbering more than twenty warships and transports, the fleet departed Bermuda on 3 August and rounded Cape Charles, Virginia, where it was sighted on the morning of the 16 August by U. S. Navy lookout Joseph Middleton.[18] Stationed at the Pleasure House, a popular seaside inn near Cape Henry, Middleton recorded the details of the fleet as it entered the Chesapeake Bay. An express rider carried Middleton's report to Norfolk, to be relayed thence to Washington. Other lookouts around the Chesapeake dispatched similar reports as the British ships entered Hampton Roads and swung north into the bay. By early evening on the 17th, Cochrane's fleet anchored at the mouth of the Potomac, where it was joined by the two dozen ships already stationed in the bay under his second in command, the feisty Rear Admiral George Cockburn. Thomas Swann, a volunteer observer for the U.S. Army at Point Lookout on the Potomac, counted fifty-one ships near the mouth of the river and sent his report to Washington, seventy miles away.[19]

Ordered by Bathurst to create a diversion, Cochrane sent Captain James A. Gordon up the Potomac with a squadron of sloops and ordered Captain Sir Peter Parker, a first cousin of Lord Byron, to probe the central coast of the Chesapeake in his frigate *Menelaus* so as to suggest that Cochrane was interested in more than Washington alone. As the British force disembarked on 19 August at Benedict, Maryland, on the Patuxent River, the capital, forty-five miles to the northwest, remained largely undefended.

Except for Commodore Joshua Barney's squadron of small gunboats on the Patuxent, there were no American naval defenses in the region. The frigate *Constellation* was still blockaded at Norfolk, while a new *Argus*, 18, and *Columbia*, 44, were still under construction in the Washington Navy Yard. As for land forces, U.S. troop strength around the capital amounted to no more that 380 regulars, 120 marines, and Lieutenant Colonel Jacint Laval's 125 light dragoons. There were, in addition, garrisons at Fort Warburton on the Potomac, just below Washington, and at Fort McHenry at Baltimore, as well as two forts at Annapolis. For the most part, Washington and Baltimore depended on their militias for their defense, which were drawn largely from the cities' clerks, civil servants, shop keepers, and self-employed professionals. Most were poorly equipped and poorly trained—no match for the 4,500 hardened veterans of the Napoleonic Wars coming ashore at Benedict.

President Madison had been concerned about an attack on Washington in the aftermath of Napoleon's defeat that spring, and on 1 July 1814 he put thirty-nine-year-old Brigadier General William Winder in charge of assembling the defense of the city. The choice of Winder was typical of Madison's military assignments—the candidate's lack of qualifications was offset by the appointment's political expediency. A Baltimore lawyer, Winder had little military experience beyond being captured at Beaver Dams on 24 June 1813. Released in early 1814 to travel to Washington to negotiate an exchange of prisoners, Winder had the good fortune of being in town just as Madison needed an officer to organize the defense. And he had the even better luck to be the nephew of Maryland's Federalist governor, Levin Winder, whose support Madison would need if the capital were attacked.

Although some officials believed the British would never attack the capital—conventional wisdom had the British attacking Annapolis and then promptly leaving—the energetic Winder assumed the worst and set about cobbling together a defensive force. He received little support from Armstrong, who was convinced that Washington was safe. The secretary of war assumed that the British shared his contempt for the new capital city, in which he, a cosmopolitan New Yorker by marriage, was stuck. He insisted that at most "there might be what he called a 'Cossack hurrah'—a quick hit-and-run strike." His proposal was to stuff the capital with armed troops who would leap out and attack at the moment of greatest peril. "On the success of this plan I would pledge both life and reputation," Armstrong assured the president.[20] Other members of the cabinet were less sanguine. Navy Secretary Jones summoned to Washington all of the naval forces blockaded in nearby ports. He urged Commodore Rodgers to bring three hundred men down from Philadelphia. He told Captain David Porter, stranded in New York, to bring as many men as he could. And he pulled Oliver Hazard Perry out of Baltimore, where he was overseeing the construction of the *Java*.[21] With Madison's support and encouragement, Winder worked tirelessly, though not always effectively, calling up the militias of the District of Columbia, Virginia, and Maryland, and assembling them into an organized force that could defend the city against an enemy whose intentions and strength were as yet unknown.

On 20 August, Secretary of State James Monroe—fifty-four years old and a combat veteran of the Revolutionary War—left his office to assume the role of chief scout, riding with a small party of cavalry through the Maryland countryside in search of Ross's force. The sixty-three-year-old president—perhaps sensing that the city's military command left much to be desired—rode east with his aides to Long Old Fields, Maryland, where Winder had assembled his three thousand infantrymen and four hundred cavalry. Accompanied by the secretaries of the army and navy, Attorney General Richard Rush, and a couple of aides, Madison reached Winder's encampment that evening, spent the night at a nearby farm house, and met with the general at dawn.

Madison believed that Ross would soon return to his ships and leave the region. Winder disagreed, expecting the British to march to the southwest, attack Fort Washington on the Potomac, and then march north to the city. Unconvinced, Madison and his entourage returned to Washington. On 23 August, Ross ordered his troops to march west to Bladensburg, Maryland, from which they intended to cross the Eastern Branch of the Potomac (now the Anacostia River) and drive south to the capital.

Ross's Chesapeake force comprised some of Britain's most experienced regiments, but with only 4,500 men and no supporting cavalry or artillery, it was well short of what conventional military strategy deemed sufficient for an assault on a major target far from home. After Ross and Cockburn had begun the march to Washington, Cochrane apparently urged them to turn back. Ross was inclined to obey, but Cockburn was committed to taking the capital and persuaded Ross to ignore Cochrane's request. So they proceeded.[22]

Two days earlier, as Winder waited at Long Old Fields, Brigadier General Tobias Stansbury of the Maryland militia moved his enthusiastic but poorly trained force of just over 1,300 down from Baltimore to occupy the town of Bladensburg. They were soon to be joined by the 950 men of the "Dandy" Fifth Maryland Infantry Regiment, made up of "Baltimore's most fashionable young blades"[23] and commanded by Lieutenant Colonel Joseph Sterrett. Among the Fifth Infantry was Private John Pendleton Kennedy, who had brought with him a pair of dancing pumps to wear at the anticipated Victory Ball at the President's House.[24]

Still trying to determine Ross's whereabouts and intentions, Winder ordered Stansbury and Sterrett to defend Bladensburg as long as possible. If pressed by a superior British force, they were to retreat across the Eastern Branch and move south to Washington. As Stansbury attempted to arrange his tired force to fulfill Winder's conflicting orders, a rumor that Winder was missing and believed captured began to circulate. It stemmed, perhaps, from Winder's riding day and night from one outpost to another to organize the American defense. Monroe added to the confusion when he rode into Stansbury's camp late in the evening of 22 August[25] and confirmed the rumor of Winder's disappearance. He urged Stansbury to attack Ross's rear, though neither man had any idea where that rear might be. Confused and worried by conflicting orders, Stansbury did nothing. Winder correctly suspected that Ross was leading his force against him at Long Old Fields so he ordered his men to retreat to Washington across the Eastern Branch bridge, which Commodore Barney and his sailors and marines were ordered to defend.

Stansbury soon abandoned his position in Bladensburg and pulled his militia back across the bridge to the west bank of the Eastern Branch, where they would rest, prepare a much needed meal, and, perhaps, establish a new defensive position against the expected British attack. Winder exploded in anger when he learned of Stansbury's retreat, but there was little he could do about it. Stansbury feared Ross more than he feared Winder, and he had no intention of meeting the former from anything other than the most secure position he could find.[26]

As Winder's force of about 2,000 men marched north from Washington to Bladensburg, Monroe raced ahead to help Stansbury prepare for the attack. Although Stansbury's military training and experience were limited, he had deployed his 2,200 militiamen in a serviceable defense of the river crossing at Bladensburg by digging them in on the high ground above the river and the bridge and placing his artillery units where they could lay down an effective cover fire against the attacking forces coming over the bridge or fording the river. About fifty yards behind the front line, Stansbury hid three regiments, including Sterrett's Fifth, in an apple orchard, where they could quickly move up and plug any gaps, block a British breakthrough, or secure a shaky flank. Monroe, however, had other ideas. Without informing Stansbury, he ordered the three Baltimore regiments in the orchard to redeploy 500 yards to the rear, where they would be of no value at all.[27]

Hours later, when the 800 militiamen from Annapolis arrived at the front, Monroe intercepted them, ordering them to hold a hill nearly a mile behind the front before Stansbury could add them to his left flank.[28] And when Laval, a veteran of the battle at Sackets Harbor, arrived with 125 cavalrymen,[29] Monroe placed them, along with 250 additional riders who arrived soon after, in a ravine well to the rear, where they too were certain to be of no value in the coming fight.

Soon after Stansbury had deployed his Marylanders in front of the bridge, Winder brought his substantial force into the area, deploying them as ineptly as Monroe had rearranged Stansbury's initial defensive line. Walter Lord observes,

> The country to the north and west [of the Bladensburg bridge] was largely a tangle of woods, and with the river a barrier to the south, Bladensburg did function as a sort of funnel through which anyone bound for Washington from the east would have to go.... Nearly everyone except General Winder saw this clearly.[30]

Rather than establishing a defense that would compensate for the Americans' lack of experience by challenging the British when they were most vulnerable—while crossing the river on a narrow bridge or fording it through shallow water—Winder deployed his line about a mile behind Stansbury's front line force, which was already weakened by Monroe's blundering rearrangements. Summing up the defensive strategy confronting the British that day, one historian remarks, "None of the lines was in a position to support any other line; indeed, the first two did not know that the third was behind them."[31] Among the many mistakes the Americans made that day, the worst was the failure to destroy the wooden bridge that crossed the river from Bladensburg to Stansbury's first line of defense.

Wearing a pair of dueling pistols given to him by the secretary of the treasury, George Campbell, Madison set out on the morning of the 24th with his aids from the White House to review the points of defense that had been established around the capital. Stopping first at the Eastern Branch bridge, Madison and Armstrong were confronted by an angry Commodore Barney, who raged at the folly of leaving him and his formidable force of tough sailors and marines out of the coming fight. Madison concurred, and Barney led his

500 men to the front, leaving a small force behind to destroy the bridge if necessary.

The British had started out at five o'clock that morning from Melwood, Maryland. After a forced march of fifteen miles through the humid heat of August, the advanced guard arrived at Bladensburg around noon, exhausted and hungry, with the rest of the army still straggling in from behind. Always cautious, Ross worried about the vast American force dug in across the river with its huge advantage in cannon (he had only four). He wanted to delay the attack until the whole army was in place and a battle plan devised. Cockburn and Colonel William Thornton, however, wanted to attack immediately with the 1,100 men of the colonel's First Brigade, believing they faced only untrained militiamen who would run at the first sight of a British bayonet. Ross reluctantly agreed, and Thornton raced his men from behind the hill, through the town to the bridge, and to the shallow fords to confront a larger and entrenched force that was just as tired as his. Elting describes the condition of the troops Thornton's men encountered:

> Only one thing was certain: these Americans—militia, regulars, flotillamen and marines—were hard-used men. For four days they had endured forced marches, half rations, comfortless bivouacs, and little sleep. They were half-sick from August heat, dust, salt rations snatched half-cooked or raw. Worse, they had been hurry-scurried back and forth by generals who all too obviously did not know what they were doing and were afraid of the enemy to boot. Those redcoats across the river were Wellington's "Invincibles." But to the honor of the United States, most of them would stand and fight.[32]

For an hour, anyway. The battle opened with the British shooting dozens of Congreve rockets across the river at the American defense. None came anywhere close to hitting its mark, but the rockets nevertheless frightened the inexperienced defenders huddling behind their barricades waiting for the attack. As Thornton's force approached the bridge and river bank, American artillery and muskets opened up on them with deadly accuracy, killing and wounding many and sending the rest running for cover behind nearby buildings and walls. Momentarily pinned down, and with momentum shifting to the Americans, Colonel Thornton reined his horse toward the bridge and, flattening himself along the animal's back, galloped across the wooden planks with his startled troops running behind, trying to catch up and defend the honor of the regiment.[33] The American artillery laid into the crossing force, and eight or nine of the redcoats following Thornton fell. More followed, though, and when the American fire paused as muskets and cannons were reloaded, scores of British troops stormed over the bridge, and hundreds more waded across the shallows of the river and rushed up the banks to attack the American position along its entire front.

As the British soldiers swarmed up the west bank of the Eastern Branch with gleaming bayonets leveled, Stansbury's Maryland militia fired off a few rounds but quickly abandoned its front line defenses in an unruly rout. Within minutes, the redcoats' frontal assault was pouring over the Americans' abandoned defense works. Others, who had forded the river to the north and south of the bridge, were closing in on both flanks and approaching the second line of defense, five hundred yards behind on the Washington Pike, where the three Baltimore militia regiments, under Sterrett, Ragan, and Shultz, were waiting, guns loaded and ready to fire. Winder ordered Sterrett's Fifth to mount a counter-offensive against the British, who had taken cover in an abandoned apple orchard, and ordered Ragan's and Shultz's regiments to cover Sterrett's flanks.

But as Sterrett's force advanced, the British fired off another barrage of Congreve rockets, the sight of which sent Ragan's and Shultz's regiments into a disorganized retreat and left Sterrett far out in front with no support. Nevertheless, Sterrett's men kept up their fire, and their example led a few other scattered remnants of the American front line, and Burch's artillery on the distant right flank, to join the fight. Had there been intelligent and experienced leadership on the American side, Sterretts's determined stand would have encouraged the American's to bring forward the considerable force that was well to the rear—including Barney's flotillamen, Captain Miller's marines, and Captain Smith's Washington militia—but no such leadership was on the field that day.

Instead, Winder issued a series of conflicting orders to the exposed Sterrett, first ordering him to retreat, then to hold his position, and then to fall back, all within the space of several minutes. With no confidence in their leadership, the men and officers of the Fifth Regiment fell back as ordered. The retreat soon turned into a running rout, however, as the militiamen of Baltimore followed in the footsteps of their comrades in Ragan's and Shultz's regiments, who had long since fled the field in panic. Within minutes, the retreating militia ran through Laval's waiting cavalry, still stationed, unused, in the ravine where Monroe had deployed them. As the tidal wave of frightened soldiers plunged through the men and horses assembled there, panic spread. Laval and his horse were crushed against a caisson, breaking the colonel's leg. He was left with only about fifty men from his original force of more than four hundred—the rest having joined the race back to Washington.

Well to the rear, President Madison and his entourage surveyed the developing disaster and quickly understood how hopeless and vulnerable their position was. While Monroe stayed on at the collapsing front to offer his views to whomever would listen, Madison and Rush rode back to the White House to save whatever they could of the American government.

All that remained was the third and last line of defense, anchored by the Washington militia under Captain Smith on the left, the flotillamen under Barney and Colonel William Scott's regulars in the center, and Colonel William Beall's Maryland militia, which had come in that morning from Annapolis, on the right. Ever the aggressive leader, Colonel Thornton led his light infantry over the creek south of the Tournecliff's bridge and attacked the gap between Barney and Beall on the American right. But he more than met his match in Barney, who led his hardened sailors and marines in a vicious counter-attack that left Thornton badly wounded and sent Britain's Eighty-fifth Foot running back to the creek. Sensing trouble, Ross and Cockburn raced to the scene of the fight and ordered up reinforcements, whereupon one of Ross's favorite Arabians was shot out from under him.[34]

Barney's men pulled back to restore their line and prepare for the next attack. Winder, meanwhile, ordered Brigadier General Smith's considerable force of Washington militiamen to fall back, leaving Barney and Beall alone on the hill. The British Forty-fourth and Fourth overwhelmed Barney's men in a fierce attack. The commodore received a nasty wound in his thigh and his horse was killed. Beall believed his position was hopeless and decided to retreat. Now alone, Barney and his men held their ground, earning the respect of the British, who soon dislodged them and drove the remaining defenders back to Washington. One British officer recalled, "Not only did they serve their guns with a quickness and precision that astonished their assailants, but they stood till some of them were actually bayoneted with fuses in their hands; nor was it till their leader was wounded and taken, and they saw themselves deserted on all sides by the soldiers, that they left the field."[35]

Badly wounded and weak from loss of blood, Barney ordered his remaining troops to save themselves. Sitting beside the road, with sailing master Jesse Huffington at his side, the commodore waited for the British to take him captive.

> It was a Corporal of the 85th Foot who first found him. Barney, always a stickler for rank, told the man to get an officer so he could surrender. The corporal bought back Captain Wainwright of the *Tonnant*, who looked so young Barney thought he was a midshipman. That straightened out ... Wainwright rushed off and soon returned with both Admiral Cockburn and General Ross.... After a brief huddle with Cockburn, Ross then told Barney he was paroled on the spot and asked where he wished to be taken. Barney picked a tavern near Bladensburg. The General ... called a surgeon to dress the Commodore's wounds, and told off a party of soldiers to act as stretcher-bearers. Not to be outdone, Cockburn detached Captain Wainwright to go along and see that every attention was paid to the Commodore.[36]

Several days later in a letter to Naval Secretary Jones, Barney wrote, "Capt. Wainwright first Capt. to Admiral Cochrane remained with me and behaved to me as if I was a brother—During the stay of the enemy at Bladensburgh I received the most polite attention from the officers of the Navy & Army."[37]

As Ross rested and reorganized his force, panic ruled in Washington. Most of the defeated American army had come down the Washington Turnpike and through the city on its way to temporary safety in Georgetown, a few miles to the west. As rumors spread of a British victory, Dolley Madison was urged by the mayor and by her staff to leave immediately. She refused until she received a note from her husband, at the front, urging her to flee.

Piling as many valuables as she could onto a wagon, the first lady famously insisted on saving Gilbert Stuart's full-length portrait of George Washington. Its frame screwed into the plaster and lathe, the painting resisted all efforts to detach it from the wall. Urged to forget the painting and save herself from capture, Mrs. Madison refused to leave until the portrait was safely removed. The frame was eventually chopped to pieces with an ax, and the canvas and stretcher were removed.[38] She committed Washington's portrait to the staff for protection, grabbed a few more items—silver, some of her husband's papers, and the ornamental eagles in the drawing room—and left the grounds of the President's House in a carriage, her personal maid Sukey beside her.

Thirty minutes after her departure, President Madison and his entourage returned to the White House. He rested for an hour with his colleagues, commenting on the limits to which an untrained militia could be relied upon in combat against professionals: "I could never have believed that so great a difference existed between regular troops and a militia force, if I had not witnessed the scenes this day."[39] The opinion was shared by Lieutenant George Robert Gleig, a British officer on the field that day: "They seemed country people who would have been much more appropriately employed in attending to their agriculture occupations than in standing with muskets in their hands on the brow of a bare green hill."[40]

But neither Madison nor Gleig was quite correct. While there is much to be said for professionalism and training in the ranks, there is no substitute for good leadership. On that day, the American soldiers were poorly served by their leaders. The problem began with Madison, who, to his discredit, blamed others, including the hundreds of ordinary men who chose to stand and die that day for their country. A couple of weeks later, near Baltimore, a well-led militia would prove how wrong both Madison and Gleig were in their assessment of the ordinary American men who served in the militia.

Much of the blame for the disaster falls on Madison, whose inept cabinet was unsuited for the challenge confronting the nation and who failed to rise above the crassest partisan politics in appointing a military commander to lead the defense of the capital. Henry Adams's assessment of the feckless Winder was scathing:

> When he might have prepared defenses, he acted as scout; when he might have fought, he still scouted; when he retreated, he retreated in the wrong direction; when he fought, he thought only of retreat; and whether scouting, retreating or fighting, he never betrayed an idea.[41]

Ross resumed his march at six o'clock and entered Washington near the capitol at nightfall on 24 August 1814, the Fourth Foot leading the column. Snipers hiding in Robert Sewall's house fired at the approaching British, killing one and wounding three; Ross's horse was also a victim. The snipers were not caught, but Ross ordered Sewall's house burnt to the ground.[42] While Ross secured the neighborhoods around the capitol, seven blocks to the south, on the banks of the Eastern Branch near its juncture with the Potomac, Captain Thomas Tingey of the U.S. Navy ordered the buildings and supplies in the Washington Navy Yard destroyed to keep them out of British hands. The nearly completed frigate *Columbia* and the recently finished sloop of war *Argus* were also put to the torch.

Although Ross ordered all private buildings spared, there were some exceptions—Sewall's house being one of them. Also torched within the first hour or two was Tomlinson's Hotel, standing across First Street from the Senate (where the Supreme Court building stands today). Walter Lord says the hotel was destroyed because arms were found there,[43] but the real explanation may be simple revenge for an earlier insult: In December 1812, Tomlinson's Hotel was the site of a raucous celebration of America's early naval victories over the British fleet. The flags of the defeated frigates were presented to Dolley Madison as the band played patriotic tunes and the crowd roared its approval.

Unsure whether the capitol was occupied by armed defenders, Ross ordered the Third Brigade to shoot out its windows. There was no return fire, so Lieutenant Sir George de Lacy Evans led a party into the building to prepare its destruction. Cockburn took a bound copy of a Treasury report as a souvenir, and someone else stole the portraits of Louis XVI and Marie Antoinette. As the looting proceeded, British soldiers piled smashed furniture, ripped curtains, and wooden doors into huge piles of kindling mixed with rocket powder to generate a blaze hot enough to destroy the masonry structure. Ross and Cockburn had at first wanted to blow the building up, but neighbors protested the death and destruction that the explosion would inflict on nearby residences. Under orders to spare the civilian population and its property, Ross and Cockburn instead put the building to the torch. Four neighboring residences—including two on North Capitol Street built by George Washington—were ignited by sparks from the burning capitol. Three thousand volumes in the Library of Congress were also sacrificed in the flames.[44]

Around ten thirty, Cockburn led about 150 men west on Pennsylvania Avenue toward the Treasury and the President's House, where they found the dining room table set for forty, covered with plates of sliced cold meats, and cider and wine cooling in buckets of ice.[45] After a quick meal, Cockburn acquired a few souvenirs before setting the house on fire. One officer took Madison's medicine chest, another his rhinestone shoe buckles. The president's sword was stolen as well. Captain Harry Smith replaced his filthy, sweat-soaked shirt with one of Madison's. Cockburn, however, was interested in novelty, not value. He "chose an old hat of the President's and a cushion off Mrs. Madison's chair—joking that the latter would remind him of her *seat*, or so a letter written three days later delicately implied."[46]

Only a few officers and men were allowed into the President's House, and Ross and Cockburn joined them in smashing the furniture into kindling. With the White House in flames, the British turned to the brick Treasury building next door, which was soon ablaze. With the three most important structures in the U.S. capitol burning brightly, Ross called it a night, returning to Mrs. Suter's rooming house, where earlier that day[47] he had instructed the landlady to have a meal ready for him and his staff that evening. After dinner, Cockburn and Ross set off in search of the offices of the virulently anti-British newspaper the *National Intelligencer*, with the intention of burning it to the ground. But again, neighbors intervened, fearing that the burning office would take their houses with it. Cockburn again relented, agreeing simply to wreck the paper's offices the next morning, which he did in front of an angry crowd. As the soldiers smashed the press and type, one bold bystander yelled to Cockburn. "If General Washington had been alive you would have not gotten into the city so easily." Cockburn retorted, "No Sir, if General Washington had been president we should never have thought of coming here."[48]

A small force of 200 men was ordered to destroy what remained of the American fort at Greenleaf's Point, where the Eastern Branch met the Potomac. The fortifications had been destroyed but not the 150 barrels of gunpowder in the magazine, which the British dumped into the fort's well. The water, however, was insufficiently deep. As smashed barrels of the explosive black powder piled up in the close confines of the well, a spark or flame from a careless soldier ignited them in an explosion of immense violence that killed as many as thirty soldiers and badly wounded another forty-four. The injured were taken to a makeshift hospital in a series of buildings called Carroll Row (now the site of the Library of Congress) near the smoldering capitol.

Ross, who had accomplished more than he had ever expected, gave orders to prepare for the return to the ships still anchored at Benedict. At eight o'clock on the evening of the 25th, the British force began quietly to slip out of Washington, leaving fires blazing at their encampments and a few sentries to create the impression of occupation. On the march back to Benedict, 111 of his men disappeared—some to loot the countryside, others to seek a new life in a new country. Several suspected looters were seized by a group of Upper Marlborough citizens led by Dr. William Beanes, who a week earlier had shown the British unwarranted hospitality as they marched on Washington. One of the captive redcoats got away and alerted a British cavalry patrol, which returned to the town, arrested the sixty-five-year-old Beanes, and took him to Ross at Nottingham. Angered at what he considered to be Beanes's egregious breech of manners, Ross had the elderly doctor imprisoned in the hold of one of Cochrane's ships.[49]

The next day Ross's men boarded the troop ships, which they would occupy for a week, both to prevent them from deserting and to allow the infantrymen to rest and recover while their leaders argued about what to do next. According to some accounts, Cockburn wanted to attack Baltimore, whose brazen privateers in their nimble "Baltimore Clippers" had seized millions of dollars of British shipping. But Ross worried that the Americans, after losing Washington, would be better prepared to defend Baltimore and would be emboldened by a victory there. He wanted to return to Bermuda to prepare for the more lucrative attack on New Orleans and is reported to have sent his deputy adjutant captain, Harry Smith, back to London to inform Bathurst of the decision to avoid Baltimore.[50] Other witnesses report that Ross supported the attack on Baltimore, while Cochrane and Codrington opposed it.[51] The final decision fell to Admiral Cochrane, who again sided with Cockburn. Baltimore it would be. With a population of more than forty-six thousand, Baltimore was the third-largest city in the United States. Its capture would be a major blow to the young nation's morale and its struggling economy.

Anchors hoisted and steered by light winds, the British ships drifted downriver with the current to the Chesapeake Bay and into the mouth of the Potomac. There they waited for Gordon's squadron, which returned on 10 September from its mission of plunder at Alexandria, Virginia. The city's worried and accommodative leaders had surrendered the city (twice) and offered no serious objection when Gordon looted it of 16,000 barrels of flour, 1,000 hogshead of tobacco, 150 bales of cotton, and wine valued at $5,000. "*Niles Register* called the British action base and barbarous, and branded the Alexandria reaction cowardly."[52]

While Gordon's diversionary assault up the Potomac was both successful and profitable, Captain Sir Peter Parker's diversion along the Chesapeake Bay was neither. The son, grandson, and great grandson of British admirals, the aggressive Parker was the beneficiary of favorable treatment that made him a lieutenant at sixteen and a captain at twenty. Parker was "immensely spoiled and a merciless disciplinarian," writes Walter Lord, "but he had great dash, resourcefulness, and took to independent command."[53] A midshipman on Parker's earlier cruises on the bay, Frederick Chamier, wrote,

> If by any stretch of argument we could establish the owner of a house, cottage, hut &c. to be a militia-man, that house we burnt, because we found arms therein; that is to say, we found a duck gun or a rifle. It so happens that in America everyman must belong to the militia; and consequently, every man's house was food for a bonfire....[54]

While Ross and Cockburn marched on Washington, Parker and his small squadron probed Annapolis then sailed up the Patapsco toward Baltimore, taking soundings of the river and channel that Cochrane could use if he attacked the city. On his return to Cochrane's anchored fleet on the Patuxent, Parker picked up rumors that a substantial force of militia had assembled near Chestertown, Maryland, on the Sassafras River—an opportunity, thought the ruthless captain, "for one more frolic with the Yankees."[55]

Waiting for nightfall and probably depending on unreliable American guides whom he had pressed into service, Parker led 124 sailors and marines to assault the encamped militia. The militiamen, however, seem to have known of, and perhaps even encouraged, his attack and had prepared an ambush. When Parker attacked, the center line of the waiting militia pulled back as if in retreat, inviting Parker to pursue. Eager for a victory, he marched his small force to Caulk's Field. As he closed, the Maryland militiamen fired from the front and both sides, sending the British into a headlong retreat that left thirteen dead and twenty-eight wounded.[56] Among the dead was Parker himself, whose femoral artery was severed by a load of buckshot, most likely fired by a farmer from his hunting rifle. Another forty sailors and marines were reported to have taken advantage of the confusion and the dark of a hot August night to desert.[57] If so, only a third of Parker's force remained after the skirmish with the Maryland militia.

Months later, Parker's bereaved family called upon his first cousin, the poet Byron, to pen some tender words of remembrance for the fallen warrior. Byron responded with one of his less memorable works, "Elegiac Stanzas on the Death of Sir Peter Parker, Bart.," which included the lines,

And, gallant Parker! thus enshrined
Thy life, thy fall, thy fame shall be;
And early valour, glowing, find
A model in thy memory.

Byron later confessed that he hardly knew the man and "should not have wept melodious except at the request of friends."[58]

News of Washington's capture and destruction reached England on 27 September. Despite the deep animosity that the war had created between the people of the two great English-speaking countries, the response in Britain to news of the sacking of the capital was measured and equivocal, in contrast to the reaction to earlier victories over the Americans. Captain Harry Smith later wrote, "I had no objection to burn[ing] arsenals, dockyards, frigates building, stores, barracks, etc. ... but we were horrified at the order to burn the elegant Houses of Parliament."[59] Some in Britain agreed with Smith. The *Annual Register* complained that the arson was "more suitable to the times of barbarism. If there is such a thing as humanized war, its principle must consist in inflicting no other evils upon the enemy than are necessary to promote the success of warlike operations."[60] The editor of the *Statesman* wrote, "The Cossacks spared Paris, but we spared not the Capitol of America. Is it certain, that the destruction of the public edifices for destruction sake alone, is a legitimate method of warfare?" And in the House of Commons, on 4 November 1814, the wealthy brewer Samuel Whitbread said that the burning of America's capitol "was abhorrent to every principle of legitimate warfare."[61]

Britain's military leaders in North America took a different view, however. In a letter of 18 July 1814 to his commanding officers, Cochrane advised, "You are hereby required and directed to destroy & lay waste such Towns and Districts upon the Coast as you may find assailable; you will hold Strictly in view the conduct of the American Army towards its unoffending Canadian Subjects."[62] Yet the raid to which Cochrane alluded—across Lake Erie to Long Point on 14 May 1814, which destroyed several houses, a distillery, and flour mill—was never authorized by the U.S. government, and the officer that led it—Colonel John Campbell—was subsequently court-martialed and censured.[63]

Writers to the *Naval Chronicles* felt a similar awkwardness at the news of the destruction in Washington and struggled to put an acceptable face on it. A correspondent to the *Chronicle* wrote,

> This vast destruction of edifices, not devoted to the purposes of war, would tarnish the glory of our victory, and fix an indelible stain on our national honour, if the American military commanders, during their invasion of Canada, had not set a frightful example, in wantonly burning, plundering and destroying the defenceless farms and villages that lay in their way: which violations of the laws of war, and the dictates of humanity, have never been disowned by the executive government, nor the commanding officers punished.[64]

But another *Chronicle* writer contended,

> Its effects in America cannot be otherwise than powerful and decisive. It will appall the government, and destroy its power—or strengthen its arm, calling into action everything fierce and vindictive in their nature, and give birth to irreconcilable hatred and interminable war. It has also supplied a test that will decide the character of the present race of Americans.[65]

This writer got it mostly right, but the consequences would fall somewhere in the middle. The American response was not vindictive, but it was fierce. As Cochrane consolidated his force on the Potomac, thousands of armed American men—from Virginia and Pennsylvania, from the streets and shops of Baltimore, and from the farms in the Maryland countryside—streamed into Baltimore, ready to test their character, and determined that such a humiliating defeat would not be repeated.

III

As the British fleet stood at anchor at the mouth of the Potomac on 7 September, waiting for Gordon's return, an American sloop sailing down the bay from Baltimore was given permission to approach and allowed to disembark its two passengers—John Skinner, the U.S. agent for the exchange of prisoners, and Francis Scott Key, a Georgetown lawyer, an aide to Brigadier General Walter Smith, and a family friend of Dr. Beanes—who had come to petition General Ross for the release of the elderly physician. That night, over what was probably a sumptuous meal of stolen food served in the admiral's dining room on the *Tonnant*, the two Americans made their case to Cochrane, Codrington, and Ross. In the end, Ross agreed to release Beanes, largely in appreciation of the care the Americans had given to the British wounded left behind in Washington. But there was a catch: knowing the fleet's intentions, Skinner, Key, and Beanes would not be allowed to leave the ship until the attack on Baltimore had been concluded.

When Gordon returned, the British fleet weighed anchor and sailed north to the mouth of the Patapsco, arriving on the evening of Sunday, 11 September. As the massive fleet came into view, a series of three American cannons stationed near the mouth of the river were fired to alert the citizens of Baltimore that the enemy had arrived. In contrast to Washington, which had been unprepared, Baltimore was ready. On the day the British stormed over the Eastern Branch at Bladensburg, Baltimore had established the Committee of Vigilance and Safety, naming Mayor Edward Johnson its chairman. In turn, the committee offered the command of the city's defenses to Samuel Smith, "a major general in the Maryland militia, United States senator, Revolutionary War veteran, Federalist, and outspoken opponent of the Madison administration."[66] Astutely aware of the counter-productive influence of Republican politics on issues of national defense, Smith made his acceptance contingent upon the approval of Maryland's Federalist governor, Levin Winder, uncle of General William Winder. Nominally in command of the military district that included

Baltimore and Washington, Governor Winder marginalized his nephew by assenting to Smith's command. The chain of command was now clearly established; General Smith and nearly everyone in the city began to prepare for Ross's arrival, which the cannons down the Patapsco had just announced.

> The committee resolved to draft every white male between the ages of sixteen and fifty years of age, and to provide him with a firearm and accessories.... [E]lderly men "who are able to carry a firelock and willing to render a last service to their country and posterity" were invited to form a company. Exempt citizens were asked, on hearing a fire alarm, to go to the station and give aid. "This request becomes the more necessary as members [of the fire squads] generally are engaged in military duty." The doctors of the city who were not already militia surgeons were asked to join some corps which had no surgeon....[67]

Major George Armistead—who commanded the six hundred regulars at Fort McHenry, a massive hulk of brick and stone guarding the entrance to Baltimore harbor—had been preparing for this moment for more than a year. The previous summer, when Admiral Cockburn was attacking small towns on the Chesapeake Bay, Armistead began strengthening the fort's defenses against a British attack on Baltimore. When the attack seemed imminent, he reviewed his careful preparations and found one thing missing. Armistead reported to General Smith:

> We, Sir, are ready at Fort McHenry to defend Baltimore against invading by the enemy. That is to say, we are ready except that we have no suitable ensign to display over the Star Fort, and it is my desire to have a flag so large that the British will have no difficulty in seeing it from a distance.[68]

Armistead's superiors agreed with him about the need for a suitable flag, so they contracted with Baltimore's Mary Young Pickersgill, a widowed seamstress specializing in flags for the city's many merchant ships, to sew a banner for the fort. Mrs. Pickersgill's flag measured thirty-two by forty-two feet, one of the largest ever made, hand-sewn with an estimated 350,000 stitches. Some question whether a mother and her young daughter could have completed the task in the six weeks allotted, and Mrs. Pickersgill's three nieces, a slave, and a free black woman in her household may have helped.[69] If Mrs. Pickersgill's massive banner was flying over Fort McHenry that day (the fort also flew a smaller "storm flag" for inclement weather), it would have been visible to Ross's four thousand soldiers and one thousand armed sailors when they disembarked at North Point, fourteen miles downriver from Baltimore.

Certain that Ross would approach from North Point, Smith devoted much of his manpower and Baltimore's civic energy to building a massive earthen fortification just east of the city at Hampstead Hill. The network of trenches, battlements, and redoubts stretching south from the Philadelphia Road to the edge of the Northwest Branch of the Patapsco would be filled with as many as ten thousand militiamen. Here and there along the line and down the Northwest Branch's banks to where Fort McHenry protected its egress to the Patapsco, artillery batteries manned by sailors under Commodore John Rodgers were tucked into earthen redoubts. Smith requisitioned dozens of merchant vessels, loaded them with rocks, and sank them in the narrow stretch of water where the Patapsco joined the Northwest Branch and Baltimore's harbor, keeping the British fleet and its powerful frigates far from the city proper and its main line of defense at Hampstead Hill. On the west side of the channel stood Fort McHenry, bristling with cannon, and on the eastern edge, at the *Lazaretto* (a former hospital for victims of contagious disease, named for Lazarus),[70] a three-gun battery under the command of Lieutenant Solomon Frazier of the navy stood ready to fire on any British ship that attempted to penetrate the line.

This formidable defense at the edge of the city was, in Smith's plan, only a last resort. He intended to challenge Ross and his redcoats many miles to the east as they made their way to the city. Smith therefore sent his immediate subordinate, Brigadier General John Stricker—another Revolutionary War veteran who had served as a captain of artillery under General Washington—to establish a front line of defense in the open fields several miles to the east. There Stricker and 3,200 militiamen would challenge the British with three lines of defense, each separated by 300 yards, and each standing in a tight line on an open field.[71] In the pine woods and bramble in front of his first line, Stricker placed 150 or so skilled riflemen to harass the approaching British, exacting a heavy price for every inch of Maryland soil they attempted to possess.

Stricker's front-line troops would play a critical role in the city's defense, and Smith selected them carefully:

> Smith chose to risk the best he had, his "City" (or 3rd) Brigade, made up of Baltimore citizens who literally would be fighting for their hearth and homes.... One of the infantry regiments, the 5th, and the riflemen were veterans of Bladensburg; they had learned something in combat and had reputations to refurbish.[72]

Well over fifteen thousand militiamen had streamed into the city from Maryland, Virginia (2,600 men), and Pennsylvania (1,200),[73] and Smith's army greatly outnumbered the attacking British, who may have numbered no more than 5,000, perhaps fewer.[74] But Smith's men were mostly amateurs. The commander needed a strategy that would take advantage of his numerical superiority and offset Ross's advantage in skill, discipline, determination, and training. Smith and Stricker believed that the multiple lines of defense they had established provided just that advantage. The militiamen on one line knew that the line right behind them would back them up and offer refuge if the tide of battle turned against them. These ordinary men, meagerly trained but devoted to their families, their city, and their country, were prepared to stand their ground against one of the world's most fearsome armies.

By eight o'clock on the morning of 12 September, Ross's force was on the march to the city. Cochrane's smaller ships with shallow draft sailed up the Patapsco to Fort McHenry, prepared to bombard the American fortifications into rubble. Ross had advanced seven miles toward Baltimore when his advance guard met sporadic fire from the riflemen Stricker had hidden in the woods before him. As Ross's force approached, however, a rumor swept through the ranks of the riflemen that they had been outflanked by a British landing behind. Most of them retreated, but some remained in their hiding places—including, according to legend, the eighteen-year-old apprentice saddlers Daniel Wells and Henry McComas—to take what shots they could at the advancing British.

Reaching Stricker's line with his reconnaissance force and surveying the militia arrayed before him in the open field, Ross determined that a column of light infantry should lead the assault, and he rode back to the main body to order them forward. Returning to the front to lead the assault, Ross came into the sights of an American rifleman—some say young Wells or McComas, the history of Ross's Twentieth Regiment identifies the sniper as Aquila Randall. The rifleman squeezed the trigger, flint hit steel, sparks fired powder, and a shot of heavy lead crashed through Ross's arm and lodged in his chest. Mortally wounded, the general fell from his horse and was found lying on the field by the advancing light infantry he had just ordered into battle. By nightfall Ross was dead, as were Daniel Wells and Henry McComas.[75]

Colonel Arthur Brooke assumed command from the fallen Ross. He thought he was confronting six thousand regulars and cautiously waited until his whole force had come up before attacking Stricker's line. The Baltimore militia held its ground against the brave British advance for about an hour, knocking holes in the enemy line and sending some units running for cover. But Stricker knew that the well-trained British infantry would ultimately prevail on an open field of battle, and he devised an orderly retreat. Moving his valuable artillery back to the second line of defense, Stricker ordered his militia to wait for a bayonet charge, fire a last round into the closing line of redcoats, then run back to the next line.

Though the Americans had surrendered the field, Stricker's clever defense had ensured that the British success was costly. In addition to General Ross, forty-six British soldiers were killed and 273 wounded on the first day of the battle, a heavier toll than at Bladensburg. Thanks to Stricker's leadership and orderly withdrawal, American losses were half that of the British—twenty-four killed and 139 wounded, with fifty taken prisoner.[76] His force battered and exhausted and the day coming to an end, Brooke chose not to pursue but ordered his men to camp for the night. Stricker marched his still considerable force back to Baltimore, where they joined the ten thousand or so militiamen, regulars, and sailors dug in on the Hampstead Hill line. Along the way, his men felled trees to obstruct the roads that Brooke would have to use on his way to the city.

The next day, 13 September, Brooke resumed his march to the city, and the British ships that could maneuver in the shallow waters of the Patapsco began the bombardment of the forts guarding the entrance to the Northwest Branch and Baltimore Harbor. If Fort McHenry and the smaller force dug in at the Lazaretto could be taken out and a path cut through the line of vessels sunk at its mouth, the Northwest Branch would be open, and Cochrane's frigates and bomb ships could move close enough to ravage the city proper and the defending line of militia.

Struggling through the obstacles that Stricker's men had laid in his path, Brooke approached the Hampstead Hill line that evening and rested his troops in preparation for a night attack. The defenders had dug themselves into a formidable line of earthen works. Tough sailors manned the series of redoubts, ready with enfilading cannon fire for any British regiment trying to cross the line.

As night fell, it was becoming apparent to the British that their day-long bombardment had made little progress in subduing the defiant Fort McHenry and the Lazaretto. The expected victory seemed to be slipping away because of the fierce resistance from the citizens of Baltimore. Cochrane and his staff considered several options. By ten o'clock, the admiral had settled on a diversionary amphibious attack behind Fort McHenry, to be quickly followed by a massive frontal assault on the American line by Brooke's entire force.

At midnight, three hundred men set out in twenty barges and boats led by Captain Charles Napier (son of Colonel Charles Napier, who led the tragic raid on Hampton, Virginia, the previous summer). The flotilla approached the second barrier of sunken hulks, which extended south from Fort McHenry across the river to Cromwell's Marsh, near the entrance to the Ferry Branch and the American batteries at Forts Babcock and Covington.[77] Aided by a vigorous bombardment of Fort McHenry from the frigates and bomb ships, Napier probed the black water until he found an opening in the line of sunken hulks. Meanwhile, eleven of his twenty vessels had failed to keep up or got lost in the dark. Napier and his diminished force slipped through the line and continued west into the harbor. As planned, the British bombardment ceased as Napier approached the rear of Fort McHenry, which was Brooke's signal to launch the main attack on the American line.

The alert Americans manning the guns at Fort Babcock realized that the inexplicable halt in the bombardment probably indicated the presence of British forces who otherwise might be hit by friendly fire. Scanning the waters before them, they detected the silhouettes of Napier's squadron and fired a barrage of solid shot and grape at the attacking force. The guns at Forts Covington and McHenry and the Lazaretto soon joined the fight, and in minutes Napier and his men were being pounded by dozens of cannon from the north, east, and west.

Sensing danger, Cochrane renewed the naval bombardment. Napier fought back with the few pieces of artillery mounted on his barges and held his own for more than an hour, hoping to trick the Americans into believing that he was the main attack. No one knows if any Americans fell for his ruse, but after an hour of fighting, Napier's magazines were empty. He launched a blue rocket, the signal to Cochrane that he was turning back.

On shore, Brooke sensed that something was wrong. When there was no diminution in the Americans' return fire and the line before him showed no sign of panic,[78] Brooke concluded correctly that Napier's diversion had failed and that his land assault against the earthen works before him would receive the undivided attention of the vastly more numerous defenders. Cochrane sent a message to Brooke that the navy could do no more against the forts. After consulting with his officers and Cockburn, Brooke decided that his attack was likely to fail and that his losses would be severe. He wrote back to Cochrane, "Under these circumstances and keeping in view your Lordship's instructions, it was agreed between the Vice-admiral and myself that the capture of the town would not have been a sufficient equivalent to the loss which might probably be sustained in storming the heights."[79]

Brooke left a few sentries behind to keep the campfires blazing and maintain the pretense of a continued British presence and, at two o'clock in the morning, ordered his men back to North Point. Cochrane maintained his bombardment for another five hours before turning his fleet back down the Patapsco. Brooke's army quickly boarded their troopships, and by the end of the day the British force had left the Baltimore area.

As the new day dawned and the British guns fell silent, the bleary-eyed American defenders wondered if the siege was really over or if it was just a pause before the final, savage assault. The same thoughts were in the minds of Francis Scott Key and his companions, including the paroled Dr. Beanes, as they stood wondering and worrying on the deck of their Norfolk packet at North Point. But as the smoke cleared and the sun rose, Key saw that the city remained unconquered. There are many moving and eloquent descriptions of that moment, but the British naval historian G. J. Marcus's is as fine as any:

> The British were falling back to their ships; and in the first light of day the two Americans saw the great flag still floating defiantly

above Fort McHenry. It was then, with swelling heart, that Key wrote down on the back of an old letter the famous lines with which his name will always be associated.

O! say can you see by the dawn's early light,
What so proudly we hailed at the twilight's last gleaming,
Whose broad stripes and bright stars through the perilous fight,
O'er the ramparts we watch'd, were so gallantly streaming?

Though it was unknown to Key and his contemporaries, the war which was welding the people of the United States into a nation had also given them a national anthem. One thing, however, was certain: Baltimore was saved.[80]

Two days after the battle, Cochrane's fleet sailed into the Chesapeake to wait for a favorable wind for the voyage south to Hampton Roads. On 19 September, Cochrane sailed for Halifax and Cockburn for Bermuda. A small squadron under Rear Admiral Pulteney Malcolm, and the troop ships, maintained a British presence in the Chesapeake until 14 October, when Malcolm was ordered into the Atlantic. Off the northwest coast of Jamaica he rendezvoused with the grand fleet assembling there for the attack on New Orleans.[81]

The cargo of the departing fleet included the pickled remains of Britain's fallen hero, Major General Robert Ross. In the hold of the *Royal Oak*, Ross's corpse—stripped, washed, and eviscerated—was preserved in a cask of 129 gallons of Jamaican rum for burial in Halifax. Sir Peter Parker's corpse was similarly preserved, though in the lead-lined coffin he carried with him on the *Menelaus*. The American poet Charles L. S. Jones honored the preservation process with his song "Sir Peter Parker," sung to the tune of "Maggy Lauder." The last stanza runs,

But most his tongue thy praises rung,
Jamaica's lively liquor;
And swore, 'twas fit to enliven the wit
Of laymen or of vicar:
So not in fun

To be outdone,
They sent this gallant speaker,
Well seasoned, home,
In his favorite rum,
The far famed Peter Parker.[82]

A perceptive correspondent to Britain's *Naval Chronicle*, writing in October, appreciated the implications of the defeat at Baltimore:

> The effects of the failure of our attack on Baltimore, and the events in Canada, have already produced consequences in America very different from those calculated on the advocates for this unnatural and dangerous war; whilst at home the public feelings are vehemently and variously agitated. Some of our leading journals are for crushing all the United States at once, by sending the Duke of Wellington and fifty thousand troops there! We fear other work may too soon be cut out for that Hero and his army much nearer home, and that this ruinous contest will continue till we become again involved in a new war, with a power we need not name.[83]

The unnamed power, of course, was France. Upon his surrender in April 1814, Napoleon Bonaparte was allowed to maintain the title of emperor and to rule over the tiny island of Elba at an annual pay of two million francs—an arrangement that the allies viewed as something between a bribe and a pension. But by October, it was rumored that the emperor was restless and that something dreadful was about to happen. Four months later, Napoleon fled Elba and returned to France, proving the prescience of the *Chronicle*'s correspondent.

As soon as he returned to Baltimore, Francis Scott Key sought fresh sheets of paper on which to transcribe the lines he had scrawled on the scraps of paper available aboard the *Tonnant*. He had already had in mind a tune to which his verses could be sung—the popular drinking song "Anacreon in Heaven," to which he had set an earlier poem he had written in honor of Commodore Stephen Decatur.[84] Key showed his poem to a few friends and relatives. The verses made their way to the *American and Commercial Daily Advertiser*, where they were printed on a handbill with a description of their origins, the suggested tune, and titled "Defence of Fort M'Henry."

> [T]he song caught Baltimore's fancy right away. Key's words somehow conveyed perfectly the strange combination of fear, defiance, suspense, relief, and sheer ecstasy that went into that desperate night. The Fort McHenry garrison adopted it—every man received a copy—and the tavern crowds took it up. Resuming publication after a ten-day lapse, the Baltimore *Patriot and Evening Advertiser* ran it in full on September 20, proclaiming that it was "destined long to outlast the occasion, and outlive the impulse that produced it."
>
> It quickly spread to other cities too, as the whole nation rejoiced in the news from Baltimore. Within a month papers in towns as far away as Savannah and Concord, New Hampshire, were running Key's stirring lyrics. Everywhere they struck the right chord—the rare sense of exultation people felt about this totally unexpected victory.[85]

IV

The defeat at Baltimore did not appear to chasten the British government, which was unrelenting in its demands at Ghent. Indeed, while Gallatin and the other American negotiators hoped for an agreement based on the *status quo ante bellum* (that is, what both sides held prior to the hostilities), the British still insisted on the principle of *uti possidetis*, by which Britain would keep the territory it had gained in the war. "The state of possession must be considered as the territorial arrangement which would revive upon a peace, except so far as the same may be modified by any new treaty,"[86] argued Lord Castlereagh, Britain's foreign minister. In July 1814, the British looked forward to further conquests by their reinforced armies. A treaty based on *uti possidetis*, they anticipated, would yield northern Maine and New York, Vermont and New Hampshire, both sides of the Niagara River, Mobile, and New Orleans. The Northwest Territories would revert to the local Indian tribes, with whom the United States would be required to sign a peace agreement.

The government of Canada pushed Britain to insist on harsh terms. The Treaty of Paris, which ended the War of Independence, neglected Canada's interests, in their view, and ceded too much to the Americans. The British officials in Canada intended to rectify that wrong. In addition to Britain's territorial demands, they wanted complete control of the Great Lakes, the restitution of the Louisiana Territory, and the establishment of the Ohio River as the boundary between the United States and the Indian lands in the northwest. When the news arrived in early autumn of the capture of Washington, Britain's goals seemed to be within reach. Powerful British armies were on the march in Maine and New York and in the Niagara and Chesapeake regions. Cochrane's proposed attack on New Orleans was approved on 10 August 1814. It was only a matter of time, presumably, before the United States would surrender and huge stretches of territory would revert to Britain. But in late October, news of a different type began to arrive from the United States and Canada, and that attitude would soon change.

Reports of the staggering September losses began to arrive by ship in England in mid-October. Drummond's failed assault on Fort Erie (17 September) with a great loss of life left the Americans in control of strategic Canadian territory. Downie's death, the loss of the entire Lake Champlain squadron, and Prevost's ignominious retreat (11 September) left New York and New England securely in American hands. Cochrane's failure to take Baltimore (14 September) and Ross's death quickly reversed the exultation that followed the sacking of the capital. In Mobile Bay, American cannon in Fort Bowyer turned back a British naval assault (15 September), sinking the frigate *Hermes* and battering the *Sophie* and the *Carron*.[87] Within the space of a single week, British land forces and their naval support in North America had suffered severe setbacks, often against local militiamen drawn from the country's shipyards, workshops, counting houses, and small farmsteads. Less than two months later, on 7 November, Andrew Jackson seized the Spanish fort at Pensacola, denying the British a valuable base for the assault on New Orleans, Britain's last bargaining chip.

On top of the U.S. victories in North America, the American navy and privateers continued their raiding in Britain's home waters and along the trade routes that connected it to its empire. Trade was disrupted, valuable cargos were lost, and insurance rates soared. British merchants and ship owners began to lobby the government for a quick end to the destructive war.

As costly as the war was for the merchants who bore both high costs and high taxes, the consequences for government were even worse. Lord Liverpool, the prime minister since 1812, observed: "Looking to a continuance of the American war, our financial state is far from satisfactory.... [T]he American war will not cost us less than £10,000,000, in addition to our peace establishment and other expenses. We must expect, therefore, to hear it said that the property tax is continued for the purpose of securing a better frontier for Canada."[88] Henry Adams summed up England's shifting mood when he wrote:

> The war had lost public favor. Even the colonial and shipping interests and the navy were weary of it, while the army had little to expect from it but hard service and no increase of credit. Every Englishman who came in contact with Americans seemed to suffer.... The tone of the press showed the same popular tendency, for while the *Times* grumbled loudly over the Canada campaign, the *Morning Chronicle* no longer concealed its hostility to the war, and ventured to sneer at it....[89]

The situation in America was even worse. The country confronted financial ruin as expenditures soared while tax revenues declined, forcing the government to borrow vast sums of money. Expenditures on the army and navy have been estimated at $93 million. Another $16 million was paid in interest on the debt incurred to finance the war, while veterans' benefits ultimately reached $49 million. The national debt, which had been reduced to $45 million by 1815, stood at $127 million at the end of 1815.[90] As the resources required to prosecute the war against the British became increasingly scarce, President Madison notified his peace commissioners in Ghent that a treaty based upon the *status quo ante bellum* would now be acceptable to his government.

On 17 October, as the British cabinet debated the specific terms that would be enforced through the policy of *uti possidetis*, news of Downie's defeat and death and of Prevost's retreat reached England, provoking both defiance and concern. On 19 October, the *Times* declared, "This is a lamentable event in the civilized world ... an event to which we should have bent and must bend all our energies. The present American government must be displaced, or it will sooner or later plant its poisoned dagger in the heart of the parent State."[91] But the *Times* did not speak for all. A somewhat confused peace commissioner Henry Goulburn wrote to Bathurst from Ghent, "The news from America is very far from satisfactory. Even our brilliant success at Baltimore, as it did not terminate in the capture of the town, will be considered by the Americans as a victory and not as an escape.... If it were not for the want of fuel in Boston, I should be quite in despair."[92]

Goulburn's tempered optimism did not last. The losses at Plattsburgh, Lake Champlain, Fort Erie, Baltimore, and Mobile Bay forced the British to reconsider their stubborn insistence on *uti possidetis*. In late October, their negotiators reduced their demands to the possession of Fort Niagara, Mackinac Island, and Moose Island, but the American commissioners refused to agree to even these concessions.

Britain's setbacks in North America also influenced the more important European negotiations at the end of the Napoleonic Wars. As the French, Prussians, British, and Russians met in Vienna, Castlereagh "found himself unable to make the full influence of England felt, so long as such mortifying disasters by land and seas proved her inability to deal with an enemy she persisted in calling contemptible."[93] Desperate for a resolution to the conflict, Lord Liverpool wrote Wellington on 4 November offering him the entire command in Canada. The general replied,

> I have already told you and Lord Bathurst that I feel no objection to going to America, though I don't promise myself much success there.... In regard to your present negotiations, I confess that I think you have no right, from the state of the war, to demand any concession of territory from America.... You have not been able to carry it into the enemy's territory, notwithstanding your military success and now undoubted military superiority, and have not even cleared your own territory on point of attack. You cannot on any principle of equality in negotiation claim a cession of territory excepting in exchange for other advantages, which you have in your power.... Then if this reasoning be true, why stipulate for the uti possidetis? You can get no territory; indeed, the state of your military operations, however creditable, does not entitle you to demand any.[94]

Perhaps influenced by Wellington's harsh assessment of the British position, the foreign ministry abandoned all territorial claims in late November. Now it was the Americans' turn to slow down the negotiations as the pursuit of regional interests—British navigation rights on the Mississippi and access to

British fisheries off Canada—led to discord among the American commissioners. In the end, both sides agreed simply to an end to hostilities, with the other issues to be settled later.

The peace treaty was signed on 24 December 1814, and copies were sent to the respective governments for approval, a process that took considerable time in an age when global communication was dependent upon the vagaries of wind, currents, and storms. Indeed, it was nearly two months before the Christmas Eve agreement arrived in New York on 11 February 1815. C. S. Forester nicely captured the nature of the interminable delay when he wrote:

> Seven weary weeks elapsed before H.M.S. *Favorite*, bearing the treaty of peace and a British chargé d'affaires, clawed her way across the Atlantic in the teeth of westerly gales and reached New York, but fast horses carried the vital papers from there to Washington, and only six days passed before the treaty was ratified and the war officially ended, the Senate raising singularly few difficulties. Almost two years, from March 11, 1813, to February 17, 1815, had passed since Mr. Madison's nomination of commissioners to treat for peace.[95]

Yet as a consequence of these delays and the difficulty in conveying information to military forces scattered around the globe, intense conflict would continue for many more months.

CHAPTER TWENTY-ONE

CHALLENGING THE BRITISH BLOCKADE

Despite major victories on the lakes, the U.S. Navy was hobbled during much of 1814 by a massive British blockade of American ports from Boston to New Orleans. The navy's few warships were often stuck in port for long stretches of time by Britain's suffocating offshore presence, which challenged any American ship, merchant or navy, attempting to run for open water. Commodore Stephen Decatur had returned to New London, Connecticut, in December 1812 with the frigate *United States* and the captured *Macedonian*, but the tight British blockade kept both ships bottled up in the Thames River through all of 1813 and 1814.

Decatur repeatedly challenged the blockading force with invitations for ship-to-ship duels with the *United States* and the now repaired *Macedonian*, but the British commander, Captain Sir Thomas Hardy, demurred. A stalemate that neutralized two of his enemy's powerful warships at no cost in British lives or ships was very much in his country's interest. When Decatur proposed to lead the *United States* and *Macedonian* in a two-on-two fight with the frigates *Endymion* and *Statira*, Hardy rejected half the offer, arguing that *Endymion* was no match for the muscular American super frigate *United States.* But he agreed to a duel between *Macedonian* and *Statira*. Decatur declined on the grounds that *Statira* would enter the fight with a picked crew drawn from the seven ships of Hardy's squadron, and so the stalemate continued.[1]

With no hope of escaping Hardy's blockade, Decatur moved the two frigates up the Thames, where their masts, spars, sails, and rigging were dismantled and stored below against the weather. Hardy's rejection of the *Endymion-United States* match reflected both professional caution and a respect for the capabilities of the American super frigates. *Endymion*, one of the fastest and strongest British frigates, was built in 1797 along the lines of the captured French *Pomone* (taken by Sir John Borlase Warren in 1794). Her eighteen-pounders had been replaced with twenty-four-pound guns in 1813, and she had been given two additional thirty-two-pound carronades to better match the American frigates she was expected to fight.[2]

Elsewhere on the east coast, *Constellation* entered its second year locked up at Norfolk on the Elizabeth River, while the *John Adams* and *Congress* remained stuck in port. From Halifax the British kept watch on Boston and the coast of Maine with two ships of the line, four frigates, eleven sloops, and one schooner. Two frigates were stationed off Nantucket, while two ships of the line, one frigate, and two sloops kept watch on Decatur off New London. In the Delaware Bay, two frigates kept watch on Philadelphia while a razee and a frigate secured the waters off New York City. In the Chesapeake, two ships of the line, two frigates, one sloop, and one schooner stood guard, while the Carolina coast was covered by a razee and three sloops. Along the Gulf Coast a frigate, two sloops, and two schooners kept watch on Mobile and New Orleans.[3]

Commerce ground to a halt, and America's once prosperous economy collapsed, bringing misery to the citizens of port cities dependent on trade. Henry Adams wrote:

> In August [1813] superfine flour sold at Boston for $11.87 a barrel, at Baltimore for $6.00, and at Richmond for $4.50 . . . . Rice sold at Philadelphia for $12.00 a hundredweight; in Charleston and Savannah for $3.00 . . . . No rate of profit could cause cotton, rice or wheat to be brought by sea from Charleston or Norfolk to Boston . . . . Sugar which was quoted at nine dollars a hundred weight in New

> Orleans, and in August sold for twenty-one or twenty-two in New York and Philadelphia, stood at forty dollars in December.... The exports of New York, which exceeded $12,250,000 in 1811, fell to $209,000 for the year ending in 1814. The domestic exports of Virginia diminished in four years from $4,800,000 to $3,000,000 for 1812, $1,819,000 for 1813 and $17,581 for the year ending September 30, 1814. At the close of 1813 exports, except from Georgia and New England, ceased.[4]

By 1814, even the nimble privateers had trouble getting out to sea and back again. Only a few of the navy's warships were able to escape to the ocean, often having to wait weeks or months for a storm to blow the blockading force out to sea. When Bainbridge returned *Constitution* to Boston in February 1813 after his victory over *Java*, the fifteen-year-old frigate was in desperate need of repair because of the rot and decay that afflicted even the best cared-for wooden ships. Bainbridge wrote to Navy Secretary Jones that *Constitution* would require new beams, waterways, decks, ceilings, and knees, that her copper sheathing needed to be replaced, and that new sails and rigging were needed.[5] Now the commandant of the Boston shipyard, Bainbridge supervised substantial repairs to the frigate. Bad weather delayed the work, and the ambitious ship-building project on Lakes Erie, Champlain, and Ontario left Boston with a shortage of skilled workmen.

All the repairs except for the re-coppering had been completed by June 1813, when Captain Charles Stewart was transferred from the *Constellation*, still blockaded at Norfolk, to the *Constitution*. Stewart, who formally took command of the ship on 18 July, worked with Bainbridge to complete the repairs and enlist a new crew to replace the men who had been sent to the Great Lakes. The *Constitution* was finally ready in early December to run the blockade and head for sea. On the 31st, with the British blockading force nowhere to be seen, Stewart sailed into the Atlantic and set a course south for the water around Barbados, where he took a few prizes of limited value. Stewart's efforts to engage British warships were unavailing, as their captains were under orders to avoid the big American frigates unless both sides were evenly matched. Off the coast of Guyana on 23 February 1814, Captain Frederick Lewis Maitland of HMS *Pique* (formerly the French *Pallas*), 36, made all sail to escape once he realized the identity of his opponent.[6]

Finding little to prey on in the Caribbean, Stewart sailed north, looking for quarry near Bermuda. A substantial crack in his mainmast, however, and an outbreak of typhus and scurvy among the crew forced him back to port, and he approached Marblehead at dawn on 3 April. Heading into port, the *Constitution* was set upon by two of the blockading frigates, the *Junon* and the *Tenedos*. As the latter vessel closed on him, Stewart dumped fresh water and other provisions and managed to outrun his pursuer. The British broke off the chase as *Constitution* slipped into the protected harbor of Salem. *Tenedos* and *Junon* hovered offshore for the next two weeks, but they soon lost interest and departed, leaving Stewart free to continue to Boston.

Boston, however, was not the refuge he expected. A critical report on Stewart's voyage by Bainbridge provoked a court of inquiry to examine why an early return to port was necessary when the ship had just undergone what Bainbridge described as repairs "of the most ample kind."[7] The inquiry exonerated Stewart and removed the threat of a court-martial. He kept his command of the *Constitution*, which remained blockaded by a substantial British force led by Hardy's flagship, the *Ramillies*, 74.

II

Despite the blockade and the dimming prospects for a naval offensive, the U.S. government launched nineteen warships in 1814, including three "heavy sloops of war" that served as commerce raiders against British shipping. Built as three-masted, flush-decked ships armed with twenty thirty-two-pound carronades and two eighteen-pound long guns, they were the *Frolic*, 22 (Boston), the *Wasp*, 22 (Newburyport), and the *Peacock*, 22 (New York). The first to sea was *Frolic*, commanded by Master Commandant Joseph Bainbridge, the younger brother of Captain William Bainbridge. In March 1814 she came across a Carthaginian privateer that refused to surrender. Bainbridge ordered a broadside from *Frolic*'s carronades, and within minutes the privateer slipped below the waves, taking as many as a hundred crewmen with her.[8] A month or so later, on 20 April 1814 while cruising near the Bahamas in search of convoys bound for the British Isles, Bainbridge came upon the British frigate *Orpheus*, 36, under Captain Hugh Pigot, and the schooner *Shelburne*, 12, under Lieutenant David Hope (formerly of the *Macedonian*), both to leeward. Outgunned nearly three to one, Bainbridge tried to escape. The faster *Shelburne* soon weathered *Frolic* but did not close with the more powerful sloop, waiting instead for the slower *Orpheus* to close the distance. The chase lasted thirteen hours, during which Bainbridge did everything he could to lighten his ship and increase her speed. Water was dumped, anchors cut away, and finally the heavy guns were pitched over the side. But to no avail. *Orpheus* continued to close, and without any means of defending his ship, Bainbridge struck and was taken prisoner.[9]

A month later, on 12 March, the *Peacock*, 22, sailed from New York on her maiden voyage under Master Commandant Lewis Warrington. A thirty-two-year-old Virginian and a graduate of William and Mary, Warrington entered the navy in 1800 as a midshipman. *Peacock* was his first command, and he was determined to make the most of it. Heading south in search of British convoys, on 28 April *Peacock* found three merchantmen out of Havana[10] headed for Bermuda under the protection of the brig sloop *Epervier*, 18, commanded by Captain R. W. Wales. *Epervier* carried a shipment of specie valued at $118,000. As Warrington closed, the merchantmen made all sail to flee on their northeasterly course, while *Epervier* turned south on a port tack to meet *Peacock*. As the two ships closed on parallel courses—*Peacock* sailing north, *Epervier* south—Warrington tried to maneuver *Peacock* into a raking position, but Wales thwarted the move by turning his helm. Minutes later the two ships exchanged broadsides, causing some damage aloft, especially to *Peacock*, which lost her head sails and the ability to maneuver.

As *Peacock* continued north, the only course her damaged rigging allowed, *Epervier* tacked, came around, and ran alongside the American sloop. The ships exchanged a series of broadsides over the next forty minutes—*Peacock* from her starboard guns, *Epervier* from her port—the British vessel receiving far more damage than she inflicted on the American. Wales's ship was badly battered and taking on water, several of his guns were out of action, and his ability to maneuver was limited by damaged rigging. His only chance against the superior gunnery of *Peacock* was to board her and fight hand-to-hand. The British naval historian William James describes the end of the battle:

> As a last resource, and one which British seamen are generally prompt to execute, Captain Wales called the crew aft, to follow him in boarding. These dastardly wretches replied,—"She is too heavy for us." There was no alternative but to strike the colours, to save the lives of the very few remaining good men in the vessel.... The

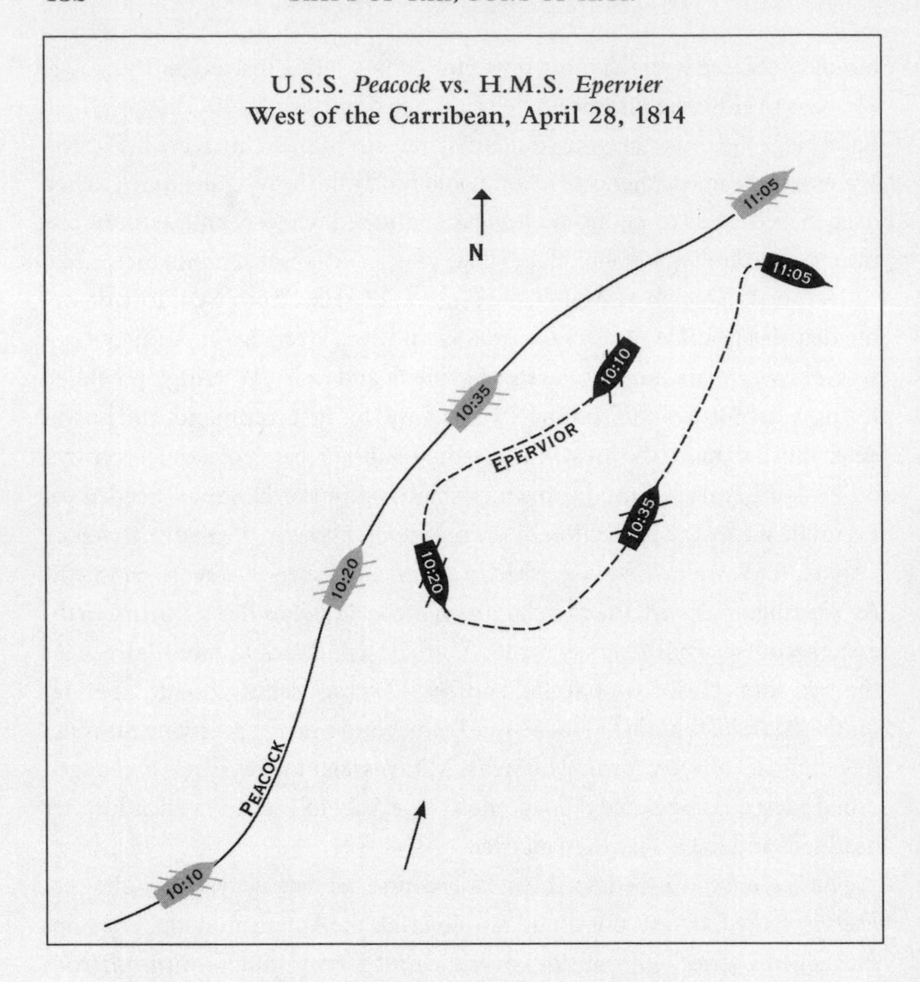

> *Epervier* ... had but three men in a watch, exclusive of petty-officers, able to take helm or lead; and two of the men were each 70 years of age! She had some blacks, several foreigners, lots of disaffected, and few even of ordinary stature: in short, a crew that was a disgrace to the deck of a British man of war.[11]

Apart from the early damage to her foreyard, *Peacock* was relatively unscathed, and casualties amounted to only two slightly wounded men. *Epervier*, however, suffered severely with forty-five holes in her hull, five feet of water in her hold, and twenty-three casualties, including her first lieutenant, who lost an arm and took a nasty splinter wound to his hip. Hasty repairs kept *Epervier* afloat, and on 1 May the prize, later sold to the U.S. Navy, entered Savannah harbor under the command of Lieutenant Nicholson. *Peacock* came into port a few days later for a month of repairs to her battered masts, yards, sails, and rigging. Savannah's leading citizens hosted Warrington and his officers to a public dinner, and Congress later awarded silver medals to him and his officers and swords to the midshipmen.[12]

Warrington and his crew were back at sea again on 4 June and resumed their commerce raiding at all points on the Atlantic Ocean. Over the next five months *Peacock* would prowl the Grand Banks off Newfoundland, the Azores, the Irish Channel, Cape Finisterre, and then back across the Atlantic to Barbados before returning to New York on 29 October 1814. Counting *Epervier*, *Peacock* took fifteen prizes during the voyage, and tied with *Wasp* for the most ships taken by an American vessel during 1814.

The *Wasp*, 22, was the last of the new sloops of war to sail, leaving Portsmouth, New Hampshire, on 1 May 1814 under the command of thirty-three-year-old Captain Johnston Blakely. Born in Ireland, Blakely emigrated to North Carolina when he was an infant, and at age nineteen he joined the navy as a midshipman. By 1811 Blakely had advanced quickly to become the commander of the *Enterprise*, a position he held until 1813. Eluding a tight British blockade off the coast of New Hampshire, Blakely took the *Wasp* due east to the English Channel, where he captured and destroyed several merchant vessels during June. In the early hours of 28 June, while chasing two merchantmen, the *Wasp*'s lookouts spotted a sail on the ship's weather-beam and determined it was a British warship in hot pursuit.

HMS *Reindeer*, 18, commanded by Captain William Manners and armed with twenty-four-pound carronades, was outgunned by *Wasp*'s thirty-two-pounders. As dawn broke, Manners prepared his ship for battle and made sail for the American intruder, his audacity earning rare praise from Theodore Roosevelt:

> Captain Manners must have known well that he was to do battle with a foe heavier than himself; but there was no more gallant seaman in the whole British navy, fertile as it was with men who cared but little for the odds of size or strength.[13]

The wind that day was light, and hours passed while *Reindeer* closed the distance. As the British ship drew near about noon, Blakely hauled up and prepared for Manners's arrival. At a quarter past one, as *Wasp*'s drums beat to quarters, American sailors and marines took their stations and ran out the guns while the ship's boys brought up powder from the magazine deep in the hold. Over the next two hours Manners and Blakely skillfully maneuvered for the advantage of the weather-gauge—Manners keeping it, Blakely never getting it—until seventeen minutes after three, when *Reindeer* came up on *Wasp*'s weather quarter and began firing a mobile twelve-pound carronade. No more than sixty yards separated the two ships. Manners was able to get off five unanswered shots until Blakely, realizing that the smaller *Reindeer* had no intention of coming on his beam, slowed *Wasp* as he "put his helm a-lee and luffed up, firing his guns aft forward as they bore"[14] on the faster-sailing *Reindeer* coming up under the American broadside.

Guns blasting, both ships sailed on parallel course no more than twenty yards apart. Grape and round shot flew across the water, ripping through wood and flesh as both crews loaded and fired, straining on decks slippery with blood and obscured by smoke. Early in the fight, both of Manners's calves were shot away, and soon after grape shot from *Wasp* passed through both of his thighs, severing veins and arteries and knocking him to the deck. Though badly wounded—one London newspaper claimed he sustained "14 wounds"[15]—Manners got up and resumed command as the ships came closer together and the carronades and top men on both ships continued their lethal fire.

The ships closed together, and Blakely ordered his marines and crew aft to board the *Reindeer* once contact was made. "As the vessels came grinding together the men hacked and thrust at one another through open port-holes, while the black smoke curled up between the hulls."[16] One British seaman was shot through the head with a ramrod but continued to man his gun. His mates begged him to go below for treatment, but the sailor refused, proclaiming, "If all the wounded of the *Reindeer* were as able to fight as I am, we should soon make the Americans strike."[17] The gravely wounded Manners, sword in hand, rallied his men for a counter-offensive:

> He called to his men, "Follow me, my boys, we must board them"—While climbing into the rigging, two balls from the tops penetrated his skull and came out beneath his chin. Placing one hand on his

> forehead, the other convulsively brandishing his sword, he exclaimed—"Oh God!" and dropped lifeless on his own deck.[18]

The Americans swarmed over *Reindeer*'s bulwarks, nets, and hammocks and beat back the British in a short but furious fight "til the decks were a sheet of blood."[19] Manners's clerk, the highest British officer left standing, surrendered the ship at 3:44 PM, twenty-seven minutes after the first shot was fired. Eleven men from the *Wasp* were killed or mortally wounded, and another fifteen were wounded. More than half of the battered *Reindeer*'s crew of 118 were casualties—thirty-three dead or mortally wounded and another thirty-four wounded. The ship herself was damaged beyond saving, so Blakely removed for his own use the mobile carronade that had harassed him early in the fight and set fire to the *Reindeer*. The wounded were placed on a neutral vessel for return to England, and the rest of the prisoners were disembarked at L'Orient, France, on 8 July 1814.

Blakely remained in L'Orient for seven weeks, repairing damage, buying supplies, and adding to his crew from the American privateers in the port. *Wasp* sailed out into the Channel on 27 August and over the next three days captured two prizes. Four days later she fell in with a convoy of ten merchantmen bound for Gibraltar and escorted by HMS *Armada*, 74. Over the next several hours the nimble *Wasp* played a game of cat and mouse with *Armada*—coming in close ... chased away ... coming in again ... chased away ... until finally, in the afternoon, *Wasp* succeeded in cutting out and capturing one of the merchantmen loaded with iron, brass, cannons, muskets, and other military stores.

Wasp got safely away with her prize before the lumbering *Armada* could intervene. Back on the prowl later that afternoon, she sighted in the distance a line of six ships strung along the port and starboard sides of her bow. Blakely set a course for the most weatherly of them, the British brig-sloop *Avon*, 18, commanded by James Arbuthnot.[20] Heading on a southwest course with the wind blowing in on the port beam, the ships closed on a parallel course. It was half past nine in the evening when *Wasp* came up close enough on *Avon*'s stern to fire the *Reindeer*'s twelve-pound carronade, and Arbuthnot responded with his stern-chasers and a few of the port guns that could bear. Fearing that *Avon* may try to escape, Blakely put his helm up to gain a stronger wind, crossed under *Avon*'s stern, and came up on her starboard quarter, where he unleashed a full broadside as each of *Wasp*'s larboard guns came to bear on the target.

Avon answered with a broadside of her own, and over the next twenty-five minutes, in the blackness of night, the two ships battered each other as they sailed on a southwesterly course. Four round shots smashed into *Wasp*'s hull in several places, killing two sailors, but as the fight continued, the fortune of war shifted to the Americans as *Wasp*'s guns pounded away at *Avon* with punishing accuracy. According to Theodore Roosevelt,

> The *Avon*'s gaff was shot away at almost the first broadside, and most of her main-rigging and spars followed suit. She was hulled again and again, often below the water-line; some of her carronades were dismounted, and finally the main-mast went by the board. At 10:00, after 31 minutes of combat, her guns had been completely silenced.[21]

Blakely called across the water to ask if she had struck, but there was no reply except for a few random shots. *Wasp* commenced firing at the disabled brig, and a few minutes later hailed *Avon* again with the same question, "Have you struck?" *Avon* this time answered in the affirmative, but as *Wasp* lowered a boat to take possession, the British brig *Castilian*, 18, was sighted bearing down on them from the northeast. As Blakely readied *Wasp* for a second round of combat, lookouts sighted two more sail coming in from the same direction. Blakely put *Wasp* before the wind to gain speed and allow time to repair the ship's damaged braces before combat resumed. As the Americans worked frantically to ready their damaged ship for further battle, *Castilian* closed and fired her lee guns. The shot flew high over *Wasp*'s quarterdeck and did but little damage to the rigging. But as *Castilian*'s Captain Braimer prepared a second barrage, urgent signals of distress from the sinking *Avon* forced him to break off, allowing *Wasp* to escape.

Wasp's depredations in Britain's home waters, her defeat of *Reindeer* and *Avon*, and her escape from four pursuing warships were troublesome signs of British naval inferiority. A few feisty American captains sailing tight little sloops-of-war, superior to whatever the Royal Navy could put against them, provoked an outcry among the British public. One correspondent to the *Naval Chronicle* recounted the fate of the *Avon* despondently:

> On board the *Avon* were forty-one persons killed and wounded; the main-mast was shot away; and she received so many shot in her hull, that she was actually sinking, and some accounts say that she had struck, when providentially the *Castilian* hove in sight ... to the relief of the gallant crew in the sinking vessel. The captain was wounded in both his legs but not dangerously. The first lieutenant, Mr. Pendergast, who was dangerously wounded, died the next day.... A neutral vessel has since landed at Downs the masters of three of our merchantmen, that were prisoners aboard the *Wasp*, during the engagement, who have reported that she had only two men killed and three wounded during this long and desperate battle: to us this assertion appears incredible, and shews the necessity of immediately building vessels capable of carrying more men, and heavier metal, as the present disparity is truly discouraging to both sailor and officer.[22]

Recovered from her modest injuries, *Wasp* sailed south, taking several prizes, which she destroyed, and in late September took the brig *Atalanta*, 8, and sent her to Savannah with a prize crew under Midshipman Geisinger. On 9 October, well off the west coast of Africa in the Atlantic, *Wasp* boarded the neutral Swedish brig *Adonis* and removed a couple of the officers from the defeated *Essex* on their way to England from Brazil. Geisinger brought the *Atalanta* safely into Savannah's harbor on 4 November 1814. The *Wasp*, however, was never seen again, presumably lost in an accident or a storm. In her six or so months at sea, *Wasp* tied *Peacock* for the most prizes of any ship that year, fifteen.

III

Back in Boston, the second round of repairs to the *Constitution* were completed and she was ready to sail in July 1814. HMS *Nymphe*, 38, patrolling the entrance to Boston Harbor, reported that the big frigate was ready for sea and that Bainbridge's shipyard had launched the *Independence*, a seventy-four-gun third-rater and the largest ship in America's little fleet.[23] Captain Stewart was prepared to bide his time, confident that as summer turned to fall and fall to winter, New England's harsh weather would make it difficult for the British to maintain the blockade. As cold rain, sleet, and snow lashed the harbor, *Constitution* remained on the alert, ready to leave at a moment's notice.

On the morning of 18 December, with a good breeze blowing in from the northwest and no British ships in sight, *Constitution* sailed out of Boston Harbor and past Cape Cod. When she reached deep water, she turned south to confront the blockaders stationed at the Delaware and the Chesapeake. The British, however, credited rumors that *Constitution* would join with Decatur's *President*, out of New York, and the *Congress*, from Portsmouth, for a raid on the waters of the British Isles. Thus, much of the blockading force off Boston sailed east to intercept the non-existent squadron supposedly on its way across the Atlantic.

Commodore Rodgers took over the new seventy-four-gun *Guerriere* in the spring of 1814, opening up the command of his former ship, the *President*. The *United States* and the *Macedonian* were bottled up in New London, so Decatur took advantage of Rodgers's move and assumed command of the *President*, which was docked in New York. The *Hornet*, which Captain Biddle managed to slip out of New London, and the *Peacock*, under Warrington, joined Decatur in New York. The small squadron was ready to sail at the first opportunity that the weather or the British offered.

The obstacle to Decatur's departure, it turned out, was not the enemy but his own government, which wanted his squadron kept where it was to protect New York from the thousands of British troops streaming over to North America after the fall of Napoleon. But by late 1814, following British losses at Baltimore, Plattsburgh, Mobile, Pensacola, and Fort Erie, the threat of invasion had diminished, and Decatur was allowed to sail. On 14 January 1815, a month after Stewart left Boston and three weeks after a peace agreement had been signed in Ghent, Decatur took advantage of a winter snow storm to sail his squadron out of New York Harbor for a commerce raiding cruise to the East Indies.

The *President*, 52; *Hornet*, 20; and *Peacock*, 20, were accompanied by the brig *Tom Bowline* and the merchantman *Macedonian*, both of which carried supplies for the long voyage around the Cape of Good Hope to the Indian Ocean.[24] Waiting for Decatur outside the harbor were five British warships under Captain Hayes, who commanded the razee *Majestic*, 52. With him were the frigates *Endymion*, under Captain Henry Hope, *Pomone*, under Captain Lumly, and *Tenedos*, under Captain Parker, as well as the brig *Dispatch*. Hope was eager for a shot at Decatur and the *President*, and when rumors spread that the Americans were about to leave the harbor, Hope saw an opportunity to answer the challenge that Hardy had declined when their blockade had Decatur bottled up in New London in early 1814.

Hope was probably eager for a little vindication, as well, following an unpleasant encounter with an American privateer off Nantucket a few months earlier. Under the command of Captain Jean Ordronaux, the 310-ton, seventeen-gun brigantine *Prince de Neufchatel* was returning to New York after an exceptionally successful voyage of plunder. In her hold were stolen goods worth $300,000, plus thirty-seven prisoners who had been taken off her many prizes. Though she normally sailed with a crew of 150, the departures of sailors to man the many prizes she taken had reduced her complement to just forty men when *Endymion* sighted her off the coast of Nantucket on 11 October 1814. The *Prince de Neufchatel* fled, and *Endymion* made sail to pursue. The chase soon stalled, though, when a dead calm settled over the waters of the Atlantic.[25]

Undeterred by the absence of wind, Hope armed 111 of his crew and launched them in five boats under the command of Lieutenant Abel Hawkins toward the becalmed privateer, which prepared herself for the attack by stringing thick rope netting above the bulwarks and loading her guns with grape and bullets. As *Endymion*'s boats came in range, Ordronaux ordered his guns to fire at will, but the determined British seamen pressed on through the storm of iron and lead and were soon alongside the undermanned *Prince de Neufchatel*.

Clambering up the privateer's side, British officers, sailors, and marines confronted a rain of lead musket balls and the slashing steel blades of axes and cutlasses hacking at them though the protective netting of the brigantine. One by one the British attackers fell back, bleeding and disfigured, into the wet bottoms of their small boats, while others pressed on in their place, only to suffer the same fate. A few British seamen managed to hack their way through the netting, but they were quickly cut up and killed when they reached the privateer's deck. Within minutes, one boat was sunk, three others drifted away with their dead and wounded, and the fifth was captured along with her surviving crew. According to Theodore Roosevelt:

> The slaughter had been frightful, considering the number of combatants. The victorious privateersmen had lost 7 killed, 15 badly

> and 9 slightly wounded, leaving but 9 untouched! Of the *Endymion*'s men, James says 28, including the first lieutenant and a midshipman, were killed, and 37, including the second lieutenant and a master's mate, wounded: "besides which the launch was captured and the crew made prisoners".... [O]f the prisoners captured 18 were wounded and 10 unhurt.... It was a most desperate conflict, and remembering how shorthanded the brigantine was, it reflected the highest honor on the American captain and his crew.[26]

The *Prince de Neufchatel* slipped away with her captured goods and a complement of British prisoners outnumbering her surviving crew three to one. No wonder that three months later Henry Hope and the *Endymion*'s surviving crew thirsted for the revenge that the capture of the *President*, *Hornet*, or *Peacock* would represent.

Their opportunity came on 14 January 1815, when a snowstorm moving in from the west with strong winds gave Decatur the perfect cover to escape New York Harbor. Visibility was poor, and the strong westerly wind, Decatur presumed, would blow the blockading ships off station and well to the east. His plan was for the ships of his squadron to sail separately—*Tom Bowline* and *Hornet* would follow when ready—and rendezvous at the Tristan da Cunha, an island in the south Atlantic about eighteen hundred miles west of Cape Town, South Africa.

But disaster struck early when *President*, leaving her anchorage off Staten Island, and accompanied by the store ship *Macedonian*, ran aground off Sandy Hook, New Jersey. Apparently one of the beacon ships that marked the channel and the edge of the sand bar was misplaced, and the pilot on *President* mistook the direction of the channel. Sailing onto the bar, the heavily laden *President* became lodged while the ebb and flow of the waves, tides, and currents battered the ship's bottom against the unyielding sand bar. It took the crew two hours to extricate the ship, but the *President* had "become much broken-backed, and otherwise strained, breaking several of her rudder braces, displacing a portion of her false keel, and otherwise receiving, as it was apprehended, considerable injury."[27] The damaged *President* finally broke free of the bar that night at ten o'clock, but the wind, blowing from the northwest, made it impossible to return north to New York City for repairs. With no choice but to continue on the voyage, Decatur turned east and sailed close along the Long Island shore for fifty miles before setting a course east southeast in the belief that the British blockading force, struggling to hold its position in the storm, would be somewhere behind him in the west.

But the blockading force had not held its position with the success Decatur assumed and was blown far to the east:

> They had drifted to the very point where Decatur thought they ought not [to] be; and with the early dawn, at five o'clock in the morning, three ships were descried right ahead, not more than two miles off, and standing east-north-east on a wind. But for the unhappy delay of two hours on the bar, the *President* would have been at least twenty miles outside of them. Decatur immediately ordered the helm of the *President* put to starboard, and hauled her by the wind on the larboard tack, with her head to the northward, toward the east end of Long Island. By daylight, four ships were discovered in chase under a press of sail; one on each quarter and two astern.[28]

By eleven o'clock the next morning, the lumbering *Majestic* was close enough to fire a few shots, but to no effect, and soon fell behind as *Endymion* gained on *President*. All things equal, *President* was the faster ship, but with the damage incurred on the bar and the hogging of her keel, the frigate had lost her edge in speed and was being overtaken by the well-armed *Endymion*. Around noon, with the wind light, Decatur kept his sails wet from the royals down, and lightened the frigate by starting his water, and throwing overboard the anchors, boats, cables, spare spars, and provisions. But when a fresh wind finally came up, it filled *Endymion*'s sails first and let her close the distance before it filled *President*'s. *Endymion* opened up with her bow guns, and *President* responded with her stern chasers. Little damage was done, but by late afternoon, with both ships on a northeasterly course, Hope had taken a position a quarter-mile off Decatur's starboard quarter where none of *President*'s guns could be brought to bear, but from which *Endymion* could maintain a devastating fire that ripped up *President*'s spars, sails, and rigging.

Unable to bring his guns on his pursuer, Decatur altered his course in an attempt to bring *President* alongside *Endymion*, board and seize the British frigate, scuttle *President*, and in the faster British ship sail away from the pursuing *Majestic*, *Pomone*, *Dispatch*, and *Tenedos*. Hope anticipated the move, and as Decatur changed course, so did he, maintaining his position off *President*'s quarter and away from her guns. Hope recorded in his ship's log for that day:

> At 5.10 gained the enemy's starboard-quarter, and preserved the position; evidently galling him much.... At 5.30 the enemy brailed up his spanker and bore away, showing a disposition to cross our bow and rake us. Put the helm hard a-weather, to meet this manoeuvre; and brought the enemy to close action in a parallel line of sailing.[29]

Decatur next attempted to bring *Endymion* to battle by turning south from his northeasterly course, bringing the wind on his starboard quarter and *Endymion* on his starboard beam. By this change, Decatur brought Hope on his beam. The two ships, with roughly comparable firepower, now fired at each other with cannon and musket as they sailed south on parallel courses. Casualties ran high as the powerful guns of both ships found their mark. *President*'s first lieutenant, Babbit, had his leg blown off below the knee by a thirty-two-pound shot from a carronade. Teetering on the leg that remained, Babbit tumbled down the wardroom hatch, fracturing what remained of the damaged limb in two places.

> He survived nearly two hours, calmly dictating his last messages of affection to his friends, removed from his neck the miniature of the young lady to whom he was betrothed, with a request that it might be delivered to his mother, and in like manner sent his watch, as a parting memorial, to his brother.[30]

Decatur himself was knocked over when a splinter struck his chest. When he regained his feet, he was struck again in the forehead by another splinter, which opened a torrent of blood. Undeterred, the commodore continued to command from the quarterdeck, and during the engagement *President*'s marines fired as many as five thousand cartridges at their adversaries.[31] As the battle continued, casualties mounted. Fourth Lieutenant Archibald Hamilton, who as a midshipman two years earlier had presented *Macedonian*'s colors to Dolley Madison, fell dead when a load of grape pierced his chest, though another account says a twenty-four-pound shot cut him in half.[32] Lieutenant E. F. Howell was shot in the head as he commanded the fifth division of guns on *President*'s quarterdeck.[33] Three of Decatur's four lieutenants now lay dead, and his exhausted crewmen had been at their posts for thirty-six hours.[34]

The *President* was severely battered by the two hours of broadsides, but *Endymion* also suffered considerable damage. By eight o'clock in the evening, gunfire from the British frigate slowed, as much as a minute passing without a shot. Most of her sails were shot away, and many of her larboard guns were dismounted or disabled. With *Endymion* seemingly beaten and out of action, Decatur wore ship and returned *President* to the northeasterly course, presenting to the British frigate an undefended stern. *Endymion*, by some accounts, could not take advantage of this vulnerability,[35] but Hope's log book claims that he fired a broadside into the *President*'s exposed stern.[36] It was now near nine o'clock, dark and cloudy, and Decatur hoped the night would hide him from the remaining three ships of the British squadron. But an opening in the clouds around eleven o'clock allowed enough of the moon light through to reveal the squadron, still in pursuit and now within gunshot.

The small frigate *Pomone* came up on *President*'s larboard side and let loose a broadside that killed and wounded several men. She then used her speed to race ahead and take a raking position off the sluggish *President*'s larboard bow as *Tenedos*, two cables' length distant, took a raking position off the starboard quarter as the fifty-two-gun *Majestic* and the brig *Dispatch* followed. Sensing the hopelessness of his situation, Decatur ordered his men below, out of harm's way, as he attempted to surrender by lowering the stern light as a signal of capitulation. Misreading the signals, *Pomone* fired another broadside, but as Decatur recalled his men from below to meet the challenge, the British frigate ceased fire and allowed the surrender to proceed. With *Endymion* disabled and lagging behind, *Pomone* and *Tenedos* took possession of *President* and supervised its surrender. In the wee hours of 16 January, *Endymion* and *Majestic* caught up with *Pomone* and *Tenedos*, and around three o'clock Decatur, in full dress uniform, was rowed to *Majestic* to present his sword to Captain John Hayes. Hayes refused it, remarking that "he felt proud in returning the sword of an officer, who had defended his ship so nobly."[37]

Casualties ran high on the *President*: twenty-four men were killed and fifty-five wounded compared with eleven killed and fourteen wounded on *Endymion*. After a few hours of sleep aboard the *President*, Decatur again donned his full dress uniform to preside over the burial of his fellow officers, Lieutenants Babbit, Hamilton, and Howell.

> The three bodies, shrouded in their country's flag, were placed side by side in the gangway. The surviving officers, dressed in uniform, gathered around all that was left of mess-mates who had won their respect by their high and valuable qualities.... Decatur, standing on the gun-slide next to the gangway, read the burial service.... Their bodies were committed to the deep, honored with appropriate volleys from British marines, forming part of the prize crew.[38]

Two days later, on their way to Bermuda for repairs, *President* and *Endymion* were both dismasted in a storm. So precarious was their state that the British frigate had to throw overboard all of her spar deck guns to remain afloat.

The details of this sea battle and the question of how the leaders fulfilled their duty have been the subject of considerable historical controversy. Many American historians, but not all, were complimentary of Decatur's performance, arguing that he did as well as could be expected with a disabled ship confronting four opponents. Theodore Roosevelt was one of the exceptions, though: "... I regret to say that I do not think that the facts bear out the assertions, on the part of most American authors, that Commodore Decatur 'covered himself with glory' and showed the 'utmost heroism.'"[39]

A number of British historians attempted to present the fight as a one-on-one battle that *Endymion* won fair and square without help from *Pomone* and *Tenedos*. William James downplays the involvement of the two other British frigates, which forced the surrender while *Endymion* was well behind and dead in the water repairing her sails and rigging. Contemporary correspondents to the *Naval Chronicle* saw the British victory in a heroic light:

> Our hopes have been honourably realized in the capture of the United States ship *President*, Commodore Decatur commander, by the British frigate *Endymion*; and we most cordially congratulate Captain Hope, his officers and men, on the merited success of their

> gallantry and skill, in so bravely maintaining the reputation of their country.[40]

While in Bermuda, Decatur was treated with every courtesy, including a dinner hosted by Admiral Sir Alexander Cochrane (who stopped by on his return from the British defeat at New Orleans). News of the 24 December treaty ending the war arrived in New York aboard HMS *Favorite* on 11 February. The U.S. Senate ratified the treaty six days later. Decatur did not know that the war had ended until the admiral of the blockading fleet (presumably awaiting orders to disband and return home) gave him the news. Within weeks, he was paroled, and on 21 February HMS *Narcissus* landed him in New London. Decatur requested a court of inquiry into the loss of his ship. The court convened on 11 April and reported its findings to Secretary of the Navy Benjamin Crowninshield on 17 April. The report exonerated Decatur and his officers, noting that "in this unequal conflict, the enemy gained a ship, but the victory was ours...."[41]

IV

As Decatur was fighting *Endymion* and *Pomone*, Captain Stewart and the *Constitution* were in the Caribbean chasing a brig. One of her crewman fell overboard, Stewart halted his chase to rescue the seaman, and the brig got away. Stewart had enjoyed only modest success on this cruise, though the prize he did take, the merchantman *Lord Nelson*, provided the Americans with what they most needed—food. Boston merchants were unwilling to accept the depreciated United States currency, so the frigate had set out with insufficient rations. *Constitution*'s chaplain, Assheton Humphreys, described in his journal the crew's delight at discovering the *Lord Nelson*'s bounteous provisions:

> Upon overhauling the invoices of the schooner she proved to be a perfect slop ship and grocery store, very opportunely sent to furnish a good rig and bountiful cheer for Christmas, and never more opportune could Fortune have played her freak—there was lots of meats tongues, corn beef in rounds, smoked salmon, dried beef and cod fish ... fine apple cheeses & barrels of loaf sugar of the most superior kinds, pipes of best brandy, gin and port wine, chests

> of imperial and gunpowder tea, barrells of flour, hams inferior not even to Smithfield Virginia [*sic*] .... No loss of time occurred in gutting the schooner of these desirable valuables, more precious than the diamonds of Golconda, and ere the Christmas sun was low it shown no longer on the hull of Lord Nelson ....[42]

Lord Nelson's captain at first thought that *Constitution*—bearing a white gun stripe and flying the Union Jack for deception—was a British ship and had volunteered his convoy's next rendezvous before realizing he had been overtaken by an American. Followed by *Lord Nelson*, Stewart sailed to that point—east of Bermuda—but found nothing. Turning south again to a position where his ship could intercept home-bound British merchantmen laden with cargo from the West Indies, Stewart again found nothing. Turning south, they hunted the West Indies sea lanes and weathered a severe winter storm. It was here that Stewart was forced to give up on the brig he was chasing when the seaman fell overboard.

Sailing well to the west of the Canary Islands, Stewart still found his prey elusive. He took advantage of a chance encounter with a French brig to unload the captured crew of *Lord Nelson* for a safe voyage home and turned his ship north to prowl Britain's home waters off Cape Finisterre. On 8 February, Steward boarded a Hamburg barque, whose crew informed him of rumors of a peace agreement between the United States and Britain. Over the next several days, French and Dutch ships provided confirmation that a peace treaty had been signed and that the document was on its way to Washington for ratification.[43] Perhaps Stewart was mindful that no treaty was in force until ratified by the Senate, for *Constitution* continued her patrol off the west coast of Spain. The harsh winter weather made life aboard the damp and unheated ship miserable and service aloft in the cold, wet wind almost unbearable. Indeed, Stewart had several times upbraided his lookouts for thinking more about their comfort than about the ship's safety. As Assheton Humphreys tells it, *Constitution* was better protected by an officer's pet dog than by the weather-battered lookouts. A Portuguese frigate, *La Amazonas*, materialized out of the bad weather:

> A terrier dog (named Guerriere) belonging to Lieut, Hoffman, from the very great sagacity with which he was gifted had become

> a great favorite with all hands officers and men. So a display of almost natural faculties did he exhibit that many were of the opinion that he would talk were it not for that he feared he would be set to work.... Guerriere who was playing about the heels of Lieut. Ballard appeared uncommonly frisky and was rather troublesome, at length becoming an encumbrance he attracted the particular attention of the Lieut., perceiving which he jumped upon the hammock clothes and stretching his head to windward began to bark almost vehemently;—upon looking to discover what attracted his notice lo! And behold! There was a large frigate standing down before the wind under a press of sail, which the gentlemen at the mast head had not yet discovered, fearing perhaps to look to windward lest "the winds should visit their cheeks too unduly" as my friend Hamlet the dane, says.[44]

The sea was too choppy to board *La Amazonas*, so the two ships soon parted, and *Constitution* continued to search, without much success, for British prizes off Lisbon. The British, however, got wind of *Constitution*'s presence and came out in pursuit. *Elizabeth*, 74, was joined by the frigate *Tiber*, 38, under the command of Captain Richard Dacres, who was eager to avenge his loss of *Guerriere* to *Constitution* two and a half years before. While the warships searched for her, *Constitution* captured the merchantman *Susanna*, bound for Liverpool from Buenos Aires, on 19 February, seizing her valuable cargo of hides, vicuna wool, and nutria pelts (plus two jaguar cubs) valued at $75,000. Captain Ross of the *Susanna* attempted to keep the cubs from the Americans, asking Stewart "in his Scottish dialect if he 'wad na restore him his pet kie [kitties]', roundly asserting that he had paid a considerable sum for them and that they were his own, and he could hardly be convinced that he was lying when the letters advising the owners they were on board were produced for him."[45]

Several days later, after setting out with Russian and Portuguese merchant vessels, whose neutrality protected them from seizure, Stewart sent the *Susanna*'s crew home on the Portuguese ship; a prize crew sailed the *Susanna* and her cargo to New York.[46] On 20 February, with a northeast wind behind him, and having spent the past ten days making a nuisance of himself off Portugal, Stewart thought it best to get out of the British-controlled waters and head southwest toward Madeira, where more prizes might be found. Shortly after noon, however, "a sail was cried from the mast head as being on the weather bow; hauled up for her under all sail, shortly after another sail was descried on the lee bow and word from aloft that the ship to windward had bore up for us...."[47]

These were the frigate-built corvette HMS *Cyane*, 24, under Captain Gordon Thomas Falcon, and the ship sloop HMS *Levant*, 18, under the Honorable George Douglass, which were part of a trailing force out of Gibraltar to cover the rear of British convoys headed to the West Indies. Certain that they were British and worried that they might flee and seek refuge in the falling night, Stewart set all sail and took up the chase. As *Constitution* closed the distance, she tested the range with a shot from her bow chaser, but the shot fell well short. Twenty minutes later the bow chaser was fired again and the shot fell within range. But just as the distance was short enough for serious combat, *Constitution*'s main royal mast cracked and gave way. Repairs took about an hour—a spare spar was substituted for the broken mast—and with her main royal filling with wind, the distance between *Constitution* and her British quarry again began to narrow.

Around six o'clock, lookouts on *Constitution* saw the two British ships come within hailing distance as the weather ship crossed under the other's stern and minutes later began to reduce sail for the coming fight. All three ships beat to quarters. Decks were sanded, powder brought up, shot stacked, sails trimmed, boarding weapons placed on deck, matches smoldered in their tubs as gun crews opened the ports, pulled off the tompions, and wheeled out the iron barrels of the big guns.

Having hauled in their lower sails in preparation for battle, the British apparently had second thoughts upon discovering that their adversary was one of America's big frigates. They set all sail and hauled close to the wind, endeavoring to weather their opponent and "delay action till dark, so as to get the advantage of manoevering."[48] But their attempt at flight was to no avail against the faster *Constitution*, and at ten minutes after six the big American frigate ranged up on the windward side of the British. Pulling past the trailing *Cyane* and sailing on a parallel course, *Constitution* took a position between the two, *Cyane* off her larboard quarter and *Levant* off her port bow. With everybody in range, *Constitution* hoisted her ensign, the British responded by setting theirs, and Stewart opened the fight by firing a single shot between the two.

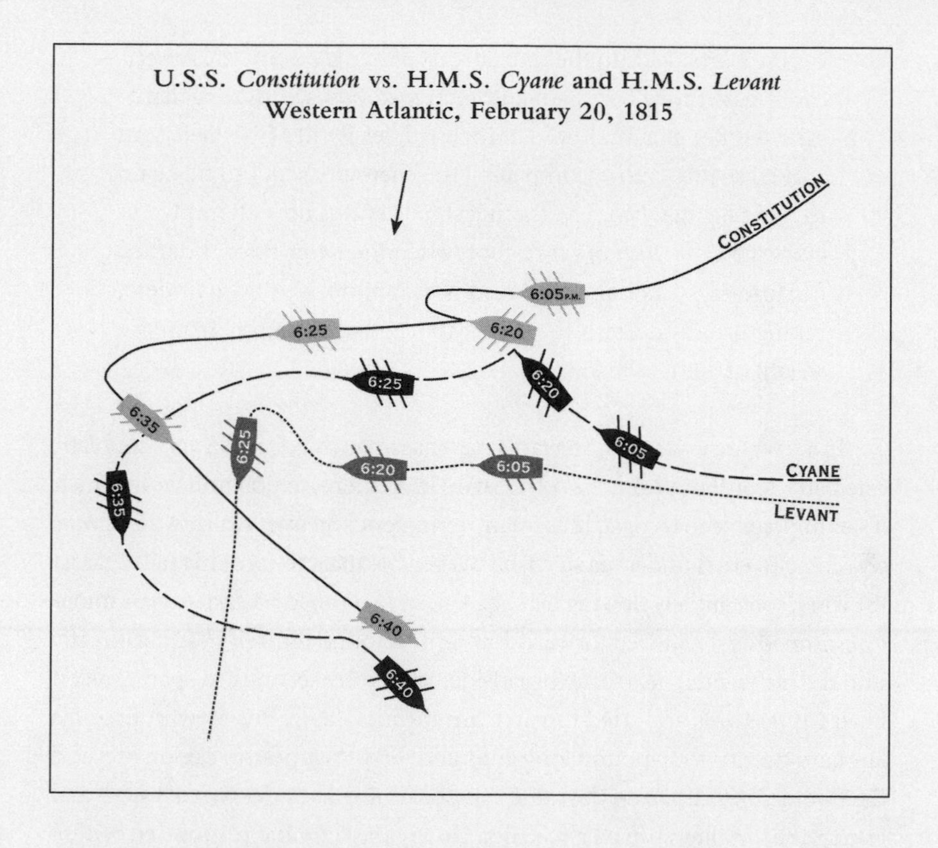

As the dark winter night settled on the combatants, both sides fired with their big guns while marines in the tops and on the shrouds kept up a withering musket fire to clear the decks. A British shot got two Americans in the waist, continuing on to smash the boat that held the two jaguar cubs, killing both.[49] Dense smoke from the guns soon impaired visibility for all combatants. With no targets in sight, the guns fell silent on both sides. Minutes later, after the smoke had dissipated in the gentle breeze, Stewart found *Levant* off his larboard bow and *Cyane* behind, luffing her sails in preparation to tack and cross under *Constitution*'s stern, hoping to rake the frigate at her most vulnerable point.

Recognizing the threat, Stewart ordered a broadside against *Levant* and immediately took steps to thwart *Cyane*'s attack in what may have been the most extraordinary few minutes of sailing of the entire war. James Fenimore Cooper describes it, perhaps with some technical help from his friend Isaac Chauncey:

> Giving a broadside to the ship abreast of her [*Levant*], the American frigate threw her main and mizzen-topsails with topgallant-sails set, flat aback, shook all forward, let fly her jib-sheet, and backed swiftly astern, compelling the enemy [*Cyane*] to fill again to avoid being raked. The leading ship [*Levant*] now attempted to cross the *Constitution*'s fore-foot, when the latter filled, boarded her fore-tack, shot ahead, forced her antagonist to ware under a raking broadside, and to run off to leeward to escape from the weight of her fire.[50]

In a few short minutes, Stewart's clever seamanship foiled a very sophisticated attack and put both his adversaries in a defensive position from which it was impossible to recover. In layman's terms, once Stewart realized that *Cyane* was going to cross under his stern, he twisted his spars to force his sails against the wind, substantially slowing his ship. Falcon had timed his tack to pass under *Constitution* as she moved forward, but he now found himself heading directly into the big frigate's fearsome broadside. With only seconds to spare, Falcon filled *Cyane*'s sails and tried to run from the inevitable. But Stewart fired his larboard twenty-four-pound long guns and forty-two-pound carronades and then wore *Constitution* on the same course, coming in under *Cyane*'s stern and raking the smaller ship as she sailed slowly past. *Cyane* responded with a broadside of her own, but as Stewart's powerful frigate came up on the corvette's weather quarter and threatened to blast her to splinters, Falcon struck at 6:50 PM. Stewart sent Second Lieutenant Hoffman over with an armed party to take possession of the ship.

Meanwhile, the smaller *Levant*, which suffered damage to her rigging from *Constitution*'s earlier raking broadside from behind, had sailed away from the fight to make repairs. Apparently unaware of *Cyane*'s surrender, Douglass took his sloop back into the fray about eight o'clock under the dull moonlight that pierced the cloud cover. Coming at each other on opposite tacks, *Levant* and *Constitution* fired broadsides as they passed. Realizing that *Cyane* was no longer in the fight and that his sloop was no match for *Constitution*, Douglass "crowded all sail to escape,"[51] but was quickly overtaken by the faster frigate. After a couple of obligatory shots from his bow chasers, Douglass struck and *Constitution*'s Third Lieutenant William B. Shubrick was sent over to take possession of the defeated sloop.

When the news of the defeat reached England, one correspondent to the *Naval Chronicle* remarked, "It is with considerable mortification and regret, that we state the capture of the *Levant*, 24, ... and the *Cyane*, 24, ... by the American frigate *Constitution*. They were captured early in February, on the coast of Africa, after a very sharp action."[52]

Casualties were relatively light on both sides: *Constitution* suffered three men killed and twelve wounded, three mortally. No official report for the British ships exists. It is estimated that *Cyane* saw twelve men killed and twenty-six wounded, several mortally. Roosevelt says seven men aboard the *Levant* were killed and sixteen wounded, but Cooper, drawing on Stewart's report,[53] says that the death toll on *Levant* may have been as high as twenty-three, an estimate more in keeping with some of the eyewitness accounts. After noting that *Cyane* had five feet of water in her hold and that "her masts tottering and nothing but the smoothness of the sea [were] preventing them from going over the side," Chaplain Humphreys added: "The *Levant* in a condition somewhat better, her spars having generally escaped, but her hull pretty well drilled and her deck a perfect slaughter house, in fact so hardly had she been dealt with on deck that her men by the acknowledgement of their Officers twice went below from their quarters."[54]

A midshipman accompanying Lieutenant Shubrick onto the captured *Levant* recorded, "The mizen mast for several feet was covered with brains and blood; teeth, pieces of bones, fingers and large pieces of flesh were picked up from off the deck."[55] Damage was light on the *Constitution*: aloft, only her foretopgallant yard was lost and a few lines cut. Her hull was hit hard by about a dozen thirty-two-pound shots, but all were held tightly embedded in the stout oak of her scantlings. In a few hours' time, prisoners were secured, prize crews assigned, and enough repairs made to allow the three ships to get underway on a southerly course that took them away from British patrols that might threaten them. It was a course that took them toward a sea lane where earlier reports from *Susanna* suggested a valuable British prize might be found.

The captive British officers seem to have been unpleasant guests for the American officers, duty-bound to host them with sympathy and respect aboard *Constitution*. They complained about their accommodations—especially the toilet facilities, and the *Constitution*'s log for 25 February records that "they did not conduct themselves below, like gentlemen, being in their language indecent, vulgar, and abusive to each other."[56] Assheton Humphreys recalled,

> The loss of their vessels appeared to give them no uneasiness nor did they appear at all to feel the least mortification from being taken by an inferior force, though they frequently resorted to manly recrimination in mutually accusing each others ship as the cause of their being here.[57]

Captains Falcon and Douglass were apparently no less abrasive than their subordinates and were often found arguing with each other as to who bore responsibility for the defeat. According to one account, on returning to his cabin from the quarterdeck, Stewart found Falcon and Douglass in a heated argument over who was at fault for the loss. Tyrone Martin sums up the incident:

> Stewart listened to the acrimony for a few moments, then reportedly told them, "Gentlemen, there is no use in getting warm about it; it would have been all the same whatever you might have done. If you doubt that, I will put you all on board again and you can try it over." The offer was not accepted.[58]

On 6 March, *Constitution* and her captive consorts arrived off Cape Verde Islands and the next day anchored in the harbor of Porto Praya on the larger island of Sao Iago. Stewart transferred his prisoners to a British brig already in harbor, and sent a party of seventeen ashore to buy fresh supplies for the voyage back to the United States. But as the transfer and loading continued through the next day, Lieutenant Shubrick caught sight of many masts poking out through the fog off shore and correctly surmised they belonged to a British squadron in search of *Constitution*. The frigates *Leander*, *Acasta*, and *Newcastle* had been part of the Boston blockading force that in late December 1814 hastily sailed off to protect the British Isles from the rumored attack squadron of *Constitution*, *President*, and *Hornet*. After fruitlessly pursuing *Constitution* in the Channel and off Spain and Portugal, they followed rumors of the big frigate's presence in the south to the Cape Verde Islands. On 11 March 1815 they finally had her, or so thought their commander, Captain Sir George Collier on the *Leander*.

Stewart understood that he was especially vulnerable to the three frigates in the confines of the harbor, where there was no room for maneuver. Within four minutes of sighting the British, the *Constitution* was on her way out of the harbor on a course that would give her the weather gauge for the long chase which he expected to ensue. Behind him followed *Cyane* under Lieutenant Hoffman and *Levant* under Lieutenant Ballard. They had left behind the few British prisoners, who in turn responded to their good fortune by seizing Porto Praya's fort and turning its guns on the fleeing Americans, though without success. The fleeing ships crowded on as much sail as they could. As the chase progressed and *Acasta* closed on the trailing *Cyane*, Stewart signaled Hoffman to tack to the northwest, which he quickly did, escaping his pursuers and safely arriving in New York on 10 April 1815.

Acasta, *Leander*, and *Newcastle* closed on *Levant*. Stewart responded by ordering Ballard to tack to the northwest, but this time all three British ships tacked with him, perhaps calculating that they had no chance of catching the speedy *Constitution*, so they might as well settle for whatever was nearest. The unfortunate *Levant* was soon overtaken, and she surrendered after several broadsides. This consolation prize, however, scarcely satisfied the pursuing British squadron. Collier, says Martin, "was never able to provide a satisfactory explanation for his actions that day; the fact that he had allowed *Constitution* to escape eventually led to his suicide in 1817."[59]

James Fenimore Cooper offered this assessment of the moonlit fight:

> The manner in which Captain Stewart handled his ship, on this occasion, excited much admiration among nautical men, it being an unusual thing for a single vessel to engage two enemies, and escape being raked. So far from this occurring to the *Constitution*, however, she actually raked both her opponents, and the manner in which she backed and filled in the smoke, forcing her two opponents down to leeward, when they were endeavoring to cross her stern or fore-foot, is among the most brilliant manoevering in naval annals.[60]

Theodore Roosevelt adds,

> [I]t would have been simply impossible to surpass the consummate skill with which she was handled.... The firing was excellent, considering the short time the ships were actually engaged, and the fact that it was at night. Altogether, the fight reflected the greatest credit on her, and also on her adversaries.[61]

"If [Stewart's] adversaries can be said to have done anything 'wrong,'" writes Martin, "it would have to be having the temerity to challenge him in the first place. On *that* day, in *those* circumstances, *Constitution* and the crew simply were unbeatable."[62] Yet not every American commentator was as enthusiastic as Cooper, Martin, and Roosevelt. Henry Adams concludes,

> Either separately or together the British ships were decidedly unequal to the *Constitution*, which could, by remaining at long range, sink them both without receiving a shot in return ... the *Constitution* was built of greater strength; the two sloops had only the frames of their class.... In truth, the injury inflicted by the *Constitution*'s fire was not so great as might have been expected. The *Cyane* lost twelve killed and twenty-six wounded.... Neither ship was dismasted or in a sinking condition.... On the other hand, the *Constitution* was struck eleven times in the hull, and lost three men killed and twelve wounded, three of the latter mortally. She suffered more than in her battle with *Guerriere*—a result creditable to the British ships....[63]

After escaping Collier's squadron, Stewart headed south and west in search of the richly laden *Inconstant*, which *Susanna*'s captain said was crossing the Atlantic to England. Finding nothing, on 4 April 1815 Stewart unloaded his 225 prisoners at Sao Luis, Brazil, and headed north to the U.S. mainland, searching for prizes along the way. Stopping at San Juan, Puerto Rico, Stewart received confirmation that the U.S. Senate had ratified the Treaty of Ghent. "but because it had a 'time late' clause built into it to provide time to communicate that fact to the far-flung naval units on both sides, *Constitution*'s capture of *Cyane* and *Levant* stood as valid wartime conquests. The British recapture of *Levant*, however, technically was after the fact."[64]

Constitution continued on to New York City, arriving off the battery on 15 May. Stewart, his officers, and his crew were honored by the city and later by the nation with speeches, accolades, dinners, medals, and prize money. This time, however, there was a slight difference in the praise. The nation had come to realize that the *Constitution*—this great oaken beast of war—was herself as important as the men who sailed her. A century later, the historian Charles Francis Adams, borrowing a phrase from George Canning, eloquently described the *Constitution* as having "had occasion ... to 'assume the likeness of an animated thing, instinct with life and motion'; to ruffle its swelling plumage; to put forth its beauty and its bravery; and, collecting its scattered elements of strength, to prepare again to 'awaken its dormant thunder.'"[65]

After a week or so in New York, *Constitution* set sail for her home port of Boston, where a local paper reported that "this glorious Yankee vessel was welcomed by federal salutes. Captain Stewart landed under a salute; and was escorted to the Exchange coffee-house, by troops, amidst the repeated cheers of citizens of both sexes, who filled the streets, wharves, and vessels, and occupied the houses. A band of music played national airs...."[66]

V

Although *Constitution*'s post-treaty battle is among the greatest of the war, she was not the only American warship still at sea, and naval conflict between American and British ships continued into July. When Decatur set out from New York on 14 January 1815, he led a formidable squadron that would follow him out a few days later and rendezvous at Tristan da Cunha in the south Atlantic. Unaware that Decatur and *President* had been taken by the British on 15 January, *Peacock* and *Hornet* sailed from New York on the 22nd but became separated several days out. Each sailed independently to the island. *Peacock* and the supply ship *Tom Bowline* arrived first on 18 March but were blown off station by a strong gale. *Hornet* arrived five days later, on 23 March, and was preparing to anchor off the north coast of the island when her lookout sighted a sail off to the southeast headed on a westerly course.

The sail belonged to the British brig-sloop *Penguin*, under the command of Captain James Dickenson. Armed with ten guns and sailing out from the Cape of Good Hope, Dickenson was in search of the American privateer *Young Wasp*. But he found *Hornet* instead, and the two ships came at each other as the marine drummers beat to quarters and the crews prepared for battle. With *Penguin* holding the weather gauge, Biddle yawed and wore to keep from being raked. At 1:40 PM, *Penguin* hauled to wind on a starboard tack and raised her British colors, while Biddle put *Hornet* on the same tack and raised the Stars and Stripes. Sailing on converging parallel courses, *Hornet* and *Penguin* traded broadsides while the marines in the tops blasted away at each other's officers and crew with their muskets and rifles.

As Dickenson ordered his helm put aweather to bring *Penguin* into a position to board *Hornet*, he received a mortal wound. Lieutenant McDonald assumed command and crashed *Penguin* into *Hornet*'s starboard side as Biddle attempted to cross her bow and rake the British brig with his carronades. *Penguin*'s bowsprit pierced the space between *Hornet*'s main- and mizzenmasts, and for a brief moment the two ships were tied together. The American crewmen armed themselves with cutlasses and pikes for the expected melee, but the British ignored the opportunity and remained on their ship. Eager for a fight, the Americans wanted to board *Penguin*, but Biddle refused, believing that *Hornet*'s superior gunnery would soon beat *Penguin* into submission with greater certainty and fewer casualties than hand-to-hand combat.

In her collision with *Hornet*, *Penguin*'s bowsprit ripped away *Hornet*'s mizzen shrouds, stern davits, and spanker boom,[67] severely damaging both ships' rigging and maneuverability. Once separated, neither ship was in a position to bring its guns to bear against the other, and the conflict was momentarily limited to the small arms on the decks and in the rigging. The ships were no more than thirty feet apart, and musket shots peppered the air between them. The Americans thought they heard a shout from *Penguin* indicating surrender, but when Biddle stood upon the taffrail to confirm *Penguin's* intentions, two British marines fired, wounding him in the neck. Return fire from *Hornet* killed both marines, and minutes later *Penguin*'s bowsprit broke off and her foremast toppled over the side. Free of *Penguin*'s impaling bowsprit, Biddle put his stern into the wind, crossed *Penguin*'s bow, and came under on her larboard side ready to blast the brig to splinters. But *Penguin*, her rigging badly damaged, mainmast tottering, hull pierced in many places, and a third of her crew dead or wounded, struck her colors before Biddle could deliver his devastating broadside.

The battle had lasted twenty-two minutes, and in that brief time the British suffered fourteen killed and twenty-eight wounded. Two were killed and eight wounded on *Hornet*. *Penguin* was too badly damaged to keep as a prize, so Biddle had her stores taken onto *Hornet* and her crew imprisoned below before scuttling her. As *Penguin* slipped below the water, sails were spotted over the horizon. They turned out to belong to *Peacock* and *Tom Bowline*, returning to station after being blown off by a strong gale several days earlier. The prisoners were loaded onto *Tom Bowline* and taken to Rio de Janeiro, where they were released. *Hornet* and *Peacock* cruised off Tristan da Cunha, waiting for the arrival of Decatur and *President.* The war was over by now and Decatur had already rejoined his wife in New London, but neither Biddle nor Warrington knew of the treaty. By 13 April they had given up on *President* and followed their orders by sailing east past the Cape of Good Hope and into the Indian Ocean, where they were expected to raid British merchantmen going to and from India.

On 27 April, southeast of Port Elizabeth (now in South Africa) and just into the Indian Ocean, the two ships spotted a sail to the southeast and went in pursuit. *Peacock*, the faster of the two, pulled ahead of *Hornet* and got closer to the quarry, only to discover that it was not a cargo-laden Indiaman but the seventy-four-gun *Cornwallis*. The British two-decker turned quickly on the two American brigs and came down in hot pursuit, showing surprising speed for a large, heavily armed ship. The *Peacock* got away, but the slower *Hornet* was not so lucky. *Cornwallis*, taking the weather gauge, targeted the slower brig for the chase and gradually closed the distance. As the chase continued into the evening, the gap narrowed. Biddle hoped to pick up speed by lightening his ship and began throwing overboard all of the excess stores taken from *Penguin*. But the *Cornwallis* was the faster ship, and as day turned to night and then to day again (it was now the 29th), the *Cornwallis* was ahead of the *Hornet* off her starboard beam. Now within range of her guns, *Cornwallis* fired, but the shots were poorly aimed and no damage was inflicted.

Biddle continued to lighten his ship by dumping more supplies, his anchors, cables, extra spars, shot, ballast, boats and all but one of his guns,[68] and for a while the lightened *Hornet* pulled ahead and out of range. But a shifting wind negated the advantage, and soon the *Cornwallis* came close enough to fire another volley. Again the poorly served guns did little damage, though they scared the crew.

> The shot that fell on the main deck ... struck immediately over the head of one of our gallant fellows, who had been wounded in our glorious action with the *Penguin*, where he was lying in his cot very ill with his wounds; the shot was coming through the deck, and it threw innumerable splinters around this poor fellow, and struck down a small paper American ensign, which he had hoisted over his head....[69]

By afternoon, the wind shifted in *Hornet*'s advantage and the gap widened through the night. Deprived of any supplies and guns after a chase of nearly forty-eight hours, *Hornet* gave up her mission and worked her way back to New York, stopping along the way at São Salvador, Brazil, where Biddle sought relief for his wounded men. There he learned that a treaty had been signed and the war was over.[70]

Warrington, on board the *Peacock*, knew nothing of the treaty. Having escaped *Cornwallis*, he continued into the Indian Ocean, where he captured four valuable merchantmen before coming upon a convoy protected by the fourteen-gun British brig *Nautilus* under Lieutenant Boyce. *Nautilus* sent over a boat to advise Warrington that the war was over, but Warrington denied receiving the message. As *Peacock* approached the brig, Boyce hailed him with the same news of peace. Warrington took this to be a deception and demanded that Boyce surrender, but honor required Boyce to refuse. Against a more powerful enemy, the British captain prepared his ship for battle. After one or two broadsides that killed seven of his men and wounded another eight, he struck his flag to the American. And on this confused note, the naval conflict between the United States and Great Britain came to an end.

CHAPTER TWENTY-TWO

NEW ORLEANS—PEACE AT LAST

As British and American peace commissioners closed in on an agreement to end the war in the autumn chill of Ghent, British troop ships carrying fifty-seven hundred seasoned infantrymen from the battlefields of Europe were converging off the western tip of Jamaica for the invasion of America's Gulf coast. Their plan was to rendezvous at Negril in mid-November 1814 and, accompanied by more than a thousand sailors and marines, sail north to attack and seize Mobile and New Orleans. November 20 was the date set by the Admiralty for the fleet to embark from Negril, but the late arrival of several of the convoys bringing the troops from Bermuda, the Chesapeake, and Europe—slowed, perhaps, by the nasty fight in the Azores a month earlier with the American privateer *General Armstrong*—delayed the sailing until the 26th.

An attack on New Orleans offered a number of opportunities to undermine the power and influence of the troublesome Americans. Napoleon had seized the Louisiana Territory from Spain. His sale of the "stolen goods" to the United

States in 1803 had given the Americans control over a huge, productive land mass and river valley that threatened Britain's remaining power and influence in North America. Capturing New Orleans would allow Britain to moderate this threat by returning the city and territory to its ally Spain. Control of New Orleans could hobble the development of America's frontier west of the Appalachians by blocking access to the city's port and thus the global economy. The capture of New Orleans would also push the Americans out of the Caribbean. Finally, Admirals Cochrane, Cockburn, and Malcolm were keenly aware that the huge stores that had accumulated in the city's warehouses during the blockade promised prize money of epic proportions.[1]

II

New Orleans had been under the United States' control for little more than a decade, and the loyalty of its largely French and Spanish population to their new Anglo-American rulers in Washington was suspect. Whereas thousands of ordinary citizens in Baltimore and Washington had risked their lives to save their city, the British expected little opposition from the inhabitants of New Orleans. It was the most polyglot city in North America, and the British presumed that its diversity of races and loyalties would hinder American efforts to defend the city. Immigrants from Portugal, Germany, Italy, and Ireland had added to New Orleans' ethnic mix. Many Anglo-Americans had recently arrived, including a former mayor of New York, Edward Livingston, whose political career had ended in financial scandal. And of course, many people in New Orleans were not white:

> There was also a big black population, mostly slave but including a big population of free blacks. If they were native to the mainland the blacks were also Creoles, as were the Spanish descendants of native-born settlers.... Mixing had produced a kaleidoscope of color: mulattoes, quadroons, and octoroons, that led to outbursts such as the New Orleans housewife who called quadroon women "*Heaven's last, worst gift to white men.*"[2]

The frigate *Vesta* arrived in the Chesapeake in early September 1814 with a dispatch from London advising Cochrane that seven thousand fresh troops under

Lord Hill were on their way to America and would rendezvous with Cochrane's fleet on 20 November at Jamaica for the assault on the Gulf coast. Cochrane withdrew from Baltimore on the 14th. En route to the Caribbean, Cochrane wrote, "I have it much at heart to give them a complete drubbing before peace is made, when I trust their Northern limits will be circumscribed and the Command of the Mississippi wrested from them."[3]

Fortunately for the United States, Britain's plan to attack along the Gulf was one of the worst kept secrets of the war. Walter Lord describes the stream of hints and leaks:

> As early as August, Albert Gallatin warned from Ghent that a big expedition was fitting out, Louisiana the objective. In September James Monroe sent a separate warning to the district military commander, Major General Andrew Jackson. That same month Jean Laffite, leader of the freebooters operating out of Barataria Bay, reported a visit from a Royal Navy captain seeking his cooperation. And if Laffite was a bit of a chameleon, there was the proclamation issued by Major Edward Nicolls, the battle-scarred Royal Marine officer in charge of recruiting Indians, blacks and other dissidents.[4]

Nicolls's proclamation read:

> Natives of Louisiana! On you the first call is made to assist in liberating from a faithless, imbecile government your paternal soil: Spaniards, Frenchmen, Italians, and British, whether settled or residing for a time in Louisiana, on you, also, I call to aid me in this just cause: the American usurpation in this country must be abolished, and the lawful owners of the soil put in possession.[5]

In response to the many warnings, President Madison appointed Andrew Jackson to the command of the Seventh Military District on 28 May 1814. In September, Secretary of State James Monroe—now also serving as secretary of war following Armstrong's forced resignation—sent messages to the governors of Georgia, Tennessee, and Kentucky asking them to call up their militias, and he advised General Jackson that as many as twelve thousand militiamen would be provided by these states alone. In Louisiana, Governor Claiborne called up the state's militia, placed them at various points vulnerable to a British attack, and sent a note to Jackson welcoming him to New Orleans. Jackson, however, expected the main British attack at Mobile Bay. As he marched his troops to Mobile, Cochrane left his anchorage at Negril with fifty ships and fifty-seven hundred infantrymen and set sail for America.

Though New Orleans was the prime target, one of Britain's planning options allowed for an initial attack at Pensacola or Mobile. Once the British controlled the eastern Gulf coast, the Indian forces that Captain Hugh Pigot of the Royal Navy and Nicolls had been cultivating might join them. The combined force would march west across the coastal flatlands of Alabama and Mississippi and cut off New Orleans from northern reinforcements. The people of the city were expected to rally to the British and withhold their support from the Americans, while Cochrane's powerful force swept in from the east. Surrounded by the British on land and sea, New Orleans would capitulate without a fight. Under ordinary circumstances, it would have been a good plan. But the presence of Andrew Jackson on the field of battle made the circumstances anything but ordinary.

Notwithstanding orders to the contrary (which in any case he did not receive until after the war[6]), Jackson anticipated the British plan, which he intended to thwart by seizing the Spanish fort at Pensacola. Jackson was eager to destroy the last remaining European presence on the Gulf coast. Another motive was revenge. Earlier in the year the Spaniards had sent their congratulations to the Creeks on their capture of Fort Mims, and now they were harboring Josiah Francis, Peter McQueen, and other Creek renegades at Pensacola.

Marching his army east from Mobile, Jackson arrived at Pensacola on 7 November 1814 with a force of four thousand men—some of them regulars, the rest Tennessee and Mississippi volunteers. After a few brief skirmishes, both the city and the fort surrendered. Jackson's capture of Pensacola and a lack of confidence in their Indian allies persuaded the British that their only option was a direct attack on New Orleans from the sea.

But Jackson did not foresee the change in Britain's plans. As Malcolm's fleet prepared to sail directly to the Mississippi coast, Jackson found himself two hundred miles east of an undefended New Orleans. Despite evidence to the contrary, he still believed that Mobile would be the first target. He hedged his bet by ordering Colonel John Coffee and his Tennessee Mounted Volunteers to camp at Baton Rouge, from which they could sweep down to New Orleans

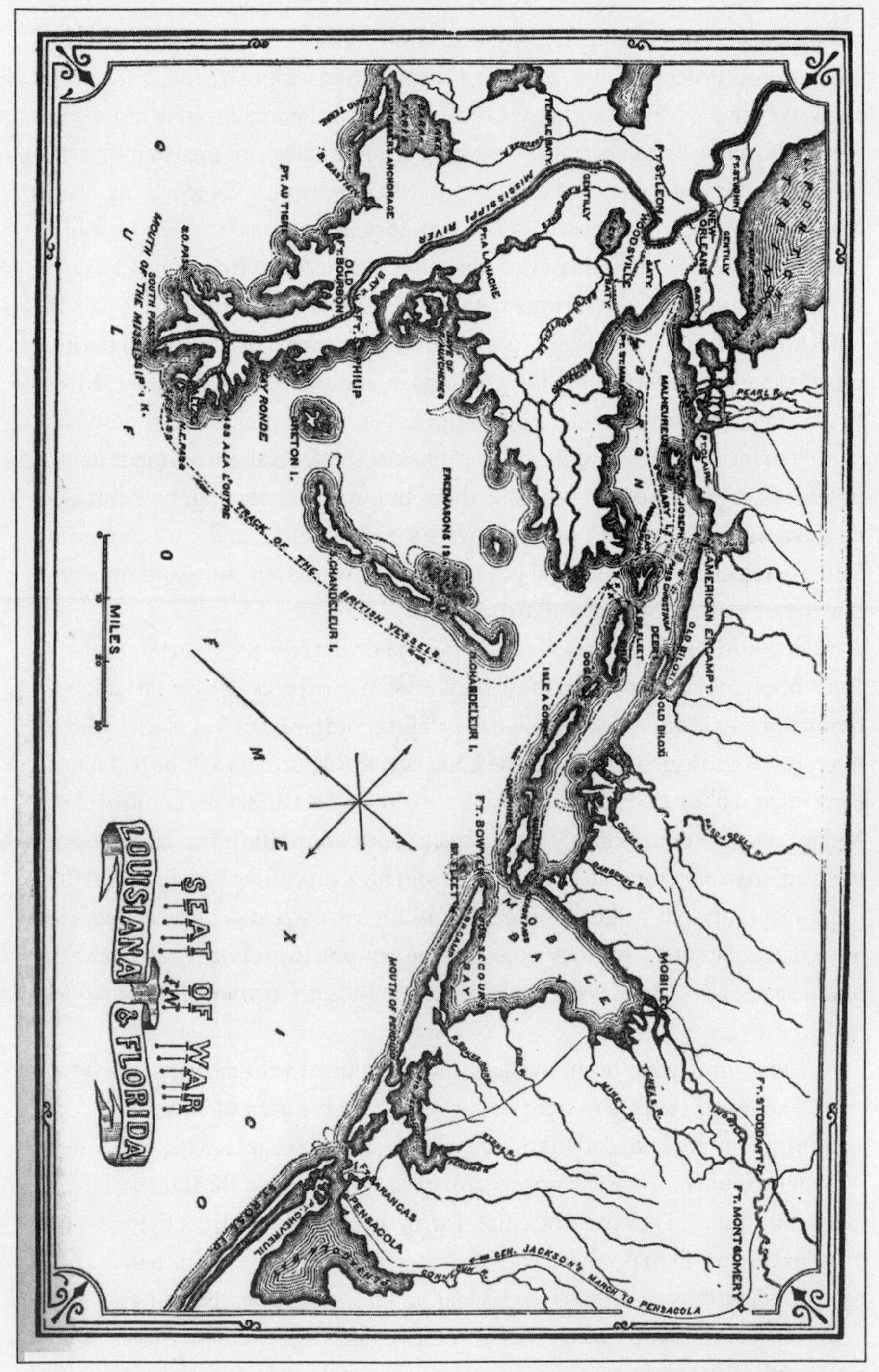

Courtesy of *Lossing's Pictorial Field Book of the War of 1812*

if the attack occurred there or move east if Mobile or Pensacola was the target. Jackson also ordered Major Thomas Hinds's Mississippi Dragoons to camp midway between Mobile and New Orleans, where they could readily move east or west once the British revealed their intentions. Regulars of the Forty-fourth Infantry were sent to New Orleans by sea, while Jackson, still recovering from a broken arm from his duel with Benton, traveled by land to New Orleans, arriving on 2 December "dirty, unpolished and emaciated from long illness."[7]

In the meantime, the various state militias summoned by Monroe slowly made their way to New Orleans. In late November, twenty-five hundred poorly supplied militiamen left Nashville, floating languidly down the Tennessee River to the Ohio, then south on the Mississippi to New Orleans. Kentucky raised its complement of twenty-five hundred men, but the federal government never provided the promised boats to take them to Louisiana, leaving the Kentuckians to fend for themselves. Arms too were slow in coming, and it was not until early November that the federal government shipped four thousand muskets downriver from its arsenal in Pittsburgh.

The battle of New Orleans would be one of the few occasions in the war when black soldiers served on the American side. Governor Claiborne had recommended to Jackson two battalions of militia composed of free blacks, which were authorized by a special act of the Louisiana legislature. One of the battalions comprised refugees from Saint-Domingue (now Haiti) under the command of Major Louis D'Aquin. Major Pierre Lacoste commanded the other. Jackson sent them an invitation, through Claiborne, to join him, promising equal pay and the same 160 acres that white volunteers would receive when the war ended. He offered his guarantee "that they would not be exposed to improper comparisons or unjust sarcasm."[8] In his letter to the governor, the slave-owning Jackson wrote,

> Our country has been invaded, and threatened with destruction. She wants soldiers to fight her battles. The free men of colour in your city are inured to the Southern climate and would make excellent Soldiers. They will not remain quiet spectators of the interesting contest. They must be either for, or against us—distrust them, and you will make them your enemies, place confidence in them, and you engage them by Every dear and honorable tie to the interests of the country who extends to them equal rights and privileges with white men.[9]

Jean Lafitte offered eight hundred of his pirates and privateers for the defense of New Orleans. The British had made overtures to Lafitte (who made his living seizing cargo-laden Spanish ships in the Caribbean under the dubious authority of a letter of marque issued by the fictitious Republic of Cartagena), but he remained noncommittal. Lafitte was interested in a pardon that would untangle his affairs, and it was important that he end up on the winning side. Perhaps he sensed that the Americans would ultimately prevail. Indeed, he had engaged as legal counsel the disgraced but influential Edward Livingston, who had managed to work his way into Jackson's confidence, becoming a close aide to the general.

Supplementing Jackson's growing land force, two U.S. warships under the command of Captain Daniel Patterson lay at anchor in the Mississippi. The small schooner *Carolina* carried fourteen guns and a crew of ninety-five. The *Louisiana,* a ship sloop or corvette, carried twenty-two guns and 170 seamen.[10] The crews of these vessels were as diverse as the eclectic land force. According to Theodore Roosevelt, the *Carolina* was

> manned by regular seamen, largely New Englanders. The ... newly-built ship *Louisiana*, a powerful corvette, ... had of course no regular crew, and her officers were straining every nerve to get one from the varied ranks of the maritime population of New Orleans; long-limbed and hard-visaged Yankees, Portuguese and Norwegian seamen from foreign merchantmen, dark-skinned Spaniards from the West Indies, swarthy Frenchmen who had served under the bold privateersman Lafitte....[11]

As Jackson reconnoitered the terrain around New Orleans in search of vulnerabilities and likely attack routes, the British approached by sea from the south, landing on 8 December at Ship Island, about eighty miles due east of New Orleans near what is now Biloxi. There Cochrane discovered that the promised flat-bottomed boats needed to transport his men though the shallow coastal waters and bayous had not been provided. He would have to transport more than five thousand men across miles of shallow water in the few small boats and cutters stored on the decks of his ships.

The Mississippi River was too narrow and twisting to navigate safely, and the entrance to Lake Ponchartrain was defended by Fort Petite Coquilles.

Cochrane's only option, therefore, was to sail as far into Lake Borgne as its depth would permit and from there row his men in the small boats the remaining sixty miles across the lake and up the bayous to a landing site eight miles south of New Orleans. Because there were far more troops than the small boats could accommodate, the landing would be an excruciatingly slow enterprise.

As the massive British fleet moved east in the cold and damp December weather, a small squadron of five American gunboats, accompanied by the schooner *Seahorse* and the sloop *Alligator*, moved to block Cochrane's seaborne attack. Commanded by Lieutenant Thomas ap Catesby Jones, the squadron had 185 men serving twenty-three guns. When the fleet's destination was apparent, Jones moved his force east ahead of them and anchored his small ships in a mile-long line over shallow water from Malheureux Island to Pointe Claire on Lake Borgne. Springs on their cables allowed Jones's ships, which were anchored by the stern, to turn and bring their broadsides to bear on any target. On the morning of 14 December, Cochrane sent forty-five boats manned by twelve hundred sailors and marines under Captain Nicholas Lockyer to attack the American squadron.

Although they had been rowing their packed boats over the open waters of Lake Borgne for thirty-six hours, the British seamen came directly at Jones's seven vessels, suffering severe casualties as a consequence. Outnumbered nine to one in vessels and six to one in men, the Americans stood firm amid the furious gunfire. The British sailors and marines gradually hacked and slashed their way onto the seven defending boats and ships, and by noon all seven vessels had been taken and their crews captured, though at enormous cost to the attackers. The bloody fight left seventeen British dead and seventy-seven wounded. Six Americans were killed and thirty-five wounded.[12] While the fight delayed the British advance by several days, all of the American ships fell into British hands and were quickly converted into troop transports able to navigate the shallow waters of Lake Borgne and its bayous.

III

News of Cochrane's fierce attack on Jones left no doubt that New Orleans was the target and that the attack would come from the west or south. Word was sent to Colonel Coffee in Baton Rouge and to Major Hinds in Mississippi to come immediately to New Orleans. Two days later, Jackson wrote again to Coffee:

> I need not say to you, to reach me by forced marches, it is enough to say that Lord Cochrane is on our coast with about eighty sail great and small, and the report says he has taken all our gun Boats in the lakes.... I am astonished the T. & Kentucky Troops are not up. If heard from please to detach an express, to them to proceed night and day until the[y] arrive....[13]

The day Jackson wrote to Coffee, the British disembarked on Isle aux Pois (Pea Island), near the entrance to Lake Pontchartrain, and set up a primitive camp for six thousand men. The men shivered in thin tents and dirty uniforms, and the frigid weather left a thick layer of ice on the camp's water tubs. As the two forces slowly closed, the bad weather played havoc with both sides. From Baton Rouge, Colonel Coffee wrote to his wife that on the ride from Mobile "it rained on us twenty days Suckessively [*sic*] and heavier rain than you ever saw."[14] Of the 2,000 men with him when he left Mobile, only 1,250 were fit to march to New Orleans, and 400 fell out during the three-day march covering 135 miles. The 850 men who entered the city on 20 December were a less than imposing sight: "They did not impress the city folk very much, dirty as they were, unshaven, their hunting shirts and pants of home-dyed dingy color, their skin caps with tails on, and belts of untanned deerskin. But each man carried a tomahawk, a hunting knife, and a long rifle."[15]

Carroll's force from Tennessee arrived on the 21st. The next day, Lieutenant Colonel William Thornton, accompanied by Major General John Keane, led a floating column of 1,850 British infantrymen from Isle aux Pois up the Bayou Mazant to the estate of Major Gabriel Villier. Upon landing, they quickly captured the thirty or so inattentive militiamen supposedly on guard. Villiere, however, escaped, and warned Jackson of Thornton's presence eight miles from the city. The small British force debated whether to continue the advance and surprise the city's few defenders or wait for the rest of the force to be shuttled up the bayous in an arduous trek covering more than seventy miles.

Jackson, however, wasted no time in debate but scrambled to assemble a force to attack the approaching British before they got settled. He sent Majors Latour and Tatum ahead with a small scouting force to reconnoiter the British camp. Plauche and his New Orleans militia were summoned from their encampment to the north at Bayou St. John to join Coffee's exhausted men. Jackson took between 1,600 and 2,000 men, including a few Choctaw warriors, from the defenders trickling into the city and arrived near the British camp a few hours after sunset. Thornton and Keane, contemptuous of American capabilities and ignorant of Jackson's reputation, had taken few precautions. Most of their cold, wet, and exhausted troops slept while the campfires blazed brightly. The American force crept closer, and the armed schooner *Carolina*, carrying fourteen guns and ninety-five men under the command of Captain John D. Henley and Commodore Daniel Patterson, slipped down the Mississippi and anchored offshore.

Surveying Thornton's encampment with Coffee, Jackson formulated a plan of attack. Coffee's Tennesseans on the left would penetrate deeply into the camp and then turn east toward the river, rolling up the British right flank. As the British struggled to defend their right, the rest of Jackson's force would push down from the center and along the water, while *Carolina*'s guns pounded the British left flank and rear.

Jackson's men took up their positions, and *Carolina* furled her sails, dropped her anchors, set her springs, and swung her broadside to face the British camp. The battle opened when British sentries discovered the menacing *Carolina* and attempted to hail her without any response. They fired several muskets at her, but still the schooner maintained her silence. Near eight o'clock, British Lieutenant George Robert Gleig heard a voice yell from the ship, "Give them this for the honor of America!" The ship's cannons opened up with grape shot, sending hundreds of little iron balls ripping through the canvas tents of the sleeping camp.[16] The *Carolina* continued her bombardment for an hour, and around nine o'clock Jackson launched his ground attack. In the first minutes of the battle, the Americans had the upper hand against the surprised British, but group by group and in the dark, the well-trained British infantry organized themselves into formidable pockets of resistance. Under the skilled leadership of their sergeants and officers, they stood firm as the battle swirled around them. Much of the fighting was at close quarters. Desperate men in the blackness of night wielded bayonets, knives, rifle butts, and tomahawks. Theodore Roosevelt vividly describes the intensity of the fight:

> Many a sword, till then but a glittering toy, was that night crusted with blood. The British soldiers and the American regulars made fierce play with their bayonets, and the Tennesseans, with their long

> hunting-knives. Man to man, in grimmest hate, they fought and died, some by bullet and some by bayonet-thrust or stroke of sword. More than one in his death agony slew the foe at whose hand he himself had received the mortal wound; and their bodies stiffened as they lay, locked in the death grip.[17]

Exactly when the battle ended is in dispute. Some say nine thirty. Others say Jackson did not signal a retreat until the wee hours of the next day, when the fog rolled in and made an effective attack impossible. Casualties were severe on both sides: the British had forty-six dead, 167 wounded, and sixty-four missing or captured, while Jackson's force suffered twenty-four dead, 115 wounded, and seventy-four missing or captured.[18] Wandering about the battlefield the next morning in search of a fellow officer, Gleig "noted that the dead and wounded appeared more grisly than usual, due to the high incidence of cut and thrust wounds."[19] In his memoirs, Gleig recalled, "Friends and foes lay together in groups of four to six.... [S]uch had been the deadly closeness of the strife, that in one or two places, an English and American soldier might be seen with the bayonet of each fastened in the other's body."[20]

When the smoke cleared, some in the British force delighted in their successful repulse of the Americans, while others saw in the unexpected attack a harbinger of trouble. Gleig recalled, "Instead of an easy conquest, we had already met with vigorous opposition; instead of finding the inhabitants ready and eager to join us, we found the houses deserted, the cattle and horses driven away, and every appearance of hostility."[21]

Once again the British command quarreled among themselves about how swiftly to launch a counter-attack, and again the cautious Keane overruled the impetuous Thornton and opted to stay put. Although Jackson now had fewer than two thousand defenders at the city, local residents and captives told the British that as many as twenty thousand armed American fighters were entrenched at New Orleans. Uncertain of the size and nature of the force he would confront, taken aback by Jackson's bold night attack, and unable to get any reconnaissance teams past the frontier sharpshooters and the Mississippi Dragoons who patrolled the woods, swamps, and fields outside his camp, Keane decided to wait until the full force of six thousand men were in place and the supplies brought up before moving on the city. It was another two weeks before the British were ready, and the long delay gave Jackson plenty of time to prepare a defensive line and to receive the reinforcements that each day straggled in from Tennessee, Kentucky, and Mississippi.

The day after the fight, Jackson marched his force two miles closer to New Orleans, stopping in the open fields of the Macarte plantation on the banks of the Mississippi at Chalmette. There, where the dry, solid ground connecting the British camp with the city narrowed to several hundred yards between the river on the west and swamps on the east, Jackson began to build an earthen entrenchment behind the Rodriguez Canal, perpendicular to the river and continuing into a densely wooded swamp that began about six hundred yards to the east. It was Christmas Eve. While slaves, citizen soldiers, and regulars hacked at the damp earth of the bayou with picks and shovels, American and British peace commissioners across the Atlantic Ocean signed the treaty that, upon ratification, would end the war.

By late December Jackson had received most of the forces promised him. The entrenchment at Chalmette was completed, and the diverse units of his army were assigned their place on the battle line. Beginning in the west, the redoubt was held by a company of the U.S. Seventh Infantry while elements of the Forty-fourth manned the guns. Behind them were sharpshooters from Thomas Beale's New Orleans Rifles, drawn mostly from the city's white-collar class. Moving east along the line, several more companies of the Seventh Infantry under Major Henry Peire held the line between Batteries 1 and 2, the former of which was manned by dismounted Mississippi Dragoons under Major Henri de St. Geme. West of Battery 2, manned by crewmen from the *Carolina*, the rest of the Seventh Infantry was placed along the earthen wall as far as Battery 3, which was manned by Baratarian pirates.

Continuing east along the line, the space between Batteries 3 and 4 was filled by New Orleans militiamen under Major Jean Plauche and by Major Pierre Lacoste's battalion of free men of color. Battery 4 was manned by another contingent from *Carolina*, and the line from there to Batteries 5 and 6 was held by the free blacks under Major Louis D'Aquin and the rest of the Forty-fourth Infantry, elements of which manned the guns of Battery 5. A group of French nationals under Lieutenant Etienne Bertel worked the gun at Battery 6. From there through Batteries 7 and 8 the line was held by the combined force of General Billy Carroll's Tennesseans and Brigadier General John Adair's

Kentuckians, who covered the line to the edge of the woods and swamp. East of Adair, John Coffee's Tennessee Volunteers held the muddy flank up to its western tip, where Captain Pierre Jugeant commanded a force of Choctaw warriors. As the battle neared, Jackson worked his way down the line, greeting the Tennesseans by name, stopping for a cup of coffee with Dominique You and his pirates, and encouraging the men who constituted the most unusual military force the United States had ever assembled in her defense.

Andrew Jackson may have been the only commander then alive capable of assembling and molding such an army into a disciplined fighting force. Much taken by the frontiersmen of the early nineteenth century, Theodore Roosevelt describes the challenges of leading this eclectic force of men:

> Accustomed to the most lawless freedom, and to giving free rein to the full violence of their passions, defiant of discipline and impatient at the slightest restraint, caring little for God and nothing for man, they were soldiers who, under an ordinary commander, would have been as fully dangerous to themselves and their leaders as to their foes. But Andrew Jackson was of all men the one best fitted to manage such troops. Even their fierce natures quailed before the ungovernable fury of a spirit greater than their own; and their stubborn, sullen wills were bent at last before his unyielding temper and iron hand.[22]

As Jackson's force dug in, Keane kept to his camp several miles south, waiting for reinforcements and for the arrival of the operation's commanding officer, General Sir Edward Michael Pakenham, the duke of Wellington's brother-in-law and a distinguished veteran of the war in Spain. On Christmas Day the Americans at Chalmette heard a hearty cheer roll down the flat plains of the Mississippi delta from the British encampment. General Pakenham had finally arrived with Major General Sir Samuel Gibbs and Admirals Cochrane and Malcolm to take the lay of the land and plan the attack on New Orleans. Some maintain that Pakenham expressed skepticism and concern about the project and the position he inherited,[23] but there is no proof of that.

One of the first tasks confronting the British was to rid themselves of the damaged but still lethal *Carolina*, which continued to menace them from the river channel. Under the command of Lieutenant Colonel Sir Alexander Dickson, a shot furnace was built near the artillery, and red hot balls of iron were fired into the immobile American schooner until it burst into flames and exploded on the morning of 27 January. Dickson then turned his attention to the larger and better armed *Louisiana*, but her captain warped the ship out of range and moved it upriver to better support Jackson's entrenchment at Chalmette.

On 28 December, with eight thousand men under his command, supported by what little artillery the sailors could row and muscle to the camp, Pakenham marched north toward New Orleans—one wing under Keane, the other under Gibbs—only to be surprised by the stout defense work that Jackson had erected just a few miles north of the British camp. As the redcoats came into range, American artillery emplaced at the eight batteries along the entrenchment, supported by the twenty-two guns of the *Louisiana*, fired at the oncoming columns. The *Louisiana* alone fired eight hundred rounds during the seven-hour bombardment. One by one, Pakenham's gun emplacements were blown to bits. Most of his assembled troops had laid themselves flat on the ground to avoid the lethal iron shot that crisscrossed the open field. After several hours of incessant bombardment, Pakenham ordered his humbled force to withdraw out of the range of the American cannon to the La Ronde plantation, just south of the field.

During the next three days British sailors were put to the back-breaking work of rowing heavy replacement cannons from the ships across Lake Borgne, up the muddy bayou to Pakenham's camp at La Ronde, and then to the line facing Jackson's entrenchment. The new guns aimed and primed, the British assault began at dawn on New Year's Day as two columns of infantry moved forward with orders to assault the openings in Jackson's earthen entrenchment that the heavy guns would create. Caught off guard on parade in the field behind their entrenchment, the Americans scrambled back to their positions and aimed their guns at Pakenham's new emplacements as the redcoats assembled behind them. "Within 40 minutes, American cannon fire had wrecked 5 English pieces, and disabled 8 more. By afternoon the British artillery was all but silenced, and Pakenham had to issue the humiliating order to withdraw without guns."[24]

Back at La Ronde, Pakenham now waited for the sixteen hundred men being brought to the campaign by General John Lambert. With artillery shot in short supply at the front because of the difficulty of transporting it from the ships to the encampment, each arriving infantryman was required to include in his knapsack a twenty-four-pound iron ball to be delivered to the front. "One unfortunate boatload of soldiers thus burdened with cannon balls in their knapsacks turned over during its passage across Lake Borgne, and they all disappeared below the waves without a sound."[25]

Pakenham moved his men forward on 7 January. He planned to attack at four o'clock the next morning, hoping that the dark would diminish the effectiveness of the frontier marksmen at the center of the line. Dickson's artillery was to batter holes in the Americans' entrenchment while three columns of infantry attacked Jackson's line. As the main assault was underway on the east bank of the river, Thornton was to take a force across the river, seize the right flank from its few and poorly armed defenders, and bombard Jackson's line from behind.

The first infantry column attacking the entrenchment would be led by Lieutenant Colonel Robert Rennie. He was to move along the riverbank, seize the redoubt, and turn its guns left to enfilade Jackson's line. The second column, 1,200 men under Keane, was to come up along Rennie's right. Keane would have the option of assaulting the American right with Rennie if Thornton seized the guns across the river or wheeling right and exploiting the expected success of Gibbs's main force of 2,100, who would attack the American left. Behind them, Lambert held a reserve of 1,400 men ready to exploit whatever opportunities emerged during the battle.

Despite the two weeks of preparation, several key figures failed to fulfill their responsibilities under the plan of attack. Thornton was late getting across the river with only a fraction of the intended force, while on the right flank a disgruntled Lieutenant Colonel Thomas Mullens, who was to lead Gibbs's main attack on the American left, had failed to bring up the fascines (bundles of sticks to fill the canal) and ladders needed to assault the earthen wall. As a result, Gibbs's main force was briefly stalled midfield while men searched the rear for the missing equipment. When the attack resumed and the British came within five hundred yards of the American line, Jackson ordered the artillery to open fire on the massed troops and the gun emplacements supporting them. Dozens were mowed down as grape and solid shot ripped through the crowded ranks.

On the British left, the aggressive Colonel Rennie moved his men forward to attack the redoubt as cannon from Battery 1 blasted at his men. With

Thornton bogged down on the other bank, Commodore Patterson's artillery across the river fired at will into Keane's left flank, while Batteries 2, 3, and 4 targeted Pakenham's guns, which had been hastily placed the night before. Further to the right, Batteries 5 through 8 fired into Gibbs's stalled troops, while the Kentucky and Tennessee infantry hit them with a wall of musket fire. As the British came within range of the long rifles carried by the regulars and militia, Jackson ordered the artillery batteries in the center to halt "so their smoke would not spoil the aim of the keen-eyed woodsmen."[26]

> With orders to aim just above the breastplate, paying particular attention to mounted officers, the riflemen fired as one, a sheet of orange flame rippling down the length of the line. The first rank then stepped back to reload while the second rank took its place, then the third, then the fourth. Thus a steady fusillade tore apart the approaching British columns.[27]

As the two British columns struggled toward the American line, Rennie rushed forward at the head of his force, jumped the ditch, and scrambled up the earthen wall and onto the parapet of the redoubt that anchored Jackson's right flank at the river. Within minutes he had cleared the fortification of its American defenders, but before he could consolidate his victory and turn the redoubt's guns on Jackson's line, Thomas Beale moved his New Orleans Rifles into the action. Along with soldiers from the Seventh Infantry, they laid down a withering barrage of musket and rifle fire on the momentarily triumphant British soldiers in the redoubt below. Rennie took a ball through the eye and fell back dead as the American riflemen annihilated the British infantry, still clustered in the crowded parapet. In minutes the Americans retook the redoubt as the British retreated.

Realizing that Patterson's artillery fire on his columns from the other bank meant that Thornton had not secured the western side of the river, Keane initiated the second option and ordered his Highlanders, led by Lieutenant Colonel Robert Dale, to the right to aid Gibbs's stalled effort. But marching his men to the right across the American line exposed his left flank to the cannons, muskets, and rifles of the defenders. Within minutes Dale was shot dead while scores of his officers and men fell dead or wounded under the murderous fire from the four-deep Kentucky and Tennessee militia behind the breastwork at the center of the American line. As the American shot and grape filled the air, the remnants of Dale's force gave up on their mission of relief and hugged the ground for survival, having already suffered hundreds of casualties in their failed attempt to cross the field.

Gibbs's force now finally moved forward but inexplicably stopped again as it neared Carroll's Kentucky militia and began firing at the American line. Sharp-shooting frontiersmen blasted back with deadly accuracy, forcing many of the infantrymen to drop and hug the ground. Gibbs led more than two thousand men to the field, but only two units made it to the embankment and up to the parapet, which they briefly held before all were killed or captured.

> A Kentucky soldier reported that "the smoke was so thick" the dawn was like darkness. He wrote that "our men did not seem to apprehend any danger, but would load and fire as fast as they could, talking, swearing, and joking all the time." After the first volley "everyone loaded and banged away on his own hook." The massacre of the Kentucky militia at River Raisin in Michigan in 1813 seared the memories of many....[28]

Seeing his troops stagger from the massed rifles and huddling on the ground for protection, General Gibbs spurred his horse and galloped to the front to rally his men by example. Many responded to his entreaties, and the force inched forward, but the heavy toll on the officers often left the beleaguered troops without leaders or orders, so many simply stayed where they were until a superior ordered otherwise. Even then, many soldiers simply refused to expose themselves to the certain death of the murderous fire erupting from the American line. Packenham ordered Keane to bring the rest of his force across the field to aid Gibbs, and then rode to the front to rally his men. A blast of grapeshot from one of Jackson's batteries shattered Packenham's knee and killed his horse. Wounded but undeterred, the general took another mount and threw himself back into the fray until another bullet pierced his arm. With Major Duncan Macdougall leading his horse, Packenham raised his hat with his good arm and cried out "Come on, brave Ninety-third!" just as another volley from Jackson's line ripped through his neck and stomach and spine. The leader of the British force was dead before his men could lay him down in the shade of an oak tree away from the fighting.

On Jackson's far left, where Coffee commanded the Tennessee Volunteers and a force of Choctaw warriors, the British attempted a flanking action but were turned back after a brief skirmish with many wounded and a dying commander. Coffee realized that this was probably the last flanking action and that the British were pinned down to his right, so he wheeled his Volunteers and Choctaws through the woods to the edge of the field and began firing into the flank of Gibbs's already battered force.

As the fight continued, Gibbs was hit by four bullets and fell from his horse, dying in agony the next day. Keane, too, was wounded, with a shot to the groin, and was carried off the field but survived the battle. With most of the officers dead or wounded, the attack stalled, and many of the British soldiers began a slow retreat from the worst of the gunfire. Command of the British force now devolved to the most senior surviving officer, General John Lambert, still in command of the reinforcements, who themselves had become pinned down when they attempted to aid their comrades at the front. Stunned by the appalling destruction before him and certain that any further offensive effort was futile, Lambert halted the attack and pulled his force back from the edge of battle and out of harm's way. It was now about eight o'clock in the morning, the winter sun hung low in the sky, "and Jackson's men could look over their parapet and see a once-brown field now red with the bodies of over two thousand British troops, many still living, though horribly wounded."[29]

IV

Though many mark this victory as a hollow one, occurring as it did two weeks after the adversaries had agreed to the terms of peace, many of the issues that had brought the two sides to war and had prevented peace earlier remained unresolved by the Ghent agreement. Disputes over the status of the Indians in the northwest, fishing rights along Canada's coast, and navigational rights on the Mississippi, among others, were expected to be negotiated to a satisfactory conclusion in the months and years to come. But this decisive victory for the Americans—and stunning defeat for the British—tilted those future negotiations in America's favor. One of Jackson's biographers concludes, "The Battle of New Orleans was one of the most important ever fought in the New World and its effect on world affairs was not insignificant. It effectively ended the British threat to Young America.... The United States had proven to the world that it had come of age and was here to stay."[30]

There were some in Britain who understood this shift in power. In mid-March 1815, when the full extent of the defeat at New Orleans reached England, "Albion" wrote in the *Naval Chronicle*:

> Thus has ended in defeat all our attempts on the American coast, and thus have the measures and inadequate force provided by our government brought disgrace by their irresolute, and contemptible conduct, thrown victory into the lap of America ... and concluded a peace far from glorious to Britain; certainly it must be allowed we have not conquered a better one; an inglorious, unsuccessful war must naturally end in such a peace as America chose to give; for assuredly we have now done our worst against this infant enemy which has already shewn a giant's power. Soon will the rising greatness of this distant empire (and its distance is, perhaps, fortunate for Europe) astonish the nations that have looked on with wonder, and seen the mightiest efforts of Britain, at the era of her greatest power, so easily parried, so completely foiled.[31]

In a war in which many battles were swiftly carried by one side or the other, and where casualties fell disproportionately on the vanquished, the outcome at New Orleans was in a class by itself. Both sides fielded armies of similar size—the British sent about 5,800 men into battle against an estimated 4,300 on the American side[32]—yet the outcome was both devastating and lopsided for the British infantry and many of its officers. Among the British force, 192 were killed, 1,265 wounded, and 484 missing, while the American dead totaled just thirteen, with another thirteen wounded and nineteen missing. When the guns were silent, Lambert asked Jackson for an armistice. The American commander agreed, provided the British did not use it to reinforce their position across the river. The Americans watched from behind their earthen ramparts as the British dead were collected and buried and the wounded carried back for treatment. Pakenham's corpse, like that of Major General Ross after the battle of Baltimore, was stripped of its bloody uniform, washed, eviscerated, and stuffed into a cask of Jamaica rum to preserve it for the long voyage home and burial in his native land. Lambert remained in sight of Jackson's force for almost another three weeks, allowing time for his wounded to recover while the able-bodied men carved a more secure route back to Lake Borgne. On 27 January 1815, the British army marched to the water's edge and were rowed the sixty miles to their transports, where they would remain another week before the wind turned favorable.

V

It took almost a month for news of Jackson's victory to reach Washington. Word arrived on 4 February 1815, preceding news of the Treaty of Ghent by ten days.[33] Citizens thronged the streets to catch whatever information they could about the stunning victory, and the *National Intelligencer*, still suffering from Cockburn's vandalism, struggled to get the news into print. Burning candles glowed from every window, and the raucous sound of joyful singing spilled from the doors of the city's taverns. Thirty-five miles to the north in Baltimore, Fort McHenry celebrated the victory with an artillery barrage that rolled across the harbor and down the Patapsco River to the Chesapeake Bay, now free of the marauding British fleet.

Not every American gained by the peace, and fortunes were won and lost as news of the war's conclusion swept financial markets. Prices of imported products like tin, tea, cotton fabric, and sugar plunged on the expectation of a resumption of trade, while the price of domestic products like wheat, flour, and bulk cotton soared on the prospects of unhindered export. There were winners and losers in the market of politics as well: "Half the influence of the Hartford Convention was destroyed by [the Battle of New Orleans]; and the commissioners, who were starting for the capital, had reason to expect a reception less favorable by far than they would have met had the British been announced masters of Louisiana."[34]

Thanks to an enterprising newspaper willing to pay for timely information, Boston knew about the treaty before Washington. Henry Adams wrote:

> While the government messenger who carried the official news to Washington made no haste, a special messenger started from New York at ten o'clock Saturday night, immediately on the landing of the government messenger, and in thirty-two hours arrived in Boston.... Reaching the *Centinel* office, at Boston, early Monday morning, he delivered his bulletin, and a few minutes after it was published all the bells were set ringing; schools and shops were closed, and a general holiday taken; flags were hoisted, the British with the American; the militia paraded, and in the evening the city was illuminated.[35]

Up and down the Atlantic coast and into the frontier, entire towns turned out for the celebrations that greeted first the news of the victory and then the news of the peace treaty that would finally end the long and costly war. In New York, Walter Lord writes, "The citizens vied with each other in producing complicated illuminations. Most agreed that Dr. MacNoon took the honors with an 'elegant transparency' depicting a Tennessee rifleman shooting two redcoats labeled respectively 'Booty' and 'Beauty'—reputed to have been Admiral Cochrane's watchwords at New Orleans."[36] "Schools in Boston were closed, people left their jobs, and the legislature adjourned. In the boisterous celebration that followed, bells were rung, the city was illuminated, troops turned out to fire a salute, and cartmen formed a procession of sleighs, parading around the city with the word 'peace' on their hats."[37]

Outside the major metropolitan areas of the young nation, the celebrations continued with equal fervor, albeit on a different scale. George Johnston describes one such event in his history of Cecil County, Maryland:

> The court was in session at Elkton when the news reached that place, and so great was the joy of the people that it immediately adjourned, and everyone repaired to Fort Hollingsworth to celebrate the auspicious event.... [T]he patriotic people of the town, who had a grand feast, at which they had roasted an ox which they had decorated and driven through the streets with a board placed

on his horns, containing the following verse, said to have been composed by George Ricketts of Elkton:

My horns, my hide, I freely give,
My tallow and my lights,
And all that is within me too,
For free trade and sailors' rights.[38]

EPILOGUE

The men who served in uniform and in positions of political leadership during the War of 1812 became a nineteenth-century version of the "Greatest Generation." A few were still prominent almost fifty years later during the Civil War.

Seven participants in the war became president of the United States: James Monroe, Andrew Jackson, Zachary Taylor, John Quincy Adams, William Henry Harrison, John Tyler, and James Buchanan. At least two—Davy Crockett and Jim Bowie—died at the Alamo on 6 March 1836, and another two—Stephen F. Austin and Sam Houston—played major roles in the establishment of the Republic of Texas. When war between the United States and Mexico broke out in 1846, Winfield Scott and Zachary Taylor led the American armies. Scott landed an expeditionary force at Vera Cruz in March 1847 and in September captured Mexico City, winning for the United States vast new western territories (the future states of California, New Mexico, and Arizona, and parts of Colorado and Nevada).

When the Civil War began in April 1861, an elderly Winfield Scott was in command of the Union army. David Glasgow Farragut and his foster brother, David Porter (son of the *Essex* captain), were leading officers in the navy and played pivotal roles in the Civil War.

Many of the lesser figures in the War of 1812 became leaders in the nation, their states, and in their communities. The historian Donald R. Hickey offers one example:

> The Battle of the Thames, which became a kind of Bunker Hill in western legend [and in which three thousand Americans participated], helped create one president, one vice president, three governors, three lieutenant governors, four senators, and twenty congressmen. In addition, countless other participants in the battle were elected to lesser offices.

For the naval heroes, however, postwar life was not always as happy. Oliver Hazard Perry had his share of disputes with other officers and with the leadership of the navy. In 1819 he contracted yellow fever while on a mission to Venezuela and died. Thomas Macdonough came down with tuberculosis during the war, and the disease limited his service in the years that followed. He died in 1825. David Porter was embroiled in a series of disputes in the post-war era. After he was suspended from the U.S. Navy, he accepted an offer to head the Mexican navy. He eventually returned to the U.S. diplomatic corps, dying in 1843 while serving in Turkey.

Despite his loss of the *President* in one of the final naval battles of the war, Stephen Decatur remained a national hero, and his reputation was enhanced by a successful cruise against the Barbary pirates in 1815. But the return of James Barron (who had been suspended from the navy after the loss of the *Chesapeake*) inflamed old wounds. Decatur and Barron agreed to settle their differences in a duel at Bladensburg, Maryland, on 22 March 1820. A wound to the groin left Decatur dead by the end of the day.

After his victory over the *Guerriere*, Isaac Hull spent much of his remaining naval career on land, interrupted by post-war commands in the Pacific and the Mediterranean, where he met up with James Richard Dacres. The two were seen amicably arguing what-if scenarios of their epic confrontation in the North Atlantic. Hull died in 1843.

William Bainbridge also spent much of his later career serving on land and fell into disputes with Hull, Stewart, and Decatur.

Another naval man who spent most of his post-war years on land was Charles Stewart. He remained in active service until 1861 and died in 1869. Uriah Levy, nominally an officer on *Argus*, was captured by the British while taking a prize to France and confined in the infamous Dartmoor prison, where he organized a *minyan* among the Jewish prisoners. Levy remained in the navy, rising to the rank of commodore, and used his influence to end the practice of flogging. An admirer of Thomas Jefferson, Levy acquired the badly deteriorated Monticello in 1834, restored it, and left it to the United States upon his death in 1862.

Several of the ships have survived, albeit through many rebuilds and reconstructions. Thanks to Oliver Wendell Holmes Sr., *Constitution* was spared the demolition that the navy was contemplating in 1830 and has remained in service ever since. Lovingly restored and exquisitely maintained, the great frigate is docked at Boston and open to the public. She is still in commission and crewed by members of the U.S. Navy. After a number of rebuilds and modifications, the frigate *Constellation* is now anchored in Baltimore Harbor as a museum.

The brig *Niagara*, Perry's second command at Put-in-Bay, was later sunk in the shallow but cold water of Lake Erie in an attempt to preserve her from the natural deterioration that afflicts all wooden ships. She was occasionally raised for patriotic celebrations, but by the early twentieth century it was apparent that time and rot had taken their toll and not much would be left for the future. The remains were surveyed in detail by naval architects and the information used to build an exact replica, completed in 1963, incorporating some of the original timbers. That too fell into disrepair and a second replica *Niagara* was completed in 1988 and is now docked at the Erie Maritime Museum. She is open to the public, and in warm weather tourists can book passage for a cruise of the lake.

As for the famed Baltimore Clippers, many went on to serve as merchant vessels in the Caribbean. One of these was renamed *Amistad* and became the object of a landmark court case when the slaves she was carrying revolted and seized the ship. In the 1970s Maryland financed the construction of a detailed replica of a Baltimore Clipper—named the *Pride of Baltimore*—and her successor (*Pride of Baltimore II*) can be visited in Baltimore Harbor when she is not on tour. Finally, after her capture, the *Chesapeake* was taken into British service but later decommissioned. She was broken up and her timbers sold for scrap. Some ended up as the structure of a flour mill in Wickham, England, where they can be seen today.

Many of the battlefields have been preserved. Among them are Chalmette (New Orleans), Sackets Harbor (New York), Fort McHenry (Baltimore), Fort Niagara (New York), Tippecanoe (Indiana), and Fort Meigs (Ohio). In Canada, Fort George, Queenston Heights, and Fort Erie (all in Ontario along the Niagara River) are among the many sites that have been preserved and restored. Readers interested in visiting these and the many other sites may want to consult *Guidebook to the Historic Sites of the War of 1812* by Gilbert Collins (Toronto: Dundurn Press, 1998), or the 1868 classic *Lossing's Pictorial Field Book of the War of 1812* by Benson J. Lossing (Gretna, LA: Firebird Press, 2003).

ACKNOWLEDGMENTS

A book of this scope has several core benefactors who have given selflessly of their time, assistance, and advice to help bring it to print. First among the many are the staff and librarians at the Library of Congress, the Library of the Naval Museum, the Library of the Historical Society of Washington, D.C., the Martin Luther King Jr. Memorial Library of the District of Columbia, the Paterno Library at Penn State, the Senate Historical Office, the Erie Maritime Museum, the Arlington County Public Library, and the Central Rappahannock Regional Library for all of their assistance in helping me track down resources and facts. Kudos also to the Naval Institute Press in Annapolis, Maryland, for publishing a motherlode of valuable resources on the War of 1812 over the past many decades.

Many thanks also to the leadership of my former employers—Ed Feulner, Phil Truluck, Stuart Butler, and Alison Fraser of the Heritage Foundation—for giving me time to research and write this book while on the clock. Thanks also to my former Heritage colleagues Bob Moffit and Pat Fagan for their very valuable help, advice, and intervention along the way.

Special thanks to Mitch Muncy, now with the Alexander Hamilton Society, for bringing an early draft of this book to the attention of the publishing community and for his initial edits and advice on how to make it better. And thanks go to Thomas Spence, senior editor at Regnery History, whose careful editing has greatly improved the readability of the manuscript, and whose efforts have saved me from innumerable errors.

A bigger debt is owed to my family, starting with my children Josh, Yael, and Micah, who believed their dad could actually do it, and especially to Josh, whose voluminous readings in American history kept me focused on what today's readers are looking for in a book about history. And best of all was the help and support from my soul mate and lovely wife Michele, who proofread the drafts and offered a keen critique that led to many improvements.

But most of my thanks go to my parents—the late Fred Keener Utt and June Virginia Utt—who probably had more to do with this book than any of the others whose help I value. My father, Fred, spent the best years of his life as a radioman in the U.S. Navy during World War II and repeated that service when, as a young father, he was called back to duty during the Korean Conflict. But mostly the origins of the book can be traced to my mother, June, who many decades ago read poems each night to her little boy to help send him off to sleep, among which was his favorite, "Old Ironsides" by Oliver Wendell Holmes Sr.

Ay, tear her tattered ensign down!
Long has it waved on high,
And many an eye has danced to see
That banner in the sky;
Beneath it rung the battle shout,
And burst the cannon's roar;—
The meteor of the ocean air
Shall sweep the clouds no more.

Her deck, once red with heroes' blood,
Where knelt the vanquished foe,
When winds were hurrying o'er the flood,
And waves were white below,

No more shall feel the victor's tread,
Or know the conquered knee;—
The harpies of the shore shall pluck
The eagle of the sea!

Oh, better that her shattered hulk
Should sink beneath the wave;
Her thunders shook the mighty deep,
And there should be her grave;
Nail to the mast her holy flag,
Set every threadbare sail,
And give her to the god of storms,
The lightning and the gale!

NOTES

CHAPTER ONE

1. F. Alexander Magoun, *The Frigate Constitution and Other Historic Ships* (Dover Publications Inc., New York, 1987), p. 71.
2. Benjamin Larabee, et. al., *America and the Sea: A Maritime History* (Mystic Seaport Museum, Mystic, CT, 1998), p. 198.
3. Alan Schom, *Trafalgar: Count-Down to Battle 1803-1805* (Atheneum, New York, 1990), p. 327.
4. Dudley Pope, *Life In Nelson's Navy* (Chatham Publishing, 1981), p. 109.
5. Ibid., p. 131.
6. Brian Lavery, *Nelson's Navy: The Ships, Men and Organization* (Naval Institute Press, 1994), p. 318.
7. Ira Dye, *The Fatal Cruise of the Argus: Two Captains in the War of 1812* (Naval Institute Press, 1994), p. 46.
8. Lavery, *Nelson's Navy,* p. 143.
9. Pope, *Life in Nelson's Navy* , p. 95.
10. Reginald Horsman, *The War of 1812* (Alfred A. Knopf, 1972), p. 7.
11. Ibid., p. 55.
12. Robert Gardiner, ed., *The Naval War of 1812* (Caxton Pictorial Histories,

Naval Institute Press, 1998), p. 16, and Larabee, *America and the Sea: A Maritime History* , p. 196.

13. Donald R. Hickey, *The War of 1812: A Forgotten Conflict* (University of Illinois Press, 1990), p. 11.
14. Hickey, *Don't Give Up the Ship!*, 21
15. Tyrone G. Martin, *A Most Fortunate Ship* (Naval Institute Press, 1997), p. 90.
16. Samuel Eliot Morison, *The Oxford History of the American People* (Oxford University Press, 1965), p. 372.
17. Nicholas Tracy, ed., *The Naval Chronicle: The Contemporary Record of the Royal Navy at War, Volume IV, 1807 – 1810* (Stackpole Books, Chatham Publishing, 1999), p. 98.
18. James Boswell, *The Life of Samuel Johnson*, Vol. I, notes by John Wilson Croker (James B. Lyon, 1889), p. 282.
19. Lavery, *Nelson's Navy*, p. 26.
20. Nicholas Tracy, ed., *The Naval Chronicle: The Contemporary Record of the Royal Navy at War, Volume V, 1811 – 1815* (Stackpole Books, Chatham Publishing, London, 1999), p. 71.
21. Tracy, *The Naval Chronicle*, Vol. IV, p. 99.
22. Larabee, *America and the Sea*, p. 198.
23. Hickey, *The War of 1812: A Forgotten Conflict*, p. 11.
24. Robert Gardiner, *Warships of the Napoleonic Era* (Naval Institute Press, 1999), p. 110.
25. Howard P. Nash Jr., *The Forgotten Wars* (A.S. Barnes and Co., 1968), p. 113.
26. Robboti, *The U.S. Essex and the Birth of the U.S. Navy*, 146
27. Spencer Tucker, *Stephen Decatur: A Life Most Bold and Daring* (Naval Institute Press, 2005), p. 23.
28. Dye, *The Fatal Cruise of the Argus*, p. 70.
29. Tucker, *Stephen Decatur*, p. 142.
30. Dye, *The Fatal Cruise of the Argus*, p. 69.
31. Ibid., p. 68.
32. Robboti, *The U.S. Essex and the Birth of the U.S. Navy*, p. 130.
33. Claude G. Bowers, *Jefferson in Power: The Death Struggle of the Federalists* (Houghton Mifflin, 1967), p. 430.
34. Larabee, *America and the Sea*, p. 198.
35. Horsman, *The War of 1812*, p. 38.

36. Ibid., p. 93.
37. Ibid., p. 121.
38. Edwin G. Burrows and Mike Wallace, *Gotham: A History of New York City to 1898* (Oxford University Press, 1999, pp. 411–12.
39. Barra Foundation, *Philadelphia: A 300 Year History* (W.W. Norton & Co., New York, 1982), p. 213.
40. Robboti, *The U.S. Essex and the Birth of the U.S. Navy.*
41. Gardiner, *The Naval War of 1812*, p. 20.
42. Morison, *The Oxford History of the American People*, p. 379.
43. Joyce Appleby, *Inheriting the Revolution: The First Generation of Americans* (The Belknap Press, 2000), p. 43.
44. Gardiner, *The Naval War of 1812*, p. 21.
45. Lewis, *Famous American Naval Officers*, p. 136.
46. Henry Gruppe, *The Frigates* (Time Life Books, 1979), p. 67.
47. Horsman, *The War of 1812*, p. 3.
48. John K. Mahon, *The War of 1812* (Da Capo Press from University of Florida Press, 1972), p. 134.
49. John Buchanan, *Jackson's Way: Andrew Jackson and the People of the Western Waters* (John Wiley & Sons, Inc., New York, 2001), p. 90.
50. Ibid.
51. Hickey, *The War of 1812: A Forgotten Conflict*, p. 72.
52. Morison, *The Oxford History of the American People*, p. 333.
53. Horsman, *The War of 1812*, pp. 3, 40.
54. Ibid., pp. 15–16.
55. John R. Elting, *Amateurs to Arms: A Military History of the War of 1812* (Algonquin Books, 1991), p. 21.
56. Morison, *The Oxford History of the American People*, p. 381.
57. Ibid.
58. Hickey, *The War of 1812: A Forgotten Conflict*, p. 25.
59. Ibid., p. 26.
60. Ibid., p. 25.
61. Charles A. Beard, and Mary R. Beard, *The Rise of American Civilization* (Macmillan Co., 1930), p. 411.
62. Gruppe, *The Frigates*, p. 67.
63. Beard, *The Rise of American Civilization*, p. 415.
64. Elting, *Amateurs to Arms*, p. xv.
65. Charles Oscar Paullin, *Commodore John Rodgers 1773 – 1838* (Naval

Institute Press, 1909 & 1967), p. 223.
66. Tracy, *The Naval Chronicle*, Vol. V, pp. 28–34.
67. Paullin, *Commodore John Rodgers 1773 – 1838*, pp. 232, 234.
68. Martin, *A Most Fortunate Ship*, p. 134.
69. Thomas A. Bailley, *A Diplomatic History of the American People*, Third Edition (S. F. Crofts & Co., 1947).
70. Michael A. Lofaro, *The Life and Adventures of Daniel Boone* (The University Press of Kentucky, 1986), p. 126.
71. Christopher Hitchens, "The Medals of His Defeats," *Atlantic Monthly*, April 2002, p. 137.
72. Elting, *Amateurs to Arms*, p. 2.
73. Jack Murphy, *History of the US Marines* (Exeter Books/Bison Books Corp, 1984), p. 2.
74. Gruppe, *The Frigates*, p. 77.
75. Hickey, *The War of 1812: A Forgotten Conflict*, p. 42.
76. William S. Dudley, ed., *The Naval War of 1812: A Documentary History*, Vol. I (Naval Historical Center, 1985).

CHAPTER TWO

1. John R. Elting, *Amateurs to Arms*, p. 28.
2. J. Mackay Hitsman, *The Incredible War of 1812* (updated by Robin Bass Studios, 1999, original University of Toronto Press, 1965), p. 77.
3. Elting, *Amateurs to Arms*, p. 30.
4. Hickey, *The War of 1812: A Forgotten Conflict*, p. 82.
5. Alan Taylor, *The Civil War of 1812* (Alfred A. Knopf, 2010), p. 165.
6. Hickey, *The War of 1812: A Forgotten Conflict*, p. 84.
7. Pierre Berton, *The Invasion of Canada: 1812-1813* (Anchor Canada, 1980 & 2001), p. 191.
8. Elting, *Amateurs to Arms*, p. 35.
9. Berton, *The Invasion of Canada: 1812-1813*, p. 191.
10. Ibid., p. 193.
11. Ibid., p. 194.
12. Elting, *Amateurs to Arms*, p. 34.
13. Berton, *The Invasion of Canada: 1812-1813*, p. 194.
14. Elting, *Amateurs to Arms*, p. 34.
15. Mahon, *The War of 1812*, p. 67.

16. Horsman, *The War of 1812*, p. 82.
17. Ibid.

CHAPTER THREE

1. Dudley, *The Naval War of 1812: A Documentary History*, Vol. I, p. 136.
2. Ibid., p. 160.
3. Ibid., p. 161.
4. Moses Smith, *Naval Scenes in the Last War* (Gleason's Publishing Hall, Boston, 1846), p. 21.
5. F. Alexander Magoun, *The Frigate Constitution and Other Historic Ships*, p. 72.
6. Ibid., p. 73.
7. Morris says only one was used in his autobiography: Charles Morris, Jr., *The Autobiography of Commodore Charles Morris* (Naval Institute Press, 1881), p. 161.
8. Theodore Roosevelt, *The Naval War of 1812* (The Modern Library Edition, 1999), p. 48.
9. Tyrone G. Martin, *A Most Fortunate Ship*, p. 149.
10. Roosevelt, *The Naval War of 1812*, p. 49.
11. Magoun, *The Frigate Constitution and Other Historic Ships*, p. 73.
12. Ibid., p. 50.
13. C. S. Forester, *The Age of Fighting Sail* (Chapman Billies, 1956), pp. 55–56.
14. Dudley, *The Naval War of 1812: A Documentary History*, Vol. I, p. 208.
15. Martin, *A Most Fortunate Ship*, p. 2.
16. Edward L. Beach, *The United States Navy: 200 Years* (Henry Holt and Company, 1986), p. 11.
17. Ibid., p. 12
18. William Gilkerson, *The Ships of John Paul Jones* (The United States Naval Academy Museum, 1987), p. 74.
19. Virginia Steele Wood, *Live Oaking: Southern Timber for Tall Ships* (Naval Institute Press, 1981), p. 24.
20. Ibid.
21. Henry Gruppe, *The Frigates*, p. 39.
22. Daniel DeFoe, *Robinson Crusoe: An Authoritative Text, Contexts, Criticisms*, Second Edition, ed. Michael Shinagel (W.W. Norton &

Company, 1993), p.15.

23. Martin, *A Most Fortunate Ship*, p. 3.
24. Irvin Anthony, *Decatur* (Charles Scribner & Sons, 1931), p. 28.
25. Dudley, *The Naval War of 1812: A Documentary History*, Vol. I, p. 458.
26. Martin, *A Most Fortunate Ship*, p. 4.
27. James Henderson, *The Frigates* (Wordsworth Press, 1970), p. 15.
28. Ibid.
29. Martin, *A Most Fortunate Ship*, p. 5.
30. Ibid. , p. 140.
31. Ibid., pp. 5–8.
32. Gardiner, *The Naval War of 1812*, pp. 160–61.
33. Ibid., p. 161.
34. Magoun, *The Frigate Constitution and Other Historic Ships*, p. 101.
35. Beach, *The United States Navy*, p. 33.
36. Wood, *Live Oaking: Southern Timber for Tall Ships*, p. 61.
37. Ibid., p. 28.
38. Martin, *A Most Fortunate Ship*, pp. 11, 375.
39. Barra Foundation, *Philadelphia: A 300 Year History*, p. 398.
40. Martin, *A Most Fortunate Ship*, pp. 8–9.
41. Ibid., p. 11.
42. Ibid., p. 17.
43. Linda M. Maloney, "Isaac Hull: Bulwark of the Sailing Navy," in James C. Bradford, ed., *Command Under Sail: Makers of the American Naval Tradition 1775-1850*, (Naval Institute Press, 1985), p. 253.
44. Ibid., p. 251.
45. Martin, *A Most Fortunate Ship*, p. 65.
46. Henderson, *The Frigates*, p. 140.
47. Hershel Parker, *Herman Melville: A Biography*, Vol. I: 1819-1851 (Johns Hopkins University Press, 1996), p. 259.
48. Henry Adams, *The War of 1812* (Cooper Square Press Edition, 1999), p. 41.
49. Beach, *The United States Navy*, p. 87.
50. Smith, *Naval Scenes in the Last War*, p. 28.
51. Ibid., p. 29.
52. Magoun, *The Frigate Constitution and Other Historic Ships*, p. 74.
53. Smith, *Naval Scenes in the Last War*, p. 30.
54. Forester, *The Age of Fighting Sail*, p. 62.

55. Adams, *The War of 1812*, p. 41.
56. Magoun, *The Frigate Constitution and Other Historic Ships*, p. 74.
57. Gruppe, *The Frigates*, p. 95.
58. Smith, *Naval Scenes in the Last War*, p. 32. By some accounts, one of the Americans remained at his gun; see Richard Woodman, *The Sea Warriors* (Constable London, 2001), p. 299.
59. Magoun, *The Frigate Constitution and Other Historic Ships*, p. 75.
60. Gruppe, *The Frigates*, p. 84.
61. Magoun, *The Frigate Constitution and Other Historic Ships*, p. 74.
62. Gruppe, *The Frigates*, p. 84.
63. Martin, *A Most Fortunate Ship*, p. 156.
64. Charles Francis Adams, "Wednesday August 19, 1812, 6:30 PM: The Birth of a World Power," in *The American Historical Review*, Volume XVIII, April 1913, No. 3, p. 519.
65. Smith, *Naval Scenes in the Last War*, p. 33.
66. C. F. Adams, "Wednesday August 19, 1812, 6:30 PM," pp. 519–20, from Edmund Quincy, *Life of Josiah Quincy*, p. 264.
67. Ibid., p. 520.
68. Magoun, *The Frigate Constitution and Other Historic Ships*, p. 75.
69. Dudley, *The Naval War of 1812: A Documentary History*, Vol. I, p. 246.
70. Martin, *A Most Fortunate Ship*, p. 158.
71. Roosevelt, *The Naval War of 1812*, p. 52.
72. Gruppe, *The Frigates*, p. 89.
73. Magoun, *The Frigate Constitution and Other Historic Ships*, p. 75.
74. Lewis, *Famous American Naval Officers*, p. 84.
75. Martin, *A Most Fortunate Ship*, p. 159.
76. Smith, *Naval Scenes in the Last War*, p. 35.
77. Gruppe, *The Frigates*, p. 90.
78. Smith, *Naval Scenes in the Last War*, p. 35.
79. Quincy, *Life of Josiah Quincy*, p. 264.
80. Gruppe, *The Frigates*, p. 90.
81. Magoun, *The Frigate Constitution and Other Historic Ships*, p. 76.
82. Martin, *A Most Fortunate Ship*, p. 165.
83. Dudley, *The Naval War of 1812: A Documentary History*, Vol. I, p. 238.
84. Ibid., pp. 238–42.
85. Eliza Susan Quincy , *Memoir of the Life of Eliza S. M. Quincy*, 1861, p. 163.

86. Available at http://www.contemplator.com/america/constitutn.html.
87. Martin, *A Most Fortunate Ship*, p. 167. See Forester, *The Age of Fighting Sail*, p. 75, for a different interpretation of the switch.
88. Maloney, "Isaac Hull: Bulwark of the Sailing Navy," in Bradford, *Command Under Sail*, p. 260.
89. Dudley, *The Naval War of 1812: A Documentary History*, Vol. I, p. 244.
90. Tracy, *The Naval Chronicle*, Vol. V, p. 113.
91. Roosevelt, *The Naval War of 1812*, p. 55.
92. Dudley, *The Naval War of 1812: A Documentary History*, Vol. I, p. 245.

CHAPTER FOUR

1. Roosevelt, *The Naval War of 1812*, p. xxix.
2. Alan Taylor, *The Civil War of 1812*, p. 187.
3. John R. Elting, Amateurs to Arms, p. 43.
4. Reginald Horsman, *The War of 1812*, p. 46.
5. Elting, *Amateurs to Arms*, p. 47.
6. Ibid., p. 49.
7. Donald R. Hickey, *The War of 1812: A Forgotten Conflict*, p. 88.
8. Ibid.
9. Ibid., p. 90.

CHAPTER FIVE

1. Samuel Leech, *A Voice from the Main Deck: Being a Record of the Thirty Years Adventures of Samuel Leech* (Chatham Publishing, 1999), p. 70.
2. Benjamin Larabee et al., *America and the Sea*, p. 213.
3. Ira Dye, *The Fatal Cruise of the Argus*, p. 84.
4. James Henderson, *The Frigates*, p. 59.
5. James Tertius deKay, *Chronicles of the Frigate Macedonian 1809-1922* (W.W. Norton and Co., 1995), p. 85.
6. Theodore Roosevelt, *The Naval War of 1812*, p. 62.
7. de Kay, *Chronicles of the Frigate Macedonian*, p. 51.
8. John Masefield, *Sea Life in Nelson's Time*(Sphere Books, Ltd., 1905, 1972), p. 89.
9. Brian Lavery, *Nelson's Navy*, p. 216.
10. Patrick O'Brian, *Master and Commander* (W. W. Norton & Company,

1970), p. 93.

11. Leech, *A Voice from the Main Deck*, p. 71.
12. Ibid., p. 72.
13. de Kay, *Chronicles of the Frigate Macedonian*, p. 70.
14. Ben Birindelli, *The 200 Year Legacy of Stephen Decatur, 1798-1998* (Hallmark Publishing Company, 1998), p. 52.
15. Irvin Anthony, *Decatur*, p. 184.
16. Alexander Slidell Mackenzie, USN, *Life of Stephen Decatur: A Commodore in the Navy of the United States* (Little Brown, 1848), p. 172.
17. Spencer Tucker, *Stephen Decatur: A Life Most Bold and Daring* (Naval Institute Press, 2005), p. 4.
18. Tyrone G. Martin, *A Most Fortunate Ship*, p. 3.
19. Roosevelt, *The Naval War of 1812*, p. 28.
20. Mackay, *Extraordinary Popular Delusions and the Madness of Crowds*, p. 647.
21. Anthony, *Decatur*, pp. 103–4.
22. Ibid., p. 81.
23. Mackenzie, *Life of Stephen Decatur*, p. 123.
24. Anthony, *Decatur*, pp. 155–56.
25. Tucker, *Stephen Decatur*, p. 26.
26. Anthony, *Decatur*, p. 98.
27. Larabee, *America and the Sea*, p. 190.
28. Morison, *The Oxford History of the American People*, p. 363.
29. Tucker, *Stephen Decatur*, p. 48.
30. Larabee, *America and the Sea*, p. 191.
31. Anthony, *Decatur*, p. 153.
32. Birindelli, *The 200 Year Legacy of Stephen Decatur*, p. 40.
33. Dye, *The Fatal Cruise of the Argus*, p. 79.
34. Larabee, *America and the Sea*, p. 218.
35. Robert Gardiner, *Warships of the Napoleonic Era* (Naval Institute Press, 1999), p. 37.
36. Lavery, *Nelson's Navy*, pp. 80, 82.
37. Hershel Parker, *Herman Melville: A Biography*, Vol. I: 1819-1851 (Johns Hopkins University Press, 1996), p. 258.
38. de Kay, *Chronicles of the Frigate Macedonian*, p. 73.
39. Leech, *A Voice from the Main Deck*, p. 84.
40. Magoun, *The Frigate Constitution and Other Historic Ships*, p. 71.

41. Tom Wareham, *The Star Captains: Frigate Command in the Napoleonic Wars* (Naval Institute Press, 2001), p. 163.
42. Leech, *A Voice from the Main Deck*, p. 73.
43. Parker, *Herman Melville: A Biography*, p. 259.
44. Leech, *A Voice from the Main Deck*, p. 73.
45. Roosevelt, *The Naval War of 1812*, 62
46. Ibid., p. 62.
47. Mackenzie, *Life of Stephen Decatur*, p. 173.
48. Leech, *A Voice from the Main Deck*, p. 73.
49. Ibid., p. 74.
50. Roosevelt, *The Naval War of 1812*, p. 62.
51. Leech, *A Voice from the Main Deck*, p. 76.
52. Ibid.
53. Dudley., *The Naval War of 1812: A Documentary History*, Vol. I, p. 549.
54. Mackenzie, *Life of Stephen Decatur*, p. 176.
55. Leech, *A Voice from the Main Deck*, p. 83.
56. de Kay, *Chronicles of the Frigate Macedonian*, p. 90.
57. Mackenzie, *Life of Stephen Decatur*, p. 179.
58. Gruppe, *The Frigates*, p. 98.
59. Anthony, *Decatur*, p. 191.
60. Gruppe, *The Frigates*, p. 100.
61. Mackenzie, *Life of Stephen Decatur*, p. 178.
62. Birindelli, *The 200 Year Legacy of Stephen Decatur*, p. 56.
63. de Kay, *Chronicles of the Frigate Macedonian*, p. 98.
64. *National Intelligencer* (Washington DC), December 10/12, 1812.
65. Edward L. Beach, *The United States Navy*, p. 95.
66. C. S. Forester, *The Age of Fighting Sail*, p. 142.
67. Mackenzie, *Life of Stephen Decatur*, p. 188.
68. Forester, *The Age of Fighting Sail*, p. 142.
69. Mackenzie, *Life of Stephen Decatur*, p. 189.
70. Ibid.
71. *National Intelligencer* (Washington DC), December 10/12, 1812.
72. Birindelli, *The 200 Year Legacy of Stephen Decatur*, p. 56.

CHAPTER SIX

1. John K. Mahon, *The War of 1812*, p. 66.

2. John R. Elting, *Amateurs to Arms*, p. 59.
3. Ibid., p. 58.
4. Reginald Horsman, *The War of 1812*, p. 84.
5. Harry L. Coles, *The War of 1812* (University of Chicago Press, 1966), p. 116.
6. Elting, *Amateurs to Arms*, p. 62.
7. Coles, *The War of 1812*, p. 116.
8. Elting, *Amateurs to Arms*, p. 62.
9. Mahon, *The War of 1812*, p. 130.
10. Adams, *The War of 1812*, p. 57.
11. Pierre Berton, *The Invasion of Canada*, pp. 300–1.
12. Donald R. Hickey, *The War of 1812*, p. 86.
13. Elting, *Amateurs to Arms*, p. 63.
14. Roosevelt, *The Naval War of 1812*, p. 251.

CHAPTER SEVEN

1. Frances D. Robboti, *The U.S.Essex and the Birth of the U.S. Navy*, p. 20.
2. Craig Symonds, "William S. Baindridge: Bad Luck or Fatal Flaw?" in James C. Bradford, ed., *Command Under Sail: Makers of the American Naval Tradition 1775-1850* (Naval Institute Press, 1985), pp. 99–100.
3. Benjamin Larabee et al, *America and the Sea: A Maritime History*, p. 185.
4. Symonds, "William S. Baindridge: Bad Luck or Fatal Flaw?" *op cit.*, p. 102.
5. Ibid., p. 109.
6. Ibid.
7. Henry Gruppe, *The Frigates*, p. 62.
8. Tyrone G. Martin, *A Most Fortunate Ship*, p. 169.
9. Moses Smith, *Naval Scenes in the Last War*, p. 38.
10. Martin, *A Most Fortunate Ship*, p. 169.
11. Theodore Roosevelt, *The Naval War of 1812*, p. 39.
12. F. Alexander Magoun, *The Frigate Constitution and Other Historic Ships*, p. 100.
13. Brian Lavery, *Nelson's Navy*, p. 175.
14. Herman Melville, *White Jacket*, p. 8.
15. Ibid., p. 9.
16. *OECD in Washington*, July-August 2001, p. 2.

17. Edwin G. Burrows and Mike Wallace, *Gotham*, p. 477.
18. Magoun, *The Frigate Constitution and Other Historic Ships*, p. 103.
19. Ira Dye, *The Fatal Cruise of the Argus*, p. 106.
20. Joyce Appleby, *Inheriting the Revolution*, p. 206.
21. Ibid., p. 189.
22. Burrows and Wallace, *Gotham*, p. 405; and Appleby, *Inheriting the Revolution*, pp. 209–11.
23. Appleby, *Inheriting the Revolution*, p. 215.
24. Magoun, *The Frigate Constitution and Other Historic Ships*, p. 77.
25. Robboti, *The USS Essex and the Birth of the American Navy*, p. 59.
26. John Masefield, *Sea Life in Nelson's Time*, p. 74.
27. Lavery, *Nelson's Navy*, p. 217.
28. Masefield, *Sea Life in Nelson's Time*, pp. 74–75.
29. W. Jeffrey Bolster, "To Feel Like a Man: Black Seamen in the Northern States, 1800-1860," *Journal of American History*, Vol. 76, No. 4 (March 1990), p. 1176.
30. Gerald T. Altoff, *Amongst My Best Men: African-Americans and the War of 1812* (The Perry Group, 1999), pp. 18–19.
31. Michael J. Crawford, ed., *The Naval War of 1812: A Documentary History*, Vol. III(Naval Historical Center, 2002), p. 116.
32. Ibid., p. 689.
33. Altoff, *Amongst My Best Men*, p. 22.
34. William C. Nell, *The Colored Patriots of the American Revolution, with Sketches of Several Distinguished Colored Persons: To Which is Added a Brief Survey of the Condition and Prospects of Colored Americans* (Boston, 1855), p. 314.
35. Roosevelt, *The Naval War of 1812*, p. 76.
36. Symonds, "William S. Baindridge: Bad Luck or Fatal Flaw?" *op cit.*, p. 114.
37. Ibid.
38. Ibid.
39. Martin, *A Most Fortunate Ship*, p. 171.
40. Dudley, *The Naval War of 1812: A Documentary History*, Vol. I, p. 640.
41. Lavery, *Nelson's Navy*, p. 62
42. Richard Woodman, *The Sea Warriors* (Constable London, 2001), p. 304.
43. Ibid.
44. Roosevelt, *The Naval War of 1812*, p. 68.

45. Dudley, *The Naval War of 1812: A Documentary History*, Vol. I, p. 641.
46. Gruppe, *The Frigates*, p. 101.
47. Woodman, *The Sea Warriors*, p. 305.
48. C. S. Forester, *The Age of Fighting Sail*, p. 118.
49. Dudley, *The Naval War of 1812: A Documentary History*, Vol. I, p. 641.
50. Roosevelt, *The Naval War of 1812*, p. 70.
51. Martin, *A Most Fortunate Ship*, p. 178.
52. Gruppe, *The Frigates*, p. 102.
53. Dudley, *The Naval War of 1812: A Documentary History*, Vol. I, p. 647.
54. Ibid.
55. Woodman, *The Sea Warriors*, p. 306.
56. Martin, *A Most Fortunate Ship*, p. 176.
57. Beach, *The United States Navy*, p. 97.
58. Martin, *A Most Fortunate Ship*, p. 178.
59. Beach, *The United States Navy*, p. 97.
60. Nicholas Tracy, ed., *The Naval Chronicle*, Vol. V, p. 159.
61. Roosevelt, *Naval War of 1812*, p. 73.
62. Gruppe, *The Frigates*, p. 104.
63. Tracy, ed., *The Naval Chronicle*, Volume V, p. 150.
64. Gruppe, *The Frigates*, p. 133.
65. G. J. Marcus, *A Naval History of England 2: The Age of Nelson* (George Allen and Unwin Ltd., 1971), p. 459.
66. Dudley, *The Naval War of 1812: A Documentary History*, Vol. II, 1813, p. 183.
67. Horsman, *The War of 1812*, p. 56.
68. Martin, *A Most Fortunate Ship*, p. 178.
69. Symonds, "William S. Baindridge: Bad Luck or Fatal Flaw?" *op cit.*, p. 118.
70. Martin, *A Most Fortunate Ship*, p. 179.
71. Woodman, *The Sea Warriors*, p. 306.
72. Dudley, *The Naval War of 1812: A Documentary History*, Vol. I, p. 648.
73. Woodman, *The Sea Warriors*, p. 306.
74. Martin, *A Most Fortunate Ship*, p. 179.
75. Ibid., p. 180.
76. Symonds, "William S. Baindridge: Bad Luck or Fatal Flaw?" *op cit.*, p. 119.
77. Martin, *A Most Fortunate Ship*, p. 180.

78. Ibid.
79. Symonds, "William S. Baindridge: Bad Luck or Fatal Flaw?" *op cit.*, p. 119.
80. Woodman, *The Sea Warriors*, p. 307.

CHAPTER EIGHT

1. J. Mackay Hitsman, *The Incredible War of 1812*, p. 131.
2. Ibid., p. 132.
3. John R. Elting, *Amateurs to Arms*, pp. 92–93.
4. John K. Mahon, *The War of 1812*, p. 142.
5. Ned Myers, in Jon E. Lewis, ed., *Life Before the Mast: An Anthology of Eye Witness Accounts from the Age of Fighting Sail* (Carroll & Graf Publishers, 2001), p. 357.
6. Donald R. Hickey, *The War of 1812*, p. 129.
7. Ibid.
8. Jeanne T. Heidler and David S. Heidler, eds., *Encyclopedia of The War of 1812* (ABC-CLIO, 1997), p. 569.
9. Elting, *Amateurs to Arms*, p. 118.
10. Henry Adams, *The War of 1812*, p. 60.
11. Hickey, *The War of 1812*, p. 135.
12. Mahon, *The War of 1812*, p. 160.
13. Ibid.
14. Ibid., p. 161.
15. Adams, *The War of 1812*, p. 61.
16. Elting, *Amateurs to Arms*, p. 106.
17. Harry L. Coles, *The War of 1812*, p. 119.
18. Alexander Slidell Mackenzie, *The Life of Commodore Oliver Hazard Perry*, p. 141.
19. Elting, *Amateurs to Arms*, p. 122.
20. Ibid., p. 123.
21. Hickey, *The War of 1812*, p. 130.
22. Ibid.
23. John Buchanan, *Jackson's Way*, pp. 199–200.
24. Mahon, *The War of 1812*, p. 200.

CHAPTER NINE

1. Frances D. Robotti, *The USS Essex and the Birth of the American Navy*, p. 164.
2. William S. Dudley, *The Naval War of 1812: A Documentary History*, Vol. I, p. 625.
3. Robotti, *The USS Essex and the Birth of the American Navy*, p. 166.
4. David F. Long, "David Porter: Pacific Ocean Gadfly," in James C. Bradford, ed., *Command Under Sail: Makers of the American Naval Tradition 1775-1850* (Naval Institute Press, 1985), p. 177.
5. Charles Lee Lewis, *Famous American Naval Officers*, pp. 100–1.
6. Ibid., p. 103.
7. Long, "David Porter: Pacific Ocean Gadfly," p. 174.
8. Ibid., p. 175.
9. Lewis, *Famous American Naval Officers*, p. 106.
10. Long, "David Porter: Pacific Ocean Gadfly," p. 176.
11. Edwin G. Burrows and Mike Wallace, *Gotham: A History of New York City to 1898*, p. 416.
12. Henry Gruppe, *The Frigates*, p. 110.
13. Burroughs Wallace, *Gotham*, p. 416.
14. Robotti, *The USS Essex and the Birth of the American Navy*, p. 149; and Lewis, *Famous American Naval Officers*, p. 109.
15. Frederick C. Leiner, *Millions for Defense: The Subscription Warships of 1798* (Naval Institute Press, 2000), p. 183.
16. Robert Gardiner, *Warships of the Napoleonic Era*, p. 37.
17. Robotti, *The USS Essex and the Birth of the American Navy*, p. 154.
18. Roosevelt, *The Naval War of 1812*, p. 46.
19. Dudley, *The Naval War of 1812: A Documentary History*, Vol. I, p. 171.
20. Ibid., p. 172.
21. Ibid., p. 174.
22. Ibid., p. 174.
23. Ibid., pp. 175–76.
24. Robotti, *The USS Essex and the Birth of the American Navy*, p. 140.
25. Ibid., p. 137.
26. Ibid.
27. Gruppe, *The Frigates*, p. 110.
28. Ibid., pp. 111–12.
29. Robotti, *The USS Essex and the Birth of the American Navy*, p. 162.
30. Roosevelt, *Theodore, The Naval War of 1812*, p. 122.

31. Robotti, *The USS Essex and the Birth of the American Navy*, p. 177.
32. Ibid.
33. Ibid.
34. Gruppe, *The Frigates*, p. 118.
35. Ibid.
36. Long, "David Porter: Pacific Ocean Gadfly," p. 178.
37. Thomas Kessner, *Capital City: New York City and the Men Behind America's Rise to Economic Dominance, 1860-1900* (Simon & Shuster, 2003), p. 10.
38. Robotti, *The USS Essex and the Birth of the American Navy*, p. 217.
39. Tom Wareham, *The Star Captains: Frigate Command in the Napoleonic Wars*, p. 121.
40. Robotti, *The USS Essex and the Birth of the American Navy*, p. 189.
41. Gruppe, *The Frigates*, p. 117.
42. Robotti, *The USS Essex and the Birth of the American Navy*, p. 183.
43. Ibid., p. 191.
44. Lewis, *Famous American Naval Officers*, p. 114.
45. Gruppe, *The Frigates*, p. 117.
46. Jon Latimer, *1812: War with America* (Belknap Press of Harvard University, 2007), p. 240.
47. Long, "David Porter: Pacific Ocean Gadfly," p. 179.
48. Robotti, *The USS Essex and the Birth of the American Navy*, p. 194.
49. Ibid.
50. Long, "David Porter: Pacific Ocean Gadfly," p. 183.
51. Ibid., p. 182.
52. Gruppe, *The Frigates*, p. 119.
53. Long, "David Porter: Pacific Ocean Gadfly," p. 180.
54. Porter, *Journal of a Cruise* (Naval Institute Press, 1986), p. xxi.
55. Ibid., p. 295.
56. Ibid., p. xvii.
57. Gruppe, *The Frigates*, p. 120.
58. James Fenimore Cooper, *The History of the Navy of the United States of America* (Naval Institute Press), p. 300.
59. James Henderson, *The Frigates*, p. 163.
60. Robotti, *The USS Essex and the Birth of the American Navy*, p. 203.
61. Porter, *Journal of a Cruise*, p. 478.
62. Michael Crawford, *The Naval War of 1812: A Documentary History*,

Vol. III (Naval Historical Center, 2002), p. 721.
63. Ibid., p. 722.
64. Ibid., p. 714.
65. Lovall Farragut, *Life of David Glasgow Farragut* (D. Appleton and Company, 1879), p. 39.
66. Robotti, The USS Essex and the Birth of the American Navy, p. 206.
67. Roosevelt, *The Naval War of 1812*, p. 166.
68. Farragut, L., Life of David Glasgow Farragut, 41
69. Richard Woodman, *The Sea Warriors*, pp. 314–15.
70. Farragut, *Life of David Glasgow Farragut*, p. 40.
71. Ibid., p. 45.
72. Ibid., p. 42.
73. Gruppe, *The Frigates*, p. 128.
74. Henderson, *The Frigates*, pp. 166–67.
75. Farragut, *Life of David Glasgow Farragut*, p. 42.
76. Gruppe, *The Frigates*, p. 129.
77. Robotti, *The USS Essex and the Birth of the American Navy*, p. 231.
78. Ibid., p. 231.
79. Henderson, *The Frigates*, p. 166.
80. Woodman, *The Sea Warriors*, p. 315.
81. Robotti, *The USS Essex and the Birth of the American Navy*, p. 235.
82. Ibid., p. 236.
83. Crawford, *The Naval War of 1812: A Documentary History*, Vol. III, p. 754.
84. Robotti, *The USS Essex and the Birth of the American Navy*, p. 238.
85. Gruppe, *The Frigates*, p. 131.
86. Roosevelt, *The Naval War of 1812*, p. 92.
87. Robotti, *The USS Essex and the Birth of the American Navy*, p. 238.

CHAPTER TEN

1. John R. Elting, *Amateurs to Arms*, p. 107.
2. Ibid.
3. John K. Mahon, *The War of 1812*, p. 164.
4. Ibid.
5. Reginald Horsman, *The War of 1812*, p. 102.
6. Elting, *Amateurs to Arms*, p. 109.

7. Mahon, *The War of 1812*, p. 165.
8. Mark O. Hatfield and Wendy Wolff, eds., *Vice Presidents of the United States: 1789 – 1993* (Senate Historical Office, United States Government Printing Office, 1997), p. 122.
9. Ibid., p. 123.
10. Elting, *Amateurs to Arms*, p. 110.
11. Mahon, *The War of 1812*, p. 182.

CHAPTER ELEVEN

1. James Fenimore Cooper, *The History of the Navy of the United States of America*, p. 277.
2. Ibid., p. 278.
3. Theodore Roosevelt, *The Naval War of 1812*, p. 90.
4. C. S. Forester, *The Age of Fighting Sail*, p. 132.
5. Joseph Bryan Icenhower, *American Sea Heroes* (Hammond, 1970), p. 24.
6. Henry Gruppe, *The Frigates*, p. 134.
7. Icenhower, *American Sea Heroes*, pp. 23–25.
8. William C. Nell, *The Colored Patriots of the American Revolution*, p. 314.
9. Richard Woodman, *The Sea Warriors*, p. 307.
10. Roosevelt, *The Naval War of 1812*, p. 96.
11. Ibid., pp. 93–94.
12. Woodman, *The Sea Warriors*, p. 307.
13. Gruppe, *The Frigates*, p. 134.
14. Roosevelt, *The Naval War of 1812*, p. 96.
15. Forester, *The Age of Fighting Sail*, p. 126.
16. Nicholas Tracy, ed., *The Naval Chronicle*, Volume V, p. 151.
17. Ibid.
18. Forester, *The Age of Fighting Sail*, p. 128.
19. Peter Padfield, *Broke and the Shannon* (Hodder and Stoughton, 1968), p. 126.
20. Ibid.
21. Edward L. Beach, *The United States Navy: 200 Years*, p. 99.
22. Gruppe, *The Frigates*, p. 135.
23. Beach, *The United States Navy: 200 Years*, p. 113.
24. Padfield, *Broke and the Shannon*, p. 151.
25. Ibid., p. 143.

26. Beach, *The United States Navy: 200 Years*, p. 102.
27. Roosevelt, *The Naval War of 1812*, p. 101.
28. Ibid.
29. Woodman, *The Sea Warriors*, p. 317.
30. Padfield, *Broke and the Shannon*, p. 102.
31. Tom Wareham, *The Star Captains*, p. 160.
32. Forester, *The Age of Fighting Sail*, p. 161.
33. Padfield, *Broke and the Shannon*, p. 139.
34. Spencer C. Tucker and Frank T. Reuter, *Injured Honor: The Chesapeake-Leopard Affair* (U.S. Naval Institute Press, 1996), p. 82.
35. Padfield, *Broke and the Shannon*, p. 183.
36. Tucker and Reuter, *Injured Honor: The Chesapeake-Leopard Affair*, p. 82.
37. Robert Gardiner, ed., *Warships of the Napoleonic Era*, p. 148.
38. Cooper, *The History of the Navy of the United States of America*, p. 305.
39. Beach, *The United States Navy: 200 Years*, pp. 106–7.
40. Ibid., p. 107.
41. Ibid.
42. Padfield, *Broke and the Shannon*, p. 144.
43. Roosevelt, *The Naval War of 1812*, p. 101.
44. Padfield, Broke and the Shannon, 146
45. Nicholas Tracy, ed., *The Naval Chronicle*, Volume V, p. 162.
46. Wareham, *The Star Captains*, p. 159.
47. Padfield, *Broke and the Shannon*, p. 148.
48. Ibid., p. 149.
49. Ibid., p. 155.
50. Beach, *The United States Navy: 200 Years*, p. 102.
51. Padfield, *Broke and the Shannon*, p. 156.
52. Ibid., p. 157.
53. Ibid., p. 161.
54. Ibid., p. 160.
55. Woodman, *The Sea Warriors*, p. 318.
56. Cooper, *The History of the Navy of the United States of America*, p. 306.
57. Padfield, *Broke and the Shannon*, p. 168.
58. Ibid., p. 169.
59. Woodman, *The Sea Warriors*, p. 320.
60. Roosevelt, *The Naval War of 1812*, p. 104.
61. Cooper, *The History of the Navy of the United States of America*, p. 307.

62. Woodman, *The Sea Warriors*, p. 319.
63. Roosevelt, *The Naval War of 1812*, p. 104.
64. Padfield, *Broke and the Shannon*, p. 180.
65. Roosevelt, *The Naval War of 1812*, p. 104.
66. Ibid., p. 106.
67. Tracy, ed., *The Naval Chronicle*, Volume V, p. 160.
68. Gruppe, *The Frigates*, p. 138.
69. John Brannan, ed., *Official Letters of the Military and Naval Officers of the United States During the War with Great Britain in the Years 1812, 13, 14 & 15 With Some Additional Letters and Documents Elucidating the History of that Period* (Washington, 1823), pp. 179–81.
70. Beach, *The United States Navy: 200 Years*, p. 111.
71. Dudley, *The Naval War of 1812: A Documentary History*, Vol. II, 1813, p. 192.
72. Tracy, ed., *The Naval Chronicle*, Vol. V, p. 171.
73. Wareham, *The Star Captains*, p. 201.
74. Gruppe, *The Frigates*, p. 138.
75. Padfield, *Broke and the Shannon*, p. 186.
76. Mahon, *The War of 1812*, p. 124.
77. Beach, *The United States Navy: 200 Years*, p. 114.
78. Padfield, *Broke and the Shannon*, p. 182.
79. Wareham, *The Star Captains*, p. 201.
80. Tracy, ed., *The Naval Chronicle*, Volume V, p. 154.
81. Padfield, *Broke and the Shannon*, p. 194.
82. Ibid., p. 195.
83. Tracy, ed., *The Naval Chronicle*, Volume V, p. 161.
84. Woodman, *The Sea Warriors*, p. 321.
85. Wareham, *The Star Captains*, p. 91.
86. Ibid., p. 59.
87. Gruppe, *The Frigates*, p. 138.
88. Padfield, *Broke and the Shannon*, p. 218.

CHAPTER TWELVE

1. Hickey, *The War of 1812*, p. 152
2. Adams, *The War of 1812*, pp. 79-80
3. Ibid., p. 137

4. Philip Haythornthwaite, *Nelson's Navy*, (Osprey Publishing, UK, 1993), p. 75
5. William M. Marine, *The British Invasion of Maryland, 1812 – 1815*, (Heritage Books, Inc., A Facsimile Reprint, 1998), p. 42
6. Dudley, *The Naval War of 1812: A Documentary History*, Vol. I, p. 320
7. Mahon, *The War of 1812*, p. 111
8. Thomas C. Gillmer, *Pride of Baltimore: The Story of the Baltimore Clippers*, (International Marine, Camden, ME, 1992), p. 26
9. *The Naval Chronicle,, Volume V*, p. 177
10. Marine, *The British Invasion of Maryland*, p. 32
11. *The Naval Chronicle, Volume V*, p. 178
12. George Johnston, *History of Cecil County, Maryland*, (Regional Publishing Co., Baltimore, 1972), p. 417
13. Marine, *The British Invasion of Maryland*, p. 33
14. Ibid., p. 39
15. *The Naval Chronicle, Volume V*, p. 180
16. Elting, *Amateurs to Arms*, p. 79
17. Marine, *The British Invasion of Maryland*, pp. 39–40
18. Johnston, *History of Cecil County, Maryland*, p. 418
19. Ibid., p. 421
20. Christopher T. George, *Terror on the Chesapeake: The War of 1812 on the Bay*, (White Mane Books, 2000), p. 36
21. Adams, *The War of 1812*, p. 131
22. Marine, *The British Invasion of Maryland*, p. 23
23. Ibid., p. 23
24. Adams, *The War of 1812*, p. 134
25. Elting, *Amateurs to Arms*, p. 80
26. George, *Terror on the Chesapeake*, p. 42
27. Dudley, *The Naval War of 1812: A Documentary History*, Vol. II, 3 p. 13
28. Mahon., *The War of 1812*, p. 119
29. George, *Terror on the Chesapeake*, p. 42
30. Cooper, James Fenimore, *The History of the Navy of the United States of America*, p. 302
31. Mahon., *The War of 1812*, p. 119, and Hickey, *The War of 1812*, p. 154 (but Adams says 1,500)
32. Mahon., *The War of 1812*, p. 120, (but Adams says seven hundred men in fifteen boats, 134). Captain Hanchett has sometimes been

erroneously described as an illegitimate son of King George III. See *Harper's Monthly Magazine*, vol. 103 (June–November 1901), p. 662.

33. George, *Terror on the Chesapeake*, p. 46
34. Ibid., p. 46
35. Ibid. p. 47
36. Elting, *Amateurs to Arms*, p. 80
37. George, *Terror on the Chesapeake*, p. 47
38. Ibid., p. 48
39. Mahon., *The War of 1812*, p. 120
40. Marine, *The British Invasion of Maryland*, p. 25
41. Adams, *The War of 1812*, p. 135
42. Dudley, *The Naval War of 1812: A Documentary History*, Vol. II, p. 362
43. Ibid., p. 41
44. Hitsman, *The Incredible War of 1812*, p. 160
45. Elting, *Amateurs to Arms*, p. 80
46. Marine, *The British Invasion of Maryland*, p. 25
47. Hitsman, *The Incredible War of 1812*, p. 160
48. Latimer, *1812: War with America*, p. 160.
49. Marine, *The British Invasion of Maryland*, p. 55
50. Ibid., p. 57
51. George, *Terror on the Chesapeake*, p. 64

CHAPTER THIRTEEN

1. Ira Dye, *The Fatal Cruise of the Argus*, p. 109.
2. Ibid., p. 111.
3. Ibid., pp. 118–19.
4. Ibid.
5. James Fenimore Cooper, *The History of the Navy of the United States of America*, p. 315.
6. James Inderwick, *Cruise of the U.S. Brig Argus 1813* (New York Public Library, 1917), p. 16.
7. Dye, *The Fatal Cruise of the Argus*, p. 267.
8. Ibid., p. 17.
9. Ibid., p. 19.
10. Ibid., p. 272.
11. James Inderwick, *Cruise of the U.S. Brig Argus 1813*, p. 19.

12. Dye, *The Fatal Cruise of the Argus*, p. 274.
13. Theodore Roosevelt, *The Naval War of 1812*, p. 114.
14. Henry Adams, *The War of 1812*, p. 148.
15. C. S. Forester, *The Age of Fighting Sail*, p. 170.
16. Dye, *The Fatal Cruise of the Argus*, p. 277.
17. Cooper, *The History of the Navy of the United States of America*, p. 316.
18. Roosevelt, *The Naval War of 1812*, p. 115.
19. Dye, *The Fatal Cruise of the Argus*, p. 279.
20. Inderwick, *Cruise of the U.S. Brig Argus 1813*, p. 21.
21. Dye, *The Fatal Cruise of the Argus*, p. 282.
22. William S. Dudley, *The Naval War of 1812: A Documentary History*, Vol. II, p. 223.
23. Cooper, *The History of the Navy of the United States of America*, p. 317 (footnote).
24. Ibid., pp. 315–16.
25. Roosevelt, *The Naval War of 1812*, p. 114.
26. Richard Woodman, *The Sea Warriors*, p. 310.
27. Inderwick, *Cruise of the U.S. Brig Argus 1813*, p. 20.
28. Ibid., p. 22.
29. Ibid., p. 14.
30. Ibid.
31. Nicholas Tracy, ed., *The Naval Chronicle*, Volume V, p. 164.

CHAPTER FOURTEEN

1. John Sugden, *Tecumseh: A Life* (Henry Holt and Company, 1997), p. 237.
2. Ibid., p. 238.
3. Ibid., p. 240.
4. Henry Adams, *The War of 1812*, p. 110.
5. Reginald Horsman, *The War of 1812*, p. 218.
6. Albert James Pickett, *History of Alabama* (re-published by River City Publishing, 1851, 1962), p. 512.
7. Ibid., pp. 512–13.
8. Sugden, *Tecumseh: A Life*, p. 254.
9. Adams, *The War of 1812*, p. 114.
10. John K. Mahon, *The War of 1812*, p. 232. According to Henry Adams, McQueen had come into possession of the letter from the English that

Little Warrior had tried to deliver to Pensacola, urging the Spaniards to arm the Creeks (Adams, *The War of 1812*, p. 115).

11. John Buchanan, *Andrew Jackson and the People of the Western Waters* (John Wiley & Sons, Inc., 2001), p. 217.
12. Adams, *The War of 1812*, p. 116.
13. Pickett, *History of Alabama*, p. 530.
14. Horsman, *The War of 1812*, p. 218.
15. Adams, *The War of 1812*, p. 116.
16. Pickett, *History of Alabama*, p. 532.
17. Buchanan, *Andrew Jackson and the People of the Western Waters*, p. 222.
18. Pickett, *History of Alabama*, p. 533.
19. Ibid., p. 535.
20. Ibid.
21. Ibid., pp. 536–37.
22. Donald R. Hickey, *Don't Give Up the Ship!*, p. 69.
23. Buchanan, *Andrew Jackson and the People of the Western Waters*, pp. 224–25.
24. Ibid., p. 206.
25. Ibid., p. 227.
26. Ibid.

CHAPTER FIFTEEN

1. C. S. Forester, *The Age of Fighting Sail*, p. 150.
2. Joseph Icenhower, *American Sea Heroes*, p. 27.
3. John K. Mahon, *The War of 1812*, p. 165.
4. Donald R. Hickey, *The War of 1812*, p. 131.
5. Alexander Slidell Mackenzie, *The Life of Commodore Oliver Hazard Perry*, Vols. I & II (Harper and Brothers, 1840), p. 15.
6. Icenhower, *American Sea Heroes*, p. 26.
7. Ibid.
8. Mahon, *The War of 1812*, p. 166.
9. Richard Dillon, *We Have Met the Enemy*, p. 55.
10. Harry L. Coles, *The War of 1812*, p. 123.
11. John S. D. Eisenhower, *Agent of Destiny: The Life and Times of General Winfield Scott* (The Free Press, 1997), p. 57.
12. Forester, *The Age of Fighting Sail*, p. 98.

13. Ibid., p. 158.
14. Horsman, *The War of 1812*, pp. 98–99.
15. Coles, *The War of 1812*, p. 122.
16. John K. Mahon, "Oliver Hazard Perry: Savior of the Northwest," in James C. Bradford, ed., *Command Under Sail: Makers of the American Naval Tradition 1775-1850* (Naval Institute Press, 1985), p. 130.
17. Gerald T. Altoff, *Amongst My Best Men: African-Americans and the War of 1812* (The Perry Group, 1996), p. 36.
18. Ibid., p. 37.
19. Ibid.
20. Alexander Slidell Mackenzie, *The Life of Commodore Oliver Hazard Perry*, p. 190.
21. Ibid., p. 198.
22. Ibid., p. 208.
23. Ibid., p. 148.
24. Icenhower, *American Sea Heroes*, p. 29.
25. Mahon, "Oliver Hazard Perry: Savior of the Northwest," p. 131.
26. Ibid. And Dillon, *We Have Met the Enemy*, p. 126.
27. Emily Pritchard Cary, "The Flag that Helped Captain Perry Win the Battle of Lake Erie in 1813," *Pennsylvania*, Vol. 7, No. 4, April 1988, pp. 62–63.
28. Mahon, "Oliver Hazard Perry: Savior of the Northwest," p. 131.
29. Mahon, *The War of 1812*, p. 170.
30. Mahon, "Oliver Hazard Perry: Savior of the Northwest," p. 132.
31. Ibid., p. 201.
32. Ibid.
33. Cooper, *The History of the Navy of the United States of America*, pp. 386, 392.
34. John Sugden, *Tecumseh: A Life* (Macmillan, 1999), pp. 355–56.
35. Ibid., p. 356.
36. Coles, *The War of 1812*, p. 126.
37. Mackenzie, *The Life of Commodore Oliver Hazard Perry*, p. 222.
38. Icenhower, *American Sea Heroes*, p. 29.
39. Ibid., p. 30.
40. Gerald T. Altoff, *Oliver Hazard Perry and the Battle of Lake Erie* (The Perry Group, 1999), p. 37.
41. Theodore Roosevelt, *The Naval War of 1812*, p. 146.

42. See http://www.brigniagara.org/log.htm.
43. Mackenzie, *The Life of Commodore Oliver Hazard Perry*, p. 241.
44. Altoff, *Oliver Hazard Perry and the Battle of Lake Erie*, p. 42.
45. Ibid., p. 243.
46. Ibid., p. 43.
47. Henry Adams, *The War of 1812*, p. 69.
48. Altoff, *Oliver Hazard and the Battle of Lake Erie*, p. 44.
49. Roosevelt, *The Naval War of 1812*, p. 148.
50. Ibid., p. 146.
51. Altoff, *Oliver Hazard Perry and the Battle of Lake Erie*, p. 50.
52. Adams, *The War of 1812*, p. 68.
53. Mahon, *The War of 1812*, p. 173.
54. James Fenimore Cooper, *The History of the Navy of the United States of America*, p. 390.
55. Dillon, *We Have Met the Enemy*, p. 144.
56. Adams, *The War of 1812*, p. 68.
57. Altoff, *Oliver Hazard Perry and the Battle of Lake Erie*, p. 52.
58. Mackenzie, *The Life of Commodore Oliver Hazard Perry*, p. 252.
59. Mahon, *The War of 1812*, p. 174.
60. Mahon, "Oliver Hazard Perry: Savior of the Northwest," p. 136.
61. Hickey, *The War of 1812*, p. 133.
62. Mackenzie, *The Life of Commodore Oliver Hazard Perry*, p. 264.
63. Altoff, *Oliver Hazard Perry and the Battle of Lake Erie*, p. 54.
64. William S. Dudley, *The Naval War of 1812: A Documentary History*, Vol. II, p. 555.
65. Adams, *The War of 1812*, p. 69.
66. Dudley, *The Naval War of 1812: A Documentary History*, Vol. II, p. 561.
67. Ibid., p. 563.
68. Ibid., p. 564.
69. Ibid., pp. 561–62.
70. Victor Suthren, *The War of 1812* (Galafilm Inc., 1999).
71. Mahon, *The War of 1812*, p. 175.
72. Ibid.
73. Nicholas Tracy, ed., *The Naval Chronicle: The Contemporary Record of the Royal Navy at War*, Vol. V, p. 172.
74. Altoff, *Amongst My Best Men*, p. 40.
75. Mahon, *The War of 1812*, p. 176.

76. Dudley, *The Naval War of 1812: A Documentary History*, Vol. II, p. 560.
77. Ibid., p. 559.
78. Mackenzie, *The Life of Commodore Oliver Hazard Perry*, Vol. I, p. 291.
79. Ibid., p. 292.
80. Ibid., p. 53.
81. Ibid., pp. 54–55.
82. Ibid., pp. 58–59.
83. Ibid., p. 60.
84. Ibid., pp. 73–74.

CHAPTER SIXTEEN

1. John Sugden, *Tecumseh: A Life*, p. 356.
2. Ibid., p. 357.
3. Ibid., p. 358.
4. Ibid., p. 359.
5. Ibid., p. 360.
6. Ibid., p. 362.
7. John K. Mahon, *The War of 1812*, p. 182.
8. John R. Elting, *Amateurs to Arms*, p. 111.
9. Mahon, *The War of 1812*, p. 182.
10. Sugden, *Tecumseh: A Life*, p. 373.
11. Henry Adams, *The War of 1812*, pp. 73–75.
12. Mahon, *The War of 1812*, p. 183.
13. Adams, *The War of 1812*, p. 75.
14. Mark O. Hatfield and Wendy Wolff, eds., *Vice Presidents of the United States: 1789–1993*, p. 126.
15. Adams, *The War of 1812*, p. 75.
16. Donald R. Hickey, *Don't Give Up the Ship! Myths of the War of 1812*, p. 68.
17. Victor Suthren, *The War of 1812*.
18. Hickey, *The War of 1812*, p. 148.
19. Elting, *Amateurs to Arms*, p. 167.
20. Hickey, *The War of 1812*, p. 148.
21. John Buchanan, *Jackson's Way: Andrew Jackson and the People of the Western Waters*, p. 237.
22. Ibid.

23. Ibid.
24. Reginald Horsman, *The War of 1812*, p. 220.
25. Buchanan, *Jackson's Way*, p. 241.
26. Ibid., p. 243.
27. Elting, *Amateurs to Arms*, p. 168.
28. Buchanan, *Jackson's Way*, p. 245.
29. Horsman, *The War of 1812*, p. 221.
30. Ibid.
31. Buchanan, *Jackson's Way*, pp. 257–58.
32. Elting, *Amateurs to Arms*, p. 169.
33. Buchanan, *Jackson's Way*, p. 259.
34. Elting, *Amateurs to Arms*, p. 169.
35. Buchanan, *Jackson's Way*, p. 266.
36. Elting, *Amateurs to Arms*, p. 170.
37. Buchanan, *Jackson's Way*, p. 273.
38. Ibid., p. 277.
39. Ibid., p. 278.
40. Horsman, *The War of 1812*, p. 223.
41. Hickey, *The War of 1812*, p. 149.
42. Elting, *Amateurs to Arms*, p. 172; and Horsman, *The War of 1812*, p. 224.
43. Buchanan, *Jackson's Way*, p. 285.
44. Ibid., p. 287.
45. Elting, *Amateurs to Arms*, p. 173.
46. Donald Braider, *Solitary Star: A Biography of Sam Houston* (G.P. Putnam Sons, 1974), p. 33.
47. Ibid., pp. 34–35.
48. Buchanan, *Jackson's Way*, p. 293.
49. Ibid., p. 294.
50. Ibid.
51. Hickey, *The War of 1812*, p. 151.
52. Horsman, *The War of 1812*, p. 225.

CHAPTER SEVENTEEN

1. Reuben Elmore Stivers, *Privateers and Volunteers* (Naval Institute Press, Annapolis, 1975), p. 66.
2. Donald Barr Chidsey, *The American Privateers* (Dodd, Mead & Co.,

1962), pp. 89–90.

3. Stivers, *Privateers and Volunteers*, p. 60.
4. Ibid., p. 59.
5. G. J. Marcus, *A Naval History of England, 2*, pp. 460–61.
6. Stivers, *Privateers and Volunteers*, p. 132.
7. Chidsey, *The American Privateers*, p. 114.
8. William Gilkerson, *The Ships of John Paul Jones*, p. 31.
9. Ibid., p. 34.
10. Samuel Eliot Morison, *John Paul Jones: A Sailor's Biography* (Naval Institute Press, 1999, first published 1959), p. 205.
11. Ibid., p. 238.
12. John Buchanan, *Jackson's Way*, p. 322.
13. Chidsey, *The American Privateers*, p. 15.
14. Donald A. Petrie, *The Prize Game: Lawful Looting on the High Seas in the Days of Fighting Sail* (Naval Institute Press, 1999), pp. 40–41.
15. Chidsey, *The American Privateers*, p. 10.
16. Stivers, *Privateers and Volunteers*, p. 61.
17. Chidsey, *The American Privateers*, pp. 53–54.
18. Petrie, *The Prize Game*, p. 166.
19. Chidsey, *The American Privateers*, p. 71.
20. Ibid., p. 79.
21. Henry Adams, *The War of 1812*, p. 159.
22. Stivers, *Privateers and Volunteers*, p. 58.
23. Robert J. Brugger, *Maryland: A Middle Temperament 1634- 1980* (Johns Hopkins University Press, 1988).
24. Larabee, *America and the Sea: A Maritime History*, p. 223.
25. Stivers, *Privateers and Volunteers*, p. 109.
26. Ibid., p. 110.
27. Gerald T. Altoff, *Amongst My Best Men*, p. 29.
28. Ibid., p. 30.
29. Nicholas Tracy, ed., *The Naval Chronicle*, Vol. V, p. 168.
30. See Chidsey, *The American Privateers*, for the text of the contract governing the privateer.
31. Chidsey, *The American Privateers*, p. 93.
32. Adams, *The War of 1812*, p. 153.
33. Thomas C. Gillmer, *Pride of Baltimore: The Story of the Baltimore Clippers* (International Marine, 1992).

34. Adams, *The War of 1812*, pp. 153–54.
35. Gardiner, *The Naval War of 1812*, p. 65.
36. Gillmer, *Pride of Baltimore*, p. 36.
37. Ibid., p. 26.
38. Ibid., pp. 29, 38.
39. Chidsey, *The American Privateers*, pp. 115–16.
40. Larabee, *America and the Sea: A Maritime History*, p. 223.
41. Lavery, *Nelson's Navy*.
42. Larabee, *America and the Sea: A Maritime History*, pp. 225–26.
43. Tracy, ed., *The Naval Chronicle*, Vol. V, p. 237.
44. Stivers, *Privateers and Volunteers*, p. 56.
45. Tracy, ed., *The Naval Chronicle*, Vol. V, p. 237.
46. Adams, *The War of 1812*, p. 155.
47. F. Alexander Magoun, *The Frigate Constitution and Other Historic Ships*, p. 108.
48. Stivers, *Privateers and Volunteers*, p. 77.
49. Chidsey, *The American Privateers*, p. 4.
50. Ibid., p. 6.
51. Theodore Roosevelt, *The Naval War of 1812*, p. 187.
52. Chidsey, *The American Privateers*, p. 7.
53. Roosevelt, *The Naval War of 1812*, p. 188.
54. Beach, *The United States Navy: 200 Years*, p. 137.
55. Gillmer, *Pride of Baltimore*, p. 82.
56. Stivers, *Privateers and Volunteers*, p. 60.
57. Adams, *The War of 1812*, p. 160.
58. Gardiner, *The Naval War of 1812*, p. 67.
59. Adams, *The War of 1812*, p. 161.
60. Stivers, *Privateers and Volunteers*, pp. 116–17.
61. Adams, *The War of 1812*, p. 161.
62. Stivers, *Privateers and Volunteers*, p. 61.
63. Altoff, *Amongst My Best Men*, p. 28.

CHAPTER EIGHTEEN

1. Henry Adams, *The War of 1812*, p. 85.
2. Ibid.
3. Ibid., p. 90.

4. John R. Elting, *Amateurs to Arms*, p. 135.
5. Robert Allen Rutland, *The Presidency of James Madison* (University Press of Kansas, 1990), p. 122.
6. Elting, *Amateurs to Arms*, p. 119.
7. Ibid., p. 3.
8. David S. Heidler and Jeanne T. Heidler, eds., *Encyclopedia of The War of 1812* (Naval Institute Press, 1997), p. 555.
9. Elting, *Amateurs to Arms*, p. 141.
10. Ibid., p. 59.
11. Donald R. Hickey, *The War of 1812*, p. 144.
12. Adams, *The War of 1812*, p. 91.
13. Elting, *Amateurs to Arms*, p. 136.
14. Ibid.
15. Hickey, *The War of 1812*, p. 106.
16. Ibid.
17. Rutland, *The Presidency of James Madison*, pp. 149–50.
18. Hickey, *The War of 1812*, p. 145.
19. J. Mackay Hitsman, *The Incredible War of 1812*, p. 188.
20. Elting, *Amateurs to Arms*, p. 146.
21. Ibid., p. 147.
22. Ibid.
23. Hitsman, *The Incredible War of 1812*, p. 189.
24. Adams, *The War of 1812*, p. 86.
25. Ibid., p. 99.
26. Elting, *Amateurs to Arms*, p. 150.
27. Hitsman, *The Incredible War of 1812*, p. 192.
28. Elting, *Amateurs to Arms*, p. 175.
29. Ibid., p. 177.
30. Walter Lord, *The Dawn's Early Light* (W.W. Norton & Company, 1972), p. 33.
31. Hitsman, *The Incredible War of 1812*, p. 214.
32. Ibid.
33. Elting, *Amateurs to Arms*, pp. 154–55.
34. John S. D. Eisenhower, *Agent of Destiny*, p. 78.
35. Elting, *Amateurs to Arms*, p. 180.
36. Eisenhower, *Agent of Destiny*, p. 78.
37. For alternative views on this issue see Hickey, *The War of 1812*, p. 185;

and Elting, *Amateurs to Arms*, p. 187.

38. Elting, *Amateurs to Arms*, p. 181.
39. Adams, *The War of 1812*, p. 176.
40. Elting, *Amateurs to Arms*, p. 182.
41. Ibid., p. 186.
42. Adams, *The War of 1812*, p. 176.
43. Elting, *Amateurs to Arms*, p. 186.
44. Adams, *The War of 1812*, p. 178.
45. Ibid., p. 179.
46. Ibid., p. 183.
47. Elting, *Amateurs to Arms*, p. 194.
48. Hitsman, *The Incredible War of 1812*, p. 229.
49. Adams, *The War of 1812*, p. 188.
50. Elting, *Amateurs to Arms*, p. 197.
51. Adams, *The War of 1812*, p. 187.
52. Ibid., p. 194.
53. Hickey, *The War of 1812*, p. 189.
54. Ibid.
55. Adams, *The War of 1812*, p. 196.
56. Ibid., p. 197.

CHAPTER NINETEEN

1. Donald R. Hickey, *The War of 1812*, p. 282.
2. Henry Adams, *The War of 1812*, p. 8.
3. Hickey, *The War of 1812*, p. 283.
4. Ibid., p. 285.
5. Ibid., p. 289.
6. David Curtis Skaggs, *Thomas Macdonough: Master of Command in the Early U.S. Navy* (Naval Institute Press, 2003), p. 99.
7. Victor Suthren, *The War of 1812* (Galafilm Inc., 1999), p. 240.
8. John R. Elting, *Amateurs to Arms*, p. 282.
9. See Eliot A. Cohen, *Two Centuries of Battles Along the Great Warpath That Made the American Way of War* (Free Press, 2012).
10. C. S. Forester, *The Age of Fighting Sail*, pp. 233–34.
11. Hickey, *The War of 1812*, p. 143.
12. Edward K. Eckert, "Thomas Macdonough: Architect of a Wilderness

Navy," in James C. Bradford, ed., *Command Under Sail: Makers of the American Naval Tradition 1775-1850* (Naval Institute Press, 1985), p. 150.

13. Ibid., p. 152.
14. Ibid., p. 155.
15. Ibid., p. 156.
16. Skaggs, *Thomas Macdonough: Master of Command in the Early U.S. Navy*, p. 53.
17. Ibid., p. 55.
18. Ibid., p. 57.
19. Eckert, "Thomas Macdonough: Architect of a Wilderness Navy," p. 157.
20. Skaggs, *Thomas Macdonough*, p. 69.
21. Hickey, *The War of 1812*, p. 144.
22. J. Mackay Hitsman, *The Incredible War of 1812*, p. 161.
23. Ibid.
24. Ibid.
25. William S. Dudley, *The Naval War of 1812: A Documentary History*, Vol. II, p. 513.
26. Eckert, "Thomas Macdonough: Architect of a Wilderness Navy," p. 158.
27. Theodore Roosevelt, *The Naval War of 1812*, p. 197.
28. Skaggs, *Thomas Macdonough*, p. 95.
29. Ibid., p. 97.
30. Ibid.
31. Hitsman, *The Incredible War of 1812*, p. 252.
32. Ibid., pp. 214–15.
33. Roosevelt, *The Naval War of 1812*, p. 197.
34. Hitsman, *The Incredible War of 1812*, p. 250.
35. Adams, *The War of 1812*, p. 202.
36. Ibid., p. 204.
37. Hitsman, *The Incredible War of 1812*, p. 254.
38. Suthren, *The War of 1812*, p. 240.
39. Ibid., p. 255.
40. Hitsman, *The Incredible War of 1812*, p. 254.
41. Ibid.
42. Ibid.
43. Suthren, *The War of 1812*, p. 240.
44. Adams, *The War of 1812*, pp. 205–6.

45. Ibid., p. 205.
46. Hitsman, *The Incredible War of 1812*, p. 254.
47. Skaggs, *Thomas Macdonough*, p. 114.
48. Ibid., p. 123.
49. Adams, *The War of 1812*, p. 207.
50. Skaggs, *Thomas Macdonough*, p. 114.
51. As reproduced in Ibid., pp. 119–20.
52. Ibid., p. 118.
53. Ibid., p. 119.
54. David G. Fitz-Enz, (Col.), *The Final Invasion: Plattsburgh: The War of 1812's Most Decisive Battle* (Cooper Square Press, 2001), p. 99.
55. Ibid.
56. Skaggs, *Thomas Macdonough*, p. 118.
57. Roosevelt, *The Naval War of 1812*, p. 214.
58. Ibid., pp. 208, 210.
59. Skaggs, *Thomas Macdonough*, p. 127.
60. Ibid., p. 214.
61. James Fenimore Cooper, *The History of the Navy of the United States of America*, p. 410.
62. Fitz-Enz, *The Final Invasion*, p. 156.
63. Skaggs, *Thomas Macdonough*, p. 129.
64. Fitz-Enz, *The Final Invasion*, p. 153.
65. Cooper, *The History of the Navy of the United States of America*, p. 416.
66. Fitz-Enz, *The Final Invasion*, p. 156.
67. Roosevelt, *The Naval War of 1812*, p. 217.
68. Cooper, *The History of the Navy of the United States of America*, p. 411.
69. Fitz-Enz, *The Final Invasion*, p. 160.
70. Hitsman, *The Incredible War of 1812*, 261
71. Fitz-Enz, *The Final Invasion*, 161
72. Eckert, "Thomas Macdonough: Architect of a Wilderness Navy," pp. 147–48.
73. Hitsman, *The Incredible War of 1812*, p. 262.
74. Adams, *The War of 1812*, p. 211.
75. Ibid., p. 263.
76. Roosevelt, *The Naval War of 1812*, p. 218.
77. Ibid.
78. Ibid., p. 219.

79. Skaggs, *Thomas Macdonough: Master of Command in the Early U.S. Navy*, pp. 134–35.
80. Eckert, "Thomas Macdonough: Architect of a Wilderness Navy," p. 164.
81. Forester, *The Age of Fighting Sail*, p. 244.
82. G. J. Marcus, *A Naval History of England, 2*, p. 481.
83. Hitsman, *The Incredible War of 1812*, p. 263.
84. Adams, *The War of 1812*, p. 211.
85. Suthren, *The War of 1812*, p. 246.
86. Ibid., p. 264.
87. Nicholas Tracy, ed., *The Naval Chronicle: The Contemporary Record of the Royal Navy at War*, Vol. V, p. 263.
88. Hitsman, *The Incredible War of 1812*, p. 267.
89. Skaggs, *Thomas Macdonough*, p. 145.
90. Hickey, *The War of 1812*, p. 193.
91. Roosevelt, *The Naval War of 1812*, p. 219.
92. Tracy, ed., *The Naval Chronicle*, Vol. V, p. 2263.

CHAPTER TWENTY

1. J. Mackay Hitsman, *The Incredible War of 1812*, p. 289.
2. Ibid., p. 240.
3. John R. Elting, *Amateurs to Arms*, p. 267.
4. Donald R. Hickey, *Don't Give Up the Ship!*, p. 92; and Hitsman, *The Incredible War of 1812*, p. 248.
5. Reginald Horsman, *The War of 1812*, p. 162.
6. Elting, *Amateurs to Arms*, p. 269.
7. Walter Lord, *The Dawn's Early Light* (W.W. Norton & Company, 1972), p. 37.
8. Hitsman, *The Incredible War of 1812*, p. 237.
9. Nicholas Tracy, ed., *The Naval Chronicle: The Contemporary Record of the Royal Navy at War*, Vol. V, p. 209.
10. Hitsman, *The Incredible War of 1812*, p. 237.
11. John K. Mahon, *The War of 1812*, p. 312.
12. Hitsman, *The Incredible War of 1812*, p. 238.
13. Elting, *Amateurs to Arms*, pp. 201–2.
14. Mahon, *The War of 1812*, p. 293.
15. Ibid.

16. Lord, *The Dawn's Early Light*, p. 38.
17. Ibid.
18. Ibid., p. 19.
19. Ibid., p. 20.
20. Ibid., pp. 81, 82.
21. Richard Dillon, *We Have Met the Enemy*.
22. Donald R. Hickey, *The Rocket's Red Glare* (Johns Hopkins University Press, 2011), p. 148.
23. Lord, *The Dawn's Early Light*, p. 111.
24. Anthony S. Pitch, *The Burning of Washington: The British Invasion of 1814* (Naval Institute Press, 1998), p. 34.
25. Elting, *Amateurs to Arms*, p. 210.
26. Ibid., pp. 212–13.
27. Ibid., p. 214.
28. Mahon, *The War of 1812*, p. 299.
29. Pitch, *The Burning of Washington*, p. 66.
30. Lord, *The Dawn's Early Light*, p. 110.
31. Mahon, *The War of 1812*, p. 299.
32. Elting, *Amateurs to Arms*, p. 216.
33. Lord, *The Dawn's Early Light*, p. 126.
34. Pitch, *The Burning of Washington*, p. 83.
35. Adams, *The War of 1812*, pp. 225–26.
36. Lord, *The Dawn's Early Light*, pp. 138–39.
37. Michael J. Crawford, ed., *The Naval War of 1812: A Documentary History*, Vol. III (Naval Historical Center, 2002), p. 208.
38. Pitch, *The Burning of Washington*, p. 87.
39. Lord, *The Dawn's Early Light*, p. 151.
40. Mahon, *The War of 1812*, p. 299.
41. Adams, *The War of 1812*, p. 229.
42. Elting, *Amateurs to Arms*, p. 219.
43. Lord, *The Dawn's Early Light*, p. 162.
44. Pitch, *The Burning of Washington*, p. 109.
45. Nicholas Tracy, ed., *The Naval Chronicle: The Contemporary Record of the Royal Navy at War*, Vol. V, p. 242.
46. Lord, *The Dawn's Early Light*, p. 169.
47. Pitch, *The Burning of Washington*, p. 122.
48. Ibid., p. 133.

49. Ibid., p. 148.
50. Lord, *The Dawn's Early Light*, p. 225.
51. Mahon, *The War of 1812*, p. 307.
52. Ibid., p. 303.
53. Lord, *The Dawn's Early Light*, p. 55.
54. Christopher T. George, *Terror on the Chesapeake*, p. 29.
55. Mahon, *The War of 1812*, p. 304.
56. Elting, *Amateurs to Arms*, p. 229.
57. Mahon, *The War of 1812*, p. 304.
58. Lord, *The Dawn's Early Light*, p. 210.
59. Pitch, *The Burning of Washington*, p. 104.
60. Mahon, *The War of 1812*, p. 310.
61. Hitsman, *The Incredible War of 1812*, p. 244.
62. Crawford, ed., *The Naval War of 1812: A Documentary History*, Vol. III, p. 140.
63. Adams, *The War of 1812*, p. 217.
64. Tracy, ed., *The Naval Chronicle: The Contemporary Record of the Royal Navy at War*, Vol. V, p. 241.
65. Ibid., p. 242.
66. Mahon, *The War of 1812*, p. 307.
67. Ibid., p. 308.
68. Lord, *The Dawn's Early Light*, p. 274.
69. Irvin Molotsky, *The Flag, the Poet & the Song: The Story of the Star-Spangled Banner* (Dutton, 2001), pp. 73–74.
70. Ibid., p. 88.
71. Adams, *The War of 1812*, p. 236.
72. Elting, *Amateurs to Arms*, p. 230.
73. Pitch, *The Burning of Washington*, p. 185.
74. Adams, *The War of 1812*, p. 236.
75. Molotsky, *The Flag, the Poet & the Song*, p. 118.
76. Adams, *The War of 1812*, p. 237.
77. Elting, *Amateurs to Arms*, p. 241.
78. Ibid., p. 242.
79. Adams, *The War of 1812*, p. 237.
80. Marcus, *A Naval History of England*, pp. 2, 477.
81. Mahon, *The War of 1812*, p. 311.

82. William M. Marine, *The British Invasion of Maryland*, p. 129.
83. Tracy, ed., *The Naval Chronicle: The Contemporary Record of the Royal Navy at War*, Vol. V, p. 244.
84. Molotsky, *The Flag, the Poet & the Song*, p. 95.
85. Lord, *The Dawn's Early Light*, pp. 296–97.
86. Adams, *The War of 1812*, p. 237.
87. Horsman, *The War of 1812*, p. 233.
88. Adams, *The War of 1812*, p. 339.
89. Ibid., p. 341.
90. Hickey, *The War of 1812*, p. 303.
91. Adams, *The War of 1812*, p. 338.
92. Ibid.
93. Ibid., p. 339.
94. Ibid., p. 341.
95. Forester, *The Age of Fight*

CHAPTER TWENTY-ONE

1. Spencer Tucker, *Stephen Decatur: A Life Most Bold and Daring*, p. 133.
2. Robert Gardiner, *Warships of the Napoleonic Era*, pp. 55, 107.
3. John K. Mahon, *The War of 1812*, p. 249.
4. Henry Adams, *The War of 1812*, p. 129.
5. Tyrone G. Martin, *A Most Fortunate Ship*, p. 181.
6. Theodore Roosevelt, *The Naval War of 1812*, p. 160.
7. Martin, *A Most Fortunate Ship*, p. 188.
8. Roosevelt, *The Naval War of 1812*, p. 172.
9. James Fenimore Cooper, *The History of the Navy of the United States of America*, pp. 324–25.
10. William James writes that it was Jamaica. See William James, *Naval Occurrences of the War of 1812* (Conway Maritime Press, 2004), p. 171.
11. Ibid., pp. 171–73.
12. Jeanne T. Heidler, *Encyclopedia of The War of 1812*, p. 543.
13. Roosevelt, *The Naval War of 1812*, p. 178.
14. Ibid., p. 179.
15. James, *Naval Occurrences of the War of 1812*, p. 177.
16. Roosevelt, *The Naval War of 1812*, p. 179.
17. Nicholas Tracy, ed., *The Naval Chronicle: The Contemporary Record of*

the Royal Navy at War, Vol. V, p. 245.

18. James, *Naval Occurrences of the War of 1812*, p. 178.
19. Tracy, ed., *The Naval Chronicle*, Vol. V, p. 245.
20. Roosevelt, *The Naval War of 1812*, p. 182.
21. Ibid.
22. Tracy, ed., *The Naval Chronicle*, Vol. V, p. 237.
23. Martin, *A Most Fortunate Ship*, p. 191.
24. Alexander Slidell Mackenzie, *Life of Stephen Decatur*, p. 210.
25. Roosevelt, *The Naval War of 1812*, p. 189.
26. Ibid.
27. Mackenzie, *Life of Stephen Decatur*, p. 211.
28. Ibid., p. 212.
29. James, *Naval Occurrences of the War of 1812*, p. 214.
30. Mackenzie, *Life of Stephen Decatur*, p. 217.
31. Tucker, *Stephen Decatur*, p. 144.
32. Ibid.
33. Mackenzie, *Life of Stephen Decatur*, p. 219.
34. C. S. Forester, *The Age of Fighting Sail*, p. 263.
35. Tucker, *Stephen Decatur*, p. 145.
36. James, *Naval Occurrences of the War of 1812*, p. 214.
37. Mackenzie, *Life of Stephen Decatur*, p. 226.
38. Ibid., p. 227.
39. Roosevelt, *The Naval War of 1812*, p. 224.
40. Tucker, *Stephen Decatur*, p. 147.
41. Ibid., p. 151.
42. Assheton Humphreys, *The USS Constitution's Finest Fight, 1815: The Journal of Acting Chaplain Assheton Humphreys, US Navy*, ed. by Tyrone G. Martin (The Nautical & Aviation Publishing Company of America, 2000), pp. 10–11.
43. Ibid., pp. 15–16.
44. Ibid., p. 20.
45. Ibid., pp. 25–26.
46. Martin, *A Most Fortunate Ship*, p. 195.
47. Ibid., p. 27.
48. Roosevelt, *The Naval War of 1812*, p. 231.
49. Martin, *A Most Fortunate Ship*, p. 196.
50. Cooper, *The History of the Navy of the United States of America*, p. 423.

51. Roosevelt, *The Naval War of 1812*, p. 232.
52. Tracy, ed., *The Naval Chronicle: The Contemporary Record of the Royal Navy at War*, Vol. V, p. 288.
53. Cooper, *The History of the Navy of the United States of America*, p. 424.
54. Humphreys, *The USS Constitution's Finest Fight*, p. 30.
55. Martin, *A Most Fortunate Ship*, p. 199.
56. Ibid., p. 201.
57. Humphreys, *The USS Constitution's Finest Fight*, p. 31.
58. Martin, *A Most Fortunate Ship*, p. 202.
59. Ibid., p. 205.
60. Cooper, *The History of the Navy of the United States of America*, p. 425.
61. Roosevelt, *The Naval War of 1812*, pp. 232–23.
62. Martin, *A Most Fortunate Ship*, p. 200.
63. Adams, *The War of 1812*, pp. 354–55.
64. Martin, *A Most Fortunate Ship*, p. 200.
65. C. F. Adams, "Wednesday August 19, 1812, 6:30 PM The Birth of a World Power," in *American Historical Review* 18 (April 1913), p. 520.
66. James, *Naval Occurrences of the War of 1812*, p. 234.
67. Roosevelt, *The Naval War of 1812*, p. 237.
68. Cooper, *The History of the Navy of the United States of America*, p. 437.
69. Tracy, ed., *The Naval Chronicle: The Contemporary Record of the Royal Navy at War*, Vol. V, p. 293.
70. Cooper, *The History of the Navy of the United States of America*, p. 438.

CHAPTER TWENTY-TWO

1. John K. Mahon, *The War of 1812*, p. 339.
2. John Buchanan, *Jackson's Way*, p. 313.
3. Ibid., p. 304.
4. Walter Lord, *The Dawn's Early Light*, p. 324.
5. Buchanan, *Jackson's Way*, p. 305.
6. Mahon, *The War of 1812*, p. 350.
7. Ibid., p. 352.
8. Buchanan, *Jackson's Way*, p. 318.
9. Ibid., p. 319.
10. Mahon, *The War of 1812*, pp. 358, 361.
11. Theodore Roosevelt, *The Naval War of 1812*, p. 255.

12. Ibid., p. 253.
13. Buchanan, *Jackson's Way*, p. 329.
14. Ibid., p. 330.
15. Mahon, *The War of 1812*, p. 351.
16. Buchanan, *Jackson's Way*, p. 338.
17. Roosevelt, *The Naval War of 1812*, p. 258.
18. Mahon, *The War of 1812*, p. 359.
19. Ibid.
20. Buchanan, *Jackson's Way*, p. 341.
21. Ibid.
22. Roosevelt, *The Naval War of 1812*, p. 255.
23. Mahon, *The War of 1812*, p. 360.
24. Ibid., p. 364.
25. Harry L. Coles, *The War of 1812*, p. 222.
26. Ibid., p. 229.
27. Ibid.
28. Buchanan, *Jackson's Way*, p. 357.
29. Coles, *The War of 1812*, p. 231.
30. Buchanan, *Jackson's Way*, p. 361.
31. Tracy, ed., *The Naval Chronicle: The Contemporary Record of the Royal Navy at War*, Vol. V, pp. 281–82.
32. Mahon, *The War of 1812*, p. 365.
33. Adams, *The War of 1812*, p. 347.
34. Ibid.
35. Ibid., p. 348.
36. Lord, *The Dawn's Early Light*, p. 338.
37. Donald R. Hickey, *The War of 1812*, p. 298.
38. George Johnston, *History of Cecil County, Maryland*, p. 423.

BIBLIOGRAPHY

Adams, Charles Francis. "Wednesday, August 19, 1812, 6:30 PM, The Birth of a World Power." *American Historical Review* 18, no. 3 (1913): 513–21.

Adams, Henry. *The War of 1812.* New York: Cooper Square, 1999.

Albion, Robert Greenhalgh. *Forests and Sea Power: The Timber Problem of the Royal Navy, 1652–1862.* 1926. Reprinted as *Classics of Naval Literature.* Annapolis, MD: Naval Institute Press, 2000.

Altoff, Gerald T. *Amongst My Best Men: African-Americans and the War of 1812.* Put-in- Bay, OH: The Perry Group, 1996.

———. *Oliver Hazard Perry and the Battle of Lake Erie*, Put-in-Bay, OH: The Perry Group, 1999.

Anthony, Irvin. *Decatur.* New York: Charles Scribner's Sons, 1931.

Appleby, Joyce. *Inheriting the Revolution: The First Generation of Americans.* Cambridge, MA: Belknap Press of Harvard University Press, 2000.

Astor, Gerald. *The Right to Fight: A History of African Americans in the Military.* Cambridge, MA: Da Capo, 2001.

Bailey, Thomas A. *A Diplomatic History of the American People.* 3rd ed. New York: F. S. Crofts & Co., 1947.

Bancroft, George. *Oliver Hazard Perry and the Battle of Lake Erie.* Newport, RI: Mercury Publishing Company, 1912.

Beach, Edward L. *The United States Navy: 200 Years.* New York: Henry Holt, 1986.

Beard, Charles A., and Mary R. Beard. *The Rise of American Civilization.* New York: Macmillan, 1930.

Bernier, Olivier. *The World in 1800.* New York: Wiley, 2000.

Berton, Pierre. *The Invasion of Canada: 1812–1813.* Canada: Anchor Canada, 1980, 2000.

Berube, Claude, and John Rodgaard. *A Call to the Sea: Captain Charles Stewart of the USS* Constitution. Washington, DC: Potomac, 2005.

Birindelli, Ben. *The 200 Year Legacy of Stephen Decatur, 1798–1998.* Gloucester Point, VA: Hallmark, 1998.

Bolster, W. Jeffrey. *Black Jacks: African American Seaman in the Age of Sail.* Cambridge, MA: Harvard University Press, 1997.

———. "To Feel Like a Man: Black Seamen in the Northern States, 1800–1860." *Journal of American History* 76, no. 4 (1990).

Borneman, Walter R. *1812: The War that Forged a Nation.* New York: HarperCollins, 2004.

Braider, Donald. *Solitary Star: A Biography of Sam Houston.* New York: Putnam, 1974.

Brannan, John, ed. *Official Letters of the Military and Naval Officers of the United States During the War with Great Britain in the Years 1812, 13, 14 & 15 With Some Additional Letters and Documents Elucidating the History of that Period.* Washington, DC: 1823.

Brugger, Robert J. *Maryland: A Middle Temperament, 1634–1980.* Baltimore: Johns Hopkins University Press, 1988.

Buchanan, John. *Jackson's Way: Andrew Jackson and the People of the Western Waters.* New York: Wiley, 2001.

Buckley, Gail. *American Patriots: The Story of Blacks in the Military from the Revolution to Desert Storm.* New York: Random House, 2001.

Budiansky, Stephen. *Perilous Fight: America's Intrepid War with Britain on the High Seas, 1812–1815.* New York: Knopf, 2010.

Burrows, Edwin G., and Mike Wallace. *Gotham: A History of New York City to 1898*. New York: Oxford University Press, 1999.

Cary, Emily Pritchard. "The Flag that Helped Captain Perry Win the Battle of Lake Erie in 1813." *Pennsylvania* 7, no. 4 (April 1988).

Chant, Christopher. *The Military History of the United States: Limited Wars*. Tarrytown, NY: Marshall Cavendish, 1992.

Chidsey, Donald Barr. *The American Privateers*. New York: Dodd, Mead, 1962.

Coles, Henry L. *The War of 1812*. Chicago: University of Chicago Press, 1965.

Cooke, Timothy, ed. *History of the Modern World: Revolution and Change*. Tarrytown, NY: Marshall Cavendish, 2000.

Cooper, James Fenimore. *The History of the Navy of the United States of America*. Annapolis, MD: Naval Institute Press, 2001.

Cordingly, David. *Women Sailors and Sailor's Women: An Untold Maritime History*. New York: Random House, 2001.

Crawford, Michael J., ed. *The Naval War of 1812: A Documentary History*. Vol. III. Washington, DC: Naval Historical Center, 2002.

Davis, William. *The Pirates Lafite: The Treacherous World of the Corsairs of the Gulf*. New York: Harcourt, 2005.

DeKay, James Tertius. *Chronicles of the Frigate* Macedonian *1809–1922*. New York: Norton, 1995.

Dillon, Richard. *We Have Met the Enemy: Oliver Hazard Perry: Wilderness Commodore*. New York: McGraw Hill, 1978.

Donovan, Frank. *The Tall Frigates*. New York: Dodd, Mead, 1962.

Dudley, William S., ed. *The Naval War of 1812: A Documentary History*. 2 vols. Washington, DC: Naval Historical Center, 1985, 1992.

Duffy, Stephen W. H. *Captain Blakley and the* Wasp*: The Cruise of 1814*. Annapolis, MD: Naval Institute Press, 2000.

Durand, James R. *Life and Adventures of James R. Durand: During a Period of Fifteen Years, from 1801–1816, In which time he was Impressed on Board the British*. Carlisle, MA: Applewood, 2005.

Dye, Ira. *The Fatal Cruise of the* Argus*: Two Captains in the War of 1812*. Annapolis, MD: Naval Institute Press, 1994.

Eckert, Edward K. "Thomas Macdonough: Architect of a Wilderness Navy." In *Command Under Sail: Makers of the American Naval Tradition, 1775–1850*, edited by James C. Bradford. Annapolis, MD: Naval Institute Press, 1985.

Eisenhower, John S. D. *Agent of Destiny: The Life and Times of General Winfield Scott*. New York: Free Press, 1997.

Elting, John R. *Amateurs, To Arms! A Military History of the War of 1812*. Chapel Hill, NC: Algonquin, 1991.

Endel, Rufus. *Dartmoor Prison*. St. Teath, UK: Bossiney Books, 1979.

Farragut, Loyall. *Life of David Glasgow Farragut*. New York: D. Appleton, 1882.

Fitz-Enz, David G. *The Final Invasion: Plattsburgh, The War of 1812's Most Decisive Battle*. New York: Cooper Square, 2001.

Fitzpatrick, Donovan, and Saul Saphire. *Navy Maverick: Uriah Phillips Levy*. New York: Doubleday, 1963.

Fleming, Thomas. *Liberty! The American Revolution*. New York: Viking, 1997.

Footner, Geoffrey. *USS* Constellation*: From Frigate to Sloop of War*. Annapolis, MD: Naval Institute Press, 2003.

Forester, C. S. *The Age of Fighting Sail: The Story of the Naval War of 1812*. New York: Doubleday, 1956.

Furnas, J. C. *The Americans: A Social History of the United States 1587–1914*. New York: Putnam, 1969.

Gardiner, Robert, ed. *The Naval War of 1812*. Annapolis, MD: Naval Institute Press, 1998.

———. *Warships of the Napoleonic Era*. Annapolis, MD: Naval Institute Press, 1999.

Geiringer, Karl. *Haydn: A Creative Life in Music*. London: George Allen & Unwin, 1947.

George, Christopher T. *Terror on the Chesapeake: The War of 1812 on the Bay*. Shippensburg, PA: White Mane Books, 2000.

Gilkerson, William. *The Ships of John Paul Jones*. Annapolis, MD: U.S. Naval Academy Museum, 1987.

Gillmer, Thomas C. *Pride of Baltimore: The Story of the Baltimore Clippers*. Camden, ME: International Marine, 1992.

Gough, Barry. *Fighting Sail on Lake Huron and Georgian Bay*. Annapolis, MD: Naval Institute Press, 2002.

Gruppe, Henry. *The Frigates*. New York: Time-Life Books, 1979.

Hanks, Jarvis, Amasiah Ford, and Alexander McCullen. *Soldiers of 1814: American Enlisted Men's Memoirs of the Niagara Campaign*. Edited by Donald E. Graves. Youngstown, NY: Old Fort Niagara Association, 1995.

Harvey, Robert. *Cochrane: The Life and Exploits of a Fighting Captain*. New York: Carroll & Graf, 2000.

Hatfield, Mark O. *Vice Presidents of the United States: 1789–1993*, edited by Wendy Wolff. Washington, DC: U.S. Senate Historical Office, 1997.

Haythornthwaite, Philip. *Nelson's Navy*. Oxford, UK: Osprey Publishing, 1993.

Heidler, David S., and Jeanne T. Heidler, eds. *Encyclopedia of the War of 1812*. Annapolis, MD: Naval Institute Press, 1997.

Henderson, James. *The Frigates*. Chatham, UK: Wordsworth, 1970.

Hickey, Donald R. *The War of 1812: A Forgotten Conflict*. Urbana, IL: University of Illinois Press, 1990.

———. *Don't Give Up the Ship: Myths of the War of 1812*. Urbana, IL: University of Illinois Press, 2006.

———, and Connie D. Clark. *The Rockets' Red Glare: An Illustrated History of The War of 1812*. Baltimore: Johns Hopkins University Press, 2011.

Hitchens, Christopher. "The Medals of His Defeats." *Atlantic Monthly* (April 2002): 118– 37.

Hitsman, J. Mackay. *The Incredible War of 1812*. Rev. ed. Toronto: University of Toronto Press, 1999.

Horsman, Reginald. *Causes of the War of 1812*. New York: Barnes, 1961.

———. *The War of 1812*. New York: Knopf, 1972.

Hunt, Gaillard. *As We Were: Life in America 1814*. Stockbridge, MA: Berkshire House, 1993.

Icenhower, Joseph. *American Sea Heroes*. Maplewood, NJ: Hammond, 1970.

Inderwick, James. *Cruise of the U.S. Brig* Argus, *1813*. New York: New York Public Library, 1917.

Ireland, Bernard. *Naval Warfare in the Age of Sail: War at Sea, 1756–1815*. New York: Norton, 2000.

James, William. *Naval Occurrences of the War of 1812*. London: Conway Maritime Press, 2004.

Johnston, George. *History of Cecil County, Maryland*. Baltimore: Regional Publishing, 1972.

Kessner, Thomas. *Capital City: New York City and the Men Behind America's Rise to Economic Dominance, 1860–1900*. New York: Simon & Schuster, 2003.

Lambert, Andrew. *War at Sea in the Age of Sail*. London: Cassell, 2000.

Langguth, A. J. *Union 1812: The Americans who Fought the Second War of Independence*. New York: Simon & Schuster, 2006.

Larabee, Benjamin, et. al. *America and the Sea: A Maritime History*. Mystic, CT: Mystic Seaport Museum, 1998.

Latimer, Jon. *1812: War with America*. Cambridge, MA: Belknap Press of Harvard University Press, 2007.

Lavery, Brian. *Nelson's Navy: The Ships, Men and Organization*. Annapolis, MD: Naval Institute Press, 1994.

Leech, Samuel. *A Voice from the Main Deck: Being a Record of the Thirty Years Adventures of Samuel Leech*. London: Chatham, 1999.

Leiner, Frederick C. *Millions for Defense: The Subscription Warships of 1798*. Annapolis, MD: Naval Institute Press, 2000.

Lewis, Charles Lee. *Famous American Naval Officers*. Essay Index Reprint Series (1924, 1945). New York: Farrar Strauss, 1971.

Lewis, Jon E., ed. *Life Before the Mast: An Anthology of Eye Witness Accounts from the Age of Fighting Sail*. New York: Carroll & Graf, 2001.

Lofaro, Michael A. *The Life and Adventures of Daniel Boone*. Lexington, KY: University Press of Kentucky, 1986.

London, Joshua E. *Victory in Tripoli*. Hoboken, NJ: Wiley, 2005.

Long, David F. "David Porter: Pacific Ocean Gadfly." In *Command Under Sail: Makers of the American Naval Tradition, 1775–1850*. Edited by James C. Bradford. Annapolis, MD: Naval Institute Press, 1985.

Longridge, C. Nepean. *The Anatomy of Nelson's Ships*. Hertfordshire, UK: Nexus Special Interests, 1961.

Lord, Walter. *The Dawn's Early Light*. New York: Norton, 1972.

Lossing, Benson J. *Pictorial Field Book of the War of 1812.* 2 vols. Gretna, UK: Firebird, 2003.

Luxon, Norval Neil. *Niles Weekly Register: News Magazine of the Nineteenth Century*. Westport, CT: Greenwood, 1970.

Mackay, Charles. *Extraordinary Popular Delusions and the Madness of Crowds.* New York: Harmony Books, 1980. First published 1841.

Mackenzie, Alexander Slidell. *Life of Stephen Decatur: A Commodore in the Navy of the United States*, Boston: Little, Brown, 1848.

———. *The Life of Commodore Oliver Hazard Perry*. 2 vols. New York: Harper & Bros., 1840.

Magoun, F. Alexander. *The Frigate* Constitution *and Other Historic Ships*. New York: Dover, 1987. First published 1927.

Mahan, Alfred Thayer. *Admiral Farragut*. New York: Appleton, 1892.

———. *Sea Power in its Relation to the War of 1812.* 2 vols. Boston: Little, Brown, 1905.

Mahon, John K. *The War of 1812*. Gainesville, FL: University of Florida Press, 1972.

———. "Oliver Hazard Perry: Savior of the Northwest." In *Command Under Sail: Makers of the American Naval Tradition, 1775–1850*. Edited by James C. Bradford. Annapolis, MD: Naval Institute Press, 1985.

Malcomson, Robert. *Warships of the Great Lakes: 1754–1834*. Annapolis, MD: Naval Institute Press, 2001.

Maloney, Linda M. "Isaac Hull: Bulwark of the Sailing Navy." In *Command Under Sail: Makers of the American Naval Tradition, 1775–1850*. Edited by James C. Bradford. Annapolis, MD: Naval Institute Press, 1985.

Marcus, G. J. *A Naval History of England*. Vol. 2, *The Age of Nelson*. London: George Allen & Unwin, 1971.

Marine, William M. *The British Invasion of Maryland, 1812–1815*. Berwyn Heights, MD: Heritage Books, 1998. First published 1899.

Martin, Tyrone G. *A Most Fortunate Ship*. Annapolis, MD: Naval Institute Press, 1997.

———, ed. *The USS* Constitution*'s Finest Fight, 1815: The Journal of Acting Chaplain Assheton Humphreys, U.S. Navy*. Mt. Pleasant, SC: Nautical & Aviation Publishing Co., 2000.

Masefield, John. *Sea Life in Nelson's Time*. London: Sphere, 1972. First published 1905.

Melville, Herman. *White-Jacket, or The World in a Man-of-War*. In *Melville: Redburn, White-Jacket, Moby-Dick*. New York: Modern Library, 1983.

Molotsky, Irvin. *The Flag, the Poet & the Song: The Story of the Star-Spangled Banner*. New York: Dutton, 2001.

Morison, Samuel Eliot. *John Paul Jones: A Sailor's Biography*. New York: Time-Life, 1964. First published 1956.

———. *The Oxford History of the American People*. New York: Oxford University Press, 1965.

Morris Jr., Charles. *The Autobiography of Commodore Charles Morris*. Annapolis, MD: U.S. Naval Institute, 1881.

Murphy, Jack. *History of the U.S. Marines*. Lincoln, NE: Bison Books, 1984.

Nash Jr., Howard P. *The Forgotten Wars: The U.S. Navy in the Quasi-War with France and the Barbary Wars, 1785–1805*. London: A. S. Barnes, 1968.

National Museum of American Jewish Military History. *An American, a Sailor, and a Jew: The Life and Career of Commodore Uriah Phillips Levy, USN (1792–1862)*, Washington, DC: 1997.

Nell, William C. *The Colored Patriots of the American Revolution, with Sketches of Several Distinguished Colored Persons: To Which is Added a Brief Survey of the Condition and Prospects of Colored Americans*. Boston: Publisher unknown, 1855.

O'Brian, Patrick. *Master and Commander*. New York: Norton, 1970.

Padfield, Peter. *Broke and the* Shannon. London: Hodder and Stoughton, 1968.

Parker, Hershel. *Herman Melville: A Biography*. Vol. I, 1819–1851. Baltimore: Johns Hopkins University Press, 1996.

Patton, Robert H. *Patriot Pirates: The Privateer War for Freedom and Fortune in the American Revolution*. New York: Pantheon, 2008.

Paullin, Charles Oscar. *Commodore John Rodgers, 1773–1838*. Annapolis, MD: Naval Institute Press, 1967. First published 1909.

Petrie, Donald A. *The Prize Game: Lawful Looting on the High Seas in the Days of Fighting Sail*. Annapolis, MD: Naval Institute Press, 1999.

Pickett, Albert James. *History of Alabama*. Montgomery, AL: River City Publishing, 2003. First published 1851.

Pitch, Anthony S. *The Burning of Washington: The British Invasion of 1814.* Annapolis, MD: Naval Institute Press, 1998.

Pope, Dudley. *Life in Nelson's Navy*. London: Chatham, 1997.

Pope, Stephen. *Dictionary of the Napoleonic Wars.* New York: Facts on File, 1999.

Porter, David. *Journal of a Cruise.* Annapolis, MD: Naval Institute Press, 1986.

Preston, Antony, David Lyon, and John H. Batchelor. *Navies of the American Revolution.* Upper Saddle River, NJ: Prentice-Hall, 1975.

Quincy, Edmund. *Life of Josiah Quincy of Massachusetts.* Boston: Ticknor and Fields, 1867.

Quincy, Eliza Susan. *Memoir of the Life of Eliza S. M. Quincy*. Boston: J. Wilson & Son, 1861.

Remini, Robert V. *Andrew Jackson and His Indian Wars.* New York: Viking, 2001.

Reuter, Frank T., and Spencer C. Tucker. *Injured Honor: The* Chesapeake-Leopard *Affair.* Annapolis, MD: Naval Institute Press, 1996.

Robotti, Frances Diane, and James Vescovi. *The USS* Essex *and the Birth of the U.S. Navy*. Holbrook, MA: Adams Media, 1999.

Roosevelt, Theodore. *The Naval War of 1812.* New York: Modern Library, 1999.

Rutland, Robert Allen. *The Presidency of James Madison.* Lawrence, KS: University Press of Kansas, 1990.

Schom, Alan. *Trafalgar: Countdown to Battle, 1803–1805.* New York: Atheneum, 1990.

Skaggs, David Curtis. *Thomas Macdonough: Master of Command in the Early U.S. Navy.* Annapolis, MD: Naval Institute Press, 2003.

Smith, Moses. *Naval Scenes in the Last War*. Boston: Gleason's Publishing Hall, 1846.

Stivers, Reuben Elmore. *Privateers and Volunteers.* Annapolis, MD: Naval Institute Press, 1975.

Sugden, John. *Tecumseh: A Life.* New York: Henry Holt, 1997.

Suthren, Victor. *The War of 1812.* Toronto: Galafilm, 1999. CD.

Symonds, Craig. "William S. Bainbridge: Bad Luck or Fatal Flaw?" In *Command Under Sail: Makers of the American Naval Tradition, 1775–1850.* Edited by James C. Bradford. Annapolis, MD: Naval Institute Press, 1985.

Taylor, Alan. *The Civil War of 1812: American Citizens, British Subjects, Irish Rebels & Indian Allies*. New York: Knopf, 2010.

Toll, Ian W. *Six Frigates: The Epic History of the Founding of the U.S. Navy*, New York: Norton, 2006.

Tracy, Nicholas, ed. *The Naval Chronicle: The Contemporary Record of the Royal Navy at War*. Vols. IV (1807–1810) and V (1811–1815). London: Stackpole Books, 1999.

———. *Nelson's Battles: The Art of Victory in the Age of Sail*. Annapolis, MD: Naval Institute Press, 1996.

Tucker, Spencer. *Stephen Decatur: A Life Most Bold and Daring*. Annapolis, MD: Naval Institute Press, 2005.

———, and Frank Reuter. *Injured Honor: The* Chesapeake-Leopard *Affair, June 22, 1807*. Annapolis, MD: Naval Institute Press, 1996.

Wareham, Tom. *The Star Captains: Frigate Command in the Napoleonic Wars*. Annapolis, MD: Naval Institute Press, 2001.

Weigley, Russell F., ed. *Philadelphia: A 300-Year History*. New York: Norton, 1982.

Whitehorne, Joseph A. *The Battle for Baltimore, 1814*. Mt. Pleasant, SC: Nautical & Aviation Publishing Co., 1997.

Wills, Garry. *James Madison*. New York: Times Books, 2002.

Wood, Virginia Steele. *Live Oaking: Southern Timber for Tall Ships*. Annapolis, MD: Naval Institute Press, 1981.

Woodman, Richard, *The Sea Warriors*. London: Constable, 2001.

INDEX

B

BELAYING PIN ARRANGEMENT AT THE PORT RAIL

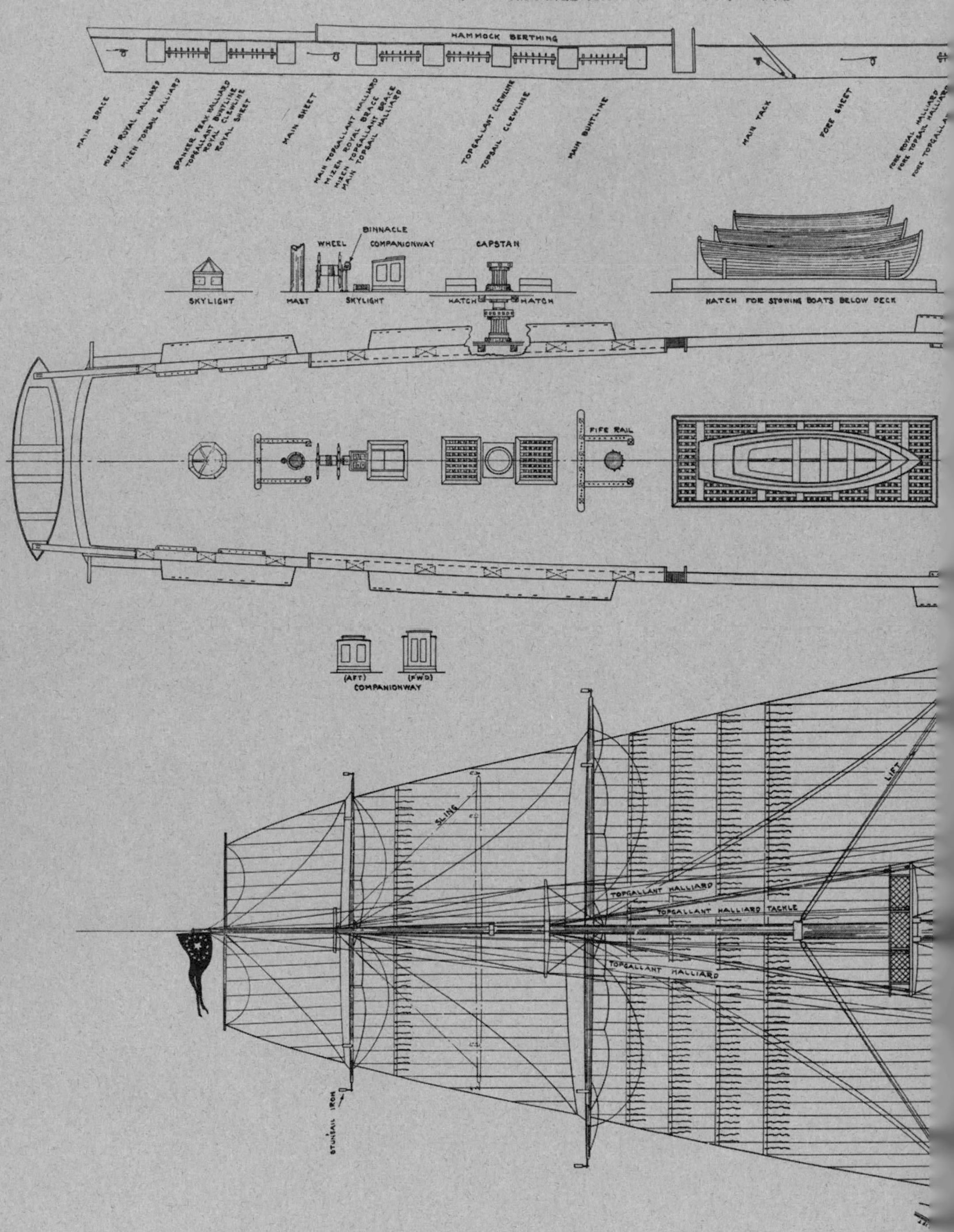